SECOND EDITION

BUSINESS ETHICS

THE MORAL FOUNDATION OF EFFECTIVE
LEADERSHIP, MANAGEMENT, AND ENTREPRENEURSHIP

Part I: Philosophical Ethics: The Moral Foundation of Business
Part II: Applied Ethics: The Moral Imperative of Business Leadership

FRANK J. CAVICO

BAHAUDIN G. MUJTABA

Custom Publishing

New York   Boston   San Francisco

London   Toronto   Sydney   Tokyo   Singapore   Madrid

Mexico City   Munich   Paris   Cape Town   Hong Kong   Montreal

4-28-9

Cover Art: *Twisti1*, by Barry Cronin.

Frank J. Cavico and Bahaudin G. Mujtaba
Nova Southeastern University
3301 College Avenue
Fort Lauderdale FL 33314
Phone: (954) 262-5000 Or (800) 672-7223 / (800) 338-4723
Email: *Cavico@huizenga.nova.edu* and *Mujtaba@nova.edu*

Printed in the United States of America

10 9 8 7 6 5 4 3 2 1

2008160514

CO

**Pearson
Custom Publishing**
is a division of

HF 5387 .C385 2008

Business Ethics

www.pearsonhighered.com

ISBN 10: 0-555-03606-5
ISBN 13: 978-0-555-03606-8

Peer Review Comments

Authors Cavico and Mujtaba have made ethics interesting! This well-written, easy to interpret book presents useful information succinctly summed up for the ethical novice or expert. Concepts are readily applied to corporate cultures and everyday dilemmas, which are often rooted in historical theory. This is one of the most thought-provoking texts I have ever read.

—*Gina H. Harris, Director of Claims, ProAssurance Corporation*

As a business owner, this book is a tremendous resource for creating an ethics-centered business and becoming an effective leader and manager. The principles discussed in "*Business Ethics: The Moral Foundation for Effective Leadership, Management, and Entrepreneurship*" are extremely valuable to all stakeholders. From ethical and legal issues to moral accountability, this book speaks to all leaders in any and every type of business. In a time where ethics and morality are needed more than ever in business, this book is one you will refer to repeatedly. This book enables you to prosper while maintaining your integrity.

—*Silvano Ferrari, Owner, Ferrari Auto Services, LLC d/b/a Precision Tune Auto Care, 15–35, Lauderhill, Florida.*

A 'must read' for the business professional, student, and/or public service professional. Drs. Cavico and Mujtaba have produced a comprehensive, readable text that speaks to the pursuit of ethical applications within any organizational framework. . . . a 'home run.'

—*Craig Inabnet, CEO of Strategic Employer Services, LLC, a Human Resources Consulting and Professional Organization, Houston, Texas.*

In reviewing "*Business Ethics: The Moral Foundation for Effective Leadership, Management, and Entrepreneurship*," I found a treatise on the "real life" application of philosophical and ethical theory to a business setting, particularly focusing on leadership within organizations. Part I of the book provides readers with a critical review of philosophical and ethical theory by reviewing the salient concepts of some of the world's great thinkers regarding their ethical theory and methodology. Part II of the book extends and synthesizes this information in an applied sense by relating the concepts to modern day organizations and the leadership within the organizations. In addition, the authors have specifically addressed various functions within organizations, the purpose for the functions, and the ethical and moral considerations in each of these areas. Based on the state of some of our top CEOs under indictment in recent years, as well as several who have been convicted of crimes against their companies and stakeholders, this book should be required reading for all their contemporaries so that the "bar can be raised" and ethics becomes a natural consideration in decision-making.

—*Douglas G. Buck, Retired Vice President of Human Resources, NSU*

The content seems to be very good! Ethics texts are usually boring, but it's like the authors are having a dialogue with the reader. The authors have made it easy to understand the legal dimensions of ethical accountability and responsibility . . . a practical interpretation of the philosophy of Ethics and its relevance in business practice.

—Rose Marie Hinds, Banker in Jamaica; The University of the West Indies

The depth and breadth of coverage in the book from philosophical to applied ethics provide a timely and handy tool for users resolving most ethical dilemmas. The book clearly illustrates the goal of business ethics education and practice: to enrich professionals with the tools of ethics that enable them to understand, synthesize, analyze, and resolve daily ethical issues comprehensively and objectively. I highly recommend this book to all undergraduate and graduate students and professionals who seek to improve on their moral reasoning skills for greater success backed by virtue and integrity.

—Akwasi A. Ampofo, Assistant Director of Accounting and Financial Reporting.

This text acts as a 'user manual' enabling business managers and executives to identify legal and ethical "red flags" that arise in everyday domestic and international business transactions, and timely refer the matters to competent legal counsel for guidance.

—Stephen C. Muffler, Attorney, Law Professor, Practitioner, and Advisor.

Dedication

Frank J. Cavico

Dedicated to the memory of my Mother and Father.

Bahaudin G. Mujtaba

Dedicated to my Mother and Father.

Presented to
Eastern University
by

Daniel & Grace Rohrer

in Honor of

D. Ryan Rohrer

Table of Contents

Table of Contents

Table of Contents

Table of Contents

Preface

This is a book about morality, philosophical ethics, and applied ethics. It is for those individuals who wish to become acquainted with moral philosophy, ethical reasoning, and especially the application of ethics to business and management. The book aims to introduce the reader to ethical theories and concepts that are relevant to resolving moral problems confronting business. The book is designed to be useful to both employees and managers as well as entrepreneurs and business leaders who want to integrate moral concerns into their decision-making process.

The book also will prove interesting to those who already possess some knowledge of ethics, perhaps from the perspective of a single discipline, such as law or political science, and who wish to explore the subject further in a systematic, practical manner. This book does examine certain laws regulating business from an ethical paradigm, but this book is not a law book; it is an ethics book. For a comprehensive examination of the laws regulating business in a global context, the authors refer the reader to their book, entitled *Legal Challenges for the Global Manager and Entrepreneur* (2008).

Business ethics courses now have been instituted in many colleges and graduate programs. Business ethics books, however, generally suffer from substantial limitations. They either provide very little substantive philosophical material or they are very far removed from any practical application of ethics to the moral problems confronting business. Comprehensive and sustained philosophic works in the area of applied business ethics have been surprisingly scant. Many current academic and popular works contain a great deal of verbiage on "business ethics," yet very little explication and analysis of the actual ethics involved.

This text, however, is not a book about the scholarship of moral philosophy; rather, it is about the problems which that scholarship addresses. The pages that follow, therefore, contain relatively few citations and footnotes. This omission should not be taken as suggesting that what others have written lacks significance. If there are too many references to other authors, however, a book will end up as a book devoted to other books, which is an appropriate approach for a purely academic audience, but not the one chosen here. The book, moreover, does not discuss all problems of moral philosophy, although it touches on enough of them to warrant titling the book an "ethics" one. References and other source materials have been used, of course, and they are gathered in a separate bibliography section.

This book grew out of a graduate business ethics course the authors developed and have taught for the last two decades at the H. Wayne Huizenga School of Business and

Entrepreneurship of Nova Southeastern University. The book is thus a partial payment of debt and gratitude to our graduate students, who most have inspired us to learn about the subject and to apply the knowledge to the "real world" problems of the business community. The authors are also indebted to Professor Richard T. DeGeorge, who in his seminal work, *Business Ethics*, "took ethics out of the philosophy department and put it in the schools of business."

The objective, then, as now, is not only to teach ethics, but also to do ethics; that is, our purposes are not merely to pass on information, but also to stimulate and assist the student and reader to do better, be clearer, and to acquire more reasoned thinking about moral questions; and to impart the analytical skills needed to apply ethical concepts to business decision making. We hope to present a sound work that provides readable philosophic materials, substantive and workable ethics, and relevant, practical, business and management applications.

The material is designed for people who already are largely within a moral world; that is, people who possess decent instincts, display a genuine concern for others, and have a basic disposition to obey moral norms. The book presupposes that business leaders are neither immoral nor amoral entities, but moral beings who want to do the "right" thing.

We recognize that no one book can suffice to turn a scoundrel into a virtuous human being. The discourse that follows, therefore, is neither aimed at people who probably will not listen to it; nor is it intended to control the "enemies" of the moral community, or its shirkers. The goal, rather, is to reassure, strengthen, and give insight to those who probably will listen to the discourse; and much can be done in the way of character formation when the reader is motivated by a desire to be a "good" person, even if one's prior education was morally deficient or neutral.

Yet, even presuming that people are in some general sense committed to thinking in moral terms, there often is a great deal of confusion as to what actions and practices are morally appropriate. The book, therefore, provides ethical reasons to people already disposed to hear them; and thus it helps to create, promote, and sustain a community held together by that same "moral" disposition.

The conceptions of morality, as well as the ethical theories addressed in this book, are aspects of the best work achieved in the history of moral philosophy. The book, therefore, hopefully also will be an exercise in recollection, whereby the reader may recall perhaps forgotten parts of ethical knowledge. The reader then may come to realize that he or she already possesses ethical resources to make contemporary moral judgments.

The study of ethics enables the reader to perceive moral issues that he or she otherwise might ignore. The reader then will find that moral dilemmas are susceptible to rigorous ethical analysis, rational argumentation, and ultimately resolution.

By ethically resolving moral problems confronting business, a manager will be better able to understand and classify his or her own moral beliefs and be better equipped to develop a critical and reflective personal morality. People frequently seek reasons for the goals they are considering pursuing and for the decisions they are contemplating making. They also often desire to place their lives in a meaningful larger picture. Ethics can provide intelligible reasons for one's decisions, direction for one's goals, coherence to one's existence, significance to one's life, and a satisfaction that one has lived as one ought.

This book, in addition to providing an introduction to moral philosophy, closely examines its relationship to business and management. It is written from a business management perspective. Moral issues are treated not only as philosophical questions, but also as fundamentally important, practical, business questions for managers. It is difficult to imagine a business manager, leader, or entrepreneur who has not at one time or another had occasion to appeal to morality or to question and discuss whether a course of action is moral. Yet, undeniably, there is a gap between the level of discussions of moral philosophy in university philosophy departments and the level of discussions of particular moral problems as they are encountered by business managers. A manager probably does not indulge in philosophical speculation about the meaning of morality; he or she may even hesitate to use moral terminology and concepts. Yet the literature on moral philosophy, ethics, and morality is immense; morality long has been an object of academic analysis discussion.

This practical perspective of the book, therefore, is an attempt to bridge the gap between philosophy and business. The content and case demonstrates the importance of philosophical issues and aspires to make them come alive for business managers. These moral issues not only should be of "academic" interest to philosophers, but also of practical interest to business managers.

Many people who confront moral issues, in business or otherwise, either ignore them or treat them superficially. Why do people have difficulty in dealing with moral issues? Perhaps it is because philosophers and academics, who traditionally have dealt with moral issues, tend to be highly theoretical and abstract. Often, very little practical information is imparted. One tends to get bogged down and ultimately frustrated when reading much philosophical academic literature.

This material is not designed to be a philosophical treatise; and the authors certainly do not want to compete with professional philosophers. The material discussed is meant for the non-specialist; it presupposes no formal study in philosophy. Fundamental moral issues and ethical theories are discussed, of course, but in lay terms. The philosophical jargon found in most of the literature has been eliminated to the greatest extent possible.

Yet, there are certain philosophical theories, concepts, and problems that do require treatment when dealing with moral issues that arise in business. The book, therefore, raises in a nonphilosophical manner fundamental moral issues that are important to business managers. It selects ethical views for explication that historically are important and that also help to illuminate the relationship between moral philosophy and business. The book does not oversimplify moral issues; but it deals with them in such a way that their significance is apparent. The book strives to make ethics accessible to business managers. There is no reason why the stimulating and challenging subject of moral philosophy should be the exclusive preserve of the philosophers and academics who claim to specialize in it.

The study of ethics is not a new concern. What is new is the development of "business ethics" into a field of study in its own right and not as a peripheral subject to be added to existing philosophy, law, or even business works and courses as time and interest permit. In the past, philosophers and academics provided the leadership for the field. Today, thanks to pioneering efforts of Richard T. DeGeorge and others, business administration scholars are located in business schools, and they are conducting research, teaching courses, and writing books. There are now business ethics books, and at times they actually have something to say about ethics and morality. Yet, what is needed is a comprehensive and systematic, yet clear and readable, account of morality, ethics, and applied ethics for business managers. This book fulfills that need.

The field of business ethics now has secured a position on important moral issues affecting society. To be successful in this effort, the field must take seriously its own ethical content. When managers do become aware of the ethics involved in business ethics, they will realize ethics' limitations, but they also will come to recognize its strengths.

This work is the second edition of the authors' ethics book, *Business Ethics: Transcending Requirements Through Moral Leadership*. The first edition has been very well received; and the authors accordingly are most grateful and honored. Based on the comments and recommendations of faculty colleagues, other professors, students, and managers using the book, the authors have made some refinements and additions to the second edition, including a change to the subtitle to the book. This second edition is now called *Business Ethics: The Moral Foundation for Effective Leadership, Management, and Entrepreneurship*. The authors made this title change to make more explicit the critical correlation between ethics and management, entrepreneurship, and leadership as well as to underscore the additional coverage accorded to this significant relationship. Note that the basic structure, approach, and core elements of the second edition of the book remain the same. That is, the first part of the book is an explication of ethics as a branch of philosophy and also provides illustrations of how ethical theories and principles can be applied to business controversies. The book then demonstrates in a variety of important business subject matter contexts how ethics can be applied to resolve specific moral challenges confronting business. The book also includes a discussion of the value of corporate social responsibility as well as an expanded discussion of the correlation of ethics and morality to successful leadership, entrepreneurship, and management. The authors have materially expanded the discussion of corporate social responsibility and have included more examples of social responsibility, especially in a global context. The authors also have expanded the discussion of corporate governance and have added a new chapter subsection dealing with a legal and ethical analysis of age discrimination. Furthermore, for this second edition the authors have provided at the end of each substantive subject matter chapter a series of questions based on the material in each discrete chapter that can be used for discussion and/or review purposes. Finally, the authors have provided several new and very recent and controversial case studies that will provide opportunities for ethical analysis and fervent, though principled and reasoned, debate on many significant moral issues affecting business and society. Some of the new cases have been contributed to the second edition by faculty colleagues and former students of the authors. The authors are most appreciative of their contributions; and the authors are also most grateful for all the support and encouragement to publish the second edition and particularly for the many most helpful suggestions for improving the second edition of the book. We sincerely hope that you also enjoy this second edition; and find it similarly useful and beneficial—academically and practically—as well as intellectually stimulating, thought-provoking, and challenging.

Furthermore, by using this book you are contributing to the *Business Ethics and Global Social Responsibility Scholarship* which has been established at Nova Southeastern University to support scholarly research and coursework by students that will advance the fields of business ethics and global social responsibility. This scholarship was conceived and created by the authors of this book, and Huizenga School professors, Dr. Frank J. Cavico, J.D., LL.M, Professor of Business Law and Ethics, and Dr. Bahaudin G. Mujtaba, Associate Professor of Management. Professors Cavico and Mujtaba are co-funding this academic scholarship initiative with the support of the H. Wayne Huizenga School of

Business and Entrepreneurship and Nova Southeastern University. Professors Cavico and Mujtaba, the co-authors of this book, are continuing to provide funds to this scholarship from the royalties from the sale of this book, *Business Ethics: The Moral Foundation for Effective Leadership, Management, and Entrepreneurship*. Thank you for exploring and leading discussions, and advancing knowledge on morality and ethics in the world of business management, entrepreneurship, and leadership!

Frank and Bahaudin

Acknowledgements

Many individuals provided valuable input toward the preparation of this second edition, as well as the first edition, and, as authors, we would like to extend our gratitude and heartfelt appreciations to everyone.

First and foremost, we thank our Nova Southeastern University colleagues and friends for their guidance, valuable input in the review of this material, and for making the doors of learning open to thousands of individuals throughout the world. In particular, Dean Randolph Pohlman at the Huizenga School has consistently emphasized the importance of value creation for all stakeholders in the long-term which runs shoulder to shoulder with business ethics. Also, Preston Jones, Executive Associate Dean of the Huizenga School, has energized us all to think of various ways for creating managers and leaders that leave our school with the requisite skills to effectively compete in the global market. Such encouragements of long-term value creation and effectively competing in the business environment, while maintaining high integrity, are moral imperatives for good business. As such, their leadership, guidance and encouragements were the basis for this book on business ethics.

Second, we thank our spouses Nancy Cavico and Lisa Mujtaba for their thoughts, guidance, and caring orientation in the preparation of this material. Their love, support, patience, encouragement, and wisdom have sustained and inspired us in an enduring partnership of marriage.

Third, we thank and acknowledge the following individuals for generously sharing their thoughts, suggestions, and contributions on business ethics related issues from various perspectives around the world in the preparation of this book on business ethics.

- A. George Petrie
- Akwasi Ampofo
- Cagri Tanyar
- Cuneyt Oskal
- Crystal Gomez
- Dana Tesone
- Don Ariail
- Don Valeri
- Doug Buck
- Elizabeth Danon-Leva
- Gary Waldron
- Gimol Thomas
- J. Preston Jones
- Joseph Durden
- John Wayne Falbey
- John W. Palma Jr.
- Laura Yanez
- Josephine Sosa-Fey
- Laura Yanez
- Matthew Kenney

- Miguel A. Orta
- Miguel Valdez
- Randolph A. Pohlman
- Regina Harris
- Rose Marie Hinds

- Stephanie Ferrari
- Stephen C. Muffler
- Tiffany Cullens
- Trevor Pendleton
- William Freeman

Fourth, we thank the thousands of graduate students that have taken our business ethics courses since 1988 and those who have provided valuable input for ethical issues and concepts during each term. In addition, we thank hundreds of doctoral candidates and management development seminar participants that have provided us valuable learning laboratories to sculpt and fine-tune our business ethics philosophy and approach.

Finally, we especially thank you for reading this second edition on business ethics. We have been very pleased and most grateful that our first edition has been so well received; and we sincerely hope you also enjoy the second edition and find it even more useful, rewarding, and thought-provoking. We wish a life of integrity and value-creation for you, your family, and humanity.

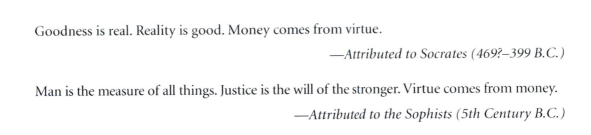

Goodness is real. Reality is good. Money comes from virtue.

—Attributed to Socrates (469?–399 B.C.)

Man is the measure of all things. Justice is the will of the stronger. Virtue comes from money.

—Attributed to the Sophists (5th Century B.C.)

Purpose, Approach and Format of the Textbook

This work is a treatment of philosophical subjects that are of intellectual and practical interest. The book explains the nature, aims, and usefulness of moral philosophy, ethics, and morality; it demonstrates the relationship between philosophy and business. The book clarifies the meaning of such basic concepts as happiness, justice, law, duty, and freedom. The book examines a variety of ethical views that are relevant to resolving moral problems confronting business managers. The book addresses such seminal issues as to whether people and business are capable of acting morally; and, if so, whether people and business should act in a moral manner. In particular, the book is concerned with ethical and moral ideas as they are relevant in today's business world.

One aim of the book is to transform what first appears to be a chaos of differing ethical opinions into an orderly set of clearly defined points of agreement and disagreement. The book provides reasons for the positions advanced as well as reasons for the disagreements. As the future resolution of moral problems depends upon sustained, rational, intellectual efforts, the book strives to encourage and to facilitate rational debate.

This document, although not a "survey" type work, does introduce the reader to several distinct ethical theories that help one to understand the meaning of morality and thus to think about what a moral life might be. It provides guidance in resolving perplexing moral problems and points out reasons for acting morally that most rational people should be willing to accept. This work, however, is not a dogmatic moralizing preachment, but rather, in the spirit of Socrates, a searching inquiry. An honest search for moral truth, however, because of the better understanding that ensues, very likely will lead to an improvement in behavior itself.

1. Approach

This work has a non-philosophic orientation in the sense that it does not undertake to develop a new moral philosophy. It is less concerned with what moral philosophers have said than with what may be learned from what they said. It is neither the book's intent to supply an exhaustive, systematic analysis of morality and ethics, nor to spend a great deal of time in examining technical, arcane, philosophic questions. Yet basic philosophical issues are addressed; there is a philosophical content to the book. The textbook does explore certain, select, important ethical areas within the broad field of moral philosophy, and it also applies ethical theories to present-day business problems. The object of the book is not only to introduce the reader to ethics but also to practice ethics.

The material discussed is neutral in the sense that it does not seek to convey a set of moral "truths." Rather, in a sustained effort to be impartial, it treats many different ethical points of view. The goal is to encourage and to educate the reader to think carefully about moral issues that arise in personal and business life. The idea is not to impart "right" answers, but to make the reader more perceptive in seeing moral issues, better acquainted with moral philosophy, and better equipped to reason ethically about moral issues. What matters most is not whether one agrees or disagrees with a moral conclusion, but whether one ends up with more ethical knowledge and with an enhanced moral reasoning capability.

The book, on the other hand, is not neutral because it involves more than ethical exploration and explication; it also contains critical ethical analysis that is designed to test the soundness of the ethical views discussed. Philosophic ideas are treated seriously when they are subject to demanding critical appraisal. Consequently, the book views morality as a problem to be critically investigated, instead of something to be embraced and vindicated more or less as it is received. To learn the most from philosophy, one must be aware of certain deficiencies in assumptions, methodology, reasoning, and conclusions. One must rectify these problems, while preserving and building upon fundamentally sound philosophical structures.

The book, therefore, does provide the reader with some account of the authors' own attitudes toward ethical theories, assessments of the merits of conflicting claims, and at times, the authors' own solutions to some of the recurring problems in business ethics.

2. Format

One cannot achieve an adequate understanding of morality and a fair assessment of ethics unless one broadens one's ethical views. Accordingly, the first part of the book introduces the reader to basic ethical theories and methods of reasoning; they are presented, not as mere historical curiosities, but as viable, defensible, workable doctrines that efficaciously can be employed to analyze and resolve moral dilemmas that arise in business.

The second part of the book is the application of the ethics. Ethical theories and methods are applied to specific moral issues confronting business. Part two deals with more narrow questions that relate to specific business practices and relationships; and it is based on the philosophic foundation built in the first part.

PART I

Philosophical Ethics:
The Moral Foundation of Business

CHAPTER 1

Introduction to Ethics and Ethical Concepts

A. Terminology and Methodology

Business ethics is a specialized study of moral right and wrong. It concentrates on the application of ethical principles to business practices, policies, and institutions. Business ethics, in addition, is the study of how ethical principles apply to the conduct of individuals, especially managers, involved in business.

Business ethics is a form of applied ethics. The field encompasses not only an analysis of ethical theories and principles, but also the application of this analysis to the behavior of people and organizations in business settings.

Many people, admittedly, are skeptical about morality, particularly as it pertains to business. This skepticism derives in part from an assumption that moral considerations are not appropriate for business. The argument is raised that business is, and should be, amoral; that is, that ethics and morality have no application to business and management, that the business of business is to make money; and that although morality and ethics may pertain to one's personal life, they are irrelevant to one's business life and one's role as a business manager. There may be lurking in this "amoral" view, moreover, an implication that business and business managers are immoral; that is, the assumption that it is not always better in business to be "better"; that business demands take precedence over moral concerns; and that immorality itself may be necessary for business survival and success.

There are a variety of reasons for this "amoral" view. It is easier for business people to deal with economic and legal judgments as opposed to moral ones. Managers are more comfortable in discussing business issues in terms of their economic and legal impact, rather than their morality. Most business people are not well trained in ethical analysis. Managers generally are not cognizant of ethical theories; they are not familiar with ethical principles and moral terminology; and they cannot argue moral questions from an ethical point of view.

The real problem, therefore, is not that business people are amoral or immoral, but that they are ignorant ethically. Since the problem, in fact, emerges as ethical ignorance, then the solution, as proposed in this work, is to expose business people to ethical theories, principles, and reasoning. The object is to heighten the reader's moral awareness, help managers recognize the moral ramifications to business activities, and particularly to provide business people with the ethical tools needed to answer questions of morality.

For ethics to be taken seriously by business people, it must be related to business and management activities and, most importantly, to business performance. Otherwise, ethics at best will be perceived as nothing more than a mere "academic" exercise and at worst as an impediment to success. The challenge is to link business ethics to business performance. An important aim of the book, therefore, is to reconcile the requirements of morality with claims of business, management, and personal self-interest. The perceived conflict between morality and self-interest lies at the heart of ethics; and this relationship is addressed in this book, as it must be in any true "ethical" endeavor.

1. The Importance of Definitions and Terminology in Ethics

It is very important for an ethical practitioner to look for, ascertain, and pay special attention to definitions and terms. When one initially encounters the field of ethics, one is confronted with some confusion due to a lack of an agreed-upon terminology and set of definitions.

Yet, if one is going to understand how ethics works, there must be some agreement on, and some insight into, the structure within which ethics works. There is, therefore, a need for words, terms, and definitions with precise meaning. Definitions can function as the first ethical principles of moral reasoning. If one defines terms carefully at the start or knows the appropriate definitions and one applies them consistently, one can draw moral conclusions deductively from these incontrovertible first ethical principles. One, therefore, can use definitions and terms to decide what to do in particular cases.

2. Philosophy

Philosophy is the study and analysis of such deeply problematical and fundamental question, such as the nature of reality, conduct, and thought. The field of philosophy traditionally is divided into three parts: the metaphysical, the political and ethical, and the philosophy of knowledge.

Metaphysics is philosophy in the "macro" sense. It is the attempt to understand and to explain the ultimate nature of the world in which human beings live. Political and ethical philosophy is philosophy in a more practical and "micro" sense. It is the study of human beings, their nature, place in the world, and their relations with others. It is an attempt to formulate systematic doctrines to determine the best way of living. The philosophy of knowledge is the attempt to determine what knowledge is, what it is ultimately based on, and what correct mental processes.

A philosopher is a person with the conviction that beneath the apparent chaos, multiplicity, confusion, and change in the universe, there exists an underlying permanence, unity, stability, identity, and fundamental truth that reason may discover. A philosopher is a person who seeks this truth.

3. Moral Philosophy

Moral philosophy is the philosophical study of morality; it is the application of philosophy to moral thinking, moral conduct, and moral problems. Moral philosophy encompasses various theories that prescribe what is good for people and what is bad, what constitutes right and wrong, and what one ought to do and ought not to do. Moral philosophy offers ethical theories that provide a theoretical framework for making, asserting, and defending a moral decision.

There is not one determinate set of ethical theories. Moral philosophy embraces a range of ethical perspectives and spends a great deal of time in analyzing the differences among these ethical views. Each ethical theory, however, does underscore some ultimate principle or set of principles that one is obligated to follow to ensure moral behavior and the good life.

The philosophical study of morality is distinguished by the general, systematic, and logical nature of the endeavor. It is the effort to systematize ethically moral judgments and to establish and defend ethically moral beliefs and standards. Moral philosophy develops ethical frameworks for evaluating the merits of asserted moral positions. Moral philosophy attempts to establish logical thought processes that will determine if an action is right or wrong and seeks to find criteria by which to distinguish good from bad conduct. Moral philosophy endeavors to prove its claims through ethical arguments that can demonstrate that the ideal thought, conduct, life, and morality are in fact ideal. The ultimate aim of moral philosophy is to answer Socrates's fundamental question: how *should* one live?

Specifically, moral philosophy attempts to answer the following questions: What is the nature of morality and the meaning of good and bad and right and wrong in human conduct? How is one to know the good from the bad? How can moral judgments be established or justified? Can they be justified at all? What is the nature of the good life? What should one seek in life? Is there a highest good for human beings? What are one's moral obligations? Why should one be moral?

A study of moral philosophy also reveals the question as to just how far purely rational inquiry can take one in answering the preceding questions.

4. Ethics

Ethics is the theoretical study of morality. Ethical theories are moral philosophical undertakings that contain bodies of formal, systematic, and ethical principles that are committed to the view that an asserted ethical theory can determine how one should morally think and act. Moral judgments are deducible from a hierarchy of ethical principles. It is the moral philosopher's task to articulate such ethical principles and to insist upon their proper application. Ethics is the sustained and reasoned attempt to determine what is morally right or wrong. Ethics is used to test the moral correctness of beliefs, practices, and rules. Ethics necessarily involves an effort both to define what is meant by morality and to justify the way of acting and living that is being advocated.

Ethics proceeds from a conviction that moral disagreements and conflicts are resolvable rationally. There is one "right" answer to any moral dispute, and this answer can be reached through reasoning. The purpose of ethics is to develop, articulate, and justify principles and techniques that can be used in specific situations where a moral determination must be made about a particular action or practice.

There are, of course, problems in this ethical attempt to formulate principles to resolve concrete moral problems. To what extent is ethics a source of objective, determinate, and reasoned principles rather than merely personal, political, cultural, legal, or religious "answers" to moral questions? Presuming ethical principles are objective and reasoned, how are they justified? Is there some independent, overarching, principle or mechanism that can arbitrate among various moral philosophies and validate the correctness of ethical principles? Even if people agree on general ethical principles, the application of those principles to specific moral problems also causes controversy.

5. Morals and Morality

There is, of course, a relationship between ethics and morals in the conduct of human affairs. When something is judged good or bad, right or wrong, or just or unjust, the underlying standards on which the judgment is based are moral standards. Moral standards include not only specific moral rules but also the more general ethical principles upon which the moral rules are based. When a decision involves a moral component, the decision necessarily encompasses moral rules and ethical principles.

Morals are beliefs or views as to what is right or wrong or good or bad. Moral norms are standards of behavior by which people are judged and that require, prohibit, or allow specific types of behavior. Moral rules are action-guiding or prescriptive statements about how people ought to behave or ought not to behave.

Ethics deals with matters that are of serious consequence to human beings. Ethics affects human welfare and fulfillment in significant ways. People will be positively or negatively affected by moral decisions. Ethics, therefore, is concerned with conduct that can benefit or harm human beings.

Morals fundamentally convey norms to human life. Moral standards enable resolution of disputes by providing acceptable justification for actions. If one bases a decision on a moral rule, and if the moral rule is based on and derived from an agreed-upon ethical principle, the decision should be publicly acceptable. Ethics then can identify certain behaviors as better or worse than others by endowing these determinations with normative moral force. Ethics and morality thus perform a directive role, encouraging or discouraging ways of conduct, living, thinking, and choosing. People can then pursue their conception of the good life in such a way as not to conflict with the ways of life of others. There obviously must be constraints on the manners in which people pursue their chosen ways of life; morality emerges as an important delimiting factor.

Although ethical theories and ethical principles are propounded principally by moral philosophers, morality is not an invention of philosophers; rather, it is part of the make-up and outlook of almost all people. A moral judgment, however, is a particularly important type of deliberation. It is a reasoned ethical conclusion directed toward what one ought or ought not to do. Morality, therefore, properly and accurately should be understood as a development of the ethical.

6. Beliefs and Knowledge

Beliefs and knowledge are criteria of thought and ways people think about given concepts. Moral beliefs are views as to what is right or wrong. Beliefs support norms; but there is no action involved and no overt behavior toward others.

Knowledge, however, consists of self-evident truths known with certitude; beliefs based on knowledge or logically connected with knowledge; beliefs definitely proven by scientific methods; beliefs based on sufficient evidence and authority and supported by reasons to outweigh any contrary beliefs.

Thus, a belief is a judgment that cannot be proven or tested completely to be true or erroneous. As a consequence, all such beliefs must be held only provisionally as hypotheses, subject to revision and rejection, in the light of advancing knowledge. A growth of knowledge consists of transforming beliefs into knowledge through validation or disproof of beliefs. If a belief is far from a body of knowledge, one must treat it as arbitrary and lacking logical compulsion; one entertains such beliefs at one's own risk.

7. Values

Values are rankings or priorities that a person establishes for one's norms and beliefs. Values express what the chief end of life is, the highest good, and what things in life are worthwhile or desirable. As per Values Theory, deeply held values drive behavior.

One very difficult problem is placing values in proper relation to one another. Values often are controversial because the norms and beliefs that one person holds in high esteem conflict with different norms and beliefs that another person holds in equally high esteem. Moral values are the rankings or priorities that a person establishes for one's moral norms and moral beliefs.

A distinction is made between two types of values: instrumental and intrinsic values. Instrumental (or extrinsic values) are good because of their consequences. They are desired as a means to an end. Their worth is not in their own right, but because of what they can bring in the way of other values, for example, economic values. Intrinsic values are good in and of themselves. They are an end in themselves and desired for their own sake. They are values that claim appraisal in their own right. They are, or claim to be, of absolute worth, such as pleasure (to a hedonist), power (to a Machiavellian), knowledge, or self-realization. Moral values are generally held to be intrinsic.

There are theories of ethics that depend upon some theory of intrinsic value. That is, in order to determine if something is good or right, one first must determine which things are worth seeking without regard to their consequences. Whose intrinsic good, however, should be promoted? To an egoist, one should promote one's own greatest good; but to a utilitarian, one should promote the greatest good for everyone.

8. Judgments

There are two types of judgments: descriptive or factual judgments, and prescriptive or normative judgments. Descriptive judgments deal with matters of fact. They describe or interpret objects and things as actual existences in the environment. They attempt to make clear to people the nature of reality. A descriptive judgment tells one what does or does not exist and what are or are not the characteristics of existing things.

Prescriptive (or normative) judgments appraise, appreciate, or evaluate objects and things. Prescriptions are not concerned merely with objects as actually existent facts, but rather what objects might be and are not. For example, the following statement is prescriptive: "The chair is ill-proportioned." The statement, however, is in some sense descriptive too. The difference largely is one of emphasis; but it is an important one because it provides a basis upon which rests the distinction between normative philosophy and the descriptive sciences. Prescriptive judgments answer questions of value. They provide standards of behavior by which people are judged. They lay down standards or norms of conduct, expectations of proper behavior, what ought or ought not to be done, ways people should act, and answers to questions of right and wrong.

Prescriptive (or normative) judgments often are thought of as purely subjective, that is, wholly relative to one's individual preferences. A finding is objective if all, or virtually all, of those investigators, regardless of ideological or other preconceptions, would be bound to agree to it. A finding, however, can be construed as objective if it is reasonable; that is, if it is amenable to and accompanied by a persuasive, though not necessarily an absolutely convincing, explanation.

Moreover, when one judges that an object has worth (for example, that a deed is "generous"), one feels that the judgment is by no means an arbitrary one; and that there is something in the object so judged that makes the judgment necessary (for example, that the deed in its own right is generous). There is, therefore, an aspect thereto that is deemed worthwhile and that is independent of individual preferences; there is some quality in the object that calls out these preferences.

9. Summary

In order to respond intelligently to moral controversies, one must be familiar with basic philosophic terminology. One must be familiar with the different types of moral philosophy and the ethical principles that are derived therefrom. Of course, there is no one simple, uncontroversial definition of what morality is. There are many rival moral philosophies, each expounding a different ethical conception of what it means to live morally.

A definitional approach, however, draws attention to "moral" language and thus helps one to think about ethics and a moral life expressed in ethical terms. One must recognize that moral understanding needs a dimension of definitional explanation. As the highest knowledge is the knowledge of good and bad, the subject, as Socrates said, deals with "no small matter," but how one ought to live.

B. Principles, Rules, Conventions, and Personal Taste

1. Ethical Principles

A distinction exists among ethical principles, moral rules, social conventions, and matters of personal taste; and the differentiation is significant. Ethical principles are very general, pervasive, basic, and fundamental standards that are used to evaluate the rightness or wrongness of behavior and to determine the truth or falsity of moral issues. Ethical principles are the source or grounds of moral rules. Ethical principles establish, justify, and underlie moral rules; they interpret a rule, determine its scope, and justify exceptions to a moral rule. An example of an ethical principle is the principle of utility, which evaluates the morality of a practice in terms of the net social benefits it produces.

2. Moral Rules

Moral rules are propositions that a certain kind of action is morally right or wrong. Moral rules, however, must be understood with a qualification. They generally or usually state what is right or wrong. A moral rule may not apply in all circumstances. It is generally morally wrong to lie, for example, but not always wrong. It may be morally justifiable to break a moral rule against lying if, by giving a truthful response, one would cause severe pain or injury to another. It is, however, immoral to violate a moral rule without a legitimate reason. An act that violates a moral rule requires justification-ethical justification.

Moral rules, as well as exceptions thereto, are established by means of ethical principles. If a moral rule cannot be derived from the application of an ethical principle, it cannot be justified. Lying, for example, is morally wrong because of the negative consequences that would ensue if everyone lied. Moral rules are not isolated or independent of each other; they are connected because they are established through the application of ethical principles. If moral rules should conflict, moreover, ethical principles supply the criteria for deciding or mediating between them.

3. Social Conventions

A convention is an accepted usage or an established practice. "Social" entails living with others in a community and encompasses the lives, welfare, and relations among human beings in a community. Social conventions are the usages, practices, and habits of the members of a social group or a society. There are, of course, various practices peculiar to different groups and societies. Customs are social conventions regarded collectively.

Many factors produce a society's social conventions. Physical circumstances and local conditions, religious and moral beliefs, and traditions and shared history all help to produce social conventions. Cultural conditioning, learning by precept and example, and internalized, unconsidered "learning" influence one to view certain conduct as socially acceptable and unacceptable. An example of a social convention is a society's funeral and burial practices.

There are important differences between social conventions and moral rules. Social conventions depend on local circumstances and conditions; moral rules are the precondition for any society or community at all. As pertaining to a society, its conventions are neither right nor wrong; they exist. One need not feel obligated to provide objective reasons why a particular society's social conventions are better than another's. Moral rules, however, are either right or wrong based on ethical analysis. One must provide objective reasons for one's moral conclusions.

The diversity in social conventions may be attributable to the different aspects of community life. There thus may be less disagreement about moral beliefs than there appears to be. One should not conclude that because social conventions differ, there can be no agreement about moral rules.

Social conventions, however, do have an initial claim to acceptance. Unless a convention violates an ethical principle or moral rule, or unless the conditions that brought a convention into existence change, a social convention should be regarded as binding. A social convention is a practice or usage accepted by a particular group; the members of the group expect and depend on other members to act in accordance with its conventions.

4. Personal Taste

Expressions of personal taste are the personal preferences, likes and dislikes, and subjective opinions of a person concerning objects and actions in question. An example is a person's choice of ice cream flavors.

There is no need to have a reason for one's personal predilections. There is no such thing as rationally defending one's like or dislike of coffee ice cream. There is no way of investigating an expression of personal taste to determine its validity. It is not meaningful to say that a matter of personal taste is true or false. There is simply no point in arguing about matters of personal taste.

So long as one is accurately reporting his or her tastes, what one says must be true. One merely is making a statement about oneself. There is no implication that anyone else should feel the same way.

When one, however, says that an action is morally right or wrong, one not only needs reasons but also reasons that are based on ethical principles and reasoning. If the reasons are sound, a rational person must acknowledge their force. If there is no good reason behind one's "moral" expression, people will reject it as an arbitrary, unfounded, and subjective opinion and pay no attention to it.

One must be careful in crossing the border between matters of personal taste and morality when one makes an assertation that others should behave as a particular matter of taste prescribes. If one demands that others ought to do, or not to do, something, logically and legitimately others will ask why or why not.

C. Ethics Compared to the Sciences and the Law

1. Ethics v. Science

A) INTRODUCTION

The issue of objectivity arises in moral philosophy from an interest in comparing ethical beliefs, knowledge, and assertions of truth to claims of other types, particularly with scientific beliefs. Such a comparison raises certain fundamental ethical questions: Is there such a thing as scientific moral knowledge, and can ethical principles and moral rules be tested and confirmed in the manner scientific ones can?

B) SCIENCE

1) Definitiveness of Knowledge

"Scientific" knowledge, in the sense of being objective and definitive, properly belongs to science. Science seeks to resolve questions by means of scientific observations, experimentation, and testing. Science deals with facts and seeks to make determinations of objective truth. "Objective truth" signifies that all, or virtually all, of those who have examined a question agree to a particular answer. Facts can be observed and confirmed by empirical techniques. As soon as a field of inquiry yields determinations, they are subject to exact formulation and validation.

Scientific beliefs can assert a strong claim to objectivity because they are capable of being verified. Scientific judgments, therefore, can rightfully be regarded as true or false. As a consequence, science is composed of a large body of established truth, which no competent scientist would dispute and which beginners patiently must master.

2) Scientific Advancement

The field of science has made remarkable progress. Scientific knowledge always seems to grow, improve, and expand. Science is based on a corpus of learning, dealing with facts and experience, that increases steadily and is enlarged upon by people concerned with that particular body of learning. Scientific progress is not illusory. An increased understanding of the world is evidenced by the enhanced ability to affect what happens in the world.

3) Morally Neutral Stance

Science is morally neutral. It is concerned simply with knowing what is, not what should be. Science assures people what they can perform, not what they should perform. Science seeks truth and avoids falsehood; but the truths are not necessarily what one would term morally good and the falsehoods morally bad. Science is concerned with knowing the real; not seeking the ideal.

c) ETHICS

1) The Search for Definite Knowledge

Ethics attempts to resolve difficult and contentious moral issues by methods that resemble scientific methods. Ethics is based on theories of moral philosophy. Ethical principles and moral rules are used to establish and explain particular decisions. Principles and rules can be tested by appealing to moral determination that certain actions are right or wrong.

The scientific world, however, is amenable to observation, testing, and resolution in a way that the moral world is not. Ethics is not accurate in the same sense that a scientific theory must be accurate if it is to be accepted. An ethical theory is not necessarily, or even usually, confirmed or disproved by clear and indisputable evidence.

Consequently, many moral questions do not have clearly demonstrable "correct" answers; and many moral issues are highly controversial. Competent moral philosophers may disagree even about fundamental moral matters.

Yet, if ethics is not scientific, how does one ultimately resolve moral disputes? Are there any agreed-upon, objective ethical truths to be discovered? If there are objective ethical principles, can they be used to formulate moral rules governing conduct? Some moral philosophers, such as Plato, emphasized the scientific objectivity of moral judgments. They posited a "moral order" in the world waiting to be discovered. The faculty of reason will disclose immutable "moral facts" that will enable one to discover what is good and bad and thus to regulate one's life accordingly. For most moral philosophers, however, it is sufficient that an ethical theory, and the set of more or less general principles that compose it, is acceptable for the most part, on the whole, and in actual experience.

2) Ethical Advancement

Since there is little in ethics that is analogous to scientific methodology, nothing in ethics is known in a scientific sense. Ethics, therefore, has not made any definite "advances" in the sense of ascertainable and provable discoveries. One, for example, can say definitely that Aristotle's commentary on astronomy is wrong; but one cannot say, in the same sense, that Aristotle's ethical views are right or wrong. One advantage, however, to this lack of scientific ethical advancement is that an ancient treatise on ethics is not necessarily inferior to a modern one.

3) *The Moral Stance of Ethics*

Ethics is not morally neutral. A moral philosopher is not content to merely state the facts; he or she also attempts to obtain worth and value. Ethics asks not only what is the good, but also how one can be good. Ethics not only describes the world but also evaluates the world and represents it the way one wants it to be. Moral judgments are the core of ethical analysis.

d) CONCLUSION

Managers should be comfortable with scientific methods. Gathering data, analyzing data, corroborating data, and arriving at a conclusion are standard managerial practices. A manager should be more sure of himself or herself when making a provable factual statement.

Managers, however, may not be so comfortable with resolving moral issues. While managers certainly recognize the necessity of confronting moral issues and making moral determinations, a manager may find it difficult to analyze ethically and to justify a moral decision. Most managers simply are not trained to conduct an ethical analysis and to argue about morality in a reasonable "scientific" manner.

2. Ethics v. the Social Sciences

The social sciences, sociology and anthropology, for example, are similar to ethics. Anthropologists and sociologists study the various positions individuals, groups, and societies take, and have taken, on various questions, including value judgments and moral beliefs. Social scientists attempt to develop accurate descriptions and explanations for people's views. Their purpose, however, is primarily descriptive. Social scientists do not seek to determine whether or not particular views, especially moral ones, are correct or incorrect. A sociologist, for example, determines whether a certain society practices bribery and whether the society's members believe it is right or wrong. He or she would not raise the issue as to whether bribery is in fact right or wrong. The moral philosopher, however, is concerned with, and does seek to ascertain, the rightness or wrongness of bribery.

The purpose of ethics goes beyond merely reporting and classifying the various views that people have, and have had, as to what is good and bad. Ethics attempts to ascertain what the true good really is. The moral philosopher's challenge is to provide some ethical theory to determine as far as possible whether a particular moral judgment is correct. Ethics does not treat moral and value judgments neutrally, as the social sciences do; it attempts to determine if they are right.

3. Ethics v. Law

A) DEFINITION OF LAW

Law is the set of public, universal commands that are capable of being complied with, generally accepted, and enforced by sanctions. Law describes the ways in which people are required to act in their relationships with others in an organized society. One purpose of the law is to keep people's ambitions, self-interest, and greed especially in a capitalistic society, in check and in moderation.

Positive law is the law of a people's own making; it is the law laid down by legislative bodies, courts, and other governmental organs. Whenever any mention of "law" is made, the term customarily refers only to positive law, unless clearly stipulated otherwise. This is so because law also may mean "natural" law. Consequently, there are two theories of ethics that claim that morality depends on law: positive law and a natural law theory.

B) CHARACTERISTICS OF LAW

1) Public

Law must be declared publicly. It must be published and made accessible in advance to all so that people can know that they are bound. Trained professionals, however, may be necessary to interpret and explain law.

2) Universal

Law must treat equally those with similar characteristics who are similarly situated.

3) Command

There is an aura of insistency and inevitability to law. It must define what one must do and forbear from doing. The law is not composed of expectations, suggestions, and petitions to act in a certain way. The law requires one to act in a certain way. Most laws, however, are negative; that is, they require one not to act in a certain way.

4) Accessibility, Comprehensibility, and Compliability

Law must be accessible to the people who are to be bound by it. Laws are not legitimate if they neither can be found nor understood by people. Laws, moreover, are not legitimate if they do not clearly specify in advance what actions lie under the domain of those laws.

Law cannot be so incomprehensible that no one can obey it. It also cannot be inconsistent. Legal requirements, for example, that contradict each other cannot be termed "law" because people obviously cannot obey both.

5) Acceptability

Law generally must be obeyed. It cannot be so contrary to dominant public opinion that virtually no one will either obey or enforce the law. Most members of a society must voluntarily obey the law.

6) Sanctions

Law consists of commands enforced by sanctions, political, physical, and economic, that the officials of the state are able to, and disposed to, inflict on those who fail to comply. The essence of law is coercion. The law also relies on persuasion, but ultimately on force.

The purpose of legal sanctions is to motivate compliance. People must be made to understand that they will be compelled to obey the law or suffer some loss. If law is not enforced, or enforced so rarely that people forget about it, the law degenerates into a mere trap for the unwary or unlucky.

As ethics is based predominantly on rationality, and excludes force, ethics relies on persuasion to "enforce" moral rules. The characteristic "sanctions" in a moral system encompass blame, loss of esteem, and disassociation, as well as first-person reactions such as guilt, self-reproach, and remorse.

c) SUMMARY

Many business practices, for example, bribery, can be cast as either legal or moral questions, or both. Managers probably are more comfortable with such questions posed as legal issues, since managers have familiarity with, experience with, and access to the law, the legal system, and lawyers. The problem, of course, is how and when the manager decides whether it is best to formulate a question as a legal issue and turn it over to the legal department to decide or to formulate it as a moral issue and turn it over to the ethics department, perhaps, to decide.

D. Methodology

1. Introduction and Overview

How does the moral person determine the truth or error of a given judgment and thereby acquire knowledge of what morality and justice are? He or she uses reason. Reason is the property which all people are endowed. It is instrument by which people can fashion a better life. Reason places the emphasis on objectivity over passion, impartiality over prejudice, and intellect over revelation.

There are two parts to reason: an inquiry into what things one knows with certainty; and a determination of propositions which one should accept as true in practice, although they have only probability, and not certainty in their favor.

The degree of assent one should give to any proposition depends on the grounds of probability in its favor. One must not entertain any proposition with greater assurance than the proofs it is built upon will warrant.

One also must realize that there are limitations to reason. One must often act upon probabilities that fall short of certainty. Thus, the rational person will hold "opinions"; that is, particular doctrines perhaps offered as "truth," but with some measure of diffidence. He or she will avoid dogmatism and will display forbearance. Truth, of course, is difficult to ascertain, and reason does not yield absolute certainty. Yet one should not scorn reason; it is the best one can expect in this life.

There are certain requirements for a valid inquiry into objective truth. The inquiry must be a disinterested search. It must be based upon impersonal observations and inferences and free from temperamental and local biases (or as much as possible for human beings). The inquiry must be intellectually honest. It must not place limits on the pursuit of truth. It must examine all preconceptions. It neither can assume in advance that certain beliefs are true or false, nor proceed on the assumption that one already knows the conclusions to be reached. The inquiry must avoid rationalizations; that is, by pretending (or convincing or deceiving oneself) to judge by purely theoretical and neutral standards and to objectively and logically follow a line of argument; when one in fact is twisting the analysis to lead to an already-arrived-at result.

One, finally, cannot devise superficially rational justifications for an action and then conveniently forget these same reasons when it is in one's interest to so forget. What if one denies the possibility of finding ultimate truths, yet still attempts to prove something by something else? All arguments either will be circular or an endless chain hanging from nothing. Thus, nothing can be, or will be, proved. There are, however, certain tests to determine the truth. There is the Self-Evident (or Obviousness) Test. This main test of truth is based on the obviousness or indubitability of a judgment. There are some judgments that are so obviously true that they cannot be doubted. These judgments must be accepted as true (as well as those judgments that are obvious logical steps connected with those judgments whose truth is indubitable). The Self-Evident Test is the foundation upon which all knowledge is based; it stems principally from the thinking of French philosopher, Descartes.

There are two additional tests of a judgment's truthfulness. There is the Coherence or Consistency Theory, which holds that a test of a judgment's truth is consistency between the judgment and other relevant judgments. A true judgment is one that is consistent with, or inferable from, a body of knowledge, or implied by a body of knowledge. The Pragmatic (or Satisfactory Working) Test holds that proof of a judgment's truth occurs when the judgment works satisfactorily in experience. A true judgment, therefore, is one that is verified practically.

2. Deductive Reasoning

In order to ascertain objective truth, one must concern oneself with method. Method involves theory, logic, and practice and entails two principal types of reasoning: deductive and inductive. Deductive reasoning involves reasoning from general principles or definitions. One starts with a clearly defined general principle which is, or is deemed to be, self-evident. One takes the general principle and applies it to a particular set of facts. One then reasons to draw a conclusion. One thereby can make successive approximations to the truth. Each new stage can be warranted as true given the validity of the premises and prior steps from which it is derived. It is possible, therefore, to discover truths about the world by first noting what is self-evident and then using deductive logic.

It is important to note that the ultimate deductive conclusions, although not necessarily self-evident, are derived from clear steps of reasoning from acceptable and uncontroversial first principles or definitions. The deductive method, moreover, not only enables one to ascertain the truth, but also enables one to demonstrate it persuasively to others.

3. Inductive Reasoning

Inductive reasoning starts with careful observation of particular facts. One collects data through experience and interprets this data by the study of likenesses and differences among things, codifying the materials rationally. One then moves, by using reason, from the numerous bits of data to conclusions that will explain the data collected. The conclusions serve as a basis for general principles. One, finally, renders the general principles into a consistent and unified whole. It therefore becomes possible to discover the "laws" of the world by using particular examples to point to some general principle.

4. Joint Methodological Approach to Ethics

Both the deductive and inductive approaches are necessary to the development of a realistic, orderly, "scientific" ethics. Deductive ethical reasoning starts with abstract ethical theories from which are derived general ethical principles. When these ethical principles are applied to specific cases, one can deduce answers to specific moral questions. These answers form the basis of concrete moral rules. As one moves down from the ethical hierarchy of theories, principles, and rules, and as one moves from theory to practice, the answers to moral issues and the resulting moral rules become more specific and concrete.

The deductive method does allow for general ethical principles and also provides a conceptual framework for the resolution of moral problems. It is, however, too little supported by experience; it does not create a practical scheme; and it is incapable of providing determinate answers to specific moral problems. The solution is to test and prove general principles inductively by examining their various applications. The inductive method does provide a frame of reference from which moral reasoning begins; it does organize a person's moral thinking; it points a person's thought in a particular direction; serves to narrow the field of morally relevant factors; and serves to extract general ethical principles from particular moral judgments.

Yet, one's frame of reference may be tainted by emotions or social conditioning; the technical empirical bias therein too easily is detached from the human context. The solution requires inductive moral conclusions to be measured against external, invariable, ethical standards; if they "pass," then they can be called upon as a means to the solution of different moral problems.

In order to relate factual information to a moral rule and arrive at a moral determination, one must accept as valid a general ethical principle. A moral rule or standard is needed if there is to be a logical connection between the factual information and the moral decision based on these facts. Without an ethical principle, and the resulting moral rule, the factual information, even if accurate, relevant, and complete, would have no logical relationship to the moral determination.

5. The Justification Problem with Ethical Reasoning

Moral judgments may be justified internally by moral rules, and the rules justified by ethical principles within a particular moral philosophy. Yet, this justification process cannot continue indefinitely. At some point, one will reach the highest, most general, most fundamental, and most theoretical justifying level that is required for the validity of all other principles, rules, and judgments. This level cannot be justified by any further internal appeal. If disagreement still exists when the final moral philosophical level is attained, one must proceed outside this particular moral philosophy for further justification.

How does one justify an entire system of moral philosophy, ethical principles, and moral rules? When differing moral philosophies result in conflicting moral judgments, which system is the true and correct one to apply? Some external justification is necessary to ground an entire system of moral philosophic thought and reasoning, including the ethical theory, principles, and rules that are a part of the system. The problem, of course, is where to find the external theory, principle, standard, or rule to justify rationally an entire system of moral philosophy.

The validity of any moral judgment can be tested and measured only by another standard independently formed but bearing on the same point. If the first judgment is corroborated by the standard, it is considered valid. The standard, of course, will demand verification and so on. No final test of correctness can be attained until one exhausts all justifying levels from which a given judgment can be measured. The validity of a single moral judgment, therefore, depends upon its place within a system and hierarchy of judgments.

The validity of a system, moreover, can be proven rationally by its internal coherence; that is, the fact that a system is constructed of components—judgments, rules, standards, principles, and theories—that do not conflict, that sustain and necessitate one another, and that exhibit a moral order as a coherent whole.

6. Summary

The goal is to develop a coherent, rational, moral whole. To ascertain this objective truth, one must first concern oneself with methods. By adherence to a reasoned methodological approach, one will acquire habits of carefulness, accuracy, and truthfulness. One will be able to distinguish the sound from the unsound in ethical reasoning. One will be able to make and systematize moral arguments based on connected and coherent rules and principles.

Theoretical studies and a sustained methodological approach will lead to knowledge. Yet knowledge unapplied is mere academic theorizing. Knowledge cannot be divorced from its use, experience, and results. One's conceptions must be tested by reference to experience.

Reasoning can lead people not only to accept new beliefs, rules, standards, and goals, but also to reject some antecedent ones. The object is to provide such a convincing, reasoned argument in support of certain beliefs that people actually will change their behavior to conform to these prescriptions. The ultimate goal is to inspire a way of life.

E. Socrates and the Socratic Method

Socrates' philosophy focused attention on the problems of human life as opposed to the speculations about the nature of the physical world that had been prevalent in Greek philosophy. Socrates stressed the importance of comprehending what it means to be a human being, how one should live in the world, and for what purpose.

In making the change from natural to moral philosophy, Socrates confronted a great deal of confusion in the moral thought of his time, particularly the wide variety of general terms used that purported to express moral notions. Socrates' main contribution to philosophy was to "bring it down from the skies"; that is, to demand precise, workable definitions, and to enunciate a procedure for formulating such definitions.

1. Socrates versus the Sophists

Socrates believed it was extremely harmful for people to use continually a wide variety of very general terms, especially terms intending to describe moral ideas. Even more dangerous were the Sophists, who taught an extreme personal relativism. Socrates deplored the Sophists' declaration that moral terms, such as "justice," had no basis in reality and that whatever any person thought was just was "just" for him or her. Yet, if one really needed a definition of "justice" the Sophists could supply one: "Justice is the will of the stronger." The lack of any fixed meaning, the inability of people to provide proper explanations, the individualistic, expedient decision-making, and the Sophists' emphasis on rhetoric and persuasion engendered relativism, skepticism, and a great deal of confusion, particularly in the meanings attached to moral terms.

Perhaps the Sophists were right and the terms had no meaning; but if so, then people should not use them. Yet, if the terms do have permanent, objective meaning, then the people who do use them ought to be able to say what they mean. It is not only wrong but also quite unhelpful to discuss whether a person's conduct was just or unjust, moral or immoral, or good or bad unless there is some agreement as to what justice, morality, and goodness are. If there is no agreement, people are using the same words to mean different things. They then will be talking at cross purposes and their discussions will make no progress, either intellectually or morally. Only confusion, skepticism, chaos, and perhaps even conflict will ensue.

The Sophists maintained that knowledge was impossible; they viewed life as a contest in which one must be prepared to win. Socrates held that knowledge was attainable; he viewed life as a positive, common search for knowledge, but one that could begin only if the confusing, misleading, and dangerous tendencies were eliminated, and people understood the right way to achieve the goal. The Sophistic outlook was for Socrates not only intellectually incorrect but also morally harmful. He would make it his life work to combat such "Sophistry." He would seek the clear meanings and shape them into definitions, principles, and rules, always for a moral purpose; and life would be better for knowing and acting by these definitions. "Goodness is real; and reality is good," declared Socrates; and "money comes from being virtuous," he said.

An example of the Sophist's contrary advice that "virtue comes from having money" could be the case of John D. Rockefeller, who had a very bad reputation during the Gilded Age as a monopolist and "robber baron," until a public relations person told him that civic and charitable donations could help salvage his damaged image. Similarly, Andrew Carnegie was known as one of the greatest philanthropists in the U.S., because he was involved early on in his career in very socially responsible activities, especially funding libraries. The interesting, and paradoxical, point about Carnegie is that he apparently enjoyed giving away his money, and being regarded as a benefactor to society, so much that he engaged in even more ruthless, monopolistic, illegal, and unethical business actions, such as industrial violence, bribery, price-fixing, and tax fraud, so as to make more money so he would have more wealth to distribute and thus burnish his reputation as a benefactor to society. He thus did "bad" to do "good." So, the question emerges: Did the Carnegie "means" justify the "ends"?

2. The Socratic Method

Socrates realized that many people have strong opinions on moral issues; but he also recognized the serious problem caused by the fact that most people are capable neither of adequately justifying their opinions nor of defining their essential terms. For Socrates, morality must be subject to a rigorous scientific method that would reveal ultimate knowledge and universal truth.

Yet before this scientific philosophical inquiry can commence, one must question one's own beliefs. Socrates consistently maintained that he knew nothing. The only way in which he was wiser than others was that he was conscious of his own ignorance, while other people were not.

An essential aspect of the Socratic Method was to convince people that although they think they know something, in fact they do not. The conviction of ignorance is the necessary first step to the acquisition of knowledge; because no one is going to seek knowledge on any subject if one is under the delusion that one already possess it.

Socrates did not think knowledge was unobtainable, and he thought the search for knowledge is of the utmost importance. Socrates is remembered, however, not primarily for any philosophical positions, but for the primacy he accorded reason in philosophical reflection and for a method of philosophical analysis that bears his name.

How is one to go about acquiring this knowledge, for example, of what justice and morality are? Not by playing the role of an advocate, seeking to persuade others of the correctness of one's opinions, but rather by questioning people and examining the ways in which they use words, such as "just" and "unjust," and in the process progressing from particular instances to universal definitions.

The Socratic Method is a means of obtaining knowledge in three stages: questions and answers, inductive argument, and general definitions. Socrates asks a general question, for example, "What is justice?" The answer provided by the respondent will be an instance where justice was or was not present. Socrates then proceeds to refute each instance by offering a counterexample designed to show that the respondent's answer was too narrow or broad, uninformed, or wrong. Once the answer is negated, a new, more precise answer must be given to cover this instance.

The next step is to collect the instances where the parties can agree that the word under consideration, "justice," for example, can be applied. The collected instances, of "just" actions, for example, are examined to discover in them some common quality or essence by virtue of which they have that name. This common quality, or group thereof, constitutes their nature as "just" acts. A general definition of justice can be abstracted from the shared characteristics that belong to each of the examined just acts individually.

By means of questions and answers and inductive reasoning, one's mind is "led on" from the observation of individual instances, assembled and examined collectively, to grasp a general characteristic shared by all members of a class, and finally to comprehend a common, general definition. Learning, therefore, is the bringing into full consciousness the knowledge that a person already possesses but has been unable to formulate or use.

To arrive at a general meaning and to express it in a definition is to make explicit the standards by which one previously had been unconsciously or imperfectly acting. To define a term is to express one's understanding not only of what it is but also of what it is not. Definition is the remedy for confusion, relativism, and skepticism. One's life will be for the better by one's acting pursuant to known, explicit, and reasoned standards.

3. Virtue as Knowledge

Socrates' solution to the intellectual and moral skepticism of the times was to embark on a reasoned, common search for knowledge. He equated virtue with knowledge. To know the good is to do good; and to do good is to do well, since said Socrates, "money comes from being virtuous." It was self-evident to Socrates that if people could be brought to see what was right, they automatically would choose the right.

No one does wrong willingly, maintained Socrates. If virtue is knowledge, then vice is merely due to a lack of knowledge. If one does do a wrong act, one does it with the misperception that it would result in some good or benefit. Wrongdoing is due only to ignorance.

Only knowledge, therefore, is necessary to make people virtuous. By knowing the good, no one voluntarily will choose the bad. What is essential is to educate people how to find out what the right is and then to encourage them to take the time and trouble to determine what is truly good. Right action automatically will follow the knowledge of what is right.

4. Problems with Socrates

Even assuming one can obtain true knowledge of the good, there is no guarantee that one will act on it and thereby do what is right. There are many irrational forces assaulting people that combat reason, such as emotions and instincts. One may recognize the right way to act, but be unwilling or unable to do so because of a superseding desire or a weakness of will.

Although part of Socrates' "mission" was to convince people of their ignorance, he was markedly different from the Sophists by holding that knowledge was possible. Once people cleared their heads of misleading notions, and once they understood the proper method to attain the goal, he was ready to embark on a common search for true knowledge. For underlying Socrates' emphasis on methodology, procedure, and reasoning is the conviction that knowledge exists, that goodness is real, and that reality is good.

F. Descartes: Cartesian Doubt and Method

The French philosopher, Descartes (1596–1650), also insisted on beginning philosophy anew. His procedure to achieve this goal is his famous "method of doubt." In order to have a firm foundation for philosophizing, one must resolve oneself to doubt everything. Accept nothing as true unless one clearly, distinctly, and without any doubt recognizes it as true. The objective is to reach down by way of doubt to what can be demonstrated with certainty. Taking this process as far as it would go, Descartes reached a point where there remained something he could not doubt. What remained beyond all doubt, even as to the existence of his body, was the fact that he was doubting, that is, thinking. The unmistakable truth thus appeared as: "I think, therefore I am." From this truth, Descartes found his first principle of philosophy as well as the means to explore, create, and rebuild himself and the world.

To remake oneself and the world, Descartes advised to divide each problem or difficulty under examination into as many parts as possible. Next, commence the analysis by focusing on the parts or objects that are simplest and easiest to understand; and then rise by degrees to an understanding of the most complex. One, finally, must ensure that the analysis is so complete, thorough, and general as to be certain that nothing was omitted.

Descartes' method of critical doubt is of great philosophic importance, not only in counteracting skepticism, but also for the positive results it can achieve.

G. Ethics as Religion

A religious ethics theory defines morality in terms of God's will. What is morally right is commanded by God; what is morally wrong is forbidden by God. Moral standards, therefore, are the set of laws or commands sanctioned by God. What ultimately makes an action right or wrong is its being commanded or forbidden by God. Religion once had, and still does in some spheres, the authority to regulate people's affairs, including their business activities, in accordance with their spiritual welfare.

1. Problems with Ethics as Religion

Atheists obviously would not accept a religious-based standard for ethics. Questions about religious ethics are interesting and useful only if one believes in God; if not, any important moral issues must involve human beings.

A serious problem, even for the believer, is how to establish "the" convincing truth. How can one claim to have a conduit to a divine being so that one can be an authoritative spokesperson for revealed truth and a definitive interpreter of scripture? A religious theory of ethics is certainly a triumph of faith. It takes the world on trust, but diminishes human thought and endeavor. Why should the faith of any being, even God, in and of itself make an act right? Are God's commands to be regarded as arbitrary because God could have given different commands? If good is "good" or honesty is "right" because God commands it, then God could have commanded the opposite. There is, then, for God, no difference between right and wrong. Thus, it is no longer an accurate and significant statement to say that God is good; all one can say is that God is God and likes himself or herself the way he or she is, which seems rather trivial.

A theologian would defend a religious ethics standard by declaring that God is good and that God desires worship and obedience since He or She is morally perfect. God's decrees, moreover, are not arbitrary because they are inspired by God's goodness. God's will constitutes whatever moral qualities there are to an act.

Does God, however, command what is good and right because it is good and right, or is an act good and right because God commands it? The problem with the theologian's defense is that it implies a standard of goodness independent of God. That is, the defense makes sense only if one understands the concept of moral perfection before one relates it to God. There then must be some notion of goodness antecedent to God's decrees that has led God to make these decrees rather than any others. Socrates asserted that God wills an action because it is right. The standard of right and wrong, therefore, logically is independent of God. Goodness and rightness exist prior to God's commands, and the goodness and rightness in and of themselves are the reasons for God's commands. Yet, if goodness is good, and God merely recognizes this fact, the logical conclusion is that morality does not depend on God, but rather on ethics.

Ethics is an autonomous discipline, depending solely on reason that can be studied, discussed, and applied without any reference to religious beliefs and without any reliance on religious supports. The moral determinations that prevail are the ones with the best reasons on their side.

2. Summary

Modern ethical efforts to moralize business are radically different from those of religion. Moral philosophers derive their authority from neither revelation nor godly commandments; rather, ethical appeals are based on rational argumentation. Moral philosophers attempt to answer ethically moral questions that theologians may have answered religiously.

H. Ethics as Conscience and Intuition

Ethics as conscience and intuition is a notion radically dissimilar from any "scientific" version of ethics. The content of ethical principles and the answer to moral questions are determined not by the application of reason and rational argumentation, but through the operation of one's conscience and intuition.

According to this ethical interpretation, people possess inborn, instinctive knowledge of morality and are able to apprehend moral truths merely by consulting their moral sense. One's conscience and intuition are unfailing, trustworthy, and self-vindicating guides to good and bad conduct. Consequently, one need only follow one's conscience and intuition, as opposed to one's reason, in order to be right. Moral truths, moreover, not only instantly are discerned, but also are evident for reasons that cannot, and need not, be explained further. Yet reasons may be given for an action, but they are "merely" the after-the-fact rationales offered to support a "heart-felt" determination.

1. Problems with Conscience and Intuition as Ethics

Intuitionists can err by taking for intuited moral truth mere subjective feelings as to value. One is skeptical of an ethics in which no reasons are provided to support one's conscience-motivated and intuited beliefs. Appeals to conscience and intuition alone are notoriously untrustworthy. One's conscience and intuition may turn out to be mere impulse or whim. One's intuited moral "truth" may turn out to be the mistaken product of prejudice or bad habits. Ethics as conscience and intuition emerges as a theory that can legitimize any type of behavior, including the most basic conduct, by means of a "conscience was my guide" rationalization.

Presuming people to have a conscience, how can one's conscience tell one to do what appears to be a highly questionable action? Such a scenario may not be surprising if one considers that one's conscience has been altered since adolescence, often unconsciously, by many factors, circumstances, and outside forces. Yet, can one say that one possesses a special faculty that sends clear and correct moral signals from this conscience? People who do claim to receive such infallible moral messages often disagree about their meaning, and the nature of this moral sense has never been sufficiently explained. These claims are simply contrary to most people's experience and render ethics as conscience and intuition an implausible and untenable doctrine.

The theory seems to amount to nothing more than the expression of strongly held subjective beliefs. Since consciences vary greatly, and since one person's intuition appears as good as the next, ethics becomes merely a matter of individual preference. A wide diversity of moral opinions results, as people intuit different, and at times contradictory, "true" moral conclusions.

The theory obviously lacks a single objective standard by which the divergent promptings of conscience can be evaluated as correct or incorrect; there is no standard to test the validity of moral judgments; there are no criteria to expose a bad conscience or flawed intuition. Ethics as conscience and intuition, therefore, is useless to resolve moral uncertainty, which is an area of disagreement where resolution is most needed.

The capacity to defend rationally one's moral beliefs is an important intellectual capability and has the significant advantage of laying open sources of confusion and error. Ethics as conscience and intuition, however, means a complete cessation to ethical reasoning and an abandonment of critical moral thinking. The theory discards reason and rational argumentation and justification; conscience and intuition cannot be countered; no justification is called for beyond the assertion of one's intuited moral truth.

Even assuming a good, conscientious person possesses some instinctive truth, it is hardly teachable and transmissible because it is not reasoned truth stemming from and connected to prior knowledge and lucid principles and rules. One's moral instinct, moreover, may fail at a critical moment. There is no guaranty that it will respond dependably to each new moral dilemma. Only a well-reasoned, unified, and methodological ethical knowledge, illuminated by ethical principles and moral rules, can aspire to solve all the moral questions arising in life. Such knowledge, principles, and rules are transmissible and teachable and are quite natural subject matters for instruction and elucidation.

Ethics, in addition, frequently is called upon to reply morally to issues that are more comprehensive, complex, and consequential than matters to which one instinctively might respond. When legal, business, and public policy questions arise, an appeal to conscience and intuition ordinarily is not an adequate answer. In private life, however, such an appeal may have a proper place because the solution to a problem may involve the operation of values, such as love and friendship, which are difficult to define, explain, and measure.

The law as an institution, for example, requires public coherence and justification. Insoluble conflicts cannot be countenanced. The law, therefore, needs a recognized and accepted general methodology for resolving any discrepancies and dissension that arise. If anyone properly is contemplating a legal issue, he or she is thinking about the reasons to support a particular conclusion. Perhaps this conclusion is one that the person's intuition initially informed him or her was correct, but surely one would not permit one's intuition or conscience to form wholly the foundation for one's legal position.

In the business environment, how does one know intuitively whether it will be profitable to buy or sell, to increase or decrease output or requirements, to produce a new product line, enter into a new type of business, or make the multifarious management decisions upon which the survival of business depends and the prosperity of business demands. The advanced, complex, extensive, and rapidly changing modern business environment compels the prudent business person to base decisions on objective surveys, professional advice, accurate information, reasoned knowledge, and considered policies, and not mere intuitive impulses or the urgings of conscience.

The critical problem with ethics as conscience and intuition is that the theory explains nothing; what people already know about ethics militates against accepting this theory that says there is no need for reasoned knowledge and thus there certainly is not going to be any ethical explication. Yet even a professed intuitionist invariably deems it necessary to support his or her moral insights with rational arguments. Such a defense, however, ought to not be required and is in fact improper, if one's moral philosophy is ethics as conscience and intuition.

I. Cognitive Moral Development and Ethical Thought Leaders[1]

Until the work of Jean Piaget and Lawrence Kohlberg, the genesis of moral development was understood to be external; that is, social expectations, religious commandments and beliefs, and laws dictated the "morality" of the individual. However, it is with seminal scholarship of Jean Piaget and Lawrence Kohlberg that the notion of individual cognitive moral development, in addition to environmental influences, was understood as the basis for moral decision-making. Accordingly, the Cognitive Moral Development theory has become a central concept in the field of moral psychology as well as philosophical ethics. Further, Piaget and Kohlberg, as the "parents" of cognitive moral development, support the belief in "dynamic consistency" that holds a person will behave consistently in accordance with a set of morals that are innate.

Jean Piaget (1896–1980). One of the earliest researchers in the area of moral reasoning was 20th century philosopher Jean Piaget. Through his research comparing moral judgments of younger children to older children, he found that as a child matures, he or she progresses from a pre-moral to an autonomous morality stage. Piaget and his colleagues used two methods to investigate moral development. They observed children playing games such as marbles, and they interviewed children about situations involving moral issues such as lying, obedience, and responsibility.

Piaget found that as the boys aged, their understanding of rules changed according to a pattern. He noted that young children tend to conceptualize morality in terms of obedience to adults; older children tend to conceptualize morality in terms of cooperation with peers. Because Piaget found that many children display aspects of both orientations, he developed the idea that moral development proceeds in stages.

Lawrence Kohlberg (1927–1987). In his 1958 doctoral dissertation, Kohlberg replaced Piaget's scenarios with a set of nine hypothetical moral dilemmas. In his best-known dilemma, a husband named Heinz is faced with the predicament whether or not to steal an overpriced drug to save his dying wife. Kohlberg presented this dilemma to a sample of 84 boys, asking them what they thought the characters should do, and then he asked deeper questions to determine the basis of their decisions. His primary interest was not their particular moral choices; rather, his goal was to understand the motives of their choices—the "why" behind their decision.

Kohlberg spent a decade gathering empirical data to support dynamic consistency, and concluded there was a relationship between the moral reasoning stage and the performance of moral actions. Specifically, there is a difference between how one thinks and how one acts. Kohlberg followed a sample of 58 of the original interviewed boys, re-interviewing them every few years for more than twenty years. This long-term study became the foundation for his stage-based theory of moral development.

Kohlberg and Cognitive Moral Development. Kohlberg expanded upon Piaget's work to encompass the moral reasoning capabilities of young adults. Although Kohlberg did not link his work to sequential phases in a process of ethical decision-making, he claimed to have elucidated a universal structure as a measure of ethical judgment. Kohlberg maintained that people move through a linear sequence of age-related stages of moral reasoning linked to their cognitive development.

---

[1]Contributed by Dr. William Freeman, Nova Southeastern University.

Table 1—*Kohlberg's Stages of Cognitive Moral Development* (Kohlberg, 1969)

Stage	Ethical orientation	Definition
Level 1: Preconventional Level		
1	Will I be caught? *The punishment and obedience orientation*	Right is blind obedience to rules and authority, avoiding punishment, and not doing harm.
2	What will I get out of it? *The instrumental relativist orientation*	Right is serving one's own or others' needs and making fair deals in terms of concrete exchange.
Level 2: Conventional Level		
3	Be a good person. *The "good boy-nice girl" orientation*	Right is playing a good (nice) role, being concerned about other people and their feelings, keeping loyal and trust with partners, and being motivated to follow rules and expectations.
4	Laws promote societal welfare. *The "law and order" orientation*	Right is doing one's duty in society, upholding the social order and the welfare of the society or group.
Level 3: Post Conventional Level		
5	Societal standards through consensus apply. *The social-contract legalistic orientation*	Right is upholding the basic rights, values and legal contracts of a society, even when they conflict with the concrete rules and laws of a group.
6	Ethical principles chosen regardless of society. *The universal ethical principle orientation*	Guidance by universal ethical principles which all humanity should follow.

Kohlberg's model is based on three levels of morality, each subdivided into two stages for a total of six stages of moral reasoning. The construct is based on "justice" as the foundation of morality. The stages are as follows:

Kohlberg's theory of moral development hypothesized that individuals move sequentially from stage to stage in a unidirectional progress from lower to higher levels of morality. Kohlberg's theory assumes the moral philosophy position of Kant, in particular likening stage six reasoning to Kant's Categorical Imperative, specifically, the universal moral law principle, which will be examined in Chapter 8.

Kohlberg developed the Moral Judgment Interview (MJI) as a device to assess an individual's cognitive moral development. In his original instrument, the test-taker was presented with three moral dilemmas. Each situation dealt with a value conflict that tested the participant's moral reasoning. Respondents were persuaded to discuss their responses and to provide an explanation of what he or she believed was the ethical action of choice. The goal of the MJI was to determine the reasoning behind the respondent's ethical choice.

James Rest (1941–1999). Kohlberg's work was followed by that of James Rest, who concurred with the majority of Kohlberg's theory. However, unlike Kohlberg, Rest purported that individuals could use a combination of a variety of moral reasoning capabilities simultaneously. Rest took exception to the major theories of moral development including the cognitive-development, the social learning, the psychoanalytical, or social psychology's approach. Rest believed that each of these theories was faulty because of their limited focus on some particular aspects of moral thinking; and they consequently failed to develop a more holistic composite of morality. In response, he developed a four-part model of the major component processes involved in making moral decisions.

Rest and his colleagues at the University of Minnesota proposed a four-component composite paradigm of ethical decision-making. Rest held that moral behavior is the manifestation of four intercognitive-affective processes. Distinctive cognitions and affects are involved in each of the processes. They are as follows:

Component One: To interpret the situation in terms of how one's actions affect the welfare of others. This facet involves empathizing with the other parties involved in any situation and weighing the consequences of actions.

Component Two: To determine what action would best meet a particular moral ideal; that is, what ought to be done. This component involves two schools of thought. The first is that social norms govern how a moral course of action is to be defined. The second tradition is the cognitive-development approach. Here, the focus is on the rationale for establishing cooperative agreements and how each of the participants in cooperation are reciprocating and mutually benefiting.

Component Three: To decide what one actually intends to do by selecting among competing values. This facet involves the process of choosing what action to pursue and recognizing that each action represents potentially competing motives.

Component Four: To execute and implement what one intends to do. This facet involves persisting along a course of action in spite of obstacles.

Unlike Kohlberg, Rest's component structure is not a stair-step, linear, decision-making model. While Kohlberg asserted that individuals proceed through his Cognitive Moral Development model in one direction, Rest held that each factor had an affect on other factors, creating a complicated web of cognitive decision-making. James Rest termed the ability to think in a principled manner, "fairness judgment."

The Defining Issues Test (DIT-1 and DIT-2)

From Kohlberg's six stages of moral judgment, Rest developed the Defining Issues Test (DIT) in 1974. Originally published in *Developmental Psychology,* the DIT measured the level of one's moral development and the reasons behind an individual's moral decisions. One of the differences between Kohlberg's research and that of the DIT can be found in the data collection methodology. Kohlberg used a qualitative method to collect his research; a painstaking process often taking hours of interview time for each test-taker. Rest developed a quantitative method to analyze moral reasoning and to discover a person's level of moral maturity based on the Kohlberg scale. While both Kohlberg and Rest employed the ethical dilemma methodology comprised of stories of individuals facing moral challenges, Rest's quantitative test is a self-administered pen-and-pencil test that can be completed in approximately 25–35 minutes.

The DIT presents a series of scenarios and offers the test-taker with solutions based on different rationales. Even though two individuals may arrive at the same response, their reasoning may reflect substantial differences in moral development and levels of critical thinking. These scenarios and responses represent deep-seated, underpinnings of social thought, instead of the fine descriptions of specific concepts and ideas. Reasons for the decision are scored according to Kohlberg's stages of moral development.

Table 2—*Average P Score for Selected Groups* (White, 2002)

Group	Average P score
Moral philosophers and theologians	65.2
Seminarians in Protestant seminary	59.8
Advanced law students	52.2
Practicing medical doctors	49.5
Staff nurses	46.4
Graduate business students	42.8
Average college students	42.3
Average adults in general	40.0
Average senior high school students	31.8
Adults with senior high school education	28.2
Prison inmates	23.5
Average junior high school students	21.9
Delinquent 16-year old boys	18.9

Respondents rate and rank arguments (12 for each problem) that they consider important in coming to a decision about what they would do. The arguments reflect the conceptually distinct reasoning strategies that people use to justify their actions. The scores reflect the number of times the test-taker prefers each strategy. The most widely used score, the "*P*" index (where "*P*" is for "post-conventional" thinking), describes the number of times a respondent selects arguments that correspond to moral ideals (i.e., the Kantian Categorical Imperative). The test does not draw conclusions about what specific Kohlberg stage a subject falls into, but uses the "*P*" score that places the test-taker along a moral reasoning continuum. The "*P*" score measures the percent of time that people use universal principles in their decision-making. A "*P*" score of 40 means the highest stage is used about 40% of the time, with lower stages being used the remaining 60%. In this way, the DIT is a test that provides a non-stage-based index of development.

The DIT has been used extensively in more than 1,200 studies, in over 40 countries. Given the DIT's breadth of use with thousands of subjects, a profile of select groups has been captured.

In 1999, the original DIT was updated and revised to the DIT-2. The changes of the DIT-2 include updated dilemmas, a shorter test, and clearer instructions. In its 32-year history, DIT research has reinforced Kohlberg's key belief that moral judgments are cognitive and developmental. The relationship of Kohlberg and Rest to the field of philosophical ethics is very important since at the apex of the Kohlberg moral cognition or moral maturity scale is the person, as determined by Rest's DIT, who makes moral decisions pursuant to self-selected and self-imposed universal and objective ethical principles.

J. Summary

If one views morality as not to be intuited, but to be rationally ascertained, then one must determine what moral standards to adopt. The moral conclusions reached will reflect one's ethical reasoning and also may encompass any moral conscience or intuition. Moral beliefs, if urged by conscience and sensed by intuition, may provide a starting point for the application of a principled ethical theory. One's conscience, for example, could present a person with a number of proscriptions against unconscionable behavior. One would then reflect on these insights in a critical ethical manner and apply a principled ethical theory to insure that one's intuited moral beliefs are really right.

Discussion Questions

1. How did this chapter help you in defining ethics?
2. What institutions do you see as needing the principles of ethics most?
3. How would you develop a university level ethics 101 course?
4. Do you think that ethics should be a requirement course for all high school students to graduate in America?
5. What connection do you see in ethics and morality?
6. How would you incorporate the chapter material into an ethics course? Be specific.
7. What was the major theme that you learned from your assigned chapter, and how can you incorporate that theme into your personal life?
8. What aspects of the concept of ethics had the most impact on you and what you learned in this course so far?
9. What can we do individually to promote ethical principles and analysis in the United States? What about globally?
10. How will you use what you learned about ethics in your future jobs?
11. How does religion relate to ethics and how does ethics relate to religion?

CHAPTER 2

Plato: The Doctrine of the Forms, Organizational Ethics, and the Just Person

A. The Doctrine of the Forms

1. Introduction

Plato formulated one of his principal ethical theories, the Doctrine of the Forms, in direct response to two related tendencies of his times. One was an intellectual skepticism that denied the possibility of true knowledge and the existence of any ultimate eternal reality; the other was the ethical relativism and subjectivism of the Sophists, who denied the existence of any permanent, objective, and universal moral truths.

Plato maintained in the Doctrine of the Forms that reality did exist, that the objects of reality, including knowledge and goodness, could be defined, and that they are called Forms. Plato unequivocally affirmed that the Form of Goodness was an aspect of reality itself; that it provided an absolute standard of morality existing outside of human beings, and that morality was not changeable by human choice or convention.

2. The Forms

There is a real world, declared Plato, beyond the imperfect, changeable world of surface phenomena and particulars perceived by one's senses. This true world is the world of the Forms. The Forms are perfect, permanent, unchanging, and absolutely true entities. They are not mere concepts of thought; they are concrete and real and exist outside of and independently of people's minds, yet they can be conceived of by means of thinking and reasoning.

The world that one sees, senses, and experiences is not real but rather a copy of the real world. It is a copy because it owes its presence to the pressure of the Forms on matter, which creates an impression of the real world by the stamp of a perfect Form as matter. This visible world is one of many imperfections, mistakes, and mutations. It is malformed because it is impossible to impress a Form perfectly on matter because matter is imperfect and to some extent distorts the Form.

The functions of the Forms are to establish the objective, universal qualities and criteria that define and evaluate things and concepts, to provide an absolute standard that one can use in making particular decisions, and to afford a perfect purpose and paragon toward which one can evolve.

Whenever a number of particular things or natural species have a common name, such as chair, tree, or horse, they possess common qualities shared by the entire class, and they also possess a common Form. One recognizes individual chairs, trees, and horses as single entities, but one also is cognizant of a concept that enables one to define, use, and assess the terms "chair," "tree," and "horse." This awareness exists because in the real world of the Forms, there is an absolutely perfect chair, tree, and horse of which all chairs, trees, and horses are imperfect copies. The same analogy, in addition, exists for human beings. There is a Form of person, of whom actual people are imperfect and unreal copies. The analogy, finally, holds for concepts, such as equality. There is a Form of Equality, which is equality itself, which is identified with absolute equality, and which is distinct from any particular equals in the visible world. When one sees things as equal, they are not perfectly equal but only imperfectly so. One can see them as equal, even in an imperfect sense, because of the standard supplied by the Form of Equality.

3. The Form of the Good

Plato's most significant explanation of the Doctrine of the Forms regards the ethical Form of the Good. The Forms exist in a hierarchical pyramidal structure, from the many least universal to the few most universal, from the most concrete to the most abstract, and from the Forms of inanimate physical things to the Form of the Good, the highest Form at the apex of the pyramid.

The Form of the Good is the final expression of the Forms and the absolute source of goodness and morality. It is the source and explanation of the other Forms; it alone gives intelligibility, truth, and goodness to the other Forms. The Form of the Good is the end, fulfillment, and purpose for which all things exist.

Plato compares the Form of the Good to the sun. The light of the sun makes the things of the world visible, and the sun is the source of life, growth, and value.

Since the Form of the Good is eternal, unchanging, absolute, and universal, it serves as an external, objective, real standard by which actions, persons, ideas, and institutions are to be judged. By relying on the Form of the Good, one can seek a definition of morality because of the presence of a common ethical principle.

Yet how is the Form of the Good revealed? Plato argues that the Forms, including the Form of the Good, are knowable with absolute certainty. By means of mental activity, thought, and reason, one moves toward knowledge of the Forms. One can identify a range and variety of forms—from artifacts, such as beds and chairs, to lowly things, such as apples and dogs, to relations such as similarity and equality, and ultimately to values, such as beauty and goodness. One can analyze the forms, see their relationship to one another, comprehend their meaning, establish their truth, and organize them into a single structural order ascending to the Form of the Good.

One also can use one's insight and intuition in realizing the Forms. The fact, for example, that one can perceive imperfections presupposes a knowledge of perfection. If knowledge of perfection is not attained by reason or experience, yet one is simply reminded of it by example, then one must possess some instinctual knowledge.

The true moral philosopher exhibits a certain indifference to ordinary affairs. He or she, for example, is interested in the one true Form of the chair, tree, and horse, and not merely in the many chairs, trees, and horses found in the mundane sensible world. The true philosopher subdues worldly desires, sets free his or her mind, rises above the world of sensory experience, and attains by intellectual vision an awareness of the Forms. The true philosopher's ascent is made possible by a love of the good and the true, which enables the philosopher to reach the highest reality and ultimate truth, the Form of the Good.

The task of a moral person is to strive to secure knowledge of the Form of the Good. As one becomes more familiar with the Form of the Good, one will be impelled to pursue and promote morality. One will seek to perform actions, to create relationships, and to set up organizations that participate to the fullest extent humanly possible in the Form of the Good.

4. Problems with Plato's Theory of the Forms

Plato's theory certainly is an intellectualist doctrine. The object is to train and work one's mind to reach the real world of the Forms. The theory, perhaps, relies too heavily on pure contemplation, which may degenerate into mere daydreaming. There is an assertion that the world of sense experience, including the body, is a harmful, corrupt, and distorting medium which distracts the philosopher from the pursuit of the truth. There is also an implicit rejection of empirical knowledge and an aversion to scientific observation and experimentation as methods for the attainment of truth.

Leisure, of course, is necessary for the contemplation of the Forms. Acquiring knowledge and truth, therefore, will be difficult for those who have to work for a living. Only those with independent means, or who are relieved by the state from the anxieties as to their subsistence, can sustain the demanding, perplexing, and continual mental activity essential to contemplate the Forms.

B. Organizational Ethics: Justice and the State

1. Introduction

Plato's *Republic* is an attempt to define justice. Plato believed that if one wanted to obtain a view of individual justice and morality, it is preferable to examine it first at the organizational level of the state, the state being comparable to an individual displayed large.

2. The Good State

A) INTRODUCTION

The good state consists of three parts or classes, each performing a vital function on behalf of the organizational totality. The three classes are the rulers or guardians, the military or auxiliaries, and the producers.

B) THE RULERS

The outstanding characteristic of the rulers is their intellectual ability, which corresponds to reason in an individual human being. They are knowledgeable, wise, and specially trained in philosophy as well as the science and art of ruling. They are nourished and protected by the other classes in order to pursue the truth. They are capable of knowing the Forms.

The rulers' function is to govern the state, guided by the insights of philosophic reason. They plan and direct policy; regulate trade, commerce, and industry; and they always are careful to prevent any excessive individual wealth or poverty. They themselves are trained by ascetic discipline to restrain private ambitions and desires. They will find their happiness in the governance and appreciation of a perfectly ordered good state.

The rulers' authority is not to be questioned by the other classes. Since the rulers are trained and disciplined and since they have knowledge of the Forms, especially the Form of the Good, they understand what is right, will do it without question, and will rule justly.

C) THE AUXILIARIES

The auxiliaries' or military's outstanding characteristics are courage, ardour, and fierceness, which correspond to emotions in a human being.

Their functions are to assist and supplement the guardians. They are responsible for the defense of the state. They are drawn from people who strive for success by assertive and bold actions. The auxiliaries, however, are under the direction and control of the rulers, who channel their natural emotions and aggressiveness, so that instead of erupting into acts of lawlessness, the auxiliaries serve to uphold the integrity and stability of the state.

D) THE PRODUCERS

The producers are the most numerous class. They are engaged in trade, commerce, industry, agriculture, and crafts. Their outstanding characteristics are desire and acquisitiveness, which correspond to the appetite element in human beings.

Their function is to produce and to provide for the economic and material needs of the state. They are drawn from people who enjoy the fulfillment of the senses, who live for getting and spending money, and who take pleasure in acquiring possessions. The producers are the only class permitted to hold private, although limited, wealth. It is important to underscore, however, that this class does not rule. Plato seeks to avoid what he perceived as one of the worst evils in political life, the material greed of politicians. Plato's objectives, therefore, are to divorce political from economic power and to obtain a class of rulers whose sole ambition is to govern well.

E) ONE'S POSITION IN A CLASS

Each person has certain talents and abilities for which he or she is best fitted by nature to perform. In a good and well organized state, its members will be placed in a class suited to their talents. This placement will be determined largely by one's heredity and environment.

There is, however, the possibility of movement between classes. Accordingly, machinery must be provided whereby gifted persons can move up to the ruling class.

3. The Just State as the Harmonious State

The just state is based on all three classes discharging the work to which nature and aptitude best adapted them. No class interferes with the others; all cooperate. Each person accepts his or her proper task and keeps to his or her own function. If one is doing one's assigned job to the best of one's ability, one will be happy and develop to the fullest extent.

Such an organization produces a highly harmonious, coordinated, and efficient entity. Every part is in place, fulfilling its appropriate function, and doing what it does best. The result is the avoidance of civil strife, the production of civil harmony, and the creation of the best possible state and society.

Plato's emphasis, of course, is on the good of the whole. Life in the organization requires the concession of some part of the individual's autonomy to the common good. The organization survives and prospers in its competition with other groups because of its unity and power, which are based on the ability of its members to cooperate for the common ends. Harmony is the objective of the just state, and it is the goal that any state and society must seek and achieve if it would have life.

4. The Creation of the Just State

How does such a just state come about? Essentially, it needs a good governing class. To be a good ruler and govern well, one must attain wisdom and gain knowledge of the Form of the Good.

How do the rulers obtain such knowledge? The rulers must undergo a long, rigorous education and training. They are subject to the strictest intellectual, moral, and physical discipline. Only after such a test will the rulers be fit to rule. The rulers also are impelled by a sense of duty to develop the just state. They certainly will be obligated to do more than philosophize all day and contemplate the Forms.

The ruling class will view political power as a necessary burden, shouldered for the good of the community, and not as a tempting opportunity of self-aggrandizement. The ruling class will not be the most materially fortunate class, but, because of its enlightenment, the most happy.

5. Problems with Plato's Organizational Ethics

Plato's organizational ideal evidences a distrust for democracy. The many are regarded as lacking the knowledge, intelligence, and discipline needed for governing. They are unstable, unpredictable, and easily manipulated, and they care only for materials things. The presumption is that a definable section of the citizenry will be wiser and better in theory and practice than the body politic as a whole.

Consequently, the state is governed by an elite group. This elite rules with practically unchecked power. Plato's doctrine, therefore, inclines too strongly to oligarchic authoritarianism.

Who is this elite? The implication is that only a very few people possess the necessary intelligence and discipline to come to know the truth and perform selflessly the governing duty. The difficulties, of course, are how to find these superior people and how to turn the government over to them and then to trust that their rule, even if a despotism, will be a benevolent one. Plato's conception of the just state is a repudiation of individualism. The individual is treated as a mere part or instrumentality who fulfills his or her appointed place in the overall order. There is a negation of individual rights. Plato denies to the mass of people the right to deliberate and to choose their rulers. The supreme values are public duty, efficiency, and harmony, not individual rights.

C. The Just Person

1. Introduction

Plato used his conception of the just state to determine what a just person is. There are three parts to human nature, said Plato, which are analogous to the three parts of the state; and there is a merit attached to each part. There is a rational element, the ability to think and deliberate, whose merit is knowledge and wisdom. There is an emotive element, embodying emotion, spirit, ambition, and assertiveness, whose merit is courage and righteous anger. There is an appetitive element, the natural desire for physical satisfactions and material welfare, whose merit is impulse, instinct, and acquisitiveness.

These three qualities are found in all people, but in varying degrees. Some people are the essence of knowledge and reason. They seek knowledge and truth and not goods, power, or conquest. They are satisfied with contemplation and understanding, as opposed to victory in the business world or battlefield. If there is too much emphasis on ideas and meditation, however, these people risk the "intellectual" label. Other people are emotional and assertive rather than thoughtful or acquisitive. They pride themselves on power rather than contemplation or possessions. They stress the striving, the achieving, and the ultimate victory. If they possess too much in the way of feeling, however, they risk becoming fanatics. Some people, finally, are acquisitive and restlessly absorbed in material pursuits. They emphasize the "getting and spending" and as a consequence dominate commerce and industry. If their appetites are too excessive, however, they risk being consumed by insatiable desires.

2. The Unjust Person

Identifying individual justice and morality with equilibrium and balance is a central tenet to Plato's ethical teaching. Injustice and immorality are a kind of disease, characterized by instability, disharmony, and conflict.

An imbalanced and psychically unhealthy person is one whose emotion and appetites are beyond the control of reason. Such a person is victimized by all-powerful emotions and insatiable desires that reason cannot control. Consequently, the lack of inner harmony disintegrates one's personality, engendering failure, unhappiness, and immorality.

3. The Just Person

A just, good, moral, and healthy person is one in whom all three parts of human nature are working together in proper harmony, order, and balance. Each part is fit in place, each makes a cooperative contribution to behavior, and there is a proper subordination of the parts to the whole.

Individual justice and morality consist of knowing and maintaining the balance between one's rational and irrational elements. In the proper hierarchy, reason commands the highest position, then the emotive element, and then the lowest element, the appetitive element.

The proper function of the appetitive element is to sustain the nourishment of the body. The body must be satisfied and remain healthy and strong. The emotive element drives a person to activity and achievement. The spirit gives one the courage to achieve one's objectives in action. The rational element commands, controls, and directs one's emotions and appetites.

There is a harmony of all parts to the whole. Each part has a place appropriate to itself in the totality of things. One's desires, activated by emotions, are guided by knowledge. If there is a conflict between reason and desires, for example, the function of the spirited element is to side with reason.

As a consequence of such wholeness and unity, one is mentally healthy. One's appetites and emotions are under the control of reason, and one is organized for the best possible method of living. One is a successful person because harmony and unity translate into strong, effective, individual action, and ultimate success. One, in addition, is happy because balance and harmony produce inner peace. Since one is living in the best way, one cannot fail to be happy. One, finally, is just and moral since this inner harmony cannot fail to express itself outwardly in the performance of just and moral actions.

4. Problems with Plato's Ethics

Plato's ethical doctrines describe ethics in an organizational, individual, and internal sense, but how is this organizational and individual morality related to ethics in the more ordinary sense, that is, ethics concerned primarily with the activities of a person or organization in relation to others?

What is the exact nature of the moral obligations one must assume to others? What is the stringency of these obligations when they seem to conflict with one's own or one's organization's inner needs or nature? Plato, unfortunately, has very little to say about this important aspect of morality.

Not all immoral persons, moreover, are of the type Plato contemplates. A moderate immoral person, for example, is one whose reason restrains vice today in the interest of greater vice in the future. Even assuming that total dishonesty is inconsistent with mental health, happiness, and success, what about measured deceit and other moderate vices? They may not be so at all!

5. Summary

According to Plato, the ultimate good in human life is not asceticism, pleasure, material possessions, success, or power. The good, rather, is a certain form, an ordered management, and a right relationship among parts.

Each part in its right place, properly discharging its function, brings about harmony, organic unity, and the purposes of the whole. The harmony of parts and their direction to their proper end equals justice and morality, in the individual as well as the organization.

D. Plato: Corporate Applications

Plato's conception of the just state and just person has relevance in the modern corporate context. The corporation is a powerful economic and social organization that dominates people's lives and serves as a community. The corporation, moreover, is regarded by the law as an artificial "person."

The traditional model of the corporation is that of the "rational actor." The structure is one of formal relationships designed to achieve economic objectives with maximum efficiency. A fundamental corporate reality is the hierarchy of authority, identified in the organizational chart, which represents the various official positions and lines of authority. Formal bureaucratic systems of rules and procedures link the positions and activities of individual members of the corporation so as to achieve corporate objectives.

At the apex of the corporate entity stands its governing and policy making body—the Board of Directors, the CEO, and their staffs. The Board makes general policy and issues general commands, which then are explicated and implemented by corporate officers and middle management until these Board determinations reach the operating level as detailed work instructions. The determinations of the Board are designed to achieve the economic goals of productivity and profit. The Board must master complex coordination and control problems. It must ensure that corporate employees are provided with promised economic supports and suitable working conditions.

The middle part of the corporation consists of its officers and middle managers, who administer corporate policy, direct the component below them, and in turn are directed by those above them in ascending formal lines of authority.

The operating level of the corporation is composed of its employees and their immediate supervisors, who provide the basic labor to produce the goods and services that are the essential outputs of the corporation. The conventional role of the employee is not to effectuate change; rather, it is one of obedience, loyalty, and diligence in pursuing corporate goals.

Plato's discussion of the just state and just person anticipated the modern notions of entrepreneurship and corporateness, as well as the concomitant policy making, "scientific" management, and production elements. There do exist corporate parallels to the just state and the just person. For a just, good, moral, "healthy," and successful corporation to exist, all three corporate components must perform their proper function and make their contribution to the whole without interfering, conflicting, or usurping the role of the other classes. Once all corporate parts are attuned in harmony and balance in a hierarchical entity, the corporation will be a whole community working together as an organic unity to attain the common good.

The corporation, therefore, based on Plato's ethical doctrines, is more than a legal and economic entity; it is also a moral entity. If a state or individual can be conceived as a moral association, the corporate entity and artificial "person" can also be approached from an ethical point of view.

E. Summary

This chapter focused on many topics, mainly concentrating on organizational ethics and the just person. It began with Plato's principle of ethical theories, the Doctrine of the

Forms, which was formed in direct response to an intellectual skepticism that denied the possibility of true knowledge and the existence of any ultimate eternal reality; as well as to the ethical relativism and subjectivism of the Sophists, who denied the existence of any permanent, objective, and universal moral truths. Plato maintained in the Doctrine of the Forms that reality did exist, that the objects of reality, including knowledge and goodness, could be defined, and that they are called Forms. Plato unequivocally affirmed that the Form of Goodness was an aspect of reality itself, that it provided an absolute standard of morality existing outside of human beings, and that morality was not changeable by human choice or convention. The chapter ended with a discussion of organizational ethics, justice, and the state, as well as the application of "the just person" principle to the corporate environment.

Discussion Questions

1. Do all three of Plato's components of a corporation have to work without interfering with the others to succeed?
2. Can a ruling class be trusted to be moral and ethical without measures being put in place to guard against them?
3. Would Plato be writing "self-help" books today?
4. Should there be a class that we rely on to be philosophers?
5. Would we be better off if we had a class that was trained to lead?
6. Are corporation's moral entities?
7. Does environment make some more just than others? Is it easier to be just if you are fulfilled?
8. How do we balance our rational and irrational elements?
9. Should a corporation only strive for economic efficiency? Does it have a greater obligation?
10. Is there an unchanging ethic we all should strive to, or is it ever changing?
11. Can anyone really ever know the Forms?
12. Within Plato's ruler class, what is one of the worst evils in political (ruler) life?
13. What should a ruler be striving for?
14. How do the three classes within a "Good State" relate to a "just" person?
15. What is the main driving force to the creation of a "Good State"?
16. Relate the driving force from the previous question to a failure within American history.
17. Do you feel it is possible to setup a "Good State" within today's government or corporate environment and, if so, please give examples?
18. According to Plato, the ultimate good in human life is not asceticism, pleasure, material possessions, success, or power. Do you agree with Plato's statement? Please explain.

19. Within Plato's Doctrine of the Forms, are we living in a perfect world? Please explain.

20. Today we see cultural differences throughout the world. Do you feel the "American" culture could be classified as a "Good State"?

21. Analyzing your own life, what things do you feel you need in order to bring your life into a perfect harmony, to be a "just" person?

CHAPTER 3

Aristotle: The Doctrine of the Mean and Virtue Ethics

A. The Good

1. Introduction

Aristotle firmly believes that there can be knowledge of what is good for a human being. This good can not only be known but also rationally determined. This good is intrinsically desirable.

Aristotle's approach is to define the good and then to ascertain what actions ought to be performed to attain the good. The good, said Aristotle, is what a person by nature seeks. One seeks happiness. Therefore, happiness is the good and the ultimate goal for a person.

2. Happiness

The aim of everything in the universe is to realize itself to the fullest. Each thing is different from all others, with distinct attributes, abilities, and talents. Happiness is realizing these abilities and talents to the fullest. Self-realization, therefore, is happiness. Self-realization is achieved by living at one's best and at the highest level. It is achieved by fulfilling the best aspect of one's nature and by engaging in activity that most completely expresses and actualizes one's nature.

3. Realization

The distinguishing feature of human beings is reason; human beings alone possess this characteristic. The vegetative element is found in everything living; the appetitive element exists in all animals; but rationality is specific to human beings.

The peculiar excellence of human beings is their power of intellect. The development of this faculty has enabled human beings to surpass and rule over all other forms of life.

The highest good for a person, the supreme condition of happiness, therefore, is the complete realization of reason. The goal is a life devoted to contemplation, thought, and the exercise of one's mental faculties. The intellectual virtues, therefore, are ends, possessing intrinsic value; whereas the practical virtues are means, having intrinsic value and bringing only a secondary kind of happiness. The object, of course, is to use the practical virtues to enhance the rational element in one's nature.

The highest manifestation of reason, according to Aristotle, is the study and pursuit of philosophy. What is one philosophizing about? One is thinking, exercising the intellectual virtues, and using one's reason to discover the supreme truths of the universe.

4. Problems with Aristotle's Conception of the Good

Aristotle's conception of the good approaches that of an ideal. In fact, such a "virtuous" life will be extremely difficult for a person. Only a handful of people possess the intellectual capability, the time, and the economic sufficiency to engage in the sustained contemplation essential to the achievement of happiness.

Very few people are that clearly self-sufficient. One may be able to exist, that is, to survive, in isolation and solitariness, but not live, and certainly not live well. To satisfy one's material and social needs, people need other people, and some sort of community thus is required. A community immediately introduces ethics, since there is a need for objective moral rules to govern people's relations with one another.

In an Aristotelian community, however, the vast majority of people are merely means to sustain the philosophizing few. Can one regard such a community as morally fair? Is it morally satisfactory to confine the "best" things to the few and require the rest to be content with second best?

Reason, moreover, is only part of human beings. There are also feelings, desires, and appetites. Is not the good life one wherein all these characteristics are realized in perfect harmony with reason ruling? Will not reason, if only contemplation without the help of emotion and appetite, fail to lead to any practical activity?

Should a person be practical or withdraw from society and live for thought? One can live for reason, but reason has two aspects: a theoretical part which seeks to ascertain the truth, and a practical side that seeks to direct action in accordance with what is true and right.

Aristotle certainly believes in activity, but primarily intellectual activity that does not necessarily express itself in external action.

5. Summary

Although Aristotle does present contemplation, reason, and the cultivation of philosophy as the highest form of human activity and as a goal toward which one must aspire, he is realist enough to realize that the practical necessities of community life demand reference to a "practical" principle of ethics. This practical, rational, ethical principle is the Doctrine of the Mean.

B. The Doctrine of the Mean

1. Introduction

Aristotle's practical, rational, ethical principle is the Doctrine of the Mean. It serves not only as the means to determine good from bad, but also as a guide to excellence, virtue, and the good life.

The idea that morality and virtue are a mean is anything but a novelty, even for Aristotle, who essentially took over the Greek notion of moderation. The Doctrine of the Mean clearly reflects the traditional ancient Greek way of thinking, with its emphasis on measure, proportion, opposites, and balance, as well as a common sense view that in both feelings and actions, one can distinguish between the opposites of excess and deficiency.

2. The Doctrine of the Mean

The Doctrine of the Mean holds that the virtuous or moral choice is a rationally determined mean between two extremes of deficiency and excess, each of which is a vice. As a consequence, all faults and wrongs consist in a deficiency or excess, which if present in a moderate degree will be a virtue.

A morally virtuous person is one who chooses the mean between the two extremes, which constitute the corresponding vices. Moral virtue lies in cultivating moderation and aiming at the mean.

3. The Triads

This "Mean" principle can be applied to a great range of human qualities, characteristics, and activities. As demonstrated in Table 3.1, pursuant to the "Mean" doctrine, all qualities of character are arranged in triads; the first and last categories will be extremes (vices); and the middle category will be means (virtues).

4. Ascertaining the Mean

One determines the mean by making a choice that lies in the mean or middle point between the two extremes. The choice is neither subjective nor personal, but rational and objective. The choice is not arithmetical, that is, reducible to strict mathematical calculations, but rather prudentially calculable. Morality and virtue, in essence, are determined by the use of reason and disciplined objective judgment.

The choice, however, is based upon a consideration of all the facts in a particular situation. The mean, therefore, is not the same for all persons and all circumstances; it is relative to persons confronted with widely differing conditions.

5. Attaining the Mean

Attaining the mean presupposes both the right state of character and the right intellect.

A right state of character is a virtuous state of character. A virtuous person is not one who happens to do certain isolated good acts. Rather, good acts must flow naturally from this source and must come spontaneously from a person. This virtuous state of character is acquired by self-discipline, training, and learning how to choose the mean. The repeated performance of right acts and the avoiding of the extremes will cause one to form habits of virtuous conduct.

One also seeks and follows the teaching, advice, and examples of a person of "practical wisdom." These are gifted, skillful, and experienced people who have the capability of finding the mean when facing complex situations. They teach how to develop the right character, and their opinions should be followed.

Aristotle is saying that it is permissible to use opinions in ethics, so long as these are the opinions of people of "practical wisdom." These are the experts with the requisite background, patience, training, and knowledge. The use of opinions, however, is not an endorsement of relativism or subjectivism because Aristotle offers an objective general principle of ethics—the Doctrine of the Mean—and an objective standard—the virtuous person—by which to determine and measure right conduct. Aristotle's "opinions" do not bring Aristotle into the camp of the Sophists, who also said that ethics was based on opinion, and inferred from this that ethics was doomed to utter subjectivity and relativity. For Aristotle, ethics remains as an "objective" science.

6. Problems with the Mean

Some virtues do not seem to fit into Aristotle's scheme. Does the doctrine apply to intellectual contemplation, which is the "best" of all activities? Probably not, as one can maintain that the doctrine is intended only to apply to the practical virtues, not to those of the intellect.

Table 3.1—An Example of the "Mean" Principle

Activity	Vice (Deficiency)	Virtue (Mean)	Vice (Excess)
Facing Death	Rashness (too little fear)	Courage (right amount of fear)	Cowardice (too much fear)
Bodily Function	Abstinence	Temperance	Self-indulgence
Giving Spending Money	Stinginess (miser)	Generosity (good steward)	Extravagance (spendthrift)
Claiming Honors	Humility	Pride	Vanity
Social Relations	Quarrelsomeness	Friendliness	Obsequiousness
Social Relations	Bashfulness	Modesty	Shamelessness
Social Relations	Moroseness	Wit	Buffoonery
Social Relations	Deferential	Respectful	Arrogant
Achieving	Sloth—inactivity	Ambition (strong desire to succeed)	Greed—grasping
Acting	Impulsiveness (too little self-control)	Self-Control	Indecisiveness (too much self-control)
Corporate Social Responsibility	Profits only—no good deeds ("Chainsaw" Al Dunlap)	Profits and prudent good deeds (Target)	Good deeds over profit (Ben & Jerry's)

Does the doctrine apply to truthfulness? Aristotle says the "mean" is between mock modesty and boastfulness, but this applies only to truthfulness about oneself. Perhaps truthfulness is a mean between secrecy and loquacity. Yet what is the mean, that narrow line, between untruthfulness and truthfulness? It is one thing to accept Aristotle's general principle; it is quite another to know what the mean is in specific cases.

7. Summary

As a consequence of the Doctrine of Mean, Aristotle brought ethics "out of the clouds" and anchored it in the fact of everyday life.

For Plato, it is always "the" right thing to do, "the" good to be realized. Any understanding of right or wrong depends upon recognition of the single good, the transcendent substance of the Form of the Good. As a result, ethics is a branch of metaphysical philosophy. Only the true philosopher can know what right conduct is, can know "the" truth. Experience can not teach right or wrong; the facts of experience are not truth itself but only a distorted image of it.

For the Sophists, there is no objective right or good at all. Everything is relative. For Aristotle, however, there is good and right. Yet there is not just one thing, "the" good, and not a single ideal standard appropriate under all circumstances; rather, there is a right relative to a person, that is, good for a person now, contemplating a type of action now, in a particular set of conditions. This right depends upon one's circumstances, which vary from individual to individual and from occasion to occasion.

The aim of ethical study, therefore, is practical, and not metaphysical. The object is not to know virtue, but to become virtuous. The aim is not to know "the" truth, which is unattainable, but to make people and their actions better. Thus, the "right" in ethics and moral conduct equates to the "right" in mathematics and science; that is, that which is correct, fit, and works best to achieve the best results.

The doctrine, however, is not an exact scientific instrument and the mean is not a rigid arithmetical middle; rather, it is a kind of provisional principle, the implications of which can only be made clear by working them out in detail. All that can be done is to give some practical rules, which having been arrived at empirically, probably will work. Yet, the result of inculcating the mean, learning the mean, adhering to the mean, and living the mean is not only good conduct but also personal happiness.

C. Virtue Ethics

1. Virtue as Character

A virtuous person is one who possesses the ability and the disposition to make the right choice between the extremes. Virtue is thus a character trait of a certain type; that is, a fixed disposition or habit to choose what is morally right. A virtuous person is one who is habitually good at choosing the mean to the end of morality and well-being.

Morally good habits are developed by experience, careful nurturing, training, education, and practice. People acquire moral capabilities when they are taught persistently by their teachers, families, and communities to think and behave in morally appropriate ways. The exercise of a virtuous disposition requires judgment. It is little use to have a virtuous character if one is unable to decide when, where, how, and why one should be moral. True moral excellence lies not only in possessing virtue, but also in the astuteness with which the virtue is applied.

2. Ethics of Virtue v. Ethics of Principle

Aristotle's conception of ethics emphasizes the virtuous traits of character that a moral person should possess and cultivate. These character-centered qualities then are exemplified in conduct. Moral conduct is based on the type of person one should aspire to become. The "good" is what a virtuous person does, and is not some defined standard of morality. Moral actions stem from virtuous people who habitually do good and do not need to follow a set of moral rules.

Aristotle conceives of ethics not as the promulgation of principle and rules but rather as the development and cultivation of dispositions and traits of character. He is more interested in moral education and the development of moral character than in ethical argumentation. He expresses ethics primarily in terms of virtue and the virtuous, rather than in terms of what is right or obligatory. His is an ethics of virtue and not of duty, an ethics based on being rather than doing.

Kant and the Utilitarians, however, express ethics in terms of action, or, what the moral person ought to do, and not character, or, the kind of person one ought to be. They focus on the logic and moral argument and offer rational determinations that actions are right or wrong. They develop ethical principles and prescribe moral rules that ought to be followed. Their judgments are duty-entered and their ethics is action-guiding.

3. Problems with Virtue Ethics

If a person possesses a virtuous character, does that mean that his or her acts are automatically morally appropriate? The fact that a virtuous person performs a certain action does not in itself make the action moral. The action may be misguided or unknowing, yet it may be performed with the best of intentions by a virtuous person.

What if the virtuous person acts "out of character"? If one can pick out the virtuous person's acts as good or bad, then one must be using some independent criterion as a moral standard.

Since a theory of virtue ethics does not focus on the quality of actions, how can it be used to determine if an action is right or wrong? Even presuming a person is virtuous, is it certain that such a person's actions will be moral? The virtuous person may act incorrectly, may not know what proper course of action to take, or may fail to act at all. Virtue ethics does not provide any basis for ascertaining the moral quality of an action, except by judging the moral character of the person.

Virtue ethics also fails to establish what moral obligations one owes to others and what moral rights people possess. Morality is not discussed in terms of obligations and rights, but in terms of character. Yet if rights and obligations are excluded from an ethical theory, one certainly could question its adequacy in expressing a moral point of view. Virtue is underscored assuredly, but virtue, dispositions, and traits that are conducive to one's own good. What about the general good? Should not an ethical theory urge conduct that contributes not only to the good of the individual, but also to the society to which the individual belongs?

The emphasis on the virtues that are deemed to characterize a moral person is surely an appropriate component of an ethical theory. A viable ethical theory, however, requires an ethics of virtue and an ethics of principle. They complement each other and are linked in practice. A virtuous person is known through his or her actions; yet for virtues to be meaningful, they must be linked to actions; and principles are needed to judge the morality of actions. An ethics of virtue and an ethics of principle should be not rival types of ethical theories, but complementary aspects of a vibrant and workable ethical doctrine.

D. Summary

Aristotle draws a basic distinction between the powers of reason. There is theoretical reason, deployed in philosophizing, and practical reason, represented by the "mean" principle and manifested in applied thought and action. Aristotle, therefore, presents a choice: Does one do best to retire into philosophic isolation, contemplation, and a life of pure thought, or does one plunge into political life, practical matters, and the world of experience?

This dichotomy exists not only within Aristotle, but also between Aristotle and Plato, and also within Plato! Reason, for Aristotle, is, of course, the characteristic work of human beings and the faculty central to a good and moral life. Aristotle, however, at times appears to emphasize the use of reason in abstract studies. The risk of such contemplation, however, is that it can degenerate into daydreaming. Perhaps Aristotle is saying that one may find happiness in an active, practical, political life, but if one's capacities are not fit for such a life, one should look for happiness in a life of active thought and contemplation.

The attainment of excellence, moral or otherwise, requires an integrated life of thought and action. The best life requires action, but action directed by reason and motivated by philosophic insight. Contemplation will make one aware of the greater ends for humanity; action, if it is to have any value, will be directed to fulfilling the end of human well-being.

A good person is one who habitually acts in conformity to the "mean" principle, but the best possible person is one who makes the time to engage in contemplation and who does so in an excellent fashion, and who uses these insights for good in practical and political affairs. Human excellence, therefore, as well the goal of moral philosophy, is not only knowledge but also practice.

Aristotle, as well as Plato, founded morality on the well-being of the individual. They taught that virtue is not an imposed, external obligation, but the true fulfillment of one's personhood. They worked out a theory whereby the attainment of order, balance, and equilibrium was the ideal and best condition for the individual as well as the state. Most importantly, they laid the foundation for a universal, objective, normative, and prescriptive ethics. The idea of such an ethical order, superior to civil law and social custom, is one of the greatest contributions to moral philosophy.

Discussion Questions

1. Do the means always justify the ends? In virtue ethics, can one's virtuous intentions or disposition justify an unethical action?

2. According to Aristotle's conception of a virtuous life, can anyone ever be truly virtuous without society to provide a standard for which to compare?

3. Can a person be virtuous in one culture, but not another?

4. How does culture determine the triads? Provide an example of a triad that transcends cultures and one that does not.

5. In regards to the Doctrine of the Mean, explain how the mean can be different at different times in one's life? Provide an example.

6. Morally good habits are developed by experience, careful nurturing, training, education, and practice. Describe how the determination of what is morally good can change over time.

7. Aristotle believes that self-realization is achieved by living at one's best and at the highest level. Do you think that Aristotle really intended for anyone to reach this ideal, or is it simply a tool to drive individuals to improve their moral disposition?

8. In order to ascertain the mean, one must consider the situation and environment. Can you think of an example where the different decisions were made based on the situation or environment alone?

9. How can management perpetuate a virtuous character amongst employees?

10. How much can a person's disposition affect his or her ability to make sound moral decisions?

CHAPTER 4

Psychological and Ethical Egoism

A. Psychological Egoism

Psychological egoism is a doctrine based on human psychology that has significant ethical implications. A psychological egoist believes it is necessary to understand the nature and limits of human psychology in order to make an ethical evaluation of a person's behavior. Psychological egoism functions as a descriptive doctrine regarding human nature; as well as asserting a universal thesis that characterizes the motives of all human beings under all circumstances.

Psychological egoism, however, is neither an ethical nor a normative theory. It is a psychological theory of human nature and human emotion that explains how people in fact do act; it does not tell people how to behave or provide a justification for human conduct. A moral philosopher is interested in understanding ethical principles in order to ascertain the rules of right conduct. A psychological egoist is interested in studying and understanding human nature and developing theories of human motivation, regardless of where they lead. For a moral philosopher, it is no defense if one does not do what one morally ought to do because of some countervailing desire.

B. Psychological Egoism versus Ethical Egoism

Ethical egoism is a normative ethical theory that assumes that people have a choice; that is, one is not always psychologically bound to act in one's self-interest. Pursuant to ethical egoism, however, one is morally obligated to promote one's self-interest. One is permitted to promote other's welfare, but only if such an action serves one indirectly or in the long term. Prudence and reason afford one with sufficient egoistic reasons for acting. Ethical egoism, therefore, provides a justification for human conduct.

Psychological egoism, however, provides an explanation for human conduct. It is a theory about how decisions are in fact made, not about how decisions should be made. A psychological egoist assumes that people are naturally egoistic. If psychological egoism is true and people are so constituted that they can only act to advance their own interests, it is redundant and ridiculous to advise what ethical egoism recommends. That is, it is pointless to tell a person that he or she is morally obligated to do an egoistic action, when he or she psychologically cannot avoid doing the action anyway.

C. Typical Formulations of Psychological Egoism

According to psychological egoism, all people always act to promote their own perceived self-interest or to do what pleases them. Ego satisfaction is the final aim of all activity as well as the fundamental motivating force in every individual. People are not capable of being unselfish or altruistic. They cannot act voluntarily against what they believe to be their own interest. Everything a person does is ultimately in some sense an act of self-advancement or self-fulfillment. The overwhelming concern for one's self-interest lies at the heart of any apparent unselfish behavior. All actions, including those done for sup-posed "moral" reasons, are motivated by the pursuit of pleasure or self-interest. One, moreover, cannot avoid the pursuit of self-interest in order to do what may be the theoret-ically "right" thing to do. Acting to advance someone else's interests, promoting the gen-eral welfare, and devoting oneself to the good of society are all contrary to human nature and thus psychological impossibilities.

A psychological egoist cannot acknowledge the existence of an altruistic act in any case. People may appear to perform acts that on the surface seem to be totally disinter-ested, unselfish, and self-sacrificing. If one, however, probes deeply enough beneath the surface, one will find a self-centered motivation. One responds to the needs of others only because one expects, consciously or unconsciously, some reward in return. An apparently altruistic person simply may believe that seemingly unselfish acts will best advance his or her own interests in the short or long term. The true aim of an apparently altruistic act may be to gain the pleasure of knowing, and being known, as someone who helped another, or to avoid the guilt or recrimination one might confront for not having done so. One may pity others because of the possibility of being in the position of those pitied. One simply may want the future help of others, rather than their disapproval and hostil-ity. Ultimately, one is motivated to please oneself and to advance oneself.

Psychological egoism, therefore, presents a serious challenge to moral philosophy. Moral philosophy presumes that people can choose to be moral and to pursue moral and altruistic objectives, even when these conflict with self-interest. Yet if human beings, because of their psychological constitution, always act in their self-interest, there can be no purely moral and altruistic motivation; it is pointless, useless, and absurd even to ask them to act contrary to self-interest since they cannot do otherwise.

D. Hobbes and Psychological Egoism

1. Introduction

A plausible foundation for the doctrine of psychological egoism is attributed to the British philosopher Thomas Hobbes (1588–1679). Although his work is difficult to interpret, a common theme permeating his thought is that all human action is selfishly motivated.

His persistent and explicit references to the selfishness of human beings serve as a theoretical foundation for psychological egoism.

2. Hobbes: Good and Bad and Human Nature

Hobbes built his philosophy on two principal doctrines: a denial of the existence of any absolute, true, universal good and bad; and an extremely pessimistic view of human nature.

Hobbes described human motivation as consisting of mere appetites and aversions. One moves toward an object or one moves away from an object. Whatever the object of one's appetite or aversion, all that can be said is that one is attracted to it or repelled from it. Hobbs, therefore, reduced human motivation to little more than the fact that people do what they want to do.

People are by nature primarily selfish, said Hobbes. Their desires are directed to obtaining pleasure and avoiding pain and to preserving their life and security. Even supposedly unselfish acts are merely aspects of self-interest. Happiness is continual success in obtaining those things that a person desires and avoiding those things that a person dislikes. Any effacement of self-interest is unnatural because it tends to diminish pleasure, increase pain, and make one the victim of others.

The concepts of "good" and "bad," declared Hobbes, merely refer to the objects of appetite and aversion for the individual who uses such "moral" terms. There is nothing absolutely and truly good or bad. Self-interest determines what is good and bad. The content of one's appetites and aversions, on which one usually bases an ethical judgment, is irrelevant. There is no higher good than satisfying one's appetites and avoiding what is contrary to one's desires. Traditional concepts of morality, moreover, may be contrary to human nature and self-interest. "Good" is what one promotes for oneself.

3. Hobbes: State of Nature, the Social Contract, and the State

A) State of Nature

The state of nature is the conditions that existed (or would exist) before there was any state, government, law, or means of preserving the peace. Self-interest definitely would not ensure a peaceable society. People would possess the same selfish motivations and similar powers. Everyone would desire to preserve one's own life and freedom, to promote his or her own interests, and to acquire control over others. People continually would be worried by a fear of others and plagued with the anxiety of suffering harm.

As a result of being in a condition of constant insecurity and fear, people would be full of distrust, enmity, and meanness. They would engage in a never-ending struggle for security and power, which would degenerate into conflict, war, and anarchy. Since the only purpose in life would be to preserve one's life, there could be no industry, property, culture, or any of the advantages of civilization. Life would be, said Hobbes, solitary, poor, nasty, brutish, and short, thus rendering the state of nature a detestable state.

B) The Social Contract

How do people escape from the state of nature? The state, government, and society come about because of fear, a need for order, and a desire for the benefits of civilization.

Reason dictates that peace, preservation, security, and civilization can only and finally be secured by a state and government.

In order to escape the state of nature, people come together and make a contract among themselves; they agree to choose a sovereign who will exercise almost absolute authority over them. The agreement allows this common power to make and enforce laws and thus put an end to the state of nature.

Although the social contract is not thought of as a definite historical event, Hobbes used it to explain why people submit, and should submit, to central authority and limitations on personal freedom.

c) The Sovereign

The sovereign, whether individual, group, or assembly, is the supreme power and the essence of the state and government. When the sovereign is chosen, the government exists and functions according to the sovereign's will and preference. The sovereign lays down and enforces whatever laws it deems necessary to preserve the peace. Whatever rights the people have are those the sovereign may find it expedient to grant. Any property is created by the sovereign, which ultimately controls it.

The sovereign owes no responsibility to its subjects, except to maintain the peace. Once the people contractually agree to give power to the sovereign, there is no right to rebel, unless the sovereign does not do what it was set up to do. That is, so long as it is maintaining peace and security, its subjects should be passive and obliged to be satisfied. The sovereign may be despotic, but the worst despotism is better than the war and anarchy of the state of nature.

4. Summary

Psychology is very important in Hobbes' ethics. He infused ethics with an egoistic psychology according to which people only do what they agree to be in their self-interest. He psychologized ethics as a form of self-interest and reduced morality to egoism as its ultimate basis.

E. Problems with Psychological Egoism

1. Selfless Behavior

Psychological egoism is particularly vulnerable to refutation by counterexample. The doctrine does not equate with everyday actions one actually witnesses involving human conduct. Every day one clearly observes people in fact acting contrary to their self-interest. There are a significant number of actions—routine, dutiful, altruistic, saintly, and heroic—that plausibly cannot be comprehended as motivated solely by selfish desires.

It is natural for a person to feel the demands of duty, just as one feels the demands of particular selfish desires; and to perform an action because one believes the action ought to be done, even if one does not want to do it. One's interests may conflict with the interests of others; both may not be able to be satisfied, yet one may opt for advancing the interests of others regardless of self-interest and without expecting anything is return. One may act impulsively to aid another, without any thought of reward, because helping another is the instinctually right thing to do. People perform saintly and heroic acts where the degree of self-sacrifice is so great that the action can only be understood as a preeminently unselfish one. Human behavior that one actually witnesses, therefore, shows the theory of psychological egoism to be false. People, in addition, frequently praise selfless virtuous actions performed in the very distant past and in remote locales; by no means can this approval be accounted for by the self-interest of the speaker.

People may be self-interested, but their selfish side is tempered by feelings of sympathy, concern for others, and propensities of benevolence. People are charitable. They may derive satisfaction from their charitable acts, but they also may possess a genuine concern for the welfare of others. People can care about others for their own sake and have selfless desires for their happiness.

People, therefore, are not as psychologically egoistic as Hobbes supposed. It is a mistake to assume that people always are motivated by self-interest as the sole end of all human action.

2. Desire v. Selfish Desire

The mere fact that a person acts on a desire does not necessarily mean that a person is acting selfishly. The key fact is what a person desires, one's own good or another's good. If one wants others to be happy and acts on that desire, then the action is not selfish. One must be careful not to assume fallaciously from the fact that all acts are motivated by desires of the self that all acts originate in selfish desires.

To say, moreover, that a person desires satisfaction from performing an action is markedly different from saying that something is solely done for the sake of the satisfaction. The fact that one derives self-satisfaction from performing an unselfish act does not make a person selfish. The unselfish person is precisely the one who derives satisfaction from helping others, whereas the selfish person does not. One must be careful not to confuse the necessity of having some self-motivation with the necessity of having some self-interested motivation.

3. Unconscious Desires

People at times state that their actions are motivated by selfless desires. To cling to the doctrine of psychological egoism in the face of these assertions, the psychological egoist is compelled to cite unconscious or subconscious self-interested motives. Such unconscious motives, of course, are not readily apparent, and they cannot be proven. One can always contend that some unconscious desire motivated a person to do a particular action. Yet, if one is driven to assume the existence of unconscious selfish desires in order to save the doctrine of psychological egoism, one is construing the doctrine as a dogma, rather than a legitimate, empirical theory about human nature that can be proven or unproven. This retreat into the unconscious, therefore, renders psychological egoism vulnerable to criticism, particularly by people who hold other assumptions about human nature.

4. Summary

One must admit that an honest reflection of one's own motivations and careful examination of the motivations of others reveal complex and mixed motivations for the significant actions that an individual undertakes. The question, however, is not whether egoism or self-interest is strong in human nature, but whether an individual can have any selfless desires, concerns, or interest for the welfare of others.

People are interested in the welfare of others; they frequently perform acts for the sake of other people's interests; they desire to do the "right" thing, regardless of personal consequences. To attribute to such selfless actions some unconscious egoistic motives is not a plausible approach. One must be very cautious in positing the existence of unconscious motives, and especially wary in inferring an ethical conclusion from a psychological one.

The most dangerous consequence of psychological egoism, however, is the moral malaise and cynicism that is engendered by a doctrine that grants total dominion and legitimacy to self-interest.

F. Ethical Egoism

Ethical egoism is the ethical theory that holds that a person ought to act to promote the greatest balance of good for himself or herself. Ethical egoism is a normative theory that counsels how one should act. The theory claims that each person is under a moral obligation to pursue exclusively his or her self-interest. An act contrary to one's self-interest is thus an immoral act.

An ethically egoistic person is a discerning evaluator who assesses the "pros" and "cons" of each prospective action and performs the act promising the most personal good. One may, in fact, tell the truth and keep promises, but only to the extent that one reasonably believes that "honesty is the best policy" to promote one's advantage. Similarly, a person associates with others, participates in group activities, undertakes responsibilities, and obeys the laws only because it benefits one to do so. When conformity to law and group standards is no longer an advantage, one contravenes them (presuming one reasonably can avoid punishment). One can even break away from the group and any and all responsibilities.

Ethical egoists agree that people ought to pursue their own good, but they disagree as to the type of good one should be seeking. For example, one can identify the good with money, knowledge, power, self-realization, pleasure, excitement, self-esteem, comfort, or happiness. In business decision-making, of course, the "good" is viewed as money. The self-interest of business is based on monetary profits, Ethical egoism, therefore, emerges as the conventional ethical theory by which business is measured; consequently, the egoistic moral obligation of business is to maximize profits.

G. Limitations on Ethical Egoism

1. Long-Term View

An enlightened, prudent, ethical egoist thinks in terms of what inures to his or her self-interest in the long run. One suppresses any immature, immoderate, spontaneous impulses to do an act that gives one the most immediate short-term pleasure. Rather, by employing foresight, one pursues assiduously one's long-range interests. One is willing to endure present pains or forsake present small gains for the promise of greater future advantages, even if they are rather distant in time.

2. Selfless Selfish Behavior

An ethical egoist is not always an egoistic or selfish person in the everyday sense of the terms. The theory does not mean that the ethical egoist never takes the interests of others into consideration; it does not always sanction narrow-minded and obviously selfish behavior. A person can act consistently with ethical egoism by performing actions that one definitely would not designate as egoistic or selfish. Treating people well, helping others, respecting their rights, and evidencing concern for their welfare, for example, may be in fact the best policies for an ethical egoist to follow in order to promote his or her own self-interest in the long run. One's interest can coincide with the interests of others; assisting others can be an efficacious means to aiding oneself. Ethical egoism does not forbid such actions; on the contrary, it may demand them. Any benefit to others, however, does not make the action "right"; rather, it inures to one's own good.

Business, therefore, is not prevented from performing acts that benefit others. Improvements in working conditions for employees or contributions to the community, for example, very well may earn the ethical egoist's approval because they can improve "bottom-line" performance by decreasing turnover, improving productivity, and enhancing the reputation of a firm. To illustrate, Costco, which provided higher wages and provided better benefits to its workers than its competitors, has more productive workers and less "turnover" problems than its competitors, which offset the higher expense in the long-term, and "Wall Street" is finally beginning to notice the good financial results from Costco's "good" behavior. Another example of egoism involves Texas Instruments, which has developed an online course to help employees cope with caring for their parents. The course teaches the employees how to relax, how to provide care-giving, and how to deal with doctors and other family members. The company is doing this not only because it is concerned with the well-being of its employees, but also because it sees a "potential payoff" in productivity from diminished stress and enhanced "wellness."

H. The Defense of the Doctrine

It often is argued that people, as well as business, ought to act egoistically because to do so will promote the general interest in the long term.

A non-egoistic defense of egoism was advanced by the physician Bernard Mandeville (1670–1773). In the *Fable of the Bees*, Mandeville argued that not only is society founded on the fact that each person seeks his or her self-interest, but also that the public good ultimately is based on selfishness. An overriding concern for self, manifested, for example, by a desire for money, possessions, pleasure, sensual satisfaction, luxury, power, and other such "vices," actually produces employment and livelihoods for many, injects money into the economy, and thus emerges as an effective means to social prosperity. Private vices, according to Mandeville, add up to public benefits, whereas conventional "virtues" are destructive of the social good.

Perhaps the best known defender of ethical egoism is Adam Smith (1723–1790). In the *Theory of Moral Sentiments*, Smith accepted people as they are, noted that the real workaday world ran on motives of self-interest, and concluded that satisfying one's own desires and self-interest is a very laudable principle of action. Such an egoistic motivation, argued Smith, is the basis for society's well-being. For example, there is no denying that

Bill Gates is a very socially responsible person by funding the Bill and Melinda Gates Charitable Foundation with many billions of dollars. Yet it is conceivable that not only the average person but also society as a whole has benefited, and will benefit more, from Gates' profit-seeking, indeed "monopolistic," activities at Microsoft than from all his and his wife's charitable endeavors.

In the *Wealth of Nations*, Smith advanced his famous "invisible hand" theory. If each person is left free to pursue and promote his or her own self-interest in a free market, the general welfare inevitably will be served by an invisible hand, even though the well-being of society is not part of anyone's intent. People will work harder and contribute more to society when they pursue their own self-directed goals. As a consequence of acquisitiveness, competition, and freedom of exchange, a range of goals is achieved: the wants of others are satisfied, productive efficiency increases, public affairs are regulated, prices are lowered, resources are conserved, and society naturally progresses and prospers. Individual ambitions and self-interest are thus "handily" channeled into activities that benefit society as a whole.

People, therefore, are under a moral duty to pursue their own self-interest; they also are morally obligated to place their own interests over the interests of others.

I. Problems with Ethical Egoism

1. Foreseeing and Acting upon the Good

A major problem for a person who subscribes to ethical egoism is ascertaining which course of action, of the many open to a person in any given circumstance, will produce the most personal benefit. Predicting long-term consequences is a difficult undertaking at best. Even when consequences can be discerned, one does not always act on the information. One, for example, may choose a lesser immediate good in preference to a more distant greater good.

2. The Absence of Impartiality

Ethical egoism certainly is not a disinterested point of view. The ethical egoist promotes his or her self-interest over others. Yet why is the egoist so special? What differences exist among the egoist and others that warrant placing the egoist's interests in a priority category? If there are no relevant rational differences, the theory is unacceptably arbitrary.

The ethical egoist, moreover, may not want everyone to act in the manner in which he or she acts. Perhaps for the egoist, the best state of affairs is one where the egoist can break the rules with impunity but others do not. This obviously is not a disinterested point of view; if a moral point of view is to be impartial and unbiased, ethical egoism is not a valid ethical doctrine.

3. The Absence of Logic

Ethical egoism is attacked as being inconsistent internally. If two people, for example, desire to do the same act, but only one can, can the same act be both morally right and morally wrong? If, moreover, an act is in one party's interest, that party ought to do the act, but if that same act is against another party's interest, then the act ought not be done; consequently, two contradictory judgments ensue: the act ought to be done, and the same act ought not to be done.

4. The Non-Egoistic Defense of Egoism

The standard defense of ethical egoism, exemplified by Adam Smith, is that if each person pursues his or her own self-interest, the general welfare will be served. This defense, however, implies a different, non-egoistic criterion for the morality of an action. Promoting the general welfare, bettering society, and overall good consequences are not factors that an egoist supposedly is concerned with; rather, the fact that an action results in advantageous consequences for society as a whole is the key factor in the utilitarian ethical analysis.

The evident problem for ethical egoists, therefore, is that the major defense of their theory is a utilitarian one. The concept of ethical egoism inevitably collapses into utilitarian ethical philosophy.

5. The Presence of Conflict

According to ethical egoism, a person must designate something "good" when it is the object of one's desires, and "bad" when it is the recipient of one's disfavor. These definitions, however, supply no objectivity to "good" and "bad." When people differ in their desires, ethical egoism does not provide any mechanism for settling their differences; whereas one might suppose a satisfactory ethical theory would. How is one to decide among conflicting desires, except perhaps by the strength of those desires? Since ethical egoism reveals no "truth" as to what is right or wrong, one risks being laid open to the harsh creed that "might makes right."

The majority of people are far more interested in their own welfare than in that of others. People in any society, in addition, possess different interests and many of these interests are in direct conflict. It is unlikely that what is in one person's interest or advantage will always coincide with what is in another person's interest or advantage. If everyone is acting egoistically, it appears reasonably certain that many cases of conflict will take place. One person, for example, will covet property, thereby thwarting another's acquiring the property he or she wants; another person craves power over others, thus interfering with the freedom that others demand.

Yet pursuant to ethical egoism, parties in a circumstance of conflict morally ought to pursue their own self-interest ceaselessly, exclusively, and energetically.

Such a situation is not tolerable. Disagreements soon resolve themselves into contests for power. Disputes are decided by emotional appeals, propaganda, force, or, in the ultimate resort, war. Clashing egos produce hatred and violence.

Ethical egoism is a completely unregulated system. If one or more interests begin to prevail, any domination threatens the ability of all others to pursue their self-interest. Although some persons momentarily might advance their interests, no one would have any real security from the aggression of others; even the strongest would succumb to a coalition of the weaker. A continual struggle to emerge victorious could engender a complete breakdown of society.

Ethics is necessary because people's desires do conflict. Yet ethical egoism not only fails to provide a solution to conflict, but also further exacerbates the problem.

6. Problems with the Invisible Hand Theory

For the "invisible hand" to work, each person must be prepared to treat others solely in terms of their contribution to one's own goals. Accordingly, nonaltruistic behavior supposedly causes the "best" overall results. It is only to the extent that individuals are prepared to act with a certain detachment, not to say in a mercenary manner, with respect others that the market as a whole presumably will manifest its munificent proclivities.

Yet would not cooperation better promote the general welfare? In a world of limited resources, would not cooperation make more sense and produce even greater sustained growth? Would not cooperation also treat people with dignity and respect? It seems clear that all economic systems depend on people in society possessing dispositions that reach beyond self-interest.

Any theoretical causal connection between self-interested conduct and overall social good can be maintained only so long as self-interest functions within certain prudential limits. Relentlessly self-interested people, however, will not respect any limits. They will coerce, steal, lie, and break promises as soon as it is in their interest to do so; they will breach contracts, waste resources, engage in monopolies, and hire and fire arbitrarily and capriciously under complete freedom of contract.

Yet unless people possess some assurance that their persons, property, and contracts will be maintained and respected, they have no reason to involve themselves in production and exchange. Without some constraints on the operation of self-interest, society soon collapses into chaos. The theory of absolute free competition, therefore, must be, and has been, modified to impose limitations on conduct.

7. Defining the Individual's Good

Ethical egoism calls for an individual to fulfill his or her desires, but provides no guidance as to the proper content of those desires. Which aspirations count as personal benefits to a person and which do not? What general principle, fundamental rule, or objective criterion enables one to differentiate between personal advantages and other possible aims?

In the business realm, the successful pursuit of profit, while clearly essential to a business entity, alone may not be sufficient to provide the total satisfaction a business manager may desire as a human being. There may be other goals also worth pursuing—goals that are within a manager's power and ability to pursue.

8. Summary

The chief criticism of ethical egoism is that it simply is not acceptable for a supposed ethical doctrine to determine right and wrong wholly in terms of an individual's desires or advantage. Ethical egoism, therefore, makes no real contribution to ethical philosophy since it asserts that a person ought to act on what are regarded as nonmoral considerations.

J. Hedonism

1. Introduction

Hedonism is an egoistic theory that holds that all desire is properly the desire for one's own pleasure. Pleasure is the "good" end to be attained. A good action, therefore, is one that produces a preponderance of pleasure over pain for the individual actor.

Pleasure, that is, one's own pleasure, emerges as the only intrinsic good. A hedonist does not dispute the fact that many things are desirable. He or she denies, however, that there is anything other than pleasure that is intrinsically good. Knowledge and money, for example, have value, but not as ends in themselves, merely as the means to obtaining pleasure. Knowledge and money are only instrumentally good. They are valuable because pursuing them may be a pleasurable activity and securing them may be very satisfying to an individual.

2. Epicurus

Epicurus (342–270 B.C.) is the most prominent proponent of a hedonistic philosophy, as well as the founder of a school of philosophy known as Epicurianism. He made pleasure the only conceivable, and altogether rightful, end of action and life. The aim of his philosophy is to attain that pleasure. Epicurus himself sought a life of tranquility and serenity. His philosophy, however, came to be regarded as meaning something quite different.

3. Pleasure for Epicurus versus "Epicurean" Pleasure

Pleasure for Epicurus includes physical and sensual pleasures. The good life, however, cannot be achieved if one preponderately embraces physical pleasures. A life focused on fulfilling the needs of the body is bound to be unsatisfying. The "price" of gratifying bodily senses often produces long-term pain. Do not of necessity spurn pleasures, counsels Epicurus, but be more selective in choosing pleasures. Avoid coarse indulgence of the senses, master the "low" senses by the "higher" ones, and cultivate the preferred arts as the means to the end of a pleasurable good life. Aesthetic pleasures, intellectual stimulation, knowledge, wisdom, and friendship, for example, are the superior practices to be encouraged and nurtured.

Ironically, the term "epicurianism" has come to embody a way of life against which Epicurus would disapprove strongly. It is commonly and mistakenly identified with a vain, frivolous, excessive, indulgent, and debased delight in food, drink, and sex.

While some "epicureans" view life as an extremely enjoyable, exquisite gourmet feast, this version of Epicurianism is a vulgar rendering of Epicurus' ideas.

4. Epicurean Tranquility

Epicurus is an exceedingly rational ethical egoist; he counsels prudence in the pursuit of pleasure. His advice is to live moderately, engage in the more refined pleasures, regulate one's activities, and maintain oneself in a state of equilibrium. The object is to attain a balanced, tranquil, serene, and happy life.

5. Problems with Epicurianism and Hedonism

Epicurus and his adherents affirm that pleasure and the "good" are the same. When they attempt to explain the aspects of, and means to, this pleasurable good life, it becomes evident that some pleasures are more desirable than others and that other things may be even more desirable than pleasure. The dilemma, of course, is that in order to maintain any sort of differentiation or ranking, the Epicureans are compelled to rely on some standard of goodness other than pleasure in and of itself. One cannot find in Epicurianism any objective basis for classifying pleasures as "higher" or "lower," nor for establishing that what some people deem as pleasurable should be regarded so by others.

Yet individuals obviously do differ in their desires. What is desired by one person may not be desired by another. Desires and pleasures vary from person to person, from time to time, and from circumstances to circumstances.

There does not exist within Epicurianism or any hedonistic theorizing a point of reference to determine the relative desirability of rival desires. Which desires should one pursue to their logical conclusion? Perhaps all, or perhaps, since desires are very inconsistent, the strongest desires will emerge victorious.

The principal problem with hedonism philosophy, therefore, is that it ultimately is exposed as a completely subjective notion. As the good is equated to pleasure, the theory logically and inevitably must conclude that what is deemed good by one person because it gives him or her pleasure is in fact "good."

6. Summary

Despite the relativistic termination to hedonistic philosophy, one does discern in the doctrine, especially in Epicurus' explication, the idea of making the most of one's existence by living a rich, full, and abundant life. A good life is realizable and should be one's goal, Epicurus would emphasize. It would be a "crime" not to seize eagerly the precious, brief gift of life before it passes away, and a life without pleasure and happiness would be a tragic farce.

K. The Sophists

1. Introduction and Background

The word "sophist" originally carried neither negative connotation nor disparaging reference. It merely meant teacher, professor, intellectual, disseminator of ideas, or practitioner of wisdom.

The Sophists emerged with distinction in the latter decades of the fifth century B.C. in Greece, a period marked by substantial political and social transformation. Democracy was politically rising, but the affluence and authority of the old aristocratic families had not yet receded. The ascendance and expansion of democracy afforded many political opportunities, provided one possessed not only intelligence and ambition but also the knowledge and skills to prevail over one's adversaries.

The Sophists traveled from city to city, offering schooling and supplying education to those who could afford to pay. They professed a wide variety of skills and knowledge; those essential to success in law and politics were most in demand.

As the Sophists journeyed throughout Greece and the Mediterranean, they came to know of and report on the many peoples and cultures of the ancient world; they perceived diverse customs, practices, religions, governments, laws, beliefs, and values. The Sophists' own views were far from uniform, but one can sense a predilection toward relativism permeating their thinking. To Socrates, the Sophists conveyed ideas which he believed should be condemned as false and dangerous.

2. The Sophists as Teachers

The Sophists did not establish any particular philosophical school or even hold one set of opinions; rather, they came into prominence as a profession of itinerant teachers. Some were, in fact, well versed in philosophy, others knew science, astronomy, mathematics, music, rhetoric, language, grammar, and memory training.

In fifth century B.C. Greece there were no universities, law schools, colleges, adult education centers, and no public provision for education. There were no professional lawyers. The parties to a lawsuit appeared in person and made their own presentation and argumentation to a panel of judges composed of lay persons chosen by lot. There clearly was a need for professional instruction.

The Sophists were the first professional teachers in Greece. The emphasis in their teaching was to impart practical knowledge and to inculcate practical skills, especially in the areas of law and politics. They taught material that would be useful to their fee-paying students. They concentrated on the knowledge and skills that were essential to advance one's position in society. Rhetoric, for example, was a leading subject for aspiring politicians and potential "lawyers."

The methodologies of the Sophists also varied. Some conducted conventional classes; others gave lectures to large or small groups; others employed discussion groups or seminars; and some held question and answer sessions. They spoke on prepared themes from a written text, invited questions and commentary from the audience, and conducted rhetorical exercises (especially structured to show how the most unpromising position could be maintained).

Many young ambitious adults with the means to pay attended their presentations and were educated in this new "school" of self-awareness, self-satisfaction, and self-realization.

3. Rhetoric

The study of rhetoric was particularly useful in a society where a great deal depended upon the ability to influence public opinion and to advocate a position in the law courts. Persuasive public speaking was, and still is, an essential component to success, advancement, and the attainment of power. Rhetoric, therefore, was one subject that practically all the Sophists taught. They stressed the important lesson of speaking and arguing with equal clarity and cogency on both sides of an issue. The Sophists instructed their students to see both sides to a question, to recognize the virtues and defects of each position, to approve and disapprove with commensurate vigor, and especially to bolster up the weaker side so that it would seem stronger.

Although the Sophists emphasized the art of disputation, they did not restrict their teaching to mere form and style. In showing how to argue for or against any position, the Sophists also treated the substance of what was being disputed, but only to the extent that such substantive knowledge would be efficacious to the art of argumentation.

The Sophists were convinced that people could be persuaded of anything. The emphasis on rhetoric flowed naturally from this cynical sounding and potentially subversive belief. Yet today, one very well might assign to rhetoric the place now occupied by advertising. As the ancient Greeks had the Sophists and "schools" of rhetoric, modern society has its business schools and courses in marketing and advertising.

Although the Sophists were cognizant of ethics and philosophy, their ultimate objective was neither to make the student "good" in the moral sense of the term, nor to assist the student in searching for and attaining the "truth" on any matter. Their aim was to help the student become a good speaker and a good debater and to master all the skills that would make the student successful and dominant in whatever sphere he or she endeavored to enter. The Sophists, viewed in this "sophisticated" light, conceivably can be pictured as the first business consultants, political promoters, and public relations specialists!

4. The Sophists as Relativists

Protagoras (born 500 B.C.), an important figure in the Sophist fellowship, is credited with the saying: "Man is the measure of all things." This statement was interpreted to mean that everything is relative to each individual person; that everything is as it seems to each individual person; and that each person has the right to determine for himself or herself what is good and bad; and that what one considers good, another may consider bad.

Such an interpretation leads one down a relativistic path. Morality is relative to the particular perceiver. There are no absolute values, general principles, fundamental rules, or objective standards as to what is right and wrong. When people differ on moral issues, there are no impersonal criteria to decide whom is right and whom is wrong.

Such relativism engenders a profound mistrust in the possibility of ever attaining absolute knowledge and truth. If there are no rational grounds for knowledge and truth, how can one expect to find any absolute moral values and standards? One consequently becomes skeptical, and skepticism was in fact an attitude shared by the Sophists. If knowledge and truth are only relative to the perceiving subject, then all truth is ephemeral and no one knows anything for certain. Truth, moral or otherwise, is individual and temporary, not universal and eternal. Truth for any person is simply what he or she believes for the moment or what he or she could be convinced of, and the Sophists maintained that it was possible to persuade anyone of anything.

Skepticism led some Sophists to cynicism. If right and wrong, good and bad, and just and unjust are subjective and unreal concepts, they are simply empty words; the Sophists counseled that at times it is prudent and expedient to act as if these notions actually existed. One now can discern the more modern definition of the term "sophist" emerging, with its negative connotations of overly clever but false argumentation and disingenuous reasoning.

Relativism, however, did lead some Sophists to more conventional ethical theories. Ethical relativism, a morality based on custom and convention, with moral rules relative to the group that believed in them, can be traced to Sophist thinking. Legal positivism, a morality based on the laws promulgated by a particular group, with the laws serving as the arbiter as to what to accept and observe, also can be traced to the Sophists.

5. Justice as Power

Thrasymachus, a Sophist described in the first book of Plato's *Republic*, was defiant toward all conventional opinions of justice. He denied that morality and law have anything to do with justice. He admitted that law exists; but what is law, said Thrasymachus, but a set of rules that the ruler (or ruling few or class) imposes on its subjects. Even in a democracy, the law is simply what the majority decides. In every situation, the ruler, whether individual, few, class, or majority, prescribes the law, composes it in its own interest and advantage, and enforces the law with its power.

As a consequence, Thrasymachus claimed that there is no justice except the desires and interests of the stronger. In essence, "might makes right." Power becomes the highest virtue; and there are no impersonal objective standards to which to appeal in the struggle for power. Thrasymachus, therefore, repudiated all accepted views of law, morality, and ethics, as well as obedience to a law made only in the interests of the stronger. Act in one's own interest, if one can, and regardless of the law, advised Thrasymachus. The stronger one is, the surer one is of obtaining what one wants.

What about the people who do act conventionally good and do abide by the law? They are stupid or weak. Mere conformity, in the sense of submissive obedience, exposes defects in intelligence or character. These people cannot or will not see that morality and law do not serve their interest. They thus should violate moral and legal norms when it is advantageous, expedient, and safe to do so. Get what one can, and get what one can get away with; and then worry about one's reputation, since "virtue comes from having money," which is the "ethics" of the Sophist Thrasymachus.

L. Summary

As one can perceive, the Sophists shocked people, especially people for whom philosophy, ethics, morality, and law were a way of life closely tied to religion. To many people, the Sophists seemed to be overly clever and cynical contrivers who made use of specious and disingenuous disputations. To some people, they appeared as utterly immoral; and these perceptions, perhaps, were the origins of the odium that the Sophists incurred and the reasons for the negative connotations of the term "sophistry."

The Sophists, however, did demonstrate intellectual merit. They vigorously pursued their studies, setting aside what was traditionally thought as morally, culturally, and legally edifying. They wanted people to think for themselves and to follow a line of thought wherever it might lead. This thinking, particularly about standards for right and wrong, frequently did lead to skepticism. Yet the Sophists did point out and address fundamental issues in ethics, such as the meaning of "good" conduct and the preference for being good or being strong. They did display an intense honest effort to ascertain whether there is any objective basis for morality. Even though ethics as a field of study properly begins with Socrates, a very important stimulus was provided by the Sophists.

Discussion Questions

1. What is the best theory of operation for corporate America?

2. When should we not operate under the law of self-preservation?

3. Does the fact that a person acts on desire mean he/she is acting selfishly? Explain.

4. What is your philosophy of operation?

5. How can one operate under the philosophy of psychological egoism and remain ethical?

6. How can a business operate under the philosophy of ethical egoism?

7. When should a business ever choose other factors over profits?

8. What are the differences between pleasure and the "good"?

9. How can people be moral and choose to pursue altruistic objectives?

10. How do morality and law relate to justice?

11. What follows from the Sophists' view that moral determinations are neither objectively right nor wrong? Are the Sophists' beliefs as to the subjectivity of morality consistent with the moral experience of most people?

12. Can one be a psychological egoist and be truly altruistic too? Why or why not? Provide business examples.

13. Hobbes appears to indicate that traditional notions of morality and ethics are contrary to one's self-interest? Do you agree with Hobbes? Why or why not? Provide business examples.

14. What constraints are placed on the Doctrine of Ethical Egoism? Do these restraints make this egoistic theory a more acceptable doctrine? Discuss, providing business examples.

15. What is the "conflict" problem inherent in ethical egoism? How can it be resolved? How should it be resolved? Discuss, providing business examples.

16. Are morals, ethics, and justice totally subjective and relativistic concepts as the Sophists argue? Why or why not? Provide business examples.

CHAPTER 5

Machiavelli and the Ethics of Empowerment

A. Background

1. The "Conflict" Problem in Ethical Egoism

Ethical egoism generates conflict when people pursue their own, often clashing, interests, but ethical egoism does not resolve these contests. As a consequence, life deteriorates into a long series of conflicts, with each person struggling to win. What then is the "solution"? Do one's very best to prevail! Consequently, any resolution occurs not by the application of any objective moral rules, but by one person "winning" the struggle.

Actions, therefore, are not good or bad in themselves but only relatively as they augment or diminish one's power. Virtue and power thereby become one.

2. The Sophists

Thrasymachus, in Plato's *Republic*, declares that justice is the interest of the stronger. There are no objective, universal, true standards of good or bad, but merely what the person using these words desires. In a case of conflict, the strongest person's desires predominate. In practice, and whatever the moral truth, the world is driven by a contest for power. One merely needs to remember the Chinese proverb that states "Be not afraid of growing slowly; be afraid only of standing still."

B. Introduction

Niccolo Machiavelli (1469–1527), the Italian political philosopher, set out to discover, from history, contemporary events, and his own experience, how principalities are founded, won, held, and lost. Machiavelli's philosophy is regarded as "scientific" in the sense that it is empirical, pragmatic, and rational. For the first time in political theorizing, Machiavelli attempted to look at his materials from a scientific perspective.

His attention clearly is on the "what is." What he is accused of leaving out is the "what should be," that is, ethics and morality. His focus is on the manner in which people behave and how society is run, not on expounding the good way to behave or how society should be run.

His purposes were to discover how principalities are won, how they are held, and how they are lost; how one becomes a ruler and how a ruler must behave if the ruler wishes to survive and prosper.

Machiavelli's most notable work, *The Prince*, is a disturbing book, both for what it says and for the deliberately provocative way Machiavelli says it. *The Prince*, although pre-figured in the thinking of the Sophists, is rightfully regarded as a post-medieval philo-sophical assault launched against traditional ethics and morality.

C. Machiavelli's Two Questions

In *The Prince*, Machiavelli poses two seminal questions: First, what do people strive for? This aim, whatever it is, is their "good." Second, what acts will produce this good? These acts, whatever they are, are "virtues."

Machiavelli's answer to the first question is "power." Ultimately, the question becomes one of power. Reality is power. Everyone endeavors to obtain, maintain, and expand one's power. This aim, then, is the "good." Machiavelli does not expect the work of founding a principality or any great enterprise to be undertaken from purely unselfish motives; rather, the impetus stems from the desire for power and the success, fame, and glory that power can achieve. To attain any significant end, power of one kind or another is essential, although this evident fact often is concealed by philosophical slogans to the effect that right, good, and justice will prevail.

As to the question, what are the best techniques for securing and maintaining one's power? Machiavelli sets forth and describes the "virtuous" means to the assigned end, regardless of whether the means are considered traditionally good or bad. In order to ascertain these means, it was necessary for Machiavelli to examine human nature.

D. Machiavelli's Conception of Human Nature

Machiavelli's conception of human nature is an important postulate in his theorizing and an essential aspect of his view of public affairs. Machiavelli's major premise is that people are predominantly egoistic and selfish, unscrupulous and treacherous, envious and greedy, fearful and cowardly, passionate and irrational, and, above all, short-sighted, gullible, and stupid. These are the characteristics that one must take into account when founding a principality or attempting any great enterprise.

Machiavelli replaces an optimistic view of human nature with a pessimistic one; human nature is treated, at least for the purpose of public affairs, as "bad." Since people are incapable of governing themselves intelligently, and since their self-seeking drives spawn only disharmony, a strong power is necessary to guide and regulate people and to prevent them from destroying themselves and others.

E. The Traditional Virtues

Observation of the real world in which people live, particularly the world of public affairs, disclosed to Machiavelli so much upheaval, strife, and injustice as to amount to a "moral jungle." A traditionally good virtuous person simply cannot survive, let alone prosper, in a world where most people are not good. Moral standards, therefore, are merely snares for fools. A founder can not succeed, and a ruler cannot endure, if he or she is always traditionally good. The traditional classical virtues, such as good faith, integrity, temperance, forbearance, charity, and even at times prudence, are contrary to self-interest. They are severe hindrances when dealing with those who ignore any constraints on their self-interest.

Machiavelli, consequently, repudiates traditional morality and justice, especially when the conduct of a founder or a ruler is concerned. Machiavelli, in essence, converts the traditional virtues into vices, a "vice" appearing as any behavior that impedes, diminishes, or destroys power. One who pursues the "good" goal of power by moral means in bound to fail.

F. The Machiavellian Virtues

Machiavelli's advice to a founder or ruler, particularly an aspiring one, is to employ the Machiavellian virtues of astute, sharp, cold-blooded calculation of self-interest, readiness to take a risk, and use of whatever means are available to promote the acquisition and maintenance of one's power. One, for example, can use deceit, disguise one's character, and employ hypocrisy. Break promises; do not keep faith when it is against one's interest. Engage in manipulation and propaganda; play upon the passions and stupidity of human beings. Manage others so as to serve one's advantage. Win people over. Persuade them that the one is devoted to their welfare, yet avoid making any real concessions. Above all, appear more virtuous than one's rivals. If all else fails, make oneself feared, even at the risk of being hated (which is nonetheless better than being loved). Force, of course, is "expensive"; so use other means first, but always be prepared to back them up with force and to deal very firmly with those who are not easily deceived or readily manipulated. Only by these "virtues" can the "good" end of power be secured.

G. The Instrumental Nature of Virtue

Pursuant to Machiavellian ethics, a "virtue" is a means to effectuate a given end. No means is rejected if it is necessary to achieve the desired result; any means that diverts or hinders one from pursuing the objective is rejected. The result is a consequentialist type of ethics. If the end is "good," then one must use whatever means is required to achieve a successful result, regardless of how many ethical principles are violated and regardless of whether the means are designated conventionally as good or bad.

Any fastidiousness about the means employed is not only inappropriate, but also may be a dereliction of duty. The "means" issue must be treated in a purely pragmatic manner. A "bad" means is nothing more than an ineffective or inadequate one; a "good" means is an efficacious one.

H. The Test of Success

For Machiavelli, the only relevant moral criterion for an enterprise is success. Success is right; failure is wrong. Attainment of purpose, acquiring power, wealth, prestige, continuing strength and prosperity, personal and organizational dominance, and, ultimately, fame and glory measurable by the historian, are all part of the Machiavellian value of success.

I. Public v. Private Morality

Machiavelli does draw a distinction between public morality, appropriate for great enterprises, and private morality, suitable for personal relations. When dealing with personal relationships, such as family and friends, one's egoism, in principle, can be transcended. One is assumed to regard the good of others as a sufficient reason for acting or not acting. These relationships are based on recognized commitments, distinct duties, and special values; they may claim a measure of altruistic conduct. One may be called upon to suspend or even to sacrifice one's own good for the good of these special others.

In the public sphere, however, individuals predominantly are valued only as means to certain ends. These ends, however, may not solely pertain to one person, because if one is involved in public affairs and is undertaking public responsibilities, these ends can, and should be, in the interests of the community. A person acting in a public policy capacity, therefore, shoulders an enlarged burden because the consequences of public policies are more weighty, are more enduring, and affect a greater number of people than mere personal interactions. Accordingly, one playing a public role is obligated to support, protect, and advance the interests of those whom one in some sense represents.

As a result, it may be stupid and irresponsible to apply to public action the traditional moral standards that are appropriate for private life and personal relations. Public policies are evaluated by their outcomes and not by the innate quality of the actions necessary for their successful implementation. The tenets of traditional morality, therefore, may not apply to a public person. Since he or she serves the community as a whole, he or she is empowered to do whatever is warranted to fulfill and to further the community's objectives. The need for unscrupulous tactics may arise in the public arena. If one is unable or unwilling to be manipulative, deceitful, ruthless, and coercive in pursuit of public policy goals, one is betraying the trust of these people who have placed their fate in the hands of their representative.

J. Business Applications

1. The Political Corporation

A corporation is perceived as an organized, structured, rational, goal-oriented, and efficient entity. There is a great deal of corporate behavior, however, that is highly politicized. These political features of the corporation reflect a more Machiavellian view of the corporation. Corporate officers and employees, for example, may be engaged in intrigues for influence, struggles for career advancement, controversies over corporate goals, and disagreements concerning strategies. There may be feuding among cliques, battles for corporate benefits and resources, and disputes regarding management.

The corporation, therefore, can be considered a system of competing individuals and groups who enter into power coalitions and who engage in power tactics, both formal and informal and overt and covert, to exert their influence over others and to advance their aims. As a result of these power arrangements, the goals of the corporation actually may be those established by the most powerful and dominant individual or group.

2. The Fundamental Corporate Reality

The fundamental corporate reality, therefore, emerges as power. Power is the capability of an individual or group to control the behavior of others within the corporation. In addition to the formal system of controls and rewards and punishments, the corporation contains many informal avenues and sources of power that do not appear on the corporation's organizational charts, and the uses of this power may be covert and perhaps not recognized as legitimate.

Serious moral questions arise with regard to the acquisition and exercise of corporate power. What moral limits are there, if any, on the use of power within the corporation? What moral constraints should be placed on the use of power within the corporation?

The Machiavellian answer to these questions is clear. A person should seek power. One should aim for power in one's life, including, and perhaps especially, one's corporate life. Power emerges not only as a tool for the successful corporate manager, but also as the goal of a manager intent on advancing his or her career. The means to acquiring this "good" end of power, and the application of power for one's benefit, are justifiable according to Machiavellian empowerment ethics.

3. Entrepreneurial Applications

In the modern world, founding a political principality or conquering a kingdom is a problematic undertaking. Entrepreneurship and corporate empire building, however, are excellent opportunities for a person with "princely" ambitions. Machiavelli's "lessons" for aspiring entrepreneurs are clear: be tough, smart, single-minded, and dedicated; be cruel and exploitative if forced to; bend and break the rules if necessary; pursue business success and attain the ultimate goals of wealth, fame, and glory; and do not be overly concerned with traditional notions of ethics and morality.

In *The Prince*, Machiavelli discusses at length and attempts to solve the problems confronting as aspiring "founder." This examination makes Machiavelli's book very relevant to an enterprising individual. The many practical examples Machiavelli cites for founding a political entity can be translated into modern entrepreneurial and corporate terms. Machiavelli's commentary on the manipulation of people, and the orientation and tactics employed by manipulators, certainly are subjects the aspiring entrepreneur should be motivated to study. The entrepreneur can start a business, as the prince could found a principality; an entrepreneur can conquer markets, as the prince could subjugate cities. How should the entrepreneur manage a taken-over firm? The same way the prince handles subject cities. Machiavelli recommends the interjection of clusters of adherents, acting as small management teams, to represent the prince. These supporters will be capable, loyal, and indebted to the prince. Those displaced will be few and easily removed from the scene; everyone else will be docile and anxious to avoid the same fate. Machiavelli advises the prince to either treat people well or destroy them, because people can and will retaliate for less serious injuries, but they cannot avenge themselves of the more serious debilitating ones. The entrepreneur, therefore, instead of demoting taken-over top executives, should discharge them outright. Furthermore, the entrepreneur as well as any business leader should never trust a sycophant. The worst and most dangerous advisor is the "yes man" or "yes woman," because all he or she can offer the leader and entrepreneur is fawning information which prevents one from making realistic and wise decisions.

4. Corporate Power Tactics

In the pursuit of corporate power, conduct within the corporation can readily become "Machiavellian." Abusive tactics, such as deception, manipulation, and exploitation, can be employed to advance individual interests at the expense of organizational or group interests. Such tactics also can seriously harm those who themselves possess little or no power, knowledge, or expertise.

One, for example, can sabotage the careers of one's co-workers by anonymously making false charges on the firm's ethic's "hot line," by acquiring control of scarce resources needed by others, or by withholding, distorting, or overwhelming a party with information. In order to obtain information about one's competitors, one can create and advertise for a fake job position, meet with the "duped" applicants, and get them to talk about their employers; and the reverse is also true, that is, one can interview with a job at a rival company go gain information about the firm. One can feign power, expertise, friendship, concern, favor, or respect and thereby manipulate others to show deference, loyalty, indebtedness, and trust and persuade them to perform actions for one's benefit that they ordinarily would not do. One can exploit particular personal vulnerabilities, such as vanity, gullibility, sense of responsibility, or generosity, that unknowingly can place a person in a position of dependency and servility. One can associate with the influential, ingratiate oneself with one's superiors, build one's image, and develop a base of support for one's ideas. If competitors challenge entrepreneurs, attack the competitors, blame them for any failures, and denigrate their accomplishments as unimportant, self-serving, poorly timed, or just lucky. Undo, obliterate, or minimize one's own association with policies that are failing. Always remember, appearances are essential; one must seem to be important, intelligent, confident, honest, ethical, sensitive, personable, and popular.

In the Hewlett-Packard "spy" case of 2006–2007, any corporate power tactics appeared justified, and viewed as "good," to preserve stability and to maintain power. The company was under suspicion that several employees, as well as members of the company's board of directors, were leaking very sensitive and highly confidential information to the media. The nature of the leaks suggested that the leaks were occurring at a very high management and governance level in the company. So, in true Machiavellian fashion, the executives resorted to "any and all" means available to find the "traitors." The fact that the investigation utilized certain illegal and unethical tactics to uncover the source of the leaks was not germane. Since the tactics were construed as absolutely necessary, the conventionally "immoral" nature of the means was not an issue. These tactics were necessary to protect the organization; and the constituents of the organization could well expect that the leaders would take these actions to protect the company. Invading people's privacy, assuming their identity, deceiving them and others, all were perceived as necessary, and thus "good" actions to preserve the collective entity, though these actions traditionally have been condemned as "bad." However, Machiavelli would also advise, of course, that if one is going to use "Machiavellian" tactics, such as "pre-texting" (fraudulently assuming people's identities in order to obtain private phone information and computer records), to ascertain which members of the company's board of directors and management were "leaking" confidential information to the media, one should do so very, very carefully, or else one (for example, H-P's former CEO and ethics officer) might find oneself indicted for fraud, identity theft, and illegal use of computer data. The true Machiavellian response would be to do what was necessary to find the leak, but not, as Machiavelli counseled, be "hated," that is, in the H-P case, not being prosecuted and being condemned as unethical. Unfortunately, here, at least in the Machiavellian context, the HP investigative tactics were exposed, the company was fined, the company's top executives were implicated, and were held accountable in the criminal justice system as well as the "court of public opinion," in the Hewlett-Packard "spy scandal."

5. Machiavellian-Based Business Leadership

A Machiavellian leader strives to attain power, riches, rank, fame, and above all, personal eminence and grandeur.

In order to achieve these lofty and exalted goals, the Machiavellian leader first must be cognizant certainly as to the true nature of people. Most people, stressed Machiavelli, are ignorant, unmindful, and stupid, self-interested, selfish, and petty, suspicious and envious, ungrateful, disagreeable, and malcontented, readily deceived and misled, merely satisfied and even impressed by superficial appearances and show than substance and reality, and too weak and disabled to be either completely good or bad, though venal and easily corruptible and more prone to evil.

If anarchy is to be avoided, and order and progress are to be obtained, the majority obviously cannot rule; but rather the people need a strong leader to discipline and control them and to convince, persuade, manipulate, command, or frighten them into acting prudently for their common good.

In order to be a successful leader of the people and to secure one's own position, wealth, and glory, the Machiavellian leader must be well aware that leadership definitely does not consist of adhering to any objective, universal, veritable, or ethical code, law, or principles of leadership. True leadership, rather, is a relative, situational, contingent, suitable, adaptive, and amoral conception; that is, the leader must do, and has the right to do, depending on the circumstances, whatever the leader deems necessary, fit, and proper to get the people to perform correctly, to maintain the leader and to advance the leader's objectives, and to achieve the leader's greatness. The leader, moreover, must do whatever it takes to fulfill these purposes, repudiating any notion of any higher law as well as eliminating any questions as to the conventional rightness or wrongness of the means used. Leadership, therefore, is simply a matter of expediency, which Machiavelli advocates as the one true and inviolable principle of leadership.

In purely private matters, for example, dealings with family and friends, the conventional virtues, values, and moral standards perhaps can be sustained, but when one enters the domain of public affairs and concerns, one must leave behind any notions of conventional morality, goodness, or rightfulness, because such "good" thoughts and precepts are irrelevant, and perhaps even "bad," for the ambitious leader, who must take on an amoral approach.

The overriding issue for the leader, therefore, plainly is not whether a particular action is good, right, or moral, or bad, wrong, and immoral; rather, the overruling principle is whether the circumstances require the use of a specific efficacious means. Any traditional "badness" of the proposed method must be weighed carefully against the anticipated desirable consequences of achieving the objective. It is thus quite possible that a customarily "bad" means will be outweighed by the prospects of securing a sufficiently "good" end, as defined and calculated by the leader, of course. Immorality and vice, as well as morality and virtue, all have their uses, and the sharp leader keenly can alternate between good and bad. Such actions as fraud, deceit, dissimulation, manipulation, cunning, intrigue, stratagem, disrespect, and abuse are not necessarily bad; rather, they are merely instruments to be used if the situation demands their use, and they actually may rise to the level of laudable virtuous actions, depending on the "good" ends they serve. If the situation requires, for example, that the leader's followers (or perhaps employees in a corporate setting), be lied to, misused, or even betrayed, and these "bad" actions are indispensable to the leader's personal success, then so be it! Machiavelli counseled, for example, that a reputation for morality is an important ingredient to the leader's formula for mastery; and if it is necessary for the leader to deceive the people as to the leader's true character, such deception not only is permissible, but good too! The goodness or badness of any action just depends on the particular circumstances and consequences involved; traditional moral norms are irrelevant; and actions become disassociated not only from moral standards but also from the actors performing them. The leader thereby is licensed completely to perform actions that do not conform to the exemplar of the virtuous ruler, and also is enjoined not to render conventionally good deeds if to do so would thwart the leader's "good" purposes. Good and bad are merely seemingly good or bad, and the leader is not bad by using an expedient "bad," that is, good, means. To illustrate, Daimler-Chrysler Chairman Jurgen E. Schrempp admitted that he had lied to Chrysler executives and employees regarding their status in the merged company; and specifically that he had never intended the combined auto company to be "a merger of equals"; rather, he stated that he chose to be "misleading" for psychological reasons since if he had been truthful there would have been no merger, and he could not have made Chrysler into merely another Daimler operating unit. Since lying was absolutely necessary to get the deal done, lying was moral, at least according to Machiavellian "ethics." Yet, the way things worked out between Daimler and Chrysler, with the former selling the latter at a considerable loss in 2007, perhaps it would have been better for chairman Schrempp to have told the truth!

Intelligence, reason, judgment, and prudence thus emerge as truly virtuous qualities for the successful leader. Realizing that traditionally good acts neither may serve the public good nor the "princely" good, the astute and calculating leader cautiously will alternate between good and bad, virtue and vice, and moral and immoral. The leader may have to use a means, traditionally classified as "bad," which due to its efficaciousness in a particular situation now may be deemed a good action. In certain circumstances, for example, it may be counterproductive to be kind and compassionate, and thus good to be severe and cruel. If innocent people have to be dishonored, betrayed, or abandoned for a greater good, so be it. Yet, Machiavelli warns that the leader must be careful, circumspect, and proportionate in employing conventionally bad means. Do not indulge or tolerate disproportionate or pointless badness, admonishes Machiavelli, or else one will become subject to hatred and contempt and one's purposes ultimately will be frustrated. Bad means are temporary expedients that must be used in appropriate, direct, and expeditious ways and to accomplish great goals, of course. The leader, moreover, who is obliged to apply bad methods naturally should attempt to appear as conventionally good, and otherwise actually may be quite conventionally good, but always ready and willing to change to the contrary if circumstances dictate.

Carefully alternating between good and bad and eschewing extremes, however, does not mean that the leader should give way to feeble half-measures, weak compromises, and granting concessions. Irresolution, vacillation, and continually choosing the middle course must be rejected. Such signs of weakness and indecision surely will undermine the leader's power. The leader, instead, should opt for a bold course of action; and plan it and execute it well. Such a Machiavellian leader hence will be able to cause change, whether by reason and common sense, persuasion and manipulation, or command and coercion.

A fundamental question concerning a Machiavellian approach to leadership is whether Machiavelli really is teaching evil. Machiavelli, in fact, does abjure traditional moral virtue and goodness, and instead sanctions the Machiavellian virtues of ambition, expedience, and the prudent use of good and bad. Yet, for the leader to attain and maintain power and authority and ultimately to achieve great glory, must not the leader also consider the needs and aspirations of the leader's followers, the community, as well as society as a whole? That is, must not the leader's personal ambitions and "princely" goals be advanced and achieved fully in the context of benefiting the public; and, therefore, does not the common good become the ultimate, almost utilitarian, criterion for the Machiavellian leader?

Perhaps the arrival of a crisis allows a leader to act in an absolutely Machiavellian manner. A leader confronting an emergency may be impelled to take swift, decisive, strong, even draconian measures to save the organization; and in such a situation the leader must do quickly whatever is necessary to ensure survival, without the consultation or participation of followers or managers, even though the leader's determination directly affects them, and without the niceties of ethical evaluation or moral justification. Yet, if there is a true crisis and the leader has forged bonds of trust with his or her followers, then one's followers will rely on the leader's judgment and accept, and perhaps welcome, the leader's prompt unilateral exercise of power.

In the short term, however, it may be expedient for a leader to be Machiavellian, but is it efficacious in the long term for a leader to be Machiavellian in the sense of being deceptive and manipulative and disrespectful and abusive? Dissimulation cannot be concealed forever, and eventually one will run out of people to mistreat; and this type of "raw power," coercive, intimidating leadership ultimately will fail as it cannot sustain itself indefinitely. People simply will neither follow nor labor for individuals they mistrust or detest; and thus such a Machiavellian immoral or amoral "boss" will not be able to motivate or direct activity.

A leader, therefore, must be very careful in asserting Machiavelli's rationales as the pretense for expedient, short-term, or crisis-caused authoritarian conduct. Once one acknowledges that Machiavellian behavior is acceptable, one risks falling into the trap of portraying present circumstances as fittingly critical, problematical, exceptional, or tactical for swift, arbitrary, "tough," Machiavellian handling, and thereby steadily sanctioning autocratic conduct. Moreover, regardless of the unsettled, troublesome, or exiguous nature of a situation, is it ever morally permissible or appropriate for a leader to act in a despotic and tyrannical manner?

It is never permissible nor appropriate to mistreat, disrespect, betray, deceive, manipulate, or exploit people. It is always immoral to behave in such a wrongful manner and to contravene fundamental natural rights and no crisis, real or perceived, no short-term advantage, can ever justify such misconduct. True leadership, as well as successful long-term leadership, is built on certain fundamental, inviolable ethical principles, such as integrity, honesty, trust, and respect, which are constant, permanent, noncontingent, and categorical norms. Effective leadership, of course, will require at times course corrections and changes in strategy and tactics, yet leadership also demands steadfast adherence to ethical principles and moral rules.

A person who is ethically deficient thus lacks the necessary predicate for successful leadership, and when such a person confronts a crisis or is tempted by short-term advantage, or for that matter, simply faces the unavoidable problems of authority and administration, he or she will act in such a way as to destroy any leadership effectiveness.

A leader who is demanding, and even exacting, may well be acceptable as well as efficacious, but one who is abusive and coercive is never acceptable, and in the long term such leaders will be failures. Trying to lead by fear, suspicion, and manipulation hinders genuine communication and interaction, breeds apathy and mistrust, suppresses motivation, undermines commitment and loyalty, prevents empowerment, and eventually engenders serious problems and wrong decisions.

If leading by fear, manipulation, and paternalism is neither morally acceptable nor practically efficacious, are there feasible leadership techniques for the results-oriented individual? Successful, long-term leadership always comes down to certain essential attributes—morality, honesty, and integrity. Treating one's followers and one's employees with dignity and respect, trusting and empowering them, as opposed to coercing and controlling them, will create not heedless, mindless, enervated automatons, but rather knowledgeable, energetic, and motivated associates who wholeheartedly believe in the leader and who are enthusiastically committed to achieving the leader's vision. Such leadership is principle centered, values based, and vision inspired; and the only type of leadership capable of producing and sustaining transformational and beneficial change.

6. Summary

Machiavelli would view the acquisition of corporate power as the "good" objective to be attained by any means. Power drives the corporate manager and the entrepreneur because power is not only an end but also a means, because if one uses and wields power correctly, one will be rewarded with success, wealth, fame, and glory.

K. Problems with Machiavelli

The risk of underscoring the value of power is that that power becomes an end in itself. This goal of power, however, may be unattainable. Possessing and maintaining power over others may require one to constantly strive to increase the power that one possesses. The power that one has thus cannot be used to achieve any notable purposes; rather, it is merely a means to obtain more power, which is the means to secure every further power, and so on indefinitely. The result is an incessant, repetitive, naked power struggle with an endless deferring of goals.

The liberation from traditional moral restraints and the granting of moral legitimacy to self-interest may make some people more energetic and creative, but a concomitant decline in moral standards might engender increasing malaise, suspicion, distrust, perfidy, social disunity, and inevitably anarchy.

A personal acting in a public affairs capacity should be able to do whatever he or she desires, Machiavelli counsels, so long as the action is for the community as a whole, and not solely for that person's own satisfaction and aggrandizement. How realistic is such a scenario? Machiavelli himself saw the problems with his own reasoning. He notes how difficult it is to find a good person willing to employ bad means, even though the ultimate goal is good. He also observes how infrequently a bad person, after having acquired power, is willing to use it for good ends. If a person cannot succeed by moral means, perhaps it is preferable that he or she not succeed at all, because if successful the objective would no longer be the same cause for which the person initially sought to attain.

Perhaps Machiavelli is too much the realist and gives too much emphasis to material and "scientific" factors. His "crime" may not be one of amorality or immorality, but an underestimation of the moral factor in public and business affairs.

One also must consider the long-term consequences of using "Machiavellian" tactics on oneself, others, and an organization. Prolonged use of such tactics can engender debilitating outcomes. One who exercises power in such a manner, and aggressively seeks to secure and use even more power, can find himself or herself corrupted thereby. The use of power can routinize not only the control, but also the undignified and abusive treatment of less powerful individuals. Those controlled and so treated perhaps feel like failures and may regress to a depressed and apathetic state or perhaps feel frustrated and become aggressive and hostile. Capable corporate employees might leave the organization, or their performance could deteriorate, when a manager uses unscrupulous tactics over a prolonged period of time. An organization can become plagued by ruthless competition, antagonistic rivalries, and conflict. A society's economic and social health, as well as the livelihoods of many people, are too dependent on business to regard business as some type of Machiavellian power game.

Admittedly, building a power base is important in establishing or conducting a business, but gaining power as one's ultimate goal is not a license for the practice of a spurious or specious code of ethics. There is not a separate set of moral standards for business or for a manager acting in a corporate capacity. One is not relieved of moral responsibility by acting in a public affairs or business capacity. One cannot hide behind and attempt to operate under a separate, unique, and dual system of ethics applicable only to business and public affairs. There should be one system of ethics, one set of moral rules, and one ethical code that applies to everyone alike, including business. A pernicious potential consequence of a "dual system" type of thinking is the acceptance or acquiescence by some in the business and political community that the "public" system or code can be, is, and should be, morally inferior to the "private" code.

L. Summary

Machiavelli is regarded as a well-known exponent of public morality and power tactics. His name is used to symbolize a sinister "real-world" view. Machiavelli, however, does expose the internal contradiction between traditional morality and real business and public "ethics." Comprehending this contradiction and resolving it is not merely an abstract theoretical challenge, but a very concrete and practical one.

It is simplistic, however, to use Machiavelli as a synonym for wicked realism. Machiavelli does recognize traditional moral standards; he does not deny the intrinsic value of moral rules and virtues. He also recognizes, and wants his readers to understand, that the real world of values is not a homogeneous one. There is not just a world of moral values that alone exists in reality. Recognizing this fact does not mean that the Machiavellian solution is simply a matter of recommending deception, manipulation or coercion; rather, Machiavelli is urging that people confront the real world, know what real-world tactics they and others are using, and realize that some of these tactics are evil.

Machiavelli never regards "badness" as a tactic to be used continually and regularly, but rather as a temporary means to secure and maintain power more firmly. In the real world, it will be impossible to act in compliance with traditional moral standards at all times and all places. Such compliance is contrary to human nature and hardly a new discovery. Machiavelli's point is that the contravention of traditional morality (though in a moral sense adjudged as "bad"), can act as the necessary means, in certain concrete circumstances, to effectuate a greater "good."

Machiavelli clearly recognizes and it is extremely important for his readers to recognize, that certain means, although regarded as necessary, are in fact bad and immoral. The moral character of the means remains unchanged, even though they are used for a good purpose. One must not only recognize a bad means as a bad means, but also only the extent necessary to employ such means. Then one can dispose of the bad means as soon as the good end is achieved. One must be true and honest to oneself and others, admit that one does not have "clean hands" by having used such means, and ought to accept that reality.

The acquisition of power and the assumption of a public affairs role affords one the opportunity to change others lives on a large scale. Since power possesses instrumental as well as intrinsic value in Machiavelli's scheme, one can use power for "good" ends, such as establishing one's authority in moral matters and using power to administer standards of right and wrong to people. Power and public affairs entail enlarged responsibility, accountability, and gravity in the use of power. Significant potential public consequences thus compel one to formulate carefully and seriously, calculate cleverly, intelligently justify, and prudently implement public policies.

Discussion Questions

1. In your opinion, do the ends really justify the means?
2. The chapter suggests that holding to your personal moral virtues is more likely to occur in situations where you are interacting with friends than in the public forum. Do you behave with a different set of values in the public forum than in your personal relationships?

3. Machiavelli has a very pessimistic view of the individuals within a society. Do you agree with his view or are you more optimistic about individuals?

4. Do you think that Machiavelli would draw the same conclusions about the attributes of most members of society today as he did so long ago?

5. Describe a situation where you feel it would be acceptable to manipulate or coerce someone into doing something that benefits you?

6. Machiavelli suggests that it is important for a leader to have the appearance of being virtuous, not necessarily for the leader to actually be virtuous. Can you draw parallels between recent corporate and political scandals and "Machiavelli's virtuousness"?

7. Does the diversity present in today's society lend support to Machiavelli's recommendation that personal ethics stay out of public decision-making?

8. Describe a situation where your morals had to be put aside for the "greater good."

9. Which group do you feel falls within Machiavellian principles—Politicians or Business Leaders?

10. Why do you think that Machiavelli stated that being feared, or even hated, is better than being loved?

CHAPTER 6

Ethical Emotism, Ethical Relativism, and Legal Positivism

A. Ethical Emotism

Ethical emotism is a theory of ethics founded on feelings and emotions. Moral judgments are based on and express the feelings and emotions of the people making the judgments. Displays of emotion, such as "bribery, boo," and "privacy rights, yeah," are moral determinations.

The Scottish philosopher David Hume (1711–1776), is one of the principal sources for an emotist theory of ethics. Hume believed that morality is based on sentiments and feelings. Morality is ascertainable only if one attends to one's own emotional reactions to situations where one assigns "good" and "bad" as moral norms. According to Hume, morality must be perceived by means of some emotional impression or sentiment that enables one to distinguish between right and wrong.

1. Feelings v. Reason

Hume and the ethical emotists deny that moral distinctions are derived from reason; they deny that good consequences or conformity to a moral code determine morality; they deny that morality and immorality are properties of actions themselves, independent of one's feeling toward them; and they deny that rightness and wrongness are objective universal features of reality.

To perceive an act as right or wrong is merely to have feelings of approval or disapproval toward it. An act is deemed moral for the emotion that inspired, sustains, and approves it. Moral sentiments are merely a subclass of feelings.

Reason may be required to guide and direct one's emotions so as to achieve one's purposes, but ultimately, said Hume, sentiment itself, and not reason, is the only true means to judge between good and bad. One's feelings of approval and disapproval determine one's moral judgments, and not rationally determined prescriptive and proscriptive norms.

Ethical emotism, therefore, is a totally subjectivist attack on a rationalistic ethics that places reason in the prime position in determining morality. For Hume and the emotists, morality is not cognitive, but emotional.

2. The Power of Feelings

One must admit that feelings do play a part in moral judgments. Morality is something most people feel deeply about and argue emotionally. Strong feelings concerning a moral issue are frequently a sign of seriousness. To be emotionally in favor of something "good," moreover, is to want it to happen; to be emotionally opposed to something "bad" is to want it stopped. Reason may be incapable of supplying the motivation to act in the "right" manner. Firm moral feelings, however, readily can translate into action.

3. Hume's "Generalized Feelings"

Morality is based on feelings, said Hume, and moral feelings stem from human beings associating with each other, pursuing common ends, and evoking a natural sympathy for their fellow human beings.

Morality is based on the fact that people possess a sentiment of morality, said Hume. People are so constructed that they feel a weak, general sympathy for others. In the course of the socialization process, they acquire stronger feelings, their feelings are shaped, and they come to view certain types of conduct as good or bad. Moral feelings, therefore, are based on social and public feelings. The consequence of this line of emotist thought, however, is that morality is not subjective; it is based on generalized feelings of a society regarding what is and is not morally acceptable. Presuming people possess normal sentiments and sympathies and live in similar ways, with common historical memories and local conditions, people, as Hume in fact argued, should tend toward agreement and harmony on moral issues. The problem with this line of reasoning, for an emotist, is that it looks like ethical relativism and not ethical emotism.

Pleasure and pain form the foundation of human feelings. One seeks pleasure and avoids pain. One's sympathy for others is derived from the recognition that people have similar feeling to oneself. One desires, even weakly, what is beneficial and causes pleasure for one's fellow human beings. Such sentiments are common to all people and are founded upon a common human nature. People are not entirely selfish; there is some benevolence, however small, in human beings; morality, said Hume, is based on this sentiment of benevolence or fellow feeling. The presence of such a sentiment means that one approves actions, such as trustfulness and cooperation, which produce pleasure for oneself and others. Moral feelings, therefore, are based on beliefs about the general tendencies of actions to affect positively oneself and others. An ethics of promoting human pleasure and diminishing human pain is certainly noteworthy and arguably appropriate, yet the problem with this version of emotism is that it resembles very closely the principled ethical theory of utilitarianism. After examining the ethical theory of emotism, one wonders whether its principal exponent, Hume, is even an emotist.

4. The Consequence of Ethical Emotism

A) MORAL INFALLIBILITY

If one is an ethical emotist, one can never be wrong in one's moral judgments. One's feelings and emotions cannot be true or false, and so long as one accurately expresses one's feelings of approval or disapproval, it is not clear how one ever could be mistaken in making a moral judgment.

Yet how can ethical emotism account for the fact that people often do call moral judgments true or false? People are not perfect. One may be mistaken even if one expresses a feeling sincerely. People accuse themselves, and others, of making mistakes on moral issues; but based on ethical emotism, one could never disagree with anyone regarding the morality of an action. Each person's moral expression is equally right because it is based on feelings. Yet people do disagree with others concerning moral issues, and these disagreements are argued in rational as well as emotional terms.

B) MORAL SUBJECTIVITY

Pursuant to ethical emotism and its emphasis on individual feelings, relativism is extended into the field of ethics and morality becomes completely subjective. If a person sincerely feels it is good and right to steal, then, for that person, it is moral to steal. Another person's feelings may tell him or her that stealing is immoral. Based on ethical emotism, both these feelings and concomitant moral conclusions are correct.

One thus cannot tell another person what is right or wrong, what moral beliefs to accept or reject, or how to live one's life. No objective morality can be possible, no universal standards of right or wrong can exist, and no one can assert rationally or defend a moral position. Moral judgments are arbitrary, personal, and subjective; therefore, the logical conclusion to ethical emotism is moral anarchy.

C) THE RELIABILITY OF FEELINGS

Feelings and emotions obviously exist, but feelings are not necessarily perceptions of the truth. Feelings, regardless of how powerful, may be the irrational products of selfishness, prejudice, or social and cultural conditioning.

D) CHANGING ONE'S FEELINGS

As human nature is variable and people have different feelings at different times, ethical emotism is rendered an even more relativistic ethical theory. At one time, one felt one way about an action or person; now, one feels another way. Perhaps one once felt that adultery was wrong, and now one feels it is right. Can one change one's moral judgments by simply changing one's feelings? Yes, according to ethical emotism, by simply expressing a different feeling about an action.

E) RESOLVING MORAL DISPUTES

If ethics is merely the expression of feelings and emotions, then moral disagreements are irresolvable. Since reason does not play any significant role in moral inquiry and justification, people can argue and argue without reaching any moral agreement. One cannot say which of two competing moral judgments is right or wrong. Since there is no way of deciding which is which, it even may be arrogant to claim either as right or wrong. One may feel so strongly about a moral issue, one may assume knowledge of the "truth" and not even consider any contrary arguments. In either case, ethical emotism emerges as an impediment to discovering any moral truth.

People, however, do make moral judgments and provide a rational defense therefor. People do attach praise and blame to others for their actions by judging the quality of the actions, not merely by expressing their feelings. Ethical emotism, therefore, does not correspond to the normal experiences of people.

f) Ethical Reasoning

Frequently, it is true that people simply like or dislike something, without having a reason, giving a reason, or feeling compelled to give a reason; yet what makes an inquiry a typically philosophical one is the intelligent reflection involved and the rational argumentation presented. Hume and the emotists, therefore, can be criticized for accepting too sharp a dichotomy between reason and emotion. Their reliance on feelings leaves very little place for reflective ethical thought, reasoning, and judgment.

Yet, when a person contemplates an activity, one often asks and attempts to explain, why one should do the act and whether there are good reasons for doing it. People often want to understand themselves, and the reasons that motivate them, before they determine what course to follow. People adopt particular moral opinions based on the results of their ethical reasoning; they offer rational arguments for the positions they have taken; and they seek to answer arguments for opposing views; all of which indicates that people believe there are reasoned right and wrong answers to moral questions.

If another person, moreover, says that a certain action is "wrong," it seems quite logical to ask "why" and to expect that the person's answer will be based on a reason, and that this reason will consist of more than the expression of mere feelings. If no reason is given, or the "reason" does not consist of relevant and rational facts, arguments, and alternatives, one very likely will disregard the normative characterization of the action.

People have not only feelings but also the capability to reason. Moral truths are the truths of reason. The "correct" answer to a moral question is the answer with the weight of reason on its side. Moral truths are objective; they are true independently of what one might feel. One cannot make something good or bad by expressing a feeling or changing an emotion. One must be ruled by reason. Morality is consulting reason, and the morally right thing to do is a rational determination.

g) Summary

Although there is an irreducible element of emotion in moral decisions, a moral judgment is more than the mere expression of strong and transitory feelings. One must use one's reason to organize one's feelings into some coherent whole of reasoned preferences that can withstand rational scrutiny. Morality is neither subjective, solitary, personal, nor unsubstantiated; rather, it is a reasoned determination and part of a moral life that to an important degree is shared by other rational beings.

Hume and the ethical emotists may provide an account of what people actually approve as good, but they cannot account for what is really good. They may tell people what an individual will do, but cannot provide a good reason for people to take an individual seriously. Only a reasoned normative ethics that rationally establishes and defends standards of good conduct can tell people authoritatively what is worthy of moral approval and adoption. Only a reasoned ethics retains the authority to play a role in public, social, and individual life.

B. Ethical Relativism

The Skeptics, a group of ancient Greek thinkers who founded a philosophical school, were struck by the diversity of peoples, customs, beliefs, and schools of thought. The exposure to all these conflicting circumstances and views, together with an emphasis on relativism (acquired from the Sophists) and a healthy personal skepticism as well, led the Skeptics to conclude that it would be quite futile to seek any rational grounds for preferring one set of conventions or "explanations" over others. Rather, since there is no way of telling what customs and theories are correct and true, the proper, prudent, and practical approach is to conform to the customs and beliefs of whatever country or society one inhabits. Follow the local customs, the Skeptics recommended, be content with appearances, and surely do not waste one's time seeking absolute "truth." From the thinking and attitude of the Skeptics arose the ethical theory of Ethical Relativism. Ethical relativism can be exemplified by two sayings, one very, very old, and the other, as related to one of the authors of this book by one of his graduate students doing business in an African nation, relatively new. The first is "when in Rome, do as the Romans"; and the second is "why hire a lawyer, when you can buy a judge."

1. Basic Tenets

Are there objective, universal moral rules upon which one can construct an absolute moral system? Are there moral rules applicable to all peoples, in all societies, and at all times? An ethical relativist denies the existence of any universal truth in morality. There are no universal standards by which to judge an action's morality; morality is merely relative to, and holds for, only a particular society at a particular time.

Morality is a societal-based phenomena. Morality is nothing more than the morality of a certain group, people, or society at a certain time. What a society believes is right is in fact right for that society. The moral beliefs of a society determine what is right within that society; if the prevailing moral view says an action is "right," the action is right. Society is the source of all morality.

Different societies, of course, have different conceptions of right and wrong. What one society thinks is right, another society may conceive as wrong. The same act, in fact, may be morally right for one society and morally wrong for another. For example, as related to one of the authors of this book by a Japanese student, it is considered immoral for a manager in Japan to move from firm to firm; rather, the moral norms of that society is lifetime employment with one firm.

Since pursuant to ethical relativism there are no moral standards that are universally true for all peoples, in all societies, and at all times, and since there is no way of objectively showing that one set of beliefs is to be preferred, the only way to determine an action's morality is to ascertain what the people in a particular society believe is morally right or wrong.

2. Effect on Business People

Because different societies have different customs and beliefs, the absolutism or relativism of morality is an important issue that a global business person inevitably will encounter. An ethical relativist would advise the business person who operates in different countries, and who thus confronts societies with different moral beliefs, simply to follow the moral standards prevalent in whatever society he or she finds himself or herself. For example, if the issue arose as to whether it is moral to use nudity in a product advertising campaign, the ethical relativist would counsel that if the campaign was focused in Italy or France, where nudity is acceptable in advertising, by all means use nudity as it is morally sanctioned by those societies.

Following the host country's morality is certainly a convenient approach to take, but the doctrine of ethical relativism probably has persuaded more people, particularly business people, to be skeptical about ethics than any other line of thought.

3. Justification

There is some rational justification for respecting some set of conventional moral beliefs. Some moral prescriptions are necessary in the area of social relationships; and people are, and should be, inclined to respect those prescriptions that have survived and that have a history of respect.

It is, moreover, well and proper to know something of the customs of other peoples, so as to more rationally judge one's own customs and to avoid thinking that everything contrary to one's own beliefs and conventions is wrong. Ethical relativism can appeal to tolerance of every kind of society; it militates against being "judgmental" toward other groups of persons.

It is one thing, however, to say that certain societal practices deserve a degree of respect and tolerance, and quite another to suggest that they are morally right and ought to be protected and prolonged, especially if overriding reasons of a rational kind argue against these prevailing societal conventions.

4. Cultural v. Ethical Relativism

Cultural relativism is a purely descriptive doctrine. It intends to report as a matter of fact the customs and beliefs of different societies and cultures. The doctrine seeks to relate the fundamental and unique beliefs of a society and how these beliefs differ from those of other societies. The doctrine, however, is purely descriptive and in no sense normative. It merely informs; it neither prescribes nor evaluates.

Ethical relativism does more than report cultural differences. It is a prescriptive theory. Although an ethical relativist denies there are absolute, universal moral standards, an ethical relativist views morality as societal-based. That is, once a society approves certain conduct and beliefs as right, these moral determinations are right for that society and thus contain prescriptive and evaluative elements. While there may be no way under ethical relativism to justify a single societal morality as the correct one, a society will approve certain types of conduct and beliefs as right and will disapprove others as wrong. Certain types of immorality will be proscribed by law; others will be discouraged by public opinion and personal feelings of shock, repugnance, and disapproval.

It is not possible for a reasonable person to deny the well-known variations in human conduct and beliefs in different societies and at different times, including the diversity of moral beliefs and conduct. Societal customs and beliefs, moreover, do merit some respect. Conformity to the established traditional conventions of one's society is essential to the survival and welfare of the society. It is wrong to heedlessly ignore and contravene the practices and beliefs of those around one, simply because this will offend people needlessly and evince a lack of respect for their beliefs and values. For example, Nike found itself in difficulty in China for airing a commercial in which a U.S. basketball star was shown fighting and beating a Chinese Kung Fu master and a pair of dragons, viewed as sacred symbols in traditional Chinese culture. The Chinese government, after a public outcry, barred the ad, condemning it as an affront to Chinese culture and disrespectful to Chinese dignity. Another example, also involving China concerned Hong Kong Disneyland, where Disney, in an effort to accommodate Chinese culture, planned to serve shark's fin soup, but later decided to forgo the practice when environmentalists condemned the practice as immoral.

The existence of diverse societal-based customs and beliefs, in addition, is quite compatible with nonrelativistic ethical theories, such as utilitarianism. Not all cultural relativists are ethical relativists. Variations in moral beliefs can be construed as merely a statement of descriptive morality, a fact for history, anthropology, or sociology that does not entail ethical standing. One can accept the unmistakable fact of cultural relativism, even as applied to morality, while adhering to the position that only one morality can be justified ethically as true. It is very difficult, therefore, to make the radical and monumental transition from cultural to ethical relativism.

5. Problems with Ethical Relativism

A) DEFINING "SOCIETY"

A fully realized and individualized society is at best a rare phenomena. Even within relatively simple societies there are diverse cultures, subcultures, social classes, and kinship and work groups. These fragments constantly confront one another and interact, and in so doing exchange and modify conventions and beliefs. A united and distinct group, which one reasonably could term a society, might even tolerate a great diversity of practices and beliefs. Regardless of how small and socially homogeneous the group, there still will be some divergence in moral opinion.

In large, complex, heterogeneous social systems, the "society" will contain myriad small "subsocieties" that co-exist, yet that reflect different standards and attitudes. Definite moral beliefs also can be ascribed to many of these "subsocieties." An individual, moreover, can simultaneously belong to distinct sub-societies, cultures, and groups, all with different moral norms and beliefs.

In a heterogeneous world, filled with heterogeneous societies, the presence of too much diversity offers a serious challenge to the ethical relativist. What constitutes a society for the purposes of ethical relativism? What are the boundaries of a society; how does one determine where one society ends and another begins; and whose beliefs and practices form the core of values for the society? Particularly in an age of multinational business and the increasing "globalization" of economic activity, the doctrine of ethical relativism presents so many serious problems as to render the theory practically unworkable.

An individual ethical relativist, in addition, can make the same charges and use the same arguments as a societal-based ethical relativist. A distinct subgroup within society with different moral views is not "wrong" according to ethical relativism because of its smaller size. It should be viewed as a society in its own right, with an equally valid set of beliefs. What about a dissenting group within this minority; and what about a dissenting individual within this dissenting group? Pursuant to ethical relativism, each subgroup, dissenting group, and individual can be viewed as a "society," thus possessing a set of moral beliefs that are right. The logical progression to the theory of ethical relativism, therefore, is an individual, personal, subjective "ethics," soon degenerating in moral anarchy.

B) COMPARATIVE MORAL JUDGMENTS

One obvious drawback to ethical relativism is that no comparative moral judgments are possible. Since there are no external, universal, objective moral standards, there is no impartial way of evaluating and deciding among different practices and beliefs. One cannot say that any practice or belief is better or worse from a moral perspective than any other. No matter how seemingly reprehensible or praiseworthy a society's practices and beliefs, nothing correctly can be adjudged wrong or right because comparative judgments require absolute moral standards, which the ethical relativist denies. For example, if the Europeans view corporate executive compensation "packages," including Golden Parachutes and stock options, as excessive, unseemly, unjust, immoral, or even obscene; but Americans view such compensation as "good old-fashioned" entrepreneurial capitalism; then, according to ethical relativism, both moral views are right.

C) SOCIETAL AGREEMENT

The norms in one society very well may differ from the norms in effect in another society. What is right and what is wrong will not always be the same in different societies; but under ethical relativism, what is right for a society is right for that society. As a consequence of taking this ethical relativistic perspective, two bizarre and contradictory results ensue: agreement on morals is, in principle, impossible; and no societal disagreements are possible. Since each society has its own true "right" view, no two societies, in principle, can disagree as to the morality of an action.

D) CRITICIZING A SOCIETY

If one is an ethical relativist, it makes no sense, and it would in fact be wrong, to criticize the practice and beliefs of other societies so long as they adhere to their own standards. One can no longer say that the customs of other societies are morally inferior to one's own. One's own society has no special status; it is merely one among many.

There is certainly no place for moral reformers. One must cease condemnation of other different societies, regardless of how "atrocious" their practices are. It would be arrogant to evaluate the practices of a society and attempt to persuade the other society to change its view. Rather, one should adopt an attitude of tolerance. All one can, and should, do is report what a society believes about an action. So, if the Chinese believe it is morally appropriate to "harvest" human organs from executed prisoners who presumably gave their consent, and then sell and transplant the organs to wealthy foreigners, then the practice is moral pursuant to ethical relativism and beyond reproach morally.

If one accepts ethical relativism, it is also wrong, and makes no sense, to criticize the practices and beliefs of one's own society. If right or wrong is relative to a society, it must be relative to one's own society too. Consequently, one's own established standards are correct and any attempt to reform them must be taken as "mistaken." Since right or wrong are determined by the standards of a society, one cannot propose changes for the "better" because there is no way to judge the reforms as better.

Yet people do recognize that moral standards of their own society, as well as other societies, are wrong; and this judgment implies that the moral standards that a society accepts are not the exclusive criteria of right and wrong. The idea, for example, that the practice of slavery cannot be evaluated ethically across societies, cultures, and times by a common moral standard appears not only mistaken but also quite ridiculous.

E) ILLOGICAL APPROACH

Common sense informs one that conventions and beliefs do differ among societies, cultures, groups, and times. Yet, the culturally relativistic fact that societies have different beliefs, including moral beliefs, does not logically mean that all societal-based moral beliefs are equally acceptable and right.

The ethical relativist's approach is a flawed one. He or she argues from the fact of societal diversity to a conclusion about the lack of any universal, objective, and true morality. The approach is not logically sound because the conclusion does not follow from the premise. Even if the premise is true, the conclusion may be false. To say that morality derives from societal norms and beliefs is not to say that whatever is customary is right and true. One cannot infer logically from the fact of societal diversity that there is no way, and can never be any way, to establish one view as correct. One should not be tempted to conclude from the fact of diversity that there are not any true moral standards to resolve differences in beliefs. When two societies have different moral beliefs, all that logically should follow is that one of them probably is wrong.

F) UNIVERSAL MORAL STANDARDS

The fact that there are differences in moral positions among societies does not mean that there are no universal moral standards and rules. There are reasons to think that all societies actually do share the same basic moral norms. The underlying similarities of human beings the world over, the actual, well-established, normal habits of people, revealed in their conduct and language, and the similar conditions necessary for survival and advancement, are all evidence of common human needs, dispositions, and aspirations. Human beings share a belief in fundamental human rights that apply to all people, in all places, and at all times. People, moreover, speak out whenever and wherever universal human rights are denied or violated.

There are moral standards that unmistakenly are universal and that have been, and are, esteemed by the peoples of every society. There is agreement, commonalty, and invariability concerning a core of moral rules that forms a part of the ethical system of all societies. Standards, for example, that treat murder, stealing, lying, treachery, cruelty, uncontrolled aggressiveness, unregulated sexual practices, self-indulgence, selfishness, and laziness as immoral vices are universally held. Standards that treat honesty, promise-keeping, faithfulness, loyalty, kindness, self-control, and industry as moral virtues are accepted by all societies. These standards are constant and universal and do not depend on societal variation. It makes no sense to say that a rule against causing unnecessary suffering, or a rule respecting property rights, may be held for one group of people and not for another. These universal norms recognize that people are social beings, that cooperation is necessary for survival, and that people need moral rules and prohibitions to lead a common life.

These moral norms are the minimally necessary preconditions for any society to exist at all. There are certain basic moral rules that must be followed in each society if a society is to survive and its members are to interact with each other effectively. Norms, for example, against killing or injuring the members of the society, taking their property, and using language untruthfully when communicating with them, form part of this moral minimum. If these norms are not complied with, if there is not some protection for persons, property, representations, and promises, then the social system will not survive and there will not be any society at all. One cannot avoid these minimal moral obligations, not to murder, steal, and lie, without removing oneself from society altogether.

Societal moralities, despite surface differences, do converge on a common core, and thus are not so diverse as the ethical relativists contend. One can recognize "different" moralities as being one universal morality through their common, invariable, and constant core.

G) Factual v. Moral Disagreement

Are moral disagreements among societies really disagreements about facts? That is, are disagreements based not on differing moral beliefs, but on nothing more than the attempt to apply universally recognized moral rules to specific factual situations? The apparent diversity of beliefs among societies may be only apparent. Societies do agree on certain fundamental moral standards. Different views on specific moral issues do not reflect deep differences in fundamental moral beliefs, but instead are reflections of differing factual circumstances.

H) Universal Moral Rules v. Universal Practice

Although people from different societies actually may not agree on all moral norms, this automatically does not mean that there are not ultimate, fundamental, moral norms that everyone ought to believe. Fundamental moral rules are universal, but they may not be universally practiced. Members of one society, for example, will agree that they should not kill, steal, and lie to one another, but they may think it permissible to inflict these actions on members of other societies. Morality, therefore, is not relative; it simply is not practiced universally. Nonetheless, in the business world, one of the biggest challenges for a global company is to achieve consistent compliance with its ethics code and its "universal" moral standards since the moral beliefs of its employees are often rooted in cultural and societal differences. For example, Italian employees might balk at mandatory whistleblowing provisions due to their country's experience with collaborators during World War II.

I) Experience

People's own experiences contradict ethical relativism. People do make comparative moral judgments and people do marshal ethical arguments in support of their moral criticisms. Trans-societal moral judgments can be, are, and should be made. If ethical relativism is true, such judgments, criticism, and arguments are doomed to failure. Moral reformers, moreover, certainly would have no place in an ethically relativistic universe.

The fact that moral judgments are made, however, does not imply that there is a single and complete ethical theory to answer satisfactorily all moral issues and that it is always easy to ascertain what is right and wrong. Ethical analysis does mean that societal rules, actions, and beliefs can be determined to be right or wrong based on reasoning from ethical principles. Ethical principles do allow one to dismiss certain societal "moral" rules as inadequate. One pernicious consequence of ethical relativism, with its emphasis on culture, custom, and convention, is to short-circuit the ideal of the universal-absolute-good out of human consciousness. The challenge, rather, is to establish consistent ethical methods to rationally raise, discuss, and resolve moral issues, to classify actions as right and wrong, and to make the classification universal and operational.

6. Summary

Moral beliefs may be in part the internalized reflection of the views of one's society, transmitted by one's parents and other societal influences. The resulting moral norms can be prescribed, explained, and reinforced by the society's customs and conventions. The norms, in addition, can function as instruments for maintaining social cohesion and stability. Following the customs of one's society, therefore, does provide an explanation for performing an action.

Adherence to social convention, however, does not provide a justification for engaging in an activity. Acceptance of societal norms generally is not the product of logical ethical reasoning. Moral norms need justification. Rational arguments are necessary to establish what a societal practice ought to be and to determine whether a person should be guided by an essentially nonreasoned conformity to societal convention. A too-ready disposition to conform to the practices of one's society may not be a virtue, but rather a weakness and vice.

Fundamental moral rules are not relative. Not every moral rule varies from society to society. Societies may differ in some moral beliefs, but there is agreement on fundamental rules. It is a mistake, therefore, to overestimate the amount of differences among societies, and certainly to construct an ethical theory based on these differences. Several societies have believed in the morality of the practice of slavery throughout history; yet slavery was morally wrong then, as well as now, despite societal norms.

C. Legal Positivism

An examination of business ethics at once confronts managers with a core philosophical issue: Is justice the same as legality? That is, when a person uses the presumably ethical term "just," does he or she merely mean "legal" in the sense of conformity to existing law? Hence, to be deemed a moral manager, is it sufficient for a manager simply to observe the law?

1. The Doctrine

Legal Positivism affirms "positive" law as the basis for decision making when a business manager is confronted with a moral problem. Positive law (derived from the word "posit," meaning place or lay down) is the body of ascertainable and enforceable rules promulgated by government entities to regulate conduct in a society. Acting in conformity with this law signifies that one also is acting morally. What is moral is identical to what is legal; a "moral" person is a "legal" person.

Legal Positivism rejects the view that law can be measured against any objective, universal, true moral standard. The question as to whether a law is moral or immoral thus cannot be ethically determined. Law itself supplies the standard for morality, which is an admittedly relative standard derived from the positive law prevailing at a particular time and place.

Legal Positivism does not deny that the term "morality" is employed in other ways. The doctrine however, maintains that when morality is used to express something different from legality, the meaning is hopelessly subjective. The only clear, definite, determinable, and objective criterion for morality is the law.

2. The Allure of Legal Positivism

Why not allow the law to decide moral dilemmas? Why not equate morality with legality? Relying on the law does have initial appeal. Obviously, it is a challenging task to resolve ethically what acting morally requires. The law certainly is a more facile, apparent, and convenient standard to adopt. The law also possesses the advantage of being an enforceable norm. The result for a manager is that he or she need not pay attention to ethical principles and moral rules since there are no such independent principles and rules. What is moral is determined by merely examining the law. By complying with the law, a manager is acting morally. Legal Positivism certainly simplifies moral matters.

Yet perhaps the law is too easy to embrace as a moral emblem. A person can refute an accusation of morality merely by demonstrating that no law was contravened. The absence of law may accommodate a rationalization to overlook moral issues.

In order to determine the legitimacy of Legal Positivism, one first must explore the genesis of the doctrine.

3. Hobbes and Legal Positivism

A) INTRODUCTION

The moral philosophy of the English philosopher Thomas Hobbs (1588–1679), is markedly positivist. Morality evidently is a legally oriented concept for Hobbs, who consistently denied the existence of natural law and natural rights as well as the existence of any absolute, universal, objective moral truth. Hobbes defends his proposition that morality depends on legality by attempting to describe what conditions would be like in a situation where no law existed.

B) THE STATE OF NATURE

In Hobbes's view of the "state of nature," there is neither any organized society nor any enforceable rules. People oppose each other as individuals, seeking only their own advantage. They constantly strive to accumulate power. Power is sought not to attain a better life, but simply to assure maintaining one's present existence. Yet people are roughly equal in power, so no one possesses a clear advantage. People do and suffer wrongs freely and without restraint. They cannot stand still in the race for power without risking losing everything. They are forced to compete for power. The obvious outcome is conflict. People will do anything to preserve the security of their persons and property. Any query as to morality or immorality is nonsensical. Productive work and social cooperation scarcely are present. The incessant mistrust and insecurity erode any mutual endeavors to spur economic development and to produce the benefits of a civilization.

c) The Social Contract

People, nonetheless, are rational purposive planners as well as predominantly self-interested beings. They realize that life without rules is not a human life. They seek to create some type of entity that can defend them from the injuries they inflict on one another.

Consequently, they enter into a mutual agreement or "social contract" to appoint or elect a sovereign person or assembly with the absolute authority to lay down the law and to enforce it. By virtue of the agreement, the individual members thereto surrender their "natural" right to self-rule, confer on whomever is elected or appointed their combined power, and authorize all actions of this sovereign power. The resultant contractual concentration of strength empowers the sovereign to discharge its protective duties. The credible threat of commensurate punishment by the common power deters aggression, breaches of the agreement, and rule breaking. The legal commands pronounced by the sovereign emerge not only as the code of conduct but also as the standard for justice. To be a good citizen and a moral person is to be just. To be just, one must obey the law.

d) The Nature of Morality

Since no other foundation of normative order can be built with certainty, positive law secures moral significance. Morality, therefore, depends on law (assuming that the law is enforced effectively). Rules achieve validity only when a sovereign, with the power to command and impose sanctions for noncompliance, declares the rules as law. In the absence of any power to guarantee that rules will be obeyed, any moral proposition is only subjectively and conditionally true. Law not only imparts clarity, conclusiveness, and verifiability to moral questions, but also renders morality ultimately obligatory.

This legal rendering of morality is justified in terms of prudence. One will agree to live under a state of law and to abide by the rules not only to protect oneself, but also to effectuate the conditions for mutually advantageous communal living. The considerable gains to be secured through organized civil society supersede the inconveniences that might chafe an individual by adhering to the terms of the social contract and complying with the law. The law, therefore, is the vehicle for moving from the chaos of the state of nature, to peace, civil society, and to prosperity.

e) "Bad" Law

According to the Hobbesian creed, since law is the source of morality, there cannot be an immoral law. Questions as to the justice, fairness, rightfulness, and reasonableness of the law are entirely irrelevant. Law itself makes morality. Until the rule of law exists, there is no morality at all. Measuring the law against a moral standard is nonsensical; it amounts to measuring the law against itself. Hobbes does not countenance any foolishness as to whether the sovereign is just or unjust. Whatever is authoritatively decreed by the sovereign is just and moral. There is no such thing as a "bad" law. Law is defined without any reference to its content. What law is and what it ought to be are strictly separated.

F) Summary

Pursuant to the Hobbesian version of Legal Positivism, the sovereign emerges as the final authority as to what the law says and should say. Morality does not exist outside civil society, its legal conventions, and concomitant coercive enforcement mechanisms. A significant reason for entering into the social contract and establishing civil institutions is to create enforceable moral requirements by means of the law.

4. The Law's Relationship to Morality

A) Moral Support for the Law

There seems little doubt that the law interacts with morality. Many laws are motivated by beliefs in moral rights and responsibilities and are grounded in moral convictions. Laws governing contracts, for example, formalize moral ideas concerning promise-keeping. Moral standards often are incorporated into the law. The tort of negligence, for example, legally exemplifies the moral proposition that a person should act in a reasonably prudent manner. Many laws prohibit immoral practices that are severely injurious to society. Laws against murder, theft, and fraud, for example, are based on moral convictions about killing, stealing, and lying. Laws that business finds burdensome, for example, antitrust, securities regulation, environmental, and employment discrimination laws can be traced back to "immoral" business practices.

Morality, like the law, treats subjects of the greatest social significance. Some laws formally require conduct that is the same required by morality. In China, for example, respect for one's family elders has been ingrained in Chinese culture, society, and tradition. Now, that moral norm has been embedded into a law, promulgated in 2005, called "Protecting the Rights and Interests of the Elderly," which states that support for the elderly shall be provided for mainly by their families. There seems little doubt that morality shapes, supports, and supplements the law. Hence, the law does provide a criterion to measure the morality of management practices. Conformity to the law, therefore, very well may be the leading and most commonly accepted test of morality.

B) The Language of Law and Morality

The relationship between law and morality, moreover, is reflected in their use of similar language. Law and morality both speak of obligations, duties, rights, and excuses, for example. They harness the words "ought" and "must," "right" and "wrong," and "good" and "bad." Such a lexicon endeavors not only to evaluate conduct but also to steer a course of conduct. In ascertaining the correct course, law and morality employ an analogous reasoning process.

C) Legal and Moral Reasoning

Legal reasoning exhibits the familiar pattern of reasoning whereby general legal principles and rules of law are applied to particular factual situations to arrive at a logical decision. An essential part of legal reasoning is that the principles and rules upon which resolution of a dispute is based not only are stated clearly and fully but also are available for future reference and use as precedents.

Moral reasoning is similar to legal reasoning. Ethical principles and moral rules constitute a kind of moral law. Moral reasoning often entails the logical thought processes that are characteristic of the law. Although morality is not as peremptory as the law, it is extremely efficacious and advantageous for a moral philosopher to craft carefully and to apply consistently an ethical formula whenever a moral decision is contemplated. Although the need to conform to precedent is not as imperative in moral systems as in legal systems, a moral decision should be available as an antecedent reference. Adherence to such "moral precedent" promotes predictability, continuity, and stability that contribute towards a preferred "good" way of life. Legal and moral reasoning, in addition, can bring forth rights.

d) Legal and Moral Rights

Legal rights are supported by existing legal principles and rules. They are derived from constitutions, statutes, and case law. They are accessible, ascertainable, uniformly applicable, and ultimately determinable. Legal rights also can be eliminated, for example, by lawful amendment to a constitution or the repeal of a statute.

Moral rights are derived from ethical principles and supported by moral rules. Moral rights, however, lack certain characteristics of legal rights. Ethical views not only differ but also conflict, thereby engendering inconsistent moral rules. Moral rules also are informal and indeterminate compared to legal rules. No assembly of moral authorities is empowered to promulgate authoritatively and definitely moral rights.

If rights do exist, however, then it is imperative that rights not be contravened by society and its members.

e) Legal and Moral Sanctions

A mark of the law is the presence of sanctions for its noncompliance and for the transgression of rights. Sanctions enforced by the state include actual physical force, restraint, incarceration, and the threat thereof. Morality, like law, seeks to act as a system of social regulation. Yet what are the sanctions attached to the violation of the moral law, and who enforces the moral law?

Moral sanctions are associated with certain emotions about oneself, for example, guilt, shame, remorse, and loss of self-esteem. In this sense, the "sanctions" are self-actualizing and self-imposed. When directed toward another person, moral sanctions are associated with feelings of indignation, resentment, and even disgust. Here, the sanctions are supported by social pressure in the form of blame, condemnation, disassociation, and other indications of disfavor and aversion.

What morality demands and what society commands, however, are not always the same. What is right can conflict with what most members of society believe to be "right" and thus try to enforce by means of social pressure.

f) Law and Ethical Relativism

The societal-based doctrine of ethical relativism further reveals the connection between law and morality. Law reflects the collective moral judgments fashioned by the members of a society. Law provides an insight into what is right and wrong by mirroring the moral beliefs, standards, and values of the community.

When a number of people agree on moral rules with a sufficient measure of detail, laws can be promulgated, thereby formally executing and enacting the moral rules. The law now codifies "right" conduct and elevates it to a binding obligation backed by the authority and power of state. Predictably, a society's legal and moral standards will converge. Legal duties are reinforced by conformity to what the society regards as moral duties. The conventional morality of a society reflects and complements the law's prohibitions on conduct.

5. The "Democratic" Rationale for Legal Positivism

The law in a democratic state represents the collective moral beliefs of the members of that society. Consequently, what is "right" is construed as what the state pronounces as legal. Particularly in a democratic state, the governing body can be persuaded that its law-making was wrong and as a result change the law. Determinations of right and wrong ultimately are to correspond to the majority views of the population. Until the law is changed, however, it serves as a significant guide to moral behavior.

If a person is complying with the law, he or she credibly can contend that a legal action is not wrong in any moral sense because the action complies with the moral beliefs of a majority of his or her peers. If the law is in some way "bad," it still must be obeyed until properly remade or replaced by the proper processes; otherwise, disorder ensues if every person perceives a privilege to disregard the law on moral grounds. If a group in society objects to any "immoral" business or management practice, its responsibility is to convince a majority of society members democratically to approve or modify a law that will prohibit or regulate the practice; at that time, management is constrained to conform to the law.

6. Problems with Legal Positivism

a) Introduction

Law and morality do coincide to a considerable degree. The area of overlay, however, is not complete. Law and morality do not always correspond; the law does not consume the concept of morality. It is incorrect, therefore, to view law and morality as identical.

b) Morally Neutral Laws

Some laws simply lack moral content. Laws such as left versus right side driving laws, for example, do not raise moral concerns because they do not involve serious moral matters.

c) The Limits of the Law

Not everything regarded as immoral can be rendered illegal. Telling a "little," "innocent" lie or the breaking of a social promise, for example, is considered immoral. Laws against such actions, however, are either enforceable or not worth the time, trouble, and resources to enforce.

There are, in addition, more serious moral weaknesses or omissions in the law. A misrepresentation of law (that is, lying about the existence, nature, or applicability of a law), for example, generally is not actionable as fraud because of the conventional dogma (which is obviously untrue) that "everyone is presumed to know the law." The possible consequence of such a moral "gap" in the law is that a person may be deceived and taken advantage of legally but immorally.

It is obviously unrealizable for the law to be promulgated in such a way as to cover all the complicated changing circumstances that arise in a modern society. The law, for example, easily can fall behind scientific and technological advances.

d) The Impermanence of the Law

Laws are created, changed, and repealed by the determinations of a law-making entity. Law is not as ultimate as fundamental ethical principles and moral rules. Moral rules are neither established nor remade by the decisions of any particular authoritative body. Their validity does not depend on individual or group decision making, but rather on the sufficiency of the reasoning employed to assert, support, and defend the rules. So long as this reasoning is justifiable, the rules remain permanently valid. Laws can be repealed, but a genuine moral obligation is categorical and not repealable.

e) Promoting Morality Legally

The law can dictate a person's conduct but it neither can demand obedience from any particular motive nor require that a person possess a particular purpose when obeying the law. One's inner motives and purposes in acting cannot be made part of the law.

The law can compel a person to be law abiding and to act as he or she was moral, but the law cannot make a person be moral. The power of the law to promote moral standards and ends is limited. Controversy, contentiousness, and litigation frequently accompany the legal process. Litigation focuses attention on procedural issues and the "letter" of the law rather than its substance, "spirit," and the moral justification behind the law's initial creation. Any sense of justice rapidly is lost in the diverting details and adversarialness of the process, the professional ambitions of the attorneys, and the inducements for self-centeredness in the litigants.

The parties to a legal controversy are, or soon become, adversaries, whereas the bonds of personal and social relations are strengthened by morality. Lawyers probe for moral gaps in the law for legal exploitation, whereas ethics responds sensitively to vulnerable "stakeholders" and seeks at a minimum to do no moral harm.

f) The Law as Representative of the Collective Moral Standards of a Society

There are problems in viewing the law as the reflection of the collective moral standards of a society. The moral standards themselves can be "faulty" if they are based on misinformation, emotion, or bias rather than rational judgment. Presuming the moral standards are accurate, pertinent, and reasoned, there is no assurance that they are represented correctly in the law. Moral standards are diluted by the demands of interest groups. The legal system is not only complex, cumbersome, and costly, but also subject to pressure and manipulation. Interest groups often act from nonmoral motives, such as enhancing material benefits for their membership. Not all people, moreover, or even interest groups, possess commensurate prestige, access, and influence in the formulation of the law.

The laws of a society thus can contain oppressive and even unpopular precepts, the authoritative legal status of which is not open to discussion. Slavery is a classic example. Laws also can be inadequate to prohibit oppressive conduct. A multinational corporation, for example, may be able to neglect legally its workers' safety due to the absence of laws. Legal accountability can lag behind the moral standards of a society. Employment discrimination and environmental pollution, are examples of recognized compelling moral problems only gradually remedied by the law. Changes in the law were required to cause the laws to conform to society's moral standards.

G) MORALITY AS A CRITERION FOR JUDGING THE LAW

The fact that laws are enacted does not mean necessarily that the laws are just. In analyzing law, it is important to differentiate between legality and legitimacy. A precept is legal when it is based in the positive law of a state. A law is legitimate when it is deemed as good, right, just, and moral. A concept of legitimacy discloses that law is not morally neutral.

It is difficult to dispute that laws are judged as rationally as right or wrong. In everyday business affairs, managers regard laws as good and bad. When judges interpret the law, they often take into account what the law should be. If one contends that the legal power of the state ought to be exercised in accordance with justice, one also is saying that legality is not the source of morality. Legal power achieves legitimacy and moral justification only when applied in accordance with ethical principles.

When there are rational objective moral standards by which laws are evaluated, the law then can be judged morally right or wrong. In such a context, law and morality obviously are considered as coequal systems assessing conduct.

People on the whole believe that they have an obligation to obey valid laws and to support generally the rule of law; yet why should people bother to make moral judgments about the law and act on these judgments? The answer is that moral judgments acquire great practical importance. The principal value of ethics to the law is to supply the critical ethical reasoning that serves to change the law. Laws can be criticized, eliminated, or made "better" when it becomes evident that laws contravene ethically determined moral standards. One now can contend from a moral position that a "bad" law should be invalidated or that a new law should be promulgated.

If a person does argue that a law is bad and ought to be changed or that a judge's decision ought to be reversed in the interests of justice, one is acknowledging the dependence of law on morality. By focusing on the moral rationale behind legal decision making, one enters the realm of ethical jurisprudence. The legitimacy and acceptability of an existing legal rule evermore depend on its conformity to an ethically ascertained moral standard.

If morality is synonymous with legality, one cannot morally criticize law. If one adopts legal positivism, one is precluded from attempting to change the laws by independent, rational, ethical persuasion.

H) RESISTANCE TO UNJUST LAWS

Discharging a legal duty may contrivance a moral obligation. Actions in the moral realm are rooted in rational ethical persuasion, conscience, and personal choice. These features of morality often can serve as a basis to disobey law. Accordingly, one may have a superseding moral responsibility to censure, oppose, and disobey an unjust and immoral law.

There exist many examples of laws that as transgress recognized moral standards. The historical legal reality of slavery emerges as the primary example of morally offensive law. When positive law and morality are in such serious conflict, violating the law can be declared as a defense of what is morally right. The historical cases of Mahatma Gandhi, Henry David Thoreau, Rosa Parks, Dr. Martin Luther King Jr., and Nelson Mandela are prime examples of civil disobedience to immoral laws

i) LAW AS A FOUNDATION

The law properly can be regarded as representing a minimum set of standards. Law should serve as a "baseline" constraint for management action. Moral norms and obligations, however, may demand conduct above and beyond this minimum. The requirements of the law tend to be negative, yet a moral obligation may be positive. The conventional legal doctrine of nonfeasance, on one hand, holds that generally there is no legal accountability for not acting, not rescuing, and not coming to a person's aid. The ethical principle of "last resort," on the other hand, mandates that one may have a positive moral duty to act affirmatively.

j) DELEGATING MORAL ISSUES TO THE LEGAL DEPARTMENT

If a manager believes that law and morality are virtually synonymous, he or she merely has to turn over any moral problem to the corporation's legal staff. Although the legal department does engage in defining, prescribing, and monitoring appropriate corporate conduct, a manager must recognize the difference between law and morality in the corporate setting.

The function of the corporation's legal department essentially is to protect and promote the interests of its "client," the corporation. Morality, ideally the function of a separate and co-equal corporate department-the Ethics Department, aims to protect the interests of the corporation's constituents, at times by opposing corporate actions narrowly beneficial to the corporation's own shareholders and management. The problem in delegating moral issues to the legal department is the creation of a conflict of interest. Since laws and morality serve different "clients," whose interest does the corporation's legal department serve?

7. Summary

The law is not the equivalent of morality. One cannot rest wholly on the law when countering a moral difficulty. One cannot and must not maintain that morality is synonymous with the positive law a state enforces. An absence of law, moreover, may be insufficient to excuse an action or the lack of an action.

One need not assume, however, that the dividing line between morality and legality is a precise one. There is a relationship between law and morality and the law does serve as a guide to moral decision making.

A fundamental problem with Legal Positivism is the doctrine's pessimistic and doubtful perspective. The doctrine, in essence, holds that morality makes no sense and ethics has no value. The doctrine also implies that people, particularly business people, basically are bad and will remain so. Even assuming a moral course of conduct can be ascertained, management will adhere to this proper standard only by means of legal compulsion.

A manager's subscribing to Legal Positivism, therefore, amounts to complete abdication of moral responsibility. Managers must grapple with ethics and struggle to make moral determinations. Managers must act morally based on their own ethical reasoning and moral convictions. Managers must not countenance others prompting them to moral action. If management does surrender its moral authority, external legal agents surely will impose even further restrictions on management activities.

Government has demonstrated no reluctance to resolve misconduct allegations against business. The law now regulates in detail many aspects of corporate conduct. If management fails to respond, or is unwilling, government will "legislate" morality at the expense of corporate freedom. Law creates as many problems as it solves. Laws narrow the discretionary authority of management decision makers and inhibit innovation by emphasizing sanctions rather than rewards.

If management fails to become more involved with moral issues, it is possible that the present system of corporate governance might be altered. Large, publicly traded corporations, for example, might lose control of director and officer selection.

Why then do managers retreat to the law as a standard for business morality? Perhaps managers are not educated ethically to handle moral issues. Management simply may be unclear about moral standards and unprepared to engage in the ethical process of ascertaining, clarifying, and resolving moral issues. A major purpose of this book is to supply appropriate ethical knowledge.

Discussion Questions

1. Would acting purely on what an individual feels is right make the individual morally right?

2. What effect would morality have for a global businessperson visiting a foreign country?

3. How can ethical relativism appeal to a global society?

4. Why would it be wrong for an ethical relativist to criticize the practice and beliefs of other societies?

5. What are moral universal standard based on? Give a few examples.

6. Under the definition of Legal Positivism, would it be correct to say, "A moral person is a legal person"? Why?

7. Do you believe that a person doing what he believes is morally right but lawfully wrong be prosecuted?

8. Do you believe that all laws are legal?

9. Why would certain individuals or groups engage in civil disobedience and rallies against a government?

10. What can result when law and morality comes into conflict?

11. We now know that ethical emotism says that morals are strictly based on emotions. We also know that moral decisions are also based on reason, and serious

consideration of an issue. How much is emotion actually involved in moral decisions?

12. Is there a "proper" way to make a moral decision?

13. Will the moral judgments of one person be truly comparable to the moral judgments of another person, if their moral beliefs are the same, though they may live in different societies?

14. What is an effective argument to the ethical relativist who believes there is no universal right or wrong?

15. At what point is the moral good of the society more important than the moral good of the individual?

16. Legal positivism has yielded many laws that strictly govern how businesses may act. Yet, businesses clearly act immorally or unethically in violation of those laws. What can be done to effectively implement moral standards on business managers?

17. Can business laws legislate moral behavior of those businesses?

18. What is the real cost to society by the attempt to legislate morality?

19. Moral behavior is usually instilled by the society through the parents, peers, and social customs of behavior. Can ethically centered classes for adults (managers) really make a difference in the behavior of managers, if they have not acted ethically in the past?

20. How are morality and ethics effectively taught, particularly if one had no ethical standards before?

CHAPTER 7

Utilitarianism

A. Introduction, Background, and Principal Tenets

Utilitarianism refers to a systematic theory of moral philosophy developed by the British philosopher Jeremy Bentham (1748–1832), and elaborated on and refined by his primary disciple, John Stuart Mill (1806–1873). Bentham was one of the earliest and the most influential utilitarians. He was trained in law and he originated utilitarianism from a general and intense disenchantment with the British legal system. In his *Introduction to the Principles of Morals and Legislation*, Bentham's primary objective was to provide a criterion for acceptable legislation in general and the use of punishment in particular. He made very little distinction between morality and law, basing both on utilitarianism.

The utilitarians were more than moral philosophers; they were social reformers too. They regarded utilitarianism as an objective, scientific system of ethics, not merely as abstract ethical theory.

Bentham and the utilitarians rejected any theory of natural rights, which they viewed as discredited by the excesses of the French Revolution and which served as a "license" for the masses to overturn the political order. Locke's natural law theory was viewed as a meaningless generality, which only supplied an elaborate rationalization for the privileged classes to maintain the status quo. Bentham also rejected any intuitive basis for ethics. Intuition or conscience merely reflected irrational sentiments, which lacked any objective basis. The English common law was ancient, ossified, and harshly punitive. The true purpose of the law, for Bentham, is to promote the welfare of the people, not to impose severe punishments.

In place of these erroneous beliefs and in order to reform the law, Bentham offered a new, fundamental, universal principle of ethics to determine morality and to justify changes. Bentham's doctrine would cut through the abstractness, irrationality, and partiality of the status quo. Bentham's ethics was "scientific"; it supplied an external, objective standard for morality, which is mathematically calculable and proven by empirical means.

Utilitarianism was aimed at the English middle class, who were searching for a doctrine, other than natural law or natural rights, to serve as a basis for effectuating legal and political changes.

Bentham realistically took hedonism as the governing principle of human conduct. He viewed pleasure and pain as the "sovereign masters" of human beings. From this foundational principle, Bentham derived the ethical theory known as utilitarianism.

Bentham's goal was to create as much happiness as possible, and accordingly his ethics was an attempt to bring about this happiness. The moral course of human conduct, therefore, is the one that promotes the greatest amount of happiness for the greatest number of people. Bentham's objective was to create the greatest degree of benefit for the largest number of people, while incurring the least amount of damage and harm.

Utilitarianism, therefore, determines morality by focusing on the consequences of actions. Actions are not good or bad in themselves; they are judged right or wrong solely by virtue of their consequences.

A utilitarian, after identifying the action for ethical evaluation, determines those people directly and indirectly affected by the action. The utilitarian then attempts to ascertain consequences of the action, good and bad, on the affected parties. In the most challenging aspect of this ethical theory, the utilitarian then strives to measure and weigh the good as compared to the bad consequences. If the good consequences outweigh the bad, the action is moral; if the bad outweigh the good, the action is immoral.

A utilitarian analysis of an action, private employment surveillance or monitoring, for example, would proceed as follows: Does the sum of the good attained by these actions outweigh the sum of the bad that results from them? The people and groups affected by such an action include the employer, the employees, shareholders of the employer, customers, the competition, and society. A utilitarian would require that an employer contemplating surveillance and monitoring consider the consequences not only to itself and its direct "stakeholders," but also to the interests of society. Accordingly, surveillance and monitoring at the workplace negatively can affect society as a whole because such practices may violate the right to privacy of its individual members. If employers, however, implement such practices in part to advance recognized societal agendas, such as eliminating incompetent, dishonest, or impaired employees from the workforce, one can say that society benefits.

A utilitarian would attempt to measure and weigh all the preceding consequences. To illustrate this step, one could argue that benefits or pleasure of surveillance and monitoring as outlined above may outweigh the costs or pain. If this were true, it would be moral based on the ethical principle of utilitarianism for an employer to artificially and electronically monitor and observe its employees.

B. Impartiality of the Analysis

Utilitarianism treats all people as equally important. Each person's life, happiness, pleasure, and pain has the same value; each person's good is as worthwhile as any other person's good. There are no privileged persons. No one possesses special importance; no person's pleasure or pain counts more heavily than another's. Consequently, there is to be no unequal weighing. An impersonal calculation of the good is required. A utilitarian, therefore, must acknowledge that other peoples' welfare is just as important as one's own.

Ethical egoism, however, evaluates actions in terms of the actor's own good, welfare, or preferences. The doctrine may or may not require that the actor serve another's good, and it may require that the actor do so only as a means of promoting his or her own good. Utilitarianism, however, evaluates actions in relationship to the greater good or general welfare. The doctrine requires the actor not only to consider the welfare of others, but also to serve the welfare generally and to the maximum extent possible. Utilitarianism evaluates actions in relation to the good of all those people directly or indirectly affected by the action, with each person's pleasure or pain being accorded equal weight. Utilitarianism maintains that the right action is the one that produces the greater good. This does not mean that the right action is the one that produces the most good for the person performing the action. Rather, an action is moral if it produces the most good for all people affected by the action, including, of course, the person performing the action.

C. Long-Term Consequences

When one is evaluating a particular action, one may give undue weight to considerations of pleasure and pain that seem immediately more pressing at the expense of the consequences that a more deliberate and detailed analysis would treat as possessing greater relative weight in the long-term.

Utilitarianism, therefore, underscores the long-range consequences of an action. Even though the short-term consequences are pleasurable, the long-range consequences may be quite painful. If one, for example, is contemplating breaching a promise to repay a monetary debt to a wealthy friend in order to use the money to help a needy person, the short-term pleasurable consequences emerge as more vivid; but a more reflective, long-term analysis will indicate more painful consequences, such as a loss of confidence, reliability, and an undermining of the institution of promise-keeping.

D. Foreseeing Consequences

The utilitarian ethical principle is based on consequences. It is, of course, very difficult to foresee the consequences of an action, even in the simplest of cases, and to predict the future state of affairs resulting from an action occurring in a modern, complex, rapidly changing, urban society is a challenging task, indeed. The indefinitely large number of people potentially affected, the uncertainty and indefinite extensiveness of the future, the fact that some consequences will never be fully knowable, and that others will depend on later, independent choices of people, indicate that ultimate consequences never are fully foreseeable.

Where does one draw the line in predicting consequences? Where does one stop in taking consequences into account? Even if one can estimate probabilities of foreseeable consequences, at some point probabilities will fade into guesses, and eventually the thread of causation will be broken.

Of course, if one attempts to calculate accurately the consequences of an act for the whole future, one would be so dismayed that one would never act. The utilitarians, therefore, emphasize that their ethical theory extends only to foreseeable consequences, and thus one calculates only reasonably foreseeable consequences. Frequently, one can foresee a large number of possible, if not actual, consequences. Some, moreover, may be so important as to dominate the calculation. One should know many consequences because of history and general knowledge. In judging an action, one also has the benefit of similar actions done in the past. Accordingly, when faced with a difficult moral decision, one must stop and take the time to consider the consequences. One, finally must realize that ethical determinations are subject to error, and thus moral judgments always must be subject to ethical revision and correction.

E. The "Good"

What exactly constitutes the "good" to be maximized under utilitarianism? Is the "good" an objective conception of human welfare or is it in fact a separate and independent value judgment itself?

It may be possible to reduce the "good" to money and thus make a monetary determination of the pleasurable and painful consequences. If money is the unit of measurement for quantifying pleasure and pain, then the utilitarianism calculations are relatively easy.

The aim of business, of course, is to make money, and business traditionally reduces the "good" to money. As a matter of fact, the cost-benefit analysis commonly used in business is a form of utility calculation. When a business manager uses the cost-benefit analysis as a decision-making tool, however, he or she weighs the good and bad monetary consequences as they relate to the firm, whereas utilitarians weigh the good and bad results of an action, monetary or otherwise, on everyone directly and indirectly affected by the action.

The real problem with ethically using money as the "good" is that not all benefits and costs can be expressed in terms of money. Certain things, such as human life and limb, or even job satisfaction, are not really capable of being bought and sold and therefore have no "price" on the market.

Bentham held that the ultimate good was pleasure (or the absence of pain), but pleasure in the sense of happiness and satisfaction. The "right" action, therefore, is the one that maximizes happiness and satisfaction.

Pleasure, happiness, and satisfaction are, for Bentham, intrinsic "goods." They possess value in and of themselves, for their own sake, and not for some other benefits they may produce. Intrinsic goods must be differentiated from instrumental goods, which are valuable only because they lead to other things. Money, for example, usually is viewed as an instrumental good because it is valuable as a means to other things. The possession of money, therefore, is not valued for the sake of having stacks of money, but rather because money can be used to purchase various things and services as well as provide security and peace of mind, all of which contribute to happiness.

There may be other goods that possess intrinsic value in their own right. That is, there may be certain things that are good for their own sake, independent of whether their presence produces pleasure or their loss causes pain. For example, consider the values of knowledge, beauty, love, and friendship. Are these good only because they cause pleasure, or are they worthwhile independent of any pleasure they produce? Pleasure and happiness actually may be a response to attaining a multiple of things, already recognized as intrinsically good, independently and in their own right.

Bentham believed that pleasure and pain should be calculated on the basis of a "hedonic calculus," which considers the following aspects of pleasure or pain: intensity, duration, certainty, remoteness, abundance, and purity. Bentham rejected the view that some pleasures were of a higher level or quality than others. Bentham thus presumed that pleasures are to be "ranked" only on the basis of the seven features of the "hedonic calculus."

Mill, however, thought he observed a weakness in Bentham's position and tried to correct it. Mill believed the "good" could not be defined simply as a quantity of the pleasure or pain produced. Some pleasures are of a "higher" quality than others, even though they may not be as long lasting or as intense. Pleasure, therefore, differs in quality as well as in quantity. Intellectual pleasure and aesthetic pleasure, for example, are qualitatively superior, and thus preferable, to others, such as the pleasures of eating and drinking. Mill's refinement thus introduced a qualitative element into Bentham's quantitative calculus.

The problem, of course, with Mill's "refinement" is determining how one is to rank pleasures. What if one pleasure is more intense than another, but the latter is asserted as "higher" than the former? How is one to choose between them? What are the criteria for determining the hierarchy? It will be rare to get unanimous agreement on the ranking; if the ranking is determined by the views of the majority, then the standard of morality is what most people believe, which sounds like ethical relationism!

A quality criterion implies that an action can be good or bad independently of the amount of pleasure or pain it produces. Mill's refinement, therefore, exposes an inconsistency: maintaining that pleasure is the good, yet also holding that there is something in certain pleasures that makes them intrinsically better than others. The emphasis on quality not only contradicts a fundamental tenet of utilitarianism, quantifying the good, but also compels a person, in order to define and rank quality, to go outside the utilitarian theory.

F. Distribution of the Good

By underscoring the maximization of the good, utilitarianism engenders another problem—a potential conflict between the quantity of the good and its distribution. Is utilitarianism based on an aggregative principle or a distributive principle? That is, should the emphasis be placed on the total amount of good or the number of people who share in the good? There may be two acts: one produces a greater quantity of good, but with a very narrow distribution; the other produces a lesser quantity, but with a much wider distribution. Which one should a utilitarian choose?

Bentham and Mill did not distinguish clearly between the two principles. Bentham did remark that everybody is to count for one, and nobody for more than one; perhaps these statements can be taken as a distributive principle, but they are probably more appropriately taken as an admonition that there neither be any unequal weighing nor any privileged people. Bentham, in addition, often spoke of the "greatest happiness" without reference to the greatest number, thus implying that one ought to maximize the total amount of good, regardless of distribution.

Neglecting the "just" distribution of the good, however, opens up utilitarianism to a serious criticism. Where is the ethical principle that ensures that the distribution of the maximized good is fair. The just solution may be to choose the action that produces good for more people, rather than maximizing greater good for a smaller number. Since one is supposed to promote the greatest good for the greatest number, a distributive principle widely distributes the good in the short run; and should maximize the good in the long term.

G. Measuring Pleasure and Pain

Utilitarianism assumes that one can measure on a common numerical scale the quantities of pleasure and pain produced by an action. Once one adds up the quantity of pleasure and then subtracts from it the quantity of pain, one thereby can determine whether the action produces more pleasure than pain; and when comparing actions, one can determine which produces the greatest total good (or perhaps the lowest total pain). How this numerical measuring is to be done and, indeed, whether it can be accomplished at all are highly controversial theoretical and practical ethical issues.

Bentham certainly wanted ethics to be a scientific and mathematical subject matter capable of quantitative measurement. He naturally assumed that pleasure and pain could be measured in numerical terms. In Bentham's bookkeeping or accounting approach to ethics, all one has to do is add up the good and bad consequences of an action to determine its morality.

Yet is it really possible to measure quantities of pleasure and pain? There are certainly problems with Bentham's moral accounting. There is, for example, the improbability of accurate measurement. If the greatest happiness principle is to work, pleasures and pains must be capable of exact measurement, so as to be weighed against one another. Exact mathematical measurement and quantification, however, either seems to be out of the question or so long to perform as to be impractical for determining what ought to be done in daily life.

Attempts to measure pleasure and pain and to quantify utility also unavoidably involve arbitrary and subjective assessments. How safe is it to assume that the person doing the weighing desires to promote the common good, as opposed to furthering his or her own private pleasure? Can the person doing the weighing be adequately supervised and controlled? There is, moreover, the distinct possibility of rationalization. One can act for purely selfish reasons and then conveniently (and perhaps even unconsciously) weigh the consequences in such a way so as to justify the action one desires.

The utilitarians would reply that people make utilitarian-type calculations everyday, weighing present against future utilities. In so doing, people rely on their intelligence, common sense, and past experience. The utilitarians, moreover, do not demand precise mathematical calculations. One can approximate outcomes and include these approximations in the calculations. In many cases, the consequences are sufficiently obvious; the good and bad predominate so clearly that great precision is not necessary. In difficult cases, where the calculation is not clear, and one is not sure if one is correct in moral measurement, one must be ready to revise one's calculations. Ultimately, however, all one humanly can do is to "satisfy"—which means to provide a reasonable predictability and assessment, and not perfect predictability or computerlike calculations.

H. A Utilitarian Analysis

Since utilitarianism assumes that the pleasures and pains of an action can be measured and weighed on a common numerical scale, and then added and subtracted from each other, the following detailed, "mathematical" utilitarian analysis is offered.

1. *The Action.* A utilitarian analysis first requires identification of the action to be evaluated. Here, the action is random, observed, urinalysis drug testing and the subsequent

discharge of employees who test positive. The second step is to identify parties affected by the action. This action directly affects employers and employees. Those indirectly affected are employees' families, shareholders of the employers, customers and consumers, suppliers, local communities, and society in general.

2. *The Consequences.* The final step in a utilitarian analysis is to weigh the positive and negative consequences of any action. This step of balancing necessarily implies that good and bad are capable of measurement in some quantitative manner. Although there is disagreement regarding whether values can truly be quantified and compared, people make numerous such evaluations in a fashion every day. Further, the utilitarian process of identifying alternatives and estimating their consequences may be of use to decision makers faced with ethical judgments. The purpose of assigning numbers to units of pleasure and pain is to underscore the "scientific" spirit of the utilitarian ethical philosophy to demonstrate one potential practical application of an ethical theory, and to encourage the reader to actually apply this ethical measuring procedure. The figures used in this article are not to be taken as revealed "truth," but as an illustration of applied ethics. This analysis assigns hypothetical numerical values to the relative benefit or pain for each category of person affected. These values fall on a suggested numerical scale from −5 (most pain) to +5 (most benefit). Accordingly, +1 or −1 would represent a negligible amount of benefit or pain, respectively, with +5 or −5 simplifying a considerable amount.

i. *Employers.* Positive consequences for employers who randomly test employees for drugs result from the reduction and gradual elimination of drug use from the workplace and ultimately the workforce. If employees were to become drug-free, many problems now associated with the use of drugs would be lessened. Considerable decreases, for example, in tardiness, absenteeism, poor performance, on- and off-the-job accidents, and medical costs would be likely, with a final result of more productive employees and overall enhanced profitability. Negative consequences are a diminished level of trust between employers and employees, a decrease (at least short-lived) in employee morale, and a loss of some "good" employees (drug using, privacy-threatened, or both). Overall, the good consequences appear to weigh heavily against the bad, resulting in a value of +4 for the employer.

ii. *Employees.* Employees are negatively affected in that they lose some privacy rights as a consequence of the testing program. Urination is a private bodily function; drug testing is an invasive procedure. Compelling employees to undergo the actual physical act of collecting urine under observation for analysis strains the bounds of decency.

An obvious negative consequence of drug testing to those employees who test positive is the possibility of losing their jobs. Employees who do not use drugs also may feel violated if treated as though they are under suspicion for the drug use and subject to testing. Finally, employees may believe that if they do their jobs properly, then what they do outside the company is none of the employer's business.

Positive consequences for employees are the identification of impaired individuals and their removal from the workplace, thereby providing a safer working environment for all personnel. The eliminated drug user may be a friend to many, but coworkers will no longer have to worry about drug induced substandard performance. Another good consequence of a drug testing program is the early identification of employee drug users. Early identification helps in the eventual rehabilitation of some individual users, especially if an employer's program allows for assistance to the impaired employee. Discharging the possibly good effects of drug screening for the sake of argument, employees are assigned −4 units of pain.

iii. *Families of Employees.* Discharging employees for testing positive may adversely impact their families. The families must deal not only with the loss of income but also with the emotions of the discharged employees. These negative consequences, however, can be tempered if an employee, as a result of the drug testing policy, does become drug-free. An employee who is compelled to receive help, perhaps through an employee assistance program, may be able to achieve a more balanced life not only at work, but also at home. Nonetheless, due to the foreseeable consequence of loss of family income, the families of employees are assigned a −3 pain designation.

iv. *Shareholders of Employees.* Shareholders benefit from the imposition of the testing due to the resulting elimination of poorly performing drug users. The company will reduce its liability from accidents caused by impaired employees. Diminished liability and healthier employees translates into enhanced performance, possible higher market share, and presumably a higher rate of return for the shareholders' investments. Although shareholders could be affected negatively from wrongful discharge litigation or adverse publicity stemming from a drug testing program, the overall benefit is +4.

v. *Customers and Consumers.* Purchasers and users of the employer's products and services gain substantially through surveillance and monitoring. Because employees will be more likely to perform their duties at optimum capacity, customers can expect to receive better products and services. The customers, however, may have to pay for the drug testing program, if the employer passes along costs. The result is an overall measurement of +4.

vi. *Suppliers.* Suppliers also would benefit from an employer's drug testing program. They would be protected against dealing with drug-impaired employees. Suppliers would gain, for example, in not incurring unnecessary absenteeism costs and by meeting with capable representatives of the employer. The employer's drug testing program should lead to safer, more harmonious, and economically more productive relationship with its suppliers. As an employer's costs decrease, and its efficiency and economic growth increase, suppliers will benefit from the employer's concomitant rise in purchasing power. Overall, the employer should find abundant support from its suppliers for the company's drug testing program. Consequently, because the drug testing program will effectuate better and more profitable relationships with "stakeholders," such as suppliers, who interact with and depend upon the employer, suppliers represent +4 units on the scale.

vii. *Local Communities.* The benefits to local communities rise from the decrease in the number of drug users in the workforce, including those employed in critical positions. These benefits are reduced, however, by the possibility that the community may have to support terminated employees' families through the use of public assistance. Local communities are assigned a +3.

viii. *Society.* Society will experience pain due to the diminution of privacy rights of the individual employees who must undergo testing. Society will gain, however, because elimination of drug users will reduce the possibility of defective products and negligent services, which in turn enhances public safety. Drug testing will also improve employers' productivity. As productivity increases, society's standard of living should correspondingly improve. If such a blanket program does in fact help produce a drug-free work force, it would contribute to a drug-free society, thus giving other social programs a better chance of working. There admittedly is a price to be paid for the further loss in privacy rights, but the resulting societal good outweighs the pain. Society is assigned a value of +3.

3. *Weighing the Consequences.* The consequences expressed in the assigned units of pleasure and pain are as follows: Employers +4; employees –4; families of employees –3; shareholders +4; customers and consumers +4; suppliers +4; local communities +3; and society +3. The result is –7 units of pain and +22 units of pleasure. Because the random drug testing program produced more good than bad, the action is moral under the ethical doctrine utilitarianism.

4. *Summary.* Although not "scientific" doctrine, utilitarianism can be a useful tool for making moral determinations. Individuals would benefit from familiarity with the central tenets of this ethical theory-foreseeing, measuring, and weighing the consequences of actions. A person who does focus on consequences usually is concerned with the impact of the consequences on himself. Utilitarianism, however, asks that a person expand the scope of analysis and objectively anticipate the consequences of an action on others.

I. Act versus Rule Utilitarianism

1. Introduction

A distinction is made between two versions of utilitarianism: Act and Rule. The distinction, however, is more of a 20th-century concept; it never was made explicitly by Bentham and Mill. However, since Bentham was concerned with reforming the laws of England so as to conform with the principle of utility, he often focused on justifying general rules.

2. Rule Utilitarianism

Rule utilitarianism is the utilitarian analysis applied to general and broad classes, categories, or types of actions, for example, the morality of breaking a contract or keeping one's promises. The moral result of such a calculation is framed as a rule, and individual actions then are judged right on wrong by reference to the moral rule.

Rule utilitarianism is at times criticized as an unnecessarily watered-down version of the utilitarian principle; that is, one that may give general rules a greater importance than they merit. In a particular case, for example, one may be able to bring about the best consequences by violating a rule that generally maximizes utility to follow. By not violating the rule, one would be engaging in slavish "rule worship" and thus not doing the greater good. Mill, however, at times argued that it is the contribution of certain rules to the general happiness that justifies one's adherence to them, despite what may seem the counterutility of a specific act.

3. Act Utilitarianism

Act utilitarianism subjects individual, particular, concrete actions to the utilitarian test. A specific act is evaluated by reference to its own unique consequences. For example, one must calculate the consequences of a particular lie, a particular breach of contract, in unique sets of circumstances.

It is important to note that the particular consequences may be similar to lying and breaking contracts generally, but they may be different. Generally, lying and breaking contracts results in more bad than good, but a particular lie, or the breaking of a particular contract, may result in more good than bad. Thus, a morally permissible exception to the rule may arise by means of Act utilitarianism.

There are, of course, problems with this version of utilitarianism. It is even more difficult to know in advance and with certainty the consequences of a unique and particular act, and it is not always possible to calculate the results of such an act. Act utilitarianism, moreover, can be used as a rationalization for a predetermined moral judgment. The Act principle possesses the suppleness to be "bent" in the direction one wants. There is always the temptation to think that the particular instance one is considering will be the exception to the rule, especially if one is the beneficiary of the excepted action. Although it is true that each situation is somewhat unique, it does not follow automatically that it is unique in all respects; thus that it cannot be comparable to other situations in morally relevant aspects.

4. Summary

Decision making under Rule utilitarianism is less difficult, costly, and time-consuming than the Act version. With Rule, moreover, there is less tendency for wishful thinking and self-deception. There is also less room to give oneself any undue advantage by manipulating the calculation of consequences since morality is determined by general rules rather than by case-by-case analysis. Rule utilitarianism, therefore, helps one to avoid the conflict that may arise between Act utilitarianism and commonly held and perhaps cherished moral beliefs.

Act utilitarianism, however, demonstrates that conventional moral rules should not be taken as absolute moral rules. Act utilitarianism also shows that many standard moral feelings, intuitions, and beliefs may be mistaken. Act utilitarians recognize that each situation is different and unique and that general rules serve at best only as "rough" guides. In certain circumstances, for example, the consequences of lying, breaking promises, or stealing might be more beneficial than refraining from these "immoral" actions. Act utilitarianism, it is important to note, does not reject totally a rule-based morality; rather, these general rules are used as guides. A true Act utilitarian, moreover, clearly understands that the result of the analysis is right not only for himself or herself, but for anyone in the same or similar circumstances. Act utilitarianism, finally, does what philosophy ought to do: it challenges one to rethink moral matters that one has heretofore taken for granted.

J. The "Justice" Problem with Utilitarianism

The major criticism of utilitarianism is that this ethical theory does not account for justice and may even run counter to it. The "right" or "moral" action under utilitarianism may in fact be unjust! The greater good, pleasure, and happiness very well may be maximized, but only by sacrificing justice. There always is the possibility of exploitation of the few. Benefits for the majority can be justified morally pursuant to utilitarianism by imposing sacrifices on the minority. The expropriation of the property of the "wealthy," for example, might bring substantial benefits to large numbers of people, but such an action would be "wrong" despite the benefits for the majority.

Utilitarianism also may allow the exploitation of the many. The few may benefit greatly at the expense of the many, yet the sum total of good is maximized. A slave-holding society, for example, if it provides a greater sum of goodness than one in which all people are treated equally, is moral! A more modern example emerges when a company hires illegal immigrants at very low wages to enable the company to compete.

Utilitarianism, therefore, conflicts with the principle that people have certain rights that ought not to be restricted or contravened, even when so doing results in a greater sum of total good. Utilitarianism is incapable of respecting individual rights because they always can be overridden in favor of any act that maximizes the total good. Utilitarianism, therefore, requires that one be ready and willing to commit unjust acts of the most blatant type!

Justice, however, does not depend on consequences which are irrelevant; rather, justice is treating people fairly, equitably, and giving each person his or her due. A fundamental characteristic of morally good person is that he or she recognizes that there are limits to what he or she will do to others. He or she discerns that morality involves not only maximization of utilities, but also the respecting of limits. The morally good person can use the utilitarian principle initially, but if the result contravenes justice, then a principle of justice must supersede.

K. The Value of Morality—The Utilitarian Approach

According to Richard DeGeorge, in his book, *Business Ethics*, value can be quantified using the Utilitarian approach. In order to determine the morality of an action, practice, rule, or law pursuant to the ethical theory of Utilitarianism, and with reference to the DeGeorge Utilitarian Model, one can use the following steps:

1. Accurately and narrowly state the action to be evaluated (e.g., is it moral for a particular company to. . . ?)

2. Identify all stakeholders who are directly and indirectly affected by the action (including the company's constituent groups as well as society).

3. Ascertain whether there are some obvious, dominant considerations that carry such weight as to predominate over other considerations.

4. Specify for each person or group that is affected directly or indirectly all the reasonably foreseeable good—pleasurable and bad—painful consequences of the action, as far as into the future as appears appropriate, and consider the various predictable outcomes, good and bad, and the likelihood of their occurring.

5. For each person and group, including society as a whole, measure and weigh the total good consequences against the bad consequences.

6. Quantify the good and bad consequences for each person and group on a numerical scale (for example, −5, −4, −3, −2, −1, 0 +1, +2, +3, +4, +5) representing units and extremes of pleasure and pain.

7. Sum up all the good and bad consequences.

8. If the action results in a positive number, it produces more good than bad and is a morally right action; and if the action results in a negative number, it produces more bad than good and is morally wrong.

L. Summary

Despite the problems inherent in utilitarianism, several strong arguments favor the use of this ethical theory. Utilitarianism accords with the criteria people actually do employ when making practical decisions. At the level of theory, Bentham's "science" may appear imprecise and even crude, but at the level of practice, the principle of utility is not foreign to ordinary ways of thinking and acting. It is perfectly natural that people seek pleasure and happiness and avoid pain. It also seems quite sensible to try to foresee pleasure and pain, to balance pleasure and pain against one another, and to bear a certain amount of short-term pain in order to achieve greater long-term pleasure. People, consciously or unconsciously, do make utilitarian-type calculations on a daily basis. They realize that the consequences of actions are important, they strive to foresee these consequences, they draw up a balance sheet of pleasures and pains or "pros" and "cons," and they then choose the actions that produce the most happiness. It is important to note, however, that when people choose these "good" actions, they predominantly are choosing actions that promote the most good for themselves.

Utilitarianism, moreover, accords with practical, governmental decision making. The theory matches the way government operates when deciding public policy issues and allocating public pleasures and pains. The principle of utility has had a strong influence upon the view of how a government should legislate. One purpose of present day legislative hearings, for example, is for the legislators to hear various opinions on how much happiness or unhappiness a proposed law will cause. The principle of utility itself, moreover, provides a criterion to judge legislation, law, and government. Utilitarianism measures actions against a standard of usefulness. Its values for the purposes of public policy are obvious. The doctrine shifts attention from the origin of law and government to its operation, and from precedence to consequence. The implication of this thinking is that obedience to government and law is required only if government and law are useful in producing pleasure.

The utilitarians were reformers; they wanted societal and legal reforms. They wanted their moral philosophy to be a "live," efficacious, contemporary public policy option, not simply an arcane, abstruse, theoretical relic. The utilitarians understood that reforms require more than mere "talk"; they require appropriate action on the part of those who want them. The utilitarians wanted their ethics to be judged by its efficacy as an instrument of reform. They wanted to make goodness a matter of genuine concern in the practical affairs of human beings; and, in fact, their influence was great and on the whole positive.

Utilitarianism does supply ethics with an objective component. By advancing utility as a standard, the theory substantially lessens the danger of incorporating dogma, irrationality, and pure subjectivism into ethics. Utilitarianism, consequently, may justify actions that are contrary to many peoples' feelings, intuitions, or moral beliefs.

Utilitarianism seeks to give to ethics a precise content that can be defined concretely, measured scientifically, and determined objectively. Utilitarianism is a comparatively clear, coherent, and comprehensible ethical theory that can be translated into practical terms.

Utilitarianism, moreover, is an ethical theory that places human beings at the center of morality. It is a universal, impartial, egalitarian theory that stresses the importance and equality of all human beings, not merely one person, group, or class. Utilitarianism underscores the shared capabilities of all human beings to experience pleasure and pain. No one's pleasure or pain is overlooked; nobody is excluded as unworthy. The amount of pleasure and pain is considered without favoritism.

By affording all human beings an equal moral importance, utilitarianism serves as a reminder that law, government, and the social order exist for everyone and that the general well-being and happiness always are relevant considerations. The theory embodies generous, enlightened, and humane tendencies, and it instills feelings of benevolence toward all humanity.

Although Bentham and Mill and their adherents may not have persuaded all that utilitarianism is the "right" ethical theory or a "scientific" one, they did establish utilitarianism as permanent and very influential ethical position. They also expanded dramatically the moral intelligence and sensitivity of people by drawing attention to the full consequences of actions and by emphasizing the vital happiness of all sentient beings capable of feeling pleasure and pain.

Discussion Questions

1. What is the Utilitarian Theory of Ethics? How would a utilitarian focused person act when making decisions?

2. Define, compare, and contrast the Act from the Rule versions of Utilitarianism? What are some of the advantages and disadvantages of each version?

3. Can following the Utilitarian ethical theory lead at times to an unjust result? Explain why or why not, citing a business example.

4. What are the steps in carrying out a Utilitarian, stakeholder, pleasure v. pain, numerical calculation in order to render a moral decision? Provide a business example.

5. According to Utilitarianism, can one state that bribery is always immoral? Why or why not? Cite a business example.

6. Is it possible for an economic system based on slavery to be deemed moral on Utilitarian ethical grounds? Why or why not?

7. Is taxation morally justifiable on Utilitarian grounds? Why or why not?

8. How does one go about predicting and then measuring the good and bad consequences of putting an action into effect? Discuss, providing business examples.

CHAPTER 8

Kant's Categorical Imperative

A. Introduction

The main text for the study of "Kantian" ethics is the German philosopher Immanuel Kant's seminal 1785 work—*Groundwork (or Foundation) of the Metaphysics of Morals.*

B. The Primacy of Reason

Reason, declared Kant, is the source and ultimate basis for morality. Morality wholly rests in pure, innate reason and not in intuition, conscience, law, or utility. The standard of morality, therefore, is inherent in the human mind; it is definable only in terms of the mind; and it is derived from one's innerself by direct perception. Reason, moreover, not only plays the key role in determining the origin and content of morality, but also supplies the force behind morality.

The moral "law" is binding on human beings, said Kant, simply because they are rational. Morality is derived from ethical principles that every rational person must accept. To be moral, therefore, is to be rational, and morality consists of acting rationally. Consequently a person who does not recognize or accept the moral "law" is not only immoral, but also irrational.

The proper use of reason is connected with morality. One understands and is subject to the demands of morality only insofar as one is a rational being. The purely intellectual use of reason, however, which is unconnected with morality, is mere "intellectualism" and thus a form of egoism. The right use of reason is directed to moral ends.

Kant presumes that human beings are rational and can utilize their reason. People can think, understand, give reasons for acting, and be convinced by reasons; they can act logically, consistently, and not in a self-contradictory manner. They can understand what it means to be moral, and what type of actions are appropriate for moral people. All human beings possess this reason.

C. Reason, Duty, and Happiness

The utilitarians based their ethics on the concept of happiness as the supreme good. Kant definitely rejected the assumption that morality stems from the actual desires of human beings for happiness. People, even though they do desire happiness, do not derive their dignity and worth from desiring it. Morality, therefore, must be grounded on a characteristic that gives human beings their distinctive worth and dignity. It is the ability to reason and the freedom to reason that distinguish human beings from other creatures. Morality thus is based on rationality and freedom. Consequently, one is not acting morally if one seeks to justify an action by an appeal to one's desires or even a general maximization of happiness.

Kant moreover underscores the importance of duty. He declares: disregard consequences, even "happy" ones; rather, do one's duty regardless of consequences.

Kant did not believe an ordinary, rational person needed guidance in arriving at a moral judgment. The right decision should be clear. The problem, as Kant correctly realized, is not necessarily arriving at this right decision; rather, it is possessing and maintaining the self-control and strength of character to do one's duty, that is, to do what is clearly right. As Abraham Lincoln declared in his famous anti-slavery speech at Cooper Union in New York City on February 27, 1860: "Let us have faith that right makes might, and in that faith, let us, to the end, dare to do our duty as we understand it."

D. The Categorical Imperative

1. Introduction

Kant called the supreme ethical principle the Categorical Imperative. This principle is a necessary element of human reason and the foundation upon which rest all moral judgments.

2. Hypothetical versus Categorical Imperatives

Before examining the Categorical Imperative, it is necessary to differentiate categorical from hypothetical imperatives. An imperative is a command; it gives instructions about how one ought to act. A hypothetical imperative prescribes the necessary means for attaining certain ends; that is, one must do X if one wishes to achieve Y. The imperative or command (X) is "hypoethical" because it is binding only insofar as one accepts the end (Y); if one rejects the end (Y), then the command (X) has no force.

A categorical imperative prescribes certain kinds of actions as objectively and absolutely necessary, without any regard to any end or any particular desire. One must do X, period! One, for example, categorically must keep promises, and not merely because one ought to keep promises if certain results are to be obtained; rather, one ought to keep promises without qualification and condition. There is, moreover, a moral obligation to keep promises even in the absence of any desire to keep promises. The rational moral rules that govern conduct are of this categorical kind. They are absolutely binding and unqualified.

3. The Categorical Imperative as a Formal Test

The Categorical Imperative is not a principle of action itself; instead, it ethically lays down the form a moral maxim must take. Thus, said Kant, reason indicates that a moral action must have a certain form. The ethics "test" is a formal test. An action is morally right if it has a certain form, and morally wrong if it does not have that form.

The Form, the Categorical Imperative, is the first, supreme, fundamental principle in ethics. It is the form a moral action must have; it provides the ultimate standard by which one can test actions, rules, beliefs, and standards to determine if they are moral.

4. The Three Requirements of the Categorical Imperative

There are three aspects to the Categorical Imperative. Kant claims they amount to the same thing, providing the form, matter, and complete characterization of morality. The three formal conditions that an action must have to be a moral action are: 1) the action must be possible to be made consistently universal; 2) it must respect rational beings as ends in themselves; and 3) the action must stem from and respect the autonomy of rational beings and be acceptable to rational beings. If an action or rule passes all three, it is moral; if it fails one, it is immoral.

5. The Imperativeness of the Categorical Imperative

One must be moral, regardless of circumstances, consequences and regardless of whether one wants to achieve a particular end. Acting morally is a command of reason. Since morality is derived from reason, and there is a presumption that all people are rational, a moral action is one that must be done.

E. Kantian Duty

Duty, therefore, is a central concept in Kant's ethical theory. He places a premium on the obligation, the "ought," in ethics. One ought to perform an action, regardless of self-interest, personal desires, or consequences, because it is one's duty to do so.

Morality is possible for rational beings because only rational beings have the power to act according to the idea of a moral duty. Moral worth, moreover, exists only when a person acts from a sense of duty. An act possesses only moral merit when it is performed because duty demands it. A morally good person, therefore, is one who acts conscientiously from duty.

Morality often arises as a duty or constraint because people are human beings who are subject to self-interest and personal desires. The demands of morality, however, should not be viewed as external constraints, but as self-imposed and acceptable restrictions decreed by the very autonomous and rational beings who are subject to them.

F. The Good Will

How does one determine if a person is a morally good person? It is not enough that his or her actions, even "good" actions, be intended; an action also must be motivated by a good will. A person who does an act without a good will is not a morally good person and is thus not worthy of moral praise.

Only a good will is morally valuable. It is the only thing unqualifiedly good, intrinsically good, and the only measure one needs in assessing the moral worth of a person. A morally good person is a person with a good will.

What is a good will? A good will knows what duty is; it comprehends what the Categorical Imperative commands. A good will acts solely from a motive of duty and for the sake of duty. A morally good act is one done in obedience to this duty. The motive for acting, therefore, must be in recognition of this duty.

It is insufficient morally if one performs an act out of psychological compulsion, external pressure, internal urges and impulses, or personal desires, pleasures, or rewards. It is insufficient if one acts because of self-interest, legal requirements, or social sanctions. It is insufficient to look at consequences, even good consequences. Results are irrelevant morally. Inclinations toward persons or objects are also irrelevant. If one is fond of a person and thus treats him or her well, there is no moral merit. If one is kind because of a benevolent feeling, the action is not morally good. If one does "kindly" acts because one is a "kind person," one is not worthy of moral praise. A person receives no moral credit for natural inclinations. Actions themselves, although "good" and intended, are insufficient alone to assess moral value. A "bad" person may do the "right" thing for the wrong reason; a "good" person may do the "right" thing but for the wrong motive. An act has moral worth only if one does it because it is right, because it is required by the Categorical Imperative, and because one's motive for acting is in recognition of this duty.

Human beings, of course, are not unaffected by compulsion, consequences, inclinations, desires, and self-interest. Yet, one must follow the Categorical Imperative and the moral "law" even against one's inclinations and desires. The force of the moral "law," therefore, is felt as a demand made against will, a command or imperative of reason, ordering the will to act from duty. The emphasis in Kant, accordingly, is on inner strength, constancy of purpose, self-discipline, self-control, and mastery of oneself.

G. The Three Parts of the Categorical Imperative

1. The First Test

The first test of morality under the Categorical Imperative is universality. A morally good person is one who acts only on maxims that a rational person consistently could will to become a universal "law" without any contradiction or negation.

An action or a rule is moral pursuant to Kant's first test if it is capable of being made consistently universal. What would happen if everyone took the action, and if all people followed the rule, would it continue indefinitely and remain efficacious, or would it become self-contradictory, nonsensical, self-destruct, and lead to its own demise? If the action or rule can continue and sustain itself, it is moral; if it becomes inconsistent, illogical, and collapses when made universal, it is immoral.

Lying, for example, according to Kant, is immoral. A rational person simply cannot logically will that lying become a universal law. Lying cannot be made consistently universal. Lying ultimately is self-defeating. If everyone lied, one could not rely on what people say; no one would believe anyone else; nothing would be believed. The very practice of lying, therefore, is undermined. Lying ceases to be advantageous, and the practice of lying disappears. For a lie to be efficacious, one must believe that most people are telling the truth; thus, the "success" of any lie depends on its "exceptional" character, that is, there not being a universal "law" permitting lying.

Similarly, it logically is impossible to universalize breaking promises. If there was such a universal "law," and everyone followed it, promises would cease to have any value or force; thus the institution of promising would cease to exist and the action, when made universal, necessarily destroys itself.

Other examples of actions or rules that cannot be conceived of as consistently universal "law" are killing, breaking contracts, not contributing to charity, stealing, expropriating property, and disclosing confidential information.

Kant's first test implies that a person will not regard himself or herself as special from a moral point of view. A rational person possessing a good will cannot consistently and logically think that he or she is permitted to act in ways that are forbidden to others.

There are, of course, immoral people. They not only exempt themselves from the moral "law," but also are unwilling to grant this same "privilege" to others. These people are parasites on the moral system they violate. Their immoral behavior is possible and advantageous only in an otherwise moral society. An immoral person assumes that not everyone will break the moral "law"; he or she counts on others not to act in the parasitic way he or she acts, because if everyone would engage in immoral behavior, it loses its efficacy.

It is very important here to distinguish Kant's first test from utilitarianism. Kant is not arguing that the consequences of everyone always lying or breaking promises are "bad"; rather, the results are self-defeating.

It is also important to note that when Kant is referring to universal "law," he means reasoned and self-imposed moral "law" and not any body of international law. Nevertheless, it should be underscored that there are efforts to make universal legal law. For example, the United Nations has a project called the U.N. Global Compact, wherein multinational companies voluntarily agree to join the Compact and to promise to abide by the Compact's broad principles, such as protecting human rights and workers' rights and protecting the environment.

2. The Second Test

The second test of Kant's Categorical Imperative, as well as the third, emerge as a powerful check against any residual immorality that the first test failed to prevent. The second test demands respect for rational beings as ends in themselves. In Kant's "Kingdom of Ends," each person must be treated by every other person as an "end," that is, with dignity and respect and as a valuable and worthwhile entity.

The second test recognizes the intrinsic worth of human beings. Human beings have unconditional value, just because they are human; and quite apart from whatever special advantages may accrue from birth, beauty, wealth, or status. The second test underscores one's standing as a human being in company with other human beings. A rational being is conscious of himself or herself as a person, as a valuable entity, and as an intrinsic end. He or she, therefore, must be conscious of the same worth in others.

The second test demands that people be treated with dignity and respect. They must be considered, and treated, as rational and free agents who possess the capability, freedom, and the right to set their own goals, make their own choices and decisions, and govern their actions by reason. The second test emphasizes that dignity resides in freedom and rationality.

Rational beings are capable of recognizing the moral law, understanding what the moral law requires, then acting from a sense of duty and choosing to obey the moral law. Rational human beings are the only creatures capable of performing such an action, not because it is to their advantage, but because duty requires it. Thus, rational beings have moral worth; their value is absolute; and they always are to be treated as ends, in Kant's "Kingdom of Ends."

People, of course, have personal desires and goals. Other things naturally have value for them in relation to fulfilling their desires and attaining their goals. These mere "things" have value only as a means to an end; and it is the human ends that give them value. The second test clearly forbids people to be treated as mere means. It violates the dignity of a person to treat him or her simply as an impersonal object, instrument, or "vehicle" to satisfy a desire or advance a goal. Respect entails not using and not manipulating people to achieve certain purposes, no matter how "good" these purposes are.

Lying, for example, is immoral because the liar is manipulating a person and treating him or her as a "means." Even if one lies not for one's own selfish advantage, but for a "good" reason or for the "good" of the "victim," one is telling a person that he or she cannot be trusted to understand the facts and judge for himself or herself. Lying treats people as children still under tutelage and not as free, rational adults. Lying denies people their just title and true dignity as free, rational, human beings.

Ethical egoism and utilitarianism, consequently, violate Kant's second test because they are incompatible with human dignity. Ethical egoism views people as valuable only as they promote the egoist's self-interest. Utilitarianism permits people to be used as instruments in a calculated effort to maximize the greater good. For example, even if a multinational company's foreign "sweatshop" factory produced a greater good for the company and its stakeholders as well as for the foreign society, it would still be immoral pursuant to Kantian ethics due to the exploitation of the workers.

It is important to note that Kant recognizes that people often must employ other people to achieve certain objectives. Yet even when people are employed, one never can forget that they always remain ends and do not exist as mere cogs in a mechanistic economic entity. It is, therefore, immoral to treat employees as mere objects to serve the employer's ends or, to use Kant's own example, as broken pieces of furniture to be merely discarded by the employer when no longer usable. An employer exhibits a lack of respect for an employee by not soliciting the employee's judgment or by rejecting his or her views summarily. A moral employer allows its employees the freedom to form their own reasoned judgments and grants the greatest freedom possible to perform the actions they choose, within the limits of the employment relationship, of course.

3. The Third Test

The third test, yet another way of formulating the Categorical Imperative, underscores the autonomy of rational beings. The third test invokes the idea of the rational being as a universal legislator making rules for the Kingdom of Ends. A rational human being possesses the ability to recognize the moral "law," to "give" to himself or herself the moral law, and to govern himself or herself according to the moral law.

The third test requires the universal acceptability of the moral "law." When a person is contemplating doing a particular action, he or she must ask what rule he or she would be following if the action was performed. He or she then must ask whether a rational person would be willing for the rule to be followed by everyone all the time. If a rational person would not be willing for everyone to follow the rule, then one cannot follow it.

The third test is at times phrased as the "agent-receiver" test. The agent-receiver test asks whether a rational person would accept the action or rule regardless of whether he or she was the agent (or the giver) of the action, or the receiver of the action or rule. If a rational person would not, the action or rule is immoral; if the answer is yes, then the action or rule is moral. Rational people, for example, would not want lying or theft to be universal "laws" applied to themselves as well as others.

The third test harmonizes with the second test's treatment of people as "ends." A rational person acts as an "end" when he or she prescribes universal moral laws through the autonomy of the will; and treats others as "ends" when he or she subjects himself or herself to such laws.

The third test also underscores impartiality. When a person acts on a moral rule, he or she must be willing to accept the right of everyone else to act on the same rule. Even a self-interested person must realize that the claims he or she asserts for himself or herself also will be advanced by others who are in a similar position. The third test thus emerges as a powerful "check" against selfish people who desire to make an exception for themselves to rules they would want others to adhere to.

President Abraham Lincoln exemplified certain core Kantian beliefs. Slavery was morally wrong because it violated the fundamental principle of equality by treating members of a different race as unequal. Slavery was also wrong because it was demeaning to and exploitative of human beings, who were treated because of their race as mere "instruments" or things. Furthermore, slavery was immoral because it violated the Kantian "universal law" and "agent-receiver" tests. Lincoln succinctly stated and logically explained his Kantian logic in an 1858 anti-slavery speech at Cooper Union in New York City: "As I would not be a slave, so I would not be a master." Moreover, Lincoln urged people to be of strong moral character, and to impose the moral law on themselves; that is, in the words of his immortal Gettysburg Address, to "dedicate" themselves to the struggle of freedom; and accordingly to exercise self-restraint; and not to impose on others the condition of slavery, which is a state of servitude that they surely as rational human beings would not want imposed on themselves.

H. Problems with Kantian Ethics

1. The Abstractness of the Categorical Imperative

The Categorical Imperative is, of course, an abstract principle that lacks definite content. It is "formal" in the sense that it says nothing about the precise content of moral rules. It neither directs one to perform any specific action nor proscribes one from committing any specific action.

The Categorical Imperative, especially the third test, in essence comes down to the "golden rule," which however revered and beyond dispute is just an injunction to treat a person as a "person." There certainly is room for discussion concerning the Categorical Imperative, for example, about its own validity and status, how it is to be interpreted and applied, and then what follows regarding the specific content of morality.

2. The First Test and Consequences

Kant clearly says to disregard consequences. Yet, when one attempts to apply the "consistently universal" test, one cannot avoid taking into account the consequences of an action. If the first test demands that an action be deemed immoral if the result of its universal adoption would be the self-destruction of the action, then the consequences of the action must be considered, as the morality of the action cannot be separated from the consequences of the action.

3. Conflicting Ends

A problem also emerges with Kant's second test—the "ends" doctrine—in that the test provides no means of reaching a decision when two peoples' interests conflict. If each is to be an "end," how is one to arrive at a decision for determining which "end" prevails?

One solution is to treat all with dignity and respect, but not as absolute ends; that is, one can count all equally, but also note any specific differences among people that they make some more entitled than others to a particular application of dignity and respect.

4. General v. Specific Applications of the Categorical Imperative

Kantian ethics evidences a desire to establish broad, absolute moral standards, such as "never lie." Yet, moral standards, even within a Kantian framework, need not be regarded as absolute, and Kant did not provide any explicit rationale for summarily rejecting narrower, qualified moral standards.

A problem, however, arises when stipulations and qualifications are placed in the statement of an action for the purpose of constructing a precise moral standard regarding it. In so doing, it may be possible to describe an action in such a specific way that it will pass the Categorical Imperative; yet when phrased in general terms, would violate the Categorical Imperative. For example, "lie," "bribe," and "kill" all fail the Categorical Imperative. If one attempts to universalize these actions, they become self-contradictory and self-destruct. Yet, there are more specific descriptions of these actions that allow lying, bribing, or killing but only in select particular circumstances, for example, "lie when necessary to save an innocent human life," "bribe only to save one's company," or "kill only in self-defense." These specific actions very well may be made moral; they arguably pass the Categorical Imperative.

The danger in specifically applying the Categorical Imperative is to encourage further the all too human tendency to make exceptions to general rules, especially when one's own interests are involved. It is not easy to be completely honest with oneself in stating an action. The temptation, of course, is to create a moral "rule" that allows one to do what one pleases; that is, to categorize an action so narrowly, by grafting enough specific details onto it, that one will be one of the few, if not only one, to fit within the rule.

Although subjecting specific actions to the Categorical Imperative may be necessary, one must be aware that every exception to a general rule tends to weaken it. Before one acts, one always must ask: Does one want this kind of an exception itself to become a moral rule or standard? If not, then one should abstain from making the exception; if so, then logically one must be willing for anyone in the same or similar position to take "advantage" of the exception to the general rule.

5. Conflicting Duties

A problem arises in Kantian ethics when conflicting duties oblige one to perform two or more actions when only one can be performed. That is, there may be a clash between actions that two secondary moral rules command; yet each rule passes the Categorical Imperative. Where is the formula to solve this moral dilemma?

What, for example, if it is morally wrong to do X and also wrong to do Y; there are no other alternatives and a person must choose one. "Never lie" and "never break promises," but what if one must lie in order to keep a promise? What if the only way to compensate a victim of employment discrimination involves discrimination against others? Both these actions, "compensate for past discrimination" and "refrain from discrimination," seem morally demanded. Both "pass" the Categorical Imperative; yet they clash. What about "blow the whistle on wrongdoing" and "be loyal to one's firm"? Kantian ethics leaves unresolved the issue of how one is to determine one's duty when two or more "moral" moral rules conflict.

One solution is to construct general rules that allow for the exceptions needed to resolve a given case. Another solution is to distinguish absolute moral duties and rules, which one always must comply with, from nonabsolute duties and rules, which one must comply with only if there are no other conflicting, superseding, duties and rules. Accordingly, one is to compare conflicting duties and rules and determine which take precedence. A greater moral duty will override a lesser. The process of comparing and weighing values compels one to rank moral beliefs, that is, to establish values. The comparing and weighing of duties and rules, however, also tends to incorporate utilitarianism into Kantian ethics, as the duty or rule which brings about the most "right" prevails.

I. Summary

Despite the problems with Kantian ethics, Kant's very important accomplishment was to underscore, and to appreciate, people as free, rational, moral beings, with individual rights and self-imposed duties to respect others.

Even though Kantian ethics is not concerned directly with consequences, adherence to its principles promotes a framework of formal justice that serves to preserve the integrity of society and facilitates its fair operation. Kantian ethics promotes a principled society whose members relate to one another on the basis of mutual recognition and respect for each other's freedom and dignity.

Discussion Questions

1. There have been ethical dilemmas and conflicting resolutions presented to the world's ongoing problems. All of the resolutions are presented with the reasons of each individual behind them. According to Kantian Ethics, what determines a correct moral resolution?

2. If a person performs an action knowing that he or she will be rewarded afterwards, would the person be acting with a good will?

3. Is it morally right to make a promise if you are not certain that you will be able to keep it?

4. Are actions moral if you gain happiness from them?
5. Do all people have the ability to be moral?
6. What is the Categorical Imperative? Why is it "categorical"? Why is it an "imperative"?
7. What is an example of a moral act that conflicts with the Kantian Ethics?
8. According to Kant, is morality truly "black and white"?
9. Is Kantian Ethics truly attainable?
10. What do you see as the biggest conflict with Kantian Ethics?

CHAPTER 9

Laws and Rights

I. Natural Law

A. Introduction to Natural Law

1. DEFINITION

Natural law is fundamental moral law that provides an objectives norm for human conduct. Natural law stems from the moral order in the universe and embodies a basic set of moral rules that ultimately governs the world. This moral order, which human beings did not create, is binding on all people.

2. DISCOVERING THE NATURAL LAW

The moral standards in nature are discovered by the use of one's reason in the same manner as the physical laws of nature are discovered. One proceeds in a rational manner to discover the nature of moral reality, to understand the natural, moral order of things, and to discern moral rules. One can consider, for example, the extent to which the rules of conduct that actually are recognized are due to human institutions and the norms that would endure if human institutions were eliminated.

3. EXAMPLES OF NATURAL LAW

Fulfilling obligations is an example of a natural law prescription. An obligation itself may be the consequences of an agreement made by people, yet one detects a "natural" tendency to fulfill it, even without legal compulsion; and so to abide by one's agreement is part of the natural law.

Other examples of natural law are abstaining from what is another's and making reparation for culpable wrongs.

4. Why Obey the Natural Law?

People should obey the natural law because reason commands it. Reason is the ultimate sanction for complying with the natural law. A person will do the right thing solely from the motive of rightfulness.

B. Natural Law v. the Civil Law

One must differentiate between laws that are merely the issue of government entities and laws that are grounded on the nature of things. Civil laws are rules of conduct promulgated by some individual or group, publicly commanded, and dependent for their existence on a state that possesses the power to enforce its legal resolutions by means of penalties for breach. Since people inhabit societies varying widely in history, culture, geography, and climate, distinct rules of law are required to fulfill the purposes of the civil law. Accordingly, civil law consists of relatively detailed decrees pertinent to specific societies. Individuals are protected in civil society by the constraints of the civil law. By means of the civil law, moreover, a person not only is provided protection from others, but also is afforded privileges over others; but eliminate the civil law and what protections and privileges would remain?

Natural law is the corpus of universal, constant, and enduring moral rules, discoverable and interpreted by reason, valid for all societies and states, at all times, and independent of any legal conventions, proclamations, and agreements. The body of natural law necessarily is more general than civil law since the natural law must be broad enough to hold for entire societies and divergent communities.

One cannot be released from a natural law obligation by government decree. The failure to comply with the natural law carries not a civil but a moral sanction. In essence, the natural law is an ethical rather than a juristic principle. The natural law never has appeared formally in the statute or case books, yet it influences in important ways the formal civil law that does emerge. As fulfillment of agreements is a component of the natural law, and as contractual agreements are the foundation of business, natural law is the origin of business laws.

C. The Stoics

1. Introduction

The source of the natural law theory flows from the ethical thought of the Stoic philosophers. The central concept of the Stoics was the notion of Nature; their highest good was acting in accordance with nature. According to their understanding of nature, the Stoics believed the universe behaved in accordance with law, order, and reason. Nature revealed the true law that each person not only is capable of comprehending but also of conforming his and her conduct thereto.

2. Reason

Since nature involved world reason and unveiled the true law, this natural law is valid for all people at all times, not merely as citizens of a particular state at a particular time.

As rational human beings, all people share in the reason that rules the universe. The similarity of all human beings thus depends upon the essential human capacity to reason. By means of rational analysis, for example, one can examine diverse actual laws, classify them according to what they share in common, note the specific fundamental features present everywhere, and thus discern the universal natural law.

3. The Primacy of the Natural Law

The law that took form from the ethical thought of the Stoics was the idea of a Law of Nature, which superseded state law and human conventions. Law was not merely a proclamation dictated by the state, or even an agreement entered into by people for their mutual advantage; rather, law was somehow part of the true nature of things.

This natural law also supplied a systemic, objective, universal moral standard by which to measure state law. A rational person, therefore, distinguishes between the actual civil law, which from time to time govern people's relations in and with states, and the true law, to which state law ought to conform and the perfect relations that ought to attain.

4. The Universal Community

Since all people shared the imperative characteristic of reason, the Stoics stressed the solidarity of the human race. They underscored the freedom, equality, dignity, and unity of all humankind, overriding all distinctions of state, race, class, birth, wealth, education, and position in society; they urged integrity, good faith, and mutuality of obligation, even in the absence of civil law. These ideas originated in the conception of a superior law of Nature that rational people could perceive.

The notions of nature, law, world reason, and human reason suggested to the Stoics that all people were members of a great universal community. If all actual codes of law ought to be judged against a single, universal natural law, all people everywhere ought to be equal members of one, single, great, universal community. This idea of the cosmopolis, or universal city, was a Stoic contribution.

5. Equality and Slavery

Since the Stoics maintained that all people are created equally, possessing the like faculty of reason, slavery could not be reconciled with Stoic principles. The Stoics clearly recognized that such an institution was not "natural," but merely an unjust arrangement imposed by some human beings on others. The slave is an equal human being endowed by nature with the capability of reasoning.

Differences of state, race, position, and conduct, which may appear noticeable to an unreflective observer actually are artificial and superficial. By not carefully observing, a casual onlooker might see so many separate individual entities, but mindful, intelligent analysis would compel one to behold in these varied individuals the reasoning human being, who is everywhere and at all times the same beneath any ostensible differences. For the Stoics, the universal nature of the natural law and the cosmopolitan nature of the world community erupted any theory supposing the "natural" inequality of persons.

6. Duty to Obey the Natural Law

People have a duty to obey these natural laws because they are the universal laws of nature. A rational being must subordinate oneself to the natural law and live in such a way as to serve the good of all.

7. Happiness

Happiness, for the Stoics, consisted of activity in accordance with nature, that is, in accordance with the order, reason, and law that they conceived the universe to display. Peace of mind, therefore, arrives through the acceptance of the universe as it is and a corresponding acquiescence to the worldly course of events.

8. Summary

The influence of Stoic thought and teaching was significant, lasting, and far-reaching. The idea of a single, open, equal world society, where people act in deference to the natural law, is insightful, persuasive, and most abiding. To the Stoics, more than to any other philosophic school, humanity is indebted for the conception of a universal ethical standard superseding the wills of lawmakers and the conventions of peoples. The Stoics' exposition of the natural law contributed a moral dimension to lawmaking and behavior, by demanding an ethical justification therefor, and by providing a universal criterion to which law and conduct ought to conform.

D. Locke

1. The State of Nature

The English philosopher John Locke (1632–1704), endorsed the belief in a state of nature. He viewed the state of nature as a situation where people live together according to reason, without a common superior with authority to judge among them. All people naturally live in such a state unless they are in a civil society. The historical question of the existence of such a state of nature is irrelevant for Locke. The truth he is attempting to ascertain is what the natural condition of people would be if there was no civil society.

Locke's characterization of the state of nature differed radically from Hobb's conception. In Locke's state of nature, people are equal and free by the law of nature. People are free to order their actions and dispose of their persons and possessions as they deem proper. This state of liberty is not a state of license. Locke does not describe a horde of savages, succumbing to wild, irrational, and ungovernable passions. Rather, Locke sets forth a state where people obey reason and conduct their activities within the bounds set by the natural law.

Why then do people leave the state of nature, band together, and enter into civil society? Unfortunately, there are problems with the state of nature. Some people do not live according to the law of nature. They attempt to place other people under their power and to deprive them of their natural rights. Every person, of course, can defend himself or herself from aggression, but each person not only is a judge in his or her own case, but must rely on himself or herself for vindication of rights. To avoid disturbances and to curb violations of the natural law, people agree to elect or appoint a government to protect their already existing rights and to officiate as a common judge among them. Preservation of the natural right to property, said Locke, is an important reason for the institution of government. Many material things, moreover, are wanting in the state of nature. Only a civilized society can provide the foundation for development and progress.

2. LOCKE AND THE NATURAL LAW

John Locke, in his *Treatise on Civil Government*, recognized the existence of the natural law and made it the starting point for his ethical considerations. Locke maintained that three types of law exist: the law of opinion or reputation, the civil law, and the natural law.

The law of opinion or reputation consists of those actions deemed virtuous or censorious by the several societies of the world, according to the conventions and customs of the particular place. These laws differ because societies differ. The only real sanction for violating these laws is the censure of public opinion.

The civil law is the law promulgated by the state and enforced by the legal machinery of the state. The law of opinion and the civil law, Locke noted, tend to coincide because if conduct is disapproved strongly by public opinion, a proscription likely will be enacted into the law.

Superseding both, however, is the natural law, which is the only true standard of morality. Locke held that there were laws of nature that govern human society exactly as the laws of nature govern the physical realm. Amid the diversity of manners and laws among peoples are to be found fundamental principles from the "nature of things."

3. DISCERNING THE PRINCIPLES OF THE NATURAL LAW

Locke contended that there was a natural order; this natural order contained rules of conduct that are objectively valid; human beings are rational agents and that they can use their reason, to discover, understand, and act upon these natural laws.

The world of peoples, their laws, ways, and ideas made subject to reason by rational agents will yield clear, certain laws with respect to which people in all parts of the world must agree.

4. THE NATURAL V. THE CIVIL LAW

That natural law is natural certainly does not preclude the agency of human beings in creating law. The natural law is not only independent of and superior to the civil law, but supports, guides, explains, and inspires the civil law. One can compare all other laws to the natural law to determine if they are morally good or bad. The civil law is justifiable insofar as it conforms to the law of nature.

A major purpose of the natural law is to explain the foundation and maintenance of the legal order. The true function of government is not to impose laws on its people, but to discover what the laws of nature are and to govern accordingly.

5. NATURAL LAW AND MORALITY

Since the natural laws operate in conformity to nature, natural law is the only true standard of morality and thus must govern the manner in which one behaves. The natural law supersedes any personal or public "pleasure" criterion and exists above and beyond the relativistic habits and customs of a particular group or society.

An important ethical point that Locke drew from the natural law is that reason enables a person to order his or her affairs correctly. If one reflects in a careful, rational manner, one will reach the right normative conclusion with certainty.

6. Why Obey the Natural Law?

If natural law reflects the natural order, one is under a duty, in terms of one's status as a rational person, to obey it. According to Locke, it is also in one's long-range advantage to obey the natural law since the natural law decrees what is actually productive of the maximum pleasure. One, therefore, should obey the natural law because it contains the best advice on how to maximize one's pleasure.

E. Problems with the Natural Law Theory

A basic assumption of the natural law theory is the belief that people are rational, honest, and strong-willed, and therefore can know what the natural law is and can act upon such knowledge. Such an assumption, however, does not allow sufficiently for the strength of emotion or bias or the weakness of the intellect or will.

The natural law is supposed to provide fixed, objective, normative standards of conduct. What exactly is "natural" was, and always has been, difficult to express. Locating a normative standard within nature, or even explicating it in any detail, emerges as a challenging task. The risk is that any natural law directives will be too general and too abstract for the theory to serve as an efficacious standard to guide conduct.

Whose function is it to produce the natural law? Obviously, there are no licensed natural law professionals. Establishing a tribunal capable of pronouncing authoritatively on natural law issues is a problematic undertaking. The danger in practice is that such issues, if they are important, will be decided by power, not by the natural law.

What about the concrete issues that divide people? Without some degree of social, cultural, and political homogeneity, the natural law may not be able to generate a demonstrably right or sufficiently compelling answer to difficult moral issues. If the community is too homogeneous, however, the risk is that the prevailing norms will be "natural" in the relativistic sense and the natural law will be merely a reflection of societal norms.

F. Summary

The significance of the natural law lies not in its ability to resolve definitively the complex moral issues that arise in a civilized society, but in the assistance it affords in determining what a civilized society is. The natural law, therefore, properly is viewed as a goal for reformers and morally aware people to aim at.

Natural law embraces morality as primarily and basically a human good. Its most fundamental moral precept is to promote good and avoid evil. Since the law of nature applies to all people equally, all people are equal citizens of one world community.

By using one's reason, one can discover the existence of the natural law and that the natural law encompasses certain natural rights. The theory thus has produced an ever-widening expansion of rights.

The theory seeks to provide universal, rational, objective criteria to evaluate states and their civil laws, even laws promulgated by a properly elected governing body. Consequently, one can employ the concept of a natural "higher law" to challenge existing civil law. By emphasizing the moral dimension to law, natural law proponents are declaring that ethics is a part of the law.

By constantly asserting and appealing to reason, the natural law theorists reject dogmatic "truth" in favor of discussion, accommodation, compromise, and the mutual solving of problems.

II. Natural Rights

A. Introduction to Natural Rights

The notion of "rights" arises in many of the moral arguments raised in business controversies. One type of right invoked is the concept of a natural right. The purpose of this chapter is to provide an understanding of this concept, the methods of ethical analysis that underlie its use, and the moral rules derived therefrom.

Natural rights are rights people possess and enjoy as individuals. Natural rights supersede laws, societal conventions, local customs, and any principle of the social good. They exist prior to, and independent of, what government entities recognize as rights; they are possessed by people before they enter into a state of political society; they are possessed by people because they are human beings, not because they are members of any political society. In essence, natural rights are promised on the fact that all people are equal and independent, furnished with like faculties, and living and sharing in one world community.

Natural rights are more than mere ideals; rather, they are demonstrable fundamental precepts that must be respected because they are rooted in a knowledge of the nature and proper ordering of the universe. Natural rights are self-evident and are discerned rationally by anyone whose natural reason is neither deficient nor degenerate.

B. Locke

The idea of natural rights has a long history, reaching back to ancient Greek and Stoic beliefs. John Locke (1632–1704), the English political philosopher, generally is credited with developing the "modern" doctrine that human beings have natural rights. Locke declared that people possess the right to life, liberty, and private property as "natural" rights. He based his assertion on the conviction that the natural law guarantees to every person certain inalienable rights. These rights exist for persons simply because they are human beings. Since people are rational, they can recognize the fact that each person in the state of nature is the equal of all others. These natural rights exist, Locke maintained, regardless of political organization, one's status as a citizen, and the legal rights recognized by society.

As a result of this ethical thinking, Locke not only enunciated a moral statement regarding the rights that ought to be recognized at all times and in all societies, but also provided a moral standard by which actual states and laws can be evaluated.

C. Natural Rights v. Legal Rights

A right is a person's entitlement to act in a certain manner or to constrain others to act in a certain way toward him or her. A legal right is a grant of authority from a government entity, limited to the particular jurisdiction within which the legal system is in force, and dependent for its existence on some sort of enforcement mechanism.

Natural rights are "natural." They are neither devised, created, nor granted by government nor dependent upon any particular legal system. They are entitlements derived from a fixed, objective, universal system of moral standards, stemming from the natural law, possessed and binding on all persons, and taking precedence over laws and conventions.

D. Natural Rights v. Utilitarianism

Utilitarianism explains morality as the maximization of the greatest amount of good for the greatest number of people. The natural rights doctrine defines morality as a matter of individual right. Utilitarianism focuses on the consequences of an action and how the consequences add to or subtract from the greater good. Natural rights underscores the character of an action and the manner in which the action promotes or hinders individual freedom and welfare. Pursuant to utilitarianism, a person can be treated as a means or instrumentality to achieve a socially beneficial end; whereas the natural rights doctrine emphasizes what is due to an individual and serves to protect individual autonomy against infringement by society. If a person possesses a natural right to do or to have something, or to be left alone, it is morally wrong for anyone to interfere, even though a very large number of people will gain more utility by the interference.

E. Types of Natural Rights

An assertion of natural rights frequently is made in the form of a declaration which sets forth a number of specific rights that are claimed to be "natural." The United States Declaration of Independence and the United Nations Declaration of Human Rights provide examples of expressed natural rights. Certain rights, such as life, liberty, property, and equality, properly are regarded as fundamental natural rights because they are either prerequisite or necessary conditions to the enjoyment of other rights.

The right of life thus is the paramount natural right. People must be able to rely upon not being killed in order to survive and prosper; accordingly, the right to existence must be respected as a natural right.

One's reason also informs one that everyone possesses a right to liberty and personal freedom. Such a right encompasses the ownership of one's own body and labor, as well as the right to hold some space, relations, and objects as one's own.

All people possess the natural right to own property. Something held in common in the "state of nature," such as land or creatures, becomes one's private property, said Locke, if one combines his or her enterprise and labor with it. The natural right to property stems from the natural law precept that everyone possesses the right to one's own person and body, the employment of oneself in labor, and the enjoyment of the products of one's labor. The natural right to private property also is based on the obvious commonsense rationale that a person will take care of one's own property in a considerably different manner than the property not one's own.

Equality of opportunity and treatment emerges as a fundamental natural right. Equal treatment of people insofar as they are equals is required. Equality is such a basic and self-evident principle that any departure from it demands an immediate substantive explanation. All people have the right to be accorded the dignity and respect due to them as beings. In an employment setting, people are not to be used as a mere expendable labor source or to be employed in pure mechanical travail. A business enterprise is not to be built upon the toil of cheap, degraded, and dispensable human beings.

People have the natural right to make a free employment choice. They are entitled to fair work conditions as well as equitable remuneration ensuring an employee an existence deserving of human dignity. Employees also possess a natural right to rest and leisure, including the reasonable limitation on working days and hours.

F. Problems with the Natural Rights Theory

The concept of natural rights raises several problems that must be addressed in ascertaining the ethical efficacy of the doctrine. How does one know the natural law so as to warrant a claim of natural right? Locke relies on the contention that natural law and natural rights are self-evident. All people are supposed to reason that such rights exist. Yet where are the particular arguments essential to establish the proposition that human beings possess natural rights? Everyone agrees that legal rights exist, but the status of natural rights is more perplexing. The theory may be too subjective to support claims concerning rights and obligations.

The theory also appears too indefinite to provide standards for human conduct. Morality must be based as much as possible on precise and exact norms, yet the concept of natural rights is vague and thus runs the risk of degenerating into empty and meaningless conjecturing. The theory by itself lacks precise criteria and one is compelled to venture outside it for other ethical theories and moral rules to govern conduct.

Even when a natural right is conceded with sufficient clarity, it may have to be limited in its exercise by the existence of a countervailing right.

G. Summary

Although the doctrine of natural rights appears indeterminate and inexact, it clearly is antipathetic to aggression, encroachment, and interference. One is not to injure, impair, or hinder another absent a valid justification; one is not to subjugate another or to use another as a mere instrumentality. Natural Rights thus afford people the autonomy, equality, and dignity to freely pursue their interests. The doctrine provides at least some rational basis for defending one's own conduct and for invoking the protection and aid of others.

The doctrine allows each person to prosper according to his or her capabilities and efforts; it opens up the resources of the earth on equal terms to all and supplies a maximum of stimulus. Most meaningfully, the natural rights creed holds each person sacred and entreats everyone to do as much as possible to preserve the rest of humanity.

The challenge for the business manager is to take the generally stated doctrine of Natural Rights and to use it to fashion definite natural rights in a modern-day business context. This challenge will be undertaken in a later section, "Employee Moral Rights."

Discussion Questions

1. What is natural law?
2. What is civil law?
3. What is the Stoics' theory of natural law?
4. What is the Locke theory of natural law?
5. Who is John Locke and what are his views on natural law?
6. What is the difference between natural and civil law?
7. What is the difference between Locke's theory and Stoics' theory on natural law?
8. What are the problems with natural law theory?
9. What are natural rights?
10. What are Locke's views on natural rights?
11. What are the differences between natural rights and legal rights?
12. What are the differences between natural rights and utilitarianism?
13. What are the types of natural rights?
14. What are the problems with the natural rights theory?
15. Is it a natural right for an employee to expect equal treatment in the workplace?
16. Is it a natural right for an employee to feel safe at work and not expect to be harassed?
17. Does natural law follow moral laws?
18. If natural law follows moral laws, who determines what is moral or ethical?
19. Is it possible that natural laws exist, and that is how people reasoned the creation of government and civil law?
20. Do all people in the United States have inalienable rights? What are those, and whose authority gives them?
21. Should employers abide by what is moral and ethical according to natural law or only by what is dictated by civil law?
22. Is civil law the highest standard of conduct expected of people?
23. What are some of the problems with the theory of natural law?
24. What are some of the problems with the theory of natural rights?

CHAPTER 10

Social Contract and Fatalism

I. The Social Contract Theory of Ethics

A. Introduction

The primary proponent of the theory of ethics known as the social contract theory of ethics is the French philosopher Rousseau (1712–1778). For Rousseau, the social contract not only explains the existence of the state, but also the origin and nature of morality. Rousseau draws a distinction between the natural and moral order. He describes existence before, and after, the formation of organized societies.

B. History of the Social Contract

The social contract constitutes the means to the existence of society and morality. Yet, the social contract has very little basis in historical reality. Those who are assumed to be bound by this alleged agreement have no recollection of ever making it. If such an agreement was in fact historically entered into, how can a contract previously entered into by others bind those who were not parties to it? If the "contract" is viewed as "hypothetical," in the sense that it is an agreement reasonable people would make, then how can one be bound by an agreement one never has made? It is useful to think of the social contract as an implied contract by which all by their present conduct are implicitly bound. An implied contract theory, therefore, serves to validate the social contract, which in turn explains how society and morality came into existence.

C. Rousseau and the State of Nature

What would existence be like if people lived without government, law, social organization, and societal rules, and without any commonly accepted method for enforcing any rules? Rousseau declared that people in such a natural state are characterized by sentiments of compassion rather than viciousness. Although people may not possess an idea of goodness, they are not naturally wicked. Rousseau's conception of people in the state of nature thus is different from Hobbes' view.

Why, then, do people depart from the state of nature? Human beings, explained Rousseau, are social creatures. They naturally live together in groups, wanting and needing the company of others of their own kind.

Communities, civil society, and the state come into existence to satisfy people's natural need for the conditions requisite for achieving a "good" human life: physically good at the Hobbesian sense of merely living and surviving; materially good in the Lockian sense of living well and acquiring possessions; and also morally good in the sense of gradually nourishing and strengthening moral and social instincts. Leaving the state of nature and forming a human community, therefore, are the necessary conditions to being a fully delineated human being.

D. The Social Contract and Morality

Before entry into the social contract, there is no law, ethics, morality, or moral standards, said Rousseau. When one does enter into the social contract and engages in civil relations with others, one becomes a different type of person. Human association engenders feelings of kind, producing feelings of kindness, sympathy, and conscience.

As a result of social living, an individual's power yields to the moral and then legal standards of the whole community. Morality arises when people are brought together and accept rules that are necessary for civilized social living. Morality, therefore, is grounded on certain rules that underlie society, that people agree are necessary, that enhance social living, and that create a society where everyone can have a chance to attain the good life.

Only within the context of the social contract can people become true moral agents. Morality is possible because the social contract creates the conditions under which people can afford to be moral. The contract, therefore, is the ethical means of enabling people to life together peacefully and morally in a community.

E. Rousseau: The General Will as the Standard of Morality

According to Rousseau, the body politic is a legal and ethical entity possessed of a will. The purpose of this will, the General Will, is to preserve the whole and achieve the common good. It is the source of law, justice, and morality. By participation in the social contract and the General Will, people share in the common good. In so doing, however, they submerge their individual wills to something greater, which necessarily expresses what they really want.

F. Problems with Rousseau's General Will

The General Will has great legal and moral significance, but in order for it to have any application, the General Will must be determinable. The question, accordingly, as to how the General Will is ascertained, is of enormous importance. The crucial question is what does the common good consist of and what therefore is the General Will. To presume that there is such a will, that is, there is something that people really want, as distinct from what they want individually, is an obscure, if not mystical, doctrine.

The problem with Rousseau's theory is that it invites identification of the General Will with some individual's conception of it. If the General Will exists as an ideal, its meaning is only accessible to a philosopher. If the General Will does have practical implications, it is then suited to manipulation and exploitation, particularly when the people consent to its interpretation by one or a few people. There is, of course, the potential for democratic interpretation, whereby the General Will is determined by counting votes.

G. Summary

Rousseau's social contract theory presumes that people are rational. They can arrive at a consensus regarding the rules that they will agree to adopt for their mutual benefit. The theory is designed to show the agreements and rules rational people would make, on prudential grounds, when informed by an understanding if the interests at stake, and on condition that others follow these agreements and rules as well.

II. Fatalism, Free Will, and Determinism

A. Introduction

Moral goodness is present when moral responsibility is present. Moral responsibility is the relationship between a person and his or her conduct that enables a person to be praised or blamed because of the behavior. This relationship commonly is supposed to be based on a certain independence of action on a person's part, usually denoted by the concept of freedom of will.

A free will, therefore, is a distinguishing feature of a moral person. Freedom is an indispensable element of, and a necessary postulate for, morality.

Science tends to view human beings as actors whose behavior is caused by hereditary and environmental factors. Are people free individuals who can make their choices and determine their actions without hindrance, or are people's actions determined by a fate or causal laws over which they have no control? If people's actions are fully predestined or determined, are they truly morally responsible? Is it fair that they should be blamed and punished for their wrongdoing, or praised and rewarded for their "goodness"?

B. Fatalism

1. INTRODUCTION

The Law of Fate (or Fortune or Destiny) was a prominent aspect of ancient and medieval thought. According to this "fatalistic" view, the universe is the result of fixed and unchanging laws. Every event in the universe, including human "will," is ruled by an external and immutable Law of Fate. Everything is determined through an unbroken chain of causes, and with an absoluteness that permits no break. Nothing happens by chance or choice.

2. MAJOR TENETS

There are two major tenets to fatalism: natural events are fixed absolutely, and human destiny is predetermined.

All change is according to a fixed and unalterable law, a law that is the basic and absolute principle of the universe. Every natural event is predetermined, both as to manner and time of occurrence. There can be no possible interference with this necessity.

The destiny of human beings, especially death, is eternally fixed by powers of fate. Deeds, sufferings, ideals, and character are products of the external forces of fate.

3. Consequences

As a result of this fatalistic philosophy, there can be no freedom anywhere; freedom is an impossibility; there is only an unbending necessity.

People can have no freedom of will in any true sense of the term. No one possesses any choice about what one does. All one's actions are the result of factors over which one can have no control. Fate dictates its will to helpless human beings.

4. The Stoics and Fate

The Stoics claimed to understand the universe. They maintained that there exist inevitable laws in the universe to which all things, including human beings, are subject completely. There is nothing a person can do to change his or her destiny in the least degree. There is no choice but to follow the dictates of this law.

One may not be happy about this fatalism, but one is hopeless and one must obey. One can obey graciously, or obey ungraciously, but in either case, one must obey. When one understands one's fate, one will not rebel, but accept it as inevitable. The only real freedom, declared the Stoics, is to accept one's fate.

5. The Sophists and Fate

The first departure from the ancient tradition of fatalism was paved by the Sophists. The Sophists focused their attention upon human beings and particularly upon their unrealized potentialities. It appeared to the Sophists that human beings could not be ruled totally by an inevitable inescapable, Law of Fate. It seemed simply impossible that human beings should not have some choice and influence on their own destiny.

The Sophists believed people could shape their fate. They could learn, with instruction by the Sophists, of course, to defend themselves, to succeed in the struggle of life, and to gain position and power. Whatever their eternal fate may be, people at least can influence their worldly existence to fit their objectives. People are not dictated to wholly by Fate, declared the Sophists.

6. Machiavelli and Fortune

Machiavelli maintained that two elements dominate one's destiny–Fortune and Virtue. Fortune (or Fate), asserted Machiavelli, is the ruler of one-half of one's actions. One, therefore, must accept the conditions imposed by Fortune. Not even the most intelligent and calculating individual can expect always to control the forces of Fortune. It is an incontrovertible truth proved by all history, declared Machiavelli, that people may "second" Fortune, but they cannot oppose Fortune. They may develop Fortune's designs, but cannot defeat them.

Virtue (or Excellence) is in part right knowledge, particularly the understanding that one cannot always control certain fortuitous happenings. Virtue, therefore, is the perpetual adaptation of one's life to the dictates of Fortune. Do not oppose Fortune, counseled Machiavelli; rather, conform one's actions to the conditions set out by Fortune. One's success ultimately depends upon the astute manner one suits one's actions to Fortune's circumstances. Virtue, therefore, emerges as a type of opportunism, a charge frequently made against Machiavelli.

Machiavelli represents a Renaissance interpretation of Fate. Fate (or Fortune) offers possibilities that one can put to use. Not only seize these opportunities, advised Machiavelli, but also strive to create them, and by so doing, master one's fate and attain one's own fortune.

7. CRITICISM OF FATALISM

Although one must recognize the existence in the universe of certain laws and consistencies, the universe cannot be closed so tightly that all one's actions are fully caused or determined. There is truth in the belief that every event in the universe stands somehow related to other events; that individuals are engulfed by their heredity and environment; and that these factors are of compelling significance to one's life and character.

One, however, also must take cognizance of the fact that new events are continuously happening and that time is continuously transforming the old into the new. The fate or destiny of each individual, therefore, is to a degree dependent upon what the particular individual is and does. One's ways of thinking and feeling are determining factors of one's character and life.

8. THE MORAL ARGUMENT AGAINST FATALISM

A world in which fate ruled completely would not in any sense be a good world, because one could not be held responsible for one's actions. Whether for good or bad, one's behavior would be caused by a power beyond one's control; and one, therefore, could neither be praised nor blamed.

Morality demands free will and an opportunity for real choice. A good person is one who makes the right choice through the force of his or her own free will; a bad person is one who makes the wrong choice. A denial of freedom obliterates moral choice.

9. KANT: FATALISM AND FREE WILL

Kant believed freedom of the will to be the foundation of morality. Freedom of will is crucial, maintained Kant, because a person cannot be held morally accountable if he or she is not free. If human choices are ruled entirely by fate, then free will is an illusion, and so is morality.

"Ought implies can," stated Kant. Since he held that duty, obligation, and the "good will" are fundamentally important concepts, the "can" must be; otherwise, morality is in vain. It makes sense, reasoned Kant, to tell people what they morally ought to do, only if one believes that they can do it. Morality presupposes free will, and free will provides the content of and motive for morality.

Kant attempts to solve the fatalism-free will dilemma by drawing a distinction between the sensual-appetitive-animal nature of human beings, which may be determined fully by causes subject to scientific analysis, and the thinking-reasoning-rational nature, which stands outside the compulsion of these causes. Human beings are unique because, alone among the animals, they are capable of reason. On the basis of this rationality, they can form the idea of freedom, act freely, engage in rational moral choice, and thus attain the special dignity accorded to free, rational, moral beings.

One not only can prove this freedom by theoretical reason, maintained Kant, but also by experiencing it and feeling it directly when one makes a moral choice. Freedom is a very real condition of ordinary moral experience. One feels within oneself the free activity of one's mind; one senses the mind as a center for initiative force, creative capability, and imperative power; and one feels that one is shaping reality, choosing objectives, and making true choices. Since this experience of reason is real, the choice whether to act in a moral manner is real too.

There is a real freedom, therefore, despite the fact that human beings are subject to the laws of nature, as is everything else. When one lives and acts with a free will, one discovers that certain moral insights are possible. This moral consciousness of human beings indicates that the will is free.

C. Free Will

1. INTRODUCTION AND MAJOR TENETS

One of the continuing problems of moral philosophy is whether human beings are genuinely free in their moral choices. The free will position, also called "indeterminism," accepts freedom of action and moral responsibility; and denies that human actions are determined by destiny, fate, or antecedent causes. Human beings are not constrained totally by external forces and motives. People are conscious and thinking beings and are free in their actions and moral choices, and they are, accordingly, responsible for them.

2. ARGUMENTS FOR THE FREE WILL POSITION

a) The Experience and Feeling of Freedom

Freedom of choice and the free will position are based on the experience and feeling of freedom that one has when one is engaged in moral choice. At the moment of choosing, one experiences an immediate and direct feeling that the act of choice is free and not determined or caused. One senses that the act of choosing was arbitrary; that is, that the opposite alternative, or no alternative, could have been selected.

b) Morality Presupposes Free Choice

A belief that human beings are responsible moral agents requires that an act be the product of a free and voluntary choice. In ordinary experience, people act as if they are free, and they are held morally responsible for their choices. These choices are praised and censured as their own. One also engages in self-praise and blame and evidences pride and remorse.

Any attribution of responsibility is completely unreasonable if one's choosing is not free and voluntary at the moment of decision; that is, if it did not lie in one's power to have decided otherwise.

If one discovers that an action is beyond a person's control because a person lacks the freedom to choose it, then certain types of responses indicating responsibility are inappropriate and wrong. These responses, such as praise and blame, reward and punishment, and respect and resentment, which are of central importance to human beings, must be abandoned along with all notions of moral responsibility. It is unthinkable to abandon free moral choice and responsibility because to do so would engender an epidemic of powerlessness, meaninglessness, and blamelessness inimical to individual character and societal cohesiveness.

c) The Dual Nature of Human Beings

People are human beings, yet there is a distinction between their "human" nature and their "beings" nature. "Beings" are subject to nature's laws, which are capable of being studied by scientists. For "beings," experience unfolds according to a causal sequence, which one may be able to use to one's own advantage but which also constrains a person. "Humans" are capable of reflecting on experience, formulating "laws" for their own self-rule, and freely acting on these determinations. A person's life is composed of both attributes, and it matters greatly which one is in operation in a particular circumstance.

3. PROBLEMS WITH THE FREE WILL THEORY

Even if one feels a sense of freedom at the moment of decision, it does not follow necessarily that freedom exists. This feeling may signify nothing more than ignorance of the causes actually operative within an individual. The feeling of freedom, moreover, may be not a reflection of choice, but merely a person seeing more clearly the advantages of disadvantages of alternative actions. When one does see clearly the benefits and costs of alternative courses of action, one proceeds in the direction where the balance of advantage lies.

The "responsibility" argument supporting the free will position also presents problems. One, for example, ordinarily does not attribute responsibility to persons, such as children and the insane, whose present conduct is uninfluenced by their past experiences. A will that theoretically is uninfluenced totally in its choice of the moment is, by definition, arbitrary, random, and completely irresponsible. One theoretically is no more free if an action just happens than if it is caused by factors beyond one's control. Since an arbitrary and random fate is indistinguishable from mere happenstance, true freedom requires not only that one's actions be not fully determined by external causes, but also that they are determined by a person for himself or herself based on reasons. Does any one have the experience of willing to act in a particular way, and then discovering that he or she acts differently, just like that, without any explanation or reason? A person, however, who acts in accordance with reasons, even compelling reasons, normally is viewed as acting freely.

4. CONCLUSION TO FREE WILL

Even supposing that there is an element of randomness in the universe, this does not make implausible the concept of a free will in the sense of predominantly self-caused human action. Free will thus reflects behavior that is not constrained totally by forces external to the actor. Moral responsibility, therefore, seems to require that a person has the freedom to decide how he or she will act, that one's actions be self-caused, and that the decision to act takes place in a sufficiently stable, natural, reasoned, and deterministic context.

D. Determinism

1. DEFINITION AND CONSEQUENCES

Determinism holds that everything in the universe, including human actions and choices, is determined by causes. For every event, there is an antecedent sufficient cause; that is, there is a prior set of occurrences, conditions, and circumstances that produce it by means of a continuous process.

Nothing happens purely by chance; that is, without any cause. Every event that occurs is the only one that could have occurred under the circumstances. Actions, including human choices, thus are subject to explanation and prediction.

If all one's actions are so determined, and Determinism is true, then human beings never can act differently from the way they do act. What occurs must occur. If responsibility does require the freedom to act; and this freedom is incompatible with Determinism, then responsibility is incompatible with Determinism. To complicate matters further, there are two types of determinism: "hard" and "soft."

2. "HARD" DETERMINISM

This version of Determinism holds that a person's heredity, history, environment, and character cause a person to act in a certain way. A person's will is always determined, not by wholly external forces as the Fatalist claims, but by motives, purposes, desires, and impulses that are an integral part of a person's character and that are present at the moment of choice. An action is initiated by a person's choosing yet according to "hard" Determinism, one cannot ignore the causes that lie behind and prompt the choice.

"Freedom," for a "hard" Determinist, therefore, is not an uncaused, spontaneous, act of choice among alternatives, but rather the capacity inherent in each person to act in accordance with his or her own nature; that is, to express in conduct individual character.

A person may be free to act according to his or her own desires, but those very desires, as well as the capacity to combat them, are basic elements of character, and character is fully molded by hereditary, historical, and environmental forces that a person did not choose.

As a consequence, one does not possess a truly free will, and such a situation significantly undermines fundamental moral concepts. How can one legitimately hold another to be morally responsible, blameworthy, or even praiseworthy? Such reactive, evaluative, responses are inappropriate and rationally indefensible if people do not have free will. What if one is a morally good and praiseworthy person? He or she simply is fortunate enough to inherit desirable characteristics and to be exposed to favorable environmental and historical factors, which caused him or her to develop "good" character.

If one accepts "hard" Determinism, one is compelled, for the sake of consistency, to make radical changes in one's conception of choice, responsibility, praise and blame, gratitude and resentment, and even more basic ethical concepts, such as goodness, morality, and justice.

3. PROBLEMS WITH "HARD" DETERMINISM

"Hard" Determinism appears indistinguishable from fatalism; the denial of freedom is only implied. The theory views a person as a passive object or conduit that is merely acted upon by forces that he or she cannot control. It thereby robs a person of his and her dignity and respect as a rational, responsible human being.

"Hard" Determinism also conflicts with a person's consciousness of being a moral entity. One feels or experiences a sense of freedom whenever one chooses to do one thing rather than another. One senses the experience of choosing and one immediately is aware that one could have chosen otherwise. If "hard" Determinism is true, then this common, immediate, and strong experience that there are other possibilities of action is an illusion.

"Hard" Determinism ignores self-control. The theory moves from the idea that people do not solely make themselves to the notion that people are not responsible since they have no real control over themselves. If "hard" Determinism holds true, only one course is really open to a person: one cannot do otherwise than what one does. Is it not really possible for people to control their actions? Admittedly, people do not solely make themselves; nonetheless, they have the power to control themselves and therefore can be held responsible for not exercising such control.

No reasonable person, finally, will think it at all likely that it is, or will become, possible to predict human actions and choices in any detail and with any certitude.

4. "SOFT" DETERMINISM

A "soft" Determinism believes that a person's will is free in the sense that it is uncaused. At the moment of choice, there are real alternatives and one or the other willfully may be chosen, and the actual choice very well might have been different.

A person's character, history, heredity, environment, and social conditioning, however, do exert an influence on the will, by delimiting the possibilities open at the moment of choice.

Acts are unfree only when caused in particular ways and fully determined by past causes and events. The mere fact, however, that acts are influenced does not make them "unfree." There must be necessary conditions for human actions. One's actions, therefore, are subject to influences, but the principal cause of the action lies within a person's own purposes, desires, and will.

"Freedom" for a "soft" Determinist occurs when a person expresses himself or herself by means of an undetermined choice within a limited field of possibilities. One is free because the conditions that influence one's actions operate through one's desires and decisions. An individual's action is free because it is due to neither external restraints, nor internal compulsions.

There are many arguments in favor of "soft" Determinism. An act of choosing always results from a given set of conditions. These influencing factors are not always external to the nature of a person, but can be elements within one's own character. One's character, moreover, is not laid down once and for all; one gradually can remold one's character. The set of conditions is related to one's character and the act of choice because the act springs from the set of conditions, and if set apart from which, it simply would not happen.

Moral responsibility presupposes "soft" Determinism. If one could choose indifferently, without reference to what one has done in the past and to those conditions present at the moment of choice, one hardly can be held responsible for the results. One then could claim, with some justice, that the act is not one's own, but only the product of arbitrary, random, momentary happenstance. The implication of such "choice" is that a person possesses the ability to act against everything he or she believes in and cares about.

Such behavior cannot be classified as a "choice," but rather resembles a spasm that cannot be controlled. One, in fact, would question the rationality of a person who evidences such irrational behavior.

Freedom of choice is indispensable to morality. Yet people are influenced by their entire past, by everything that entered into their nature, and by their character. Their actions, however, proceed from their "selves" as thus constituted; their actions are their actions, so they can be held responsible for them.

E. Summary

Human choices are neither fixed by fate nor by antecedent causes. "Hard" Determinism seems to mix up determinism and fatalism, causation and compulsion; and it thus incorrectly supposes that human actions are fixed eternally, regardless of what one desires or does.

Human choices, however, are not absolutely open, and free will is not limitlessly free. Actions are free only within certain bounds and amid the possibilities presented by certain sets of conditions. People normally recognize that their desires, beliefs, and character are formed in part by factors outside their own thinking and being. Certain types of provocative impact, however, can change one's character, desires, and beliefs. One, for example, can critically examine one's own character and ask why one believes, desires, and acts as one does. Moral philosophy not only reinforces the asking of "why," but also provides the systematic ethical principles of analysis. One's vital moral and intellectual interests, therefore, demand a more libertarian philosophy, and these interests should make the "fateful" choice.

Discussion Questions

1. Based on all the philosophies presented in this chapter, which one most closely matches your own view of life?

2. Can the social contract exist in a society that is not fairly homogenous?

3. What role would education play in the people's ability to form the social contract?

4. Can a soldier be morally responsible since he or she takes an oath to obey the orders of his or her commanding officer?

5. Can you describe a situation from your experience where the application of Machiavellian philosophy resulted in your success?

6. How much of your life do you think has been determined by the contributing factor of soft determinism?

7. Describe a fatalistic situation in your life when the outcome of a situation seemed to be fated.

8. Is it ethical to force someone to subjugate his or her rights for the greater good?

9. Do you think that the health of an individual depends more on deterministic or indeterministic (free will) factors?

10. What greater good and what particular philosophy or philosophies does the "American public" ascribe to?

CHAPTER 11

Becoming Moral

I. The Moral Person

A. Attributes of the Moral Person

1. Intelligence

Intelligence emerges as the most important virtue for the moral person. Thought has primacy. One must think of oneself as a thinking being in a system of thinking beings. The ethical theories discussed herein, particularly Kant's Categorical Imperative, underscore rationality as an essential element.

To construct the "good" life, one must build up one's intelligence. "Right" conduct constantly requires explicit thought and reasoning. Only the informed and rational mind can judge according to diverse circumstances and conflicting doctrines.

The rational person will get the facts correct, keep his or her mind clear, and carefully and impartially evaluate the facts and their implications. An intelligent person will accept rules of conduct and standards of behavior only after scrutinizing them to ensure they are ethically sound. He or she carefully weighs arguments, makes rational calculations, provides reasons for a decision, and supplies a satisfactory account of one's reasons.

The intelligent person does not resolve issues by appealing to what must people believe; rather, he or she strives to find the correct answer. The intelligent person depends on his or her own thinking and reasoning. He or she is willing to revise previous convictions. One follows the logic of one's reasoning and proceeds in an ascendancy of self-awareness, self-correction, and self-knowledge.

2. Self-Control

Morality also requires self-control and self-discipline. One needs intelligence to determine what is right or wrong, and one also requires the self-control to do what is morally right and never to do what is morally wrong. The moral person demonstrates a willingness to act on the results of ethical deliberation. He or she is strongly disposed to adhere to rationally ascertained moral rules and standards, particularly when confronted by considerations that are morally irrelevant, such as what most people believe is right, how one instinctively or emotionally feels about an action, or what consequences will impact on oneself.

Intelligence is accorded primacy, but one must possess the character to follow the "order" of one's intelligence.

3. Integrity

The moral person is an honorable, trustworthy, and loyal person. He or she stands up for his or her convictions, is true to himself or herself, and adheres to rules of conduct, even when inconvenient, unprofitable, or dangerous to do so. A moral person is committed to the rule of law—"legal" law and moral law.

4. Veracity

The moral person states what he or she believes is true and right, even though it may be easier to deceive others or oneself. A moral person is an honest person who does not break faith with anyone, violate engagements, break promises, and disappoint any expectations raised by his or her conduct.

5. Justice

The moral person is a just and fair person. He or she is tolerant of others, attempts to comprehend others, is open and unbiased, and judges people on their merits. He or she acknowledges the interests of all concerned in a transaction and not merely one's own apparent self-interest. The moral person treats all people with dignity and respect and does not abuse, use, manipulate, or exploit people.

6. Freedom

The moral person respects authority and obeys the legal and moral law; yet disdains authoritarianism. He or she loves and cherishes freedom—the freedom to pursue intellectual, practical, and moral excellence.

7. Accountability

The moral person is a responsible person. He or she engages in self-restraint, performs his or her duties, thinks about the consequences for his or her actions, and takes responsibility for his or her actions.

8. The Common Good

The moral person recognizes that a "good" life, in its truest sense, depends on one's community and society. A good life must be lived in a good community and in a good society and is not fully possible otherwise. Morality, therefore, is identified with eliminating injury, cruelty, and exploitation; distributing burdens, as well as benefits, fairly; and ameliorating human life.

9. Summary

Immorality, therefore, emerges not so much a matter of the traditional "vices," but rather a problem of weakness or "softness," for example, in intelligence, discipline, or community responsibility.

B. Conflict

A moral person necessarily is confronted with the existence of unavoidable conflict. There always will be a struggle between moral and prudential claims, between rules of conduct and demands of expediency, and between duty and desire. Effectiveness in action contends with integrity and honesty; candor struggles with kindness; and impartiality conflicts with loyalty.

Conflict, therefore, not harmony, is the essence of morality as the moral person ordinarily experiences it. Conflict generates difficult moral problems, and it is typical and essential that ethical reasoning should be concerned with such conflicts.

Conflict, of course, may be "softened" or glossed over. Yet, since conflict is unavoidable and ever-present, really how effective is this approach? One also could retreat from the chaos of moral conflict into certainty and order. Perhaps people, after a little freedom, actually may prefer authority, and the security, assurance, and economy of effort that it entails.

The solution for the moral person, however, is to be one's own person, and to strive to eliminate conflict rationally and ethically. In particular, one must seek to resolve apparently conflicting claims by demonstrating that they are part of a coherent system and lead back to a common basis.

C. Balance

The idea of balance represents a fundamental ethical principle. The notion of attaining a carefully arrived at balance, a "right" relationship, and a harmonious adjustment dates back at least as far as Greek tradition.

Accordingly, the moral person will strike the right balance between conflicting interests and demands. With good judgment, moral integrity, and wisdom, ethical resolutions to conflict can be found.

Balance, for a moral person, also requires effort to discern the "right" relationship between an individual and society. The purpose is to ascertain as clearly as possible the means to achieving the good life-individually and communally. The moral person, therefore, combines in right proportion not only reason and feeling, prudence and spontaneity, intellect and instinct, theory and practice, but also private and public activity.

D. Dual System of Ethics

The moral person meets moral standards arising from ethical doctrines espousing utility and justice. Accordingly, a moral assertion is valid if, and only if, it contributes to human welfare and is just. To promote good over bad, and to be willing to universalize one's actions, are the twofold criteria that the moral person uses to solve moral dilemmas.

What if utility and justice conflict? A reasonable person will acknowledge potential conflict. The goal then is to attempt to reconcile apparently conflicting moral philosophies and weave them into a harmonious whole. The moral solution, therefore, will emerge as a life composed of a mixture of ethical considerations; that is the way it should be.

E. Why Be Moral?

1. Introduction

One must recognize that life necessarily presents conflict between moral ways of acting and other types of conduct. All people will be tempted to cast aside moral concerns in favor of allowing nonmoral reasons. Even ethically well-demonstrated moral assertions will be resisted when their acceptance threatens peoples, or one's own, self-interest.

The question, therefore, as to why one should act morally, emerges as a fundamental question of moral philosophy and the ultimate problem of moral justification. Why should a rational person do what is right? Why should one recognize any distinction between right and wrong? How can the moral way of life rationally be justified, particularly since a moral way of life may conflict with self-interest? Why should one act on moral reasons rather than legal reasons, conventional reasons, or reasons of self-interest? Even if one can determine ethically what one morally ought to do, why one ought to do what is morally required? Perhaps rational people can be persuaded by reasons of self-interest to adhere to moral rules, but then their "moral" reasons to do things are ultimately reasons of self-interest. Is there an unresolvable tension between morality and self-interest?

2. Ethical Justification

How are moral rules justified? If one is an Ethical Relativist, one ought to be moral because that is what is approved by society. Societal rules are necessary if people are to coexist, cooperate, and prosper in a society. If one is a Legal Positivist, one ought to be moral for the same reason that one ought to obey the law, which ultimately is in order to avoid punishment. If one is a Utilitarian, one must be moral so as to achieve the greater good. One thus will set aside any egoistic motives in favor of moral rules that promote the general welfare. If one is a Kantian, one ought to be moral and do the moral act for no other reason than it is "moral." The "ought" in morality, therefore, has in itself an unconditional obligation for a Kantian.

3. Egoistic Justification

Why else be moral? A moral person, said Socrates, is happier than an immoral one. Acting morally produces certain harmonious results—inner peace, satisfaction, and happiness. The moral person sets goals that fit into the scheme of human development and at the same time satisfy one's own desires. The achievement of goals creates a feeling of satisfaction and pleasure, which is characteristic of happiness. Achieving goals produces new goals and thus a happy life. The moral person, moreover, does not blindly rush at every object, but sees the necessity of acknowledging limits to his or her actions and objectives. He or she progresses steadily along a demarcated path toward definite, attainable objectives. The moral person recognizes that "limits" are used in the sense of a guide, not a restraint; and that he or she will be happier for acknowledging such moral guidelines. Even if the moral person suffers through moments of disappointment, bitterness, and despair, even if he or she escapes the notice of the world or is misjudged by the world, even if he or she suffers from injustice, and even if he or she meets an untimely end, nonetheless, the moral person will be at peace with himself or herself.

Acting immorally, moreover, can be argued as acting imprudently against one's self-interest. Perhaps the immoral person can win some temporary short-term advantage; but ultimately immorality brings on social censure and sanctions, such as rejection, isolation, and ostracism. A prudent person realizes that acting morally will obviate many of the disadvantages that one would be forced to encounter if one acted immorally, not only societal sanctions, but also the incurring of personal costs such as guilt, remorse, and other psychological discomforts.

In order to convince a person to act morally, he or she must be able to envision a way of life that not only provides a satisfying life for himself or herself as an individual, but also contains the conditions necessary for a meaningful, satisfying, social way of life. The conditions for such a life for people living in social groups requires morality. Morality, therefore, has a social source and a social function. It is, moreover, to one's advantage to live in a society in which morality is accepted. One will be able to rely on people obeying certain norms; and one will feel safe and confident by so knowing. One's own compliance with moral standards, however, is the "price" one must pay to secure the compliance of others.

4. Problems with Justifying Morality

Even presuming that society needs and requires morality, and even if it is in one's advantage to have others act in a moral manner, does it follow that one should adopt a moral way of life, and does it follow that one always should act morally? Can it be demonstrated to a prudential person that it always and certainly will be advantageous for him or her to act in a thoroughly moral manner? Why should not the pragmatic person instead encourage and persuade others to be moral; and then take advantage of that fact; and at the same time avoid his or her own moral responsibilities? It may not be a satisfactory answer that one is not likely to get away with acting immorally. In all honesty, it must be admitted that there will be at least some circumstances where one can act immorally with impunity, perhaps without even detection, and quite efficaciously. Surely, if one is a Machiavellian, it would be advantageous for everyone else to be constrained by morality and for one to escape any moral sanctions by pretending to act morally, or, if one has the power, simply to flout moral standards. The Machiavellian goal is to succeed in making one's self-interest paramount, and this goal can be attained in part by inducing others to make the demands of morality paramount in their lives. Does not this Machiavellian scenario appear to be the best possible world for oneself? To this question, it is difficult to provide a completely satisfying answer of any kind.

5. Summary

In selecting a course of conduct, moral reasons and prudential ones not always will coincide. It is necessary, therefore, to demonstrate to people that morality is required for the well-being of people in general, and that morality demands that people to some extent and at some times act in ways that they cannot perceive as presently egoistically prudential. The challenge of explicating a way of life that both secures the agreement of rational egoistic individuals and provides the conditions necessary for a social life is a daunting one. One good way is to create a way of life that helps to make the advancement of one person's self-interest consistent, as far as possible, with the success of other people.

F. The Moral Business Leader, Manager, and Entrepreneur

1. Prudent Self-Interest

A moral manager manages the business with prudent self-interest. No one can make the conscientious manager do what he or she thinks is not in best interest of shareholders and other stakeholders. Society, of course, needs material wealth for the exercise of freedom and attainment of the "good life." Adam Smith, in *The Wealth of Nations,* however, noted that the freedom only can come from an intelligent and humane use of the free-market system.

2. No Self-Exoneration

Moral managers must be very careful in exonerating themselves from amoral attitudes or morally dubious practices on the basis of business "survival." The moral business manager avoids the placing of blame for moral failings on others, for example, society, government, the legal system, or the marketplace. Business ethics has no future if it is gradually suffocated by moral "compromises" of individual managers.

3. Practical Reason

The moral manager is one who predictably can be trusted to act reasonably under the circumstances. The best approach is for business managers to conceive of their task as attempting to reach the most reasonable result under the circumstances (which includes, but is not limited to, the facts of the case, the law, ethics, and economics). "Reasonableness" can be used as a standard for moral rightness. It is an appropriate substitute for other standards of absolute moral rightness. It is not a pipe dream, but a rational standard and attainable with effective commitments.

4. Impartiality

Fundamental impartiality and a consideration of others when making decisions are attributes of the moral manager. Ethics naturally becomes more relevant as managers make business decisions that affect human beings in significant ways. There must be a recognition that managers make judgments not only about the future of a business, but also about the future of society.

5. Management Ethics

Morality in business must be seen as a management responsibility. Moral questions must be effectively dealt with by business managers in order to develop an ethical philosophy that is sound; and in order to develop managers who are capable of thinking that can produce high ethical standards.

A firm philosophical foundation already exists for the moral development of business. A moral business manager, for example, can use the Doctrine of the Mean to determine moral standards. He or she can use inductive reasoning and work from current business practices. He or she then can use Utilitarianism to determine if the "mean" standard promotes greater good, and he or she can use Kant's Categorical Imperative to ensure that an action is not unjust to persons. If the act passes all three tests, the moral business manager can frame it as a rule and promulgate it in a code of ethics for the business.

6. Moral Accountability

Management and entrepreneurs must not only incorporate morality into business decision making, but also must hold itself accountable to standards of moral conduct. Managers must make a commitment to a moral course of conduct, and once they make the commitment, not abandon it lightly. A manager cannot do what he or she judges or thinks should not be done ethically.

7. Codes of Ethics

Managers and entrepreneurs must promulgate and adopt codes of ethics. A code of ethics is a set of just laws, ethical principles, and fundamental moral rules, governing how business and management are to treat one another, stakeholders, and society, and a set of subsidiary, supplemental moral rules that business people will agree to accept for their mutual benefit on condition that others follow those rules as well.

8. Trust

Management and entrepreneurs must be viewed as more than mere "business"; rather, as a trust. Business managers must take collective action to ensure that goods and services are available and accessible to all. They must take responsibility for management's moral behavior and do so seriously enough so as to monitor, discipline, and even remove business managers when standards of morality are violated.

9. Moral Leadership

A business manager and entrepreneur must be a moral leader. He or she must be a paradigm of morality and raise level of conventional morality by example. He or she must use moral power to build and sustain the moral community. He or she must implement moral concerns throughout management and business. He or she must give recognition to the fact that a business manager's task is fundamentally moral in nature. The moral manager must be an instrument of character formation. He or she must demonstrate that moral integrity and competence are inseparable and that demonstrate that moral character and trust are indispensable traits of business management as a profession.

Such a manager can bring about good in the world, in his or her own life as well as in others'. He or she can touch the better aspects of his or her own or another's human nature. By demonstrating enthusiasm, cooperativeness, self-discipline, and dedication, the moral manager can build teamwork and a moral business entity.

10. Why Should Business Leaders, Managers, and Entrepreneurs Be Moral?

Managers have considerable discretion. If moral, business managers will be able to increase their discretion by adhering to moral standards and thus winning the trust of public. As a result, management will gain greater freedom from external interference. If business managers want the freedom to conduct affairs with a minimum of outside interference, they must see themselves as moral agents.

If business leaders, managers, and entrepreneurs act in an immoral or amoral manner, the public will not trust them to take its interests into account. Consequently, any moral dimensions to business decision-making will be pursued by others, who will take action to shape management and business behavior. Government regulation, for example, will continue to be relied on to promote moral and social values. To abandon the moral debate to others is an irresponsible act by business managers; it is an abdication of responsibility.

II. Summary of Philosophical Ethics

A. Reason

What has to exist in the world for the moral point of view to prevail? The answer is reason. This book, thus far, has underscored a belief in the life of the mind, of thinking, and of reason. In this sense, the book reflects an "intellectualist" doctrine. The basis of morality is found principally in the powers of the mind that are common to all people. The paramount use of reason is ethically to establish moral standards for the effective guiding of human conduct. Properly directed ethical thinking can answer moral questions.

The aim of ethical thought is to construct a moral world. Human beings can reason logically about what is right and wrong; can arrive at demonstrably correct objective and communicable moral conclusions; and can agree as to standards of right and wrong. Human beings, moreover, can make their conduct conform to the moral results of their ethical reasoning.

Reasoning is not helpless "intellectualizing"; it is not sophistic rationalizing; and it is not a "slave" to passions, drives, impulses, instincts, and sentiments. Ethics fosters and even compels the use of reason as well as a kind of autonomy on the part of an individual, who is asked, and expected, to think out and make his or her own moral decisions.

B. Moral Education

Moral education is more than the mere transmission of a certain body of settled knowledge. It does more than teach what has been revealed. Rather, moral education reveals what can be taught; it seeks to provide insight rather than to preach.

The disesteem into which moralists have fallen is due in part to their failure to see that the true function of a moralist is not to command people to be good but to elucidate what the good is. He or she must show that the moral course of conduct advocated is not an arbitrary choice, but one that a rational person would choose if it clearly was ethically understood. The true and proper function of the moralist is to promote good conduct by ethically discovering and explaining the nature of morality. He or she must educate people to give weight to moral issues and to reason ethically to moral conclusions. This type of moral education will help make people into moral people. The process whereby a person chooses what he or she has deliberately reasoned to be the good choice inevitably will lead to a good and wise person who has determined rationally where the true good lies.

C. Certainty in Ethics and Morals

One will demand too much of ethics if one expects absolute proof of general ethics principles and indisputable certification of specific moral judgments. Although it is always appropriate to ask for an external justification of validating ethical principles, the problem arises as how to justify essential and high level ethical principles.

There does not exist now, however, nor is there likely to exist in the foreseeable future, one entirely and absolutely valid ethical theory. There are differing moral philosophies, espousing conflicting ethical principles, expressing various values, and treating differently the very complex subject of morality. Yet, unless moral questions can be "answered" by ethics, morality itself is laid open to subjectivism, relativism, amoralism, and disorder. There are distinct advantages in acting on principle and in having predetermined acceptable principles on which to act. One is rightly skeptical about a person with no principles as well as suspicious of a person of "principle" who has a new principle for each occasion.

The existence of conflicting types of normative ethical theories is both problematical and inevitable. One solution to the problem of differing moral philosophies and conflicting ethical theories is to discern the enduring part of positive truth each contributes to morality. Another solution is to attempt to justify internally an ethical theory by the degree of clarity and coherence it exhibits. Yet another solution is to seek to externally justify an ethical theory based in its ability to fulfill moral objectives.

Yet, despite the insights that each ethical theory contains, each has its problems, weaknesses, and limitations. It is simply not realistic to reduce all ethical considerations to one neat pattern, so as to provide one constant principled solution to all moral problems. Intelligent and sensitive people at times will disagree, not only as to the morally right course of action, but also as to the ethically appropriate principle to apply. Even if one admits there is uncertainty in ethics and morals, one cannot deny that people do act according to ethically established moral norms and that people, despite the uncertainties and disagreements, have agreed on ethical principles and have established sufficient moral norms to constitute themselves as a moral community. So long as absolute certainty is not required, one can use moral philosophy and ethics to render moral judgments.

D. Ethical Strategy

A satisfactory ethical approach is to base morality on a variety of ethical doctrines. First, one needs both egoistic, utilitarian, and Kantian moral philosophies. Each of these ethical doctrines offers a valuable perspective from which to reflect on morality. Although these ethical considerations do not seem to be reducible to each other, there is no reason why one should not be able to extract a great deal of value from each approach. Ethical Egoism is an ethics of action that advises one to promote prudently one's own objectives and happiness. Utilitarianism is concerned with maximizing social benefits and promoting the well-being of the community. Kantian ethics requires that one respect all people, and this duty sets strict limits to what people will allow themselves to do to others, as well as to themselves, in pursuing their ends. It seems clear that an excellent state of affairs is one in which every person has the opportunity to attain the best life he or she is capable of. In such a state of affairs, the concerns of a principle of individual action, a principle of utility, and a principle of duty will be fulfilled. That is, an ethics of personal and universal happiness is conjoined with an ethics of duty.

Secondly, an ethics of principle must be conjoined with an ethics of virtue. It is difficult to see how a principled ethical approach can be sustainable except through the development of virtuous dispositions to act in accordance with ethical principles. Ethics of principle and ethics of virtue should not be regarded as rival types of ethics, but as complementary aspects of the ethical point of view. How can one discern what virtuous character traits to develop or inculcate if one does not subscribe to an ethics of principle? For every virtuous character trait, there will be a principle defining the type of moral action in that the virtue is to express itself; and for every principle, there will be a virtue which exhibits a disposition to act in accordance with the principle.

The ethical strategy, and the solution to the ethical dilemma, therefore, is an ethical point of view that emphasizes action, utility, and duty, and that is assisted and sustained by an ethics of virtue that promotes tendencies to act in accordance with ethical principles.

E. Function of the Ethical Order

The function of the ethical order is to promote the fullest development of the capacities of all of its members. The true object of ethics is not to chain up human nature, but to maximize its expression. The "good life" largely is composed of the successful pursuit of activities that one finds beneficial and worthwhile for oneself and others. Whatever account one finally provides for the "good life," it must be sufficiently broad to allow people to determine its content for themselves. Freedom is an essential aspect of the good life. The good life, and the ethical order that makes it possible, must be conceived as a condition of freedom and not a restriction on it. A distinguishing mark of the ethical order is its commitment to moving human beings to the full realization of their capacities and powers. The ethical order also is committed to the conviction that happiness is possible and that everyone ought to be able to attain happiness.

The ethical order not only underscores freedom, expression, and development, but a harmonious development. Harmonious development may involve the necessity of discipline, self-denial, or even self-sacrifice. In such development, however, lies for each person only true happiness; that is, happiness that does not cause unhappiness in others.

F. The Social Good and the Community

Peoples' capacities should be conceived primarily in a social context and promoted with regard to their social significance and social consequences. The capacities that should be encouraged are those attuned to promoting the interests of the larger community. Social cohesion is an absolute necessity. One important purpose of ethics is to provide the moral rules required if people are to live together, develop, compete, and prosper in a community setting. A person is more likely to flourish if he or she has a degree of prudential concern for the interests of others. Morality serves to place restraints on unbridled selfishness that denies others' respect and overrides their rights. A central task of morality, therefore, is to protect the interests of persons other than the actor.

The object is to avoid a social order based on dictate, discipline, and dogma; to avoid the dissolution of the community by fostering an unrestrained, unsympathetic, selfish individualism that makes mutually beneficial cooperation improbable and conflict probable; and to secure a prosperous, stable society where personal independence and growth are encouraged and reinforced and where no more moral constraints are imposed on individuals than are absolutely necessary for the preservation of the community.

G. The Making of Morality

Morality consists of rules of conduct that restrain, guide, and determine "right" courses of action. People must decide what moral beliefs to adopt, what moral stands to take, and what moral rules to promulgate. Morality, therefore, is not to be discovered but to be made.

People possess the intellectual capacity to differentiate the morally good from the morally bad. The ethical theories examined here are the means by which morality is constructed. Ethics, therefore, is conceived as a practical as well as a remedial field. Ethics is the tool that can build and maintain a moral system of secular, objective, universal rules governing conduct. Morality serves as the means by which modifications of the actions and attitudes of people are brought about. Thoughtful people will become moral people, and an improvement in human life and social living will come from improved ethical reasoning.

H. Self-Interest

This book is an appeal not only to considerations of morality but also to self-interest. The book seeks to reconcile the requirements of morality with the well-being, happiness, and the good of the individual. It urges the creation of rules and standards of prudential self-interest.

Self-interest is not in and of itself immoral, and self-interest will characterize to a large degree one's actions and motives. A rational person, therefore, should welcome, in his or her own self-interest, a system of morality that is grounded upon long-range, practical, prudent self-interest. Moral standards and rules, if grounded in reciprocal self-interest, cohere with two fundamental, reliable, and widespread human attributes—self-interest and a sense of evenhandedness.

Since self-interest forms such a considerable part of human makeup, this book seeks an account of morality that allows egoistic concerns a significant place. If a moral system is to be practical and sustaining, it must link up with people's actual motivational capacities, which predominantly are egoistic. Otherwise, one risks formulating an abstract moral system that people will not follow consistently or at all; it is thus one that will have little affect on reality.

The goals of this book, therefore, have been to show that morality can be founded and harmonized fully with personal aspirations that have a viable and proper claim in human development, and to link the self-interest of people, particularly those who are concerned with being moral, to the broader moral interests of others and of society.

I. Balance

So far, this book has been an attempt to balance reason, morality, and self-interest, and to hopefully create a society in which one could live the balanced life, combining self-interest, social good, and justice. Prudent self-interest will satisfy the needs of the individual as well as the community; but this can only be done within the constraints of ethics.

This material presented aims to develop morally astute and strong people; that is, people whose intelligence enables them to recognize that their interests irrevocably are intertwined with those of others; and whose strength of will enables them to act on this conviction. These morally astute and strong people then can act as ethics-based business leaders, executives, and managers.

J. Summary

During the past few years, there has been a great deal of discussion regarding morality and ethics and how they interact within society and the lives of all individuals. There have been questions asking whether or not an action could be legal and still unethical. There have been questions asking if an action should take place even if it may be unethical but for the common good. Many different opinions have come forward. Chapter 11 defines what it means to become moral. This chapter breaks down the attributes of a moral person, defines the conflicts faced, the difficulty in maintaining balance, and also asks the question, "Why be moral"?

The first attribute of a moral person is intelligence. "One must think of oneself as a thinking being in a system of thinking beings." A person must be able to discern between right and wrong and use rational thinking to make decisions about behavior. This intelligent person will not solve a problem based on what the popular opinion may be. He or she will look to find the best and most correct solution.

The next attribute is self-control. Knowing the difference between right and wrong comes with intelligence, but without self-control a person will not be able to avoid doing what is wrong. A moral person will have the ability to act on what is considered right and exhibit self-control in avoiding what is wrong. A moral person will always act within the rules and standards, especially when there is no moral implication to his or her actions.

Integrity is third attribute and is defined as standing up for convictions, being true to oneself as well as being honorable and trustworthy. A moral person is committed to following the "letter" of the legal and moral laws.

The next attribute is veracity. A moral person will not break promises, violate engagements or allow his or her conduct to disappoint any expectations that may have been set. Also based on this attribute, a moral person will state his or her beliefs and stand by them, even when it may not be the most popular thing to do.

Other attributes are justice, freedom, and accountability. A moral person will be just and fair, tolerant of others, and will judge people based on merit. He or she cherishes the freedom to pursue intellectual, practical, and moral excellence. A moral person is also responsible. He or she will do what is expected and takes responsibility for their actions.

The final attribute is acting for the Common Good. A moral person considers a "good life" as one that is enjoyed by society as a whole. No one in the community or society should suffer prejudice, deceit, injury, or unevenly distributed burdens.

A moral person will inevitably be faced with conflict. Some examples are effectiveness in actions contending with integrity and honesty; candor struggling with kindness; and impartiality conflicting with loyalty. A moral person will simply be true to one's self and hold fast to the moral compass from within.

A moral person will also find a way to strike the right balance between conflicting interests and demands. With good judgment, moral integrity, and wisdom, ethical resolutions to conflict can be found.

There are several justifications to the question, "Why Be Moral?" An ethical justification is because it is what is accepted by society. The egoistic justification states that a moral person is happier than an immoral person. Acting immorally can be argued to be acting against one's own self-interest by winning a temporary short-term advantage, but ultimately will experience rejection and isolation from a moral society.

In business, a person can be defined as a "moral manager." The moral manager is one who predictably can be trusted to act reasonable under the circumstances. He or she will look for the most reasonable result from tasks. Morality in business must be seen as a management responsibility. The management sets the moral tone for the company. Management also has to hold itself accountable to a standard of moral conduct. By demonstrating enthusiasm, cooperativeness, self-discipline, and dedication, the moral manager can build teamwork and a moral business entity.

In a section titled "Certainty in Ethics and Morals," the chapter discussed the fact that there are no entirely and absolutely valid ethical theories. There are differing moral philosophies, ethical principles, and personal values that all treat the subject of morality differently. Even though each ethical theory offers insights to behavior, there is no one constant "packaged" solution that can be used to solve all moral problems.

Another section described the function of ethical order as being used to promote the fullest development of the capacities of all of its members. Ethics is not meant to bind human nature, but to open up its expression. Each person defines the "good life" differently, but it is basically composed of the successful pursuit of activities that one finds beneficial and worthwhile for oneself and others. The good life, and the ethical order that makes it possible, has to be looked at as a condition of freedom and not a restriction of freedom.

Titled "Self-Interest," one of the final sections in the chapter, stated that self-interest is not actually immoral. If a moral system is to be practical and sustaining, it must link up with people's actual motivational capacities, which are predominantly based on self-interest.

In looking at the world today, one can definitely ask, why be moral, since it would appear that no one else is practicing that philosophy. It is imperative that individuals not get "caught up" in the idea that if others in society behave a certain way, it must be acceptable for everyone, as that could be the downfall of society as we know it. As children, individuals are taught the basics between right and wrong. With that knowledge and some maturity, a person begins to figure out the moral compass within him or her. Depending on the value one places on ethical behavior, decisions between moral and immoral conduct can become blurred.

Within business, managers must determine whether or not they will behave within the code of conduct set about by the company. Depending on the direction set by the top management of the company, a middle level manager could get by with less than ethical and moral behavior. Sometimes, for a manager to do the right thing and behave morally, there has to be self-control present so that the person will always ask themselves if what they are doing is morally correct and within the code of conduct.

Discussion Questions

1. Why be moral?
2. How do you define the "good life," and how is it the same or different from the way society defines it?
3. Does management have a moral responsibility to the employees to abide by a code of conduct even if it means the company's profits could suffer?
4. Why should a rational person do what is right?
5. How can the moral way of life rationally be justified, particularly since a moral way of life may conflict with self-interest?
6. Why should one act on moral reasons rather than legal reasons, conventional reasons, or reasons of self-interest?
7. Is there an unresolvable tension between morality and self-interest?
8. Why should managers be moral?
9. How do intelligence and self-control define a moral "compass" within a person?
10. How should a conflict between moral behavior and legal decisions be handled?

PART II

Applied Ethics: The Moral Imperative of Business Leadership

Introduction to Part II: Accountability and Management

The first part of this work sought to define and differentiate key terms and concepts, such as philosophy, morality, ethics, values, and virtue, to distinguish the field of ethics from other intellectual endeavors, such as law and science, and to examine and explain several important ethical theories. Practical modern-day examples and applications were provided to illustrate the workings of the various ethical theories; and an attempt was made to use real-world, controversial, business issues. The first part concluded by underscoring the significance of philosophical ethics for rational people and the potential of ethics for the business leader.

Part II of this book examines "ethically," and in detail, several difficult, present day, problem areas confronting the ethics-based business leader, executive, manager, and entrepreneur and seeks to offer some moral solutions.

CHAPTER 12

Moral Accountability

I. Moral Accountability

A. Introduction

The purposes of this section are to enumerate and explain various types or levels of moral accountability. In order to comprehend degrees of moral responsibility, however, it is necessary first to examine causal and legal accountability.

A person is accountable casually for all the consequences of his or her actions, regardless of intent, volition, or the length and attenuation of the causation chain of events. A person, for example, is responsible casually for the actions he or she does while sleeping, or for striking a child who jumps in front of his or her car, or for an ultimate, remote consequence produced in an unusual manner by an attenuated causation chain. It is important to note, however, that even though a person casually may be accountable, he or she neither may be legally nor morally responsible.

A person is responsible legally for his or her intentional, wrongful actions, and careless, negligent, wrongful actions, as well as the foreseeable consequences thereof. Such legal liability is deemed misfeasance or malfeasance, and is legally actionable. Nonfeasance or not acting, however, ordinarily is not legally actionable. As a general rule, there is no legal duty to act (only to act carefully when in fact one does choose to act), and thus no legal liability for not acting. Consequently, a person who has not caused another's peril, or who is not in any "special relationship" with the "victim," is not under any legal duty to rescue or to come to the "victim's" aid; such a person is not liable legally for not acting and failing to help the person in need. A strong swimmer, for example, does not commit a legal wrong by refusing to rescue a drowning victim.

B. Moral Accountability for Acting

1. Moral Responsibility—The "Acting" Principle

When is a person morally responsible for having performed an action? A person is responsible morally for an action he or she knowingly and freely performed or brought about; he or she is responsible immorally when the act was morally wrong to be performed or brought about. A person also is morally responsible for the reasonably foreseeable consequences of such an action.

2. "Defenses" to Acting Immorally

Although one acts immorally, there may be circumstances that exonerate one's moral responsibility. Moral responsibility may be excused or lessened because of the actor's ignorance, inability, or lack of freedom.

Certain circumstances tend to eliminate or to lessen the required knowledge element to moral accountability. Moral responsibility is excused if the necessary knowledge element is missing completely, and it is mitigated if knowledge is less than completely present.

3. Ignorance

Moral responsibility may be lessened, or even eliminated completely, if one is ignorant of the relevant facts. A person cannot be held accountable morally for failing to meet an obligation of whose existence one was legitimately ignorant. One may be ignorant of the circumstances giving rise to a particular obligation, or one may lack knowledge of the consequences of an action, although one is deemed accountable for the reasonably foreseeable consequences of an action. One also may be ignorant because one fails to recognize the existence of moral reasons or relevant moral standards that one ought to have recognized.

Ignorance, however, does not always excuse a person. One, for example, cannot claim justifiable ignorance when one purposefully chooses not to ascertain the relevant facts, circumstances, or moral standards. One also cannot use ignorance as an excuse if one carelessly fails to become informed; that is, if one could have, and should have, known of the relevant facts, circumstances, and standards.

4. Impossibility of Action

Moral accountability concerns actions that are in a person's power. Accordingly, one morally is not responsible for performing an action that is an impossible action for one to perform. If one lacks the ability, skill, opportunity, or resources to act, one is relieved of moral responsibility. If, for example, one does not know how to swim, one cannot be held responsible morally for letting someone drown (if swimming is the only way to save); or if one is driving carefully, and a child jumps in front of one's car, making it impossible for one to stop in time, one is not responsible morally for hitting the child.

5. Lack of Freedom

Moral responsibility does not exist without freedom of action. There may be internal or external circumstances that render a person unable to do, or unable to keep from doing, something. An action is not free when one is subject to compulsion, constraint, duress, lack of control, or lack of alternatives.

An internal, irresistible, internal compulsion may arise within a person, for example, a kleptomaniac, that removes moral responsibility. One may lack control, for example, for actions done in one's sleep, or when one faints and knocks over a lamp and starts a fire. One may be subject to external force or coercion that eliminates or lessens moral responsibility. The validity of such a defense depends on the nature and degree of the threats, for example, a threat of death or physical harm, as opposed to an employer ordering an employee to falsify a report or else be discharged.

6. Summary

Performing an immoral action, or failing to perform a moral action, without a recognized excuse reflects poorly on one's moral character. One may be condemned as morally weak or stupid when one can act, should act, and yet one fails to act on the facts and reasons that one knows, or ought to know, one should be acting on.

C. Moral Accountability—Not Acting—The Ethical Principle of "Last Resort"

When does one have a positive moral obligation to act? Acting morally may involve more than merely avoiding negative harm; acting morally also may require one to perform an affirmative positive action, even though legally one may not be required to take the action.

The ethical principle of "last resort" indicates when one has a moral duty to act, to aid another, or to rescue. One morally must act when there is a need, proximity, capability, when one is the last resort or chance to avoid the peril, and when acting would not cause harm, or threaten to cause harm, equal to or greater than the original peril.

The principle is based partially on Kant's admonition that "ought implies can," that is, that one is obligated to do only what one can do. Thus, if one is unable to act and help, due to lack of opportunity, means, or resources, one is not obligated morally to act.

The "last resort" principle usually involves an obligation of immediacy and high priority posed by an emergency; it thus generates a moral obligation to act that one cannot ignore without moral condemnation. The classic example is a drowning case when the five "last resort" factors are present. The problem in successfully applying the "last resort" principle to business, however, emerges in the fourth and fifth factors. Who is the last resort for people unemployed and in need, business or government? Would business "rescuing" in fact harm the corporation, or its shareholders, or other stakeholders? A "friendly takeover," a corporation helping an employee pay his or her children's college tuition, may be praiseworthy actions, but are they morally required under the "last resort" principle? Is a corporation immoral for choosing not to act in the preceding circumstances? One example is the case of the Malden Mills Company, whose very compassionate owner rebuilt the facility after a fire without terminating any employees; but due in part to the added financial strain of keeping those employees, he forced his company to file for Chapter 11 bankruptcy protection in order to reorganize its finances, thereby resulting in a considerably, and permanently, diminished workforce. Another example concerns the large, multinational pharmaceutical companies who are providing for free or at greatly reduced cost their patented anti-AIDS drugs to African nations. Yet are they so doing because it is their moral responsibility as the "rescuer" of "last resort" or due to other social pressures? Similarly, corporations may not be the "last resort" to take care of their employees' disabled children, yet companies such as Toyota and Raytheon do provide assistance, for example, by hosting dinners with speakers and holding "networking" events, as well as expanding insurance coverage for "special needs" children. If not moral duty, what motivates these meritorious actions? A most interesting and thought-provoking example concerns Wal-Mart's very meritorious response to the Hurricane Katrina disaster in New Orleans and the Gulf Coast. Was Wal-Mart's "trucking in" tons of relief supplies (literally!) "merely" a socially responsible action, or was Wal-Mart the "last resort" to bring rapid relief to this devastated region of the country; and if the latter, what does that say about the government—all levels of government—federal, state, and local?

D. Social Responsibility

Although business may not have a moral responsibility, based on the principle of "last resort," to improve the quality of life in the community and society, business may be obligated by a standard of social responsibility to work for social as well as economic betterment.

A corporation, as well as a person, can have a nonmoral duty, the failure to perform, which is not a moral wrong; yet one can be held accountable for failure to perform a social obligation. The words "accountability" and "responsibility," of course, imply some sort of an obligation on the part of business to deal with social problems. "Obligation" suggests that society may demand that business act in certain socially responsible ways; otherwise, perhaps, society will compel business by law to fulfill its social obligations.

What exactly is a corporation's "social responsibility"? Does a corporation have a social obligation to take care of the poor, educate the public, give to charity, and fund cultural programs? Social projects and social welfare traditionally have been viewed as the appropriate domain of government, not of business. Business, of course, is taxed and such taxes may be used for social purposes. The traditional purpose of business, moreover, is the profitable production and distribution of goods and services, not social welfare. Yet by raising the issue of social responsibility, business is forced to concern itself with the "social" dimension of its activities.

A recent, and perhaps surprising, advocate of a Milton Friedman conservative view of social responsibility is the former Clinton Administration Labor Secretary, and liberal Democrat, Robert B. Reich. In an interview in *Business Week* magazine (Business Week, 2007), Reich stated that his fellow "liberals" are wrong to continually urge companies to be socially responsible. Corporations are not set up to be social institutions, Reich declared, in agreement with conservative Republican and University of Chicago professor Friedman. Corporate CEOs have not been conferred with the authority or the legitimacy to determine where the public interest lies and to set and fulfill social objectives, Reich says. Rather, elected and representative government officials should make these value determinations for society, and then promulgate specific laws and rules for private sector companies to follow and then to use and direct them to help fulfill social goals. Furthermore, in a very controversial declaration, Reich contends that in essence it really does not make sense to criticize, and even to praise, companies for being socially responsible, environmentally conscious, or a "good employer." Why? Do not believe for a moment, he states, that a company will sacrifice profits for the sake of social goals. Yet, it could be argued that Reich's profit rationale is a short-sighted one, since it very well could be argued that not only are profits not antithetical to social responsibility, but a firm's long-term commitment to social responsibility can materially enhance profits.

What is a definition of this "social responsibility?" The term may be defined as taking an active party in the social causes and civic life of one's community and society. Where, however, are the corresponding guidelines for corporate contributions? How should a corporation's resources be allocated, and exactly to whom, to what extent, and in what priorities?

The distinction between "merely" doing no moral harm based on reasoning from ethical principles and doing social "good" based on a definition of "social responsibility" was very nicely "captured" in the title of a *Wall Street Journal* article describing the social responsibility efforts of the Internet search company, Google. The very apt title to the article was "Google: From 'Don't Be Evil' to How to Do Good" (Delaney, Kevin, 2008). The article related that Google in January of 2008 announced a major philanthropic venture by which the company will contribute $30 million in grants and investments to a variety of charitable as well as for-profit organizations. Google's civic efforts encompass providing money to predict and prevent diseases, to develop solar power, empower the poor with information regarding public services, and to create jobs by investing in small- and medium-sized businesses throughout the "developing" world in order to boost employment. The essence of the *Wall Street Journal* article was that Google has "graduated" from being a company that "only" refrained from committing moral harm to a company now actively and substantially engaged in making socially responsible contributions throughout the world.

A corporation, of course, exists in a competitive environment and thus is limited in its ability to solve the multitude of social problems. If a corporation unilaterally or too generously engages in social betterment, it may place itself at a disadvantage compared to other less socially responsible business entities. Being socially responsible costs money, and such efforts cut into profits. In a highly competitive market system, corporations that are too socially responsible may lessen their attractiveness to investors or simply may price themselves out of the market. "Charity begins at home."—That was the very prudent social responsibility conclusion in a *Newsweek* article (Smalley, 2007) regarding the saga of THE socially responsible firm—Ben & Jerry's, which has long been known and lauded for its civic, community, and environmental efforts. Of course, the original former "hippies" Ben Cohen and Jerry Greenfield of Ben & Jerry's sold their interests in their company in 2000 to global consumer products giant, Unilever, which carried on the social responsibility activities of the brand to a degree; but, as *Newsweek* reported, several company franchisees, primarily small entrepreneurs, are suing the firm, contending that Ben & Jerry's treated them unfairly, for example, by not providing adequate training and assistance, by giving wholesale price "breaks" to large buyers, such as Wal-Mart and Costco, thereby undercutting them, by not sufficiently marketing their franchises, and by misrepresenting average gross sales for stores. Unilever is denying the allegations, but is working with its franchisees by waiving royalty fees, renegotiating store leases, and increasing marketing support. A representative from Unilever stated that it is an "ethic" of Ben & Jerry's to treat its franchisees well, which is all "well and good," but *Newsweek* posited that the lesson to be learned in this episode for "socially responsible" companies is that "Charity begins at home."

There is a further problem in expecting the corporation to take on the betterment of the "general welfare." Corporations already possess great power, and corporate executives neither are the elected representatives of the people nor are answerable directly to the general public. Corporate executives lack the mandate that a democratic society grants to those who are supposed to promote the general welfare. Government officials, elected by the people, rightfully are thought of as the social guardians of the people.

Social responsibility, however, at least to some reasonable degree, may be in the long-term self-interest of business. A corporation cannot long remain a viable economic entity in a society that is uneven, unstable, and deteriorating. It makes good business sense for a corporation to devote some of its resources to social betterment projects. To operate efficiently, for example, business needs educated and skilled employees. Education and training, therefore, should be of paramount interest to business leaders. A corporation, for example, can act socially responsible by providing computers to community schools and by releasing employees on company time to furnish the training. British Petroleum (BP), for example, marketing itself in Europe as "Beyond Petroleum," has been regarded as a very socially responsible firm, especially for its environmental and alternative fuel efforts. Another illustration involves the web-search company, Google, Inc., which has committed almost one billion dollars in stock as well as a share of its profits to combat global poverty and to protect the environment. Starbucks Corporation, in addition, is engaged in a variety of socially responsible activities in Guatemala, such as building health clinics, and also promising to pay its coffee suppliers a premium price if they adhere to certain labor and environmental standards.

Business also gains an improved public image by being socially responsible. An enhanced social image should attract more customers and investors and thus provide positive benefit for the firm. A corporation that acts more socially responsible not only secures public favor, but also avoids public disfavor. Business is part of society and subject to society's mandates; and if society wants more "responsibility" from business, business cannot ignore this "request" without the risk of incurring society's anger, perhaps in the form of higher taxes or more onerous government regulation. Sir John Brown, former chief executive officer of BP, astutely comprehends that society wants and expects business to be socially responsible, and that to be so is in the long-term self-interest of BP and business. An ethical egoist will surely see the value of a prudent degree of social responsibility in today's global business marketplace. Obviously, superior product and service quality and competitive pricing are essential for business success. Yet another strategic factor to success has emerged in the present business environment – social responsibility. The idea is not "only" to make profits but then to "give back" to the community by means of civil, social, and environmental efforts. Yet a strategic approach to social responsibility would combine profits and social activism; that is, the smart and social company will deliver products and services that naturally are profitable but that also serve society by, for example, saving energy and improving the environment. The idea for a strategic business approach is to incorporate the value of social responsibility into the firm's business model. Such an approach will enhance opportunities, increase profits, and expand the firm's market share. In essence, the ultimate goal is not only to contribute in a socially responsible manner to the community but to bring new socially responsible products and services into the marketplace. That degree of social responsibility is the ethically egoistic business model for today's astute business leaders. Exxon-Mobil for example, recently launched a social responsibility campaign to build schools in Angola, which (perhaps not coincidentally) is an emerging oil power. Coca-Cola Co. is very extensively involved in providing clear drinking water to the "developing world," for example, by furnishing water purification systems and lessons to local communities. This meritorious social responsibility effort is designed also to promote "Coke's" reputation as a global diplomat and local benefactor. "Coke," by the way, uses a great deal of water in producing its products.

Another example of social responsibility (and perhaps ethical egoism) concerns Microsoft's efforts to help its overweight employees. The company, which already provides free medical coverage to its employees, now has created a weight management benefit for employees. The software company will pay for 80% of the cost, up to $6000, for a comprehensive, clinical, weight loss program for employees. The program, intended for employees who are obese or clinically overweight, includes up to a year's worth of sessions with a personal trainer, behavioral and nutritional counseling, support groups, and medical supervision. Microsoft in the long-run expects to obtain a return on its health care investment for the formerly obese and overweight employees due to cost savings from less prescription drugs and fewer doctor and hospital visits.

HR Magazine (Fox, 2007), in a human resources context, clearly and firmly underscored the egoistic rationale for a company to be rightly perceived as a socially responsible one. In a constrained and highly competitive global labor market, the shrewd corporate executive will use his or her firm's social responsibility stance to attract new employees, especially top talent, as well as to engage and retain highly skilled and highly motivated current employees. To bolster its argument, *HR Magazine* pointed to a 2003 survey where 70% of North American students surveyed stated that they would not even apply for a job in a company that was deemed "socially irresponsible." However, a socially responsible firm must also be a realistic one, *HR Magazine* counseled. That is, socially responsible and environmental efforts must be sustainable economically and should have some relationship to the firm's business. Employees should also be engaged directly in the company's social responsibility activities so as to inspire them, motivate them, and thereby enhance morale and productivity. Moreover, a firm's social responsibility program does not have to be a multi-million dollar effort; rather, something as simple as an employee social responsibility "suggestion box" or as straightforward as a recycling or energy saving program will do to promote employee involvement as well as to promote and give credence to employee social values. Nonetheless, despite the size, a firm's social responsibility efforts should be publicized widely within the company, for example, in company newsletters, as well as externally, for example in company annual "social responsibility" reports. Being socially responsible, therefore, advises *HR magazine*, is a smart and sustainable business strategy, especially in a human resource context. An actual illustration of *HR Magazine's* social responsibility recommendation is the PepsiCo. The company's chairperson and CEO, Indra Nooyi, has urged companies to follow her company's approach to being a "good" global company; and by "good" she means that in addition to having a strong financial performance, a firm must value and take care of its employees and also the public's health and the environment. For example, PepsiCo has expanded its product lines to include more juices and waters as well as introducing low-sugar versions of its popular "fitness drink," Gatorade. The company is also promoting energy management, for example by reducing its water usage and creating more environmentally "friendly" packaging. One major benefit of being a socially responsible firm, PepsiCo has discovered, is that its employees are inspired and energized, thereby helping the company to retain employees.

The social responsibility of business has been heightened by the creation of social responsibility investment funds which promise to invest the participants' funds only in companies that are ethical, moral, and socially responsible. Naturally, investors want to invest in quality companies whose business will make a profit for the shareholder-investors; yet socially responsible investors want to invest in such companies only if they also are sensitive to the needs of other stakeholders, and conduct business in an environmentally responsible manner. Today, many socially responsible funds exist, including mutual funds; and the socially-minded investor has a wide choice of funds, ranging from those that stress environmental causes and workers' rights, to those that reflect ethical and religious values.

Above and beyond the responsibility to act legally and morally is this notion of social responsibility. The law defines legal accountability; ethics determines moral accountability, but ascertaining the nature and extent of social responsibility emerges as an even more challenging task. Nevertheless, there exist today several "socially responsible" investment firms to ensure investors they are investing in not only financially prudent companies, but socially responsible ones

Although there is an outcry, and admittedly a righteous one, that business should be socially responsible, one problem that has emerged is the permissible degree of pressure that a business can exert on its own employees to be socially responsible, especially when the demands entail the employee to spend his or her own money or personal time in charitable and civic-minded activities. Is it moral to pressure employees to be socially responsible? The good to the community might very well outweigh the "pain" in the form of expense and effort to the employees, and thus such "coercion" might be moral pursuant to Utilitarian ethics; but is the employee being treated as a mere "means" or instrument by his or her employer; and although for good ends, is the employee being so demeaned so as to make the employer's pressure immoral pursuant to Kantian ethics. Of course, if the employer is allowing its employees to be socially responsible on the company's time by encouraging them to participate in employer-sponsored volunteer programs, there should be no moral problem. Yet forcing employees to be socially responsible in addition to their work demands and workday duties can equate to unpaid and thus unethical overtime. Some employers will require such "volunteer" work, track the employees' time and efforts, and even assign the employee "volunteer" points on his or her performance evaluations. At the least, the employer should allow the employee, who very well may be very busy with a home life and personal commitments, to write a check to a charity as opposed to physically serving in a civic capacity. A better and more moral option, since it is not coercive, would be for the employer to have a released-time program, for example, a "charity day," in which the employees would be released from work to volunteer for certain approved charities. The employees would have some flexibility in choosing their volunteer projects, and, most importantly, the employees would be paid by the company for their charity work. Such a program would naturally benefit charity, treat the employees with respect, and, despite the expense, would benefit the employer in an ethically egoistic sense in the long-run.

The prevalence of corporate social responsibility (CSR) on a global basis was recently clearly illustrated by a survey conducted by the Society of Human Resource Management (SHRM) in 2007 (Workplace Visions, 2007). SHRM found that a majority of Human Resource professionals in the countries surveyed (United States, Australia, India, China, Canada, Mexico, and Brazil) reported that their organizations had corporate social responsibility practices in place. SHRM put forth a number of reasons for the extent of CSR. First, companies realize that they need to respond to large scale social problems before they become a threat to business. Second, on a more positive note, SHRM contends that solutions to major social problems can increasingly be viewed as new sources of business opportunities. That is, providing goods and services to the people of developing nations may be a way to enter into potentially vast markets of consumers. Similarly, "going green" and investing in environmentally "friendly" technology may be a way for companies to initially establish themselves in potentially highly profitable energy sectors. Two illustrations would be the success of Toyota with the hybrid car, and Nokia's and Ericsson's efforts to bring mobile communications technology to the developing world. CSR, SHRM thus concludes, is an active and essential component of creating competitive advantage and thereby promoting value creation for the firm and its stakeholders.

The topic of social responsibility has emerged as such a critical one for global business that the World Bank now has an Internet course on social responsibility, called "CSR and Sustainable Competitiveness," offered by its educational and training division, the World Bank Institute (World Bank, 2007). The corporate social responsibility course is designed for "high-level" private sector managers, government officials and regulators, practitioners, academics, and journalists. One major purpose to the course is to provide a "conceptual framework" for improving the business environment to support social responsibility efforts and practices by corporations and business. The course is also designed to assist companies to formulate a social responsibility strategy based on "integrity and sound values" as well as one with a long-term perspective. By being socially responsible, declares the World Bank, businesses not only will accrue benefits, but also civil society as a whole will benefit from the "positive contributions" of business to society. Although it is beyond the scope of this book to discuss in detail the World Bank's very laudable CSR educational effort, a few key elements in the course must be addressed. First and foremost, as the World Bank points out, correctly so, there is no single, commonly accepted, definition of the critical term "CSR." Nonetheless, the World Bank offers its definition, stating that CSR generally refers to: 1) "a collection of policies and practices linked to the relationship with key stakeholders, values, compliance with legal requirements, and respect for people, communities and the environment; and 2) the commitment of business to contribute to sustainable development." The World Bank also explains the key term "Corporate Citizenship," which is "the concept of the corporation as a citizen" and which is a term often used when referring to CSR. As a matter of fact, the World Bank notes, again quite correctly, that the terms "CSR" and "Corporate Citizenship" are at times used interchangeably. The World Bank, moreover, in order to fully explicate CSR, indicates several material components to that concept, to wit: 1) environmental protection, 2) labor security, 3) human rights, 4) community involvement, 5) business standards, 6) marketplace, 7) enterprise and economic development, 8) health protection, 9) education and leadership development, and 10) human disaster relief. The World Bank also offers several decision-making frameworks for companies to plan, implement, and measure CSR. An important part of the World Bank course is a segment, eminently practical for business, called "Benefits of CSR." There are, according to the World Bank, "many reasons why it pays for companies, both big businesses and small and medium enterprises...to be socially responsible and be conscious about the interest of key stakeholders." The Bank pointed to a survey conducted by its Institute that indicated that 52% of its respondents had either "rewarded" or "punished" businesses by either buying or not buying their products based on the perceived social responsibility performance of the companies. Other reasons for being a socially responsible firm are, according to the Bank, as follows: 1) obtaining a "social license" to operate from key stakeholders, 2) ensuring "sustainable competitiveness," 3) creating new business opportunities, 4) attracting and retaining quality investors and business partners, 5) securing cooperation from local communities, 6) avoiding difficulties due to socially irresponsible behavior, 7) obtaining government support, and 8) building "political capital."

Business Week published a very revealing Social Responsibility Special Report (Engardio, 2007.) that enumerated and extolled the socially responsible practices of many companies today; and then asked the seminal question as to whether these laudatory socially responsible efforts positively contributed to the companies' "bottom-line." *Business Week* listed these companies in a chart, grouped by sectors of the economy, and then detailed their social responsibility as well as "eco-friendly" activities, and under a very revealing chart sub-title, "Who's Doing Well by Doing Good." For example, Unilever, the British-Dutch multinational, has opened a free community laundry in Sal Paulo, Brazil, provides financing to help tomato growing farmers to convert to more environmentally sensitive irrigation systems, and has funded a floating hospital that provides free medical care to people in Bangladesh. In Ghana, Unilever provides safe drinking water to communities; and in India, the company's employees assist women in isolated villages to commence small entrepreneurial enterprises. As related by *Business Week*, Unilever CEO, Patrick Cescau, views the company's social responsibility effort as one of its biggest strategic challenges for the 21st century. Cescau explains that since 40% of the company's sales come from consumers in developing countries, assisting these countries to overcome poverty and to safeguard the environment is vital to the company's sustaining its competitive advantage. In order for the company to maintain its leadership role, it must be concerned about the impact its policies have on society, local communities, the environment, as well as future generations. Cescau's rationale for social responsibility underscores the ethically egoistic justification that "good deeds" will produce strategic and competitive advantages and thus inure to the benefit of the company in the long-term. Another example given by *Business Week* was General Electric, which is taking the lead in developing wind power and hybrid engines. Even Wal-Mart, perennially criticized by labor and human rights groups, was praised for its efforts to save energy and to purchase more electricity derived from renewable sources. GlaxoSmithKline was given credit for investing in poor nations to develop drugs. Moreover, the company was praised for being one of the first major pharmaceutical companies to sell AIDS drugs at cost in 100 countries worldwide. *Business Week* pointed out that such socially responsible behavior by the large pharmaceutical company worked in its favor as the company is working much more effectively with these governments to make sure its patents are protected. In addition, as noted in *Business Week*, the company's CEO, Jean-Pierre Garner, explained that the company's social responsibility efforts produce other egoistic advantages, such as motivating top scientists to work for the firm, as well as enhancing the overall morale of the company's workforce, which gives the company, stated Garner, a competitive advantage. Another example was Dow Chemical, which is developing and investing in solar power and water treatment technologies. As noted by *Business Week*, Dow CEO, Andrew N. Liveris, explained that there is a "100% overlap" between the company's business values and its social and environmental values. Toyota was cited as another illustration of a socially responsible firm due to its work with hybrid gas-electric cars. Such practices have given Toyota a very good reputation as a company that makes clean-running and fuel efficient vehicles; and *Business Week* related that this "green" reputation has given Toyota a competitive edge. Another example provided was Philips Electronics, which provides medical vans that bring doctors to remote communities, and which has developed low cost water purification technology. Business "sustainability" is the reason given by the company for its worldwide social responsibility efforts. *Business Week* also reported that the assets of mutual fund companies that invest in firms meeting social responsibility criteria have increased dramatically from $12 billion in 1995 to $178 billion in 2005.

Yet what exactly is the effect of all these social responsibility efforts on the "bottom-line"? This critical fact is difficult to ascertain due to the paucity of research as well as the need for a long-term perspective. *Business Week* also reported that several studies have attempted to discern if a causal relationship exists between social responsibility and financial performance; but noted that the results so far are "mixed." The magazine did report one thought-provoking study that concluded that if Wal-Mart possessed the social responsibility reputation of its competitor, Target, Wal-Mart's stock would be worth 8.4% more, thereby adding $16 billion to its market capitalization. The problem of determining if "doing good" translates to "doing well" is exacerbated since companies only report the value of tangible physical assets and investments in equipment and property. Social responsibility efforts are perhaps a bit too intangible for the company's accountants to quantify; and government regulators do not mandate that social responsibility, labor, and environmental practices be quantified. *Business Week* noted, however, that a company's commitment to social responsibility could constitute a valuable intangible business asset. Moreover, the magazine noted that a growing investor demand for more accurate information on the relationship between social responsibility and profits has resulted in increased research. For example, one company, called Innovest, in addition to measuring firms' performance by means of conventional financial criteria, studies a variety of different factors, such as employee practices and energy use. The problem, of course, is that ascertaining the financial consequences of being a socially responsible and environmentally conscious company requires a long-term analytical perspective; but shareholders, mutual fund companies, and "Wall Street" analysts still are predominantly focused on the short-term. Nevertheless, *Business Week* correctly counseled today's CEOs to be very cognizant of, and to be prepared to deal with in a substantive matter, the value of social responsibility in business. *Business Week* also exhorted its readers: "Imagine a world in which eco-friendly and socially responsible practices actually help a company's bottom line. It's closer than you think."

Social responsibility is a very important and relevant topic in business, and thus it is now not only an "academic" matter for business school students, but also a very real and practical concern for the global business leader, manager and entrepreneur.

E. Altruism

Altruism is taking the interests of others into account in such a fashion that one's intentions and actions give some real degree of preference to others. Altruism requires a substantial cost in time, effort, expenditure, or discomfort; it implies a degree of effacement of self-interest, even sacrifice. Who legitimately can be held accountable for performing altruistic behavior? Members of a profession, for example, may be required to engage in altruistic behavior because the profession's code of ethics may demand such conduct. A person also may choose a particular role, such as a parent, that demands selfless devotion to the welfare of others. Business certainly neither is required nor expected to engage in altruistic behavior.

F. Moral Saints and Heroes

1. Introduction

At times, a person is called a "saint," or his or her actions "saintly," yet with no religious implications. A person sometimes is called a "hero" or his or her actions "heroic." All these terms can be words of moral evaluation.

2. Saint Status

A person is deemed a saint if he or she does an act or performs a duty under circumstances in which personal inclination, desire, or self-interest would lead almost all people not to do the act or perform the duty. One also is designated a saint if he or she does an action that is far beyond the limits of one's duty, where almost all people would not do the action. An organ donation to a stranger, or even a distant family member, is an example of a saintly action. A physician who gives up a lucrative practice to devote himself or herself totally to the impoverished people of a "third world" country can be called a saint.

Saint status invariably involves great sacrifice. Poverty and unworldliness are underlying themes. Saints give up power, property, money, ease, and comfort to live for ends that seem to yield them no real-world "profit." Saints achieve their status by exercising an inordinate amount of self-control. They persevere, whereas most of all people yield to desire and personal interest.

3. Hero Status

A person is a hero if he or she performs an act or a duty under circumstances in which almost all people would not do the act because of fear and an interest in self-preservation. A person is also a hero if he or she performs an action that is far beyond the bounds of any duty. One achieves hero status by exercising extreme self-control and particularly by overcoming the natural fears to which almost all others succumb. For example, the employee driver of an armored truck who leaves his vehicle to rescue a woman passerby from a knife wielding robber very well may be a hero, but regrettably, as per an actual case, may be terminated and unemployed for violating company policy for leaving vehicles unattended.

4. Differences

Saints and heroes differ in that a saint primarily resists desires and self-interest, whereas a hero primarily resists fear and self-preservation. Saint status also usually entails a consistency in character, purpose, and deeds over a period of time, whereas a person can become a hero by the performance of a single heroic act.

5. Summary

If a person fails to comply with legal, moral, social, or even altruistic duties, he or she generally can be blamed and castigated for non-performance, but one cannot be condemned for not being saintly or heroic. Almost all people would not and could not perform at such a level. Saints and heroes combat forces that others are unable to overcome. This very inability indicates that these actions not be classified as actions that ought to be done because required by some duty. People praise saints and heroes because their actions stem from a choice that goes beyond any duty and is motivated by ideals that transcend duty.

6. Business Heroes

What are the qualities of a hero in business? He or she must possess vision; that is, he or she takes the "long view," looks beyond the next quarter, and correctly foresees the future. He or she must exhibit leadership. The business hero puts one's vision into action and successfully leads others through the future. A business hero must be innovative by breaking barriers, being imaginative, and acting as a "pioneer." He or she must be creative and successful, contribute to the world, and change the world in a positive manner. A business hero must be courageous. He or she must be willing to take risks and must be determined and persistent in achieving his or her objectives. Business entrepreneurs also possess such "heroic" characteristics. Examples of business heroes are Ray Kroc, founder of McDonald's; Dave Thomas, founder of Wendy's; Thomas Watson, Sr., the chief executive who built IBM; Walt Disney; and H. Wayne Huizenga of Blockbuster Video, Waste Management, and the Miami Dolphins Football Team.

Why doesn't one find even more "heroes" in the world of business? Perhaps business people do not see themselves as heroes, or perhaps business people have not explained to the world how much they have contributed to it, or perhaps today's short-term management orientation precludes hero status.

G. Ethical Codes

An ethical code should serve human needs; it should treat people as they are and as they can be expected to become. A code cannot demand conduct beyond the capacity of ordinary people in ordinary circumstances. An overly idealistic and thus unattainable code results in noncompliance and engenders a general breakdown in morality.

An efficacious code, therefore, differentiates fundamental moral rules to do no moral harm, which should be simply set forth and binding on all, from the higher levels of conduct, exemplified by saints and heroes. Distinguishing levels of conduct is extremely important when one attempts to hold people accountable and to exert moral pressure in the form of praise and blame. It is permissible to pressure a person to carry out a basic moral duty, such as promise-keeping, and to hold that person morally accountable for failing to comply with that duty. It is, however, highly objectionable to pressure a person to perform an act of saintliness or heroism. It would be outrageous, for example, to pressure morally a person to sacrifice his or her life for others. Saints and heroes, however, do play a worldly role. They can be used to demonstrate virtues that are worth admiring and to a degree emulating and thus they can help people learn how to live a moral life.

It is also important to differentiate levels of accountability when making demands and exerting pressure on business. There are three legitimate types of demands that can be made against a corporation. Legally, a corporation must obey the law and is held accountable for breaking the law. A corporation also is morally accountable. Morality, of course, stems from ethical principles. The essence of a corporation's moral obligation is to do no moral harm. Moral obligations, moreover, remain whether or not enacted into law and whether or not socially mandated. It is necessary to recall that a corporation does not have a moral obligation to do good, that is, to engage in "good works" and social causes, unless the ethical principle of "last resort" is applicable. What about social responsibility, that is, the corporation's taking an active part in social causes and charities and the civic life of the community? A corporation should be involved socially to a limited degree, and a corporation must be cognizant of the fact that society can impose on business certain social obligations that are neither legal (at least initially) nor moral.

H. Role Responsibility

Role responsibility, as defined by Richard DeGeorge in his *Business Ethics* book, encompasses assuming a certain position, role, or occupation in society or in an organization, or by becoming a member of a certain profession. These roles usually impose responsibilities that have a moral dimension. A parent, for example, has a moral obligation to sustain and nurture his or her child, a corporate executive has a moral obligation to be an honest and efficient manager for the benefit of the shareholders, and an attorney has a moral obligation to represent zealously the interests of his or her client.

Members of a profession frequently assume special moral obligations inherent in the profession, for example, a duty of altruism when a physician or attorney undertakes pro bono work. When a member of a profession assumes a role in an organization, he or she carries a role responsibility of the profession in addition to the role responsibility stemming from his or her organizational role. This dual role responsibility poses a potential problem for a corporate employee who is also a member of a profession. Loyalty to the corporation may conflict with responsibility to one's profession. In weighing the conflicting role responsibilities, the duty to one's profession should prevail, as the professions are grounded on codes of ethics.

When one assumes a position in a business as an employee, one takes on the responsibility of performing the functions of that role and obeying the rules of the employer. Normally, when one follows the rules and performs the work functions, one fulfills his or her obligations to the employer. Following the rules and doing one's job, moreover, is an acceptable explanation when one is called to account for one's actions. However, if an organizational rule or employer order requires one to act immorally, merely "following orders" or "obeying" the rules is not an acceptable response and does not exonerate those who hold the roles and follow the rules and orders. Role responsibility is subordinate to general moral responsibility, as determined by ethical principles.

Business people, therefore, must be careful and avoid adopting a "role morality" mentality, which may cause them to abandon their ethics in the belief that the sacrifice is necessary to succeed in a highly competitive environment. In performing the functions involved in one's employment role, it often is thought necessary, convenient, customary, or otherwise expeditious to compromise one's ethics in order to "get the job done." The challenge for an ethical person is to resist the temptation to sacrifice ethical principles to expediency, and still be successful. Clearly, it must be understood that business objectives, and even profession status, do not supersede fundamental ethical principles.

I. Agent Responsibility

A large organization, such as a corporation, usually reflects a hierarchical structure of authority, where orders and directives emanate from those higher in the organization to a variety of subordinates, or agents, at lower levels, who act on the basis of orders from their superiors. Such an organizational structure at times raises problems of moral accountability. For example, who is morally responsible, and to what degree, when a superior orders a subordinate to carry out an immoral act?

One view holds that the subordinate, even though he or she was the agent in the immoral act's execution, nonetheless is absolved from responsibility, and only the superior is accountable. It is wrong, however, to exonerate totally a subordinate employee for example, who knowingly performs an immoral act on the grounds that he or she was merely "following orders."

The superior, of course, morally is held accountable because he or she knowingly and freely brought about the immoral act through the means or agency of the subordinate. The fact that the superior used a human being as the instrumental does not alter the fact that the superior brought about the immoral act. Subordinates, moreover, even those at the bottom of the hierarchical chain, remain moral agents and cannot deny moral responsibility for their actions. There is a limit to a subordinate's role responsibility to obey the order of a superior: one is not under an obligation to obey an order that is immoral, and thus the subordinate is morally responsible for carrying out the immoral act. However, because subordinates may make an arguable case that they were "forced" to do what they on their own would not freely choose to do, their moral responsibility may be diminished.

J. Collective Responsibility

Assigning or assuming moral accountability within an organization raises the issue of collective responsibility. In a corporation, for example, the actions of the artificial legal "person" are brought about by real people and typically brought about by the joint actions or inaction of many people. Within the corporation, therefore, moral responsibility may be distributed among a number of cooperating participants in the organization, as well as the entity itself. The question thus emerges: who exactly is morally responsible for the corporation's actions?

Legally, the acts of the corporation generally are attributed to the entity, so long as the board of directors, managers, agents, and employees act with authority and within the scope of their authority. The notion of collective moral accountability, however, is ambiguous and may be interpreted in a variety of ways. The "individual responsibility" view holds that those people who knowingly and freely did what was necessary to produce the corporate act are each morally accountable. The "group responsibility" view holds that when a group of people, such as a corporate "group," jointly act to produce a result, the act is the act of the group, and thus the corporate "group" and not the individuals who compose the group is morally responsible. The "legal" view of collective moral accountability attributes responsibility to the entity itself and not to the people involved either as individuals or as a group.

Neither the "legal" nor "group" theory alone is valid interpretation of the moral accountability involved because neither accurately reflects the moral reality behind the entity's actions. People, as individuals, had to formulate and execute the particular actions of the impersonal entity. Individuals, therefore, are responsible morally for the known, intended, and foreseeable consequences of their freely chosen actions and also for joining their actions with others to produce a group result. The fact that action is deemed that of the entity, or that group decision making was involved, does not operate as a shield to deflect legitimate moral accountability. Moral accountability is attributed to the entity, the group, as well as to the individuals involved.

II. Professionals, the Professions, and Management

A. Introduction

In any discussion of business or management ethics, it is necessary to differentiate professionals from members of a profession, to determine a manager's place in these classifications, and to understand the ramifications of a manager as a member of the "management profession."

Business, of course, is inextricably and extensively linked with professionals and members of the professions. As society and business have become more complex and specialized, requiring distinctive knowledge and skills and advanced training and education, more people and groups attempt to identify themselves as professionals and as members of a profession. Serious ethical considerations, however, are raised by the use of the terms "professional" and "profession." A great deal of confusion, moreover, exists between the two terms. It first is essential to grasp a fundamental point—that all members of a profession are professionals, but not all professionals are members of a profession. Many people who are professionals, therefore, are not members of a profession.

B. Professionals

Professionals are people who work on a full-time basis, for "high" pay, and who possess considerable skill, expertise, and knowledge. Professionals have undergone specialized, systematic, and required training and learning. They are self-supervisory, tend to set their own tasks, often do not "punch" time clocks, and work as many hours as are required to do the job, often at inconvenient times. Professionals, accordingly, possess status and rank in society. Members of the skilled trades, such as electricians and plumbers, commonly are regarded as professionals, so too are people who engage in "professional" activities, such as actors and athletes. These trade and professional activities, however, do not constitute professions.

C. Professions

1. Introduction

Members of a profession are professionals who meet certain "profession" characteristics. They command prestige and respect. They have attained a superior reputation and great influence arising from their success and achievements. Members of a profession are admired and esteemed. They have advanced education and are subject to mandatory continuing education.

2. Autonomy

The professions are autonomous; they are self-governing, self-regulating, and, in essence, are state-authorized monopolies. Members of the profession control and regulate entry into the profession, set the standards and policy for licensure (which entails not only a skills and knowledge evaluation but also a moral character analysis), set the standards for practice, police the profession, and discipline and discharge members who do not live up to the profession's standards.

Why does society permit the professions to possess so much power, power that it denies to "mere" professionals and to business managers? The professions are accorded such power because society requires such people to possess specialized knowledge that is clearly useful to society, but society requires proof that these people have mastered such knowledge, and are qualified to practice, and that the members of the profession are practicing in a competent and proper manner. Another very important reason for granting autonomy to the professions is that the professions set higher moral standards for themselves than society sets for other people and groups, including professionals and business managers. These higher moral standards, moreover, are embodied in the codes of ethics of the professions.

3. Codes of Ethics

Members of a profession are bound by its code of ethics. If the profession's code is a legitimate code, that is, one that can serve as the basis upon which the profession rightfully can claim autonomy, the code must set standards beyond self-interest and beyond the law. The code must set as standards higher moral norms. These norms must serve society and not merely the members of the profession. Members of the profession are expected to adhere to these higher moral standards, and they risk sanctions and discipline, including the ultimate penalty of expulsion from the profession, for engaging in unethical conduct. For example, in Florida, the Florida Bar Association which regulates lawyers in that state now must approve radio and television commercials by lawyers. Specifically, prohibited are ads with "inappropriate" images, such as ones with sharks, wolves, crocodiles, piranhas, and pit bulls. "Professional" organizations and associations, in addition to their education and information functions, promulgate and enforce the ethical codes of conduct of the professions. Being a member of a profession also involves the taking of an oath, which is a public admission of the moral obligations assumed. It is most interesting and revealing to note that the deans of several business schools have proposed that business school graduates take an oath in which they pledge to be morally upright and socially responsible managers. Such an oath would certainly enhance the "profession" status of "mere" business "professionals."

4. The Fiduciary and Altruistic Aspects of the Profession

When one enters into a profession, one enters into a fiduciary relationship. A member of a society is compelled to rely on and trust a member of the profession, and a member of the profession can be trusted to serve interests other than the member's own. The member of the profession is expected to use his or her power, knowledge, and skills for the benefit of society.

The professions are service-oriented and not merely profit-oriented. Members of a profession are not simply sellers of expert, specialized services in the marketplace. The obligation a member of the profession undertakes to the profession, and ultimately to society, may require a degree of altruism and effacement of self-interest on the part of the member, which at times may be detrimental to the member's own economic self-interest. The trust and confidence and altruistic aspects of the professions, as well as the code of ethics involved, stand out as critical differences between members of the profession and "mere" professionals and business managers.

5. The Exemplars of the Professions

The two traditional occupations that are regarded as the best representatives of the professions are the medical and legal professions. Doctors and lawyers are bound by codes of ethics. They must adhere to the higher moral norms set by the profession. Doctors, for example, are required to treat people even if they cannot pay; lawyers likewise are required to defend people even if they cannot pay. Craft and tradespersons, however, even if deemed "professionals," as well as business managers, are not expected to work without pay. In addition to doctors and lawyers, other examples of the professions are accounting, pharmacy, engineering, architecture, and nursing. Yet, when a profession betrays the trust the public has in it, such as some elements of the accounting profession did in the Enron scandal environment, the profession will lose a degree of its autonomy, and consequently be subject to greater government regulation, for example by the Accounting Oversight Board pursuant to the Sarbanes-Oxley Act.

D. Management as a Profession

Business managers certainly are professionals, but they are not yet members of a profession. Why would management want to be regarded as a profession? Professions traditionally carry with them great prestige, respect, and especially autonomy. Society permits the professions a large degree of autonomy—power that it denies to business managers—and members of a profession function with far fewer restraints than do business managers. In return for the right to govern themselves as a profession, members of the profession must serve society, set higher standards of conduct for themselves, formalize these standards in codes of ethics, and enforce these standards by disciplinary measures.

Business managers may desire the attributes of profession status, but are they willing to undertake the special, heightened, and sustained moral responsibilities? Managers must be aware that morally and socially, more will be expected and demanded of them when they become members of the "business management profession"; and the benefits that accrue to members of the management profession are legitimate only to the extent managers conform to its higher moral code. What if the Business Management Code of Ethics demands conduct on the part of a manager that conflict with the loyalty and obedience expected by a corporate employer? Will the manager obey the higher standard set forth in the code? Is the "management profession" ultimately serving the public and promoting the public good; if so, how?

The distinction between profession status and "mere" professional status for business managers was underscored in a 2008 book by Harvard Business School professor, Rakesh Khurana. The title to the book clearly indicates Khurana's main thesis: *From Higher Aims to Hired Hands: The Social Transformation of American Business Schools and the Unfilled Promise of Management as a Profession.* Professor Khurana argues that business schools in the U.S. have deviated from their original mission of educating students to be members of the "profession" of business. Rather, today, he argues that business education, particularly MBA education, has degenerated into "mere" profession status, and especially with the remunerative aspects of being a professional. Today, he contends, the emphasis for the students is on high-paying finance and consulting jobs; and when the students become corporate managers, their emphasis is on maximizing shareholder value on a short-term basis. An MBA degree is certainly not without value, he admits, since it does indicate that a graduate is smart, productive, disciplined, and committed; and the MBA program typically provides a network of business and employment contacts. However, lost are the "profession" attributes of balancing shareholder value with stakeholder value, taking a long-term approach to maximizing value, being "good stewards" of the economy, engaging in social responsibility activities, and being true business leaders in the "profession" of business. As Professor Khurana correctly points out, obtaining an advanced degree in business is not the equivalent of graduating from a law school and a school of medicine, which in the latter cases results in entry into a true profession. He notes that the legal and medical professions certify by exams the knowledge of graduates; and that the professions require life-long learning as well as social responsibility contributions. He suggests that business schools and business in general adopt similar "profession" attributes, especially a superseding greater social mission as well as core profession virtues such as custodianship, duty, and responsibility.

The development of a code of ethics is the key factor in transforming management from "professional" to "profession" status. A code of ethically developed moral rules can act as a guide for the practice of the Management Profession, and it can serve as a link between management and the well-being of society.

Discussion Questions

1. Does an employee with no management responsibility have the right or the obligation to question a manager if he or she felt that manager was not running the department ethically or morally? Is the answer any different if the employee was not the one being asked to act unethically?

2. A corporation elects to support the Arts instead of Medical Research. Is it ethical to exclude types of charitable causes?

3. Is there a way to have one ethical standard for all corporations?

4. McDonalds used lard to blanch their fries. Is it ethical not to tell the customer why the fries taste so good? Clearly the company was built on the world wanting their fries.

5. Is it fair to require companies to give out the "company secrets" in order to protect the consumer? Or, is "buyer beware" an ethical standard?

6. You have a long-term relationship with a client or customer and you know what the company is asking you to do is not in the interest of your client/customer. Must you follow the company's request or protect the long-term relationship?

7. It is against the law to discriminate when hiring employees. Now you post a job looking for an employee to be an account manager, and it requires traveling the world on a frequent basis. One of the applicants is a 25 year old female. You interview her and find her equally acceptable as a 50 year old male who recently lost his wife to cancer. You cannot ask the female if she intends to have children, which may mean losing her just when she got well established in the position, and yet you are well aware of the potential problem. If you recommend the female over the male, and she leaves in one year, you may lose your job for your "poor" decision. Is it really possible for an employee or company to be ethical here and still make the best decision?

8. All companies want to be good corporate citizens. Why do they still, at times, commit wrongful acts?

9. You know something confidential and were instructed by your client not to say anything to the other side. You get a direct question and you are now forced to answer with a lie. Is this an ethical request on the part of your client?

10. Should a company be held legally accountable for the immoral actions of an employee if the employee acts knowingly immoral?

11. Can a person be legally held accountable for an action he or she considers to be in compliance with his or her code of ethics?

12. If you were forced to act against your moral beliefs in the work place, how would you handle the situation?

13. How would you handle this conflict in a non-work place situation? An example here could be that you have no money and you must feed your baby. Would you steal food?

14. Should a company be obligated to help in social betterment? Are the jobs and opportunities provided by the company sufficient to say that they are helping the community?

15. Do you know a business hero; if so, why do you see him or her as a business hero?

16. Do you consider yourself as a professional? Are you part of a profession?

17. If a company had to cut back on benefits for all, or terminate a group of people to avoid bankruptcy, which would be the ethical solution?

18. Can a small business ("mom and pop" shop) be held to social responsibility?

19. Explain how someone can act in what would normally be considered an immoral action, but still be seen as a hero?

20. Should business management aspire to "profession" status? Why or why not?

CHAPTER 13

Corporate Governance: Legal and Moral Issues

I. The Legal and Moral Status of the Corporation

A. Introduction

Large, publicly-held, state-created, multinational business corporations, administered by professional managers, dominate modern economies. They are the center of the capitalistic system, the instruments of production and service, the basic source of income and wealth, and a major source of government revenues. They help make the "good life" possible, yet these corporate entities raise significant moral issues globally. Consequently, these corporations are a primary target for those people and groups who condemn the immorality of business, particularly in the "developing world." Corporate managers, therefore, must be prepared to confront and to resolve moral challenges.

Since moral problems are important and unavoidable, any efficacious approach to business ethics must pay special attention to the role and function of large business corporations. This section accordingly reviews the legal and moral status and responsibility of the corporation, which today is known as "corporate governance."

B. Legal Characteristics of the Corporation

1. Corporation's Legal Status

A corporation is a special kind of entity; it is a "creature" of law, an artificial legal being. The corporation is created by government, in the United States by state government. No one can conduct business as a corporation without a grant or franchise from the state.

States generally have promulgated corporate statutes for business corporations, nonprofit corporations, professional corporations, and small, "closely held" corporations. State statutes, moreover, regulate in detail the formation and activities of the corporation. State statutes vary, although most are patterned on a uniform, "model," business corporation act developed by commercial and legal experts.

In most states, a corporation is formed by filing the appropriate document, usually the Articles of Incorporation, with the appropriate state official, usually the Secretary of State, and paying the appropriate fee. Corporate existence is deemed to begin on the date of filing as indorsed on the document. The appropriate state official, the secretary of state or perhaps the attorney general, is charged with primary responsibility for administering corporate laws.

2. Definition and Nature of the Corporate Entity

A corporation is an artificial legal entity, independent of its owners, the investors, created by the state, pursuant to a corporate charter, with powers conferred upon it by the law, and subject to the law.

A corporation is regarded as a separate legal entity, that is, an artificial person, distinct from its shareholders. The corporation is owned by its shareholders, but overall policy is determined by a board of directors chosen by the shareholders; and day-to-day management is implemented by officers chosen by the board of directors as well as employees and agents selected by top management.

A corporation can conduct business in its own name, much in the same way as a natural person does. Assets can be acquired, contracts entered into, and debts incurred, all in the name of the corporation. The corporate entity can sue and be sued, pay taxes, obtain a business license, purchase real estate, and own a bank account, all in its own name.

A major feature of the corporation, as well as a primary reason for its creation, is the limited liability of the shareholders, who are not personally and unlimitedly liable for corporate obligations beyond the extent of the shareholder's investment. The ethical justification for limited liability usually appears as a utilitarian one. The limited liability encourages the formation of corporate business, and thus the doctrine produces greater benefits for society, such as providing remunerative work for members of society, producing goods and services for social use, paying taxes for governmental and societal needs, and generating investment capital for economic development and growth.

3. "Piercing the Corporate Veil"

As a general rule, the shareholders are only limitedly liable; their liability is limited to their investment; they are not personally liable for corporate obligations. An important exception, however, arises from the "piercing the corporate veil" doctrine. If the law determines that the corporate entity is being abused or misused, the corporate entity can be disregarded and the shareholders held unlimitedly and personally liable for the organization's obligations. This exception arises when the corporation is being used to defraud, to avoid a valid obligation, to evade a statute, or when corporate separateness ceases to exist and the corporation becomes a mere shell, instrumentality, or alter ego of the principals involved. It is important to note, however, that the mere fact that the primary motive for incorporation is to secure limited liability is not enough in and of itself to trigger the "piercing" doctrine.

4. Agency-Employment Law

Since a corporation is an artificial person, it acts exclusively by and through officers, employees, and agents. Thus, agency and employment law is very important in the corporate setting, but beyond the scope of this book.

A moral problem does arise however, when the corporation's agents or employees commit a criminal act on behalf of the corporation. It is obvious that the corporation itself cannot be sent to prison, even though the corporation is a "person" legally. The corporation, of course, can be fined when it violates criminal statutes. Imposing a fine on a corporation for its criminality raises interesting and important moral, legal, and practical issues as to whether fines are sufficient to punish and deter corporate misbehavior. If criminal conduct, however, can be attributed beyond a reasonable doubt to corporate officers, employees, and agents, these individuals, as natural persons, may be held liable criminally and imprisoned for their actions.

5. Constitutional Rights

The Constitution of the United States guarantees a "person" certain protections, and a corporation is treated as a "person" for most constitutional purposes. The corporation, for example, is entitled to the First Amendment's freedom of speech guarantee. "Pure" speech, that is, political expression, is fully protected. Commercial speech, that is, advertising proposing commercial transactions, is accorded lesser legal protection. Since the motivation behind commercial speech is predominantly economic, government is allowed to regulate commercial speech, even legitimate and truthful commercial speech, if there is a substantial government interest in regulating the speech and government does so in a direct and narrow manner. The dividing line between "political" or public affairs speech and "mere" commercial speech is a difficult one to demarcate. Regrettably, the U.S. Supreme Court declined to clarify the distinction when it refused to decide whether Nike's defense, allegedly factually erroneous, of its labor practices in Asia was protected political speech or commercial speech (which must be truthful to be protected).

The corporation also is treated as a person for full protection under the Fourteenth Amendment's "equal protection" and "due process" guarantees, the Fourth Amendment's guarantee against unreasonable searches and seizures, and the Fifth Amendment's "double jeopardy" guarantee. The corporation, however, does not possess the Fifth Amendment's privilege against self-incrimination, although the corporation's officers, employees, and agents, as natural people, do possess the right.

6. Summary

A corporation is a legal person, a person under the law, and protected by most of the same rights as a real person. As the corporation is a legal entity and legal actor, and since the law treats corporations the same as individuals in most respects, the important issue arises as to whether a corporation is similarly a moral entity and a moral actor, and thus subject to ethical analysis.

C. The Moral Status of the Corporation

1. Introduction

Moral responsibility usually is ascribed to and assumed by individuals. What about the corporation? Is it a moral entity and a moral actor? Is the corporation subject to ethical analysis? Can it be accountable morally for its actions, or does moral accountability only make sense when applied to the human components of the legal entity? This chapter seeks to answer these questions and to ascertain what "moral responsibility" means when referring to corporations.

2. The Friedman or Organizational View

A conventional view of corporate accountability, advanced principally by Milton Friedman, University of Chicago economist and Nobel prize-winner, holds that the corporation is not a moral entity. At most, it is a legal entity, which is bound by the law and legally accountable. This Friedman view has also been called the "organizational" view by Richard DeGeorge in his *Business Ethics* book. Human beings, however, are not only legally accountable; they also are moral actors subject to moral accountability.

The corporation, the artificial legal person, therefore, is not a moral actor; it has no moral responsibility and it should not be evaluated ethically. The "business of business" is to make money. Moral, as well as social, responsibilities are not the proper concern of the corporation. Successful performance in the marketplace and increasing profits are "right" corporate conduct. Assuming there is any moral or social responsibility for business, it is met in terms of marketplace performance. Accordingly, there is no need to consider a corporation's moral or social responsibility other than perhaps successful economic performance, within the law, of course.

Another version of the Friedman or organizational view maintains that formal organizations, such as a corporation, do not act; rather, the human beings therein act, make choices, and perform whatever the organization needs to do. The organization itself is nothing more than a structure, perhaps a legal one. It does not make choices, act purposefully, or on its own volition. It only acts through the human beings who compose the corporate workforce. Since the formal organization does not act, this view holds that it is not subject to ethical evaluation.

3. Arguments Against the Friedman or Organizational View

Many arguments are advanced against the Friedman or Organizational view. Ethics governs the actions of rational actors when they have an effect on people. Corporations act rationally pursuant to rational, hierarchical, decision-making processes and structures. Corporations possess reasons for what they do. These rational actions, in addition, have an impact on people. Corporate actions, therefore, can be evaluated ethically from a moral perspective. Otherwise, the potential exists for moral abuse and exploitation, because actions by a human being may be branded as morally wrong, yet the very same actions by a corporation, perhaps even a closely held or even one-person corporation are neutral and morally unaccountable. If, for example, it is deemed immoral for a person to discriminate, then it should also be immoral for a corporation to discriminate. If it is wrong for people to steal, it should also be wrong for business to steal.

Corporate actions, of course, do originate and flow from the choices and actions of human beings. These real people, moreover, are morally accountable for these actions. Yet, these actions and choices are not merely personal ones; they are made for and in the name of the corporation. People within the corporation are acting on behalf of the corporation and not strictly for themselves. Since the corporation is controlled by human beings who initiate and implement corporate actions, the corporation possesses a moral status that makes the corporation subject to ethical analysis, even though the corporation may not be a moral "person" per se.

There are practical advantages, in addition, by holding the corporation morally accountable. Ethically evaluating corporate action and making moral judgments enable one to attach praise or blame to corporate actions. If a corporation is deemed to be a moral actor, one can exert moral pressure within or on the organization to rectify a wrong, change a policy, or implement an action. For example, the cessation of the use of plastic packaging by fast-food restaurants, the marketing of condensed milk as a substitute for mother's milk in the developing world, and the use of dolphin-friendly tuna nets are corporate activities that changed in response to moral pressure.

4. Individual Moral Accountability Within the Corporation

Any focus on the corporation as a moral entity must not ignore or obscure individual moral accountability. When moral accountability is ascribed to the corporation as an entity, responsibility also must be assumed by the human components of the organization. One cannot allow the corporate fiction to act as a shield to hide the individuals who underlie the entity and who are the ultimate and primary bearers of moral responsibility.

5. Summary

The corporation, as well as the people within it, have moral status. It is a moral agent, though not necessarily a moral "person." The corporation, therefore, can be held responsible morally for its actions and inaction, as well as legally responsible. In particular, the corporation is bound by the basic ethical duty not to inflict moral harm on others.

D. Corporate Moral Responsibility: To Whom Owed

1. Introduction

The current interpretation of business ethics reflects a broadening of the corporation's responsibility beyond the law into the realm of ethics, which results in moral responsibility. Assuming that the corporation is a moral actor, the question arises as to whom the corporation owes moral duties, particularly the duty to do no moral harm. The conventional view was that the shareholders as the "owners" of the corporation were the only real stakeholder group and thus the board of directors and officers had, and only had, a legal duty to examine the consequences of corporate actions on the shareholders. Today, however, in order to encourage, and perhaps legalize, board attention on other stakeholder groups, most states in the United States have adopted statutes, called corporation "constituency" laws, that allow (but do not mandate) that the board consider the consequences of corporate decision-making on other stakeholders, including the local community and society as a whole.

The principal constituent groups or stakeholders to whom the corporation owes moral duties are: shareholders, employees, customers, consumers, suppliers, the community (local and national), society (in general), and even the competition. All these groups are owed the same general ethical duty to do no moral harm, as well as specific duties due to the nature of the group. A difficult problem arises, however, when the corporation's obligations to one group are perceived as harming another group.

2. Shareholders

In any discussion of corporate moral obligations, shareholders usually are addressed first. Obviously, the corporation cannot survive if it does not serve its shareholders well. Shareholders are entitled to honest and efficient management of their investment as well as a fair return on their investment. A corporation that abuses its shareholders, for example, by paying extraordinary pay and bonuses for merely ordinary executive performance or worse, cannot expect to exist, let alone prosper, in the long run. A problem arises, however, when the corporation's effort to fulfill its moral obligation to other stakeholder groups is perceived as limiting the profitability of the corporation and ultimately harming the shareholders.

3. Employees

The corporation is morally responsible to its employees. It is immoral for the corporation to ignore the needs of its employees as human beings. Employees, accordingly, are entitled to fair employment practices, a just wage, reasonable job security, safe and healthful working conditions, and privacy from immoral employer intrusions.

4. Consumers

The corporation's moral obligation to the consumers is to produce goods that are morally safe, to provide services that are competent, to avoid deceptive practices in advertising and marketing its products and services, to provide consumers with adequate information regarding the goods and services, and to refrain from immoral and anticompetitive trade practices.

5. Community

What moral obligation does the corporation owe the local community? Generally, the corporation owes a duty to this constituent group to do no moral harm. It is important here to distinguish the corporation's moral duties, based on ethics, from its social responsibilities, such as supporting nonprofit organizations and enterprises in the community. One area that a corporation's moral obligation to the community may rise is the closing of plants. This is not to say that ethically a plant can never be closed morally. Ethics will impose a duty on the corporation, however, not to forget the community's contribution to the development of the plant and to its operation. A minimal moral obligation requires the corporation to minimize the harm the corporation's closing of the plant will inflict on the community, as well as the corporation's own employees.

Another corporate obligation involving the community involves the corporation's obligation not to harm the environment, and, in particular, not to pollute the air and water beyond morally acceptable levels.

6. Society

What is the corporation's moral duty to society at large, to the wider social community, the state, nation, world, and even to unborn generations. The general ethical obligation, of course, is to do no moral harm; accordingly, one must use an ethical decision-making process to determine specific obligations, such as not to exploit developing nations, nor to exploit resources needed by future generations.

7. Competition

The corporation, finally, has a moral obligation to its competitors not to harm them by immoral means, to prevail by superior merit and not by immoral tactics such as making questionable payments that distort the marketplace and by other abusive and predatory practices.

8. Conclusion

In order to determine the extent and nature of the moral obligation owed to stakeholders Wal-Mart now has a new corporate position, Senior Director of Stakeholder Engagement, whose job is to help the company create value for all its stakeholders, including society as a whole.

E. Moral Status within the Corporation

1. Introduction

Moral responsibility is not only attributed to a corporation, but also to people within the firm who compose the company, in particular, directors, shareholders, managers, and employees.

2. Board of Directors

Directors are morally responsible for the "culture" or tone of the corporation and for its major policies. Directors are accountable morally for the decisions they make, and fail to make, especially the selection of honest, competent, and moral managers. Directors are responsible morally for overseeing management and for ensuring that the longer-term interests of the shareholders are looked after. In so doing, as noted, the directors may take into consideration the consequences of corporate actions on the firm's other stakeholder groups, including society as a whole, and may do so on a long-term basis.

Today, in the post-Enron, intensified legal and ethical environment, assuming the role of a corporate director definitely emerges as a more daunting challenge for the concerned businessperson. Instead of honing one's golf skills, and then after a perfunctory review, merely "rubber-stamping" a CEO's policies, directors are now learning the complexities of corporate governance and financial accounting; and are being compelled to very closely examine the actions and performance of the company and its executives. The new era of responsibility was dramatically marked by the promulgation in the U.S. of the federal Sarbanes-Oxley law in 2002, which significantly increased criminal penalties for corporate fraud. Moreover, as a consequence of the Enron corporate scandals, directors were made well aware that they could be sued civilly, and personally be held liable, for the harm that resulted from their failure to fulfill their duties as directors. In addition to legal scrutiny, shareholder "activist" groups are now closely examining directors' actions regarding the compensation packages of company executives, especially "golden parachutes," which many angry shareholders have condemned as frequently so excessive and unrelated to performance so as to be unethical, even if technically legal. Directors are now in the "spotlight," and accordingly are being forced to "go back to school" to learn corporate legal, business, and accounting subject matters (and perhaps a seminar or two on ethics would be a very good idea too!). Directors also now must ask corporate executives and managers difficult, pointed, probing, and even embarrassing questions, as well as closely monitor their conduct. Directors now also must meet as a board much more frequently, particularly the audit and compensation committees of the board. Meeting eight times a year as a board and also monthly for the aforementioned committees is rapidly becoming the corporate norm. Long gone is the Enron era, where in the case of that scandal-plagued company, the board of directors rarely met, but when they did they then typically opened a board meeting with a prayer, listened (presumably attentively) to the presentations (presumably fraudulent) by the late Ken Lay and other top executives, but rarely asked them any questions—and at times none whatsoever. The result of the heightened scrutiny of directors, the additional work burdens, and the increased risk of legal liability—civil and criminal—is that many business people no longer find the "job" of being a director an attractive and beneficial business option. For example, regarding executive compensation, new rules promulgated by the Securities and Exchange Commission now require that directors not only disclose the true extent, whether salary, bonus, stock option, severance, pension, etc., as well as detailed nature of, executive compensation packages, but also explain how and why they decided to pay executives such compensation. Serving as a board member today, therefore, is certainly a more challenging endeavor; yet better educated, more involved, and better informed board members, particularly those who take a leadership role, surely should help to ensure legal as well as ethical business behavior.

3. Managers

Managers are responsible morally for keeping the directors fully informed of actions and decisions made and contemplated and the financial condition of the firm. Executives are responsible for implementing the business policies set by the board, for administering the day-to-day affairs of the company, and for selecting and supervising "top" management. Managers are accountable for selecting honest, competent, and moral employees and for "running" the company on a daily basis.

4. Shareholders

In a small or closely held corporation, the shareholders generally are the directors, executives, and managers, and thus directly are accountable morally for the corporation's actions. In a large publicly held corporation, a shareholder normally represents a very small ownership stake. He or she is separate from management and possesses no direct voice in the affairs of the corporation, only the right to vote for directors and fundamental changes pursuant to his or her proportionate shares. Nonetheless, even a small shareholder can be held accountable morally for what a large corporation does or fails to do. If a corporation acts immorally, for example, and a shareholder becomes aware of such actions, he or she is obligated morally to attempt to change corporate policy, and if not, to sell his or her stock.

F. Corporate Culture and the Moral Company

When judging people, it is appropriate to determine their integrity and moral character. What about a corporation's integrity? Does a corporation have a moral character? A corporation can be said to possess a moral character if it takes its moral responsibility seriously and continuously and seeks to act morally in its dealings with its stakeholders.

Corporate moral character, as with people, is built by the regular past and present performance of moral actions. As a result of such actions, acting morally becomes habitual and a tradition of morality arises. People composing the company take pride in their moral company. They identify with the moral history and tradition of the company. They adopt the company's moral stance, seek to continue the tradition, and help educate and mold others to the moral corporate culture of the firm.

A company, of course, can have a corporate culture that inhibits, as well as fosters, moral conduct on the part of its members. Some firms may have a strong positive moral corporate culture, yet others may evidence a negative approach, or no approach at all, to moral concerns.

The role of directors and management is essential to ensuring a rightful moral culture. Corporate culture initially is formed by, and constantly is sensitive to, the decisions of management. Management establishes the direction that the company follows. Management can act morally and can insist on morality throughout the company, especially on the part of the employees. Managers can set the moral pattern, eventually developing into a tradition of moral action on the part of the corporation and its employees, producing a company with a deserved reputation for moral excellence. Dave Packard and Bill Hewlett, for example, who created the Hewlett-Packard Company, were regarded not only as successful entrepreneurs and innovators, but also as paragons of corporate integrity who insisted on the ethical conduct of their employees. The "HP Way" came to signify this commitment to ethics. Unfortunately, HP "lost its way" in 2006 with the revelation of the HP "spy scandal" which besmirched HP's once fine reputation for ethics and integrity.

II. Corporate Ethics Programs

A. Introduction

Business managers may know the "right" thing to do and also possess the will to do it, yet they may be uncertain how to implement moral concerns throughout the corporation. The corporate structure should be designed in such a manner so that people composing the company are encouraged to act morally and so that systematic methods are in place to achieve morality.

The moral tone or character of the corporation, of course, is set by those at the apex of the corporate hierarchy—the board of directors and top managers. They must demonstrate moral conduct, insist on moral conduct, reward moral behavior, and punish immoral behavior. In addition, the corporation should have in place the components of a program designed to institutionalize the firm's commitment to morality. The key elements of such a program are a corporate ethics department, codes of ethics, the performance of a moral audit, and management ethics training programs. The purpose of such a program is to integrate morality into the normal and regular policy-making, decision-making, and work practices of the firm. A corporate ethics program also serves to gain and maintain the public's trust and credibility, to act as a guide to moral decision making and a means to resolve moral dilemmas, to bolster the notion of management as a profession and the corporation as a moral actor, and to define, address, and redress improper corporate and employee misconduct.

B. Ethics Department and Officers

If a corporate ethics program is to succeed, someone has to be given the responsibility for developing and implementing the ethics program. The responsibility may be delegated to a top-level manager in the human resources department, but he or she may not possess a sufficient knowledge of ethics; or the responsibility may be delegated to the legal department, but an attorney is trained to act legally and not necessarily morally.

Many companies, therefore, are creating a high-level department of ethics, headed by an ethics officer, typically holding a title of vice president or director, who reports directly to the board of directors or the CEO. The ethics officer advises the board and CEO on moral issues, develops, and assumes the responsibility of administering, the corporation's ethics program, raises moral issues at board meetings and high-level management meetings, and listens to and investigates employees' and other's complaints about immoral corporate activities. For example, Wal-Mart announced in 2006 that the company will create a high-level ethics position, called Director of Global Ethics, who will be responsible for developing standards of conduct and investigating violation of company policy.

The ethics officer and ethics department have the primary responsibility for promulgating the corporation's code of ethics, communicating the code to corporate management and employees, investigating violations of the code, and enforcing the code through the imposition of sanctions. The ethics officer along with the relevant parties will review and revise the code as appropriate.

Since a written ethics code cannot adequately cover adequately every contingency, employees and others will have questions regarding the morality of certain company practices. It is, of course, the duty of the ethics officer and his/her appropriate personnel to answer questions concerning ethics and morality. Employees and others should have a department where they can obtain information and clarification about corporate ethics policies and regarding moral issues not explicitly contained in the policies. Employees should be able to pursue any moral concerns at the ethics department level, obtain a fair hearing without fear of reprisal, and be given an adequate explanation to their concerns.

An employee should be able to use the ethics department without fear of negative consequences, even when the employee is contending a corporate policy or practice is in conflict with the company's code of ethics. The ethics department functions not only as a channel for employee moral concerns, but also as a mechanism whereby shareholders, consumers, community members, and members of society can raise their concerns about the corporation's moral responsibilities. The ethics officer also must act as an advocate of corporate morality; that is, he or she must argue against a corporate policy or practice if it is immoral.

Today, in the post-Enron, intensified legal and ethical environment, assuming the role of a corporate director definitely emerges as a more daunting challenge for the concerned businessperson. Instead of honing one's golf skills, and then after a perfunctory review, merely "rubber-stamping" a CEO's policies, directors are now learning the complexities of corporate governance and financial accounting; and are being compelled to very closely examine the actions and performance of the company and its executives. The new era of responsibility was dramatically marked by the promulgation in the U.S. of the federal Sarbanes-Oxley law in 2002, which significantly increased criminal penalties for corporate fraud. Moreover, as a consequence of the Enron corporate scandals, directors were made well aware that they could be sued civilly, and personally be held liable, for the harm that resulted from their failure to fulfill their duties as directors. In addition to legal scrutiny, shareholder "activist" groups are now closely examining directors' actions regarding the compensation packages of company executives, especially "golden parachutes," which many angry shareholders have condemned as frequently so excessive and unrelated to performance so as to be unethical, even if technically legal. Directors are now in the "spotlight," and accordingly are being forced to "go back to school" to learn corporate legal, business, and accounting subject matters (and perhaps a seminar or two on ethics would be a very good idea too!). Directors also now must ask corporate executives and managers difficult, pointed, probing, and even embarrassing questions, as well as closely monitor their conduct. Directors now also must meet as a board much more frequently, particularly the audit and compensation committees of the board. Meeting eight times a year as a board and also monthly for the aforementioned committees is rapidly becoming the corporate norm. Long gone is the Enron era, where in the case of that scandal-plagued company, the board of directors rarely met, but when they did they then typically opened a board meeting with a prayer, listened (presumably attentively) to the presentations (presumably fraudulent) by the late Ken Lay and other top executives, but never asked them any real questions. The result of the heightened scrutiny of directors, the additional work burdens, and the increased risk of legal liability—civil and criminal—is that many business people no longer find the "job" of being a director an attractive and beneficial business option. For example, regarding executive compensation, new rules promulgated by the Securities and Exchange Commission now require that directors not only disclose the true extent, whether salary, bonus, stock option, severance, pension, etc., as well as detailed nature of executive compensation packages, but also explain how and why they decided to pay executives such compensation. Serving as a board member today, therefore, is certainly a more challenging endeavor; yet, as noted, better educated, more involved, and better informed board members, particularly those who take a leadership role, surely should help to ensure legal as well as ethical business behavior.

C. The Ethical Audit versus the Social Audit

The ethical audit, performed by the corporate ethics department, is an attempt to measure the moral performance of the company. The audit is based on ethical principles and seeks to determine the corporation's moral obligations and to ensure that the company is acting morally. Internally, the ethical audit will determine if the company's code of ethics is complied with by the corporation and its employees. Shareholders, potential investors, and the general public, have the right to know the moral, as well as financial, position of the company. Acquiring and communicating this information very well could inure to the benefit of the corporation, as people may choose to invest and do business with a company that is acting demonstrably morally.

The ethical audit must be distinguished from the social audit, usually performed by the company's public relations department or community relations officer. This social audit is not a moral one based on ethical principles; rather, it is a report on the social performance of the firm, for example, in the area of charitable, welfare, and civic involvement and contributions, which typically are neither legal nor moral obligations.

D. Corporate Codes of Ethics

1. Introduction

Ethics codes have always been adopted by the professions. In recent years, however, they also have been adopted by corporations and businesses. Codes of ethics usually are developed for a company as a whole and form the foundation of the company's ethics program. Codes of ethics serve as the major vehicle for stating the ethical principles, core values, and moral rules the company believes in and follows.

A code of ethics helps to make managers and employees aware that moral considerations, as well as economic and legal factors, must be considered when business decisions are made. The code also demonstrates to other stakeholders that the corporation is aware of, and fully committed to, acting morally.

If the corporate code of ethics is to serve as a means by which business managers legitimately can begin to claim "profession" status, the code ideally should contain: a statement of adherence, that is, a statement that the corporation, as well as its employees, will be bound by the principles of the code; an ethical preamble, stating the fundamental ethical principles and core values motivating the code; a statement and description of the corporation's basic mission and purpose, how this mission coheres with the ethical preamble, thus demonstrating that the corporation serves an inherently moral purpose; a statement and description of the main stakeholders or constituencies to whom the corporation believes it is obligated in the pursuit of its mission; an enumeration of the specific obligations the corporation believes it owes to these groups; a listing of precise standards of conduct required, permitted, or forbidden by the code; and a statement of the types and severity of sanctions the corporation will impose upon violators of these principles, obligations, and standards.

The process by which the code of ethics is put together is very important. The initial, and ultimate, responsibility, of course, lies with the company's board of directors. It is critical, however, that employees and departments at all levels and sectors of the corporation take part in drawing up the code. The legal department, human resources, public and community relations, and ad hoc committees of employees from different departments, for example, must be drawn into the process. If a wide variety of employees are not drawn into the process, the company risks the perils of a code that does not address real concerns and that engenders a feeling by the employees that the code is not "owned" by them, but rather is merely another set of rules and regulations imposed on them.

A company should be prepared to expect certain objections to be raised to the creation of a code of ethics. A code might invite increased scrutiny of the corporation by members of the public, the press, and consumer and environmental groups. These "outsiders" now will be able to ask if the company is complying with its code of ethics and, if there have been any violations, what is being done to rectify them. An open examination of the company, however, should be encouraged, not feared. Such an examination affords the company an opportunity to explain its positions and demonstrate its commitment to morality. If a corporation desires to maintain or regain the confidence of the public, it must demonstrate that it is taking the interests of its stakeholders into account.

A code also may appear to be an act of self-condemnation on the part of the company. Of course, if the company has been acting morally, the code can be phrased as a formal embodiment of long-standing moral policies and practices. However, if the company has engaged in immoral past conduct, the promulgation of a code may appear in some sense to be an admission of responsibility. Yet, the very creation of the code clearly demonstrates that the company's problems have been confronted, that the company does not now tolerate such misconduct and intends to redress it in a formal manner, and that the company wants to signal this new attitude to managers, employees, and other stakeholders.

2. Code Format and Features

A fully elaborated code of ethics will possess a certain format and features. A code first should enunciate a statement of ethical principles in the form of a preamble. The preamble, rooted in traditional ethics, is the company's carefully articulated statement of ethical principles. The preamble provides the foundation underlying the code's moral standards and provisions. Unless the code is understood in terms of ethical principles, the company risks the code being viewed as a mere expression of rules and regulations, imposed from "above," and to be "learned" by rote. Accordingly, a prime purpose of the preamble is to persuade the employees to conform to the moral provisions of the code, rather than simply commanding the employees to follow the rules.

A great deal of care and emphasis, therefore, must be placed on the preamble. It is not to be expected that the code contain a detailed explication of ethics and ethical reasoning. The code, however, must make reference to the general ethical principles from which the code stems, such as conducting business with honesty and integrity; treating people with dignity and respect, in a fair and equitable manner, foreseeing and weighing the consequences of all those affected by an action; and seeking to do the greater good in society. Such pronouncements will help the employees and others learn not only how the code provisions were derived and are to be implemented, but also will help the employees to internalize the code's provisions. The preamble, finally, not only helps management and employees to interpret the code, but also assists them in resolving moral dilemmas not explicitly handled by the code.

A corporate code of ethics must include an adherence statement; that is, the code must specify that each individual employee at all levels of the corporation will accept his or her moral responsibility pursuant to the code. The adherence statement, in addition, must state explicitly that not only the employees but also the corporation are bound by the precepts of the code. If the code only contains a list of rules and regulations for employees to follow, the code will appear to exist solely for the company's protection and benefit.

A statement of the corporation's mission is also an important component of the code. The mission statement indicates that the corporation's business activities, its products and services, serve an inherently moral purpose. A pharmaceutical company, for example, would stress that its mission is to promote health and save lives; a food company would underscore its mission as improving nutrition at affordable price levels. The mission statement, however, must be distinguished from the "constituency" and "practices" sections of a code, because the mission statement does not direct corporate and employee conduct in general or specific circumstances.

A constituency obligation section of the code is the statement of the corporation's responsibilities to the various groups or stakeholders it serves or affects, such as the shareholders, employees, customers and consumers, suppliers, the community, and society. The constituency section also should refer to the firm's competition, because the firm owes to the competition the duty not to immorally harm it and to prevail only by superior merit. The constituency section is a recognition of the corporation's responsibility to these groups, as well as a recognition that the company has a present, continuing, and future role and stake in society. This section usually states the corporation's obligations. It describes the corporation's general commitment to these groups, rather than prescribing moral conduct for specific situations. The code's broad guidelines found in the constituency section, however, set the stage for the specific rules of conduct that will follow in the "practices" section.

The "practices" section of the code directs corporate and employee conducts in specific circumstances. It is important for this part of the code to relate the standards therein to the previously stated ethical principles, mission statement, and constituency obligations. The standards delineated in the "practice" section must give form to the corporation's mission and stakeholder obligations.

The "practices" section of the code must be regulative and "legal" in the sense that the specific standards therein are legally binding on the employees and the corporation. This part of the code renders the code not unlike government regulations in some respects; but, of course, the company's code is developed and implemented internally and thus constitutes a type of self-regulation. While ethical principles, mission statements, constituency obligations, as well as vision statements, ideals, and values are not inappropriate in a code, the code must make very clear which of its pronouncements are idealistic, persuasive, or hortatory in nature and which are precise legalistic standards subject to punitive enforcement.

The provisions in the "practices" section should be clear, specific, and detailed. If this section of the code is too general, simple, and amorphous, it will be too vague to regulate conduct and to convey the company's commitment to morality, and the code will function as a mere public relations document. It is not sufficient for the code solely to say that "fair dealing" and "integrity" are expected by all the employees; rather, the code must spell out what these terms mean, for example, when accepting gifts from suppliers or when giving gifts to customers or governmental officials. At the least, a code can use words such as "nominal," "token," or "modest value" when discussing gifts, or the phrase "unduly influences the recipient" when prohibiting a gift. These terms help to define an enforceable standard, although they themselves must be interpreted in a particular factual context.

Even though the code, especially the "practices" section, may appear as a legalistic document, it is very important that the code do more than merely restate the law. Reformulating the law may be an appropriate function of the code, but the law must be viewed as establishing minimum standards of behavior. The code must demonstrate that the corporation and its employees are willing to conduct business by standards higher than the minimum required by the law. Otherwise, the company is just promising to obey the law, which, of course, it is already legally obligated to do. There already exist legal departments and law firms to give advice as to the legality of corporate activity, but the legal department probably is not competent to render advice as to the morality of a corporate action, and a true code of ethics goes above and beyond the law and requires moral as well as legal conduct.

In order to be a true ethics code, moreover, the code must address real moral problems that the company and its employees confront when dealing with the company's various constituency groups. In particular, the code must address those practices that are at the "moral margin," that is, practices that often are legal, socially acceptable, and perhaps tolerated due to self-interest. These "shady" or "gray" areas, consisting of not quite illegal but often immoral activities, and thus pitfalls to the company's employees, must be addressed in the code.

3. Code Sanctions

The issue will arise as to whether the code should have any penalties. It may be argued that there is no need to include penalties since the employees should know they will be punished if they violate the code. An explicit "penalty" section could send a wrong message to employees. The code perhaps should have a supportive rather than a punitive character, and it should emphasize its prescriptive elements as opposed to the proscriptive ones.

However, if the code is to be more than mere "window dressing," if it is to be more than a few pieces of paper that an employee reads, perhaps signs, and then files away and forgets about, the code must be enforced with sanctions. For the code to be effective, there must be some disciplinary measures to punish violators of the code. Sanctions can range from termination, suspension, demotion, and probation, to negative appraisal comments. Responsibility without penalties for improper conduct is empty posturing. Punitive actions, therefore, must be taken against code violators, or else the time and effort taken to promulgate the code will have been wasted. The penalty for executive and management immorality, moreover, must be the same as that for lower-level employee misconduct.

A code section on sanctions and the application of penalties also will call for an internal judicial procedure to determine whether a violation of the code has occurred and, if so, to impose an appropriate penalty.

4. Communicating the Code

The distribution and communication of the code of ethics play a key role in securing the company's commitment to morality. Who should receive the code? The corporation must develop techniques for the internal and external distribution of the code. A significant number of upper-level managers probably have participated in the drafting of the code, but the corporation must communicate the code to all its employees. If the code is distributed to the employees directly from the board of directors, chairperson of the board, or the president, this method of transmittal will underscore the stature and importance of the code, as well as signal the expectations of upper-level management. The significance of the code can be reinforced further by orientation programs, training programs, further in-house communication, discussions with immediate supervisors, and letters from management.

A company also should require a written acknowledgement that the employee has received a copy of the code (and annually thereafter). The purpose of the acknowledgement statement is to emphasize the binding nature of the code as well as to provide evidence that the employee has received the document.

What about "external" distribution of the code? If the code truly is an ethics code, it will profess the company's moral obligation to its relevant stakeholder groups, and the code, therefore, should be made available for wide public distribution.

5. Code Oversight and Enforcement

If a code of ethics is to have substantive value, if it is to function as more than a public relations device, the code must be implemented as well as administered in an equitable manner. Employees, as well as the public, must know that adverse consequences will ensue from violating the code. The lack of effective oversight and compliance, or the exemption of the corporation itself, or some level or types of employees from enforcement, will bring the code into disrepute, damage internal morale, and raise suspicions as to the company's motive in creating the code.

The introduction of an ethics code into a corporate setting, therefore, requires attention to compliance. The code must be enforceable and enforced. The code must contain provisions for the bringing of complaints, by employees and others, and for applying sanctions. As the code process is a dynamic process, the code must contain a mechanism for the promulgation of code amendments in the light of experience.

In order to ensure efficacious code implementation, the corporation must pay attention to organizational structure. It must ensure it has systems and procedures to monitor and enforce the moral conduct required by the code, such as channels for receiving, transmitting, and assessing complaints, and procedures to deal with major and minor violations.

The company, for example, should have an ethics department, committee, or office to which an employee or "outsider" can report suspected violations of the code or other moral problems. The ethics department then would investigate the incident or problem, obtain relevant evidence and information, and report its results to higher levels of management, including if necessary the board of directors. A corporation also should have an "ethics hot line," that is, a communications channel through which an employee can report anonymously without fear of reprisals. Any supervisor or manager who retaliates against employees must be subject to severe punishment. Such procedures will enable the upper levels of corporate management to deal with moral problems before they become serious and potentially damaging situations.

There will be, of course, difficulties involved in the monitoring and enforcement aspects of the code process. The company certainly does not want to penalize good faith "whistle-blowers." Yet the company does not want to encourage "tattling" and the friction it would invite. It certainly wants to avoid the bringing of false allegations and the infliction of harm on employees by jealous, frustrated, disaffected, or malicious coworkers. A company, however, also must be concerned about incursions into the employees' privacy from its monitoring and surveillance activities. Potential lawsuits arising from enforcement procedures are a legitimate concern. These problems can be lessened, however, by the corporation having oversight and enforcement procedures, as well as penalties specified clearly in the code and by having all the employees accept the code, in writing, annually?

Business must be able to demonstrate that it polices its own ranks. If business is unwilling or unable to discharge its moral responsibility, how can business rightfully claim any special privileges of a "profession" from society, and how can business argue against further government regulation.

6. Summary

Although the corporation will expend time, effort, and resources in developing, implementing, and establishing its code of ethics, there are many advantages to having a code of ethics.

The code demonstrates that the company is committed to morality and that the company realizes that morality is an absolute requirement for all its employees. The code will reinforce moral conduct and should elicit a higher moral standard of behavior on the part of the employees. The code will help teach employees their moral responsibilities, and it also can be used as a document of internal "law" that employees can cite when they feel pressured to commit a morally questionable action. The code will serve to reassure the corporation's stakeholders that the company adheres to moral rules as well as to provide to the stakeholders a standard by which to measure the corporation's moral commitment. The code, finally, will help to build a shared corporate culture of morality.

E. Ethics Training Programs

One very effective way for the corporation to communicate and implement the ethics code, as well as to further institutionalize ethics into the corporate culture, is to conduct ethics training programs for managers and employees. They regularly must be made aware of the contents of the code of ethics, the company's commitment to it, and the importance of adhering to it; and they must be given sufficient training in ethics for the corporation's ethics program to succeed.

A typical type of ethics workshop or training program would encompass a discussion of moral issues arising in connection with the company's stakeholders, the gray issues that directly challenge employees, an explanation of the code and its provisions, and a demonstration of how the code can be used to resolve moral problems. The training also should underscore the further assistance the corporation affords an employee faced with a moral dilemma, such as the corporation's ethics department, officer, and ethics hot line.

The ethics workshops can be conducted by traditional training methods, such as lectures providing an overview of the code, seminars led by professional ethics trainers and the corporation's ethics officer and other managers, the discussion and resolution of real and hypothetical cases illustrating moral problems that confront employees, and group discussions exploring the moral content of corporate decision making, and how to discover better ways to make moral decisions. The ethics workshops, finally, can serve as a means to make additions and revisions to the code of ethics, thus ensuring that the code is a responsive, living, and all-embracing moral document.

F. Summary

A systematic corporate ethics program, including an ethics department and officer, ethics code, ethics hot line, and ethics training, will not only introduce morality into the corporate context, but also serve to integrate morality into day-to-day company decision-making and operations.

The ethics code, as well as the entire ethics program, cannot stand alone. The moral standards of the code must be underscored and reinforced by the commitment of the corporation, particularly its top management, to moral policies and practices. Top management must provide continual moral leadership and set a moral example by the performance of exemplary actions. When morality is integrated into all aspects of corporate life and coheres with a corporate culture of morality, the corporate ethics program will ensure corporate morality. The important fact is that a code of ethics in order to be morally efficacious cannot stand alone. This point was clearly demonstrated in a research survey conducted by three faculty colleagues of the authors. The results of the survey were reported in an article in the *Journal of Applied Management and Entrepreneurship* (Bendixen, Abratt, and Jones, 2007). The researchers studied a large multinational with a dominant position in a country's consumer goods market. Their intent was to assess the perceptions that both the suppliers to and the staff of the purchasing department of the multinational had about the ethical behavior of the company. They found that the existence and implementation of formal codes of ethics were important factors in achieving moral behavior. However, they also found that the ethics codes were but "one side to the coin." The codes are "a necessary but not a sufficient condition." Significantly, the researchers found that in addition to the codes and the standards therein the existence of "sound and candid" and "open" relationships with stakeholders was the "linchpin" that enables moral behavior. The researchers defined "candid relationships" as those embracing transparency, respect, speedy resolution of problems, clear communications, and fair (but firm) negotiations. The researchers also concluded that adopting a leadership role in terms of enacting and embracing the ethical values espoused by the business emerges as a critical factor in producing moral behavior

Business leaders, executives, and managers must recognize the moral responsibilities of business. They must also recognize that business, particularly the corporate sector, will be called into moral account. By adopting an ethics code and programs, business leaders, executives, and managers will be able to clarify, address, and solve moral issues and thus fulfill their own and their companies' ethical obligations.

III. *Whistleblowing and the Moral Corporation*

A. Definition and Introduction

"Whistleblowing" may be defined as an attempt by a member of an organization to disclose what he or she believes to be wrongdoing in or by the organization. This section focuses on whistleblowing by employees of a corporation. "Wrongdoing" entails not only conduct or conditions that the employee believes are illegal, but also behavior that the employee considers to be immoral. Whistleblowing can be internal, that is, to those higher up in the corporate hierarchy; or it can be external, that is, to the government, such as a regulatory agency, to a public interest group, or to the media.

A "whistleblower," of course, is the person, the employee, who attempts to make known the wrongdoing. He or she usually "blows the whistle" for right, as well as rightful, reasons; yet one should not always assume that the whistleblowing employee's motives are meritorious or that he or she is even correct as to the underlying premise of wrongdoing.

B. Whistleblowing and the Law

While there may exist federal and state statutes that protect public sector employees who blow the whistle from retaliation by their government employers, as well as statutes in the areas of civil rights, labor law, and health and safety law, that prohibit employers from taking retaliatory actions against employees who report statutory violations, there is no general federal statute, and little state law, extending similar protection to private sector employees, the vast majority of whom are employees and "at will." The state whistleblower protection statutes that do exist usually only protect disclosures of actual legal violations by a company and by its employees. Therefore, reports of suspicious unfounded illegality are usually not protected, nor are disclosures of immoral and unethical conduct which are also not illegal. Moreover, the state statutes are uniform in that to be protected the whistleblowing must be made to a government agency or public official and not to the media or a public interest organization.

The issue arises, therefore, as to whether ethics extends any moral protection to private sector whistleblowing employees, especially in the corporate context.

C. Morally Justifying Whistleblowing

1. Moral Free Speech and Whistleblowing versus Duties of Loyalty and Confidentiality

One recalls a problem inherent in Kantian ethics—the possibility that two secondary moral rules, both of which "pass" the Categorical Imperative, conflict! This problem is particularly apparent in a corporate whistleblowing context. It can be argued that employees have an ethically "certified" moral obligation of loyalty and confidentiality. Yet it also can be argued persuasively that employees have a moral right to free speech, which at a minimum should include a right to "blow the whistle" on wrongful corporate activities.

All these secondary moral rules theoretically pass the Categorical Imperative, yet they clash in practice. What is the ethical solution to this problem? Perhaps the solution is to qualify the general duties of loyalty and confidentiality. That is, to maintain generally that employees do owe a moral duty of loyalty and confidentiality to their employers, but also to maintain that this duty is not unlimited. The general duty can be superseded by special circumstances, such as when the employee not only has a moral free speech right, but also an obligation to blow the whistle in order to stop or prevent harm.

The issue arises, therefore, as to when whistleblowing is morally required. The whistleblowing moral rule that follows is based in part on Richard DeGeorge's formulation in his book, *Business Ethics*.

2. Morally Required Whistleblowing

In those exceptional circumstances, whereby whistleblowing is to be deemed morally obligatory, five requirements must be satisfied: 1) the corporation or its human components are doing, or threatening to do, some activity that is seriously or considerably harmful to the public or other parties; 2) the employee must make a good faith attempt to stop the wrongdoing by reporting it to his or her immediate supervisor and then through internal channels, and these attempts have failed; 3) the employee must secure reasonably clear and comprehensive evidence to substantiate or document the wrongdoing; 4) the employee must possess a reasonably good belief that blowing the whistle externally will stop or prevent the wrong; and 5) and the employee is the "last resort" to stop or prevent the harm, that is, no one else can or will act to stop the wrongdoing that the corporation is involved in or threatening to perform. If these requirements are present, then an employee is morally required to blow the whistle on corporate wrongdoing, regardless of the consequences to himself or herself.

3. Corporate Wrongdoing

Wrongdoing is the proper predicate for a whistleblowing principle. Yet what does the term "wrongdoing" encompass? Wrongdoing, or course, includes corporate activities that cause, or threaten, serious physical harm to the users of the company's products and services, the general public, and the firm's own employees, who may be harmed by unsafe work areas or practices. A definition of "wrongdoing," however, cannot be limited to actions that cause, or threaten to cause, physical harm. While one does not want to encourage whistleblowing for matters that are merely offensive, annoying, or in bad taste, physical harm is simply too narrow a foundation for a whistleblowing principle. Accordingly, "wrongdoing" must include corporate wrongs that invade fundamental moral rights, such as an employee's right to privacy, that cause psychological harm, for example by sexual harassment, and inflict financial harm, for example by embezzlement. If the company is acting illegally, moreover, such illegality is a sufficient predicate for whistleblowing, regardless of the existence or level of harm.

Although the concept of "wrongdoing" is broader than its physical harm component, ascertaining the exact type of harm may be important in determining the evidence to be secured and to whom the wrongdoing should be reported. If the wrongdoing involves illegal corporate actions, the proper recipient is the governmental entity with jurisdiction over the subject matter. If the wrongdoing is not necessarily illegal, but otherwise harmful or immoral, a public interest organization, or perhaps the media, may be a preferable recipient. They may be more concerned with a nonlegalistic type of wrongdoing and more likely to provide help and advice.

4. The Chain of Command

An employee must follow proper guidelines in reporting corporate wrongdoing. He or she must first attempt to report the wrongdoing to his or her immediate supervisor. If, however, the supervisor is the person causing the problem, or part of its cover-up, then the employee is allowed to circumvent the supervisor and proceed further "up the chain" in the corporate hierarchy.

In addition, if fully exhausting the internal corporate channels would give the wrong-doer(s) the time to destroy the evidence needed to document the wrong, then the whistle-blower is not required to proceed through the entire chain of command. Similarly, if people's health and safety are being seriously harmed, or threatened imminently, then it is not necessary to exhaust fully all internal corporate channels.

Regardless of the unique nature of the situation, the employee who is contemplating whistleblowing is advised to familiarize himself or herself with all available internal corporate channels and procedures for reporting wrongdoing. The employee also should seek to determine how other whistleblowing employees were treated by the company and what was done about the problems these employees reported. If employees were treated fairly and the problems rectified, then the employee should feel encouraged to proceed up the chain; if other employees were retaliated against, or if the problems were not corrected, then the employee is well advised to explore appropriate external whistleblowing contacts.

5. Documentation and Evidence

An employee should not blow the whistle based on a mere guess or speculation of wrong-doing, because such an action may harm innocent people. An employee, therefore, has a duty to obtain as much evidence and documentation as reasonably possible to substantiate and verify any allegation or wrongdoing. The employee should seek to gather sufficient evidence to allow others, internally or externally, to investigate the matter further; and should secure evidence that will stand up in a government proceeding. If it is not possible for the employee to secure this level of evidence, perhaps the employee can ascertain where and how additional evidence and documentation can be obtained.

If, however, the employee possesses convincing reasons to believe that wrongdoing is occurring, he or she should disclose it, even if adequate documentation and evidence cannot be obtained. An employee simply may not be in a position to obtain this type or amount of information. What if the employee is able to obtain information, but only by engaging in illegal or immoral actions himself or herself? In such a case, the employee generally should refrain from personally acquiring the information, instead informing others who would possess the necessary legal and moral authority to investigate. If the only way to obtain evidence is through illegal or immoral means, the employee must possess very good reasons to believe the wrongdoing is so severe and is causing such a substantial risk of harm to others that breaking the law and moral norms are unavoidably necessary.

6. Anonymous Whistleblowing

Can, and should, whistleblowing be anonymous? Is it necessary for the whistleblowing to be effective for the whistleblower to reveal openly himself or herself? Although the whistleblower's identity perhaps can be kept secret, except for a few corporate managers and investigators, in order for whistleblowing to be effective ultimately, the whistleblower must be identified, testify and produce evidence publicly, and perhaps put himself or herself at risk. Anonymous whistleblowing also risks violating the right of people to face their accusers. Whistleblowing, therefore, cannot, and should not, be anonymous.

7. The Whistleblower's Motive

The whistleblower's motives, or presence of mixed motives, for blowing the whistle generally should be irrelevant. There should not be imposed an additional requirement to whistleblowing that the whistleblower evince sincerity and rectitude. The essential point is not the whistleblower's state of mind, but whether the whistleblower's assertion is true or false; and if it is true, then whistleblowing may be justified regardless of motive. If, however, the whistleblower's charges are incorrect, then his or her motive may become a relevant issue.

8. False Whistleblowing

What if the whistleblower's assertions are false, incorrect, or inaccurate? If the whistleblower acted in good faith and had reasonable grounds to base his or her charge of wrongdoing, then the whistleblowing employee should not be severely penalized. Presuming the employee has brought the false charges through the corporate chain of command, then his or her error presumably has been detected and rectified before any external disclosure. In such a case, a warning to the employee to exercise greater care in the future would be an appropriate sanction. If, however, the employee lacked either good faith or reasonable grounds, he or she should be more severely punished, and if both are missing, the employee should be dismissed. The company, of course, should bear the burden of proving the accusation was false, and, if the charges are determined to be false, then the employee must show that he or she possessed reasonable grounds and acted in good faith.

9. Whistleblower Checklist

Assuming that an employee is a "good Kantian" and thus intends to comply with the moral "law" and plans to "blow on the whistle" on his or her employer's wrongdoing, the employee should nonetheless think carefully and plan accordingly. First, the employee should seek legal counsel to ascertain whether he or she is protected by a federal or state whistleblower protection statute. There are whistleblower protection provisions in the Sarbanes-Oxley Act, but they just extend to publicly traded companies and allegations of securities fraud. Moreover, a few states do have general whistleblower protection acts which protect to a limited degree private sector workers; and perhaps the morally motivated whistleblowing intending employee will also be legally protected. If there is such a statute, it would be incumbent on the employee to check it very carefully as to the particular state's requirements for legally protected whistleblowing. As previously noted, all state statutes will require that the predicate for protected whistleblowing be a legal violation; and furthermore will require an actual, as opposed to a suspicion of a, legal violation by the employer. Moreover, some statutes require that prior notice of the legal violation be given to the employer, and in some cases in writing, and also in certain cases that the employer be given a reasonable opportunity to correct the violation. Finally, as previously underscored, all whistleblower statutes—federal and state—will require that the whistleblowing to be protected must be reported to an appropriate government agency or public sector official. Second, the capability of the employee to secure sufficient evidence or documentation of a legal violation is critical to ensuring that the employee fulfills his or her legal and ethical duties, as well as to ensure that the whistleblowing actually is efficacious and results in needed changes. Third, the prudent employee should carefully examine his or her motives for the intended disclosure. Granted, legally as well as morally, the employee may be protected in a "mixed motive" situation, but acting out of an improper motive, such as spite, hatred, or revenge, may cause the employee to embellish the case, to jump to conclusions, and to unnecessarily contravene duties of loyalty and confidentiality. Finally, the employee must be fully prepared for the consequences of his or her whistleblowing, especially if the disclosure occurs in a jurisdiction where the employee is a mere employee at-will and not protected regarding job tenure by a contract or a whistleblower protection statute. Can the employee find suitable employment, especially if the employee may be "blacklisted" in the industry or profession as a "snitch," "stoolie," or "informant"? Kant would say that if whistleblowing is morally required, one should "blow the whistle," period, regardless of consequences; yet the prudent person who intends to do his or her moral duty should nevertheless seek legal counsel and "count the cost."

D. Preventing External Whistleblowing

The occurrence of whistleblowing, especially external whistleblowing, ordinarily indicates a failure in a firm's commitment to morality as well as a breakdown in its ethical structure and communication. If, however, a company has a code of ethics, an ethics department or officer, ethics training, and ethics hot lines, such a morally committed company will enable its concerned employees to raise effectively any problems within the company through clearly defined channels, pursuant to explicit standards, and to empowered individuals.

Such a company should have a provision in its code of ethics dealing explicitly with reporting suspected violations of the code, as well as other illegal or immoral actions. The provision should state that an employee who becomes aware of a violation, or believes that a violation may take place in the future, must report the matter. Ordinarily, this disclosure initially should be made to the employee's immediate supervisor. The code provision should then specify to whom else in the corporate hierarchy the employee must notify, including, of course, the ethics officer. It should state that the matter will be investigated promptly, thoroughly, and fairly, and that such reports will be treated confidentially. The code provision, finally, must state that any attempts at intimidation or retaliation against the reporting employee will be punished severely.

E. Ethical Examination of Whistleblowing[2]

As has been pointed out, there does not exist a uniform corpus of whistleblower law to protect private sector, at-will employees. There is yet no general federal law, though the new federal, securities fraud, whistleblower provision in the Sarbanes-Oxley Act is a start. There are some state statutes, but only a relatively small number of truly comprehensive state statutes. Most of these contain strict reporting requirements, and, moreover, are strictly construed by the courts. Finally, as will be seen in the chapter on employment relationships, there is a rather large, but loose, state-by-state collection of at times widely divergent, common law, "public policy" formulations that may encompass whistleblowing protections. The statutory and case law, of course, eventually will determine the legalities of a whistleblowing situation. Ethics, as a branch of philosophy, will be used to determine what is morally required in a whistleblowing situation. Ascertaining whether whistleblowing is morally permissible, or in particular, whether it is morally required, or concomitantly whether it is morally justified, is a very difficult task. Such a moral whistleblowing inquiry first necessitates an examination of the field of ethics as a branch of philosophy. Accordingly, one important moral philosophical issue that emerges is whether ethics, as a branch of philosophy, grants, or should confer, any moral protection to private sector employees, especially at-will employees in a corporate context. Do employees have the moral right, and perhaps the moral responsibility, to "blow the whistle"? Those are the seminal moral questions for ethical analysis. Employers, therefore, must look to both the law and the philosophy of ethics when deciding issues relating to whistleblowing my employee.

1. Ethical Egoism

The first ethical theory to apply to whistleblowing is Ethical Egoism. Egoism, one recalls, is a consequentialist based ethical theory; but, as the word "ego" clearly indicates, the consequences are analyzed only so far as they directly or indirectly impact oneself. Accordingly, pursuant to egoism as an ethical theory, an action is moral if it maintains or advances one's self-interest; and conversely an action is immoral if it undermines or impedes one's self-interest. The objective, of course, is to maximize one's own "good." As this ethics book has a practical business, corporate, and employment application, the principal "good" to be valued and maximized will be deemed to be money. It is very important to note two major constraints on the doctrine of ethical egoism. First, an "enlightened" ethical egoist would counsel that one should be willing to take a long-term approach to maximizing one's self-interest. Thus, a rational ethical egoist would be willing to undergo some short-term expense or sacrifice to maximize his or her greater good in the long-run. Second, even if one has a huge ego, and the power to exercise it, the "enlightened" ethical egoist would say that it is stupid to take advantage of people, exploit them, trample on their rights. Rather, a true ethical egoist would assist, sustain, and protect people, co-opt them, and make them part of the "team." The ethical egoist will do this not out of any feelings of benevolence and charity; but because typically it will inure to the individual benefit of the egoist in the long-term to treat people well. Thus, self-interest is paramount, as well as moral; but self-interest constrained by rationality and prudence.

[2]See Cavico (2004) from which this discussion is based.

The authors believe that the doctrine of ethical egoism would dictate to the logical and "enlightened" employer that the employer treat the whistleblowing employee well, that is, as a valuable asset, as part of the true "team," and definitely not as a disloyal "trouble-maker" or "informant" to be sanctioned. Ethical egoism would dictate that not only should the employer not retaliate against the whistleblowing employee; but rather whistleblowing internally should be encouraged. Surely, an egoistic employer can be made to see that it is in its own self-interest to take care of problems internally, before they wind up in the hands of government regulators or the media. Thus, as far as the employer is concerned, internal whistleblowing is moral pursuant to ethical egoism.

2. Utilitarianism

One way to address the morality of whistleblowing is to examine the consequences thereof. Of course, ethical egoism is a consequentialist type of ethical theory, but with the consequences impacting "merely" oneself. Focusing on consequences lies at the heart of the Utilitarian ethical theory too. According to Utilitarianism, a moral action is one which produces the greatest amount of good for the greatest number of people. The object is to create the greatest amount of pleasure, in the sense of happiness and satisfaction, for humankind, while incurring the least amount of pain. Utilitarianism, though another example of a consequentialist-based ethical theory, clearly is one with a much broader approach than only focusing on how the consequences of an action impact on oneself. Utilitarianism, rather, involves an examination of how the consequences of an action impact on a much wider range of constituent groups, or "stakeholders" in a business context. The Utilitarian, therefore, after identifying the action for ethical evaluation, determines those people and groups directly and indirectly affected by the action. The Utilitarian then attempts to ascertain consequences of the action, good and bad, on the affected parties. Next, the "pleasures" or benefits to be gained from the action, whistleblowing herein, must be balanced, weighed, and measured against any "pains" or harms to the "stakeholders" that may be caused by "blowing the whistle." The tasks of predicting, measuring, and weighing are, admittedly, very challenging components to this presumably "scientific," mathematical, ethical theory. The first question pursuant to a Utilitarian ethical analysis of whistleblowing is to ascertain exactly these "stakeholders." That is, who are the people or groups who are affected directly as well as indirectly by the action of whistleblowing? The major stakeholder groups for whistleblowing are as follows: employees, employers, and society as a whole; and other constituent groups that must be covered are customers, suppliers and distributors, and government and the legal system.

The employer as a stakeholder group surely will benefit, as was mentioned in the preceding ethical egoistic section, from encouraging, and even rewarding, internal whistleblowing. It may seem to the employer that it is beneficial to get rid of trouble-making "snitches," but that kind of a notion is highly fallacious, and a much too short-term rationalism. Actually, it is in the long-term interest of the employer to make its employees believe that reporting wrongdoing internally is part of their jobs. It may be painful in the short-term to expose improprieties, especially at the higher levels of the firm, but the "cost" of investigating, acknowledging, and remedying any wrongdoing internally is surely less than the "expense" of governmental inquiries and proceedings, more regulations, private law suits, and scandal and shame. These types of whistleblowing employees, who "blow the whistle" properly, and for the right reason, are the very ones that the prudent employer wants to retain, and certainly not drive away. Of course, there is always a risk that there may a lessening of perceived loyalty in the organization, or the creation of some suspicion, distrust, and strife, all of which can hinder efficiency; but if the whistleblowing employee's assertion is handled internally in a prompt, fair, objective, and non-retaliatory manner, the firm will benefit in the long-run. The employees will realize that their employer is a legal and moral one that wants to act in a proper manner, that reform can be achieved internally, and that the employer is desirable place to work. Thus, the true loyalty on the part of the whistleblowing employee will be recognized and rewarded.

Customers, suppliers, and distributors, as well as government and the legal system, also will benefit when the employer maintains compliance with the law and moral standards, learns about problems early, takes any corrective actions promptly and internally, and thereby achieves self-improvement and a self-governing status. The employer, now with a deserved meritorious reputation for legality and morality, concomitantly benefits from the increased customer base, more stable business relationships, and less government interference. Retaliating against legitimate whistleblowers clearly sends the "wrong signal" to all the firm's stakeholder groups, and consequently will harm the employer in the long-term; whereas effectively and fairly dealing with whistleblowing will produce a benefit to the company by affirming its commitment to the values of legality and morality.

The employees are naturally one of the important stakeholder groups for analysis. Employees include the whistleblowing employee, naturally, as well as his or her fellow employees. There is, of course, some real risk and danger to the whistleblowing employee, and his or her family, notably in the form of job loss, financial hardship, and career disruption, despite the existence of many specific, and some general, whistleblower protection laws. Moreover, it may be personally "painful," especially in an emotional sense, for the employee to "blow the whistle," particularly publicly, on his or her firm and co-workers. Nonetheless, the whistleblower's perceived loyalty to his or her firm must be weighed against his or her responsibility to protect fellow employees as well as to serve the public interest. Yet, if the employer has in place internal channels for whistleblowing, an atmosphere of encouragement and non-intimidation, as well as a strict policy of non-retaliation, and a corporate culture of legality and morality, the employee's concerns and fears, especially about being a "disloyal" employee, should be mitigated accordingly. The whistleblower's rectitude and courage should be duly noted and rewarded.

Concerning the whistleblower's fellow employees, they also will benefit in the long-term by the exposure of wrongdoing in their firm. They also may benefit in the short-term too, if the whistleblowing involves a company practice or policy that is harmful to the employees. However, the employees as a whole do have the legitimate concern of false accusations of wrongdoing being leveled at them by jealous and spiteful co-workers. Yet if the employer has in place policies and mechanisms to ensure prompt and impartial investigation and resolution of all whistleblowing charges, the fear of victimization should be mollified accordingly, with the employees as a whole thereby benefiting from the whistleblowing.

The final and major stakeholder group to any Utilitarian ethical analysis of whistleblowing is society as a whole. There is clearly in the vast majority of cases a benefit for society that is caused by proper whistleblowing. Harm to the public is stopped or prevented; illegalities and improprieties are exposed; fraud, gross waste and mismanagement are revealed and curtailed; obedience to law and morality is upheld; and the public interest is thereby served and enhanced. Whistleblowing thus serves a socially useful purpose, typically outweighing any perceived duties of loyalty and confidentiality to the firm.

While an action, such as whistleblowing, consequently may "pass" the Utilitarian ethical test, and thus be adjudged as moral, it nonetheless may inflict harm on an individual or "stakeholder" group. A Kantian moral philosopher would be concerned with any harm inflicted on any individual or group in a utilitarian effort to maximize the greater good.

3. Kantian Ethics

Kant's supreme ethical principle, called the Categorical Imperative, disregards consequences in determining moral judgments, a concept plainly diametrically opposed to Utilitarianism. In order to be deemed "moral" pursuant to Kantian ethics, a practice, rule, or law must "pass" the formal ethical test of the Categorical Imperative. Therefore, even if more good consequences than bad ensue from whistleblowing, one should still subject the practice to Kant's formal test and thereby perhaps reach a different view of the practice's morality. At the heart of the Categorical Imperative is the "Kingdom of Ends" principle, which demands that one treat all rational beings as worthwhile "ends" and not as mere "means." That is, people, because of their status as reasoning beings, must be accorded dignity and respect. They cannot be used as mere instrumentalities or "things." Any action or practice that is demeaning or disrespectful to human beings, or that abuses or exploits them, is immoral pursuant to the Categorical Imperative. This ethical test, however, does not mean that one cannot hire and retain employees to accomplish a business purpose; but an employer always must remember that employees, even whistleblowing employees, are human beings and not machines or inanimate objects.

Kant therefore would counsel the whistleblower to do what is morally right, for the right reason, in the right way, and, moreover, to "blow the whistle" regardless of the personal consequences to the whistleblower. The whistleblowing at-will employee thus may lose his or her job, but will keep his or her Kantian self-respect. Kantian ethics, moreover, would dictate that the whistleblower, in "blowing the whistle," possess the right motive and neither disrespect nor demean any individual. The whistleblower, however, not only must have a strong sense of ethics, Kantian ethics especially, but also the strength of character, the "good will," as Kant would say, to command oneself to do what is morally required. If the whistleblower acts in a malicious or "machiavellian" manner, makes false accusations, engages in personal attacks, and unfairly accuses fellow employees of impropriety, perhaps out of "pure" spite, or disappointment, or revenge, or maybe to sabotage another's career and remove a "competitor," then obviously the whistleblower is violating Kantian ethical norms and is acting immorally. Treating people with dignity and respect, as demanded by Kantian ethics, also would require that the whistleblower not engage in any prying and not intrude into others' personal and private lives. In addition, since whistleblowing often involves very serious accusations being made, which can irreparably harm people, the whistleblower owes a moral duty to those charged with wrongdoing to make sure that the charges are well-founded, factually grounded, verifiable, and corroborated to the fullest degree practicable. Finally, in order to meet the moral obligations imposed by Kantian ethics, the whistleblower cannot remain anonymous. Fair treatment requires that the whistleblower identify himself or herself, as well as accept full responsibility for "blowing the whistle." Disclosure of the whistleblower's identity will serve two meritorious purposes: the whistleblowing itself will be taken more seriously, since it will be coming from an identified source, possessing a motive and corroborating information that can be objectively examined; and the accused person thereby can better defend himself or herself against the charges. Making anonymous accusations and generating unacknowledged rumors are clearly immoral demeaning practices that "fail" Kantian ethics.

One problem inherent in Kantian ethics is the possibility that two secondary moral rules, both of which "pass" the Categorical Imperative, conflict. This dilemma is particularly apparent in a whistleblowing, private sector, business situation. It can be posited that employees have an ethically mandated moral duty of loyalty, confidentiality, and obedience to their firms. No duty of loyalty, however, can ever require that an employee commit an illegal or immoral act. Yet it also can be postulated that employees have in addition a moral right to free speech in the workplace. This moral right, at a minimum, should include the right to criticize one's employer as well as to "blow the whistle" on illegal and wrongful business conduct that harms society. The problem is that all these secondary moral rules theoretically "pass" Kant's Categorical Imperative; yet they clash in practice. Consequently, whistleblowing, for ethical as well as legal, practical, and emotional reasons, emerges as such a tumultuous arena of clashing duties and concerns.

Yet is there an ethical solution to this Kantian "conflict" problem? Perhaps the resolution is to qualify the general duties of loyalty and confidentiality. That is, to maintain generally that employees do owe a moral duty of loyalty and confidentiality to their employers, but also to maintain that this moral duty is not unlimited. The general duty thus can be superseded by special circumstances, such as when the employee not only has a moral right to free speech, but also an ethical obligation to "blow the whistle" to stop or prevent wrongdoing that will harm the public interest. That is, the employee's duty to society and the public interest can prevail over the employee's obligation of loyalty to the firm, even if that societal duty may involve reporting the firm's wrongdoing externally to government authorities. True loyalty to the firm, therefore, is the recognition and respect of the true interests and goals of the firm. Whistleblowing employees acting with justification thus are very loyal employees who are morally obligated to take that often difficult step to "blow the whistle" on their firms' wrongdoing. The whistleblowing employee's loyalty and duty are pledged, in the Kantian sense, to the highest ethical principle, the Categorical Imperative.

4. Morally Required Whistleblowing

The logical ethical issue arises, therefore, as to when and under what circumstances is whistleblowing morally required. In exceptional circumstances, whistleblowing can be deemed to be morally obligatory. Based on the aforementioned DeGeorge moral rule and the preceding ethical analysis, the following requirements must be satisfied: First, the business or its employees are violating the law, or threatening to do so, or they are engaging in some activity that is seriously harmful to the firm and its "stakeholders," including society. Second, the whistleblowing employee must possess a reasonable and good faith belief that the wrongdoing has occurred, or will occur, in the near future. Third, the employee must have made a good faith attempt to report in writing the wrongdoing to his or her immediate supervisor, and then through internal managerial channels to the "top" of the firm if necessary. Fourth, when these efforts at internal whistleblowing have failed, and the employee is the "last resort" to stop or prevent the wrongdoing or harm because no one else can or will do it, then, finally, the employee is morally obligated to externally "blow the whistle" on his or her firm's wrongdoing, and regardless of the consequences to himself or herself.

5. Conclusion

Three moral conclusions based on the preceding ethical analysis can be offered. First, regarding the employer, the ethical egoism (as well as legal) analysis conducted herein clearly indicate that it is in the employer's self-interest, and thus moral, not only not to retaliate against good faith whistleblowers but also to encourage them internally. Second, "blowing the whistle" by an employee may be morally justified or permitted, based on Utilitarian ethical principles so long as Kantian ethical principles are not contravened. The most difficult moral dilemma arises as to whether a moral duty can be ethically imposed on an employee to "blow the whistle." That is, can whistleblowing be mandated morally on the part of the employee, who may be exposing himself or herself to great risk, to the degree that if the employee does not "blow the whistle," and thus violates the moral duty, the employee can be rightfully condemned as immoral? Such a scenario or morally required whistleblowing can indeed arise, but only in certain aforementioned circumstances when the employee is the whistleblower of "last resort." Such a moral result is in accord with Utilitarian as well as Kantian ethical principles. Pursuant to Utilitarianism, the greater good of society is achieved, thus making the action moral under that ethical theory. Moreover, pursuant to Kantian ethics, the principle as explicated herein can be made into a universal maxim and neither demeans nor disrespects anyone. Of course, as Kant would say, does the employee possess the strength of character, the Kantian "good will," to do what the moral "law" requires him or her to do, that is, to "blow the whistle"?

Discussion Questions

1. If a corporation squanders its assets, who should be held accountable: the shareholders or the leadership of the corporation?
2. Are fines sufficient punishments for illegal and immoral acts committed by a corporation?
3. If a corporation is guaranteed freedom of speech under the 1st Amendment, should it be allowed to say whatever it wants?
4. Although the corporation is an artificial construct, can it be morally or ethically evaluated as a person could?
5. When conflicts of interest arise between shareholders, employees, consumers and possibly the general public, to whom does the corporation owe its ultimate allegiance?

6. If it is determined that a corporate culture is deemed to be unethical in nature, how can one change this to encourage moral and ethical behavior, and who is responsible for carrying this out?

7. What should be contained in a corporate code of ethics?

8. How should violations to this code of ethics be handled?

9. What checks should be put in place to ensure that the code of ethics is being ingrained in the company hierarchy?

10. What rights (if any) should be extended to protect employees of private corporations from retaliation for "whistleblowing?"

CHAPTER 14

Global Ethics and the Environment

I. Multinational Corporations and Ethics

A. Introduction and Overview

Multinational corporations are companies that conduct business extensively in more than one country, usually through divisions or subsidiaries involved in production, service, and/or marketing. In foreign "host" countries, the multinationals ordinarily will confront laws, practices, customs, and levels of development that often are much different from those of the "home" country. In particular, a multinational may encounter different moral standards in the various foreign countries in which it operates, creating a moral dilemma as to the proper moral standard to be followed and implemented.

What should the management of the multinational do? If management adheres to legal positivism, it need only obey the host country's law and its own country's law (presuming its own country has any extrajurisdictional reach). If management follows ethical relativism, it merely needs to ascertain the moral norms of the country or society in which the company is doing business and comply with those norms.

Yet, based on further ethical analysis, it may be immoral for the multinational to go along with local law and custom. A complete ethical evaluation must be conducted by the ethics department to determine if the company's actions in the host country are moral pursuant to utilitarian and Kantian ethical analysis. If an action is deemed immoral yet is legally required by the host country's law, such as the former legalized race discrimination of apartheid in South Africa, the multinational must be prepared to forego the economic opportunity or plan to withdraw from the country. If doing business in the host country involves a local custom or practice that is immoral, though not legally required, the question then becomes whether the multinational can successfully conduct business in the host country without engaging in the immoral practice; and if not, the multinational must be prepared to forego the business opportunity or plan to withdraw from the country.

B. Foreign Payments

1. Introduction and Overview

Doing business globally raises the difficult issue of payments to foreign officials. A multinational may feel pressured into paying money or transferring something of value to a foreign official in order to protect a business investment, secure a business opportunity, or to facilitate the performance of some service in the host country.

There are several types of questionable foreign payments. For example, there are outright bribes that are demanded of the multinational in order to obtain new business. These payments very well may be illegal under the host or home country's law. "Defensive" payments also may be sought. These are payments made by the multinational to protect its existing business operations from adverse actions. "Grease" payments are smaller payments made to minor foreign officials in order to facilitate a routine lawful action, such as processing goods through customs. There are, finally, political contributions, which may or may not be illegal; the multinational managers must exercise very careful legal, ethical, and business judgment before making them.

To illustrate that corruption is a global phenomena, the MBA students of the authors of this book have related many instances of questionable payments being requested by foreign officials in the course of the students' international business dealings. For example, one student related that in order to process applications for security permits in a South American country, a $100 bill would have to be attached to each application as an additional "processing fee." Another student related that it would cost $200 to have a particular small product or product part released from customs in an Asian country. Yet another student mentioned that in order to have the utility services for a business promptly turned on in a Caribbean nation, an additional payment of $3,500 would be necessary; otherwise, one would be placed on "the list." In a most unusual case, in another South American country, as related by another student, the local military commander at a check point required a fee for the prompt processing of a vehicle convoy through the checkpoint. What was interesting was that the official wanted not money, but fancy bathroom tile as his wife had remodeling plans. Finally, as reported in a South Florida newspaper, one should be prepared if one is opening a restaurant business in Mexico City to make a payment of about $1,300 to quickly secure an operating license. Actually, according to Transparencia Mexicana, which is the Mexican chapter of the global anti-corruption organization Transparency International, it is estimated that as much as 9% of Mexico's gross domestic national product is siphoned off annually to corruption. That 9% amounted in 2005 to $69 billion, which is more than Mexico spends on education and defense combined. According to the Center for Economic Studies of the Private Sector in Mexico City, one in five businesses in Mexico admits to making questionable payments; and according to Transparencia Mexicana, in 2005, more than one in ten transactions for public services involved questionable payments. In 2005, moreover, Transparencia Mexicana estimated that Mexicans paid out $2 billion to public servants in more than 115 million acts of corruption. It also should be noted that Transparency International regularly rates countries for bribe-paying and bribe-seeking proclivity as well as corruption. For example, in 2006, that organization in its Bribe Payers Index reported that Indian, Chinese, Russian, and Turkish companies in that order are the most prolific bribe-payers when doing business abroad, and Swiss, Swedish, Australian, and Austrian companies are the least likely to bribe.

2. The Foreign Corrupt Practices Act

The Foreign Corrupt Practices Act is a U.S. statute that prohibits U.S. companies from bribing foreign officials when seeking business in foreign countries. The act imposes civil and criminal liability for paying anything of value to a foreign official possessing discretionary authority if the purpose of the payment is "corrupt," that is, to influence the foreign official to act to assist the company in obtaining or retaining business.

Although the act is broadly written and has extraterritorial effect, its reach may not include the payments to government employees to perform routine ministerial or clerical duties. These payments, called expediting, facilitating, or "grease" payments, are used to get minor foreign officials to perform usual services that they might refuse to perform, or perform very slowly, without such payments. Examples of routine government actions would include obtaining permits and licenses, processing government "paperwork," such as visas, providing police protection, mail services, and inspections, providing utility and telephone service, loading and unloading cargo, and protecting goods. The act also may not reach payments to foreign corporate executives, and major shareholders of foreign firms, as well as foreign "political contributions." The act, finally, permits legitimate and reasonable payments to foreign officials, for example, for travel and lodging expenses, if the payments are related directly to a firm's explanation or demonstration of its products or services.

The Foreign Corrupt Practices Act, therefore, has the potential to legalize "bribery." Yet, assuming a U.S. multinational's ethical analysis extends, as it should, beyond legal positivism, the issue emerges as to whether it is moral to bribe legally.

3. Ethical Considerations

In order to explicate the ethical aspects of bribery in an international setting, assume a situation, as originally proposed by Richard DeGeorge, where a sales and marketing representative of a U.S. multinational in precarious financial condition is in the final stages of negotiating a contract for the sale of a substantial quantity of goods to the government of a rapidly developing foreign country. The contract is very important to the company because it provides a significant infusion of money as well as an entry to a foreign market. The contract, moreover, personally is very important to the company's marketing/sales representative and would secure the representative a promotion and substantial raise. All appears to be proceeding well—the company's offer is viewed very favorably by the foreign government and the foreign country would in fact secure a very good deal by accepting the U.S. multinational's offer to contract. The U.S. multinational's representative seems assured of success until the representative is confronted by a key foreign government official, who also looks upon the company's offer favorably but demands a large "consulting fee" to process properly the paperwork and thus secure the contract. If the fee is not paid, the official will reopen the bidding and the contract may go to a competitor. The representative is acutely aware of the critical nature of the deal, knows that the sum is immaterial when compared to the contract price and the profits to be realized, and has heard that such payments are a common and lawful practice in the foreign country, but feels that making such payments are not quite right and may be illegal under U.S. law. What is the right, moral decision for the representative to make? Such an inquiry leads one directly into the field of applied ethics.

If one is a legal positivist, one simply would advise the representative to determine the legality of the payment. If it is legal under the foreign country's law, and it is legal under the Foreign Corrupt Practices Act exception for expediting and facilitating payments for ministerial actions (such as, perhaps, the mere processing of the lowest bid), then this legal action is also a moral action pursuant to legal positivism.

If one is an ethical emotist, one would advise the representative to get in "touch" with his or her feelings. If he or she feels "bad" about the payment, then it's immoral; if "good," then it is moral. Of course, he or she can always have a change of heart by merely having a different emotion about the payment at a later, perhaps more critical, date.

If one adheres to the doctrine of ethical egoism, the analysis is twofold: is it in the representative's best long-term interest, as agent of the multinational, to pay the bribe; and is it in the interest of the multinational, as the corporate entity, for its representative to pay the bribe? The representative must calculate whether the risks to his or her career, reputation, conscience, and even freedom will supersede the potential personal benefits from paying the bribe, securing the contract, and thus the promotion and raise. The multinational must determine whether the assertion and defense of its legitimate and critical business interests in the foreign country are worth the legal risks as well as risks to the company's reputation. An intelligent ethical egoist also could argue that even if the "bribe" is deemed immoral, the fact that its nonpayment is such a dangerous threat to the company's very existence, the issue of duress as a moral defense arises to counter any charge of immorality.

An ethical relativist simply would tell the company and its representative to ascertain whether such payments are an accepted standard and locally unobjectionable practice in the foreign country; if so, paying the "bribe" may be quite moral.

A utilitarian, of course, would be concerned with the consequences of paying or not paying the bribe. If the bribe is not paid, the company, its shareholders, employees, and suppliers all will suffer a severe financial loss. If, however, the bribe is paid, all these preceding groups benefit, as well as the sales representative, who gets a promotion and raise; the foreign official, who gets the money; the foreign government, which gets a "good" price for a "good" product; and the foreign consumers, who get a quality product. If the bribe is paid, the competition does not get the contract; yet none of the company's competitors had the low bid anyway, so what is the real harm? Paying a bribe, however, usually is construed as adversely affecting the society of the "host" country. Bribery's net effect is to reduce market competition by engendering unequal competition and by erecting additional barriers to market entry. The "best" bribers thus begin to achieve monopoly status, with the distinct possibility of exhibiting the inefficiencies characteristic of monopolies, such as higher prices and lower quality. However, if this instance of bribery under consideration is viewed as an exception, and if one is an Act utilitarian, the harm to society is reduced accordingly and this "pain" is subject to being outweighed by the greater good produced for all the other affected groups and people.

Disregard these consequences, good or otherwise, of paying the bribe, a Kantian would argue. Rather, apply the Categorical Imperative to determine if bribery is moral. Applying the first test, a Kantian would argue that bribery cannot be realized as a consistently universal practice. Assuming everyone bribed in a similar fashion, the action "bribe" would no longer be able to sustain itself. Since everyone is bribing, "bribing" loses its efficacy; it contradicts itself, becomes nonsensical, and self-destructs. Bribery, therefore, is immoral.

Bribery with qualification, however, is a different matter. Bribery, in the case herein, saves one's company from financial ruin, secures a contract that is a "good deal" for the host government and country when the bribing company is in fact the lowest bidder, and induces the foreign government official to perform his or her public duty of merely awarding the contract. With such qualifications, "bribery" can be made consistently universal. Not everyone is bribing, and the bribe, because it is qualified, will secure results in the limited circumstances presented.

Although bribery qualified arguably can pass Kant's first test, the issue arises as to whether a qualified bribery action will pass the second and third parts of the Categorical Imperative. Does bribery treat all the parties involved with dignity and respect, particularly the official and the company's representative "pressured" to pay the bribe? Would paying the bribe be acceptable to a rational person if he or she did not know his or her status as the "giver" (or agent) of the action or the receiver? Would a rational person want to be placed in the role of the competition in a bribery scenario? Such questions clearly illustrate the strictness of Kantian ethics and the difficulty of even a qualified "wrongful" action passing the Categorical Imperative.

C. Plant Closings, Relocations, Outsourcing, and Offshoring

1. Introduction

Plant closings, in response to foreign competition, and plant relocations, primarily to foreign locales, impose severe costs on the relocating company's employees, community, and society, yet they may benefit other stakeholders, domestic as well as foreign. Plant closings, relocations, and offshoring may be unavoidable in a global market economy; they even may be necessary. The issue arises, however, as to whether they are moral.

2. The "Plant Closing" Law

Before discussing the morality of plant closings, the issue of the legality of such an action must be addressed briefly. The federal plant closing law, known as the Worker Adjustment and Retaining Notification Act, requires a 60-day advance notice for plant closings and mass layoffs. It is important to note that the law does not prohibit any plant closing or layoff; neither does it mandate that a company obtain the approval of a government agency, nor does it require severance pay or any other benefit. The law does not cover all employers, only those employing 100 or more employees; and the law contains an exemption for a plant closure that results from unforeseeable business developments.

The plant closing law's notice provisions do provide a "moral minimum" to the employees. Warning employees at least affords them the opportunity to begin looking for work earlier; they thus are less likely to be unemployed, and if so, for shorter periods of time. The larger moral problem arises, however, as to whether it is even moral to close the plant, especially when the plant is being relocated to a foreign locale.

3. Ethical Considerations

In order to explicate fully the moral issues that arise in a plant closing case, it is efficacious to use a case study approach. Assume a pharmaceutical company is contemplating closing one of its U.S. plants and moving the operations to a foreign locale in order to take advantage of the lower wage scales there. A utilitarian first would identify those people and groups directly and indirectly affected by the action of closing the plant. Those directly affected are the company, its employees, shareholders, suppliers, and consumers, the local community, as well as the competition; those indirectly affected are the family members of employees, labor unions, government, and society; and also affected are the potential employees in the foreign locale, as well as its government and society.

The first major stakeholder group affected by the plant closing and relocation is the company's employees. They, of course, are drastically affected. They more often than likely will experience financial losses, including the loss of wages and benefits, as well as forced relocation expenses, perhaps including a loss on the sale of a home. All these financial losses could jeopardize the employees' personal credit ratings. The employees also will experience a loss of self-esteem and emotional problems resulting from a loss of their jobs; this loss will increase their stress levels, perhaps resulting in a rise in alcoholism and domestic violence. These employees obviously are negatively affected.

The company and its shareholders, the owners, initially will sustain some negative effects from the plant closure and relocation. These include the costs of closure and relocation, securing and training personnel at the new foreign location, higher distribution costs, and perhaps some legal costs involved in the closure. These negative aspects, however, are far outweighed by the considerably cheaper labor costs the company, and ultimately the shareholders, will enjoy in the new location as profitability increases.

Some consumers may be angry at the company for abandoning U.S. workers, and some may even boycott the company, but the vast majority of the consumers will be quite pleased when they are assured that the company's products will be available at a much lower price.

The company's local suppliers will be negatively affected due to a loss of a percentage of their sales. Other local support businesses also will be negatively affected, for example, office supply stores, printers, and uniform companies. They too will lose a percentage of their income. All their pain, however, will be counterbalanced by the pleasure felt by the company's expanding foreign supplier network.

Another group directly affected is the competition. Competitors initially may experience a loss of profit due to the company's price and profit advantages, but the competition can regain its market share and profitability by also moving some of its facilities to more cost-effective foreign locales.

There are groups that are indirectly affected by the company's move. The family members of plant employees of course will be negatively affected. They must deal with a lower household income; relocation stresses, such as a change of school for children; and marital problems, especially if one spouse is forced to relocate. The local community also is adversely affected. Local merchants for example, who provided food, clothing, shelter, and other goods and services will lose a percentage of their sales as employees and others will buy in smaller quantities while other people will move away completely. Other merchants, who supply entertainment and luxury goods, should expect an even greater percentage loss of their sales. As with the suppliers, however, the pain inflicted on these merchants and the larger local community will be counterbalanced by the pleasure derived by the local community and its merchants in the foreign locale as the company expands its operations and employment base there.

Labor unions in the U.S. will lose membership dues and income as well as a loss of goodwill and power. Local government will suffer a lower tax base and a higher demand for certain costly services, such as welfare, police, and public hospital care. The federal government will likewise suffer some adverse effects, such as increased welfare and unemployment compensation claims, as well as a reduction of personal income taxes. The fact that the company will remain competitive and profitable by making the move overseas will generate increased corporate tax revenue for the federal government.

Society in the U.S. will have to absorb some of the preceding costs, yet it will benefit by having a strong, global economic "player" providing goods at competitive prices. The foreign society definitely will benefit. The move certainly will create jobs for the citizens of the foreign society. There will be an infusion of capital into the foreign economy and a boost to the foreign society as a whole.

All the preceding "pleasures" and "pains" now should be quantified and calculated in order to arrive at a utilitarian moral conclusion. In so doing, it is quite possible that the overall maximization of good will be achieved by the company closing its U.S. facility and moving the plant overseas; if that is the case, the plant relocation is moral, even though it caused a degree of pain to employees and other groups.

Utilitarianism, however, is just one ethical theory. A Kantian would apply Kant's Categorical Imperative to determine the morality of this particular action. When Kant's first test in the Categorical Imperative—the "consistently universal" standard—is applied, the act of "plant closure" appears to be self-contradictory and self-destructive. If all plants were closed, everywhere, there would not be any plants remaining to close, and the act, in its broadest formulation, would not pass the first test, and thus it is immoral! If, however, qualifications were added to the action, it would be possible to state logically that plant closings under certain limited circumstances would pass the first test. For example, if only those plants that were demonstrated by outside consultants not to be profitable were allowed to close and relocate, then this limited action could be made consistently universal. Not all plants would be closing, only certain ones, and thus the action could be performed indefinitely and still achieve results.

Kant's Categorical Imperative, one recalls, has second and third parts, devised to "check" any immoral "residualness" left by the first part. How would the action of plant closure, even with the previous qualification, face under the second and third tests? The second test requires that no one be used as a means. In this situation, the employees, as rational beings, are being used as a means to an end. They are being treated without dignity and respect and, therefore, the plant closing would fail the second test. If the act was applied to Kant's third test, the agent-receiver test, a rational person could not accept the action of closing the plant. The possibility of loss is too great to accept the risk; hence, the plant closing is immoral. The action, however, could be qualified further in order to help make the closing of the plant moral under the strict demands of the second and third tests. It is essential, as a moral minimum, that the company take steps to minimize the harmful effects of the closing and relocation on its stakeholder groups, especially the employees. The employees, for example, must be informed sufficiently about the impending closure and allowed to participate in the closure decision. Perhaps the employees can be given the opportunity to purchase the plant and operate it themselves. The company should offer the employees a feasible relocation option, as well as job retraining, placement, and counseling. The employees, finally, should be given an early retirement option and severance pay. The harm to the local community can be lessened if the company, as a moral minimum, makes a good faith-effort to sell the plant facilities and property to a new industry that would take over the site and provide a continuing employment base. By attaching all these conditions to the action of plant closure and relocation, the action can pass the Categorical Imperative and thus be deemed moral.

4. Moving Dangerous Industries Overseas

A) INTRODUCTION

To complicate the moral situation even further, assume that the industry to be relocated overseas involves a dangerous and risky type of work and that the foreign local does not require legally the same level of health and safety safeguards as required by U.S. law. By moving the plant and operating overseas without U.S. level safeguards, is the company acting morally? The discussion that follows is based on an ethical analysis in Richard DeGeorge's 2006 book, *Business Ethics*.

Risk is an unavoidable part of many types of work, and it is too facile a moral conclusion to say that it is immoral to hire anyone to do work that is in some way dangerous to life or health. Any job may be dangerous in some way, but some workplace dangers may be prevented or lessened, and a company may be condemned as immoral for exposing its employees to such risks. A company's foreign workers are especially vulnerable in this regard due to the absence in many foreign locales of safety and health laws comparable to U.S. legal requirements. The morality of the matter is often further complicated in the international setting when a foreign government attacks U.S. "moralizers" as "cultural imperialists" who do not fully understand the needs and aspirations of the people of the foreign country and who will impose moral conditions that will impede the development of the foreign country.

B) UTILITARIANISM

One ethical way to approach the problem of transferring a dangerous industry abroad is to perform a utilitarian analysis. The move is good for the U.S. company and its shareholders, particularly if the company was in financial distress, and also is good for its consumers. The move is very good for the foreign society and its economy. Since its economy is probably labor intensive and capital poor, it needs to attract foreign industry and investment. Industry will bring in tax and other revenues, provide employment for people who probably would remain unemployed and thus burdensome; and industry will provide training and help develop the potential of the workforce and the society. The company will further boost the economy by purchasing materials locally, establishing local supplier networks; its workers in turn will use their wages to buy local goods and services and thus uplift others in the economy. The foreign government that gains from an increase in revenue very well may have made a decision to allow a level of unsafe conditions by the absence of legislation as a necessary tradeoff to encourage the development of industry in the country. The foreign country workers, finally, may choose, perhaps eagerly, to work in the dangerous industry, as opposed to not working at all. There, of course, will be "pains" associated with such a move, and especially on the part of those foreign employees who are harmed by the unsafe conditions. Yet not all workers will be harmed and many will prosper (at least by local standards), and thus the conclusion under utilitarianism, particularly the Act version, may be that the "pleasure" produced by the move outweighs the "pain," and the move is therefore moral.

Yet even if more "good" than "bad" results, the move nonetheless may not seem "right" and fair, especially to the foreign workers who are having these dangerous conditions actually imposed on them, even though they may be aware of the dangers and agree to work.

c) Kant's Categorical Imperative

Is it possible to construct a moral rule that would permit ethically, pursuant to Kant's strict test, a company to relocate in the foreign locale a dangerous industry? A proposed moral rule must address four key points: informed consent, worker pay, risk minimization, and employee health care. For the company to employ foreign workers without informing them of the risks involved certainly fails the Categorical Imperative. The company must inform the prospective employees of the risk and they must freely and knowingly choose to accept that risk. Consent, even informed consent, is not alone sufficient morally because the foreign workers may be so poor that they would agree to work under any circumstances, regardless of risk and level of pay. Accordingly, a moral company must pay the workers more for the risks inherent in the work. It is not necessary that the company pay the foreign workers the same amount it would pay U.S. workers in a U.S. plant. However, it must pay a risk-premium wage comparable to that paid in other similar economies and labor markets. Assuming differences in economies in the different parts of the world, wage differences can be morally justifiable; but employees must be compensated for assuming greater risks. Even with the added element of higher pay, the company still needs to lower the danger level to some acceptable standard. It may not be necessary for the company to achieve a foreign safety standard equivalent to U.S. legal standards; but the company, in order to be moral, must observe at least minimal safety and health precautions. The company, finally, should provide a suitable level of health and safety benefits to its employees, some of whom may be injured or harmed from the dangerous work. If these four requirements are complied with, the company will be allowed to relocate a facility involving dangerous work to a foreign locale; and to do so morally pursuant to Kant's Categorical Imperative. The foreign workers are not being treated as mere "means," and a rational person would accept the action even with the possibility of playing the role of the foreign worker. This action, moreover, can be made "consistently universal" under Kant's first test.

d) Global Monitoring Efforts

In a laudatory ethical effort to ensure that workers anywhere in the world, especially those provided very little legal protection by their own countries, are treated with dignity and respect, several international organizations as well as multinational corporations have sought to devise minimum health, safety, and wage standards for workers, as well as to inspect and monitor factories to ensure that the standards are followed. The standards, for example, prohibit child or forced labor, forced or excessive overtime, too long a workweek (with standards ranging from 48 to 60 hours), "sweatshop" or unsafe conditions, as well as require that a "fair wage" or "living wage" be paid (as opposed to the legal minimum wage). The Fair Labor Association is one organization that will do random, unannounced inspections of a member company and its foreign manufacturers and suppliers. The Fair Labor Association also has a certificate process, whereby companies that agree to be monitored and adhere to the organization's standards will be granted a "stamp of approval" on their goods. Another organization is Social Accountability International, which requires its member employers to pay their employees a "living wage," which is established for each country based on the ascertaining the basic needs of workers in relation to the local living standard and the local price of goods and services. The Worker Rights Consortium is a group that has been pressuring multinational firms to release the names of all their factories; however, the Consortium states that it will not release the information to the public unless serious abuses are revealed at a particular facility. Nike, for example, after years of refusal, recently released the names of all of its factories around the world. Another international monitoring organization designed to protect workers and to enforce labor standards is the Fair Factories Clearinghouse. It is a joint effort launched in 2006 by L.L. Bean, Reebok, Timberland, Sears, Roebuck & Co., and other companies, which sets acceptable labor standards, such as the absence of dangerous work conditions and not using child labor. The objective is to obtain and share social compliance information on the many factories that the companies use to make their products. Once one plant is duly certified by an independent and reputable agency, other companies can accept the results, and use that production facility. Another goal is for the buyers to be able to bring pressure on factories in foreign lands to improve working conditions. Factories that refuse to or fail to abide by the standards are removed from the "certified" list. Of course, it is strictly voluntary for a company to join these organizations, to abide by the standards, and to agree to be inspected and monitored. Yet, one can persuasively argue that it is in the ethically egoistic interest of these multinational firms to do the "right thing" as well as the "smart thing" and to help ensure that the workers who make their products are treated with dignity and respect.

E) SUMMARY

Kant's "consistently universal" standard, of course, is not equivalent to an international legal standard. However, until there are universal, international, enforceable legal standards regarding safety and health concerns in the workplace, the moral "law," as "enforced" by global monitoring organizations and consumer pressure, must serve to ensure justice in the workplace.

5. Outsourcing and Offshoring

A) INTRODUCTION

One controversial consequence of a global economy with a diverse and knowledgeable workforce is the recent phenomena of outsourcing or offshoring, whereby, in an effort to save money, many U.S. firms are relocating a steadily growing number of employees, as well as a wider range of positions, to foreign nations, especially China and India, in order to reduce labor costs. Initially, the jobs outsourced were manufacturing positions, but now the jobs involve the service sector, especially computer and technology support positions. Even such high-tech and traditional firms such as IBM are beginning to outsource positions. Developing nations now can offer to U.S. firms a college educated workforce as well as the technology and communication connections to sustain and integrate the foreign workforce. The foreign workers, of course, are paid a fraction of what U.S. employees would receive. The negative perception is that this aspect of globalization is causing a loss of U.S. jobs, with the United States receiving nothing in return, aside from increased unemployment.

The level of outsourcing is beginning to engender a fear of an exodus of U.S. jobs and increased unemployment, thereby creating a hot political issue. Consequently, this "exporting" of U.S. jobs has produced certain legislative efforts by the states to restrict the practice, for example, by banning companies with foreign employees from having state contracts, or by requiring foreign call-center workers to identify where they are located. Moreover, changes in the tax code are contemplated in an effort to discourage the out-sourcing of U.S. jobs.

The *Wall Street Journal* reported in February of 2007 that outsourcing now is "big business," to the extent that companies currently pay approximately $68 billion annually to other firms to manage and operate their computer systems, answer customer questions, respond to customer complaints, manage employee benefits, and perform other tasks. The *Wall Street Journal* also noted that there is now so much outsourcing that a whole new industry has developed—outsourcing consulting firms. According to the Journal, the managing director of one outsourcing consulting firm explained that outsourcing attempts often confront difficulties if their focus is primarily to reduce costs, since too much a cost reduction focus may cause the quality of the outsourced work to deteriorate. Moreover, the *Wall Street Journal* reported that today there is a professional outsourcing organization, called the International Association of Outsourcing Professionals which now claims more than 600 individual and corporate members, including Johnson and Johnson and Procter and Gamble. According to the Journal, the founders of the association want to establish professional outsourcing standards similar to those for lawyers and accountants. Outsourcing professional consultants perform a variety of functions for companies, for example, determining a company's outsourcing expectations, advising as to the success of achieving outsourcing goals, evaluating outsourcing bids, conducting site visits, making outsourcing recommendations, warning of possible problems and disruptions, and trying to minimize any negative consequences from outsourcing.

B) Utilitarianism

Legislating against outsourcing could have deleterious consequences for the world economic legal order, based on international economic and trade treaties that arguably could be contravened, by any state or federal attempt to hinder or ban outsourcing. The world economy also could be impaired as the goal has been to open up economic markets, create new markets for exports, and to improve the free flow of global trade. Erecting trade barriers by means of restrictions on employment could engender retaliation from the country's trading partners, or perhaps a wider trade "war." Free trade and global economic integration are not only Utilitarian "plusses" economically, but also politically.

The U.S. economy benefits when foreign firms outsource their jobs to the U.S., for example when a foreign firm, such as an auto company builds a plant in the U.S. or a foreign firm opens an office in the United States. The benefit to the United States is increased even further when the foreign firms out-source research, design, and development positions to the United States, for example in the pharmaceutical industry. Thus, a prime beneficiary of outsourcing is the United States, itself. If the United States resorts to job protectionism in an effort to shut out foreign competition, one consequence that is predicted is that the U.S. will hinder innovation and harm the economy, thereby ultimately producing even greater unemployment. The U.S. also will benefit when foreign countries, the beneficiaries of outsourcing, grow economically, and thus become more lucrative markets for U.S. exports.

U.S. companies certainly benefit from outsourcing. In addition to the savings in labor costs, the companies can use their offshoring facilities and personnel as an instrumentality to break into lucrative foreign markets. The companies also will benefit by hiring highly educated and skilled foreign workers, especially in the technological and scientific fields. These workers will help companies develop the next phase of wealth-creating technology. U.S. firms, moreover, will benefit from using the cost savings produced by outsourcing for new development and investment, as well as to pay even more for U.S. workers with world-class skills and knowledge. Even though some U.S. jobs will be lost by means of outsourcing, others will be created or expanded, and thus productivity overall will increase.

Consumers in the U.S. also will benefit from outsourcing since, for example, foreign programmers could produce software at lower prices than U.S. workers could. The positive result would be a reduction in costs for the many users of information technology. Similarly, if the costs of computers and communications equipment were reduced by outsourcing the work, the U.S. consumer would benefit from such international efficiency and the concomitant savings that will be passed on to consumers.

Even though there plainly will be "pain" for those U.S. workers whose jobs are outsourced, the fact that companies would remain flexible with regards to employment relationships, and accordingly become more productive and profitable, should mean that companies will be able to hire more employees, which is good overall for employees generally.

c) KANT'S CATEGORICAL IMPERATIVE

Treating employees with dignity and respect would require that the beneficiaries of outsourcing, the companies and their shareholders as well as society as a whole, mitigate the "pain" caused by outsourcing. Plainly, some workers will face difficulties when confronted with the new global economic realities. In particular, Kantian ethics would demand that U.S. firms and the nation itself must provide education and job training for those displaced employees who must now expand their skills and enhance their education, especially specialized training and schooling. U.S. companies and society as a whole have a moral obligation to help these displaced and dislocated workers adjust to the new global way of doing business. The greater the degree and scope of skill and education, the easier it will be for an out-sourced worker to find another position in the new global economy. This amelioration of the employee's discomforting "painful" situation can be effectuated by taxes paid by the nation as a whole and also by imposing a charge on the companies that benefit from outsourcing. The "pain" caused by outsourcing could also be remedied by spending more money on low-performing schools and under funded research centers. These macro as well as micro amelioration efforts will help to sustain and advance U.S.

workers and improve the country's global competitiveness too. Outsourcing should produce opportunities back in the United States for workers to move up the skill and pay ladder, assuming, of course, they are properly educated and trained, which is the right thing to do pursuant to Kantian ethics, and the smart thing to do pursuant to ethical egoism.

d) Conclusion

The ethical objective is certainly not to stifle the dynamic U.S. economy or restrict the world's increasingly integrated economy, which plainly would engender more "pain" than "pleasure" overall, but rather to help the United States as well as the rest of the world to prosper, but to attain this "good" Utilitarian goal in a manner that treats all the world's employees in a Kantian dignified and respectful manner.

II. Ethics and the Environment

A. Introduction

Environmental issues not only raise difficult, practical and legal problems for business people, but also confront ethics-based business leaders with challenging moral questions. Pollution, for example, of course involves harm to others. It thus has an ethical dimension; but, is an absolute ban on pollution morally required; and if not, how much pollution abatement is needed; and who is responsible for paying the "price" for any pollution? Moreover, what is the morally permissible extent of environmental harm produced by business expansion and technological development, and who should pay for the costs of protecting and preserving the environment. At the very least, a business enterprise has a duty to report, as part of its moral audit, any pollution and environmental harm it is causing. Yet, the larger environmental moral issues, such as whether a firm should be polluting at all, to what extent and how any such pollution should be handled morally, require extensive ethical analysis.

B. Utilitarianism

Is an absolute or near absolute ban on pollution morally required by the utilitarian ethical principle? Eliminating the first large amounts of pollutants naturally will be highly beneficial to people and to society. The costs from the harm produced by this degree of pollution are substantial. Individuals are directly harmed and society as a whole is indirectly harmed. Pollution allows the producer to pass off the true external costs of producing its products to society, which in turn engenders a misallocation of resources, unfair competition, and inefficient and wasteful manufacture and distribution. Pollution seriously harms the general welfare, yet only benefits the producer and its shareholders. Such gross pollution would cause more "pain" than "pleasure" and, therefore, is immoral under utilitarianism.

An absolute or near prohibition of pollution, however, may cause more "pain" than "pleasure." It may be possible for a firm to do too much in the area of pollution abatement. The cost of eliminating all or nearly all pollutants might be greater than the benefits that would accrue, thus resulting in a lessening of total utility. Allowing a firm to pollute and in effect to harm the environment may be morally acceptable, assuming the pollution and ensuing harm is minimal. Compelling a firm to eliminate the absolute last traces of pollutants and to safeguard totally the environment may cause serious harm to the firm, its shareholders and other constituent groups. By permitting the firm to pollute to an acceptable degree, the firm and its immediate "stakeholders" benefit, because the firm will not be compelled to absorb the potentially ruinous costs of eliminating all pollution and avoiding all harm. The customers who purchase the polluting company's products benefit because the company is able to continue manufacturing products, and the company will not be charging them for all the pollution abatement costs involved in making the product. Society benefits because economic activity not only continues but is accorded some latitude to expand. There are, of course, costs that are passed on to society, and some people and communities may be harmed by the pollution, yet the pollution produces greater good and is morally permissible under utilitarianism. Beyond this point, the firm, even though acting morally under this one ethical theory, should be a socially responsible firm and mitigate any harm inflicted, by paying for the costs of those people and communities directly harmed by the pollution.

A level of pollution and environmental harm, therefore, may be moral under utilitarianism; thus it will be morally permissible to impose some of the costs of this pollution and environmental harm on unwilling people and communities. Yet, such an imposition may contravene people's rights.

C. Kantian Ethics

Can pollution or environmental harm ever be permissible under Kant's Categorical Imperative? If the harm is serious, and preventable, it is not morally permissible, regardless of any compensation, because such pollution, together with the attempt to "buy people off," certainly does not treat them as "ends" but merely as "means." Such pollution must be prevented at its source and morally cannot be allowed to continue. If a firm does pollute, it must seek to clean up the pollution before it harms or further damages anyone or the environment. The costs for such pollution abatement and control must be borne by those who caused the pollution and have benefited from these activities. Such rules are dictated by Kant's "agent-receiver" test. If the harm is not serious, compensation to the adversely affected parties may be a suitable response; for example, noise pollution near an airport, may be morally permissible, even pursuant to Kant's strict tests, because a share of the "benefits" of pollution is flowing to those who are bearing the external costs of the pollution.

D. An Ethical Analysis of the Pollution Credit Plan

Legally setting strict pollution emission standards, yet permitting companies to purchase "pollution credits" to help them meet the standards, raises interesting moral issues. Pursuant to this pollution credit plan, also known as the market-based environmental incentive system, companies that exceed the standards (that is, reduce emissions below the legal standards) receive credits or permits, representing the "shortfall," which could be sold to firms that cannot meet the legal standards. For example, an older plant, burning high sulfur coal instead of installing potentially prohibitively expensive cleaning technology, could pay a company with more modern equipment and lower sulfur coal for its credits and accordingly "reduce" its emissions to comply with the law. Companies, therefore, would be buying and selling the "right" to pollute, and eventually, a market would develop that would treat the credits similarly to stocks and bonds.

The pollution credit plan certainly is an interesting proposal, but the question emerges as to whether it is a moral one. A utilitarian would ascertain the consequences resulting from the plan, including the effectiveness of such a market-based incentive system to reduce pollution, as well as to promote the flexibility, especially by avoiding plant shutdowns of those plants that cannot immediately comply legally, but which are allowed to "buy time" by obtaining pollution permits. The "good" created by any overall pollution reduction, avoidance of plant closing, as well as the creation of a new "credit" market, however, must be counterbalanced by the "pain" caused to the people and local communities who live near the older polluting plants that are nonetheless in legal "credit" compliance, but risk becoming pollution "hot spots" potentially endangering the health of the local residents. Yet, the overall good produced by pollution reduction nationally, as well as the good to be achieved by continuing and expanding employment, may outweigh the "pain" caused to the "few" living by these older, "credit"-compliant facilities. A Kantian, of course, would object that the pollution credit proposal does not treat these "few" with dignity and respect; that is, the "market" created will distribute permits in such a way that some locales and regions would suffer considerably more "legal" pollution, while others are subject to much less. If certain qualifications were placed on the pollution credit plan, however, such as specifying a maximum time period as well as a maximum limit for "credit" use, and perhaps by using explicit credits for specific types of pollution, a rational person could find the qualified proposal acceptable under the "agent-receiver" test as well as the Kingdom of Ends test; because the harm to the local community is lessened and delimited, and is counterbalanced by a still viable local employer legitimately seeking technical, in addition to technically legal, compliance with the law.

E. Pollution and the Law

Pollution obviously has a legal dimension; yet because it involves harm to human beings, other sentient creatures, and the environment, it has a moral dimension too. Therefore, a company that wishes to be a legal and ethical firm first must conduct an environmental audit to ensure that the many environmental protection laws are obeyed. Yet even if the company is acting legally, nevertheless people may still harmed by the company's pollution; and consequently some type of reimbursement should be paid. Of course, many jurisdictions do not have bodies of environmental law at all, let alone comparable to the extensive and detailed laws that exist in the United States. This lack of law or law enforcement may mean it is legal to pollute in certain international jurisdictions. However, if the "legal" pollution causes serious harm to the local people and their environment, the company, if it wishes to be a moral one, should not pollute at all, regardless of any compensation. Now, the authors are not advocating that a company invest so much in pollution control that it bankrupts itself; and thus if the benefits of the firm's presence outweigh the pains, some pollution of a non-serious (and compensable nature) morally could be allowed pursuant to Utilitarian ethical principles; but the global manager must always be aware of the consequences of the firm's actions on human beings and the environment, and must never treat either in a degrading, demeaning, abusive, or exploitative manner. As repeatedly emphasized in this book, the authors firmly believe that it is in a firm's self-interest to do the "right thing," which in this case would be not to harm others and the environment by pollution, even if legal to do so. In such a case, the authors assert that the "right" thing to do is also the "smart" thing too. The global business leader, executive, and manager, accordingly, must recognize this duty—legal, ethical, and, yes, egoistic—to protect and preserve the global environment. Business, after all, is part of the larger global environment itself.

An example of a socially responsible as well as "smart," ethically egoistic, corporate environmentalism is Wal-Mart's laudatory effort to go "beyond the law" and to make its massive fleet of semi-tractor trailer trucks 25% more fuel efficient by late 2008. The company has already achieved a 15% increase in efficiency in 2007. The company set forth ambitious environmental goals for its fleet in 2005; and it has been praised by industry experts and environmentalists not only for reaching its objectives, but for taking the lead far ahead of other trucking operators. Even the Sierra Club, which often is allied with unions and other critics of Wal-Mart, has praised the company. Actually, a representative of the environmental organization stated that Wal-Mart's demand for more fuel efficient vehicles could prompt truck manufacturers to make more efficient models faster. Wal-Mart's truck fleet regularly ranks among the top largest fleets in the United States. The federal Environmental Protection Agency has estimated that the company's fuel efficiency achievement will reduce its fleet's emissions of carbon dioxide by about 345,000 tons a year. So, Wal-Mart is doing the "right thing" environmentally; but it is also doing the "smart thing," since the company needs to keep fuel costs capped to avoid raising prices on its merchandise, and, unlike other carriers, it cannot easily impose a fuel surcharge on customers for higher fuel prices.

F. Summary

Business and business leaders, executives, and managers are part of the environment, dependent upon the environment, and major influences on the environment. They all must recognize their moral duties not to harm the environment as well as to protect and preserve it. Today, many companies are in fact "going green" and engaging in environmental initiatives, from "slimming down" on packaging to saving on gas and energy, and developing "hybrid" cars. Yet whether these worthy actions are motivated "merely" by egoistic reasons, such as mollifying environmentalistic, pleasing customers, or maximizing profits, or whether they are caused by obedience to a "higher moral law" is a question for debate. Ascertaining the exact nature and extent of moral duties to the environment thus emerges as a most challenging, though essential, business leadership ethical responsibility.

Discussion Questions

1. What is the obligation of a company beyond not befouling the environment through poor stewardship?

2. Is the company also responsible for bettering environmental conditions simply because it may have resources to do so?

3. Is it appropriate for the United States government to try and legislate business ethics through laws reaching to foreign countries?

4. If you were a manager, how would you advise your company's senior leadership on ethical behavior? How would you develop your recommendations and on what would you base them?

5. Do corporations have "souls?" That is, should they be held to a moral code of conduct as an entity, or should accountability reside with the officers and leadership of the company?

6. Is it ethical for the individuals making unethical decisions or engaging in immoral practices overseas to largely be shielded from consequences? What would you do to rectify this situation?

7. What is the hierarchy of compliance for corporations? That is, must they always comply with the laws in the country in which they are operating first and foremost or should they comply with the laws of their "home" country above all else?

8. Particularly for U.S.-based corporations, does adhering to U.S. laws for all foreign operations create reputation damage? In other words, is compliance with U.S. laws in foreign lands merely another way a "culturally imperialistic" America seeks to impose its values on other cultures?

9. What are the ethical obligations of shareholders in setting the moral "compass" for the company?

10. Should a company identify one particular approach to determining an ethical path?

CHAPTER 15

Product Safety, Inside Information, Trade Secrets, and Advertising Ethics

I. Morally Safe Products

A. Introduction

This section ethically examines the moral responsibilities a corporation and its managers owe to consumers in the area of product safety. Specifically, it seeks to define a "morally safe" product and to determine the corporation's moral obligation for products that may harm the consumer.

B. Characteristics of a Morally Safe Product

The relationship between the corporation and the consumer of its products initially is a contractual, and distinctive moral duties arise by virtue of this contractual relationship. The corporation has a duty to produce a product that conforms to contractual terms, as well as to disclose fully and accurately the nature of the product. A corporation also has a moral duty not to harm people by its careless acts. Accordingly, a corporation has a moral duty to exercise due care in the production of its products and to ensure that consumers are not harmed by carelessly produced products. It is, however, quite possible for a company to exercise due care, for example, by maintaining extensive and elaborate quality control, testing, and inspection, yet nonetheless have a faulty product "slip through" or "run away" from such procedures and cause harm. Consequently, a corporation has a moral duty to prevent and redress harm to consumers caused by its flawed products, that is, products that were produced defectively although by an otherwise very careful corporation. Such products are easy to ascertain because these flawed products do not even meet the corporation's own standards and specifications for products of that type.

To attain the status of a morally safe product, however, a product must do more than meet contract terms, be carefully made, and reach the consumer in an unflawed condition. The product also must be safely designed. In order to determine if a product is safely designed, one must first focus on the state of the art, that is, the level of science, engineering, and technology at the time the product was manufactured. Then, one must ask the question: was it possible, given the state of the art, as well as the constraints of practical and economic feasibility, for the producer to have done more to make the product safer. If the answer is "yes," then the company has produced a defectively designed product, because the product, even though not flawed, failed to incorporate all feasible and practical safety design features, standards, and devices. Such a product is an immorally unsafe product. For example, a gun without warning trigger locks, and perhaps even "smart gun" technology, such as palm-handle coding, may be deemed a morally unsafe product. As a matter of fact, the state of New Jersey in 2002 became the first state in the U.S. to mandate that all new handguns be equipped with "smart gun" technology that would allow only the gun's owner to fire it. The law, however, does not specify what type of technology be on a "smart gun." What about "fast food" cooked with artificial "trans fat" which can raise cholesterol levels and contribute to heart disease? Is zero "trans fat" soybean oil a feasible cooking alternative? Is "trans fat" cooked "fast food" a morally unsafe product? An example of a company attempting to provide a morally safe product is the Dunkin' Donuts food chain, which in the summer of 2007 eliminated trans fat from across its menus. Trans fat is said to boost "bad" cholesterol. The company now uses alternative cooking oil. Dunkin' Donuts was the first major chain to introduce a zero-gram trans fat doughnut. Nutrition and child advocacy groups welcomed and praised the company's moral and socially responsible initiative.

Even if a product is designed safely, however, there still may be a degree of risk involved in its use. For a product to be morally safe, therefore, the level of risk must be acceptable to a rational person. A risk is not acceptable to a rational person if he or she does not know the risk exists, its severity or frequency, or how to deal with the risk, or if the risk is far out of proportion to the benefits one expects to obtain from the product. Since the product does involve a risk of harm, although an acceptable one, the morally safe product, finally, must include an adequate warning of the risks entailed in using the product. Warnings, however, are not morally required if a rational person should be aware of the danger; that is if the danger is obvious or a reasonable person should be aware that the product, for example, a scissors, glass, or loft bed, poses a generally known risk of injury if it is misused, dropped or fallen from, then a warning is not morally required.

C. Ethical Justification for the Morally Safe Product

The proposed definition of the morally safe product can be supported by both utilitarian and Kantian moral philosophies. The proposed standard requires that the producer or seller who placed the morally unsafe product into the marketplace bear the costs of injuries caused by such products. These costs then can be "internalized" as an ordinary cost of designing, manufacturing, and selling the product. These costs, moreover, can be added on to the product as a part of the price of the product, and this internalizing of costs enables the producer or seller to distribute losses among all purchasers of the product, instead of allowing losses to fall on individual users who may not be able to sustain them. A producer or seller who is fully cognizant of its responsibilities under the morally safe product doctrine should purchase insurance; and insurance will spread further the risk-cost-loss distribution. The proposed rule, finally, has a safety rationale. Since the producer or seller has to pay the costs of injuries caused by the product, it will be motivated to exercise greater care in the design, production, distribution, and sale of the product; the number, frequency, and severity of injuries will be reduced accordingly. The morally safe product doctrine underscores the value of efficiency. Societal resources are allocated and used in a more efficient manner; the social cost of injuries is reduced; and the doctrine advances the general welfare and promotes the greater good. The morally safe product doctrine treats people as Kantian "ends" and is acceptable to a rational person, regardless of his or her role as the product manufacturer or user.

D. The Manufacturer as Guarantor

Just how far can a product manufacturer morally be required to go to ensure the safety of its products? Should a manufacturer be obligated to pay for any and all injuries caused by the use of its products, regardless of due care, compliance with the state-of-the-art, level of risk, and the warning thereof? Does a manufacturer have a moral duty to guarantee against all risks that arise from the use of a product, even if they are small, low-level, or infrequent, or even if they could not possibly have been foreseen, prevented, or eliminated? Imposing such a duty in the manufacturer, in essence, forces the manufacturer into the role of insurer, in that the manufacture is guaranteeing payment of any loss caused by the product, excepting, of course, purposefully caused injuries and those resulting from product abuse. Yet such a product insurance scheme is unfair both to the manufacturer and consumer. It is unfair to the manufacture to compel it to compensate an injured party for a risk that was not foreseeable or that could not be eliminated, and it is also unfair to compel a manufacturer to eliminate all risks, because the manufacture would have to invest so much time and money in each product that it would face bankruptcy. The insurance scheme also is unfair to consumers. Products with insurance "policies" attached would become so expensive as to be priced out of the reach of most consumers, and those consumers who are forced to pay are unjustly being required to pay for the injured consumer's "insurance."

II. Inside Information and Trade Secrets

A. Inside Information

1. Introduction

The problem areas of inside information and trade secrets are closely related. Both are based on information that is not generally known, possesses economic value, and is regarded as confidential. Inside information can be defined broadly as information that someone within a company has, but that is not available to people outside the firm. This definition includes trade secrets, of course, but it also encompasses other types of information, such as the corporation's plans and strategy.

Several moral problems arise from the use of inside information. A corporate employee, or other insider, for example, can use inside information at the expense of the company for his or her own private gain. Such information can be used while the employee is still a member of the firm, resulting in the classic conflict-of-interest situation, or information can be used when the employee moves from one company to another or goes out on his or her own and takes certain information with him or her. An even more difficult problem arises when a corporate "insider" uses inside information not directly at the expense of his or her firm, but to obtain a personal advantage over those "outsiders" not in or directly involved with the corporation.

This chapter first examines ethically the moral use of inside information and then focuses on the more narrow topic of moral trade secrets. In order to address more precisely the moral issues involved in the use of inside information, the inside information part of this chapter spotlights insider trading, that is, the act of buying or selling a corporation's stock on the basis of inside information about the firm. One point about this practice should be quite clear, however. It is illegal for a corporate insider using material inside information to trade in shares of his or her own company. Yet, this legal rule does not cover much of what should be illegal, let alone immoral.

2. Defining Inside Information

Inside information may be defined broadly as information that is not available to the general public outside the corporation and that would have a material impact on the price of the corporation's stock. Specifically designating whether certain information is inside information is a more troublesome task. Of course, if the information is confidential, it is very likely to be regarded as inside information. Yet, did the recipient know, or should he or she have known, that information was confidential? Moreover, did the recipient know, or should he or she have known, that someone within the company was breaching some legal or fiduciary duty in divulging or passing along the information? Exactly how did the information come out? Was it revealed accidentally or purposefully? Finally, what is the form of the information? Is it factual or is it more in the form of questions, opinions, or predictions? Is it factual or more in the form of rumors or speculation? Clearly, the more knowingly factual, objective, scientific, and confidential the information is, together with knowledge that it was "leaked" intentionally, and in contravention of a duty, the greater the likelihood that the information will be regarded as inside.

Despite the difficulties involved, making the initial determination as to the inside nature of the information is a crucial decision, because before one can impose either legal or moral accountability for the use of inside information, the information clearly must be deemed inside. Perhaps the preferable solution is to keep the meaning broad when dealing with moral responsibility, but to narrow the definition and examine all the component factors of inside when dealing with government-imposed legal responsibility.

The leading "tippee," or alleged tipee case, has been the saga of Martha Stewart, whom the SEC proceeded against civilly for being a tipee of, and in conspiracy with, an insider, her "good friend," Dr. Waksal, the principal shareholder and CEO of ImClone, Inc. Recall that Martha Stewart was convicted of, and served her time for, perjury and obstruction of justice. The government did not prosecute Martha Stewart for the crime of trading on inside information. As noted, the burden of proof for the government in such a criminal case would be "proof beyond a reasonable doubt," which apparently the government felt it could not adequately demonstrate, since the transmission of the clearly insider tip, that the FDA had rejected ImClone's main cancer-fighting drug, was not directly from Dr. Waksal to Martha Stewart, but rather through an attenuated chain of Dr. Waksal, the senior broker, the junior broker, and then to Martha Stewart. Of course, the irony of the situation for Martha Stewart is that she now is judged as a felon, went to prison, lost her broker's license, and forfeited any right to serve as an executive of a publicly traded company, including her own, all for lying about and covering up a trade which the government felt it did not have enough evidence to prosecute as a crime, but only civilly, where of course the burden of proof is a lesser one. Yet, there is an even greater irony in that the drug that was at the center of all the controversy, upon further testing, actually may have some cancer-fighting properties, and as a result the drug has been submitted to the FDA again for approval. So, Martha Stewart, as well as Dr. Waksal, should have held on to their stock; and thus the "good doctor" would now not be in prison, and for seven years, for the crime of insider trading, as he was clearly an insider acting on inside information. Martha Stewart did not give up, however. She initially decided to fight rather than settle the civil law suit for insider trading brought against her by the Securities and Exchange Commission. Although found guilty in the criminal case, and completing in 2005 a five month civil sentence for lying under oath and obstruction of justice for lying and covering up her sale of ImClone Systems stock, she steadfastly has denied the charges that she used material, confidential, non-public information when she sold her shares of stock in 2001. Martha Stewart claimed that she acted in good faith. In addition to civil penalties and fines, the SEC's legal action, which was "stayed" (or suspended) until the culmination of the criminal trial, also sought to bar Martha Stewart from serving as a director of a public company as well as limiting her responsibilities as an officer of a public company. Ultimately, though, despite her avowals to "fight on," Martha Stewart eventually settled the civil action brought by the SEC, thereby ending, finally, the Martha Steward saga.

In another famous (infamous!) case, the Enron case, former CEO Ken Lay always contended that he was innocent of any wrongdoing. Thus, a key element to the government's criminal case against Lay was scienter, since the presence of an "evil mind" is necessary for the specific intent crimes of securities fraud and insider trading. Ken Lay's defense was known in legal circles as the classic "idiot" or "ostrich" defense; that is, that one was unaware of any wrongdoing, that one was a weak and careless manager, that one was deceived and manipulated by other "bad" people; and that one did make misstatements; but, critically, that one lacked the specific criminal intent to misrepresent material facts about the company and to trade based on inside information. Such a defense did work for Richard Scrushy, the former CEO of Health SouthCorporation, who was acquitted on similar accounting and securities fraud charges. Of course, it helped in Scrushy's case, legal experts have related, that he was tried in Birmingham, Alabama, where he was well known as the "minister's son," and where he regularly preached in, and contributed to, the African-American churches there, and where the local jury was in part composed of African-Americans. The "idiot" defense, however, did not work for Ken Lay or Jeffrey Skilling. In May of 2006, a "home town" jury in Houston found both former Enron executives guilty of securities and wire fraud and conspiracy and Skilling also of insider trading. The victory was viewed as a major victory for the government, underscoring corporate accountability, and the "grand finale" to the era of corporate scandals which culminated in the passage by the U.S. Congress of the very strict Sarbanes-Oxley Act. Sentencing for Lay was to be in late 2006. Lay, however, was still declaring his innocence until his death in early July 2006, stating to the very end that he "firmly believes" in his innocence. Skilling seemed resigned, almost stoical, saying that he was disappointed by the verdict, but "that's how the system works." An appeal was expected; and one major point on appeal is whether the federal district court judge should have moved the case from Houston, Enron's headquarters, where the publicity was overwhelming, and overwhelmingly negative, to a supposedly more neutral venue. It should be noted, not to be disrespectful to the dead or to be overly cynical, that Ken Lay, even in death, caused major problems in the effort to provide some type of material redress to the former Enron employees and shareholders as well as mutual fund and pension holders of the stock. Because Ken Lay died before he was officially sentenced, he was not technically convicted. Actually, Lay's conviction was erased by the court since he died before his appeal was effectuated. Although it is way beyond the scope of this book to deal with this unusual "twist" in criminal law, it should be mentioned that his death will bring to an end the government's attempts to seize Lay's substantial remaining property since he is not considered to be a felon. So, instead of the defrauded Enron victims receiving most of the assets, Lay's surviving spouse will be the main beneficiary of his death. Again, not to be disrespectful, but Machiavelli surely would say that at least in one respect, the Goddess Fortuna "smiled" on Ken Lay's surviving spouse. Skilling, however, was eventually sentenced to 24 years in prison.

3. *Conflict of Interest*

A classic conflict-of-interest case arises when a corporate insider, usually a management employee, officer, or director engages in a course of conduct where the insider is motivated by a private interest that is antagonistic to the best interests of the corporation. If the insider's private interest is substantial, it deflects his or her attention from the best interest of the company and warps the independent judgment that the corporation expects its personnel to exercise on its behalf. A conflict of interest will occur, for example, when an insider holds stock in a competitor, or holds a position with, or consults for a competitor. A conflict of interest also will arise when a corporate insider uses inside information at the expense of his or her firm, for example, when an insider, cognizant of the company's expansion plans, buys adjacent property and then sells it to his or her own company at a high price.

Such conflict of interests are patently immoral. The insider is harming the main stakeholder group to which the insider owes a moral duty of loyalty and honesty—the shareholders. Shareholders, not managers and employees, own the corporation, and corporate resources, including information, ultimately belong to the shareholders. Insiders are held to a moral duty to use corporate resources only for the benefit of its shareholder-owners, and the private use and gain therefrom is an immoral action, akin to theft.

To eliminate the problem of conflict of interest, a corporation should promulgate in its code of ethics detailed guidelines protecting corporate resources, for example, requiring the disclosure of "outside" financial interests, prohibiting any holdings in a competitor, or perhaps specifying the amount of stock that the corporation will permit its managers and employees to hold in supplier or purchaser companies. It should be a fundamental objective of the corporate code of ethics to evince a heightened awareness and concern, not only for the reality of conflicts of interest, but also for the mere appearance of a conflict of interest.

4. Ethical Analysis of Insider Trading

A) INTRODUCTION

What happens when an insider uses inside information to secure a personal gain, for example, in the stock market, yet not at the expanse of his or her company, but at the expense of some "outsider"? There are two competing moral rules that can govern such use of inside information.

B) TWO COMPETING MORAL RULES

One moral rule deals with insiders who use inside information to buy or sell the corporation's stock. "Insiders" can encompass conventional insiders, such as the company's directors, officers, employees, and agents, as well as "temporary" insiders, such as the firm's lawyers, accountants, bankers, brokers, and perhaps even financial printers.

Such insiders are in a confidential relationship with the corporation and by using nonpublic, confidential, inside information, they are misappropriating corporate assets, breaking their fiduciary relationship, and acting like thieves and embezzlers. They are acting immorally. Those in conspiracy with such insiders, that is, "tipees," such as family and friends, also are morally accountable if they knew, or should have known, of the fiduciary nature of the relationship and the non-public aspect to the information. This first potential moral rule to govern the use of inside information may be designated the "insider," "property rights," or narrow rule.

The second candidate for a moral rule is a broader formulation; it may be designated the "outsider" or "level playing field" proposal. Pursuant to this moral rule, all who trade in the securities markets are entitled to a level playing field; consequently, it is morally wrong for anyone to buy or sell stock based on inside information, however acquired.

The differences between the two rules are significant: the first reaches only corporate insiders and their tippees; the second covers outsiders too, such as those fortunate enough to stumble across inside information inadvertently leaked out, and more importantly, encompasses those market professionals, for example, security analysts, whose job it is to discover by legitimate means new information regarding companies. Are there moral differences between misappropriating information, and stumbling cross it, or professionally discovering it? Should ethics protect the lucky, and should it reward the smart?

C) UTILITARIANISM

"Outsiders" clearly are not to be allowed to steal inside information or to bribe insiders for it. Yet, should they be allowed morally to search out, to discover, and then use inside information? There are, of course, some negative consequences stemming from this use of inside information. The holder of the inside information possesses an advantage in any relevant transaction, which renders it not totally equable; and the parties who conducted business with the "outsiders" under such circumstances will feel "pain," perhaps tempered by the fact that they were freely willing to buy or sell the shares at a particular price anyway. Yet when more people realize that certain individuals possess inside information and thus have an advantage, they will presume that insider trading is occurring more frequently and may tend to leave the market. A smaller market engenders negative consequences because fewer buyers and sellers results in more expensive transaction cost, especially the increased cost to buying and selling stocks, producing a decline in the ability to spread risk since there are fewer buyers and sellers.

There are, however, counterbalancing positive consequences that ensue from this "smart" use of inside information. People trading on inside information bring this information to the market, and by so doing, cause the price of stock to rise or fall in accordance with the true underlying worth of the stock. As more inside information is brought into the market, the greater the indication of what the real value of stock is. Such information leads to a more accurate and more efficient market, which benefits all investors. Therefore, allowing financial analysts and other market professionals to ferret out and use inside information is a morally permissible practice pursuant to utilitarianism.

d) KANT'S CATEGORICAL IMPERATIVE

The general principle—use inside information—clearly is immoral under the first test of Kant's Categorical Imperative. The principle cannot be made consistently universal because if everyone used inside information, there would be no such thing as inside information, there would be no advantage to using this information; the principle cannot sustain itself when one attempts to make it universal; it self-destructs, it is rendered nonsensical, an absurdity; and therefore it is immoral.

The use of inside information also fails Kant's second and third tests. The practice is immoral because the transaction is not fair. The injured outsiders are the shareholders who entered into a transaction without the same level of relevant information. They are taken advantage of and disrespected, so the use of inside information fails Kant's second test. The use of inside information places those who lack it at such a pronounced disadvantage that no rational person would find the practice acceptable if he or she did know whether he or she would be the party possessing the inside information or the uninformed party. The practice, consequently, fails Kant's third test and is immoral.

A most interesting, and difficult ethical question arises, however, when one attempts to qualify the general prohibition against the use of inside information. One still can say that the use of inside information by an insider, or the tippee of an insider, or by an outsider who steals inside information, or who bribes an insider for it, is immoral. Yet, what about the financial expert who discovers or pieces together inside information, due to his or her own hard work and intelligence, and perhaps deductive speculative capabilities; and then who uses the information in an innovative, venturesome, and perhaps, risky fashion. This expert does possess in advantage produced by the inside information, but is he or she acting immorally?

A qualified inside information principle can be made consistently universal; a qualified principle will not self-destruct. Not everyone will be using inside information, because not everyone will possess the intelligence, diligence, and perseverance to produce it, and perhaps the courage to risk using it. The qualified principle thus is moral under Kant's first test. Yet, what about his second and third tests? Does this delimited type of inside trading treat people with disrespect; would a rational person regardless of role find the restricted principle unacceptable? People buy and sell stock because they desire an investment opportunity or need or want money at the moment, and many of these people have more or better information than others. When people buy or sell stock, they pay or receive whatever the present market price of the stock is, and they would not have paid or received more for their stock from others than the price obtained from or by the holder of inside information. Of course, people may regret buying or selling once the inside information becomes generally available to the public, but are they treated with disrespect; and would the rational person find this scenario objectionable. If the expert generates and uses the inside information, and all people have the opportunity to become experts or to use the services of experts, then the qualified principle should be regarded as moral. All parties will be entering into the transaction freely and openly and with an equal opportunity to secure the relevant information, to assess it wisely, and to boldly use it.

E) SUMMARY

Insiders, tipees, thieves, and bribers who use inside information are immoral. They all essentially are stealing property, taking unfair advantage of their victims, and fouling the competitive atmosphere. They are immoral wrongdoers who must be appropriately sanctioned. Yet, to ethically prohibit all uses of inside information by everyone is too extreme a moral response. One must seek a solution that promotes the maximum amount of open and free competition that is compatible with moral fairness. Such a solution allows morally the circumscribed use of inside information generated by experts but so long as people have equal opportunity to obtain and use inside information.

B. Trade Secrets

1. Introduction and Definition

A trade secret is a more narrow formulation of the inside information doctrine. All trade secrets are inside information, but not all inside information is a morally protected trade secret. Generally speaking, trade secrets are material, important, private types of information and knowledge that give a company a distinct commercial advantage, that represent a financial investment by the firm in its purchase or development, and that the company sufficiently has indicated its desire to maintain the secrecy thereof.

A common trade secret problem arises when a company's employee or agent leaves the firm and moves to another company, taking certain information and knowledge with him or her to the second firm, and then using this information and knowledge. To whom does this information and knowledge belong? When is it appropriate to use it? If the information and knowledge are not protected legally by patent or copyright law, contract confidentiality agreements, or covenants-not-to-compete, the ethical issue arises as to whether such information is protected morally. If the information or knowledge does rise to the level of a moral trade secret, it is morally wrong to knowingly and improperly acquire and use it. The key question emerges: what exactly is a moral trade secret?

A moral trade secret consists of information and knowledge that has independent economic value because it is neither generally known to the public nor readily ascertainable by competent people. Possession of the information need not be exclusive; the fact that it is not generally available to the public is sufficient. If the information is available, or it can be readily generated, then it is not a trade secret.

The types of information that could rise to the level of a moral trade secret include devices, formulas, patterns, programs, processes, techniques, compilations, lists, records, and research results. Trade secret information can also encompass a company's business and marketing plans and strategies. Such information could be highly valuable to firm's competitor, and if revealed, could adversely affect the firm's ability to compete successfully. In addition, in order to qualify as a moral trade secret, the firm must have invested or spent a material amount of money or effort to develop the information or to purchase it. Finally, a company must exercise reasonable security measures in order to maintain the secrecy of the information. The level of security, of course, depends on the circumstances, but must demonstrate that the firm wishes to keep the information secret. Appropriate security measures include explicit confidentiality instructions, "secret" and "confidential" designations, passwords, contractual secrecy provisions, as well as the conventional guards and locks security measures.

The preceding definition of a moral trade secret, although narrower than the notion of inside information, provides a sufficiently broad scope of ethical recognition, protection, and preservation to information, of actual or potential value, that a company has made an investment in and that it has deemed sufficiently important so as to institute security measures to protect. This type of information is a moral trade secret, ethically justified by utilitarian and Kantian ethics, and to misappropriate this information is to commit a moral wrong.

2. Customer Lists

Customer lists certainly may be morally protected trade secrets under appropriate circumstances. There are a variety of special factors to be considered to determine if a customer list is a moral trade secret.

If customer information is readily available through public sources, it is not a moral trade secret. However, although the identity of customers may be readily obtainable, there may be specific information regarding each customer which is not. Accordingly, to rise to the level of a moral trade secret, a customer list should include specific and unique kinds of information pertaining to individual customers. The time, effort, expense, and expertise required to compile the list are important factors to determine the moral status of the list. Evidence, in the form of a file or log, indicating the resources expended by a firm in developing and refining the list, would be especially instructive in this regard. If a customer list has been distilled from a larger list, the firm should keep records of the distillation process, as well as the effort involved in the process. The confidentiality accorded to the customer list is a critical factor. Consequently, a company should establish explicit policies regarding the secrecy of the customer list. For example, a company should inform employees that all information regarding present or future customers is strictly confidential; have the employees sign a confidentiality agreement; and conspicuously designate as confidential all customer list information.

3. Summary

Information may not be protected legally, but it may be "protected" ethically by means of a moral trade secret doctrine. If information does rise to the level of a moral trade secret, the information belongs to its developer, ordinarily the company, and an employee who sells, uses, or otherwise misappropriates such information, as well as the knowing recipient, commits an immoral act.

III. Advertising and Ethics

A. Introduction

Commercial advertising can be viewed as a form of information transmittal; one function of advertising is to provide information to consumers regarding the nature and availability of goods and services. Yet the primary purpose of advertising is to induce members of the public to buy a seller's goods and services. Advertising is an essential component of the process of selling in a competitive, decentralized, capitalistic economy, but it is not in itself immoral because of the persuasion involved, even though some false needs, "waste," and deceptive practices may be engendered.

Sellers, as well as advertisers, have a basic ethical obligation to do no moral harm. Because advertising is publicly addressed to a very large audience, it necessarily has widespread social consequences, and therefore it is ethically incumbent on sellers and advertisers to ensure that these consequences are good ones. Prospective buyers, moreover, are entitled ethically to be treated with dignity and respect, as worthwhile "ends" and not as a mere means to effectuate a commercial transaction. Accordingly, the ethical obligation to do no harm demands that a seller not only not sell any immorally unsafe products, but also that a seller, and its advertisers, not engage in any immoral advertising in order to sell its goods and services.

The inherent conflict between the informative and persuasive aspects of advertising generates moral problems. Advertising provides information to consumers about products and services; but advertising also persuades the consumer to purchase one product or service rather than another. These two functions are not always compatible. A seller or advertiser may be subject to intense competitive pressures and thereby may be tempted to engage in immoral advertising to induce sales at the expense of any legitimate consumer education pertaining to the product or service. In this attempt to persuade, sellers and advertisers may lie, misrepresent, mislead, exaggerate, conceal information, make half-truths, or use psychological tactics, such as coercive, manipulative, and suggestive appeals. This section, therefore, focuses on types of advertising that a seller may employ and attempts to determine if these methods of advertising are moral.

Two recent examples of legally and morally questionable advertisements involved beverages. In one, during the summer of 2007, PepsiCo, Inc. stated that it would change the labels on its top-selling Aquafina water bottles to state clearly that the drink comes from the same source as tap water. An advocacy group called Corporate Accountability International had condemned the marketing of the product as misleading, and consequently was pressuring the company to stop the marketing of the product. The point of contention was the blue Aquafina label with a mountain logo. The advocacy group contended that the label was deceptive in that the reasonable consumer would think that the water came from mountain spring sources. It is interesting to note that the bottles have had the initials "P.W.S." on them, but now the term "public water source" will be spelled out. Corporate

Accountability is now aiming its efforts against Nestle Waters North America since some of the water obtained for its Pure Life drinking water comes from municipal water sources. In both cases, of course, the water goes through an extensive purification process. The other beverage controversy, also occurring in the summer of 2007, is even more contentious because it involves a supposed "energy" product with caffeine—combined with alcohol. One product, made by Miller Brewing Company, is called Sparks, and it has generated a great deal of criticism since it is packaged to look like a battery container. Other companies that produce similar beverages are Anheuser-Busch and Charge Beverages Corp. Several state attorney generals are pressuring federal regulators to curb the advertising for these "energy drinks," which they condemn as misleading due to the health and safety risks posed by the beverages, especially for young people. One attorney general from Oregon, noting the popularity of non-alcoholic energy drinks with young people, went further and condemned the marketing of the beverages as unconscionable since they make an appeal to young drinkers about the stimulating properties of the beverages. One company representative defended the product by stating that it is merely a malt beverage that contains caffeine, and is clearly marked as containing alcohol. To compare, an example of legal and moral advertising would be Burger King corporation's pledge in September of 2007 to advertise only healthy products to children. Moreover, due to the concern with childhood obesity, as well as its commitment to health, the company also stated its plan to bring out in 2008 two new healthy food products for kids—a flame broiled chicken shaped like a burger and apples cut in the shape of French fries. The company is thus doing what is not only right, but also smart, since it is being praised by child health and nutrition groups for being the first "fast-food" chain to offer a child's meal that is actually very healthy.

B. Deceptive Advertising

Deceptive advertisements include false ads and misleading ads. Deceptive advertisements clearly are immoral. False ads lie, either by making false claims, for example, that the product will kill germs that cause colds, or by misrepresenting the product, for example, by describing a used model as new. A misleading ad does not blatantly lie; rather, it induces a reasonable person to reach an erroneous conclusion to his or her detriment, for example, by offering "free" goods to the consumer or by reducing the price of goods when the price has been artificially inflated to facilitate the "free" goods and the price reduction. Another example would be the famous "Made in the USA" labels and stickers on products, many of which were condemned as deceptive because a significant part of the product was not made in the U.S. but overseas. In one highly misleading case, the only "part" of the product that was made in the U.S. was the idea for the product.

Deceptive advertising is immoral under the utilitarian ethical theory. Consumers are harmed by being deceived into buying goods and services they otherwise would avoid. The competition is harmed by the unfair diversion of potential customers. Society, moreover, is harmed because the deceptive ads engender a public distrust of advertising. This distrust diminishes the value not only of advertising but also of other forms of communication upon which business and society depend. Deceptive advertising also violates Kant's Categorical Imperative. Lying and misrepresenting obviously cannot be made consistently universal, and misleading ads disrespect the consumer by contravening his or her right to choose freely and by treating the deceived consumer as a mere means to sell a product or service.

An advertiser's mere use of exaggeration or "puffery," however, does not render an ad deceptive and immoral. Such sales talk, or the use of superlative and figurative language, such as praising the product or service as the "best," "finest," or "most," is not deceptive so long as the advertiser does not intend to deceive and does not make may unsubstantiated claims. Of course, the line between lying and "puffing" is at times hard to draw. Other moral problems also can arise even when ads are not blatantly false or misleading.

C. "Half-Truth" Advertising

A difficult moral problem occurs when an advertiser does not affirmatively misrepresent or mislead, but rather omits certain information regarding the product or service. Such an ad commonly is regarded as a "half-truth" ad and will be deemed immoral if the information omitted is significant, for example, regarding safety and health concerns. The half-truth ad also is immoral if it fails to disclose other relevant and material facts that would affect the consumer's decision to purchase or use the product or service. In an example of moral and socially responsible advertising, Burger King company pledged in 2007 to advertise only healthy products to children. The announcement came as a response to the growing concern over the problem of childhood obesity and the role that advertising "fast food" has in creating that problem. Burger King stated that it would meet a set of nutritional guidelines for any product advertising aimed at children under 12 years of age. The company also agreed not to advertise its products in elementary schools and not to use licensed characters on any advertising that does not meet the new guidelines. The company establishes its own guidelines, but they must be approved by the Council of Better Business Bureaus. Other food and beverage companies, such as McDonalds, have also set advertising guidelines as part of the Children's Food and Beverage Advertising Initiative.

A company, and its advertisers, are obligated morally to provide clear, truthful, and sufficient information so the consumer knows precisely the product or service he or she is purchasing and what the terms if the sale are. Not disclosing adequate information not only undermines the societal pillar of truth telling, but also exploits the consumer by robbing him or her of a free and knowing choice.

What happens, however, when an advertiser merely fails to disclose information that may be unflattering to a product or service? As every product or service possesses many characteristics, an advertiser naturally will underscore those positive and appealing aspects and will downplay any negatives. Such an ad commonly is regarded as a selective ad because it selectively focuses on certain specific characteristics. Such an ad generally is a moral one since an advertiser is not obligated morally to disclose every fact pertaining to the product or service. Yet, if the advertiser, by emphasizing positive characteristics, conceals or obscures important information that a purchaser requires to make a safe or prudent decision, the advertiser has converted a moral selective ad into a deceptive and immoral half-truth ad. For example, a health-conscious type of ad that emphasizes the low sodium and low cholesterol nature of the product and that contains heart designs and pictures can be declared immoral if it omits the significant fact that the product is high in fat.

D. Psychological Advertising

Even though an advertisement is truthful, accurate, unambiguous, and sufficiently factual, the advertisement nonetheless may generate heightened moral concern because the ad predominantly makes a psychological appeal and thus "sells" psychological satisfaction and emotional approval as opposed to rationally selling the product or service to the reasonable consumer.

1. Manipulative Ads

A manipulative ad is one that unduly influences or excessively dominates the consumer. It plays upon the consumer's fears, psychological needs, and emotions, and it circumvents the rational thought process to manipulate the consumer's "consent" to an agreement that the consumer would not have made if he or she was acting in a rational manner. Such ads are immoral because they violate the Kantian principle to treat people as free, equal, rational beings entitled to dignity and respect. A funeral ad that takes advantage of grief-stricken, and perhaps guilt-stricken, survivors is an example of a manipulative ad. Another, and even more flagrant example, would be a subliminal ad that not only manipulates but does so at a level beneath the consumer's conscious awareness.

2. Suggestive Ads

A suggestive ad is one that communicates information about the product or service, states that the consumer will be satisfied with it, and also suggests that the consumer will receive various extraneous benefits from the product or service. The suggestive ad gives the consumer the impression that the product or service advertised will fulfill the consumer's hopes and desires and avoid his or her fears. For example, perfume ads that promote sex appeal, and automobile ads that "promise" executive status, are example of suggestive ads.

Suggestive ads generally are moral. There is, however, a fine line between suggestive ads and manipulative ones, the latter of which clearly are immoral. Using a degree of hope or fear to sell a product or service is not necessarily immoral, yet if the advertiser's use of hope or fear is so pervasive that the consumer's free will is overwhelmed, then the suggestive ad as degenerated into an immoral manipulative ad. When a suggestive ad, moreover, targets a particularly impressionable and susceptible class or audience, such as, the very young or very old, who may be subject to heightened needs, fears, and insecurities, the suggestive ad, once again, will be regarded as an immoral manipulative ad. For example, Kellogg Co., in response to moral pressure by consumer and public interest groups, announced in 2007 that it would restrict the use of licensed cartoon characters, such as Shrek in its advertising to children, and also that it would reduce the amount of fat and sugar in products it markets to children under 12 years of age. The Walt Disney Company also announced that it would limit the use of its cartoon character in marketing "junk food" to children. Perhaps not coincidentally, the Federal Trade Commission has begun to scrutinize food marketing more closely, and intends to commence public hearings to discuss advertising targeting children.

E. Poor Taste Ads

Poor taste ads are loud, vulgar, offensive, tasteless, repetitive, boring, intrusive, and irritating. They are aesthetically unpleasant, insult the consumer's intelligence, and debase the aesthetic values of society. Such ads, however, are not in and themselves immoral; they merely are in poor taste, such as a bug or rat-infested pesticide ad that regularly appears during the dinner hour. However, an advertiser must be very careful in utilizing poor taste ads because a merely insensitive ad, though generally moral, very well could "cross the line" and degenerate into an undignified and demeaning ad, which is immoral. For example, naming one's liquor product after a famous Native American war-chief or using a Chihuahua dog to market one's fast-food product to Hispanics have been condemned as immoral marketing tactics. An example of advertisement that was condemned as being way beyond "mere" poor taste, and rather was "blasted" as demeaning and disrespectful was an advertisement by Red Bull, the soft drinks company. The ad featured its caffeinated energy drink and initially appeared on Italian television. The ad portrayed a Christmas theme in which four "wise men" instead of three visited Mary and the Baby Jesus in Bethlehem. The fourth wise man bore a can of the soft drink, Red Bull. The ad also stated that "Red Bull gives you wings," which was exclaimed by angels in the animated advertisement. The ad was deplored as being disrespectful to religion, insensitive to Christianity, sacrilegious, and blasphemous, as well as insulting to Italian religious sensitivities. The company has decided to withdraw the ad.

F. Socially Responsible Advertising

In addition to being legal and moral, advertising must be socially responsible. To illustrate, as a result of the U.S. Supreme Court decisions materially expanding the First Amendment "commercial speech" rights of marketers and advertisers, even for products and services traditionally regarded as "adult" or even "vice-like" ones (though of course legal), the U.S. television networks have agreed to accept commercials for "hard liquor." The networks, however, have been concerned about a consumer "backlash." Accordingly, one network, NBC, has agreed to accept liquor ads, but only if they are cautious and "non-glitzy," and also, significantly, that they have a "social responsibility" message and a "social responsibility" theme. For example, one such ad would underscore to consumers that the viewers who do drink choose a "designated" non-drinking driver, exemplified in an ad by having a series of empty (and consumed) glasses of liquor, but one glass turned over (and unused), which is, of course, the glass for the non-drinking designated driver.

A current example of moral and social pressure being exerted to compel health warnings involves the Benihana restaurant chain, which now has started to place warnings in all its California restaurants about the presence of mercury in seafood. Health concerns and the concomitant need for warnings were first raised by a California, public health group, GotMercury. The warnings, which as of this writing are posted only in the restaurant chain's California restaurants, caution women of child-bearing age and children to limit the consumption of fish. GotMercury asserts that Benihana has a moral and social responsibility to educate all its consumers in all states where it does business as to the health dangers of mercury. Yet Benihana is not being singled out, since the California organization has been conducting an extensive campaign to pressure other restaurants as well as supermarket chains that it is their moral duty and social responsibility to post warnings about mercury, a toxin found in fish, which can harm an unborn baby's and young child's nervous system according to the federal Food and Drug Administration. One very large supermarket chain, Publix, based in Lakeland, Florida, stated that it had no plans to post signs or warnings, but it will produce and make available to customers pamphlets, which will they will be able to pick up in the seafood department, to learn more about mercury in fish. The large supermarket chains, Albertsons and Safeway, already post warnings, as they believe it is their moral and social responsibility to do so (and perhaps their ethically egoistic interest too).

G. Summary

Ethics requires that the societal good be promoted and that people be treated with dignity and respect. Ethics, however, does not prohibit every advertising appeal, only immoral ones. Accordingly, a company and its advertisers are ethically obligated to eschew immoral advertising. Advertising must appeal primarily to the perceived needs of the consumer and must treat the consumer as a rational "end" and not as a mere means or "mark" to extract a sale.

Discussion Questions

1. What are some recent examples of products that have been found to be morally unsafe?
2. What can companies do to absorb the cost of flawed products, and how does this benefit the company?
3. What is a morally serious case of someone using insider information?
4. Why is it beneficial to allow certain financial professionals to use insider information?
5. Are customer lists always considered "trade secrets"?
6. What are three types of advertising and can you list an example of each?
7. Was the Tonka Truck of the 1970s a morally safe product?
8. Is it morally right to litigate for injuries caused by the misuse of a product?
9. If new technology is available, such as air bags in cars, is it morally wrong to sell a model at a lower price without air bags?
10. How long after a product's purchase is a manufacturer responsible?
11. If I am laid-off, is it permissible to use information I acquired at my old job to help my new company succeed?
12. If I do research and analysis on a public company, putting pieces together to extrapolate company performance, is that information "inside"?

13. If I overhear a conversation in public regarding a big deal, is it insider trading if sell or I buy stock in the companies being discussed?

14. Is it a conflict of interest to own stock in my competitor?

15. If I think my product is the best is it ethically wrong to say it in advertising?

16. Is it ethically wrong to take a copy of my customer database to my new job?

CHAPTER 16

Employment and Employee Relationships

I. Employee Moral Rights

A. Introduction

Employees, as rational human beings, must be treated with dignity and respect. As important constituents and stakeholders of the corporation or other business organization, they are entitled to moral consideration by the employer, as well as treatment in its code of ethics. The code, moreover, in order to be a legitimate moral code, must contain provisions, binding on the employer itself, that go above and beyond the law. The code, consequently, must provide the employees with clear, succinct, enforceable, practical rights. These rights may restate legal rights, since a moral right also may be a legal right; and some overlap thus is to be expected. Yet ethics may demand more than the law; therefore, the employees are to be granted by the firm's code of ethics a "bill of rights," and one that encompasses "moral rights."

Paramount among these employee moral rights, and animating the "bill of rights" is the Kantian right, as a human being, to be treated with dignity and respect. Accordingly, employees never are to be treated as mere machines or as a mere vehicle to a profit. For example, they are not to be mandated to perform work that is demeaning or stultifying. Even if the necessary work is routine or even dull, a moral employer will afford the employee a reasonable opportunity for variety and advancement.

B. Basic Employee Moral Rights

Potential employees possess the right to apply for a position with a company, as well as the right to accurate, objective, fair, and equal consideration. Note, however, that based on the ethical principle of "last resort," these applicants do not have a moral right to employment with a firm, since a company, even a global corporate giant, is not the employer of last resort for these prospective employees. If any entity is to be regarded as the employer of last resort, it perhaps should be the government.

Once hired, these employees have the right to a safe and healthful workplace and to conditions consistent with their status as human beings. If there are unavoidable dangers and hazards, the employees must be informed fully of the risks, be provided with the necessary safety equipment and apparatus to lessen the risks, and be allowed to participate in and to contribute to workplace discussions regarding safety and health issues.

An employee possesses the fundamental moral right to equal treatment on the job, including the right to equal pay for equal work, as well as comparable work (that is, work of equivalent effort, responsibility, and value to the organization), and the right to be properly evaluated based on legitimate work-related criteria.

The employee possesses a moral right to receive certain information regarding the position, the company, and the potential for future development and employment. If an employee is to be treated in a moral manner, he or she has the right to accurate and thorough information concerning the conditions under which they are hired, retained, and evaluated. For example, if the position is contemplated as a temporary one, or if it entails a probationary period, the prospective employee must be so informed. If the employee will be expected to fulfill requirements beyond those explicitly stated on the job description, these conditions must be disclosed to the employee. In essence, the employer owes to the employee, prospective or current, the moral duty to make clear all the material aspects and conditions of employment, such as salary, advancement, and possible termination and grounds therefor.

Employees, as rational human beings, must be afforded the opportunity to participate in the decision-making processes relating to their job and department, and also where appropriate, their division, or corporate, or other employing entity. Similarly, they have the right to seek to redress grievances, individually or in a concerted fashion, to register complaints pursuant to a regularized procedure, and to receive a fair hearing and without fear of retaliation. An employee, moreover, who believes that he or she has been penalized, not only for complaining, but for asserting any right in the "bill of rights," must be afforded an impartial hearing, the findings and conclusions of which are to be delivered to upper-level management.

C. The "Moral Minimum" Wage

An ethical principle that employees are entitled to a "moral minimum" wage is easy to state, as well as to subscribe to, but precisely to ascertain what this moral minimum is emerges as a daunting task. There does not exist, of course, any simple, definite, precise formula for determining exactly this moral minimum, yet there are important criteria one can apply to approximate what this moral standard should be.

An examination of the "market" is the first area one must consider. The prevailing wages in a labor market, whether industry or geographic based, must be determined. The cost of living in a particular area must be taken into account. A company's financial capabilities, including its competitive position, also must be considered. Obviously, the greater the company's profit and profit potential, the more it can, and perhaps should, pay its employees. The nature of the employee's work, encompassing, for example, the risks, responsibilities, efforts required, the degree of education, training, an experience involved, as well as the nature and extent of the employee's contribution in creating value for the company and its stakeholders, are important additional considerations.

The second major area to examine in ascertaining the moral minimum is the legal system. The minimum wage law, which sets the legal minimum wage, is a focal point of this analysis, because to pay an employee below the legal minimum is immoral, as well as illegal, of course. Yet, to pay an employee merely the legal minimum may be immoral too. Other legal factors need to be examined, such as the relationship among the wages of employees who do the same and similar work, and the fairness of wage discussions and negotiations.

The third and absolutely essential consideration in determining a moral minimum wage is ethics. Ethics, especially Kant's second test, demands that employees, as rational human beings, be treated with dignity and respect. For a firm that is capable of paying higher wages, to take advantage of employees, to underpay them, simply because it is possible to do so due to the nature of the labor market, is exploitation and clearly immoral. The moral minimum is one that provides an employee with a decent living, that is, one that secures to the employee an income adequate for the employee and his or her family's needs. Decency and adequacy, however, are not determined in the sole context of the employer-employee relationship. A moral minimum wage also depends in part on the public support that government, society, and the community provide to the employee, such as health insurance or health care, public assistance benefits, social security, and unemployment compensation. For example, Starbucks Corporation has promised to buy coffee only from its Guatemalan suppliers who pay the coffee-growing farmers a "fair" price for the coffee. The challenge, of course, is to determine what a "fair" price for Guatemala coffee is.

The moral minimum, although a firm requirement of ethics, and thus a necessity, for the moral employer, is a difficult standard to enunciate. What is necessary is to balance the interests of the employer and employee, the constraints of the market and the legal system, the level of support provided by the "system" and that component that is required as ethically mandatory.

D. Moral Rights to Speech, Press, Expression, and Association

Employees possess a moral right to free speech, press, expression, and association. This right includes the right to criticize the employer; but the criticism must be truthful, nonabusive and nonmalicious, and cannot entail the disclosure of any confidential business information. In order to properly exercise this right, moreover, the employee must be able to document or substantiate that he or she used all available internal procedures before asserting any criticism "off the job." The employee's moral right also extends to criticism "on the job" so long as the employee does not foment dissatisfaction, incite unrest, interfere with normal work functions, or disrupt the orderly operations of the company, for example, by continually arguing against, challenging, and contesting management decision or standard operating and planning matters.

The employee's moral right to free expression encompasses the employee's freedom to purchase and use products and services of his or her personal choice for personal use as well as the freedom to express views contrary to the management or corporate positions on political, social, economic, civil, or cultural topics.

A respect for the employee's dignity, rationality, and freedom ordinarily precludes any employer attention to an employee's off-the-job comportment, activities, or associations. Employees hold a valid moral claim to preserve and protect their personal lives. They possess the moral right to engage in off-the-job activities and associations of their free election and choice, unimpeded by any employer dictates or constraints. Accordingly, as a general proposition, an employee should not be sanctioned for his or her off-the-job conduct, activities, or associations. However, if the employee's off-the-job behavior or associations interfere with his or her ability to discharge work duties, the employer can impose appropriate penalties. A moral right to free expression and association certainly does not permit employees to arrive for work in an incapacitated condition. Employees, in addition, must behave in a fashion that does not cast shame or inauspicious reflection on the employer. An employee's behavior or private activities and associations that vitiate the public's trust in the employer's product or service, or seriously harm the employer's reputation, warrant adverse employment action. One difficult problem that has emerged in recent years concerns employees who smoke, and not illegal drugs, but "only" tobacco. Several employers now have policies that require employees not to smoke any time and anywhere, and not merely on the job. Employees who are "caught" smoking, even at home, are subject to discharge. The employer's motivation is to reduce its healthcare costs; yet the employer must be very careful in seeking to implement this policy since too aggressive and intensive enforcement may engender an invasion of privacy—morally and legally.

E. Privacy Rights

1. Introduction

The right to privacy is one of the most cherished, fundamental, and significant moral rights. The right to privacy embodies the esteem that a civilized society holds for the values of personal dignity, integrity, and sense of selfhood. However, the right to privacy is subject to incursion in the employment sector.

Employers always have supervised their employees' work and evaluated their performance, dependability, and potential. Now an immense new array of sophisticated technology is available to the employer. Modern technology arms an employer with advanced and highly effective methods of supervision and evaluation. A greater number of employers have at their disposal the instruments necessary to engage in surveillance, monitoring, and testing of employees. Employers have the apparatus to pry into employees' personal lives and affairs with little apprehension of discovery. Modern technology not only engenders more facile, frequent, and foolproof supervision, but makes secret supervision possible.

Quite naturally, employees worry about their privacy and its vulnerability to incursion by an employer. The employees' interest in privacy often clashes with the employer's interest in controlling and efficiently managing the workforce. As technology grows in sophistication, the danger to employees' privacy interest heightens; such technology's proliferation generates a deep-seated disquietude concerning the privacy rights of employees.

The field of moral philosophy defines the scope of the employees' privacy right, yet ethics is only beginning to be applied to employment policies impacting privacy. As the controversy over employee privacy expands, the right to privacy in the workplace is emerging as a major employment issue. In resolving these moral questions, a balance must be struck between the employees' right to privacy and an employer's need to manage its workforce. Failure to address the issue of employee privacy in the workplace and to develop fair and clear principles will beget perplexity, mistrust, acrimony, and recrimination between employees and their employers.

This section examines moral rights that are arising in the developing field of employee privacy in the workplace, and strives to resolve privacy problems in a balanced, clear, and fair manner.

2. Surveillance

Employees deserve protection against the danger that surveillance technology poses to their privacy. The moral legitimacy of an employer's surveillance scheme depends upon the specific methods used, the impetus for their use, and the significance of the employee activity under observation. In determining the validity of surveillance, one must distinguish between ordinary, traditional surveillance by frontline supervisors and artificially enhanced surveillance by means of electronic devices. A second distinction exists between unconcealed surveillance versus surreptitious surveillance techniques.

An employer should not engage in any artificial surveillance or recording of an employee's actions without advance notification to the employee, in writing, that the employer practices surveillance. Ideally, an employer should give such notice upon hiring and provide details as to the nature and duration of the surveillance, the type of information compiled, and how the collected data are used. An employer must also establish the business reasons for obtaining the information.

Employers should provide employees with access to the information accumulated by surveillance. Further, the employer should give employees a reasonable time and an adequate opportunity to review the information and correct errors. Surveillance data should never form the only basis for an employer's disciplinary actions against an employee.

Even with notice, an employer's surveillance should not reach into very private sectors of the workplace, such as areas designed for employees' health and comfort. Areas such as restrooms and lounges, and areas for safeguarding employees' property, should be free from surveillance. Employers, moreover, must be very careful in adopting and especially enforcing no-dating and no marriage policies for employees. Although employers may have legitimate reasons, such as avoiding sexual harassment lawsuits and charges of "favoritism," employers have to be sure they do not violate the privacy rights—legal and moral—of their employees.

Secret, artificially enhanced, electronic surveillance techniques targeting an individual employee or small group of employees are warranted only when the employer has a serious problem, such as a crime, that cannot be solved by traditional surveillance or disclosed electronic surveillance, and the employer has well-established, specific reasons for believing that secret artificial surveillance means will detect the malefactor(s). In this case, the employer must not prolong the use of the surveillance beyond the duration necessary to identify the suspect(s) or after it becomes apparent that the surveillance technique is not effective. Additionally, the employer must destroy or discard all data not directly pertinent to the purposes of the investigation.

These surveillance rules allow for employers' legitimate interests while mitigating the adverse effects of a surveillance scheme on employees. The proposals recognize employers' concerns, but permit employees to be treated as productive and honest persons unless there is reasonable evidence to the contrary. Finally, the proposals regard secret, artificially enhanced, electronic surveillance as an immoral incursion into employees' privacy, except under special circumstances.

3. Monitoring

Monitoring can mean listening to employee conversations and keeping a watchful eye on their overall communication. Prior notice to employees of the type and extent of relevant monitoring and recording practices is a necessary component of a fair monitoring program. A prior announcement of the monitoring is not always necessary; rather employers should give notice at the inception of the employment relationship that employees are subject to explicit and definite monitoring practices. Initially informing the employees defines the monitoring as a supplemental condition to the employment relationship and diminishes the employees' expectation of privacy. The monitoring apparatus should be visible. Concealing monitoring demonstrates disrespect for employees and risks dissension and litigation when the surreptitious monitoring is revealed.

Employers might seek to advise employees, and others engaged in their telephone conversations, that they are being monitored by means of an audible, but low, intermittent beep, tone, or similar signal. "Beeper" systems, however, destroy the natural flow of the conversation and distract the parties. Thus, warning signals would interfere with the evaluation purpose of the monitoring and impede the functioning of the business. A preferable warning proposal, therefore, would include prior written notice to the employees, and perhaps a brief, recorded, explanatory notice to callers at the beginning of a telephone call.

Employers should not implement a sweeping monitoring scheme that reaches all incoming and outgoing calls by employees. Instead, the employer should monitor only those lines dedicated to business purposes. Moreover, the monitoring must cease once the employer determines that a call is personal. The employer should provide separate unmonitored phone lines in a cafeteria or rest area for the employees to receive and make personal calls. As a corollary to the preceding rules, the employer should rigorously administer a rule against the use of business lines for personal calls.

While employers should not engage in any monitoring beyond that of business calls without giving prior written notice and obtaining expressed written consent, an employer should be able to utilize nonconsensual monitoring for a precise and targeted investigative mission. This should occur only if the employer can substantiate that it possesses a reasonable and particularized suspicion that employees are involved in activity seriously inimical to the employer's interests.

Tracking employees by means of advanced technology is emerging as another contentious privacy issue. Global positioning technology, for example, placed in cell phones, and supporting software, now enable companies to more easily monitor the movements of their employees. Such technology, which is relatively inexpensive, can make assigning and scheduling employees easier; it can also present a very clear picture to employers as to how a business operation, such as a delivery system, is functioning. Such technology makes it easier for employers to manage and supervise mobile workers and thus to improve services, and at lower cost too; yet the technology also makes it more difficult for employees to "goof off." Significantly, privacy advocates point to a further incursion by employers into the privacy of their employees; and some workers have expressed their concern that they feel they now are always being "watched." The technology displays on a computer screen the location and traveling speed of all of a business' vehicles. Dispatchers can then rapidly assign or change routes, for example, to modify assignments to account for unexpected delays encountered by certain vehicles or the unforeseen difficulties in a particular job, or to assign new jobs that come in during the day. Another use would be to assign mobile employees who do not have predetermined assignments and routes to destinations closest geographically to their locations. Furthermore, non-mobile employees with global positioning technology in their cell phones can "clock in" and "clock out" of work at the beginning and end of each day, as well as for meals and "breaks," using the technology. This information will allow employers to precisely and efficiently monitor the amount of time and locations that their employees are actually working. More accurate customer billing as well as more accurate time sheets should also be positive consequences of such monitoring technology. Yet despite the benefits for employers, one negative consequence may be resistance from employees who fear that their employer is turning into a "Big Brother," which will continually monitor and record their every movement. Accordingly, although one can make an argument that the benefits of the tracking technology outweigh the harms, and thus the tracking is moral pursuant to Utilitarian ethics, one also can make the assertion that if the technology is secretive and too intrusive, it may be immoral under Kantian ethics. So, perhaps one moral approach for employers to undertake is to notify employees of the tracking system, explain the long-term benefits it will produce for the company and its stakeholders, and then, to alleviate employees' privacy concerns, to adopt a technological feature that allows employees to shut down the system for certain time periods so that their movements cannot be monitored.

Regardless of the nature of the monitoring, the employer must be able to justify the practice from its inception by establishing that the monitoring was commenced to achieve legitimate business objectives. Competent and responsible personnel should perform the monitoring. Procedural safeguards, such as affording employees access to the information collected by monitoring, are essential. Further, the employer should refrain from basing job decisions on detrimental information obtained solely by monitoring.

These proposed monitoring practices attempt to balance the interests of the employer and employee and to promote fairness. Properly planned and administered surveillance and monitoring policies should not immorally infringe upon employee privacy rights. These proposals do not contemplate a ban on monitoring as well as surveillance. Rather, they suggest better, and moral, controls on intrusive activities.

4. Searches

When an employer's justifiably motivated search intrudes on an employee's private space, the moral legitimacy of the search also rests on balancing the contending interests. Employees should not have their desks, lockers, offices, and other private spaces searched unless the employer has given the employees advance notice. The notice, preferably written, should clearly and explicitly state that the employer reserves the right to search the employees, their property, and their work areas. The notice should disclose the methods for searching the employees and their possessions, define the scope and intent of the search, and inform the employees about the employer's exact concerns and interests.

The search must be predicated on a demonstrable, justifiable, job-related reason, such as searching an absent employee's file for information essential for a management decision. It must be properly authorized and conducted in a reasonable manner pursuant to the company's guidelines. Moreover, only a limited number of designated company officers and managers should have the authority to conduct the search. A search of an employee's person is highly intrusive. Therefore, employers should base such searches only on compelling circumstances, and make a clear and substantial showing of specific, objective, and relevant facts.

Employees possess a legitimate, moral privacy interest in their persons, offices, desks, and lockers, and they rightfully expect these areas to be restricted from employer intrusion unless there is good cause and adherence to proper procedures. The moral legitimacy of employment searches depends upon a clear connection between the search and the integrity of business operations or the safety and security of employees, customers, or the public. The employer's policies emerge as a primary ingredient in determining the invasiveness of the search and the reasonableness of an employee's expectation of privacy. It is, therefore, in the employer's interest, as well as its moral duty, to develop and administer policies that define the permissive grounds for a search, the appropriate procedures, and the use of the resulting information.

5. Drug Testing

An employer should be permitted to conduct drug tests on job applicants, current employees during annual physicals, and employees who have been involved in a serious accident. The employer also may conduct postemployment drug testing based on a reasonable suspicion that an employee is under the influence of a drug that adversely affects, or could adversely affect, work performance. A "reasonable suspicion" standard requires less than absolute certainty and less than probable cause. Rather, it entails individualized, particular evidence that warrants a test. For example, an employee's frequent lapses in work performance, productivity, or his/her involvement in unsafe practices constitute grounds for a reasonable suspicion. Random testing is morally permissible only when an employee undergoes rehabilitation pursuant to an employee assistance program, or when the employee holds a safety-sensitive or high-risk position, such as an engineer at a nuclear power plant or a mass transportation employee.

The employer must ensure that test results are accurate and reliable. Regardless of the basis for the test, if the test result is back "positive," the employee should be tested again, perhaps by a second laboratory. The employee should be allowed to explain any positive finding. If the original finding is confirmed, an employee who offers no reasonable explanation ordinarily should participate in a confidential counseling and rehabilitation program. If the employee tests positive again she/he should be discharged, and the discharge will be a moral one.

Employers should warn employees in advance that the company has a drug testing program. An appropriate notice must explicitly state the manner of selecting employees for testing, describe how the results are interpreted, and warn employees of the consequences of testing positively or refusing to undergo the test. Adequate training is essential to enable supervisors to detect employees with possible drug problems, and to gather evidence necessary to meet the testing program's evidentiary standard. Employers should implement only those tests required to detect the presence of drugs. Finally, employers have a moral obligation not to reveal information obtained as a result of the testing.

The ineffectiveness of less intrusive methods to ascertain drug use, coupled with an imperative requirement to preserve public health and safety, renders drug testing under limited conditions a morally permissible means of deterring drug use among employees. Nonetheless, it remains essential to protect the employee's moral right to privacy. Employers, therefore, should design and execute circumscribed measures, such as those delineated above, tailored to minimize the extent and intrusiveness of the testing process and maximize privacy and dignity. However, drug testing, although an effective mechanism to help control employee drug use, cannot accomplish the task alone. In an employment setting, drug testing will be successful only as an integral part of a comprehensive program of employee notice, education, assistance, and rehabilitation.

6. Personal Information

The employer's initial moral obligation is to acquire and retain only such individually identical employee information that is directly pertinent to, and necessary for, effective performance, competent management, or some other appropriate business purpose. The employer generally does not possess a legitimate right to know certain aspects of an employee's personal life, such as humiliating illnesses, failure to pay debts, and details concerning an employee's sex life.

The employer should not discuss an employee's personal and family life unless the employee raises the subject, or unless the matter clearly affects the employee's on-the-job performance. For example, a manager may perceive that an employee, although consistent in productivity, seems to be psychologically "down." While concern is appropriate, the employer should not interrogate the employee or otherwise seek to gain such information unless the employee is disposed to volunteer the private facts.

The employer should register and disseminate only those telephone numbers furnished to employees and funded by the employer. Moreover, private home numbers should not be recorded and distributed without the employees' consent. The employer, of course, can collect and keep any "personal" information that is required by law. However, only those officers, managers, and employees who have an appropriate and demonstrable business need should have access to the information. Similarly, internal disclosure is permissible based on a "need to know" standard. A manager, for example, should be able to examine performance appraisals, letters of recommendation, records of awards and honors, and sales and production accounts. A supervising manager or a manager considering an employee for a new position needs to study this material in order to make an intelligent business decision. Personal information that has little or nothing to do with job performance is beyond the scope of inquiry for the supervisor or manager. Examples of this personal information may include medical benefits data, records of personal finances (such as payroll deductions, life insurance beneficiaries, and wage garnishments), payments for educational programs, and other items necessary to administer plans or implement human resource administration. This type of data should be open only to the appropriate personnel of the human resources department.

If personal information is kept, the employees should have the right to access and examine the data. Employees also should have an opportunity to authenticate the contents of the information, correct mistakes, refute misrepresentations, dispute the relevancy or necessity of the data, and challenge the employer's interpretation, especially if the information is used as a reason for a sanction. Employees, however, should not be permitted to inspect the notes and commentary concerning investigations of complaints or charges of improper conduct, although they should be able to examine specific findings and conclusions. Additionally, employees should not examine personal evaluations and commentary by other employees if such records cannot reasonably be obtained without a guarantee of confidentiality. These moral safeguards are necessary to maintain open and uninhibited employee evaluation and investigation.

Employers must implement the following moral guidelines when developing a policy for disclosure of employee information. Employers must restrict entry to, or release of, an employee's file to an "outside" individual or entity. The employer may respond to inquiries about the essential facts of employment, such as hire date or job title, but other information regarding an employee should not be divulged to an "outsider" unless the employee consents in writing, or the requester is acting pursuant to legal authority. If an external organization seeks to establish that a person works for the company, the employer should be able to reveal the employee's most recent work designation, place of work, and date of employment. This should not require contacting or informing the employee. If the outsider wants more information, such as an employee's salary or five-year job history, the employer should not disclose the information without the written consent of the employee, Similarly, attorneys, creditors, and private agencies should not be provided with information except with the employee's approval, or in compliance with legal requirements.

Because personal information concerning employees is private, the employer is under a moral obligation to keep the information secure and confidential. Accordingly, the employer should establish policies to protect the information from disclosure, and enforce rules controlling its care and use. Information must be maintained safely, whether stored in a computer or file cabinet. If kept in a computer, for example, the employer should require passwords to limit entry to authorized personnel. Those employees with authorized access must be apprised of, and educated in, security operations. Indeed, all employees must comprehend the importance of confidentiality.

Finally, employers should inform employees that the company maintains files containing personal information. Notice to the employees should include the type of data compiled, the frequency of collecting the information, the extent of employee's and other's access to the files, and the effect the information could have on performance standards and the employee's position in the firm.

7. Electronic Mail

Electronic mail (or e-mail is a computer-based system designed to facilitate communications between an employer and its employees, and among the employees themselves. It is achieving a central position in the modern workplace. Employees, however, possess a moral right to privacy regarding their personal mail; a concomitant right to privacy does pertain to some extent to their e-mail communications, which employees may believe are private communications like letters or telephone calls.

In order to avoid any e-mail moral privacy problems, the employer should reserve clearly the property right to the system. It should prohibit private communications and explicitly warn employees that the use of the system to transmit personal messages or private information is an unacceptable practice. The employer, moreover, clearly and accurately should inform the employees, preferably on the display screen, that the employer reserves the right to access and observe the e-mail and read messages to determine if communications are work related or personal.

8. Summary

The preceding privacy proposals help the employer fulfill its appropriate function of efficient management without contravening the employees' reasonable expectations of privacy. The proposals also reflect the underlying rationales of quality control as well as the avoidance of surreptitious examination of private communications to gain personal information. These proposals, finally, and most importantly, treat the employees with dignity and respect, and thus as worthwhile human beings morally deserving of privacy.

F. Summary

The employer recognition of employee moral rights, preferably in a code of ethics, not only implements the employer's moral obligation to treat its employees as worthwhile "ends" in and of themselves, but also demonstrates sound management. A company that adopts an employee "bill of rights," based on the privacy rights discussed herein, should benefit in the long-term from a more contented, loyal, and productive workforce, as well as from the enhanced public image that comes from being a moral employer.

II. The Employment at Will Doctrine and the Right to a Moral Discharge

A. Introduction

In order to achieve a just employment relationship, it is necessary to achieve a proper balance between the employer's right to manage its workforce, including the right to discharge employees, and the employee's right to be treated fairly and with dignity, which encompasses the moral right to maintain a proper degree of job security.

This section will examine the employment at will doctrine, the traditional and most significant legal doctrine ruling the employment relationship, and will question ethically the appropriateness of adhering rigidly to this conventional doctrine. This section, finally, will propose just principles to govern the job security aspect of the employment relationship, particularly the employee's right to a moral discharge.

B. The Employment at Will Doctrine—Overview and Background

The traditional general rule in the United States regarding employment at will holds that where an employment relationship is of indefinite duration, the employer may terminate an employee, or an employee may quit, at any time and for any reason, without being liable thereby for any legal wrong. The conventional legal doctrine, moreover, allows an employer to discharge an employee even for a cause that is morally wrong. Considering the evident capability for abuse that is sanctioned by the doctrine, any careful analysis demands an investigation into the doctrine's derivation. Viewing the employment at will doctrine from an ethically relativistic perspective, it is instructive to note that Europeans and Latin Americans, who are long accustomed to protections against employee discharge, find the employment at will doctrine morally "shocking."

The salient question necessarily arises as to why the legal system in the United States formulated the employment at will doctrine and then applied it systematically and energetically to employment relationships. The answer is to be found with the advent of the Industrial Revolution in the late 19th century.

The employment at will doctrine emerged because it was well suited to the favorable business-oriented economic, political, and social climate that matured its development. During that period, the legal system, bolstered by the prevailing attitudes of laissez-faire economics and freedom of contract, encouraged industrial growth by supporting actively the right of an employer to control its business, including approving the right of an employer to discharge at will.

As the United States evolved into an industrialized nation, there came the decline of the master-servant relationship and the rise of the more impersonal employer-employee relationship. The emerging capitalist employer required wide latitude in employment practices, especially license to set the size of its workforce, so as to confront growing competition and to meet changing market conditions. The employment at will doctrine promoted and protected the capitalist employer by empowering its rule over the labor force. The employer now had great flexibility to upgrade its labor force and to dismiss employees during times of reduced demand for production; the employee now had a keen motivation to maintain high performance standards to keep his or her position.

Viewing the doctrine from the employer's perspective, therefore, it would seem that any employer's objective should be to create and preserve at-will employment relationships. Yet, it is necessary first to examine carefully the assumptions animating the doctrine, as well as the arguments asserted against it.

C. The Employment at Will Doctrine—Rationales

A rationale commonly cited to support the conventional doctrine is the principle of mutuality. That is, not only can the employer not be compelled to retain an employee, but also the employee cannot be compelled to work for the employer. The employee remains free to terminate the relationship and work elsewhere. The disinclination to abolish the doctrine thus is said to be based on the need to protect employees as well as employers. In the absence of any employment contract, the counterpart to the employer's privilege to terminate at will is the right of the employee to do likewise. Employees have a strong interest in maintaining that right free employer legal interference; or else employers will be armed with a new legal weapon with which to harass any employee wishing to change jobs. Therefore, the rights of the employer and employee to decline to impose conditions upon termination benefit both, at least theoretically.

Since both parties work at will, the employment at will doctrine appears balanced and fair. In the "real world," however, the employer ordinarily is in the dominant bargaining and economic position, and thus the risk of any harm or abuse caused by the doctrine falls squarely on the employee, the usually weaker economic party. Employers, moreover, rarely sue employees and never seek to compel them to work.

D. Criticism

Although the conventional doctrine is rationalized in terms of mutuality, the relationship of an individual employee to an employer, especially a large corporate employer, is not an equal relationship. The typical employee must work in order to obtain the means to live and frequently must accept work not of his or her preference. Many employees, in addition, are bound geographically to their jobs. They have invested time and knowledge in their positions, and they do not have the financial means to change jobs freely. In reality, employees seldom quit voluntarily. Rather, they live in fear of losing their positions absent some legal grounds of assuring a secure position. Even if employees can find suitable alternative employment, they usually must pay the expensive costs involved in the job search and relocation.

The employer, however, not only has been able to select the person to be employed, but has also been able to dictate almost all the terms of the employment relationship. The employer, moreover, rarely suffers more than an inconvenience when an employee resigns. Of course, if an employer really wants to retain an employee who is contemplating resigning to take another position, the employer merely has to make its own position more appealing. The consequences of an involuntary severing of the relationship, especially if sudden, clearly threaten far greater hardships on the employee. The employment at will doctrine, therefore, is not a mutual, equal, or balanced relationship. Although the doctrine is rationalized in terms of mutuality, granting employees as well as employers the right of at will termination, it cannot be seriously contended that in reality the doctrine impacts with equal force.

Considering the wide disparity in economic power and bargaining positions between employers and employees, particularly large corporate employers, and the employer's chiefly unchecked control over the terms and conditions of the employment relationship, abuses in the treatment of employees naturally arise. The legal system, of course, will be used to protect employees from abusive employment practices; yet until the legal system can respond, ethics and the moral "law" must fill the void. As a matter of fact, the conventional doctrine is further criticized for discouraging legal and moral behavior. An employee, for example, threatened with discharge for reporting or refusing to engage in misconduct will be disinclined to do so, and an employer undeterred from such wrongful discharges may inflict them more unimpededly.

E. Legal Limitations

Recognizing the criticisms levied against the employment at will doctrine, the federal and state legislatures have intervened to qualify the traditional doctrine. The U.S. National Labor Relations Act, for example, forbids an employer from terminating an employee in order to discourage union activity. As a result, an employer defending against charges pursuant to the act is obligated to demonstrate a legitimate job-related reason for the employee's discharge; and thus the employee is removed from the terminable at will category. The employee, of course, must fall under the act's coverage of protected activities; and, moreover, not all employees are protected by the act, such as managers and supervisors who are excluded from protection.

Title VII of the U.S. Civil Rights Act further prohibits the discriminatory discharge of employees. Thus, if an employee contends that his or her discharge was due to discrimination prohibited by the act, the employer must defend itself against the discrimination charges by providing a legitimate, job-related reason for the discharge. The employee, of course, must fall into one of the act's protected classes, and not all employees, for example, employees of small firms, are covered by the Civil Rights Act.

A major legal exception to the employment at will doctrine is the common law, "public policy" exception. When an employee is discharged for a reason or in a manner that contravenes some clearly defined and fundamental public policy, the employer may be held legally accountable. The public policy exception would arise, for example, when an employer discharges an employee in contravention of a statute, for example, for serving on a jury; for pursuing or exercising a statutory right, such as seeking worker's compensation benefits; or for refusing to violate a statute, for example, by refusing to participate in an illegal activity.

Although the abuse engendered by the conventional doctrine has prompted the intervention of the legal system, nonetheless the employment at will doctrine remains in full force subject only to the specific exceptions created by statutory or common law; and, therefore, there are still a great number of employees, especially private sector managerial employees, who are ruled by the doctrine.

F. Ethical Limitations

The employment at will doctrine yields employees no rights, but the legal limitations on the doctrine do provide some limited rights. Ethics, however, requires that employees be granted a moral right to certain job security. Employees, as human beings, possess the right to be treated with dignity and respect as well as the right not to be compelled to suffer detriment unfairly or unjustly. Accordingly, as a moral minimum, ethics demands that an employee not be discharged in an arbitrary, capricious, or irrational manner. Ethics, in addition, will not countenance a malicious or abusive discharge, that is, one entailing disinterested malevolence, ulterior motive, or insulting or offensive behavior. When an employee, for example, is discharged for seeking to perform an important public function or obligation, such as testifying in a legal proceeding potentially adverse to the employer, the employer consequently should be subject to a charge of immorality.

An employer further commits a moral wrong for terminating an employee for engaging in conduct that entails an important public interest, for example, when an employer discharges an employee for seeking legal redress for or protesting unsafe conditions at the workplace. This moral conclusion may be justified ethically on the utilitarian grounds of protecting and serving the public good as well as the good of the workforce.

This public interest rationale also is related closely to the whistleblowing principle previously examined. If an employee is obligated morally to disclose wrongdoing pursuant to the whistleblowing principle, ethics also must deem it immoral for an employer to discharge an employee who complies properly with his or her moral duty. This moral limitation to the employment at will doctrine may be explained on the grounds that a discharge of a whistleblowing employee jeopardizes the interests of the employee's coworkers as well as the public's health safety and welfare.

A difficult whistleblowing discharge problem arises when the whistleblowing employee's assertion is found to be erroneous. In such a situation, if the employee nonetheless has a good-faith belief as to the existence of wrongdoing, and the employee has sought to bring the problem to management's attention, the employee should not be terminated for mistakenly blowing the whistle. The social harm in reporting in good faith a problem that after investigation turns out to be unfounded is likely far less than the harm of not revealing a questionable complaint of misconduct for fear of adverse employment consequences. The public good from investigating all potentially serious allegations of wrongdoing is far greater than the benefit to be achieved by permitting an employer to discharge an employee who properly and in good faith reports situations that later prove neither to be legally nor morally wrong.

The discharge of a government or public sector employee for asserting or engaging in constitutionally protected rights or activities very well may be an illegal act; and, similarly, the discharge of a corporate or private sector employee for asserting or engaging in the equivalent of a constitutionally protected right, for example, the moral right to free speech, very well may be an immoral and thus ethically impermissible discharge.

The discharge of an employee for acting in conformity with a code of ethics of his or her company or profession, or for refusing to violate the code, is an immoral discharge, presuming, of course, that the code is a legitimate one that prescribes standards of conduct beneficial to the public. The employee, moreover, should refer explicitly to his or her rights and responsibilities pursuant to the code.

As a moral minimum, ethics also requires that the employer sufficiently demonstrate a legitimate, job-related reason for the discharge. Employees as rational human beings ethically are entitled to be treated with dignity and respect, and certainly not as mere objects to be discarded or replaced arbitrarily, capriciously, or frivolously. Particular reasons for an employee's termination may be clearly justifiable, such as engaging in illegal activity, incompetence, absenteeism, tardiness, or economic necessity. Other reasons, though less clearly justifiable, such as a lack of respect for management, a poor attitude toward work, and incompatibility with other employees, nonetheless may rise to the level of a legitimate, job-related reason for the employee's discharge. The employee, of course, possesses the moral right to be informed of the reason for his or her termination.

Ethics requires that the employees be accorded the moral right to "due process." Prior notice of the company's rules and standards, a fair and timely hearing, and appropriate advance notice of any termination, although not legally mandated by the employment at will doctrine, are ethically obligatory as part of the moral minimum. The length of the employee's service, the size of the company, the nature of the employee's position, and the type of alleged infraction are all important factors in ascertaining precisely the extent of the employer's moral responsibility. A long-term employee, for example, with many years of acceptable service, is entitled to a more substantive and specially demonstrable reason before he or she can be discharged morally.

Providing an appropriate reason and basic "due process" are the minimal requirements for a moral discharge. Yet, a socially responsible employer who aspires to go beyond the moral minimum can implement additional procedures and options, such as informing employees of their deficiencies, progressively disciplining and rehabilitating employees, retraining and transferring employees, granting severance pay, and allowing the use of the company's facilities as a search base.

Employer appearance policies can have a detrimental though legal, effect on employees, resulting in legal but perhaps immoral discharges. For example, an employer may desire a workforce that is thin, cute, and attractive. Consequently, it may be humiliating, demeaning, and offensive not to hired, let alone to discharged, because one is overweight or not sufficiently "cute" or attractive, but it legal under the federal civil rights acts as well as almost all state civil rights acts to discriminate in employment based on weight and appearance, though there are at least two states in the U.S. as of this writing (Georgia and Michigan) that bar employment discrimination due to weight (but not appearance). Of course, an employer who intends to differentiate among employees because of their weight and appearance is well advised to proceed very cautiously, since such legal but perhaps immoral discrimination could degenerate into immoral and illegal discrimination if the appearance discrimination case can be converted to a conventional sex discrimination one (for example, by the "cute" criteria being just applied to women) or if the weight case can be converted into a conventional disability discrimination case (for example, if one is so obese that one's weight is classified as a "disability").

The "intersection" of smoking and the employment at-will doctrine also raises challenging legal and moral issues. Employers are naturally concerned about ever-rising health care costs. Smoking, of course, is not a civil right protected by the federal civil rights act. However, there are several states, primarily in the southern part of the United States— primarily the tobacco growing region, that do protect employees who smoke. In those states, an employee cannot be discharged for smoking. Under the federal law and in the majority of states, smoking is not a civil right. Thus, employees who smoke who are also only employees at-will can be discharged for smoking. Some employers, in an effort to control and reduce health care costs, now not only prohibit smoking by employees on the job but also forbid employees to smoke at any time and any place including their own personal time and "space." Presuming an employer is very careful in how it administers its "blanket" non-smoking policy, perhaps by nicotine drug testing, an employer has the legal right to discharge an employee who violates the policy. So, the employer is acting legally, but is it acting morally? In order to act in an ethical manner, an employer must in addition to giving the employees notice of the policy, provide the employees with a reasonable amount of time and help to quit smoking. Accordingly, an employer should retain the professional services of a smoking "coach" to help the employee quit. The professional help could encompass the coach working with the employee to set reduction and stop dates for smoking, to create an individual stop-smoking plan, and to check regularly with the employee to ascertain progress and to deal with any relapses and other concerns. The coach could also work with the employee and health care personnel to determine if the employee requires any medications in order to quit smoking. Finally, the employer should introduce incentives to assist the employee to quit smoking, for example, credits to the employee's health care payments, or yearly rebates. These incentives could be part of a larger health care improvement program that encompasses not only smoking but also weight issues. With such assistance and incentives, the employer will be acting in not only a legal but also a moral manner.

G. Summary

The purpose of ethically limiting the employment at will doctrine is not only to protect the interests of the employee but also those of the employer and society. The employees possess a moral right to job security as well as the right to know that they will not be terminated for reasons that contravene ethically imposed norms. Employers possess a right and interest in knowing that they can retain sufficient latitude to make necessary personnel changes so long as their conduct is consistent with morality. Society possesses an interest and a right in a stable employment market, the advancement of fundamental policies, the dissuasion of acrimony and disruption by disgruntled and dispirited employees. The challenge to the business community is to create well-crafted and precisely defined moral formulations that respect and balance the preceding interests and rights.

III. An Ethical Analysis of Mergers

A. Introduction

The recent decades have experienced a massive wave of merger, consolidation, acquisition, and takeover activity, as businesses have embarked on "megadeals" underscoring the resurgence of the merger as the momentous agent of corporate change. Motivated by long-term, global, strategic thinking, rather than short-term pressures for quick profits, these enormous deals have reshaped the business scene, in the United States as well as internationally. This merger-made restructuring, moreover, continues unabated today, driven by the keenly felt business need to combine, streamline, and concentrate so as to compete more forcibly in the international economic arena.

These mergers, however, produce profound consequences—economic, of course, but also political, legal, social, personal, and moral. The U.S. "system" was premised on the fundamental belief that vigorous competition was "good," because it leads to lower prices, more information, superior products and services, and better distribution of goods and services, and especially because it avoided the private concentration of economic power and the potential for abuse and unfairness therefrom. United States' antitrust law, in fact, was designed to foster this competition, to thwart concentration of power, and thus to protect society from economic harm and abuse. Yet, these basic rationales now are called into question, to the point of being labeled irrelevant to business in the modern global context.

This section provides a brief legal background and overview of the major federal U.S. statutes governing mergers; and then, after rendering legal conclusions as to the legitimacy of mergers, this section ethically will examine mergers, by employing principally Utilitarian and Kantian ethics, to determine the morality of this form of business activity in its modern global economic context.

B. Legal Background and Overview

1. Introduction

The post-Civil War United States beheld the growth of large, powerful, corporate business enterprises, some of which legally consolidated as "trusts" with practically monopolistic power to prevent, reduce, or eliminate competition, to control supply, divide up markets, fix prices, and to engage in anticompetitive behavior, and to restrain unfairly trade and commerce. U.S. antitrust law was a reaction to the wielding of such economic power. The law was created to preserve competition by ensuring that free, open, and fair markets would be maintained, thereby allowing the virtues of a free enterprise, capitalistic system to be realized fully. The law also was designed to preserve democracy by impeding the concentration of economic power, which could be converted to social and political power.

The two principal pieces of federal legislation in the U.S. governing mergers are the Sherman Antitrust Act of 1890 and the Clayton Act of 1914.

2. The Sherman Act

The Sherman Antitrust Act Section 1 prohibits any agreements, contracts, conspiracies, trusts, or combinations to restrain trade or commerce. The principal example of an illegal restraint of trade pursuant to anti-trust law is horizontal price-fixing; that is, colluding to set prices by competitors at the same level in the marketing chain. An example of price-fixing was the admission by British Airways and Korean Air that they conspired to fix prices on overseas flights, specifically by uniformly raising cargo rates and fuel surcharges which were added to fares in response to rising oil prices. The companies admitted their guilt and paid a $300 million fine to the U.S. government. The fines could have been substantially higher, but the companies had cooperated with the Justice Department. Nonetheless, the fine was the second largest anti-trust sanction by the Justice Department since 1995. The largest fine was the 1999 $500 million fine imposed on the vitamin company Hoffman-La Roche in another price-fixing case.

Section 2 of the Sherman Act holds that every person who monopolizes or attempts to monopolize, or who combines or conspires to monopolize any part of trade or commerce, commits a legal wrong. A prime concern of the act is a "merger to monopoly." It is important, however, to note that the Sherman Act, as interpreted, makes a critical distinction between being a monopoly and a monopolizer. Monopolizing clearly is illegal misconduct, yet acquiring a monopoly is not necessarily legally wrong. Monopolizing not only involves size and power in a relevant market, determined principally by the percentage of the market held by a firm, which in itself is very difficult to measure, but also the purposeful and wrongful acquisition and maintenance of that market share and power. Size, therefore, is not alone dispositive of the issue, and the Sherman Act does not penalize firms that through efficiency and industry, superior marketing, business foresight, knowledge, and skill, or more cost-effective, superior, or customer preferred products and services, achieve and maintain very large market shares and dominant market power. Size, however, coupled with evidence of deliberate abusive, predatory, and anticompetitive practices, such as controlling or fixing prices (for example, when a firm attempts to drive its competitors from the market by selling its product substantially below the ordinary costs of production) and excluding or taking over competitors, will transform a legal monopoly into illegal monopolizing. Monopoly legal analysis, therefore, is not a function of size or structure alone. However, by requiring additional (and difficult to obtain) proof of intentional misconduct, antitrust law in fact licenses the rise of highly concentrated markets; and it is argued, moreover, that it would be contrary to society's interests to punish every firm that secured a position of market power. Yet, such "big" business structure, even if legally acquired, portends serious practical and moral consequences. An example of the legal and moral difficulties inherent in Sherman Act monopolization analysis in an anti-trust lawsuit instituted in 2006 by the owner of a small coffee shop owner against coffee giant Starbucks. The essence of the lawsuit is that Starbucks is a monopoly company that engages in predatory, abusive, and unethical conduct to perpetuate its monopoly. In order to prevail, the coffee shop owner must demonstrate that Starbucks has a geographic (Seattle) and product (gourmet coffee) monopoly and that Starbucks wrongfully and intentionally perpetuated its monopoly by engaging in such alleged "predatory," though legal, tactics, such as long-term and exclusive-use leases, buying up coffee sellers, and opening up several stores in a neighborhood, and giving free coffee samples to consumers.

3. The Clayton Act

The purpose of the Clayton Act of 1914 was to strengthen U.S. antitrust law, specifically by targeting anticompetitive and monopolistic practices that were not directly covered by the Sherman Act. Section 7 of the Clayton Act deals with mergers, that is, those situations where previously independent business firms are united (by merger, consolidation, stock acquisition, or purchase of assets). Section 7 pronounces that a person or business cannot hold stock or assets in another business where the effect is to substantially lessen competition in a relevant market. Section 7, therefore, is the statutory authority for preventing mergers, and it is enforced by the Justice Department and Federal Trade Commission, that has enunciated guidelines indicating what mergers will be challenged. Horizontal mergers, that is, combinations of firms in direct competition that occupy the same geographic and product market, are viewed as most threatening to competition, and thus subject to government challenge. Vertical mergers, for example, the merger of a supplier and purchaser, and conglomerate mergers, for example, the merger of firms that provide unrelated products and services, are much less likely to be challenged by the government.

It is important to distinguish the Sherman Act from the Clayton Act. The Sherman Act requires the existence of impermissible size and market power as well as an exhibition of anticompetitive conduct; and it can form the basis for criminal prosecution; whereas the Clayton Act requires only a showing of a reasonable probability of a substantial lessening of competition; and it is enforced only civilly through injunctions, divestiture, or other civil relief.

Defining the relevant market, ascertaining the degree of market concentration (that is, the allocation of market shares among the various firms in the market), and thus determining a firm's market power, are essential issues to resolve. Other important factors to consider are whether the merger will further consolidate market power and restrict competition, for example, by eliminating the number of competing firms, by dissuading the remaining competitors from aggressively competing because of a fear of retaliation, by making it more difficult for potential competitors to enter the market, and by creating such a huge, powerful economic entity that it has the capability to control prices. There may be, moreover, positive economic benefits to be attained from the merger, for example, "efficiencies" to be achieved from economies of scale, or the preservation through merger of a failing firm that otherwise would be lost to the market. Examining and weighing all these criteria, the government regulators render a judgment as to whether the merger produces an economic entity whose increased market share and augmented market power substantially reduces competition; if so, the merger is presumed illegal. The definition of the relevant market will be the critical legal determination to be made by government regulators in the Sirius-XM satellite radio merger announced in 2007. Is the market a narrow one consisting of only satellite radio companies, merger partners—or is the market a broad one consisting of all audio entertainment companies, including "free" radio and Internet-based audio services? The government's definition of the market should logically lead to the ultimate merger decision.

A horizontal merger that was approved in 2007 by the U.S. government was the purchase by Whole Foods Market, Inc. of its direct competitor in the organic and natural grocery foods business Wild Oats Market, Inc. The rationale for approving the merger was the fact that the market was broadly defined to include large supermarket chains which also sell organic foods. Another merger, a major vertical one, also approved by the U.S. Federal Trade Commission in 2007, was Google, Inc.'s $3.1 billion purchase of online advertiser DoubleClick, Inc. The key to the government regulators' approval was that Google's online advertisement sales business does not directly compete with DoubleClick's ad-serving tools, which assist publishers in placing and tracking display ads. Privacy advocates had raised concerns that the combined company would have access to a huge amount of data on individual online shopping and "Web surfing" activities. It is interesting to note that the U.S. Federal Trade Commission stated that it was cognizant of the privacy issues, but it lacked the legal authority to block the merger on any grounds except on antitrust criteria.

4. Summary

Although there exists a highly developed, extensive, and complex corpus of anti-trust law pursuant to the Sherman and Clayton Acts, which this chapter has addressed only succinctly, as well as other federal and state antitrust law, which are beyond the scope of this work, there has been very little government enforcement of this law in the last decade; and some of that enforcement has been criticized as politicized. Government antitrust concern with conglomerate mergers appears to have disappeared; and very few challenges have been made to vertical mergers. Horizontal mergers, of course, remain subject to the law; and have been challenged and even prevented (for example, the merger of two of the nation's largest drugstore chains as well as the attempted merger of the nation's largest and second largest office supply "super-stores"); but even here the government regulators have relaxed their enforcement efforts considerably, to the point of sanctioning massive mergers with much larger market shares produced than previously tolerated, for example, in the communications and media, banking, and defense industries. Specifically, just to name a few, the government has approved the mergers of AOL-Time Warner, R.J. Reynolds Tobacco and Brown and Williamson, Exxon and Mobil, Phillips Petroleum and Conoco, Chevron and Texaco, American Airlines and Transworld Airlines, Capital Cities (ABC Network) and Disney, and Sears and K-Mart. The U.S. Justice Department has approved the merger of AT&T and Bell South; and approval by the Federal Communications Commission was secured in 2006. As a consequence, government antitrust regulators have been condemned for abandoning their consumer protection functions. Instead, the government regulators seem to be giving primacy to helping business achieve efficiencies and cost-savings; and thus enabling business to compete more effectively in the global market. As international economic arguments predominate, enforcement of antitrust law languishes; and government thereby "approves" mergers that otherwise would be challenged as unduly anticompetitive; "bigness" now is not necessarily "bad," at least in the legal sense. Yet, is "bigness" in business morally wrong from the ethical standpoint.

C. Ethical Analysis of Mergers

1. Introduction

Ethical Egoism first counsels a prudent, rational, long-term evaluation as to whether it is in the best interests of the principal parties to merge; that is, will the merger maximize value for these parties and also for the stakeholders, especially the shareholders and employees, that they represent directly. Ethical Egoism thus focuses narrowly on internal profit growth in the long run. Utilitarian ethics then requires that a broader stakeholder analysis, evaluating the consequences of the merger on all those people and groups directly and indirectly affected by it, be accomplished. The interests of the local communities and society as a whole, for example, would have to be examined in the utilitarian analysis in order to determine if the merger is moral. Kantian ethics, finally, demands that executives, managers, and corporations disposed to merger identify the essential moral concerns involved, particularly those embracing the dignity and respect of affected stakeholder groups; address these moral issues when making and implementing these deals; and integrate such moral considerations into the merger process. If a "good" utilitarian merger, for example, nonetheless unfairly produces some harm for an employee constituent group, which probably had little input in the merger negotiations, can these harmful consequences be sufficiently mitigated or compensated to pass Kant's ethical test. In order to explicate fully these moral points, a more detailed Utilitarian and Kantian ethical evaluation must be effectuated.

2. Utilitarianism

a) Introduction

A stakeholder or constituent group analysis is the most appropriate method to commence a utilitarian ethical analysis of mergers. The term "stakeholder" encompasses any person or group that will be directly or indirectly affected by the merger, and thus has a stake in the outcome of the merger. The stakeholders include the shareholders, of course; ordinarily they will realize considerable gains from even the prospect of a merger, but these are not the only people with a stake in the merger. The employees, managers, customers and consumers, suppliers, local communities, creditors, competitors, government, and society also have an interest in the merger. The essence of utilitarian ethics is to determine if, how, and to what degree these constituent groups will be benefited or harmed by the merger; and then to ascertain whether the merger produces more overall "pleasure" than "pain." The merger generally will benefit some parties, the merging corporate principals and their top management and shareholders, for example, but will result in losses to other parties with a stake in the deal, middle managers and employees, for example. The degree of "pleasure" and "pain" usually will vary very significantly too, with shareholders seeing dramatic stock gains, and top managers receiving bonuses or "golden parachutes," but employees confronting reassignment and relocation, and middle managers facing termination. Yet, despite the harm suffered, if the merger produces more "good," it is moral pursuant to utilitarianism.

B) MERGER STAKEHOLDER CONSEQUENCES—QUANTIFIED

(1) Shareholders

The effects of mergers on the shareholders are of course extremely important in determining the morality of mergers. The recent surge of mergers has been very successful at building value in companies. Investors as well as the stock market generally have been quite enthusiastic about all the mergers, acquisitions, and takeovers, for example, in the banking, defense, telecommunications, utility, entertainment and media, and health care industries. The enlargement in company value has been rendered into an increase in share prices. Mergers definitely have been one successful mechanism to make corporate management become more shareholder-value oriented. The threat of forced mergers, moreover, has compelled many managers to discipline themselves and to work their companies into competitive shape. Inefficient and incompetent managers are, of course, terminated and replaced.

The augmentation in value and share price can be attributed to a variety of very likely positive merger effects. Mergers have resulted in cost savings by means of the operating and distribution efficiencies and economies of scale achieved, as well as gains from improvements in productivity and cross-promotion. Mergers have produced stronger combinations that can gain larger market share and that are more competitive in the global marketplace. Mergers also often produce a large fund of available assets, as well as improved credit access, which can be used for expansion.

There should not be too many negative consequences for shareholders. If the merger fails or is blocked by the government, the shareholders may see a loss in share value. Perhaps if certain shareholders did not like the resulting combination for political or philosophic reasons, these shareholders would not be too happy about the merger. There is a risk, moreover, that the greedy or incompetent management of the stronger entity in the merger will sell off, harshly use, mismanage, or even waste or loot the assets of the weaker party.

The merger's effect on the shareholders, however, should be primarily and substantially positive. The most likely result is that the shareholders will be positively impacted by the merger because their stock will appreciate greatly in value. These good effects will out-weigh any bad consequences of the merger. The overall impact on the shareholders, there-fore, is rated as a **+4.** Even shareholders who solely seek to maximize their own profits will, as a practical, if not a moral, matter, take into account the interests of the employees and customers, without whom the company could not exist. Utilitarianism, of course, demands this as well as a more comprehensive constituent group analysis.

(2) Employees

There are divergent repercussions on the employees resulting from the mergers. There are several foreseeable good consequences. In the newly merged company, there should be more and better opportunities for advancement since the new combination will be a larger and likely wealthier entity. The existing employees may perceive the merger as an opportunity to build an all new company, particularly if management seeks the participa-tion and input of the employees. Several employees' positions may change, expanding their authority and responsibilities, and presumably increasing their salary. Surely the lat-ter will improve their morale. Many employees very likely will own stock in the merged companies, which will appreciate in value as a result of the merger. Mergers, therefore, might help to satisfy the personal ambitions and needs of the employees, especially man-agement employees.

Yet there are also several negative ramifications to the merger for the employees. One of the very bad consequences, of course, will be the inevitable layoffs due to facility clos-ings and the elimination of redundant positions, especially middle-management posi-tions. Hopefully, there will be some type of job placement program for those employees who lose their jobs. Several remaining employees may be expected to assume more responsibility, or even managerial duties, perhaps without any corresponding increase in pay. Some of the remaining employees, moreover, may suffer morale problems due to the layoffs and changes. These employees may have been used to and preferred the "ways" of the old organization and may be resistant to any change initiated by the new entity. Another possible effect of the merger, and generally a painful one, is that certain employ-ees may be transferred and relocated. Now, some employees may be quite happy about relocating, particularly if there is a promotion and raise involved, or the new location is viewed as desirable for cost of living or other factors; but for most of the relocating employees, the transition will be painful, even if it is necessary to save their jobs, because the employees' spouses, children, and maybe family members living nearby will find the move distressing. Of course, if employees are discharged as a result of the merger, family financial and personal problems very likely could be experienced, and then the merger will be quite painful indeed for the employees.

There are significant positive and negative merger consequences impacting on employ-ees. The "bad" effects, however, are more likely to occur, and to be more harsh, than the "good" effects and any counterbalancing pleasurable consequences therefrom. These more possible and painful "bad" outcomes, in addition, will adversely affect a large number of employees. Although not all employees will be terminated or relocated, and there will be some opportunities for advancement, some employees definitely will lose their jobs, and all will undergo the stresses inherent in a merger and the concomitant need to manage change. Altogether, the numerical pleasure-pain outcome for the employees is **–3.**

(3) Customers-Consumers

Mergers produce positive and negative impacts on consumers and customers. If the cost savings from consolidation, efficiency, and economy are passed on to the consumers in the form of lower prices, the consumers obviously will gain. The consumers will also benefit if the combined and now more effective entity can produce a wider array of new products, technologies, and services for the consumers. Yet if the concentration of economic power reduces diversity, innovation, and quality, the consumers surely will lose, especially if the "product" is information and ideas. Moreover, if the resulting reduction in competition effectuates monopoly type power which brings about higher prices, the consumers will be negatively impacted, but if the merger forces the competition to become more consumer focused in price and quality, the consumer will benefit.

In viewing the recent wave of mergers, it seems that the good consequences for consumers, particularly the potential for lower prices, outweigh the bad, but not overwhelmingly so, thereby resulting in a "score" of **+2** for the customers and consumers.

(4) Suppliers

The merger "picture" is also mixed for suppliers. The merged entities now may well have the size, power, and leverage to control volume and to dictate terms, especially better prices, to suppliers, particularly smaller suppliers. On one hand, there may be a redundancy in suppliers, necessitating some painful adjustments; but, on the other hand, there may be exceptional opportunities for suppliers to serve a larger and more wealthy entity, and at different levels in the production and marketing process. Overall, the benefits to be derived from the enhanced opportunities appears to outweigh slightly the pains to the suppliers from loss of leverage and position, thus bringing about **+1** units of pleasure.

(5) Competition

There are several immediate negative effects on the competition. The mergers should effectuate stronger competition against former, and perhaps larger, rivals, some of whom may lose market share if prices are lowered and not matched. If the remaining competitors are small and weak, however, they may be subject to unfair and predatory practices, and may be eliminated thereby. Mergers, moreover, should enable the combined firms to penetrate and contend effectively in international markets, thus rivaling foreign competitors. Of course, all these competitors, foreign and domestic, could be compelled by the mergers to make their own deals, alliances, and combinations to counter the power of the newly merged entities. Yet, there also may be some positive consequences for competitors. If they too merge, they naturally will achieve the cost savings and financial gains, and other benefits therefrom. If the merged firms do not lower prices, and perhaps even have to raise them to pay for the merger, the competition should benefit by keeping prices steady and thus gaining some market share. Regardless of pricing, the competition will be forced to examine closely all aspects of their business, and will have to become more focused on the consumers' needs and wants, which exercise should measurably benefit the firms. The competitors, in addition, will be searching for other ways to compete, by looking at more than just price, for example, by considering niche or segmented marketing, where they may be able to secure a competitive advantage.

The most foreseeable result of the mergers on the competition is to cause pain, presently and in the long term, but less negatively on a long-range basis. A likely outcome of the mergers is an overall reduction in prices, though not drastically, which will enable the merged firms to acquire some market share at the expense of the competition. Responding to the mergers, the competitors will attempt to reduce costs and cater more to the consumer in order to reacquire market share. If the competition cannot do this, they probably will merge themselves, or else be eliminated. Over time, the various industries will be forced to change, will "shake out," and be reconfigured with fewer, stronger competitors. Yet the mergers definitely will produce more pain for the competition, especially initially, to the extent of causing a -2 rating as a whole.

(6) Government

The government presumably is policing all these mergers to ensure they comply with antitrust law; and even, which is the usual case, when they are not prevented, the government should be watching these powerful economic combinations to ensure they are not engaging in predatory practices. All this "patrol" work is beneficial, one surmises, for government regulators, and thus "good" for government. Yet, if one purpose of government is to foster decentralized economic, and perhaps correspondingly political, power, which is supposed to represent the advantages of more competitive markets and more democratic politics, the government should be somewhat "pained" by all the recent "merger-mania." There also may be some tax advantages for the merged companies, which can be deemed another negative financial outcome for government, as will the outlay of government payments for the merger created unemployed. There are, however, some significant positive factors for government. Since these mergers allow U.S. firms to compete more effectively against foreign competition and may even preclude "buyouts" of U.S. firms by foreign competitors, the country's international competitiveness is strengthened thereby, and government benefits financially and politically, to the degree of receiving a $+4$ "score."

(7) Society

The recent steady surge of mergers portend momentous consequences for society. Mergers clearly result in the concentration of greater economic power in ever fewer giant corporations, thus threatening market domination of certain sectors of the economy. The dangers of such concentration are especially evident in the communications and media industries, where the risk of a decrease or absence of diverse ideas and viewpoints could harm the public interest.

The mergers also have resulted in layoffs, relocations, and elimination of businesses, which "pain" has caused problems for society, especially for local communities which directly must bear the burden of unemployed workers and closed businesses, as well as for society members who must pay more taxes to help ease the financial burdens. Some employees, however, may be transferred to other areas where work or more employees are needed, and some terminated workers may enhance their skills and knowledge and eventually find other, and perhaps, better jobs, but the most likely foreseeable outcome, particularly in the short term, is the negative consequence of more unemployed people in society.

Yet the mergers, though causing negative outcomes, and some very personally painful ones too, can be viewed in a larger, long-term, strategic sense of strengthening U.S. business and industry, restructuring and "toughening" the economy, enabling stronger international competitiveness, and thus inuring to the greater good of society, and meriting a rating of $+2$ overall for society.

Table 16.1—A Utilitarian Analysis of Pain and Pleasure

Stakeholder	Pain	Pleasure
Shareholders		+4
Employees	−3	
Customers		+2
Suppliers		+1
Competition	−2	
Government		+4
Society		+2
Total Scores	−5	+13
Difference in Scores	+8 (Pleasure)	

c) UTILITARIANISM—CONCLUSION

The essence of utilitarianism is to quantify consequences—good and bad—into numerical units of pleasure and pain. If there are more positive than negative consequences, the action is moral; conversely, if the negative numbers predominate, the action is immoral. The purpose of the utilitarian analysis herein is to determine whether mergers are moral. Accordingly, the numbers for the affected categories are as presented in Table 16.1.

As the result is a positive number, indicating the production of more positive consequences, the action of companies merging is moral pursuant to the Utilitarian ethical theory. Utilitarianism, however, is one ethical theory, which should be "checked" by other doctrines, particularly Kant's nonconsequentialist, formalist, ethical test.

3. Kantian Ethics

For a merger to be moral pursuant to Kantian ethics, it must pass the test of the Categorical Imperative. If one subjects the action "merge" to the first test—the Consistently Universal principle, the action, stated generally fails. "Merge" cannot be made consistently universal, because if the action is carried to its logical conclusion, that is, if all companies merged, ultimately there would be only one, a supercompany, remaining, with no other firms to merge with; and thus the action "merge" self-destructs as it loses its meaning and efficaciousness when one seeks to make it a consistently universal action. The action "merge" stated in a qualified or limited fashion, however, can be made consistently universal. For example, "merge," but only to prevent "hostile" foreign takeovers of U.S. firms, or merge, but only to enable U.S. firms to penetrate and compete aggressively in foreign markets, passes the "consistently universal" principle, because not all firms will be merging, only certain firms in response to certain specified conditions.

The second part of the Categorical Imperative demands that the merger stakeholders, as rational beings, be treated with dignity and respect. The employees who will be terminated as the result of the merger are the stakeholders most at issue under the second test. If global economics dictates, and Utilitarian ethics countenances, their downsizing, Kantian ethics demands at the very least that actions be taken to alleviate the pain inflicted on the constituent group that suffers the harshest loss. Such "dignified" steps, such as severance packages ("silver parachutes" perhaps), retraining, re-education, and job outplacement services to assist these employees in obtaining new positions, can deem the merger a Kantian "respectful" one. The preceding steps also should allow the merger to pass the third test of the Categorical Imperative—the "agent-receiver" test, because an effort is being made to cushion the negative consequences of the merger so that no one group of people bears the full brunt of the painful impact. Under the second and third tests, the merged companies should also give something back to the local communities harmed by the merger as well as society, such as the contribution of money or the time of their employees for civic and charitable purposes.

D. Summary

Merger analysis is a multifaceted task, encompassing levels of economic, legal, and ethical inquiry. As explicated ethically herein, "big" is not necessarily "bad," according to Utilitarian ethics, and with qualifications pursuant to Kantian ethics. Yet, despite all the rational arguments, the efficiencies, cost savings, new products and technologies, and the international competition, there is still a feeling of unease at the elimination of competition and immense concentrations of economic power. Historically, in more individualistic times, such concentration of power into fewer hands was viewed as dangerous and wrong, and antitrust law was supposed to protect against such concentrations, but such "wrongness" could be construed as merely a long-ago account of an ethically relativistic moral conclusion. "Bigness" may not be bad, but it is threatening, and that threat can give rise to emotions of fear and dread, which for the Ethical Emotist are sufficient "reasons" to brand mergers as truly immorally bad.

Discussion Questions

1. What is "At-Will Employment" and how does it relate to employees and managers?

2. Discuss some of the ethical challenges associated with monitoring employee's emails and computer usage.

3. Discuss the morality of monopolies in a democratic society, citing examples.

4. Is price-fixing among companies ever morally allowable? Why or why not, citing an example.

5. Develop the utilitarian arguments for and against mergers, and provide an example of a business merger in your discussion.

6. Are "golden parachutes" ever morally justifiable? Why or why not, citing a real or hypothetical example.

7. Is monitoring of computer systems moral in a business context? Discuss, providing examples.

8. Does compiling information about an employee violate the employee's moral right to privacy? Discuss.

9. Is there a moral right to employment? If so, to whom should it be asserted—to business or government, both, or neither? Discuss.

10. What is the doctrine of employment-at-will, and what are some of the moral deficiencies of the doctrine? Discuss.

11. What constitutes an ethically just reason for a discharge? Discuss, providing examples.

12. Do employees possess a moral right to free speech on the job, or off the job? Discuss, providing business examples.

13. Is post-employment drug testing ever morally justifiable? Discuss, providing a business example.

CHAPTER 17

Ethical Analysis of Affirmative Action and Age Discrimination

Part I. Affirmative Action

A. Introduction

The United States usually is viewed as an enormous "melting pot," encompassing many different peoples with diverse backgrounds, desires, goals, and philosophies. Yet, a common objective shared by most people is to take advantage of the many opportunities afforded by the U.S. democratic, free-market system and to succeed. One key measurement of success is to attain a managerial or executive position within a firm.

Regrettably, U.S. history also reveals that minority groups and women have been victimized and hindered by past discrimination and social stereotyping; in many instances, they still are being harmed by both the cumulative and current effects of racial, ethnic, and sexual prejudice. These negative effects are especially apparent in the private employment sector where, despite some achievement of workplace equality, the ranks of upper-level managerial and executive positions remain noticeably underrepresented by women and minority group members. The continuing debate over achieving racial, ethnic, and sexual equality, therefore, frequently centers on business. In the business context, moreover, attempts to achieve equality and to remedy the effects of past discrimination and social stereotyping have substantial, far-reaching, and long-lasting ramifications.

The public discourse on discrimination frequently treats the subject in moral terms. What moral choices, therefore, must business make to help redress the effects of past discrimination and stereotyping and to achieve the societal goals of equality of opportunity, social balance, and social harmony? In seeking to resolve these issues, one confronts the division and the strain between the quest for equality and the desire to protect individual rights. This conflict between two basic "American" values renders the difficult subject of discrimination particularly difficult to solve. A corporation, for example, that strives to do the "right" thing may find itself thrown into disorder by clashing values and competing claims; and no where do these contentious issues come to a greater head than in the area of affirmative action.

Virtually every large company has some type of affirmative action program, and most companies do appear to feel morally obligated to implement some form of affirmative action. Yet, what type of an affirmative action program should a company adopt, and what is the moral propriety of so doing? These questions present exceedingly difficult legal, moral, and practical problems for a firm. Accordingly, the purposes of this section are to examine current affirmative action programs and practices, and then to apply ethical theories thereto in order to make moral conclusions about affirmative action.

B. Purpose and History of Affirmative Action

As one continues reading articles (classic or current events issues) to learn more about diversity, one will notice some of the patterns and historical trends as they relate to managing diversity. One historical trend on diversity initiatives dealing with Affirmative Actions is discussed in the classic article republished in *Harvard Business Review (HBR) on Managing Diversity* (2001) titled "From Affirmative Action to Affirming Diversity" by Dr. R. Roosevelt Thomas, Jr. This article was originally published in *Harvard Business Review* in 1990. Dr. Roosevelt is very well known for his work in the area of managing diversity. Bahaudin Mujtaba met him a few times in the early to mid 1990s when working as a senior training specialist and an internal consultant for a Fortune 100 firm in Florida. Dr. Roosevelt was invited to be the keynote speaker during a four-day Leadership Conference at Disney World of Orlando. Dr. Roosevelt did an excellent job of fueling, reigniting and energizing the organization's diversity initiatives and training. The organization had developed an excellent workshop for managers that focused on awareness of diversity issues and the existing individual and societal stereotypes that can impact one's behavior, more times than not such stereotypes may negatively impact those who fall in the minority side in terms of their difference.

In his *HBR* article, titled "*From Affirmative Action to Affirming Diversity*," Dr. Roosevelt provides a good understanding of Affirmative Action, its original intention, current challenges, and solutions to effectively deal with these challenges toward providing equal opportunities to everyone, including white males. He goes on to say that while affirmative action sets the stage for a gender-blind, color-blind, and culture-blind workplace, larger percentages of minorities and women still tend to stagnate, plateau, or quit when they fail to move up the corporate ladder. As a result, everyone's dashed hopes lead to corporate frustration and a period of embarrassed silence, usually followed by a crisis and more recruitment. Some organizations may have repeated such a cycle three or more times in the past few decades of the twentieth century. The assimilation model of washing away differences (the American melting pot) is no longer useful nor valid. So, organizations are faced with the challenge of having to manage unassimilated diversity using strategies designed for a homogeneous work force to earn employee commitment toward quality and high profits. Dr. Roosevelt continues to say that the challenge for executives, leaders and managers of today's workforce is to work not merely toward culture and color-blindness but also toward an openly multicultural workplace that taps into and energizes the full potential of every employee without artificial programs, standards, or barriers. This can be achieved by learning to understand and modify ineffective organizational assumptions, models and systems, which can be a laborious challenge.

Affirmative action was stated with the several premises in the 1960s. Five of them were:

1. Adult, white males made up majority of the American business mainstream.
2. The American economic structure was a solid, unchanging institution with more than enough space for everyone.
3. Women, blacks, immigrants, and other minorities should be allowed into the workplace as a matter of public policy and common decency.
4. Widespread racial, ethnic, and sexual prejudice keeps minorities out of the workplace.
5. Legal and social coercion are necessary to bring about the needed changes in the workplace.

The article states that more than half of the U.S. workforce now consists of minorities, immigrants, and women. White men (natives) are becoming a minority as they make up only about 15% of the workforce in the year 2000. Minorities and women no longer need a boarding pass to the workplace since the major problem is no longer having entry into the workplace. Rather, the major challenge is to make better use of their potential at every level, especially in middle management and leadership positions. Affirmative action may not provide the solutions to the changing landscape of America. Affirmative Action, which focused on short-term solutions to a major problem, alone cannot cope with the challenge of creating a work setting geared toward upward mobility of all individuals, including white men. Affirmative action is a red flag to every worker who feels unfairly passed over and a stigma for those who appear to be the beneficiaries of its policies. Dr. Roosevelt offered 10 guidelines for learning to manage diversity.

1. *Clarify motivation.* Learning to effectively manage diversity will make you more competitive.
2. *Clarify vision.* Create an environment where everyone will do their best work.
3. *Expand focus.* Create an inclusive environment for all.
4. *Audit corporate culture.*
5. *Modify assumptions.*
6. *Modify systems.* Examine the process for promotion, mentoring and informal assignments.
7. *Modify models.* "Doer to Enabler."
8. *Help people pioneer.* Empowered change agents can try and discover the best solutions in their progression toward effectively managing diversity.
9. *Apply the special consideration test.* Will the system contribute to everyone's success?
10. *Continue affirmative action.* We still need a diverse workforce to deal with diverse challenges.

The purpose/goal of managing diversity has been and should be to develop everyone's capacity to accept, incorporate, and empower the diverse human talents in the organization, in the nation, and eventually in the world so everyone can be as productive as possible. Diversity is both a national as well as an international reality and we must make it our strength.

As defined by MSN Encarta, affirmative action is "policies used in the United States to increase opportunities for minorities by favoring them in hiring and promotion, college admissions, and the awarding of government contracts." Some will argue that affirmative action is "the only way to ensure an integrated society in which all segments of the population have an equal opportunity to share in jobs, education, and other benefits." Others will argue that affirmative action is reverse discrimination showing favoritism to one group while the group pays for the sins of their fathers. Now, many managers and leaders trying to do the right thing are asking the following questions:

1. Does affirmative action enable or disable a manager who is looking for the best candidate for the job?

2. If affirmative action were reversed, what would the effects be?

3. Has affirmative action become more than it was intended to be?

4. What other means do we have or can we create to ensure that equality and diversity exist in the workplace?

Perhaps the answers to such questions can be best answered by each industry and each organization depending on their hiring patterns in the history and their current workforce demographics compared to the population demographics since it is assumed that each organization wants to be fair to all individuals. Being ethical requires deep reflections and eventually doing what is right.

C. Affirmative Action-Preference/Plus Plans

1. Introduction

The term "affirmative action" represents a wide variety of programs, from one extreme of setting rigid, fixed job quotas that must be filled by women and minority group members, to the other most "mild" extreme of taking special proactive efforts to ensure that women and minority group members are included in the pool of applicants for hiring or promotion. Almost everyone morally condemns the former and morally approves the latter.

In the middle, however, is the type of affirmative action plan that takes race, ethnic heritage, or sex into account when selecting among qualified candidates and that gives such individuals a preference over equally or more qualified white men. Such a preference plan raises a loud emotional outcry, from those who praise it as just redress for past discrimination and stereotyping, to those who condemn it as immoral, "reverse discrimination." What is required, however, to resolve this difficult issue is rational ethical analysis of preference type affirmative action plans.

2. The Supreme Court's University of Michigan and Seattle and Louisville Decisions

The United States Supreme Court, in a very significant affirmative action decision in June 2003, permitted the use of race as a preference factor in the college admissions process, but the court also issued a stern warning that colleges cannot use rigid affirmative action systems that resemble quotas and that they also must adopt race neutral policies as soon as practicable.

Justice Sandra Day O'Connor, writing for a 5–4 court majority, stated that the University of Michigan Law School did not violate the "equal protection" guarantee of the 14th Amendment to the Constitution. Significantly, Justice Sandra Day O'Connor, writing for the court's majority, stated that the goal of creating a diverse student body was a sufficiently "compelling government interest" to justify the law school's consideration of race as a beneficial admissions factor. She added, however, that race-conscious admissions policies should not go on forever. Twenty-five years from now, Justice O'Connor stated, the court would expect that racial preferences will no longer be necessary.

The University of Michigan's undergraduate admissions policy—a point system that quantified the importance of race—did not survive the Court's scrutiny in another companion case. In that case, Chief Justice William Rehnquist, writing for a 6–3 majority, stated the numerical policy made race the decisive factor in admissions decisions, and thus was unconstitutional.

Justice Clarence Thomas, the court's only black member, issued a bitter condemnation of affirmative action as a well-intended but patronizing and ultimately discriminatory attempt by whites to help African Americans. Thomas' dissent began with a quote from an address by Frederick Douglas, criticizing abolitionists in 1865 for interfering with blacks' efforts to help themselves. Thomas stated that he believes that blacks can achieve success "without the meddling of university administrators." He declared that a state's use of racial discrimination in higher education admissions is categorically prohibited by the Equal Protection Clause of the Constitution.

In the majority opinion in the law school case, Justice O'Connor rejected the argument of the Bush administration that race-neutral alternatives could be as effective in creating diversity as affirmative action. The Constitution, said Justice O'Connor, does not prevent the law school's "narrowly tailored" use of race in admission decisions in order to achieve a compelling interest in obtaining educational benefits that are produced from a diverse student body. The Michigan law school uses race as a potential "plus" factor to promote diversity, stated Justice O'Connor. The goal of the law school affirmative action policy was to produce a "critical mass" of minority students on campus. She supported the decision by citing studies showing that diversity promotes learning outcomes and better prepares students for an increasingly diverse workforce, for society, and for the legal professions. Diversity is necessary, she maintained, for developing leaders with "legitimacy" in the judgment of the people. Moreover, she stated that effective participation by members of all racial and ethnic groups in the civic life of the nation is critical if the U.S. truly will achieve the goal of being one "indivisible" nation. She emphasized, in addition, that businesses have made it clear that the skills and knowledge essential in today's increasingly global marketplace can only be created through contact and experience with widely diverse peoples, cultures, ideas, and views.

U.S. Solicitor General Theodore Olsen, however, condemned the Michigan policies as a "thinly disguised quota." Some critics contended that the decisions mean that universities can still racially discriminate so long as they are not obvious about it. Civil rights advocates, however, hailed the decision as a major victory and claimed it not only strengthened affirmative action in a college setting, but also gives added impetus to the use of race in pursuit of diversity elsewhere, especially in employment.

The University of Michigan's president, Mary Sue Coleman, said she was delighted by the decision because the principle of diversity was upheld, and she stated the school would fix its undergraduate policy so that it is not construed as a mechanical quota-based system. Unlike the law school, the undergraduate school awards a specific, predetermined number of points to applicants whose ethnicity or race is underrepresented on campus, specifically a 20-point bonus on a 150-point scale where 100 points guaranteed an admission. The majority of the Court found that this resembled a quota system, a practice previously struck down as unconstitutional. The undergraduate decision also could cause employers to rethink their reliance on quantitative evaluations of job applicants and employees. While the law school decision does allow colleges to consider race as a preferential factor in making decisions, the court made clear that diversity should not be defined solely in terms of race and ethnicity. Universities, therefore, will have to look more broadly at socioeconomic factors, special talents and life circumstances, such as family background and income and education levels, in searching for a diverse student body. Justice O'Connor required that universities now must give applicants a personal "holistic" look.

The Supreme Court's University of Michigan affirmative action cases in 2003, therefore, emerge as landmark decisions with wide-ranging implications not only for education but also for business and for society as a whole, especially so because the use of race has been upheld legally as a permissible component to an affirmative action preference plan.

The very difficult and contentious issue of affirmative action again reached the U.S. Supreme Court, and also once again in the context of education. In December of 2006, the Supreme Court heard arguments in a secondary school desegregation case in which two school boards, one in Seattle, Washington, and the other in Louisville, Kentucky, were attempting to preserve voluntarily imposed race-based integration plans. The school board plans were controversial because race was used as a factor to assign students to schools in order to achieve more racially diverse schools. The school districts contended that racial integration is an essential component to a public school education; and that such an objective is a compelling government interest so as to justify a limited use of race in implementing policies that produce integrated schools. The parents that challenged the race-based school assignment plans contended that the Equal Protection clause of the 14th Amendment to the U.S. Constitution as interpreted by the Court forbids any consideration of race in school enrollment decisions. However, proponents of the plan said that the limited use of race is necessary to redress the legacy of racism and school segregation in the United States. Moreover, proponents argued that there are positive benefits for the students and ultimately for society as a whole for students to attend racially diverse schools. Achieving a diverse student body, one recalls, was deemed to be a sufficiently "compelling" interest for the Court to uphold the University of Michigan's law school's affirmative action policy in which race was allowed to be used as one "plus" factor in an otherwise "holistic" evaluation of a candidate for admission. In the Seattle case, involving a city, it is important to note, which never imposed official segregation, students are allowed to enroll in any of ten high schools. However, if a particular high school has more applicants than seats, school officials are empowered to use several tie-breaking factors, including race, in order to achieve an enrollment that approximately reflects the city-wide student population. In Seattle, whites account for 40% of the population, with blacks, Hispanics, Asians, and Native Americans accounting for the other 60%. In the Louisville case, the city once had a legally imposed dual, "separate but equal," school system, in which certain schools were reserved for whites and others for blacks. As a result of civil rights litigation, a federal court in 1975 imposed the remedy of mandatory busing in order to achieve integration of the schools. However, in 2000, a federal judge dissolved the desegregation order, finding that the schools had been successfully integrated. In order to maintain integrated schools, school officials in Louisville decided to continue the desegregation policy, which seeks to keep black enrollment in each school between 15% and 50%. A parent whose child was denied admission to neighborhood schools, because the child's enrollment would have an adverse effect on desegregation, sued because her child was assigned to a school impermissibly due to the child's race.

Even the initial questions and comments by the Justices of the Supreme Court reflected the conservative-liberal, Kantian-Utilitarian, dichotomy to the Court. For example, the "liberal" members talked in terms of the benefits of diversity and emphasized the need and desirability of local school officials to develop policies that use race to achieve diversity in school composition. Whereas the "conservative" members asserted that despite the laudable benefits of integration and diversity, the means used to attain these "good" ends must be race neutral, non-discriminatory, and thus moral ones. Of course, the key vote in, as well as author of, the Michigan law school, 5–4, decision, Justice Sandra Day O'Connor, was no longer on the Court. The key vote, according to legal experts, was Justice Anthony Kennedy, who appears to be very reticent about using race as the classifying factor in admissions decisions. Although it is always difficult to predict the Court, many legal experts nonetheless expected that the Court would enunciate a "split decision" as in the precedent Michigan case. That is, the Court would most likely strike down the Louisville plan since race is the sole factor in assigning students; but uphold the Seattle plan where race is used as "merely" one factor, granted a potential "tipping" one, among a variety of criteria employed to determine school assignments. However, in June of 2007, the Supreme Court, in a surprising, momentous, landmark, and very close 5–4 decision, struck down *both* the Louisville and Seattle affirmative plans as unconstitutional. Chief Justice John G. Roberts, Jr., writing for the majority, declared that the two school districts had failed to meet their "heavy burden" of justifying the "extreme means" the districts had chosen to classify children by means of their race when making school assignments. Chief Justice Roberts very succinctly explained, using Kantian logic, the Court's reasoning: "The way to stop discrimination on the basis of race is to stop discriminating on the basis of race." Yet the decision may not entirely eliminate the use of race as a factor in making educational decisions. Justice Kennedy, joining the majority, but also writing a concurring opinion, opined that there might be some "narrow circumstances" that would allow the use of race as a criterion in education. Justice Kennedy also declared that "This nation has a moral and ethical obligation to fulfill its historic commitment to creating an integrated society that ensures equal opportunity for all of its children. Nevertheless, the decision very likely will force educational institutions to devise race-neutral criteria, such as socioeconomic factors, in designing affirmative policies and plans. As a matter of fact, in the majority opinion, Chief Justice Roberts stated that other means aside from race should be used to promote diversity in schools. Everyone seems to agree that classroom diversity is an important educational objective, but how to achieve it fairly and constitutionally is emerging as a daunting challenge—legally, morally, and practically.

3. The Components of a Preference Plus/Plan

In order to ethically evaluate the "preference" form of affirmative action, it is first necessary to state exactly what such a plan constitutes, and what it does not. The employment context will be used to illustrate the components and workings of the preference type of affirmative action plan.

Typically, a preference plan is voluntarily adopted by an employer to integrate its workforce in order to redress past discrimination and social stereotyping. In the private employment sector, the plan normally is not preceded by any admission or finding of purposeful past discrimination by the employer. The plan is predicated, however, on a foundation. It is designed to eliminate obvious racial or sexual imbalances in the employer's workforce. That is, the number of women and minority group members in the employer's workforce is compared with the number of women and minority group members in the area labor market. If the comparison reveals a manifest imbalance, then the preference plan possesses a foundation. Of course, if a particular position requires special training or education, the comparison is made with those individuals in the area labor force that have the relevant qualifications.

The plan does not include fixed numerical quotas for hiring or promotion; rather, the plan sets forth flexible goals or objectives for women and minority group representation in the employer's workforce. All applicants and candidates are to be qualified. For moral, as well as very practical reasons, preferences are not to be extended to unqualified women and minority group members.

Presuming all applicants are qualified, the preference form of affirmative action then allows women and minority group members to be accorded a preference or "plus" factor in employment decisions. Note that under this type of plan, no person is automatically excluded from consideration; all will have their qualifications evaluated. Yet an applicant's race, sex, or "diversity" can and will be used as one "plus" factor in the applicant's file. As one clearly can perceive, the moral controversy arises when the "plus factor" dictates the hiring of a qualified woman or minority group member over an equally or more qualified white male applicant.

The preference plan, however, is not designed as an absolute preclusion to the hiring or promotion of white men; it is not an absolute principle, but a contingent one, since race or sex is merely one "plus" factor. That is, if a white male applicant is especially qualified, he certainly can be chosen over a qualified woman or minority group applicant. Yet, the employer in so doing must be aware that it has set hiring goals, and thus will be expected to make overall progress in achieving these affirmative action goals and attaining proportionate representation of women and minority group members.

D. The Morality of Preference Plans–Utilitarian Ethical Arguments

1. Introduction

The object of the Utilitarian ethical analysis herein will be to determine if the consequences of a preference type affirmative action program produce more good than harm in the long run; and hence the program will be deemed a moral one, or, if the harm outweighs the good, an immoral one. The action to be examined ethically is stated as: Is an affirmative action preference plan with a "plus" factor being awarded for "diversity" moral?

After identifying the action, a utilitarian analysis action requires an identification of all persons and groups which are directly or indirectly affected by having the action implemented. Next, the reasonably foreseeable, long-term consequences, good and bad, are ascertained and listed for each person and group enumerated. Then, the consequences are measured, weighed, and quantified. The resulting numerical conclusion yields the moral conclusion.

2. Affected Groups—The Stakeholders

The people and groups affected by the action under examination are: white men and other applicants not hired or promoted, their families, and members of nonminority groups generally; minority and women candidates given the employment preference, their families, and members of minority groups generally; shareholders and owners of business entities and firms granting preferences; employees thereof, including production and management employees; customers and consumers; the competition, the local community; government; immigrants; potential employees, including students; business and industry; and society.

3. The Consequences—Measured, Weighed, and Quantified

The consequences—good and bad—for each person and groups now must be ascertained and then measured and weighed, with a numerical conclusion, representing units of pleasure and pain (on a scale, ranging from –5 –4 –3 –2 –1 0 +1 +2 +3 +4 +5), assigned to each affected party and group.

The white men who are denied a position or promotion because of affirmative action obviously experience pain, especially if a position is granted to a woman or minority group member with less experience and qualifications. The pain represents a loss of power in hiring and promotions, some advancement restrictions, and a potential decrease in salary and status. Of course, many of these white men still will have a position and are not precluded from applying for other positions and competing against other qualified candidates; and, if they feel they were subject to illegal "reverse discrimination," they can institute legal action. The "bad" suffered by white men also may reflect the loss of the advantages that white men have had in the past, and which they still are accustomed to, but will no longer possess. White men denied positions or promotions overall receive a –4.

Their families share their pain in losing the position or promotion, as well as the reduced pay and promotion opportunities; and the families, in addition, may have to cope with the white men's disgruntlement and discontentment. The families of these white men denied a position or promotion are assigned a −2, noting that the women family members may be able to take advantage of affirmative action programs to enhance their own and their families' prospects.

White men generally will suffer pain too. They now must compete with women and minority group members whose proportional representation in the workforce is not only encouraged but also is given a preference. A loss of former privileges and position is of course negative, but there still will be many opportunities available for this group. There will be members of this group, moreover, who perceive some benefits overall from affirmative action, especially if it is viewed as an attempt to redress past wrongs inflicted on women and minority group members. Yet, overall the impact on white men will be negative, a −3 to be precise.

Women and minority group members who are hired or promoted as a result of affirmative action policies are awarded a +4. They obviously prosper from the preferences, although they may be burdened by some negative attention and pressure and perhaps by being regarded as an affirmative action employee or diversity token. Yet, once on board, these qualified women and minority group members should begin to eliminate stereotypical myths, and hopefully will improve the overall "sensitivity" of the firm. The increase in opportunities, as well as the increase in income, prestige, and power, dictate that women and minority group members who receive the tangible benefits of affirmative action be accorded a +4.

Naturally, when women and minority group members benefit, their families benefit as well. The augmented pride, confidence, and happiness to be shared and enjoyed, as well as the increased financial rewards accruing to the family indicate a +4 designation, but noting that the family may have to help its "breadwinner" cope with some new negative pressures on the job.

Women and minority group members also substantially benefit, especially due to the positive impact working and visible minority group members and women can have as role models. Leading by example always significantly influences others, and when unemployed or underemployed women and minority group members see others hired and promoted and prospering, they too will want to advance and succeed. As more and more women and minority group members are provided with more and greater opportunities, they will play a wider role and have a greater impact on the U.S. economy and society, and especially in the planning and operation of business. This group also is given a +4.

The business firms and entities that adopt preference type affirmative action programs will be affected, of course. The most efficacious method to examine the pleasurable and painful consequences for this group is to analyze the results for the affected constituent or stakeholder components. The owners or shareholders traditionally are the stakeholder group counted first. They ultimately may receive some increased profit distribution as a result of the company's commitment to diversity, as women and minority group members with new approaches and underused talents are brought into the firm, but there may be some shorter term negative impact on productivity since pursuant to affirmative action the "best" qualified person, the white man perhaps may not receive the position, which can be filled by a lesser productive but "diverse" candidate. Disgruntled white men, moreover, may impede productivity by creating a stressful work atmosphere, and they also may sue, thus further draining the firm's profits, part of which are supposed to be allocated to the owners and shareholders. Yet, overall, there should be increase in the firm's profitability based on the utilization of new talent and the enhanced "networking" and marketing opportunities presented, resulting in a +2 for this first constituent group.

The next constituent group, employees, will be examined generally and then will be subdivided into production and management employee categories and evaluated accordingly. Employees, still predominantly white men, will experience some pain as affirmative action preference plans are implemented. They will feel that their opportunities will be diminished. Women and minority group employees will perceive these plans as a positive factor. White men, moreover, also may feel threatened by the presence of assertive and hard-working women and minority group employees who now will be competing for more positions and for more advanced positions. The opening up of opportunities in the workforce will increase competition, but also will create conflict in the workplace. Employees, therefore, receive a –1.

Production employees, as well as the management employee group, are very important components of the general employee category and thus merit separate consideration and their own numerical conclusion. The production employees, ordinarily composed of white men, nonetheless may have differing reactions to the affirmative action preference plan. For those who presently aspire to a management position, the plan would be viewed in a negative light; and for those who do not have any aspirations of becoming a manager, the perception of unfairness would probably make the action feel like a negative. Yet, for those production workers who are women and minority group members, the implementation of an affirmative action preference plan surely will be received positively. The plan might be viewed as an effort to redress past wrongs as well as be considered by some employees as an added practical incentive to prepare and aim for the management ranks. White men with greater seniority who desire advancement, however, must be given greater relative weight in this analysis. They will experience pain; overall, the affirmative action plan will result in a negative impact of a –2 for production employees.

Management employees usually have worked their way up through the ranks. Many most likely have put in many years with a firm. Although the objectives of the plan will be portrayed in an admirable fashion, it is likely to be viewed by many current management employees as a negative, at least initially. Along with the "fairness" issue, managers might feel pained because of a perceived negative impact on close working relationships previously established. Adverse reactions, friction, disruption, and conflict could arise, in addition, among employees, management as well as production, when more women and minority employees are introduced into the workforce. Management, of course, must shoulder the burden of educating the workforce as to the rationales for and objectives of affirmative action, and of ensuring a smoothly functioning affirmative action program and a conflict-free workforce.

On the "pleasure" side of the equation, however, the management ranks will be enriched by the development of a diverse management staff. These underused abilities, new knowledge, and differing perspectives should improve and enrich the long term working management environment, as well as enhance the multicultural and global capabilities of managers, which should translate into overall good for management employees as a whole, thus warranting a +2 for management employees.

As a result of the affirmative action plan, customers and consumers will be introduced to products and services that may more accurately represent their needs and wants. Certainly, increased and improved communication will be effectuated with women and minority group members. Better products and services should result from the firm's commitment to affirmative action. One also can expect, however, some resentment from white male customers, but overall the result is good, specifically a +2.

Since affirmative action plans will enhance a company's access to and ability to sell in multicultural and global markets, the competition, which probably does not have a diverse workforce, will suffer some initial pain. Yet, as more competitors adopt affirmative action plans, no firm would possess a significant long-term advantage over another. The "score" for the competition, therefore, is only a −1.

The local communities in which these companies that adopt affirmative action plans are based very well may reflect racial and ethnic diversity, as well as difficulties. The size of the company as well as the local community, of course, would dictate the impact that the firm's affirmative action program would have on the local community. The improvement of employment opportunities for women and minority group members certainly will have positive effects for the local community, but if the perception exists that these opportunities were obtained at the expense of another segment of the local community, there also will be some negative reverberations. Overall, the impact is probably negligible, though a slightly +1.

As a consequence of companies implementing affirmative action plans, government very likely will find itself with more "business," in monitoring the plans and in resolving legal disputes that arise under these plans. Yet, many of these plans were initiated in, and prompted by, government, which presumably wants to ensure their success. These affirmative action plans, in addition, should help to defuse lobbying groups who have been vociferously complaining to government that they are being denied opportunities because of their race, sex, or ethnic heritage. Consequently, government will be affected by affirmative action plans to the extent of a +1.

Potential employees, including students, are obviously affected by companies adopting affirmative action plans. Women and minority group members in these categories naturally will be affected positively by affirmative action, as it will lead to greater opportunities for them; and the white men in these groups may be harmed, at least temporarily, by the diminished opportunities. Yet, some of these white men may sense a need, based on fairness and practicality, of increasing the numbers of women and minority group members in the workforce. However, since there is a larger percentage of white men in the categories of potential employees and students, a larger portion thereof will feel pain, giving this group overall a −1.

Immigrants migrate and increasingly are continuing to do so because of the greater job opportunities available in the United States. Many of these immigrants possess the diversity characteristics that are accorded preferences under affirmative action plans. These immigrants, therefore, will view the United States as an even greater "land of opportunity," thus giving this group a +2.

U.S. business and industry naturally will be affected by companies adopting preference-type affirmative action plans. The effect, moreover, generally will be positive. U.S. business and industry more accurately will reflect the population and society in which they are based and which they seek to serve. Decisions, moreover, now will be made based on the additional knowledge and experience contributed by a more diverse workforce. Affirmative action will result in more productive relationships among U.S. business and industry and sectors of the U.S. and world population, thereby enhancing domestic and global opportunities. Some U.S. business and industrial firms may have to deal with the negative practical aspects of administering affirmative action plans. Overall, however, the impact on U.S. business and industry is quite positive, specifically at +3.

Affirmative action preference plans, finally, produce many significant effects on society as a whole. When jobs and promotions are assigned to women and minority group members on the basis of criteria not directly related to competency and merit, societal productivity declines. These employment preferences, moreover, even though accorded to groups that historically have suffered discrimination and stereotyping, frequently do result in the violation of individual rights of white men, which naturally might increase their hostility to women and minority group members. Yet, these negative societal consequences should be temporary and short-term in effect, because in the long run, there will be increased opportunities for all groups. As more women and minority group members are brought into the workforce, particularly in positions of prominence, human resources previously underused will be employed more efficiently, so as to increase societal productivity. When people see that women and minority group members are equally as competent as are white men, and especially in managerial and executive capacities, old prejudices should collapse, producing a more truly egalitarian society, where distinctions are based on real merit, not sex or race. When all are competing fully and equally, not only will societal productivity increase, but so will social balance, resulting in a more harmonious, and thus more "pleasurable" society, reflected in the +3 assigned to this category.

4. The Consequences-Computed

The consequences for all the preceding groups now are enumerated and calculated to produce the overall numerical conclusion as presented in Table 17.1.

5. The Utilitarian Conclusion

As the negative consequences add up to a −14, and the positive consequences are a +29, the end result is a +15. Since greater good and pleasure are produced by the action of affirmative action preference plans, the action is therefore moral pursuant to the utilitarian ethical theory.

E. The Morality of Affirmative Action Preference Plans—Kantian Ethical Arguments

Kant's ethical theory, one recalls, is based on the belief that morality is derived formally from reason, not the presence of "good" consequences. His supreme principle, the Categorical Imperative, is "categorical" because no other ethical theories or principles are required to determine the morality of the action under examination. It is "imperative" because one must be moral regardless of the consequences, and one's will can and must compel one to do what one's mind has reasoned as the moral course of action. In order for an action to be moral pursuant to the Categorical Imperative, the action must pass three tests: it must be possible to be made consistently universal; treat rational beings with dignity and respect; and it must be acceptable to a rational person who did not know whether he or she would be the agent, that is, the "giver" of the action, or the receiver of the action. The action to be analyzed ethically pursuant to Kant's Categorical Imperative

Table 17.1—Stakeholder Utilitarian Analysis of Pain and Pleasure

Stakeholder	Pain	Pleasure
White Men and Candidates	−4	
Families of White Men	−2	
White Men Generally	−3	
Women/Minority Group Candidates		+4
Families or Women and Minority Group Members		+4
Women/Minority Group Members Generally		+4
Shareholders/Owners		+2
Employees Generally	−1	
Production Employees	−2	
Management Employees		+2
Customers and Consumers		+2
Competition	−1	
Local Community		+1
Government		+1
Potential Employees/Students	−1	
Immigrants		+2
Business and Industry		+3
Society		+4
Total Scores	**−14**	**+29**
Difference in Scores	**+15** (Pleasure)	

is: the morality of business affirmative action plans that accord an applicant or a candidate a preference or "plus" factor based on his or her sex or minority or diversity status.

The action can pass Kant's "universalization" test. If all businesses used a goal-oriented, proportionate, preference-type plan that leads to a fuller and more balanced utilization of the workforce, the action would not self-destruct due to any internal inconsistency or self-contradiction; rather, it could be continued indefinitely as the workforce and employment needs change, since the action still would produce results. Presently, the "plus" factor is being awarded to women and minorities since they are underrepresented in the ranks of middle- and upper-level business management as compared to their percentage of the available labor force. In the future, however, the "diversity" "plus" factor may be granted to applicants and candidates based on age, socioeconomic status, or educational background in order to more fully use people with these characteristics if they are underrepresented.

Pursuant to Kant's second test, however, a preference-type affirmative action plan creates serious moral problems. All applicants and candidates are qualified, of course, and no unqualified or underqualified person would be hired or promoted over a qualified person, white men or otherwise, in the interests of furthering diversity. Yet, if the applicants and candidates are qualified, and some are given a preference due to their race, sex, or other immutable characteristic, certain persons, that is, the white men, are being discriminated against because of their race or sex. Such discrimination would be immoral under Kant's second test, because it violates the rational person's basic moral right to be treated with dignity and respect, as worthwhile "ends" in and of themselves and not as mere "means," even for the attainment of laudatory societal goals. "Dignity and respect" require that all candidates be treated equally and that all be accorded the right to be judged on merit. Since a preference-type affirmative action plan effectively requires employers to engage in intentional discrimination on the basis of sex or race, the plan is immoral, even if it is temporary and is intended to remedy the effects of past discrimination. "Two wrongs do not make a right," as Kant certainly would say; and thus discrimination against white men ethically must be condemned as strongly as discrimination against women and minority group members or discrimination based on age, body size, and disabilities when one is capable of productively performing the job.

Under Kant's "agent-receiver" test, the affirmative action preference plan is subjected to the inquiry: If a rational person did not know whether he or she would be the white-male applicant or candidate, or the female or minority group one, would the plan still be acceptable to him or her? Pursuant to affirmative action, even in the form of a preference or "plus" type plan, there is no guarantee that the job or promotion will be granted in every instance to a woman or minority group member. A rational person, moreover, would recognize that there are positive values in affirmative action, such as better utilization of the workforce and increased long-term productivity, which offset the risk of being the white male "receiver" and perhaps being passed over, at least temporarily, in certain instances for a position or promotion which goes to a qualified female or minority candidate. Yet, the rational person would not want to take the risk of being discriminated against, even for laudable business and societal objectives, on the basis of characteristics that are not directly relevant to a person's capability to perform a particular job. A rational person, contemplating one's immutable white male "receiver" status would tend to believe that a preference-type plan would be detrimental to one's career opportunities and advancement. The rational person, therefore, would not want to be in the role of the "receiver"; consequently, the action does not pass Kant's third test.

Since the preference type affirmative action plan failed Kant's second as well as third tests, it is immoral, based, of course, on the application of this one ethical theory. Is it possible, though, to devise an affirmative action plan that not only is moral under the utilization ethical theory, but also passes all three formal and strict tests of Kant's Categorical Imperative.

F. Affirmative Action—Alternatives to Race and Sex-based Preference /Plus Plans

1. Preferences Based on Past Discrimination

One alternative to a preference/plus type of affirmative action plan, based on a predicate of racial or sexual "imbalance," is a plan that still awards preferences but bases them on evidence of past discrimination. Preferences, moreover, must be narrowly tailored to redress specific, identifiable instances of intentional past discrimination. Here, the preferences are necessary to correct provable past injustices; and although the preferences are not race or sex neutral, the Kantian "rational person" surely at least would recognize the compelling need for such corrective affirmative action and acquiesce in the granting of limited targeted preferences.

2. Preference Based on Socioeconomic Disadvantage

Another affirmative action alternative is to maintain the system of preferences and "plus" factors, but to change the criteria from sex and race to socioeconomic disadvantage. Such factors as the applicant's or candidate's family background, financial condition, home and social environments, and economic need, as opposed to his or her race of sex, now would "count" for (or against) an individual. An economic needs-based measurement will help disadvantaged people of every race and gender. Yet, minority groups and women should benefit disproportionately from this type of "means-tested" affirmative action program, because they are represented extensively in the numbers of the disadvantaged. "Lower" middle-class, or poor white male applicants, however, also could take advantage of such a program and thus receive a "plus" factor over an affluent, advantaged, female or minority applicant. Such an affirmative action plan, finally, would generate broader support than a race- or sex-based plan, and thus should be acceptable to a rational person regardless of his or her socioeconomic status.

3. Preference Based on Economically Distressed Areas

In this alternative, there still are preferences, but they are granted by government to business in the form of tax "breaks" or contracts, because firms have located in economically distressed communities. To qualify for the preferences, companies would have to hire a certain number of their employees from the local "distressed" community. The objectives of such an affirmative action plan are to enhance employment opportunities, but by means of neutral geographic and economic standards. Yet, such a program, will help many minority and female applicants, many of whom are deprived and who reside in the local community. This type of affirmatives action plan, based on a partnership between the private sector and government, also should generate broad support as well as provide opportunities to people who live in economically distressed areas. Government has a role to play in providing these opportunities. Government should help in restoring equal opportunities to minorities and women, since government was a contributing source to the unequal conditions of the past; and this type of neutral economic- and geographic-based program should provide those opportunities, and in a moral manner.

G. Affirmative Action—Proactive Diversity Efforts

As part of an affirmative action plan, a company can engage in various proactive diversity efforts to attract and maintain a more balanced workforce. These efforts would encompass targeted recruiting, increasing the pool of qualified women and minority applicants and candidates, mentoring, and training in diversity awareness.

One method that will enhance the diversity of a firm's workforce, and still maintain equality of opportunity and treatment, is to define those positions in the firm where diversity is a legitimate job qualification together with intelligence, personality, education, and experience. Diversity, as so defined, can be viewed as a qualifying factor for an applicant, similar to intelligence, for example, which is assessed by the employer but which never will be equal among all applicants. If diversity can be cited as a bonafide qualification on a job description, predicated perhaps on a firm's diverse customer base, then tangible business needs, such as marketing effectiveness and competitiveness, would drive the job-related diversity program; and therefore a rational person should see the practical business necessity as well as the morality of such an affirmative action plan.

Diversity awareness training not only enables a firm's employees to recognize but also to appreciate differences among individuals and to value the uniqueness in every person. This uniqueness can be derived from one's race, sex, or ethnic heritage, as well as from one's religious, education, or socioeconomic background, and one's physical appearance or color. This uniqueness, moreover, should be considered as a highly valuable source of information, innovation, contribution, and value to a firm. A company should create a corporate culture that not only recognizes these differences but that celebrates them; and should establish a work environment where every employee can realize his or her complete potential. Such a firm will be a more competitive firm due to an empowered and more effective workforce, higher morale, and a deserved reputation for being a better and moral place to work.

A company's decision to implement a diversity awareness program will benefit all the firm's stakeholders; and society will benefit as more and more companies adopt diversity awareness programs. The rich and unique ideas and ways of thinking drawn from everyone's background and culture will make the quality of life better for all.

H. Summary

A Utilitarian ethical analysis indicated that the preference type of affirmative action plan is moral, whereas a Kantian analysis deemed it immoral. Refocusing affirmative action away from race- and sex-based "plus" programs to more neutral factors, such as socioeconomic status, and to the use of diversity as a potential and legitimate job criterion, will help to ensure that affirmative action continues to produce greater good, but not at the cost of reverse discrimination toward white men. Of course, with the projected population demographics and with the steady influx of immigrants, the traditional white male will no longer be the majority in the United States; and perhaps in the next three decades, affirmative action plans may have to give "plus" factors to underrepresented white men!

Part II. Age Discrimination

A. Introduction and Overview

Age discrimination in the workplace impacts people of all nationalities, sizes, races, colors, religions, and ethnicities. Such discrimination, which can be highly unethical, is causing many managers anxiety, and is forcing many of them to court. It is no secret that age-related lawsuits are proliferating, and in the last few years age-related claims have been on the rise due to layoffs, which seem to be and is proportionally impacting older workers. Juries often side with aggrieved employees, even if the evidence is flimsy. Because of such trends, national and international companies and their managers are realizing the need to protect themselves by periodically reviewing their workforce diversity, while analyzing the data for latent signs and patterns of "unintentional" discrimination. The focus of this section is discrimination based on age. The objective is to create awareness and reduce the negative impact of stereotypes associated with "older workers." Furthermore, based on a qualitative study of 206 culturally diverse respondents, a cultural perspective of aging is discussed from the societal norms and traditions of people in Afghanistan, Jamaica, Turkey, and the United States.[3]

An "older worker," according to the laws in the United States, is a worker that is 40 years of age or older. Unfortunately, there have been many firms that have shown patterns of discrimination against "older workers" in the United States work environment. When such discrimination becomes an "unseen" part of the culture, it can hinder the organization's morale, productivity and may possibly cause many legal problems for the firm. Organizational leaders and managers therefore must be concerned about age discrimination since an increasingly larger percentage of the workforce will come from the older population as the U.S. baby boomers continue to age. According to the United States Census Bureau and the Administration on Aging, the number of Americans who are 65 years of age or older has increased by a factor of 12 since the early 1900s.

The presence of more "older workers" being active in the workforce presents many challenges and opportunities for organizations. The challenges are stereotypes and age discrimination that are widespread in the American workforce. Organizations accordingly must effectively transcend such challenges and proactively take advantage of the experienced workforce as they attempt to be globally competitive. There are many "proactive" firms, such as Publix, based in Lakeland, Florida, which employed over 130,000 employees as of 2006, that need to be congratulated for their efforts to reduce/eliminate age discrimination in the workplace.

Aging is viewed differently in different cultures depending on the stereotypes associated with aging. Such mindsets and paradigms can be seen in how societies respond to people of different ages, their customers, their norms, and opportunities provided to them. For example, the countries of Afghanistan and Turkey are not experiencing challenges in regard to age discrimination in the same manner as seen in the United States and Jamaica. As such, a perspective of age discrimination from the various cultural perspectives is explored. When it comes to age, most Afghans tend to be guided by their Afghan heritage and, thus, respect elders at home and in the workforce because older workers are seen as mentors and coaches with much wisdom due to their extra years on earth. The culture of Afghanistan, with a population of about 28 million individuals, is similar to customs and mores of Turkish people with regard to the aging population of workers.

Turkey is a Middle Eastern country with a population of 70 million people that have similar tendencies as the Afghans with regard to how they view older workers. About half of the population is in the range of 20–40 years of age. As such, Turkey may be one of the largest countries that has a high percentage of young population in the Middle East, maybe in Europe as well. Nevertheless, the government has not come up with a feasible long-term strategy to benefit from this young generation. The common sense of the Turkish culture, similar to the Afghans, is that the older a person is, the more maturely he or she will react to crisis, not only in business, but also in one's personal life. Moreover, there are plenty of common sayings that emphasize the importance of being older and experienced. For example, one's words do not count, unless one is able to grow facial hair (the

---

[3]See Mujtaba and Cavico's 2006 book entitled "*Age Discrimination in Employment.*"

sign of getting old). In comparison to the Western countries, despite the fact that the percentage of young generation is higher in Turkey, the average ages of employees in the corporations tend to range close to 40's. In other words, they are still remarkably higher in Turkey than that of other countries in Europe, and the young generation still suffers from not being able to find enough opportunities to start their professional business life. In terms of job security both in Turkey and Afghanistan, the experience of an employee that comes with age is superior to the advantages associated with youth. The common perception is that, unless the company is going bankrupt or one commits a shameful crime, most companies tend to keep employees until they retire. In government-owned sector, one has the opportunity to continue working even after the retirement age. On the negative side, so much security for an employee sometimes causes lack of motivation for productivity and a decrease in performance that usually lead to loss of profit. Due to the security of existing jobs for current employees, mostly the older employees, the younger ones do not tend to have enough opportunities to prove themselves as productive and dynamic members of the workforce. Even if they do get an opportunity to start working, they usually find themselves in the middle of conflicts or disputes with older and more experienced employees in an attempt to apply their ideas to the organization. This conflict is also considered to be one of the reasons for the migration of young Turkish workforce to other countries, such as the United States, Canada, Australia, and Europe, where the youth seem to be more appreciated. Research conducted by different universities in Turkey, such as the Middle Eastern Technical University, shows that the young workforce wants to explore the possibilities in other countries that prefer employing young individuals. Sometimes, a country's cultural preferences and conditioning for older workers can cause difficulty for the younger generation. The young generation in Turkey is trying to find alternative solutions to the existing challenge (age discrimination toward younger employees) so they can become a dominant force in the business world and in the government sector.

Jamaica is one of the many islands of the Caribbean with strong historical and cultural ties to both West Africa and Great Britain. The population, almost three million, is a diverse blend of many different races with the majority being of African descent. The advent of the information age, aided by the Worldwide Web and Cable Television, has exposed Jamaicans to various other cultures. One could assume that with the majority of Jamaicans being of African descent, as well as the British influence on their culture, Jamaicans would have very distinct ideas on social issues such as age discrimination. And, ostensibly, they do, but in reality Jamaicans seem to take their cues from the outside world—the "first world." In this regard, no single culture has impacted the Jamaican people as much as that of North America. Jamaican attitudes tend to mirror American norms, beliefs, and values more as the years progress. As has been the case in North America, there has been a trend towards age discrimination in Jamaica. While there are no specific laws governing this issue locally, and accordingly, very little public reflection on the matter, an informal review of several typical Jamaican companies reveals that persons between the ages of forty (40) and sixty-five (65) are more likely to be "downsized" or laid-off, and less likely to be hired. There is also a noticeable trend towards encouraging early retirement. As a matter-of-fact, a colleague stated that, during early 2003, her brother was forced into early retirement from his long-term employment in Jamaica because he was 55 years of age and he was boldly told it was because of his age. Although the older recruits inevitably have more experience, this is not always a requirement for the job. Recruitment managers in Jamaica indicate that they would prefer to hire younger, "brighter" workers, who are open-minded and trainable, than older workers who are *set in their ways.* Jamaican managers also cite a third "honorable and justified" reason for their preference of younger workers: this being the *"economic reality of diminishing returns."* It is believed that older workers cost more to maintain and are less energetic than younger workers. One manager actually cited his views based on "personal experience" that "a person's performance tends to peak after a number of years (roughly eight years) and after that the rule of diminishing returns sets in." The authors consider these views expressed in support of this preference for a younger workforce to be very disturbing, especially in light of the fact that many of these views are not supported by factual research, but merely on perception. It is also disturbing that managers do not see their behavior as being discriminatory.

The United States has a diverse population of about 290 million people. A culture's perspective on aging in the U.S. can be seen from their comedy, often negative. Negative views of aging, expressed by the American comedians, are common in the United States. They are representative of how the American society feels about aging and as such youthfulness is valued and "older age" is not. These mindsets are causing an increasing number of the aging "baby boomers" to constantly search for the "fountain of youth" when in reality there is no such panacea. Nonetheless, such societal views tend to impact the workplace since senior executives and managers that make hiring decisions do come from the society and they do not always check such mindsets and stereotypes associated with aging at the door. This societal conditioning is like personal "traveling luggage" that accompanies a person from one airport to another airport and from one hotel to another and finally back home. Unlike one's luggage, stereotypes and biases do not become lost, at least not automatically. They must be consciously replaced by new appropriate "luggage" or "paradigms and mindsets."

B. Age Discrimination Issues in the U.S. Workplace

Many organizations and individuals believe that the education system in the United States has failed to deliver graduates who are fully qualified to enter and meet the demands of today's labor market. Consequently, more and more organizations are trying to retain, recruit and hire older workers because of their skill, professional expertise, and accumulated knowledge.

The elderly professionals are often in the position of being fairly healthy, wealthy, and selective in terms of what they would like to do in their later years. As a result of their years of productive work in society, they tend to live in better neighborhoods and often have hobbies or community roles. As such, one barrier for attracting the elderly is that they can be selective in determining where they would like to work. Oftentimes, they would like flexible hours with options to come and go to pursue their avocations and personal community obligations. So, the fact that they do not apply to all organizations is one barrier. Another barrier is the fact that they want flexible hours with jobs that offer the opportunity to fulfill their socialization and other higher order needs for self-actualization. Some of them also may want to work in positions that do not require too much new learning or physical activity since they have been through all this before and would rather not deal with it again. So, wanting selective jobs is yet another barrier in entering the workforce. However, the most common barrier for those older workers who do apply for specific jobs in the workplace is probably the widespread stereotypes and biases on the part of interviewers which result in not hiring the elderly. Increasingly, there are more older workers in the workforce, and many are claiming that opportunities have been limited for them due to stereotypes, biases, and structures that are designed to discourage them from the work environment.

In contrast to intentional age discrimination, covert discrimination against older employees seems to be subtler in nature; and human resource managers should be aware of such subtle forms of discrimination. Research has revealed that unintentional code words are often used during the interview process, such as "we're looking for go-getters" and people who are "with-it" to describe desirable employees. Generally, "buzzwords" seem not to apply to people who are seasoned and experienced. According to a U.S. News article (Clark, 2003) titled *Judgment Day*, about two thirds of all U.S. companies use performance as at least one factor when deciding whom to lay off during "tough" economic times. Many firms use the forced ranking systems because they seem to be the "fairest and easiest way to downsize." Unfortunately, "older workers" seem to get the "worst of it" as larger portions of them lose their jobs possibly due to biases and because they earn more income and earn more benefits compared to their younger counterparts.

The Age Discrimination and Employment Act of 1967 (ADEA) in the United States prohibits discrimination in all terms and conditions of employment against all persons 40 years of age or older. This federal law covers employment practices, including hiring, discharge, pay, promotions, benefits and other terms of employment, to include forced retirement. The focus of ADEA is to promote fairness in the employment of older persons where they are evaluated based on their ability rather than their age. ADEA also helps employers and workers seek ways to combat problems resulting from the impact of age on employment. The Age Discrimination and Employment Act (ADEA) is enforced by the Equal Employment Opportunity Commission (EEOC), thereby providing the same protection to affected individuals as provided under Title VII of the Civil Rights Act of 1964.

According to EEOC, in 2004 fiscal year, the EEOC received 17,837 charges of age discrimination; resolved 15,792 age discrimination charges; and recovered $60.0 million in monetary benefits for charging parties and other aggrieved individuals (not including monetary benefits obtained through litigation). The Equal Employment Opportunity Commission reports that age discrimination claims are still a major factor; however, the percentage of such claims declined in the mid 1990s compared to previous data. Yet, it did increase again in the turn of the new century. One reason for this decline in the mid 90's is attributed to the over 40 population as being one of the fastest growing demographic segments in the United States. Age discrimination settlements and jury awards are substantially higher than those awarded for race, sex or disability cases. Individuals claiming discrimination based on age were awarded an average of $219,000 compared to the low to mid $100,000 for race, sex and disability. An increasing number of corporations have been accused of age discrimination in the years 2001 to 2003, since there have been many lay-offs due to the downturn of the economy. Even before the downturn of the economy, there were accusations of age discrimination by major corporations. For example, in 1997 First Union Corporation, a major banking institution agreed to pay $58.5 million to 239 former employees to settle an age discrimination suit, and Continental Airlines paid between $7 and $8 million to 207 employees. The Equal Employment Opportunity Commission, which administers ADEA, provides updated information on charges of age discrimination cases that have been filed with them.

A review of the EEOC data in September, 2005 for a longitudinal observation also showed that the percentage of race related charges have decreased between 1992 (from 40.9%) and 2004 (to 34.9%). The percentage of charges filed on the basis of religious discrimination has increased from 1.9% in 1992 to 3.1% in 2004, showing a huge increase. Similarly, the number of complaints or charges related to Title VII has progressively and steadily increased from 14.5% in 1992 to 25.5% in 2004. At the same time period, the data revealed that the percentage of sex, national origin, and disability related charges have pretty much remained similar from 1993 and 2004 years with small changes in between the years. While age related charges have increased in the first five years of this decade, when compared to the last five years of the previous decade, many managers still remain skeptical and believe that age discrimination is not a major problem. Yet, the data shows that it really is as it impacts people of all races, ethnicities, body sizes, genders, and disabilities. Therefore, it is critical that employers exercise extreme caution within their corporate culture to minimize any inferences of older workers being mistreated. How can this happen one might ask? It actually starts at the top. Corporate culture is shaped at the top of the corporate "ladder" by the senior executives and managers who determine how human resources are to be utilized. If key executives are entrenched in a culture that views younger people as being more successful and aggressive, and older people as being more complacent, such beliefs can create a negative climate that will permeate throughout their organization, thereby, causing subordinates to buy into the same type of behavior. Given this circumstance, senior executives and managers, as well as the entire workforce within organizations, should make every effort to ensure their corporate culture is positive and free of illegal discrimination, thereby avoiding any instances that may make older workers feel uncomfortable.

C. Cross Cultural Study and Methodology

There seems to be cultural convergence in many human resources practices among various countries as a result of technological advancements and commonalities. However, often times, employee hiring and retention practices are heavily influenced by cultural norms and mores and international managers should be aware of different practices at various localities. The purpose of the authors' qualitative study was to find out the cultural views of aging and employment practices regarding older workers from the people of the United States of America, Jamaica, Turkey, and Afghanistan. The research question was "*Is age viewed differently among the people of Afghanistan, Turkey, Jamaica, and the United States of America?*" The authors proposed that there are some cultural differences in how people view age in each country surveyed, and such cultural views regarding older workers do impact employment practices and hiring decisions. Gathering data can provide a clearer understanding of differences from the view of people in these presumably four different cultures. This factual information can be used by global employees, managers, and human resource professionals working in multinational corporations as they design procedures and policies for attracting, hiring, developing, promoting, and retaining an experienced workforce within each country.

Several years ago, the authors set out to have discussions with employees, managers, and researchers from various countries around the world regarding age and older workers. As a result, in 2005, it was decided that a structured qualitative survey could be used to formally gather information on how the people of Afghanistan, Jamaica, Turkey, and the United States view age as per their cultural conditioning and the current employment practices related to older workers in their country. A simple and straight-forward "convenience" survey was designed so it can be distributed to a sample of individuals from each country that can speak, read, and understand English. As such, the survey questions were worded so it could be easily understood by individuals whose first language is something other than English. Initially, in a pilot study, the surveys were handed out face-to-face to a sample of about 30 diverse individuals in Fort Lauderdale to see how they interpreted each question on the survey. As a result, a few of the questions were separated into several questions, and some words were changed to further clarify what was being asked. This process led to the final version of the survey which was used for this study.

The individuals who received the surveys were colleagues, friends, professional educators, trainers, staff, students, government employees, contractors, or simply members of various newsgroups that facilitate or distribute up-to-date information to subscribers. Participants were provided sufficient information about the study and its purpose on a cover letter within the electronic communication (email). To minimize confusion and simplify the data gathering process, separate links for surveys in each country were created and sent to the people of those countries. The directions provided each person a link for the survey. On the average, the survey took about ten minutes to complete. The response rate could not be determined mathematically since the number of subscribers to some of the newsgroups was not known to the researchers. However, a response rate of 20% is estimated as per the known number of colleagues and possible number of subscribers to various newsgroups that may have received the survey information. Participants in each country were given a period of three weeks to asynchronously complete the survey as per their availability, and they were encouraged to respond within the allotted time since it would only take about ten minutes. However, participants were able to complete the survey even months after the allotted time since the survey was available to them. During a given month, only individuals from one country were sent the survey for completion. During a four-month period, the surveys were sent to people of four different countries, and the responses were received electronically within this four-month period (February to May 2005). Surveys were sent first to Afghans, then to Jamaicans, Turks, and finally to people in the United States. The survey was first distributed electronically through the internet to a group of professional Afghans living in Afghanistan, the United States, and many other countries throughout the Middle East, Europe, and Asia in the early months of 2005. The participants were encouraged to complete the survey within a three-week period. A month later, the survey directions and link were sent to people in Jamaica, and they too were asked to respond within a three-week period. In the following two months, similar procedures were followed with Turkish and American populations.

There was an estimated 20% response rate (a total of 206 individuals) to the survey from the countries of Afghanistan, Jamaica, Turkey, and the United States. There were 57 respondents from Afghanistan, 42 from Jamaica, 36 from Turkey, and 71 respondents from the United States of America for a total of 206 respondents. There also was a good distribution of both genders responding to the survey: 91 male and 115 female respondents presenting their views on aging and employment practices regarding older workers. It is very interesting to note that the preponderance of respondents from the U.S. and Jamaica are female. Given the later "scores" and comments regarding the prevalence of age discrimination, it is possible that older females may feel, perceive, or observe the presence of such discrimination more keenly than males. Perhaps this is an avenue for future research in order to see if there is a relationship between gender and the perception of age discrimination.

It is also interesting to note that the representation among the age groups was more or less evenly balanced between "young" (the first two categories) and "old" (the second two), except for Turkey, where the "young" clearly outweigh the "old." Yet this disparity does show up in the Turkish scores, except perhaps for the category of "evidence of age discrimination against 'younger workers,'" where half the respondents reported seeing evidence of such discrimination.

The education level was very high for all categories, but nonetheless sizable numbers of respondents reported that they did not know whether age discrimination against older workers was illegal in their country. As a matter of fact, out of 206 respondents from the four countries, 48 "did not know" or were not sure if age discrimination was legally wrong in their country. Clearly, something may be lacking in all this advanced education with regard to hiring practices and awareness of rules. Of course, many of these so called "well educated" individuals are more likely to become managers and leaders because of their education and, thus, should receive training on age-related employment practices.

The U.S. category reported by a "vote" of 42–29 that it had diversity training, and the other categories had significant minorities reporting such training, all of which makes the fact that so much age discrimination in employment was reported even more disturbing. Perhaps the diversity training should have a much stronger age component.

All categories of respondents reported that older workers get more respect than younger ones, except notably for the U.S. (as the majority said "no") where older workers do NOT seem to get more respect from managers and employers. This is disturbing, especially considering the educational levels and educational setting of the USA respondents.

The U.S. figures were disturbing, as more than half the respondents reported that it is more difficult for U.S. older workers to get jobs in their country. Moreover, this result occurs despite the facts of U.S. age discrimination law, the awareness of such law, as well as moral norm regarding age discrimination as morally wrong, and the prevalence of diversity training.

With regard to evidence of age discrimination, the scores were close for Turkey and Afghanistan in reporting no, and also close for Jamaica in reporting yes; but yet the U.S. scores were disturbing, as by a "vote" of 45–26, the U.S. respondents reported seeing evidence of age discrimination against older workers. With regard to age discrimination against older workers being legally wrong, respondents from Turkey and Jamaica reported "no" by sizable margins, but there was a very big "do not know" "vote." Afghanistan reported yes by a material margin, but also with a fair "do not know" "vote." What is very clear is the U.S. reporting, where an overwhelming number of respondents (63) stated that such discrimination was legally wrong, with only three reporting "no" and five reporting "do not know." Yet the fact that U.S. law prohibiting age discrimination exists, and that people are overwhelmingly aware of this law, apparently does not prevent, as reported by the respondents, age discrimination against older workers from occurring in the United States. Dee Hock, CEO Emeritus VISA International, is quoted as saying "Simple, clear purpose and principles give rise to complex and intelligent behavior. Complex rules and regulations give rise to simple and stupid behavior." Perhaps Hock's statement is true in this area of age discrimination, despite the laws and so much diversity awareness training. These results provided further support for the notion of cultural conditioning being a very strong "driver" of human behavior.

In all the countries except Turkey, which had a "tie vote," the respondents reported that such discrimination was morally wrong, but with material "do not know" "votes," but for the U.S., by a 58–7 vote, with seven "do not know" "votes," the respondents reported that age discrimination was morally wrong in the United States. Once again, this presumably prevailing moral belief in the U.S. that age discrimination is morally wrong apparently does not prevent it from happening in employment. The conclusion also provides further support that cultural conditioning can be a strong influence on the behavior of individuals regarding employment practices.

As a result of the overall review of the data from each country and the respondents' comments, one could make some observations regarding cultural views about aging and its behavioral implications in the workplace of each culture. At a general level, one can make some conclusions with regard to "unearned privileges" or "unearned advantages" to various categories of workers in different cultures. *Unearned privilege* is defined as advantages given to some individuals and withheld from others, without regard to their efforts or abilities, because of their perceived difference. What is interesting to think about is that such privileges often come to one group or category of individuals at a cost to other individuals or category of workers. From a qualitative analysis of the data, one can conclude that younger workers in the United Sates of America and in Jamaica tend to receive unearned privileges simply because of their age. Such privileges to young workers mean stereotypes, biases and discrimination to those individuals who fall in the category of older workers. So, older workers in the United States and in Jamaica are at a disadvantage when they are competing for jobs against younger individuals in the marketplace. One must reflect on the fact that all younger workers will eventually become older workers, thus losing the unearned privileges to those who are seen as young.

Similarly, because of tradition and thousands of years of cultural conditioning, older workers in Turkey and Afghanistan seemed to enjoy unearned privileges. It is important to emphasize that these are simply assumptions about older workers being wise and mature until they prove themselves otherwise. It is also assumed that younger workers are not at the same level of maturity as older workers until they prove themselves otherwise. Therefore, younger workers with extremely high levels of knowledge and maturity when compared to many older workers are only given the opportunity after they have proven themselves. So, young workers might be at a disadvantage in such cultures when they are competing for jobs against older workers.

It was striking to see that the U.S. respondents, principally from the education sector, reported such a prevalence of age discrimination, and especially so considering that the U.S. has such an extensive anti-discrimination legal network, which the vast number of the U.S. respondents were aware of, and also that the U.S. respondents reported their beliefs as well as the prevailing norms that age discrimination was legally wrong, ethically and morally wrong, and, moreover, they reported that they had diversity training. So, what does the data reveal? Despite all the legal and moral norms as well as the training, the respondents still reported significant age discrimination in the U.S. Consequently, it was very clear that national and international managers, leaders and twenty-first century professionals need to effectively prepare and deal with age discrimination issues in their workplace. The data supported previous data and the conclusions of other researchers with regard to the widespread presence of age discrimination in the United States.

In order to create awareness and a culture of fair employment practices, global leaders and managers should institute relevant policies and procedures to bring about appropriate cultural changes in the organization. Overall, a mature employee's greatest assets (compared to younger demographics) are likely to be lower absenteeism, punctuality, less likelihood to change jobs, commitment to quality, superior customer service skills, better "people skills," more eagerness to learn new skills, positive attitude, and the willingness to speak their minds and to point out the flaws of the organization. The former Secretary of Labor, Elaine L. Chao, said, "Nowhere is the case stronger for tapping the strengths of older workers than with employers facing the skills gap. Everywhere I go, employers tell me they are having difficulty finding workers with the right skill sets for the jobs they have to offer." This provides a golden opportunity to turn a challenge—the approaching retirement of an unprecedented number of Americans—into a "win-win" scenario for the economy and one's workforce. Companies hire older workers because they have certain characteristics that other generations of employees may not always have; and the following are some elements cited by authors:

- Older workers thrive on quality and hard work. They believe in putting in a full day's work for a full day's pay.

- Older workers are loyal. They appreciate the opportunity to work and stick with those who give them a chance to perform and produce.

- Older workers take great pride in their accomplishments. They care about doing a good job.

- Older workers are dependable. They show up on time all the time. They take orders seriously, keep their promises and do what they say they will do.

- Older workers do not always get involved in politics. They don't play political games, have hidden agendas or harbor secret ambitions. They are not interested in "climbing the corporate ladder," so they don't have to resort to manipulation, "dirty tricks," or one-upmanship.

- Older workers have more than their share of "emotional maturity" and common sense.

Age discrimination can appear quite rational and ethical; yet it is not. Sometimes, employers feel as though they have "solid" economic reasons for not wanting to hire and train employees who will soon be retiring. Furthermore, others rationalize that people do "slip" with age. Some have stated that reasoning skills may decline with age, and the decrement is greatest in what psychologists call "fluid intelligence." While some of these myths/opinions might have been based on few factual occurrences, they were not always representative of each individual's ability to successfully complete a task regardless of his/her age. The research presented the views of nearly 206 respondents from four different countries regarding age and age discrimination. It appeared that the study supported previous research that there is wide-spread age discrimination toward older workers in the United States and in Jamaica. However, older workers in Turkey and in Afghanistan do not seem to be facing similar challenges since age is culturally respected in these countries.

D. Summary

Being viewed as an enormous "melting pot," the United States encompasses many different peoples with diverse backgrounds, desires, goals, and philosophies. Yet, a common objective shared by most people is to take advantage of the many opportunities afforded by each country's democratic, free-market system, and to succeed. This chapter analyzed the advantages and disadvantages associated with affirmative action and discriminatory practices. History reveals that minority groups and women as well as the elderly have been victimized and hindered by past discrimination and social stereotyping. In many instances, they still are being harmed by both the cumulative and current effects of racial, ethnic, age, and sexual prejudice. The continuing debate over achieving racial, ethnic, and sexual equality, therefore, frequently centers on business. In the business context, moreover, attempts to achieve equality and to remedy the effects of past discrimination and social stereotyping have substantial, far-reaching, and long-lasting ramifications.

Virtually every large company has some type of affirmative action program, and they should continue to offer relevant programs to assure equality and fairness for all employees. Accordingly, this chapter offered an examination of current affirmative action programs and practices, and applied ethical theories thereto in order to make moral conclusions about affirmative action. This chapter also examined the topic of age discrimination in employment from legal and practical perspectives, as well as reported on some very revealing age discrimination data based on a cross-cultural survey conducted by the authors.

Discussion Questions

1. What is Affirmative Action?
2. Why was Affirmative Action created?
3. What five premises in the 1960's were Affirmative Action based on?
4. What percentage of the workforce consists of white men and how has that changed over the years?
5. What are Affirmative Action-Preference/Plus plans?
6. What Affirmative Action case did Sandra Day O'Connor argue that affirmative action did not violate the 14th Amendment to the Constitution?
7. What are Utilitarian Preference Plans?
8. What are at least two negative consequences of Affirmative Action? Two Positive?
9. What can management do to ensure correct Affirmative Action procedures?
10. What is Kant's ethical theory? How does it apply to Affirmative Action?
11. Are equality of opportunity, social balance, and social harmony really societal goals?
12. How far back in history must we go to redress the "sins" of our ancestors?
13. Which American value is more important? Equality or individual rights.

14. How can minorities ever earn senior level positions when they cannot rise within the ranks to gain the experience necessary to earn these positions?

15. Are the "point" values for the utilitarian plan fair?

16. What if an affected person does not have a family, where do those points fall?

17. Would it be fair for a female to start a company and select only females for the top positions?

18. Does an employee hired under Affirmative Action have a greater responsibility to other members of its minority group to perform?

19. What additional stresses will this put upon an Affirmative Action hired employee?

20. How can females or minorities have role models if none exist?

21. When one realizes that one's place of employment does not have equal representation, does that put undue stress on the minority groups and females?

22. How much longer will Affirmative Action have a legal stance against employers?

23. At what point does a female or minority person give up and seek employment elsewhere or accept defeat?

24. Do "pushy" aggressive females "turn off" males from hiring females?

25. Do Americans understand some foreign accents better than others; thereby giving those minorities a larger advantage of being hired over others?

26. When females only have male role models do these females tend to be more aggressive?

27. If you are a white male, do you fairly compare female or minority candidates?

28. Do female managers treat their female employees differently?

29. Do minority managers treat their minority managers differently?

30. If a female intimidates a white male, does that reflect the white male's own insecurity?

31. Age discrimination in employment in the U.S. is illegal, but is it immoral too?

32. Is age discrimination morally permissible if it is sanctioned by the prevailing norm in a particular society or culture?

33. Is age discrimination based on perceptions that older workers are resistant to change and do not adapt well, especially regarding technology? Are these perceptions true?

CHAPTER 18

Ethical Business Leadership

A. The Moral Corporation

The purposes of this chapter are to underscore the fundamentally moral nature of the corporation and business, to review the basics of business leadership, to explain the concept of Value-Driven Management and its relation to the values of legality and morality in business, and to demonstrate that a solid foundation in ethics is an essential component to successful, long-term business leadership, and thus to business.

Business ultimately is predicated on values, which means that such concepts as morality, ethics, fairness, integrity, and trust are essential for business success. These traditional values now have emerged with preeminence in the post-Enron business world. These values are critical, as people now clearly realize, and they are indispensable to the "bottom-line" of business. Those corporate leaders, directors, and executives, as well as entrepreneurs, who failed to remember, neglected, or who knowingly contravened these values, are now paying a very high price indeed, legally, financially, and personally for their unethical conduct. Yet society has also paid a price for a systemic ethical lapse in business. The revelation of corporate excess and legal and ethical wrongdoing had eroded the good reputation and goodwill developed by business during the prosperous decade of the 1990s, and now regrettably these positive feelings have given way to suspicion, mistrust, and even hostility. A lethal combination of arrogance, greed, fraud, immorality, and negligent or absent oversight caused the collapse of several of the nation's largest companies and injured the mutual fund industry. Unless the traditional values of legality, ethics, morality, and social responsibility are reestablished, prominently proclaimed, and steadfastly adhered to, rising animosity and distrust on the part of the public could prove very costly to business and society. Indeed, at risk is the very core of capitalism. If the investing public ever loses faith in corporations and mutual funds, investors might refuse to invest their capital, which of course is the critical component to entrepreneurship, innovation, development, and economic prosperity. The loss of trust and investment, unless curbed, will seriously threaten the country's ability to create new businesses, expand businesses, and thus create new jobs. The solution is evident, and that is for corporate and business leaders, directors, and executives to act with integrity and to exhibit ethical and moral leadership.

In the recent past, the market in its profit-frenzied state became less and less lenient of even the merest indication of "bad news." The overbearing demands of the daily stock price engendered unethical, "borderline" accounting and in some cases even outright fraud. Of course, every upward valuation of the stock market meant massive gains for options-rich executives. Too many boards, moreover, were composed of current and former CEOs who had a vested interest in maintaining a "buddy system" that was extremely beneficial to them. Many corporate directors were lulled into complacency by ever-rising stock prices as well as their own increasing wealth. Their self-interest consequently destroyed one of the last bastions of corporate control and accountability. Moreover, too many corporate ethics officers ignored their own firms' ethics codes or blithely made exceptions to them. Of course, it was not merely the corporation and its upper-level management that were at fault. Many of the corporation's outside professionals succumbed to greed and self-interest as well, including accountants, auditors, analysts, lawyers, investment bankers, and even regulators and lawmakers. These key market "players," who are supposed to provide the essential "checks and balances" in a system of aggressive capitalism, had in many cases been compromised. Sadly, and dismayingly, far too many auditors responsible for certifying the accuracy of a company's accounts "looked the other way" so their firms could make millions in audit fees and millions more from perhaps conflicting consulting work. Some outside lawyers invented justifications, legal sophisms, for specious practices so as to win a larger share of legal fees. CEOs learned how to "buy" political influence so as to ward off probing investigations and to derail or weaken politically necessary reforms. Key business stakeholders, therefore, failed to perform their legal and ethical responsibilities; and their firms, the system, and society as a whole consequently suffered grievously.

The Sarbanes-Oxley Act (SOX) of 2002 was a Congressional response to the spate corporate scandals as exemplified by the famous (infamous) Enron collapse. SOX emerged as one of the most important modifications of federal securities laws since the enactment of the 1933 and 1934 securities acts. The main purposes of SOX are to protect investors by improving the accuracy and reliability of corporate disclosure and to increase and improve corporate accountability and governance. The Act also imposes very harsh, some would say draconian, penalties for violations of the securities laws and SOX provisions. One of the principal provisions of SOX is to require corporate chief executives to take legal responsibility for the accuracy and completeness of financial statements and reports that are filed with the SEC. Chief Executive Officers (CEO) and Chief Financial Officers (CFO) now must personally certify that the statements and reports are accurate and complete. The days of Enron CEO Ken Lay claiming "ignorance and innocence" as to the "financials" are long gone! The Act also created a new federal agency, the Public Accounting Oversight Board, which reports to the SEC, to oversee and regulate public accounting firms. Of course, the accounting profession was regarded in the "pre-Enron days" as an independent, autonomous, and self-regulating profession, governed by a code of ethics, like law and medicine; but the failure of the accounting profession to regulate itself, let alone others, brought down on itself a new federal regulatory agency to "police" the now delimited "profession."

The certification requirements of SOX are another very important and consequential feature of the statute. Section 906 mandates that CEOs and CFOs of most major companies whose stock is traded on public stock exchanges now must certify the financial statements and reports that are required to be filed with the SEC. These corporate executives have to certify that the statements and reports fully comply with SEC requirements, and, in addition, that the information therein fairly represents in all material respects the financial conditions and operations of the company. Specifically, Section 302 requires that CEOs and CFOs of reporting companies to sign the reports and to certify that they reviewed the report, and that to the best of their knowledge, the report neither contains any untrue statements nor omits any material facts. Furthermore, the signing officers must certify that their firms have established internal control systems to make certain that any relevant material information is ascertained and is placed in the report. Finally, the signing officers must certify that they disclosed to auditors and significant deficiencies in the internal control systems of the firm. Certain reports are required to be filed quarterly as well as annually with the SEC.

In addition to the certification requirements, there are other important corporate governance provisions in SOX. Section 402 prohibits any reporting company as well as a company which is filing an initial public stock offering, from arranging, extending, renewing, or maintaining a personal loan for a director or executive officer, though there are some exceptions in the Act for consumer and housing loans. The objective of this provision is to prevent companies from making personal loans to corporate directors and officers and then "forgiving" the loans to the detriment of shareholders.

Section 806 of SOX provides protections for "whistleblowers." This provision prohibits publicly traded companies from discharging, demoting, suspending, threatening, harassing, or otherwise discriminating against an employee who provides to the government or assists in any government investigation regarding activities that the employee reasonably believes constitute a violation of securities fraud laws. The whistleblowing employee is protected if he or she discloses information internally or to federal regulatory and law enforcement agencies or to a member of Congress or a Congressional committee. The employee is not protected if he or she makes a report to the media. It is important to emphasize that the SOX whistleblower protection provisions will protect an employee who has a reasonable belief of wrongdoing, even if that belief later is determined to be unfounded. To compare, some state whistleblower protection statutes, such as the one in Florida, although allowing the employee to report the violation of any law, rule, or regulation, also will require that the employee report an actual violation of the law. A belief even if reasonable as to a violation will be insufficient for whistleblowing legal protection if the employee is erroneous as to his or her "illegal" conclusion. SOX also requires that regulated companies set up confidential whistleblowing reporting systems so that employees can express their concerns about illegal accounting and auditing practices and securities fraud. Employees should be able to anonymously contact, electronically or otherwise, an independent ethics center, which will then alert the company directors, officers, executives, and managers as to a possible problem.

Section 406 of SOX deals with codes of ethics. Initially, it must be underscored that the Act neither mandates that SOX regulated companies adopt codes of ethics, nor if such codes are in existence does the Act make them legally binding. Rather, the Act does require that publicly traded firms report to the SEC whether or not the firm has a code of ethics for senior financial officers, and if not, the reasons for the lack thereof. The objective of this provision is to let the potential investor know that he or she may be making an investment in a firm that does not have a code of ethics. Moreover, SOX also requires that if a regulated company changes its codes of ethics, or makes any exceptions or waivers thereto, the company must make an immediate disclosure to the SEC as well as disseminate the information publicly by means of the Internet or other comparable electronic means. Again, the objective is to warn current shareholders and potential investors of possible problems at the firm. This ethics "exception" disclosure provision directly resulted from the Enron disaster, where the company did have a fine-sounding code of ethics, but many exceptions were made thereto by company executives.

Finally, SOX substantially increases the penalties for securities fraud and related crimes. Specifically, Section 906 holds that a CEO or CFO who certifies a financial report statement to be filed with the SEC who knows that the report or statement does not fulfill SOX reporting requirements can be subject to up to $1 million in fines and up to 10 years in prison, or both. In addition, if the CEO or CFO willfully certifies a report knowing that it is does not fulfill SOX requirements, the CEO or CFO is subject to a penalty of up to $5 million in fines and 20 years in prison, or both. Section 1106 of the Act increases the penalties for willful securities law violations of the 1934 Securities Act, in particular by increasing the fines up to $5 million and an individual's imprisonment up to 20 years. Section 1107 deals with retaliation against whistleblowing employees, although in the statute Congress used, to the dismay of the authors of this book, the pejorative term "informants" instead of the neutral term "whistleblowers." Regardless, the penalties are very severe for an employer of publicly traded firm who retaliates against a whistleblower. The Act decrees a punishment of a fine as well as up to 10 years in prison, or both, for knowingly and purposefully taking any adverse action against a person, including interfering with a person's lawful employment or livelihood, for making whistleblowing disclosures or assisting with a government investigation.

Business commentators argue that corporations now will be much more "transparent"; that is, corporations will disclose much more information and more accurate information too. Not only will investors receive more complete and better information, but so will other key stakeholder groups, such as employees, customers, and suppliers. Consequently, the recent single-minded focus on maximizing short-term profit as the sole basis for a firm's stock price will diminish, and instead companies will elevate the interests of employees, customers, and communities, and the values they believe in. Corporate ownership very likely will become more widely spread, and organizations will be as responsive to their employees and communities as they have been to their shareholders in the past decade. A truly successful company will be one that not only makes money for the shareholders, but does so in a legal, ethical, and socially responsible manner. Corporate culture will change so as to place greater emphasis on the values of legality, ethics, morality, integrity, and trust, as well as the interests of society as a whole.

The renewed "value" agenda will require greater investment in financial accountability systems, corporate governance, ethics codes and training, and participation in civic affairs. This new program for business also may require a revision of expectations so that investors are more realistic about the returns, especially short-term, a company can legitimately, appropriately, and consistently achieve in highly competitive global markets. The necessary changes will be prompted not only by more extensive government intervention and regulation, especially the Sarbanes-Oxley Act, but also by the stigma of being branded an unethical enterprise and an unethical executive.

In the profit-dominated and at times amoral, if not immoral, recent past, too many companies allowed performance to be disconnected from meaningful corporate values, particularly ethics and morality. Many conventional corporate cultures became warped, especially by emphasizing short-term profit at any cost. Now the business community, as well as the public, clearly understand that there are two key components to business leadership and success: performance and values. The Enron scandals plainly revealed that to be successful, a business cannot have one without the other, at least not in the long term. Thus, rational, prudent, and enlightened self-interest also should prompt the necessary reforms. More than anyone or anything else, ethical beliefs and standards are set and established by the firm's top executives. The values they espouse, the incentives they put in place, the culture they establish, and their own conduct will provide the lead, the direction, and the guidance for the rest of the organization.

If there is one positive, post-Enron change that is plainly present, it is the effort to make the corporation considerably more transparent. Investors as well as government regulators surely will demand the truth when it comes to corporate "numbers" and will demand clarity in corporate disclosure, or the investors simply will not invest, which will be very inimical to the economy. Transparency is also a very important concept for employees, obviously a key stakeholder group, if they are ever going to have a true sense of ownership in their company's business.

The first and most important objective in the post-Enron, Sarbanes-Oxley, ethics environment thus is to acknowledge, firmly and evidently, that a company's long-term viability now depends less on making the next quarter's "numbers" at any cost, and more on the integrity, ethics, trustworthiness, and morality of its people and practices. In the future, business leadership that preaches and practices this "ethic," and reinforces it through value-driven management, will be far more likely to gain the benefits of the rapidly changing, highly competitive marketplace, as well as secure an increasingly diverse, knowledgeable, and skilled global workforce. The challenge to business leaders and corporate executives in the coming years will be to create corporate cultures that instill, encourage, and reward ethics and integrity as much as creativity and entrepreneurship. To accomplish that goal, executives must start at the top, becoming not only exemplary leaders and managers, but also the moral foundation for the firm. CEOs must establish a culture for propriety by publicly embracing all the corporation's stakeholders and steadfastly adhering to the core values of legality, morality, and social responsibility.

A growing economy depends on free and functioning markets, entrepreneurship, investment, and innovation, and not the mere status quo and more government regulation, particularly legislation like Sarbanes-Oxley with its very draconian criminal penalties. Economic growth ultimately is premised on investors who are willing to take financial risks in firms by investing in stocks and mutual funds. Employees have to be willing to work for firms, and thus will demand to be treated in a fair manner, especially with regard to compensation and ownership. Customers have to buy products and services, and thus will have to trust that companies are not taking advantage of them. People will not work for, invest in, or deal with firms that lie, cheat, and fail to provide essential information. There must be, therefore, a moral "contract" between the corporation and its stakeholders that the corporation will act in a legal, ethical, and socially responsible manner. A primary duty of business leaders is to ensure that firms fulfill these "contractual" and societal obligations. To ascertain whether these obligations have been fulfilled, not only the government and company stakeholders, but also social activist organizations and "socially responsible" investment firms, now will carefully examine companies to make sure they are acting in a responsible manner.

B. Business Leadership

1. Creating the Vision

The business leader's principal duty is to create and to articulate a great vision for the enterprise or company and its constituent groups. The vision must be important, noble, engrossing, and achievable. It must highlight an idea or image of what the organization should do in the future, as well as display the manner in which the organization will realize its vision. The leader also must fulfill the concomitant responsibility of forming the firm's mission and core values, which, of course, must cohere with the company's vision.

The vision, together with the firm's mission and values, will supply the basis for a strong and effective enterprise. Vision, mission, and values clearly must tell the organization's constituent groups what the organization represents and what principles govern it. The vision, mission, and values, moreover, will furnish settled standards for evaluating the firm's operations and practices, as well as for bringing them into alignment with the expressed purposes and direction. The vision, mission, and values, finally, will serve as a motivating, concentrating, coordinating, integrating, and governing force for the individual employees of the company. The natural result will be a highly vitalized enterprise.

2. Communicating the Vision

Another key dimension to business leadership is the communication and explanation of the vision, mission, and values to the firm's stakeholders. Business leadership, in this dimension, is viewed as an education function, especially as some stakeholder groups may not initially or directly comprehend the necessity for change, or a longer-term viewpoint, or more expansive perspective. The business leader, in addition, not only must communicate and explain the vision, mission, and values, but he or she also must communicate the firm's commitment to its vision, mission, and values.

3. Securing Acceptance of the Vision

The business leader not only must get people to pay attention to the firm's vision, mission, and values, but also must secure, especially on the part of the firm's employees, their acceptance and adoption of the vision, mission, and values. Such acceptance and adoption best can be obtained, and voluntarily too, when the company's vision, mission, and values are in accord with the personal plans, aspirations, and principles of the employees and other constituent groups. The company stakeholders then can see clearly that their own personal growth and success are very closely connected to, and perhaps to a degree dependent upon, the firm's development and prosperity.

When the firm's employees, in essence, elect to adopt and be bound by its vision, mission, and values, which are in alignment with their own, the employees' self-interest will activate them to attain the vision, implement the mission, and articulate and act in accordance with the firm's values. The vision, mission, and values of the company thus will emerge as a real source of organizational power as well as a key criterion for decision-making.

4. Energizing, Challenging, and Inspiring Followers to Realize the Vision

The business leader's role requires that he or she focus, channel, and enliven the energies, knowledge, and talents of the employees, as well as other relevant constituents, on the firm's vision, mission, and values. The vision and mission will decide and animate the company's strategy, policy, and method; and its values will ensure the propriety and consistency of its tactics and actions. It is necessary, of course, for the leader to manifest enthusiasm, positive energy, and passion, as well to exhibit confidence, conviction, and determination.

One assured way to animate the employees to achieve the vision, accomplish the mission, and comport themselves by the values, all based on shared goals, beliefs, and principles, is to set lofty yet achievable goals, challenge and encourage the employees to reach these objectives, believe in and trust the employees to carry out their projects, and reward them for their success and accomplishments. The business leader, therefore, must create an organizational environment of opportunity, endeavor, and growth.

The business leader's job, however, is not necessarily to command, but rather to set elevated standards, and then to expect and insist on high levels of performance from the employees. Such a demanding attitude on the part of a business leader will produce superior performance, as well as personal fulfillment, on the part of the employees, which indeed will inure to the long-term success of the organization.

Truly great business leaders not only induce and motivate their employees to perform, they also inspire people to work together, sacrifice, persevere, dedicate themselves, overcome resistance, and in turn become leaders themselves in order to realize the vision and accomplish the mission. Inspiration is predicated on trust, commitment to fundamental, shared values, and a belief in people- their worth, potential, and dignity; it is produced by providing hope and meaning to people, principally by demonstrating that their goals and own personal vision can be realized through the business organization's objectives.

Henry S. Givray, CEO of SmithBucklin Corp., in an editorial in *Business Week* (Givray, 2007), emphasized the indispensable link between ethics and leadership. Givray points out that the term "CEO" is not synonymous with "leader." CEOs are measured primarily by quantitative criteria; but leaders are shaped and defined by character. CEOs make money for the shareholders; but leaders do more; they inspire and empower others to perform at a high level, thereby fulfilling their potential, and accordingly leaders build successful, enduring companies. A leader will not be successful unless he or she possesses good moral character. No one will follow, let alone be inspired by, a putative leader who is unethical. Leaders naturally are concerned with increasing sales, revenues, and profits; yet their vision extends beyond the shareholder stakeholder group to the other constituent groups that the company serves, including the local community and society as a whole. Accordingly, he underscores that it is critical when choosing and evaluating CEOs that their character and values be considered on a par with their business acumen and results achieved. He recommends a disciplined approach to investigating a CEO candidate's character, for example, by securing insights from former employees, customers, and suppliers. Attempting to ascertain character is not an easy task, of course, but it is an essential one. True success will only be achieved and sustained if character is combined with business competence, and the CEO thus emerges as a great leader.

Such inspired, vision-focused, mission-centered, and values-based business leadership surely will effectuate positive, beneficial, and necessary change.

C. Leadership and Management

There are, of course, differences between leadership and management. The chief function of a leader is to create and to communicate the firm's vision, mission, and core values, and the principal purpose of a manager is to act to achieve the stated ends in accordance with the firm's values. The business leader's role is critical to the firm's long-term success. He or she keeps the vision and mission continually and distinctly in view, provides the values-based direction, guidance, advancement, commitment, and frame of reference, builds and makes stronger the organization's people, resources, culture, and health, and deals with the firm's "top line," that is, the efficacy, results, and success of the firm's policies and practices in realizing its vision, achieving its mission, and living up to its values. The business manager, however, is more of a "bottom-line" person. He or she develops and articulates structures, policies, and procedures, organizes, coordinates, and controls people and resources, and focuses on speed, efficiency, logistics, and cost-benefit calculation in order to make systems work, complete selected work projects, and to achieve certain, shorter-term, business objectives.

Yet, the dividing line between leading and managing is not a precisely drawn one; and leading and managing are not mutually exclusive business endeavors. Business leaders are not only leaders of change, but also good managers. That is, in order to be a successful leader, one must play a critical role in implementing the vision one has created, specifically by engaging the participation of others, typically executives and high- and middle-level managers, as leaders, and by delegating to these manager-leaders sufficient power and authority for them to play a greater leadership role. They not only adopt, together with the other stakeholders, the leader's vision and firm's mission and values, but also act as leaders themselves to their own subordinates and constituent groups. Thus, these empowered leader-managers fulfill not only an implementation function, but also formulation, communication, and motivational roles. Business leadership, therefore, emerges as the highest form of management; and leadership is revealed as an inclusive, sharing, trusting, empowering, supportive, mutually rewarding, and self-strengthening endeavor.

D. Ethical Business Leadership

1. The Morality of the Vision

A principal function of a business leader, of course, is to develop and enunciate a vision. Yet the vision must reflect an ideal and worthwhile image of the future and the mission must contain high moral purposes, and the values and goals manifested in the vision must be legitimate and rightful ones. Only then will the vision be an encompassing, inspiring, transcending, and transforming one.

2. The Personal Character of the Leader

The inherent morality of the vision, the success of leadership, as well as the effective exercise of authority, fundamentally depend on the personal character of the leader. The leader not only must possess intelligence, common sense, competence, and resolution, but also integrity, honesty, trustworthiness, fairness, and morality. The successful leader, moreover, must have the personal strength of character to do consistently and diligently what is morally right. The words and actions of the leader completely must be harmonious.

If a business person or manager lacks knowledge or capability, he or she always can seek education and training; but if one does not possess and demonstrate personal integrity and justness, one never will be able to establish, or perhaps rebuild, relationships of trust, which are absolutely essential to successful business leadership. The presence, therefore, of such an ethics-centered, highly principled leader is indispensable to the success of the organization.

3. Respect for People

Leaders respect people! An essential component to leadership is that leaders adhere to the fundamental ethical principle of respect for people. Leaders treat people with dignity, as worthwhile, valuable "ends" in and of themselves, and definitely not as mere "means" or assets or resources. Leaders know that people are human beings, not just economic beings. Respect embraces concern and consideration, not only for the leader's followers, or the business leader's employees, but also for all affected stakeholders. The ethical business leader, therefore, will propose, direct, and effectuate beneficial change that is responsive to and respectful of all the firm's constituency groups, including the community and society.

Respect also entails treating people equitably and managing people by a set of just principles and fair processes. Respect, finally, involves listening to people, truly communicating with people, addressing their concerns, incorporating their ideas, developing their potential, and sharing power with them. Ethical business leaders recognize people as capable of great accomplishments. Such respect will forge bonds of trust and foster a sense of moral community and worthwhile endeavor, all necessary elements to successful business leadership.

4. Moral Law

A business leader must direct and guide individuals and organizations in accord with a demonstrable set of ethical principles and moral rules, embodied, for example, in a company's code of ethics. Such a moral law, naturally in harmony with the firm's vision and mission, not only will give people confidence, motivate and inspire them, but also empower them to make decisions and lead others in a principled manner.

5. Building Trust

Leadership requires the full inclusion and utmost efforts of followers and employees. People indeed will follow and exert themselves for those they trust, and people instinctively trust individuals who possess honesty and integrity, manifest respect for others, strive for legitimate goals, and govern themselves and others in accordance with rightful principles. Leadership emanates from trust, and trust is predicated on shared moral vision, proper common objectives, and mutual correct treatment.

6. Empowering and Leading Others to Lead

Followers and employees who trust their leader, and who are guided and governed by rightful purposes and principles, will feel authorized to achieve these worthwhile objectives. Such people will possess a sense of stewardship; that is, they will act effectively to accomplish communal goals, govern themselves and others accordingly, and convince others to lead and make a contribution. A successful leader is committed to this principle of opportunity and shared leadership; and he or she will empower, encourage, and educate followers and employees to act, to lead, to bring out the best in themselves and others, and to achieve personal and organizational success. Such a discerning, encompassing, and enabling conception of leadership is also a most efficacious one.

7. Ethical Awareness and Alignment

Ethical business leaders value themselves and value personal as well as organizational success, yet they are altogether morally astute and enlightened to subordinate themselves to noble purposes, ethical principles, rightful conduct, as well as to shared aspirations, communal values, and manifold contributions. The challenge for a business leader is to align his or her personal goals with the organization's objectives and also with the needs and aspirations of one's followers and employees, and to ensure that this alignment is centered on a crux of morality and legitimacy. Only then can a leader truly lead and thereby achieve permanent positive transformation.

E. Value-Driven Management

Value-Driven Management, a topic that is comprehensively covered by Randolph Pohlman and Gareth Gardiner in their 2000 book, is basically an integrated, philosophical approach, as well as a practical analytical and decision-making tool, that leaders, managers, and employees can use to guide actions, resolve problems, make superior determinations, and to empower themselves and their organizations. The basic purpose of Value-Driven Management (VDM) is to motivate managers and employees, when contemplating making decisions or taking actions, to consider the impact of these decisions and actions on the value of the organization over time. This determination can be accomplished only by an examination of the sets of values held by the relevant constituents (or stakeholder groups) of the organization. These encompass world, national, societal cultures and subcultures, organizational culture, the values of employees, suppliers, customers, competitors, and third parties (such as unions and government regulators), and most importantly, but not exclusively, the values of the "owners" of the organization (for example, the shareholders in a business context). What these people and groups value, drives their actions.

1. Maximizing Value Over Time

A significant goal of VDM is to maximize value over time. "Value" is a subjective term referring to something that possesses worth, intrinsically or instrumentally. In the business context, value typically is regarded in a monetary sense; but value also encompasses such notions as happiness and security as well as morality, ethics, honesty, and integrity. The goal of VDM is to maximize the value of the organization over time, especially in the sense of maximizing its long-term profitability, by creating win-win scenarios whereby the value of the organization and its constituent groups are maximized. A long-term perspective is taken, but not so long as to prevent the prediction of the reasonably foreseeable consequences of a decision or action on the organization and its stakeholders, and then the resultant impact on value maximization over time for the organization. Note, moreover, that a decision or action, although producing overall "good" value consequences, may inflict pain on one or more of the organization's constituent groups, or within a particular constituent group. In such a trade-off case, a good faith effort at damage control must be made to mitigate the harm caused. The subjectivity and diversity of value, the long-term view, and the necessity of foreseeing consequences make VDM decisions quite complex; they will require the VDM decision maker to engage in careful determinations, accurate predictions, equitable balancing and weighing, and overall to use wise judgment.

2. What Is Valued, Drives Action

A vital underlying assumption of VDM is that what causes individuals and groups to take actions are their values. If values, therefore, are not understood clearly, there will be no way to define, predict, satisfy, or even compete with value-driven actions.

3. There Are Value-Adders and Value-Destroyers

There are people, processes, and systems within organizations that add and destroy value. There are, for example, employees within organizations who destroy more value than they create, perhaps as a result of being in the wrong position with the wrong types of skills and abilities, or perhaps they are totally incompatible with their organization's means or ends. It is every employee's responsibility to seek out a role that adds value and ensures success, and it is the organization's responsibility to eliminate value destroyers by placing people in the proper jobs and instituting proper processes and systems.

4. The Eight Facets—The "Value Drivers"

- *Culture External to the Organization.* This facet encompasses world culture, national and societal cultures, and their common sets of values, which includes their legal prescriptions and proscriptions and their moral norms.
- *Organizational Culture.* Each organization has its own unique culture. Anyone within an organization making decisions or taking actions must understand the organizational context within which they must be made.

- *Employee's Values.* Each employee comes to the organization with a set of values. It is essential that the employees' values are congruent with the organization's values. The more the employee's values are congruent with organizational values, the more successful the individual will be and the more successful the organization will be. It is thus crucial for the organization's decision makers to understand what the organizational culture is, but also to understand what each employee values, and how each can be the most successful in the organization. Each employee, of course, also has the responsibility of finding an organization and role that suits their values, interest, and abilities. When one is considering making a decision or taking an action, therefore, one must think clearly about how this will affect the employees within the organization, how these consequences, in turn, will impact value maximization over time.

- *Supplier's Values.* Attention must be given to the values of the organization's suppliers in order to maximize the organization's value over time. Treating suppliers fairly, creating "partnerships" with suppliers, and acting on their other values will lead to greater value over time, for the suppliers and also the organization.

- *Customer's Values.* Clearly understanding what customers value, for example, quality of product and service and reliability, and satisfying customer value are critical to the success of any business. In order to serve customers, the values of the customers and the employees of the organization serving them must be congruent.

- *Third-Party Values.* Understanding what third parties, such as unions and government regulatory agencies value, such as authority, rules, and compliance, can be very important in making decisions and taking actions within an organization.

- *Competitor's Values.* What competitors value, such as size and market share, profitability, and image, will drive their strategy, tactics, and actions. Understanding one's competitor's values will lead one to a better understanding of one's competitors and thus will help one's own organization formulate its strategy.

- *Owner Values.* The owners, the shareholders in a corporate context, have a set of values. They value, for example, a return on assets and equity, sustained growth, a profitable investment, and prestige of the firm. Owner values are the primary focus of VDM, but the other facets cannot be ignored. Of course, when VDM is operational and working well, the values of the owners, the values of the other stakeholder groups, and the values of legality and morality will be in harmony.

5. Good Judgment

For any organization to be successful, every individual in the organization must think in terms of what the organization's constituency groups value, how the consequences of any contemplated decision or action will affect these various groups, and then how these ramifications will impact organizational value over time. It is absolutely critical not to lose the link among the understanding of what the various groups value, their expected reactions to decisions and actions, and the ultimate effect on maximizing organizational value over time.

6. The VDM Method

Every employee in a VDM organization will be involved in an estimating, weighing, and balancing act when they are considering making a decision or taking an action. Specifically, the employee first must ensure that the values of legality and morality are attained. Then, one must ascertain what facets are most important to analyze in order to determine value maximization over time for a particular situation. In so doing, for each pertinent facet one must predict and enumerate the positive and negative consequences of a decision or action thereon, as well as its short-term compared to the long-term effects. Next, determine the eventual resultant impact all these consequences will have on value maximization over time. Lastly, for any negative consequences, or unintended consequences, that possibly could occur, resolve how they could be eliminated or at the least mitigated.

7. Conclusion

The VDM model and method is a philosophical as well as a practical approach, which is simple to state in its basic form, but arduous to implement. Implementation is difficult because organizations and people are complex, values are diverse and subjective, values of constituent groups hard to comprehend, and calculating consequences and their long-range impact on value maximization are very challenging tasks. Nonetheless, if VDM is learned well and administered thoughtfully and consistently, the ultimate goals of achieving, creating, and sustaining long-term growth, surplus, wealth, and value maximization will be attained.

F. Corporate Entrepreneurship, Ethics, and Value Creation[4]

Entrepreneurs have big egos! Entrepreneurs are ethical egoists. They want to advance their self-interest; they want to create value for themselves; they want to promote their own personal good. Entrepreneurship and ethical egoism require taking action and doing. Both involve the discovery, evaluation, and exploitation of available opportunities so that a person or groups of individuals can effectively bring new goods, services, and processes to today's competitive market. Entrepreneurs and ethical egoists must be discerning evaluators who ascertain the positive and negative ramifications of prospective actions. Of course, the origins of both ethical egoism and entrepreneurship in the local and global marketplaces can be traced back thousands of years. Organizations are often founded by entrepreneurs with little or no planning. Then as the organization grows, rules and procedures are implemented that provide the structure needed for the company to flourish. However, with this growth often comes bureaucracy, which may stifle innovation, and inevitably impedes a company's ability to compete. Developing and nurturing an entrepreneurial culture will enhance a company's ability to develop innovative solutions, create value, and sustain strategic competitive advantages. However, one should recall the limitations on the doctrine of ethical egoism, which are particularly relevant in an entrepreneurial setting, both individual and corporate. First, the entrepreneur as an ethical egoist must think of what will inure to his or her interest in the long-term, and thus be willing to undergo some short-term "pain" and sacrifice, or even forgo some short-term gains, in order to achieve a greater long-term good. Second, even though the entrepreneur has an admittedly big ego, this certainly does not mean that the entrepreneur is selfish or egoistical in the narrow and pejorative connation of these terms, and consequently never takes

---

[4]Coauthored with Matthew Kenney, Kenney College of Entrepreneurship; based on a 2007 article by Kenney and Mujtaba; originally published by the *Journal of Applied Management and Entrepreneurship*, 12(3).

the interests of others into account or treats them well and fairly. Rather, the entrepreneur as a smart and prudent ethical egoist will be concerned with people's interests and welfare because such concern will inure to the benefit of the entrepreneur in the long-run.

Initially, it is important to distinguish between entrepreneurship and corporate entrepreneurship, though both naturally have egoistic rationales. Entrepreneurship is the drawing from a wide range of skills and knowledge capable of enhancement to add value to a targeted niche of human activity. The effort expended in finding and implementing such opportunities is rewarded by income and independence as well as pride in creation. Entrepreneurship is primarily viewed as an individual pursuit, and thus characteristically associated with start-up entrepreneurs; whereas corporate entrepreneurship is viewed as acting entrepreneurially within the confines of an established organization. There is no agreed upon exact definition of entrepreneurship. Entrepreneurs should be viewed as those possessing the following characteristics: initiative, imagination, creativity, risk-taking, diligence, hard work, intelligence, problem-solving, flexibility, ambition, goal-oriented, persuasiveness, integrity, and leadership. Premised on this characterization, self-employment would be deemed a manifestation of entrepreneurship, rather than a condition of it. Most companies do not have a corporate culture conducive to entrepreneurship, and consequently inhibit entrepreneurial employees by implementing policies and procedures that stifle the aforementioned entrepreneurial traits. As a result, entrepreneurial employees may leave the organizations and pursue their own ventures.

Leaders of successful companies must recognize that entrepreneurially and ethically inclined employees can be valuable contributors to a company's success if their skills and knowledge are nurtured. Converting employees with entrepreneurial aptitude into corporate entrepreneurs can deliver exceptional value to the firm's stakeholders. Corporate entrepreneurship (sometimes referred to as "intrapreneurship") is viewed as the process of stimulating innovative ideas and processes, often with a focus on value creation. There are four types of corporate entrepreneurship: 1) Corporate Venturing is the process of starting new ventures that are related to the company's core business. 2) Organizational Transformation places the focus on enhancing operational efficiencies. This is not entrepreneurial per se, but does focus on the entrepreneurial trait of efficiency. 3) Intrapreneurship entails the identification of employees within an organization that may have entrepreneurial aptitude. Not every employee needs to have entrepreneurial skills for corporate entrepreneurship to flourish; however, it is essential that those with innate entrepreneurial ability be identified and nurtured. 4) Industry Risk-Taking pertains to initiating paradigm shifts within an industry. Companies that can identify innovative products and processes can attain "first mover" status, create value, and accordingly gain market-share.

The common denominator of each ethical entrepreneurial corporation is that the organization focuses on innovation and creating something new, be it a product or process, so as to create value for the firm and all its stakeholders. To foster corporate entrepreneurship, a company must have an entrepreneurial orientation. There are six dimensions of entrepreneurial orientation: 1) Autonomy—Employees are encouraged to become a "project champion," negotiating for the ability to bring a new product to market and/or institute a new internal process. 2) Innovation—The company must be committed to investing in Research and Development, which encompasses the creation of new products that initially may not be commercially accepted. 3) Analysis—The willingness to differentiate ideas from opportunities via research and trend analysis. This dimension requires the company to have a future-orientation. 4) Competitiveness—Companies with an entrepreneurial orientation will not only willingly engage the competition, they will aggressively engage the competition to gain market-share. 5) Risk—A firm must possess a clear understanding of the business, financial, and professional risks associated with corporate entrepreneurship as well as possess the boldness to overcome fears. 6) Motivation—An important consideration for leaders and managers of the corporate entrepreneurial firm is that success cannot be achieved without an intrinsically motivated employee. 7) Integrity— No entrepreneurial endeavor will be successful in the long-term unless the purpose and practices of the venture are inherently moral and the leaders and managers of the venture are honest, virtuous, and ethical individuals.

Corporate entrepreneurship ventures can be either initiated internally or externally. However, the most common scenario involves an aspiring entrepreneur seeing an opportunity in the market, and attempting to obtain company resources to pursue it. While entrepreneurially oriented companies will facilitate opportunity recognition and pursuance, they will also impose internal barriers that challenge the aspiring corporate entrepreneurs. It is essential for managers to maintain some degree of centralization and structure as corporate venturing can result in fragmentation. It is also important for managers to recognize that they can not predict who will be successful as corporate entrepreneurs. Rather they can develop from any area within the company. Four factors (autonomy, rewards and reinforcement, time availability, and management support) are required for corporate entrepreneurial success.

Can entrepreneurship be taught? The academic community, until relatively recently, has treated entrepreneurship as a vocational trade rather than as a facet of management or organizational behavior. However, an upswing in entrepreneurship research over the three decades has led to renewed interest in the longstanding nature vs. nurture debate. Entrepreneurial aptitude can be developed through education and training. Some facets of entrepreneurship (business planning) may be more teachable than others (opportunity recognition); however, there seems to be accord within the academic community that virtually all employees can be taught to be more innovative. Nonetheless, corporate entrepreneurship can occur spontaneously within an organization or result from strategic initiatives. However, companies should not try to force entrepreneurial initiatives through training, but rather provide a nurturing environment where ideas can flow naturally. Moreover, fundamentally, ethical egoism would dictate that if one wants to get people to act as entrepreneurs, one needs to pay them as entrepreneurs. Entrepreneurs are not necessarily motivated solely by money, but they will expect to be compensated fairly for the value they have created for stakeholders. There must be alignment between the goals of the company and the corporate entrepreneur. The mission of the venture should be clearly written; the mission must be an inherently moral one; responsibilities must be ascribed to the appropriate stakeholders; and clear and measurable objectives must be determined. Value Driven Management can be used by the entrepreneur, and particularly the entrepreneurial corporation, in order to ascertain, balance, and align individual, corporate, and stakeholder values.

Entrepreneurship in a corporate setting can also be team-oriented. There are six traits of successful corporate entrepreneurship teams: 1) Start-up Orientation—Team members view themselves as part of a "start-up" company, rather than merely part of the "parent" company. 2) Empowered—Team members have a sense of autonomy; they are not unduly inhibited by organizational rules. 3) High-Performing—Team members are intrinsically motivated; they generally are high-performing prior to joining the "start-up" team. 3) Focused—Members have a clear understanding of the ventures and goals as well as available resources. The ambiguity usually associated with traditional "start-ups" is less prevalent. 4) Established Procedures—The team typically is responsible for setting up its own rules and procedures, rather than relying on the established procedures of the "parent" company; but the team always remains cognizant of the inherently moral nature of their separate venture. 5) External Relationships—The team is willing to look outside the parent company and thus to develop relationships with new stakeholders. Therefore, an important aspect of corporate entrepreneurship development is the establishment of a team-based approach. Corporate entrepreneurs are essentially leaders, thus they must avoid developing the traits of a too individualistic or unethical entrepreneur, and rather focus on building a strong team of internal and external stakeholders whose values are in alignment and whose objectives are moral as well as practical ones.

The biggest challenge facing corporate entrepreneurs may be the corporate culture itself. The corporation is a challenging setting for entrepreneurs to create, although it is an inviting setting in which to create because there are so many undiscovered and untapped opportunities lurking in every corporation. Corporate entrepreneurship is a great tool for retaining high-performing, ethical, and committed entrepreneurial employees who want to deviate from the corporate "program" and develop new ideas, new business models, and new products. Just making such opportunities available will attract and hold committed employees. To enhance corporate entrepreneurship development, training and learning should be promoted, especially if the training and learning are in something new, different, or revolutionary (that is, really distinctive) from the normal path of the existing employee. Should new ventures be located in-house, or should they be set up separately from the influences of the parent company? Most new ventures should be set up in-house. Then some determination should be made later to decide if the activity or business should become part of the business, be moved outside the firm's normal operations to another location or site, be sold to another company, or sold to the creators.

It is essential for all levels of management to "buy into" the concept of ethical corporate entrepreneurship. Entrepreneurial organizations have a diversity of people, "change agents," and managers that can be categorized as shakers, movers, housekeepers, and lifers. 1) Shakers are high profile individuals with great vision, ability and desire to take risks in order to make effective and innovative organizational changes. Change is "created" as a result of new ideas and innovative ideas that are risky but have clear opportunity for the future improvement and growth. Shakers' priorities are directly tied into the established mission/vision statement. Shakers work "out of the box" and oftentimes require having the "reins pulled in" to structure the drive. Chaos will result if a company is run by shakers but they are necessary in order to succeed and grow. There is no thinking "inside the box"; and as a matter of fact, for shakers there is no "box" at all, and the paradigms are few and far between. 2) Movers are the Upper Management Individuals that "organize" and control the ideas created by the Shakers. It is imperative to make the Shakers' sometimes radical ideas feasible and rational. Movers are more stable with the company and are considered long term employees. Change is "evaluated" and "organized" into a working set of processes and procedures while keeping sight of the Mission and Vision Statement of the organization. Movers are the strength and practical side of the organization; they must keep not only the firm's shareholders but also all its stakeholders in mind at all times. Long-term and value-creating goals are "first and foremost"; the mission and vision statements must reflect ethical value creation by means of innovation and entrepreneurship. The organization's code of ethics must keep in check existing and contemplated business practices as well as any problematical ideas that are presented by the Shakers. Change is "invited," of course, and organized into a working manner for future success and growth. 3) Housekeepers are middle managers and staff. Middle managers follow the directives set forth by the movers or upper management. They offer ideas for process and procedure improvement but generally are the "mainline" company "backbone" of "getting the job done." Change is "accepted" and the proper steps taken to enforce it might be the main task. Innovation and more radical thought processes are left up to the Shakers—who are then "prioritized" by the Movers—who then establish guidelines for Middle Managers to follow, implement, and enforce with the staff. Housekeepers are very long term employees who manage the goals and directives, keep the processes in check, and enforce established procedures in order to meet the goals and objectives set by the Movers. 4) Lifers are those individuals who are complacent and generally short-term in focus to a great degree. They follow orders but are not receptive to change, nor do they recognize the long-term goals or objectives of the organization. They are "workers" who have limited input and in fact prefer not being involved in any risk. Change is "not recognized" and oftentimes considered disruptive for Lifers. Change requires a retooling of existing processes and procedures, which take more effort than they are willing to make. There is an expected turnover that exceeds all other organizational levels, but this movement is important to have. The exit and entry of these short-term employees or "lifers" is designed to introduce new entry level employees who can offer the organization new ideas and possibly move into the Housekeeper level and then on to the Movers level with guidance and direction from the movers who act as mentors. Today's organizations need shakers, housekeepers, movers, and lifers if they are to benefit from a diversity of different ideas to remain competitive. Accordingly, having diverse employees with different personalities will provide an organization a competitive advantage in today's global business environment. Furthermore, such diversity can best be encouraged and nourished through a collaborative and ethical entrepreneurship culture, where people communicate, work, and innovate collectively as a network of complex strands placed strategically in various markets closest to their customers and communities.

Above all, entrepreneurs—individual and corporate—must be concerned with ethics. Entrepreneurship is premised on ethical egoism, of course. Yet the prudent and wise entrepreneur will want to benefit not only himself or herself and the firm, but also benefit society as a whole, and finally achieve this personal good as well as the societal greater good by not demeaning, disrespecting, or exploiting human beings and the environment. Therefore, business managers, scholars, and leaders must fully realize that only ethical corporate entrepreneurship, collaborative entrepreneurship, and corporate intrapreneurship will be the efficacious means to create long-term value in today's diverse, global, and highly competitive business environment.

G. Ethical Decision-Making Steps

Using ethical principles, each organization and individual can form a framework for ethical decision-making by following typical decision-making strategies or methods and adding ethical principles to the equation. The willingness to add ethical principles to the decision-making structure indicates a desire to promote diversity and culture, as well as to prevent any potential moral problems from occurring through "pro-activity." Therefore, companies could, and should, use ethics as a part of their decision-making framework, and accordingly follow similar steps as outlined below in the Nine Step Ethical Decision-Making Model.

Stage 1—Understand the Problem

1. Identify the problem.
   - Is there a problem personally, interpersonally, or socially?
   - What is happening?
   - Who is affected, and/or is it damaging others?
   - What is the problem or issue?
   - Does the problem have legal concerns or consequences?
2. Define the criteria, goals, and objectives for the problem.
   - What groups or people are affected by the outcome of this problem?
   - What should be happening?
   - Are people/groups being excluded, or singled-out, because of a specific need?
3. Evaluate the effects of the problem.
   - Have all the persons/groups affected by this problem been identified?
   - Is the problem worth solving?
   - What are the anticipated results of reacting to or attempting to solve this problem?

Stage 2—Make the Decision

4. Identify the causes of the problem.
   - Are there potential conflicts of interest causing problem?
   - What is causing this problem? (Why? Why? Why?)
   - Are there multiple interpretations of the problem, causing further "breakdown" of systems?
5. Frame the alternatives (solutions).
   - What solution will do the most good, and inflict the least harm?
   - What are the possible solutions to the problem?
   - Which option represents the value of all people involved?

6. Evaluate the impact of each alternative solution.
   - Are there biases in any of the options that might be seen as prejudices?
   - What are the benefits and costs of each solution?
   - What are the legal implications?
7. Make the decision by choosing the best alternative, given the situation and stake-holders.
   - Are there any religious/cultural issues impacting the problem?
   - What is the best solution based on the evaluation?
   - What option provides the common good for all people involved?
   - Does that option treat all the affected stakeholders with dignity and respect?

Stage 3—Evaluate the Decision

8. Implement the selected alternative.
   - Accept responsibility for the choice one has made.
   - What steps are needed to implement the solution?
9. Measure the impacts of the decision?
   - What was the outcome of the solution for all those involved?
   - Did the solution provide the expected results?
   - If one had to do it over again, would one do it differently?

Using the framework above, a company or individual can embark on the process of critical thinking and ethical decision-making. As one can see, the framework diverges from the standard decision-making when taking into account ethical and cultural sensitivities. It is certainly not an easy task identifying and dealing with ethical and cultural issues in today's global marketplace, but it is an area of interest that businesses will need to recognize as important for their continued growth. The implications and potential liability of not recognizing ethical issues with sensitivity and understanding are endless! Therefore, companies should make ethics and social responsibility a common thread in their businesses, create principles and guidelines for their employees to follow, and practice business in the most beneficial and respectful way possible to maximize their potential in today's global market.

H. Summary

There clearly is an ethical dimension to effective leadership. Successful leadership must be built on a foundation of morality, and the vision, mission, values, and goals, as well as the objectives and behavior of all the participants, must be inherently good. Such ethical leadership dignifies, inspires, ennobles, and elevates people and reaps a harvest of "good" prosperity. Value-Driven Management emerges as a philosophical as well as practical management tool to integrate and implement the values of leadership, morality, and stakeholder sensitivity in an efficacious business manner.

Discussion Questions

1. Is the moral corporation a "fad" or is the moral corporation here to stay? Explain.

2. What recommendations would one make to the new manager seeking upward mobility?

3. How can management keep from "slipping back" to their unethical business styles? Explain.

4. How valuable is the path towards Value-Driven Management for the modern manager?

5. In your own words, what are the steps to effective motivation? What should every manager know about this process?

6. What is the relationship between needs and behaviors?

7. What are the five needs of Maslow's hierarchy? What relevance do they have to the study of motivation?

8. In the aftermath of Enron, realistically speaking, how much progress do you believe can be expected between now and the next five years towards a more ethical business environment? Why?

9. How can top management provide the employee with the realization that his or her particular job can be accomplished with a high degree of ethics? Cite some illustrations?

10. What is meant by the term Value-Driven Management?

11. Name some companies that have acted unethically in the past, and discuss what could have been done to avoid the situation.

12. How do you instill the company's values in your subordinates?

13. How do you know what the customer's values are?

14. What do you do when a supervisor does something that is not ethical and goes against the company's values?

15. What type of "checks and balances" can be established to minimize unethical behavior?

16. Who is responsible for the company's vision?

17. How do you communicate the company's vision to its employees?

18. What does Value Driven Management mean to your organization?

19. Do you think everybody should take an ethics test as part of the application process?

20. Would you sign an ethics charter if you did not agree with everything on it?

21. What does it mean when a corporation is "transparent"?

22. How are values and ethics communicated in your workplace?

CHAPTER 19

Critical Issues for Success

A. Equable Success

An ethical business leader or manager is an economically successful one. He or she is a real capitalist who believes in producing sizable profits for the company. Yet, this successful businessperson definitely is not the archetypal profit maximizer who abuses the firm's employees and mistreats other constituent groups in an exertion to extract the largest possible monetary gain in the shortest time possible, regardless of the consequences. The ethical business leader and manager too will attempt to make enormous profits, but only if the moral interests of the employees and other stakeholders can be satisfied. He or she may have to be content with a moderate financial return, but one that is secured, and shared, fairly and ethically. The ethical business leader and manager is committed, therefore, not only to the values of success, profit making, and growth, but also to the superseding values of morality, integrity, and honesty.

B. Moral Leadership

The insightful businessperson knows that successfully leading, as well as managing, people, is in essence a moral endeavor. A leader will fail to effectuate positive change, and a manager will fail to direct productive activity, if he or she does not exhibit and adhere to basic moral values. Effective business leadership and management cannot be founded on notions of pure power, expediency, contingency, narrow selfish interests, and "situational ethics"; rather, truly leading and managing begin with an awareness of, commitment to, and practice of universal, everlasting, and cardinal ethical principles, such as achieving the greater good and respecting people.

C. Core Ethical Values

To ask only whether a contemplated objective or action is practical, profitable, and legal is not satisfactory. To provide real leadership and management one also must ask if the goal or course of conduct is a moral one. Is the considered determination the "right" one? That is, does the decision seek to promote the greater good, does it respect people and their ideas and contributions; does it treat people fairly and equitably; and does it align with such core ethical values as integrity, honesty, and dignity? The challenging task confronting the business leader and manager is to articulate and build consensus around these core values, infuse them in the organization and its personnel, and to achieve a business resolution that is practical, profitable, legal, and moral and fair to all constituencies.

D. Stakeholder Symmetry

The emphasis on constituencies or stakeholders is an essential component to the role of the business leader or manager, who must adopt an enlightened stakeholder approach in order to achieve long-term success. He or she must consider the interests, and seek to satisfy the legitimate needs of all the firm's interdependent constituency groups, for example, the shareholders, employees, suppliers, customers and consumers, local community, government, as well as society; and he or she must do so in an efficient, fair, and mutually beneficial manner. The ultimate goal is to attain win-win resolutions whereby all the firm's stakeholders receive value and the competition at the least is not immorally harmed. Value-Driven Management is an excellent means to achieve stakeholder symmetry.

Naturally, there may be conflict as various constituencies make conflicting demands, and thus the crucial challenge confronting the business leader and manager emerges. The leader and manager must recognize competing interests, to provide balance among legitimate claims, to devise an equitable, practical, and mutually beneficial solution, and also perhaps to convince stakeholders that it very well may be in their own long-term welfare to make a present private sacrifice that will lead to eventual greater reciprocal gains.

E. Transformational Change

The business leader and manager, by taking the stakeholder standpoint and by evincing an ethics-based business philosophy that is both moral and practical, will be empowered, and be able to empower loyal and willing followers, to break past habits and traditional modes of thinking, overcome resistance and disagreements, surmount present difficulties, and, therefore, to attain effective, successful, transformational, permanent, notable major changes.

Living, leading, and managing from an ethics-centered-principled basis are indispensable elements to accomplishing great changes. An ethical attitude, approach, and accountability will convince one's followers and employees that they will be governed in a moral manner and that they will share benefits, as well as burdens, in a just way. Such an ethical environment will allow the business leader and manager to convince, encourage, embolden, and empower their people that it is not only safe, but also in their own long range self-interest, to set aside their immediate private wants and to cooperate to achieve the common good. Rational people will act on knowledge that will advance their own and other's mutual self-interest; and imaginative, enterprising, and ambitious people especially will act the most forcefully; and thus people, even ordinary people, will be able to achieve extraordinary beneficial results. Effective leadership and management, individual and group initiative and effort, internal personal and organizational power, and truly transformational positive change, all are built on a foundation of ethics and a core of morality.

F. Ethical Realization and Personal Reflections

This work has sought to demonstrate that the central, successful, long-term achievements of any individual person, whether leader or manager, group or organization, whether business or corporate enterprise, are fundamentally based on an ethical foundation. Yet, economic and political systems, as well as society itself, ultimately are predicated on an ethical foundation too. If people, especially business leaders and managers, believe in, adhere to, and internalize ethical principles and moral standards and values, people and businesses will be afforded a considerably greater opportunity to continue, succeed, and flourish. The consummation will be a productive, secure, stable, harmonious, and sustaining system that serves everyone's mutual best and self-interests; but if the economic and political systems are permitted or tolerated to operate without an ethical groundwork and without moral guidance, the consequence will be an immoral, or perhaps amoral, society, which, as history certainly has shown, degenerates, disintegrates, and self-destructs.

"In oneself lies the whole world, and if you know how to look and learn, then the door is there and the key is in your hand. Nobody on earth can give you either that key or the door to open, except yourself," said an Indian writer by the name of J. Krishnamurti. Living with honor and integrity may come at the price of learning, patience, and standing for what is right, which are all virtuous endeavors. However, living with honor, by being honest and standing up for what is right, is the only way that one can remain truly happy in the long term and become successful in the business of life. Abraham Lincoln was given the title of "Honest Abe" because he did not give up when pressured to do otherwise and continued to live and grow with honor and integrity. Someone wrote: "So, they kept on talking, knowing yet not knowing—Lincoln was the green pine, Lincoln kept on growing." The Persian poet, Khushal Khan Khatak, once said, "Without honor and glory—What is the Afghan story," speaking about the integrity associated with his people and community. An Indian poet is credited for saying, "I slept and dreamt that life was beauty—I woke and found that life was duty," emphasizing that honor and glory can be earned by truthfully performing one's duties. The proceeding three poems emphasize why learning about ethics and business ethics are important for all human beings. The first poem, titled "Life Is a Bother Life Is a Hurry," was written by Charles Jarvis. The second poem titled "The Man in the Glass," was written by Dale Wimbrow. Third, the poem titled "The Race," was written by D. H. Groberg. Fourth, the last poem, titled "I Did It My Way," was written in the spirit of Frank Sinatra's song and its author is "Anonymous," as it has been recited in several graduation ceremonies.

1. Life Is a Bother Life Is a Hurry

Life is a bother, life is a hurry
Life is a busy crowded way
Good intentions go astray
I had a friend the other day.

I haven't anymore, he passed away
I meant to write, to phone, to call
I didn't do any of those at all.

I only hope that he can now see
How much his friendship meant to me
Life is a busy crowded way
Good intentions go astray.

Yet life doesn't have to be this way, and good intentions would not go astray if one is able to cherish relationships every day and take appropriate actions in the present as opposed to waiting for someday. Almost every person looks at his or her face in the glass (mirror) nearly every day, and may not be able to see one's reflection well with a guilty conscience. Also, having a guilty conscience hinders one's progress in the race of life because these individuals spend too much time making up for, or covering up, their previous actions. On the other hand, having a clear conscience due to the successful performance of one's duties with honor and integrity can greatly assist in being victorious in the race of life. With a clear conscience and moral character, you will always be able to get up each time you fall and will eventually win the race with honor and integrity. As stated in "Law of the Harvest," one usually reaps what one has sown. Law of the Harvest states:

- Sow a thought, reap an action.
- Sow an action, reap a habit.
- Sow a habit, reap a character.
- Sow a character, reap a destiny.

Mother Teresa created a destiny and the status of sainthood for herself because of her thoughts, actions, habits, and character. She is quoted as saying that "People are sometimes unreasonable, illogical, and self-centered; forgive them, anyway." She further stated:

- If you are kind, people may accuse you of selfish, ulterior motives. Be kind anyway.
- If you are successful, you will win some false friends and some true enemies. Succeed anyway.
- If you are honest and frank, people may cheat you. Be honest and frank anyway.
- What you spend years building, someone could destroy overnight. Build anyway.
- If you find serenity and happiness, they may be jealous. Be happy anyway.
- The good you do today, people will often forget tomorrow. Do good anyway.
- Give the world the best you have, and it may never be enough. Give the world the best you've got anyway.
- You see, in the final analysis, it is between you and your creator. It was never between you and them anyway.

2. The Man in the Glass

When you get what you want in your struggle for self
*   And the world makes you king for a day,*
Just go to a mirror and look at yourself
*   And see what THAT man has to say.*

For it isn't your father or mother or wife
*   Whose judgment upon you must pass;*
The fellow whose verdict counts most in your life
*   Is the one staring back from the glass.*

Some people may think you a straight-shootin' chum
*   And call you a wonderful guy,*
But the man in the glass says you're only a bum
*   If you can't look him straight in the eye.*

He's the fellow to please, never mind all the rest,
*   For he's with you clear up to the end.*
And you've passed your most dangerous, difficult test
*   If the man in the glass is your friend.*

You may fool the whole world down the pathway of life
*   And get pats on your back as you pass,*
But your final reward will be heartaches and tears
*   If you've cheated the man in the glass.*

3. The Race

"Quit! Give up! You're beaten!" They shout at me and plead. "There's just too much against you now. This time you can't succeed."

And as I start to hang my head in front of failure's face, My downward fall is broken by the memory of a race.

And hope refills my weakened will as I recall that scene: For just the thought of that short race rejuvenates my being.

A children's race, young boys, young men. How I remember well. Excitement, sure! but also fear: It wasn't hard to tell.

They all lined up so full of hope. Each thought to win that race. Or tie for first, or if not that, at least take second place.

And fathers watched from off the side, each cheering for his son. And each boy hoped to show his dad that he would be the one.

The whistle blew and off they went young hearts and hopes afire. To win and be the hero there was each young boy's desire.

And one boy in particular whose dad was in the crowd was running in the lead and thought: "My dad will be so proud!"

But as they speeded down the field across a shallow dip, the little boy who thought to win lost his step and slipped.

Trying hard to catch himself his hands flew out to brace, and mid the laughter of the crowd he fell flat on his face. So down he fell and with him hope—He couldn't win it now—Embarrassed, sad, he only wished to disappear somehow.

But as he fell his dad stood up and showed his anxious face, which to the boy so clearly said: "Get up and win the race."

He quickly rose, no damage done, behind a bit, that's all and ran with all his mind and might to make up for his fall.

So anxious to restore himself, to catch up and to win. His mind went faster than his legs: He slipped and fell again!

He wished then he had quit before with only one disgrace. "I'm hopeless as a runner now; I shouldn't try to race."

But in the laughing crowd he searched and found his father's face; that steady look which said again: "Get up and win the race!"

So up he jumped to try again—ten yards behind the last—"If I'm to gain those yards," he thought, "I've got to move real fast."

Exerting everything he had he regained eight or ten, but trying so hard to catch the lead he slipped and fell again!

Defeat! He lied there silently—a tear dropped from his eye—"There's no sense running anymore: Three strikes: I'm out! Why try!"

The will to rise had disappeared: All hope had fled away; so far behind, so error prone; a loser all the way.

"I've lost, so what's the use," he thought "I'll live with my disgrace." but then he thought about his dad who soon he'd have to face.

"Get up," an echo sounded low. "Get up and take your place; you were not meant for failure here. Get up and win the race."

"With borrowed will get up," it said, "You haven't lost at all. For winning is no more than this: to rise each time you fall."

So up he rose to run once more, and with a new commit he resolved that win or lose at least he wouldn't quit.

So far behind the others now, the most he'd ever been, still he gave it all he had and ran as though to win.

Three times he'd fallen, stumbling; Three times he rose again: Too far behind to hope to win. He still ran to the end.

They cheered the winning runner as he crossed the line first place. Head high and proud and happy; No falling, no disgrace.

But when the fallen youngster crossed the line last place, the crowd gave him the greater cheer, for finishing the race.

And even though he came in last with head bowed low, un-proud, you would have thought he'd won the race to listen to the crowd.

And to his dad he sadly said, "I didn't do too well." "To me, you won," his father said. "You rose each time you fell."

And now when things seem dark and hard and difficult to face, the memory of that little boy helps me in my race.

For all of life is like that race, with ups and downs and all. And all you have to do to win is rise each time you fall.

"Quit! Give up! You're beaten!" They still shout in my face. But another voice within me says: "GET UP AND WIN THE RACE!"

4. "I Did It My Way"

I came, I got the books. I came to classes, read the manuals and followed directions. I worked nights, I studied hard, and made lots of friends who had connections.

I worked overtime to get the rewards; and, may I say "not in a fair way," But, I am a good student and a model citizen, so I did it their way.

I learned so many things although I know I'll never use them, The topics I learned were all required, I didn't choose them.

You'll find that to survive it's best to play the doctor their way, And so I knuckled down and I did it their way.

Well yes there were times when I wondered why I had to cring when I could fly, I had my doubts, but after all I clipped my wings and learned to crawl. I learned to bend, and in the end I did it their way.

Well now I find with friends I am now a commencement professor, Where once I was oppressed and I am now the cruel oppressor.

So, lead a moral business life and have some fun. And may I say "not in a shy way," So when it ends you can say without regret "I did it my way."

G. Summary

The field of business ethics now has secured a position on important moral issues affecting society, and this role will continue to grow and hopefully guide human beings in the right direction at all times and for the right reasons. To be successful in this effort, the field must take seriously its own ethical content. When managers, leaders, and entrepreneurs do become aware of the ethics involved in business transactions, they inevitably will realize ethics' limitations when they attempt to do things "their way," but they also will come to recognize its strengths as they realize that there are many challenges in the race of successfully running a business.

The study of ethics and morality are not new, since philosophers have been exploring such issues for thousands of years. What is new is the development of "business ethics" into a field of study in its own right; and not as a peripheral subject to be added to existing philosophy, law, or even business works and courses as time and interest permit. In the past, philosophers and academics provided the leadership for the field. Today, business leaders, managers and employees, and entrepreneurs must take personal accountability and collective responsibility for their actions to make sure they are doing the right things. Today, what is required is a comprehensive and systematic, yet clear and readable account of morality, ethics, applied ethics for business decision makers, and we hope that this book has highlighted thoroughly and to some extent fulfilled that need.

This book has been about morality, philosophical ethics, and applied ethics. It attempted to introduce you (the reader) to ethical theories and concepts that are relevant to resolving moral problems confronting managers and leaders. The book was designed to be useful to employees and managers, as well as entrepreneurs and business leaders, who want to integrate moral concerns into their decision-making processes. Furthermore, it was intended for individuals who wish to be acquainted with moral philosophy, ethical reasoning, and especially the application of ethics to business and management. The authors sincerely hope that these objectives have been achieved.

By ethically resolving moral problems confronting society through individual and collective means, one will be better able to understand and classify one's own moral beliefs; and be better equipped to develop a critical and reflective morality. People frequently seek reasons for the goals they are considering pursuing and for the decisions they are contemplating making. They also often desire to place their lives in a meaningful larger picture in the society. As one may know, ethics can provide intelligible reasons for one's decisions, direction for one's goals in life, coherence to one's existence, significance to one's life, and a satisfaction that one has lived as one ought.

The conceptions of morality, as well as the ethical theories addressed in this book, have been aspects of the best work achieved in the history of moral philosophy. Many readers have come to realize that they already possess ethical resources to make contemporary moral judgments. The authors truly hope this was the case for you as well. The authors appreciate that you are concerned about ethics and morality in society and certainly welcome feedback in improving this material. The authors finally wish you, and the people you influence, total satisfaction in delivering your good intentions by making the right decisions at the right times and for the right reasons. May you live with honor and glory personally and professionally as you deliver on your good intentions as a business leader in order to be a winner in every race you face. Always remember that you are a very special person making many lives better in your own special way.

When we count our many blessings, it isn't hard to see
That life's most valued treasures are the treasures that are free.

For it isn't what we own or buy that signifies our wealth . . .
It's the special gifts that have no price . . . our family, friends, and health.

—Larry S. Chengges.

Discussion Questions

1. How can a business leader maximize company profits, but also perform ethically?

2. What factors must a manager consider when making a decision that is fair to all stakeholders of the company?

3. Do the leaders of your company possess the traits to institute transitional change? Discuss.

4. What does one gain by making decisions with ethical considerations?

5. Is it more important to do things to please others, or to make decisions that one can live with, but might cause displeasure to others? Discuss.

6. Is your company capable of winning a Business Ethics Award? Why or why not? What changes are required to win, if not? How could these changes be institutionalized?

7. What "inner strengths" do you rely on to recover from "falls," and thus win "The Race"?

8. What attributes must a leader possess to create followers and convince them to consider the common good over their own self interests?

9. How and why has the study of business ethics been transformed from an appendage of philosophy to a study of its own?

10. Do you possess the traits to be a successful manager who can lead by moral leadership? Where can you improve? Discuss.

APPENDIX A

Cases for Analysis and Discussion

1. Corporate Ethics and Social Responsibility

Case 1.1: The Legality and Morality of Slavery Reparations

Three corporations that are accused of profiting from slavery are anticipated to be the first businesses sued in what is expected to be a barrage of lawsuits by African Americans seeking compensation for abuses suffered by their ancestors. The first lawsuit names insurer Aetna, railroad CSX, and financial services firm Fleet Boston as defendants. The complaint asks for unspecified damages, restitution for unpaid slave labor, and a share of corporate profits derived from slavery.

The case arises amid growing interest in the issue of slavery reparations among lawyers, historians, moral philosophers, activists, and state and local governments.

The plaintiff is Deadria Farmer-Paellmann, a New York attorney, legal researcher, and activist who has documented links between modern-day corporations and slavery. Her lawsuit asks the court to bring the case to a jury on behalf of all African Americans who can claim slaves as forebears—the majority of the nation's 36.4 million blacks. The lawsuit reserves the right to add up to 100 more corporate defendants.

The lawsuit states that Aetna, CSX, and Fleet were "unjustly enriched" by "a system that enslaved, tortured, starved, and exploited human beings." It contends that African Americans are still suffering the harmful effects of 2 and 1/2 centuries of enslavement followed by more than a century of institutionalized racism. The complaint blames slavery for present-day disparities between blacks and whites in income, education, literacy, health, life expectancy, and crime.

Separately, Paellmann's lawyers are sending letters to 13 other companies, as well as trade groups representing the tobacco and shipping industries. The letters warn the companies they will be sued unless they fund a historical commission examining slavery and give money to a humanitarian fund to improve health, education, and child development among blacks.

Aetna has acknowledged issuing insurance policies on an undetermined number of slaves, naming their owners as beneficiaries. Fleet's earliest predecessor bank was founded by John Brown, a notorious Rhode Island slave trader. CSX owns early rail lines built by slaves. A CSX spokesperson said there was no legal basis for the lawsuit, and condemned it as an "unfortunate misuse" of the legal system to address issues over a century old at the expense of today's workers and stockholders. The CSX spokesperson called slavery a "tragic chapter in our nation's history" but said that slavery's impacts cannot be attributed to any single company or industry. Aetna, in a statement, said it has already expressed "deep regret" for issuing slave policies, and also recounted that over the past 30 years, the firm has invested more than $34 million in the African American community. Fleet has declined comment to date and said it was reviewing the lawsuit.

Moreover, defense and civil rights lawyer, Johnnie Cochran, was a member of a group of prominent black lawyers and scholars studying reparations, and he said he had been laying the groundwork for additional lawsuits. Separately, a firm specializing in historical research is offering to do background checks for companies that believe they are potential targets for reparations lawsuits. The firm that does litigation support work warns companies that such a lawsuit will be a "public relations nightmare" for the firms and may have negative financial consequences and inflict harm on the firms' reputations.

In New York, a state lawmaker has introduced a bill that would set up a commission to quantify the debt owed to black New Yorkers as a result of the suffering by slaves. The bill would force an examination of the role of the state and local governments in slavery and identify New York-based companies that profited from slavery. The bill also calls for the state to study ways to compensate African-Americans and for the creation of a holiday to commemorate the victims of slavery. Some observers of the reparations movement actually theorize that the corporate lawsuits are part of a larger strategy to force the federal government to create a legislative remedy. In California, the state Department of Insurance is expected to make public the details of its search for insurance policies issued on the lives of slaves. A California law requires dozens of insurance companies to look through their archives and to turn over to the department any evidence they issued such policies.

Legal experts, however, assert that reparations cases confront very difficult hurdles in court. Statutes of limitations have expired. Determining the class of people to be compensated would be an obstacle. It may be impossible to trace the slaves down to all their living descendants. Juries may not be convinced that slavery's effects are substantially ongoing 137 years after slavery ended. Determining the detrimental trickle-down effects on subsequent generations will be difficult. Yet, if private companies were doing the paying, as opposed to the government (and taxpayers), then reparations might be more acceptable to many Americans. Yet, is it fair to hold today's shareholders for the centuries old transgressions of long dead people. Then, there is the basic and logical legal argument that these companies technically did nothing illegal, because slavery, though immoral and unconscionable, was legal at the time. Blaming corporations that helped finance and further the slave trade, however, does echo a legal tactic that won more than $8 billion from banks and insurance companies for World War II Holocaust survivors in recent federal litigation.

Some people, however, say that African Americans really, and mostly, want the federal government to apologize for slavery in a clear, firm, and unambiguous manner.

The lead plaintiff in the current litigation, Deadria Farmer-Paellmann, began by studying previous failed efforts to win slavery reparations. She did most of her legal research at the New England School of Law in Boston, where she earned her law degree. She learned that 600,000 emancipated African Americans lobbied from the 1890s until the 1920s for what was called the ex-slave pension movement. A court case in the early 1900s sought to force the government to pay ex-slaves the cotton profits from the last few years of slavery. The case, however, died. More recently, a 1995 lawsuit against the U.S. government sought $100 million and an apology. A judge, however, ruled the government had immunity and that the statute of limitations had run out. Her research picked up considerably in 2000 when the Aetna insurance company gave her copies of policies taken out by slave owners and slaves. She then contacted other corporations, finding other links to slavery, and built a list of 60 companies that allegedly played a role in the commerce of slavery.

It is important to note that the judge hearing the current slavery reparations dismissed it "without prejudice," meaning that it could be filed again. The judge, although condemning slavery as immoral and as a historic injustice, stated that no clear link and on specific connection were demonstrated between the companies being sued and the institution of slavery. The judge also stated that slavery reparations was more of a "political" than a legal issue, and thus more appropriate for the executive and legislative branches of government to consider.

In March 2004, the descendants of slaves again filed a lawsuit in federal court asking $1 billion in damages against U.S. and British corporations, accusing them of profiting by committing genocide against their ancestors. This latest slavery reparations suit is very significant because it is the first one to use DNA to link the plaintiffs to Africans who suffered atrocities during the slave trade. The suit specifically accuses Lloyd's of London, FleetBoston Bank (now merged with Bank of America), and R.J. Reynolds Company of "aiding and abetting the commission of genocide" by financing and insuring the ships that delivered the slaves to the tobacco plantations in the United States. The previous slavery reparations lawsuit was dismissed, one recalls, but "without prejudice" so that it could be filed again. That judge ruled that the connection between the slave victims and the plaintiffs to the lawsuit was too attenuated or tenuous, in the judge's opinion, to establish liability. In this new lawsuit, however, the plaintiffs are contending that DNA testing has made a "direct connection" between the plaintiffs and the slaves, formerly members of the Mende tribe in Sierra Leone; and thus the plaintiffs assert that they should prevail legally.

In another interesting legal development, in May 2004, businesses seeking contracts with Wayne County (Detroit), Michigan, now are obligated to disclose any historic ties to slavery pursuant to a law passed by the County Commission. The law requires companies bidding on contracts of $20,000 or more to disclose whether they invested in, supported, or profited from slavery. This law emerged as part of the ongoing national debate as to the legality and morality of paying reparations to the descendants of slaves.

Also very noteworthy, though more for emotional and psychological reasons than pragmatic ones, was the decision of the Virginia General Assembly in February 2007 to formally apologize for slavery. The General Assembly, meeting in Richmond, the former capital of the confederacy, voted unanimously to express "profound regret" for the state's role in slavery. As of the writing of this book, Virginia is the only state that has apologized for slavery.

Bibliography:

McAdams, Neslund, and Neslund, Law, Business, and Society (7th edition 2004), pp. 512-13.
Atlanta Constitution, 1/26/04; Miami Herald, 2/25/07, pp. 1A, 14A; 5/7/04, 3/30/04, 4/5/02;
Sun Sentinel, 4/3/02; USA Today, 3/25/02.

Questions for Discussion:

1. What are some of the legal issues in the reparations controversy, and how should they be resolved?

2. Are these companies with historic ties to slavery morally obligated to pay reparations today? Discuss.

3. How would a socially responsible company deal with this question? Discuss.

4. How would you advise a company named as a defendant in a reparations lawsuit using the principles of Value-Driven Management?

Case 1.2: Corporate Social Responsibility: "Crisis Funds"

Business writer, Marcia Pounds, writing in the south Florida Sun-Sentinel newspaper in November 2006, reported a most interesting corporate response to hurricanes and other natural and "man-made" disasters—the formation of "crisis funds" to benefit employees. One example was the American Express Company, which has a crisis management program that allows employees to receive sufficient funds. One employee, who home was devastated by Hurricane Wilma, received enough money to cover the cost of moving to an apartment until her insurance funds were secured and the rebuilding of her house completed. American Express and other companies have established these employee "crisis funds" in order to help their employees in extraordinary situations, such as recovering from disasters, but also coping with health crises. The basic idea is to rapidly help employees with money in an emergency. JetBlue Airways also has such a program. Employee applicants to the fund can receive payments from $500 to $5000, with $5000 the most that an employee can receive in a year. One example of a distribution was to an employee, who was a mother with two children, who lost her home and her possessions in a fire. The fund allowed her to make a down payment on a new apartment as well as buy furniture and clothing for the children. Moreover, in the JetBlue program, the fund will make up the difference in what an employee receives in disability insurance payments and what the employee's salary is, to the maximum of $5000 a year. The "crisis fund" also pays for funerals of employees; the fund has paid for 27 funerals so far. The JetBlue fund is funded by crew members who voluntarily contribute to the fund, which is set up as a non-profit corporation so that contributions are tax deductible. Moreover, and quite significantly Jet-Blue matches one-half of every employee's contribution. At JetBlue, more than 70% of crew members participate in the "crisis funds" program. There is at that airline a "crisis fund" board, composed of three management members and eight "hourly" crew members, and which decides how and to whom and in what amount the funds are distributed. In a four and one-half year period, there have been almost 300 grants made to crew members. Tire Kingdom also has a fund, called "Helping Hands," from which workers are provided grants funded solely by the company, but employees if they wish can pay the company back through payroll deductions. Tire Kingdom has many young employees who often do not have enough money saved to cover an emergency or disaster. One use of the fund was to give $2000 to the widow of an employee killed in a car crash to help pay for the funeral. Another use was to give an employee $1,500 to enable her to fly back home to be with her seriously ill father.

One benefit for the company produced by having such "crisis funds" is that employees will feel supported by their employers as well as fellow employees; and accordingly will feel very loyal to their employers and work colleagues for the aid provided during the emergency. Loyalty, of course, readily can translate into staying with a company as well as being very productive therein. Another benefit is that managers and supervisors will have a tangible method to assist an employee who has suffered a disaster and resulting financial hardship. Perhaps the manager or supervisor can help the employee apply for the aid. They certainly will not feel that they could not help and that the situation was hopeless. Then, after helping the employee to secure the aid, the managers and supervisors also will feel good in that they could help a "needy" employee; and they too will feel good about their company, and again thus more likely to stay with the firm. Some companies thus form "crisis funds" to maintain good employee relations as well as to make sure employees keep working for the company. Others do it because it seems like the "right thing" to do.

The funds for the "crisis funds" come from different sources, depending on the company. Some funds are paid for by the company into an employee emergency account; and some funds are funded by employee donations, usually through payroll deductions. Others are jointly funded by the employees and the employer, as in the case of JetBlue. Yet employers underscore that "crisis funds" are not meant to be the long-term answer to an employee's problems.

Bibliography:

Pounds, Marcia Heroux, "On-the-Job Relief for Workers in Financial Need," The Sun-Sentinel, November 6, 2006, Your Business, pp. 14-15.

Questions for Discussion:

1. Discuss the legal ramifications involved with "crisis funds." Specifically, how should such "crisis funds" be funded? Discuss. What should the criteria be for an "appropriate" funding emergency; how much should be granted; and who makes the determinations as to whether an employee has suffered sufficient hardship? Discuss.

2. Is a company morally obligated by virtue of the Ethical Principle of Last Resort to provide "crisis funds" to employees? Discuss.

3. Are "crisis funds" moral pursuant to the ethical doctrines of Ethical Egoism and Utilitarianism? Discuss.

4. Are "crisis funds" an appropriate example of Corporate Social Responsibility? Why or why not?

5. Do "crisis funds" pass the "test" of Value-Driven Management? Discuss.

Case 1.3: Norway's Ethical Investment Pension Fund

The Miami Herald newspaper reported in November of 2006 that the Norwegian government has created an ethical investment pension fund. The fund aims to make that nation's immense oil wealth grow for the benefit of its citizens as well as to make the world a better place. Significantly, the $263 billion fund is governed by strict government imposed ethical guidelines to ensure that the money is not invested in companies linked to such unethical practices as weapons production, human rights abuses, environmental damage, or corruption. The goal is to ensure that only ethical investments are made on behalf of the Norwegian people. An organization, called the national Council on Ethics, oversees the fund's investments in up to 4000 companies worldwide. The leader of the Council underscored that one major purpose of the fund was to enable the people of Norway "to sleep better at night." The national Council of Ethics periodically reviews investments, then makes recommendations to the Finance Ministry; and if it agrees, the ministry orders the bank to sell its stake in the banned company within a few weeks.

Offshore oil fields have made Norway the world's third largest oil producer after Saudi Arabia and Russia. Norway as a nation donates more foreign aid per capita than any other country. Norway is a nation of 4.6 million people. It has been placing its huge oil profits into an investment fund, called the Norwegian Pension Fund—Global, which will provide a retirement pension for millions of Norwegians once the country's oil resources have been used up. There currently is no set year for disbursements from the fund to begin or the set amount to be distributed to each retiree. The fund, which is operated by the Central Bank, presently is worth almost 2.5 times the entire central government budget for 2007. In 2005, the government transferred $34 billion to the fund.

What makes the fund controversial is the government imposed ethics guidelines, first imposed in 2004. Since then, 18 companies, 12 of them U.S.-based, have been excluded; but one of them, oil and gas producer Kerr-McGee Corp, was reinstated in late 2006. Wal-Mart, the world's largest retailer, was also "blacklisted" as unethical by the fund in 2006, allegedly for labor abuses and discouraging unions. The Wal-Mart ban drew an angry response. Last year, the fund also banned Boeing, Honeywell, Northrop Grumman Corp, and United Technologies for contributing to the production of nuclear weapons. Alliant Techsystems, General Dynamics Corp, Lockheed Martin, and Raytheon Company were blacklisted because they contributed to the manufacture of cluster bombs.

The U.S. Ambassador to Norway, Benson K. Whitney, denounced the entire ethics program, calling it unfair, inconsistent, and hypocritical. He further stated that the ethical investment process was not just and contravened the values of the Norwegian people.

Norway is not the only entity to review its investments. As originally reported in the Los Angeles Times in January of 2007, the Bill and Melinda Gates Foundation announced that it would review all its investments to determine if they are morally and socially responsible, in particular that they contribute to health, housing, and the social welfare and do not contravene environmental stewardship and human rights.

Bibliography:

Mellgren, Doug, "Norway uses oil wealth to make ethics statement," The Miami Herald, Business Monday, November 27, 2006, p. 7.

Piller, Charles (2007). Gates foundation to review holdings. Sun-Sentinel, January 11, p. 15A.

Questions for Discussion:

1. Is the Norwegian ethical investment fund moral under Utilitarian ethics? Discuss.

2. Shouldn't such a pension fund be solely concerned with making as much money as possible (from legal business operations, of course) to support the retirement of Norway's citizens? Why or why not?

3. What exact ethical standards should guide the fund's investments? Why? Who should decide if such standards have been adhered to; and how should such a process work? Discuss.

4. Do you agree with the U.S. ambassador that the fund is unjust and unfair? Why or why not?

Case 1.4: Social Responsibility and Safety: The Saga of British Petroleum CEO Sire John Browne

John Browne, the former CEO of London-based British Petroleum, has always been regarded, and justifiably so, as a very socially responsible CEO, one who took the lead in taking BP to its "Beyond Petroleum" reputation, that is, as a firm that was materially involved in alternative fuels as well as environmental and civic and charitable affairs. As a matter of fact, John Browne was knighted in Great Britain, and is now referred to properly as Lord Browne or Sir John Brown, in part for his social responsibility efforts as CEO of BP. Browne's social responsibility philosophy, strategy, and tactics, and the egoistic rationales thereof, were very clearly enunciated. He believed that for BP to survive and to prosper, so must society as a whole and the communities where BP does business. Thus, he made the economic, social, and environmental health of the communities where BP did business a central feature of the company's endeavors. He also took a long-term approach to social investment. Moreover, he made commitment to social responsibility an important criterion in the compensation of BP executives and managers. The exact nature of BP's social responsibility activities is left to the discretion of the managers of the company's local business units. Then, regional social responsibility audits are conducted on a regular basis by regional executives. Some examples of BP's social responsibility efforts encompass job training, reforestation, flood control, technology transfer, providing refrigerators to store anti-malaria vaccines, small business development loans, reprocessing its own waste material into bricks for local building, building schools, and providing solar energy to schools. Social responsibility goals are set; and the local manager's performance is measured, and achievement of the goals is ascertained. In addition to BP's management at all levels, local members of the community are involved in determining social responsibility objectives in their community. There is continual monitoring, quantification, and verification of the social responsibility efforts by a major accounting firm. One recalls, perhaps, in the 2004 Presidential campaign that candidate Senator John Kerry extolled BP as an exemplar of a moral and socially responsible company. BP means "Beyond Petroleum," declared Kerry at a news conference.

The commitment to social responsibility has not impaired BP's "bottom-line," according to Business Week magazine. BP has been a very successful company under Browne's stewardship. Browne, as noted in Business Week, explains that BP's social responsibility "efforts have nothing to do with charity, and everything to do with our long-term self-interest." He also states that BP, as well as any company, must be aware of its social responsibilities limitations, in particular that "companies cannot substitute for government." Yet he underscores that companies, especially large multinationals, have a great stake in economic progress and social responsibility. Accordingly, under Browne's stewardship, BP has fully integrated social responsibility into the company's policies on governance, operation, and compensation.

Sir John Browne served as BP's CEO for 11 years; and during that time frame, according to Business Week, he transformed the company from a "middling player into an immensely competitive money machine." Browne also brought about five big merger and acquisition deals in five years, including the 1998 $62 billion takeover of Amoco as well as the 2000 $32 billion takeover of Arco.

In 2005, however, an explosion occurred at a BP refinery in Texas City, Texas, which killed 15 people and injured 140 people. Many lawsuits were instituted as a result of the explosion. In 2006, moreover, serious maintenance problems were discovered in a major company pipeline in Prudhoe Bay, Alaska. Corroding and leaking pipes caused a big oil spill, which resulted in BP cutting back production from that key oil source.

The head of the U.S. Chemical Safety and Hazard Investigation Board (CSHIB), a federal agency that oversees refineries, criticized the company, in particular its leadership, for failing to communicate the importance of prudent and safe work practices. BP also commissioned its own study shortly after the Texas accident. The company report found a demoralized workforce that did not follow safety rules; and where the safety knowledge and safety skills of the workforce, including management, were generally poor. In September of 2006, the U.S. Congress held hearings on BP; and, as reported in USA Today, several members of Congress "blasted" BP executives for the failure to prevent the Alaska oil leaks, in particular criticizing the company for ignoring safety and maintenance concerns and for harassing internal "whistleblowing" employees.

One industry expert noted that BP is less a command-and-control company, but rather a more decentralized one where lower level managers are empowered to take actions, are expected to take the initiative, and are required to use their own judgment in running BP's operations locally. That approach worked very successfully for social responsibility issues. Yet that industry expert stated, as related by Business Week, that Browne may have been culpable of being naïve in trusting local managers in Texas and Alaska to fulfill demanding financial goals without compromising on-the-ground operations.

As a result of the Texas and Alaska problems, a commission was formed, headed by former Secretary of State James Baker to examine the company's performance. The Baker Commission found significant problems at five of BP's U.S. refineries. In particular, the Baker report said that BP has not provided the necessary leadership concerning process safety. Moreover, the report criticized the company for not adequately establishing process safety as a core company value. The safety culture at BP was so poor that the company could not always ensure that sufficient funding and people were devoted to safety issues. The report also said that BP did not establish consistent standards and practices needed for proper maintenance and to maintain safety at its U.S. facilities. The report also mentioned high turnover among plant managers, a lack of resources, and poor communication, all of which contributed to the breakdowns. Now, as recommended by the Baker Commission, sweeping changes will be made at the company in the areas of safety and maintenance, and an independent body will monitor the safety practices of the company.

Browne, 58, announced in January of 2007 that he would step down as CEO, about a year and one half earlier than expected. The Baker report did mention that Browne had made BP a leader in environmental, climate control, and social responsibility issues, yet contrasted that positive record with a failure of leadership on safety.

Sir John Browne, also known as Lord Browne, the paragon of the socially responsible CEO, is now called contemptuously and with derision, "Prince John."

BP's new CEO, Tony Hayward, formerly the head of BP's exploration division, faces the daunting challenge of repairing not only pipelines and refineries but the company's now tarnished reputation; and thereby restoring the company's credibility. He stated that the company would fully embrace all the recommendations of the Baker Commission, and would agree to the outside monitor for a five year period. Presumably Hayward will continue BP's social responsibility activities.

Thus ends the saga of Sir John Browne, the clearly socially responsible, but allegedly unsafe CEO; and perhaps the "moral" to this "story" is that old maxim that "charity begins at home."

Bibliography:

Cummins, Chip, "Safety Report Will Test BP's Incoming CEO," The Wall Street Journal, January 17, 2007, p. A14; Davidson, Paul, "Congressmen Slam BP executives at oil leak hearing," USA Today, September 8, 2006, p. 2B; Franklin, Sonja, "At BP, it wasn't safety first," Sun-Sentinel, January 17, 2007, p. 3D; Garten, Jeffrey E., "Globalism Doesn't Have to Be Cruel," Business Week, February 9, 1998, p. 26; Porretto, John, "Report: BP failed to focus on safety," The Miami Herald, January 17, 2007, p. 3C; Reed, Stanley, "BP Feels the Heat," Business Week, January 22, 2007, pp. 52-53.

Questions for Discussion:

1. Do you agree with Browne's conception of corporate social responsibility as well as the rationale thereof? Why or why not?

2. Did Browne act in a socially responsible but unethical manner? Why or why not?

3. How does a business leader integrate, balance, and practice the values of corporate social responsibility with the more "mundane" values of safety and maintenance? Discuss.

4. Should social responsibility efforts be left to local managers? Should safety concerns? Why or why not?

Case 1.5: "Rebuild New Orleans and Get a Green Card in Return"

The Washington Post reported in December of 2007 on a little known but very controversial U.S. immigration program. The goal of the program is to provide a legal conduit and incentive for foreign money to be invested in economically depressed areas in the United States. As the Post noted, a foreign investor can invest in a fund "to rebuild New Orleans and get a green card in return." One example of such an investment fund is called Noble-OutReach, and is based in Gaithersburg, Maryland. The objective of this fund is to secure money to rebuild parts of New Orleans; the money is to be obtained from wealthy foreigners who are seeking a means of legal immigration status in the United States. Technically, this visa program is known as the EB-5 immigrant investor program. It is, as noted by the Post, a pilot program as well as a relatively small one. The program reserves 3000 visas a year for foreign investors who contribute at least $500,000 into to one of 17 projects throughout the U.S. which are designed to improve economically distressed areas. Other examples cited by the Post include a dairy farming business in South Dakota and an ethanol production plant in Texas. Other illustrations are a project in Pittsburgh that focuses on tourism, trade, and technology, and one in Milwaukee that deals with professional business service companies. In exchange for their investments, the foreigners receive any dividends generated by the funds, and, most significantly, permanent residence status, that is, "green cards," for themselves and members of their immediate family. The NobleOutReach program, which according to the Post, began in the spring of 2007, seeks to raise money from immigrant investors to develop office buildings, hotels, restaurants, and medical clinics in New Orleans. As of the writing of the Post article, the fund has attracted 50 investors from South Korea, China, Great Britain, and the Middle East. NobleOutReach hopes to invest $100 million in projects that it claims, according to the Post, could create thousands of jobs. The Post quoted the chairperson of an Asian business group who stated that the program would be attractive to many people in China, who now have substantial wealth, but who would seek a better "quality of life" in the U.S., especially regarding educational opportunities for their children. The EB-5 program is a pilot visa program that granted permanent residency in return for a one million dollar direct business investment in the United States. The Post reported that this original visa program was criticized as the "million dollar" visa program. So, the U.S. Citizenship and Immigration Services restructured the program in 2002 after problems arose with fraud and abuse by investors. The new program now operates more like a mutual fund. Significantly, investors no longer have to serve as day-to-day managers of the projects; rather, the daily supervision is left to others; and the investment is half as much as the original program. The money ultimately is directed to regional centers, such as New Orleans. Under both programs, the investment must create at least 10 local jobs. The Post reported that at the end of September of 2007 779 people had applied for the new visa program, which was just double the 389 who applied in 2006. The greatest number of investors has come from South Korea, China, and Great Britain. The Post reported that the amount invested last year through EB-5 visas was $500 million, and the amount is projected to rise to $800 million in 2007, and $1 billion in 2008. Yet the new program is still being criticized for affording the foreign rich an immigration "loophole." Under the program, the foreign investors initially receive two year residencies while immigration authorities monitor their investments and participation in the program. Once the foreign investor passes all immigration requirements and the regional center certifies that the investment produced 10 jobs, the foreign investor applicant is granted permanent residency in the United States. After five years and a "clean" record, a permanent resident can begin the process leading to citizenship in the United States.

Bibliography:

Kang, Cecilia, "Foreigners Invest Greenbacks in Return for Green Cards," The Washington Post, December 8, 2007, pp. D1, D3.

Questions for Discussion:

1. What are the legal, ethical, and practical implications of this investor visa program? Discuss.

2. Specifically, is it moral pursuant to Utilitarian ethics? Why or why not?

3. Is it a fair one pursuant to Kantian ethics? Why or why not?

Case 1.6: The Economist and "Good Business"

The Economist magazine in two January 2008 articles addressed the concept of corporate social responsibility (CSR) in the sense of being "good business." The Economist first provided an example of a socially responsible firm—the British retailer Marks & Spencer, which is one of Great Britain's leading retailers. At the lobby of the company's London headquarters is a giant electronic screen which describes the company's progress in fulfilling "Plan A," which sets a target of achieving 100 worthwhile socially responsible goals over a five year period. Examples include providing a better education to 15,000 children in Uganda, saving 55,000 tons of CO_2 in a year, recycling 48 million clothes hangers, tripling sales of organic food, and converting over 20 million garments to "Fairtrade" cotton. Each Marks & Spencer store has a dedicated "Plan A" champion, reported the Economist. Marks & Spencer calls their corporate social responsibility effort "Plan A," because there is no Plan B. There is also a corporate committee that monitors the Plan, called the "How We Do Business Committee."

However, the Economist does report that the connection between "good corporate behavior" and good financial performance is a "fuzzy" one at best. The magazine reported that the "latest academic research suggests that a positive link exists, but it is a weak one." Yet the Economist also underscores that "there is no evidence to suggest that CSR is destroying shareholder value." One problem, the magazine posited, may be that some companies do social responsibility, but "get it out of proportion." Also, there is a paucity of high level academic studies examining the long-term consequences of the value of social responsibility, particularly since CSR is a relatively new value for business. The Economist also warns that business, although striving to be more socially responsible, should be concerned mainly with its paramount function in a capitalistic system and that is to benefit society by creating ideas, producing and providing goods and services, and employing people. Business should not stop being business, the Economist asserts, and should not become "merely" and solely a social responsibility tool. Furthermore, the Economist warns that it is not business' responsibility to solve all the world's social problems; rather, it is the function of governments—to govern and to provide for the "general welfare."

The Economist, in reviewing corporate social responsibility, corporate citizenship, and sustainable business efforts, reported on a wide range of company activities that benefit society—from helping the poor and saving the planet, to having employees volunteer in the local community, and to the companies themselves "looking after" their own employees properly. The Economist reported a survey by its Intelligence Unit that shows that corporate social responsibility is rising dramatically as one of global executives' priorities. The result, therefore, according to the Economist, is that executives can no longer afford to ignore the value of corporate social responsibility.

The Economist also pointed out that, in Great Britain, the Parliament promulgated a Companies Act in 2006 that requires public companies to report on social and environmental issues. Moreover, as a response to societal demands for enhanced corporate social responsibility, the Economist also reported that business schools are now adding specialized courses in business ethics and corporate social responsibility in order to satisfy business schools, their students, the business community, and society as a whole. An interest in protecting one's reputation, especially as an environmentally conscious "green" firm, also emerges as a factor motivating enhanced social responsibility, especially during this time of heightened concern with climate change. Regarding reputation, the Economist points out that now many consumer and environmental organizations stand ready to point out and to decry any perceived corporate misbehavior or social irresponsibility. Furthermore, many of these interest or "pressure" groups have rating and ranking systems which report on firms' non-financial performance as well as on their financial results. As the Economist correctly noted, due to the Internet, "embarrassing" news can be communicated rapidly just about anywhere in the world. Accordingly, the Economist reported a 2007 survey by the McKinsey consulting group which found that 95% of the executives surveyed said that society now has higher expectations for business in taking on societal challenges and responsibilities than they did the year before. The Economist also noted that by maintaining a good CSR reputation business will be able to avoid any government regulatory "backlash."

The Economist also reported that investors are beginning to scrutinize companies more carefully regarding their social responsibility activities. To illustrate, the Economist noted a Columbia Business School report by Geoffrey Heal which found that $1 out of every $9 under professional management in the U.S. now involves some type of social responsibility criterion. Furthermore, the Economist noted that some very large banks, such as Goldman Sachs and UBS, now have commenced to integrate environmental, social, and governance concerns into some of their equity research. Yet the Economist did admit that the financial industry at times sends out "mixed" signals by demanding short-term good financial results as well as expressing concern for social responsibility.

The Economist, moreover, related that pressure for companies to be perceived as socially responsible ones is coming internally from their own employees. Actually, this internal pressure is so intense, declared the Economist, that being socially responsible has become part of the larger competition of attracting and maintaining as well as motivating top talent. People naturally want to work for a company viewed as a legal, moral, and socially responsible one, as those core values are ones that the majority of the people share and practice. Finally, the Economist notes that consumers will more likely want to do business with a firm known as a socially responsible one. Good corporate behavior and good corporate citizenship are a form of public relations, the Economist admits, but public relations is a part of business too.

The Economist views corporate social responsibility as consisting of three levels: The first is the most basic and consists of a firm's philanthropic and charitable contributions to the community. Yet, although such charity is viewed as "giving back to the community," and thus the "right thing" to do, other companies now are going beyond "merely" writing checks. Part of the reason impelling companies to proceed upwards is pressure from their own employees who want to be actively involved in social responsibility efforts as well as from shareholders who want to know how a firm's social responsibility activities impact the "bottom line." Accordingly, the second level of social responsibility is one the Economist calls "risk management." This level entails a firm's efforts not only to contribute to the community but to take a proactive approach to preventing environmental harm, the spread of disease, child labor, censorship, and obesity. The idea is to be a socially responsible company and thus to avoid what the Economist deems "blows to its reputation." At this level, the Economist suggests that companies commit themselves to more transparency and engage in efforts to promulgate codes of conduct and ethics. Furthermore, the Economist suggests that companies engage in such efforts jointly with their competitors in the same industry so as to try to devise and "to set common rules, spread the risk and shape opinion." At the highest social responsibility level, the Economist sees social responsibility as a means of affording a company greater business opportunities. This is, according to the magazine, the "trendiest" level of social responsibility." The idea is for a company to view social responsibility as a strategic asset that can produce value and thus inure to a company's competitive advantage. An example of such heightened social responsibility is Toyota's successful attempts to produce and sell "green" cars, which clearly provided it a competitive advantage. The Economist also noted a study from the Committee Encouraging Corporate Philanthropy that reported that in 2007 that the share of business giving that was viewed as strategically motivated increased from 38% in 2004 to 48% in 2006. The idea, of course, is to "do good and do well," and help "save the planet" as well as take care of the interests of the shareholders. The Economist concludes by emphasizing that "for most managers the only real question about CSR is how to do it."

Bibliography:

Franklin, Daniel, "Just Good Business," Special Reports, The Economist, www.economist.com, January 17, 2008; Opinion Leaders, "Ethical Capitalism: How good should your business be?" The Economist, www.economist.com, January 17, 2008.

Questions for Discussion:

1. Why should a prudent company be concerned today with social responsibility; and to what degree? Discuss, providing examples.

2. Can the impact of corporate social responsibility efforts be ascertained and measured similarly to financial performance? Why or why not?

3. Do you foresee any legal problems stemming from companies who are competitors joining together and cooperating to form industry-wide codes of conduct and ethics? Discuss.

4. Do you feel that by increasing CSR the role of governments will be diminished? Why or why not? What does any diminished role for government portend for a democratic capitalistic system? Discuss.

5. Compare and contrast the value of morality, based on ethics, to the value of social responsibility, providing examples to illustrate both values.

6. How can Value-Driven Management be used as a tool to determine and to measure a firm's social responsibilities to its broader stakeholders? Discuss, providing examples.

Case 1.7: Bill Gates' "Creative Capitalism"

Microsoft Chairman Bill Gates, in a speech in January 2008 in Davos, Switzerland at the World Economic Forum, called for a major revision of capitalism into what he called "creative capitalism," where businesses use market forces to enter untapped markets of "the poor" to address their needs, which he feels are being ignored, make a modest profit, and then to empower the poor to partake of the global economy. He believes that capitalism, which has always served the wealthy, now must serve poorer people as well. Bill Gates most certainly has not given up on capitalism, but he feels that capitalism does have a major shortcoming—its inability to serve the very poor of the world. The goal is to bring the poor into the global economy so they too can benefit from capitalism, and thereby narrow the gap between the rich and the poor. In particular, Bill Gates is concerned that technology and advances of technology are surely helping the rich, but not really helping the poor. One fundamental aspect of this new "creative capitalism" is for businesses to manufacture products and to provide services for the poor. As such, he still wants business to make a profit, but also to improve the lives of the poor people who at the moment do not fully benefit from capitalism and market forces. He also still believes in basis social responsibility, as exemplified by the very generous philanthropic efforts of his foundation—the Bill & Melinda Gates Foundation—which now has accumulated $70 billion, which Bill Gates has stated he wants to give away within 50 years of the deaths of him and his wife. Government and charities will still have a role, he admits, to provide for the very poor who cannot even partake of "creative capitalism." Yet he also wants companies to employ their most innovative and creative thinkers and planners to ascertain how to market products and services to the most needy to serve them, to empower them, to benefit them, and to still make a modest profit. The potential profitability of serving the poor is a critical element to his formula for "creative capitalism." Although transactions selling products and providing services to the poor may be small ones, since there are so many poor in the world (estimated at 4 billion poor people), the transactions, even at a modest profit, will accumulate significantly due to the fact that the poor are such a large market. In addition, a company that engages in "creative capitalism" will also benefit from receiving positive recognition for its beneficent (but profit-seeking) efforts. Recognition, asserts Gates, enhances a company's reputation, and accordingly not only appeals to customers but also attracts good people to the organization, thereby resulting, he underscores, in market-based rewards for such a firm. Right now, though, according to Bill Gates, this vast "poor" market is not being tapped. It is important to stress that, as opposed to his philanthropic foundation work, the new conception for capitalism is not "merely" a charitable endeavor, but a profit-seeking one. As an example of "creative capitalism" Bill Gates cites a Microsoft program to produce a stripped-down version of the company's software and alternative ways for the people of poor countries to buy it as well as the computers to run the software. In addition, he cites a program whereby poor coffee farmers and growers in Africa can use the Internet to find coffee buyers, especially in rich countries. The idea, of course, is to help the poor find and reach markets in rich countries. Another illustration cited by Gates is a Microsoft program to develop computers and software to enable semi-literate and illiterate people to use a computer instantly with minimal training or assistance. These examples of "creative capitalism" naturally reflect a core belief of Bill Gates that technology can solve all the world's problems, even such a massive and intractable one such as global poverty. In his speech, he stated that breakthroughs in technology can, and do, solve key problems, and for billions of people. Yet he related that such breakthroughs can only help people when people can afford to buy the technology. In order to help people afford technology, Bill Gates calls for his version of capitalism—"creative capitalism" which will make capitalism serve the poorer people as it does the wealthier ones. The idea is to harness the power of capitalism in innovative ways to empower and to benefit people and thus to improve their lives. The twin missions of "creative capitalism" are, according to Bill Gates, to make profits and to improve lives. The "creative capitalism" business hero for Gates would be what he calls a "social entrepreneur," that is, a smart, innovative entrepreneur who can devise and implement profit-making ideas for providing affordable goods and services to the poor of the world, and as a result improve their lives.

Bibliography:

Gates, Bill, "A New Approach to Capitalism in the 21st Century," World Economic Forum 2008, Davos, Switzerland, January 24, 2008, Remarks by Bill Gates, Chairman, Microsoft Corporation, *www.microsoft.com/Presspass/exec/billg/speeches/2008/01*; Guth, Robert, A, "Bill Gates Issues Calls For Kinder Capitalism," The Wall Street Journal, January 24, 2008, pp. A1, A15.

Questions for Discussion:

1. Do you think Bill Gates' vision of "creative capitalism" and "social entrepreneurship" is a feasible one? Will it "ease the world's inequities," as he said in his speech? Why or why not?

2. Do you think it is a bit hypocritical for Bill Gates, whose company was adjudged by the U.S. federal courts as well as the European Community courts to be an illegal, monopolizing, predatory, abusive, unethical antitrust violator, to now be concerned with revising capitalism and helping the poor? Why or why not?

3. Do you agree with the U.S. federal courts that Microsoft was in fact a monopolizing company, that is, a firm that possessed a monopoly which it abused in a predatory and anti-competitive manner? Why or why not?

4. Can technology solve all the problems of the world, as Bill Gates says? Why or why not?

5. Do you agree with Bill Gates that a reputation as a "creative capitalistic" company will produce tangible benefits in the sense of market-based rewards for a company in the long-run? Why or why not?

2. International Business and Bribery

Case 2.1: Cultural Change and Ethnocentricity:
Blunders in the International Arena

Cultures change at their own pace and for their own reasons. Imposing cultural change on others, based on one's own values, may not be the best way to bring about effective results in the short term. Andrea Parrot, working out of Cornell University, is one of today's many authors that write about cultural differences, their practices and the ways to best affect negative practices towards women and minorities. She is currently writing Forsaken Figures: The Global Brutalization, Oppression, and Violence against Women with fellow Cornell educator, Nina Cummings. The author of the article "Effecting Cultural Change," Joe Wilensky (2003) examines her writing. Andrea Parrot claims that "Ethics are culturally and historically determined." Every culture has its own history, and whatever triumphs or tribulations it has gone through helped to shape that culture, and helped it to form its own ideas of wrong and right. Because of this, it is very difficult for one culture to try to impose its ethics and values on another. The central theme to Parrot's article is that in order to effect change in one culture, one must understand the reasons behind their acts and work within those constraints and the people themselves in order to make it happen. She provides many convincing examples that might be extreme at times but are reality nonetheless.

In many parts of the Chinese and Indian cultures, it is a common practice to commit infanticide (feticide). Also, in both of these cultures having a male child is much more desirable for a good number of individuals because of cultural or economic implications. China has placed a one child per family policy to control the population (over 1.2 billion) from rapidly increasing. In the Chinese culture (as well as Indian and many other cultures), the son's wife is generally expected to take care of the son's parents in their senior years. In India, the son's family is provided the dowry of the new daughter in-law. Such norms not only make a son more valuable (desirable) in the eyes of many families but it also makes a daughter that much more expensive (costly). With the new technology of ultrasound equipment, many female fetuses are aborted in such cultures and unfortunately many young girls are sold in the market for slavery, etc. One might say that because of the cultural pressures, it has become common practice in the lives of many citizens, living in such cultures, to treat their daughters in harsh manners. Furthermore, for many individuals, it is probably difficult to read a statement that says "having a girl is more expensive or more costly than having a boy" which is the reality of the infrastructure in many cultures. Changing such a mindset of valuing a male child more than a female child is not easy and requires getting to the root of the infrastructure which enables this paradigm to sustain over time. There are many hidden such structures embedded into the culture that must also change in order to eliminate the incentives associated with this mindset. In reality, parts of China and India (as well as parts of many other cultures) may not be able to bring quick changes to these perceptions because of the traditions and such complex integrated network of variables that influence and condition generations of human beings.

One of the first examples is the Hippocratic Oath used by medical practitioners Wilensky (2003). The author uses this Oath to make the point that even the Western culture's values have changed in the last decade. Medical doctors agree that it has changed tremendously; however, each medical student still has to take the oath before graduating as it was witnessed at the University of Florida's graduation ceremony for a cousin named Anis Ahmadi in 2002. Another example is the general acceptance of single parenthood, the acceptance of having children without marriage, and the increasing acceptance of single men/women becoming sexually active at earlier ages. Even the things that are seen on television are signs of rapidly changing values. Take for instance reality programs such as the Bachelor, and even the Victoria's Secret Lingerie "runway show" that was aired, not on cable television, but on a major network. Back in the fifties and sixties, shows like "I Love Lucy" would not even picture Lucy and her husband sleeping in the same bed as husband and wife. Yet today, one really can't escape the visual revolution of sexual acts that are all over the television shows throughout the day.

Another example refers to how ethical concepts and beliefs change from culture to culture. Even with the next door neighbors such as Cuba, Bahamas, Mexico, Jamaica, and Canada ethical values and philosophies are different because of their historical basis. As far as healthcare is concerned, Canada's ethics is focused on equal access. In the United States, the predominant value freedom of choice; that is, freedom to decide who, what, when and where we receive treatment. Freedom is a strong value held here in the United States of America because of our traditions and history. So the question shouldn't be, "Who's more ethical, or whose values are better?" Instead, one should focus on why those ethics and values are there.

This fact leads to the main point she tries to make in her writing, which is that one culture should not hastily impose their cultural values and ethics on another without a good understanding of why those practices exist. Parrot uses her passion, women's issues, to make this point. Her insightful examples of the problems in China, India, Uganda, and Slovakia are all the more convincing because she gives not only the cultural background, but their historical significance along with it. And with that being her point, that if we understand it from their perspective, and work with genuine care of their issues, one can be seen as trying to help, rather than trying to dominate or impose one's values through ethnocentric mindsets. Parrot is right by stating that "Awareness is the first step in global change of abusive cultural practices." One could go one step further and reiterate that learning the reasons behind the practices should be the next step in the process.

Andrea Parrot's special interests within women's health are sexual assault, infertility, and teenage pregnancy. She is also currently writing a book with Nina Cummings on cultural practices and risks encountered in attempting to change them. She states that with each generation comes acceptance of things that were not acceptable in the past. Our generation does things now that our parent's generation would have looked down upon. Another point that stands out to most readers is that people may judge and act inappropriately to cultural problems because they do not understand why they are happening. The example of how people look down on countries that practice feticide is one opportunity for many in the western cultures to see how they have judged others. Parrot also makes it a point to show the consequences of cultural practices that may not be ethical in America's opinion, such as China's unbalanced gender split. She also states "Awareness is the first step in global change of abusive cultural practices." She makes the point that if people are unaware of what's going on, they will not have the knowledge and understanding to change the situation. The examples of female mutilation also stands firm in many minds. This issue is something many individuals have felt strongly about and work hard towards changing. After researching the topic and working with relevant organizations, many discover and understand the educational, governmental, religious, cultural, and civic differences in cultures that condition people to behave a certain way.

There are many practical implications for today's workforce. The practical implications in the work world would be to be aware of cultural differences, and not to judge others from information you receive without first understanding why the action is taking place. You should also always be careful not to make uneducated opinions or statements to others about a certain group of people, or to those people directly. Treat people as individuals, and respect the differences.

It is important to acknowledge and respect other's cultures, beliefs, and backgrounds. When one knows where a coworker came from and his/her cultural background, one is not as quick to make negative judgments, at least one shouldn't be. At home, this lesson is even more important because attitudes at home have far reaching effects into the community, beginning within small towns, then spreading into the cities, the state, and finally the entire country. Unfortunately, if one does not learn the blunders, ignorance can even spread internationally, leading to some of the mistakes Westerners and others in the globe have made in the past as well as in the recent events abroad—be they personal, business, professional or governmental.

Bibliography:

Wilensky, Joe (2003). Effecting Cultural Change. Human Ecology; December, Vol. 31 Issue 2, p12, 4p.

Questions for Discussion:

1. List some of the personal, business, professional, and governmental blunders that you have seen when dealing with differing values and ethical concepts in various cultures.

2. Has the Western culture done more good or bad for the international community as a whole? Be specific and provide examples.

3. Is ethical relativism becoming an anachronism? That is, is there emerging a universal world ethical culture? If so, does this ethical culture encompass global business? Discuss and provide specific examples.

4. Are there cultural practices that Western Cultures participate in that may be viewed as abusive? Do you think most people in other cultures feel this way, and do we as a culture recognize the abuse?

Case 2.2: The Bhopal Disaster in India and Its Lessons[5]

Most dictionaries state that "ethics" is telling right from wrong. Yet, most adults know it is a little more difficult than that when applied in daily activities. There are many "tough" personal choices that professionals must make each day; and they will have to make choices that they can live with the rest of their lives. Many young individuals in the society (about 45%) believe and rely on their own experience to make ethical decisions, which may not be enough when they are making decisions that affect others in the society. For example, one individual wanted to try an experiment that was very dangerous and interesting. Employees knew that if they didn't follow the order, they would lose their jobs. Almost all employees knew that the experiment was very dangerous and could put many lives in danger. They knew that the risks associated with the experiment were great. So, what did these individuals do?

In the actual case of Chernobyl, radio-active fallout in the nuclear power plant, the employees decided to stay quiet and the experiment went very wrong. In this experiment, people stayed quiet and did not speak to anyone about the possible problems and concerns in the experiment. However, on April 9th 1986, the worst industrial nuclear disaster took thousands of lives and damaged the environment around it. It was the Chernobyl nuclear disaster that affected people throughout the globe. Perhaps, this could have been avoided if people spoke up regardless of personal consequences. The boss along with the employees need to respect the reality of what can go wrong may go wrong. The Chernobyl disaster (radio-active fallout) in the former Soviet Union went wrong because people didn't have respect to see reality and the possible consequences of their decisions. Many children and people in that environment died. In the real world, what can go wrong often may go wrong. Radiation didn't stop at the borders of Soviet nation, but it spread and adversely affected others throughout the world. What is unfortunate is that another major disaster known as the Union Carbide Bhopal incident happened just two years prior to the Chernobyl disaster. Unfortunately, no lessons were learned from it, nor applied to the safety standards by the professionals working at the Chernobyl Nuclear plant. The remainder of this case discusses the Bhopal incident in hopes of preparing all professionals to take appropriate steps for ensuring safety standards in order to prevent such disasters from taking place in any country.

The country of India, like other developing nations, welcomes foreign businesses and expects them to be socially responsible in order to prevent disasters such as the Bhopal incident which hurt many individuals and the economy. The Bhopal disaster was one of the biggest catastrophes in India's history, where thousands of people were killed, injured and hurt as a result. Most Indians value life in all of its forms and believe that people's lives have the same value regardless of where they reside. Therefore, all professionals and foreign companies should ensure that their subsidiaries in India, at minimum, have the same safety standards as the plants operating in the parent country in order to prevent major disasters. A few years after the Bhopal disaster, and many hours of pain and suffering by many victims, India's economy was on the road to a slow recovery as many multinational corporations commenced to institute their subsidiaries in India (Wikipedia, 2004).

_____

[5]Coauthored with Gimol Thomas.

The Bhopal disaster occurred on December 3rd, 1984 in Bhopal, India. It killed over 3000 people and injured more than 200,000 individuals. The disaster took place at a chemical plant named Union Carbide, India, which was owned by an American parent company. The chemical plant produced Sevin, which was primarily used as an agricultural pesticide. Union Carbide, India was expanded per Indian Government's request since it would open more employment opportunities to Indians. Since the Indian government requested the expansion, the government allowed Union Carbide to own 50.9 percent, and the other 49.1 percent were owned by the Indian government. According to De George (1995), this ownership agreement was an exception based on India's Foreign Exchange Regulation Act in 1973, which stated that the maximum foreign ownership was 40 percent of the foreign companies in India. The rest were owned by the Indian Government.

Since Union Carbide offered many job opportunities after the expansion, Indian families moved into the surrounding areas of the plant, which made the city overcrowded. Methyl Isocyanate (MIC) produced Sevin, the agricultural pesticide, the MIC was kept in a tank in the plant before developing into pesticide. During 1982, Union Carbide plant in India had an inspection to monitor the safety of the plant. The inspectors found many deficiencies with the safety mechanisms and they were reported to the Union Carbide-India personnel. Then, the plant personnel reported that all the deficiencies were fixed and the plant could be operated regularly and accurately (De George, 1995). However, the safety enhancements, if there were any major ones, were not enough to prevent the unfortunate disaster that killed and injured thousands of people.

On the day of the disaster, Methyl Isocysnate (MIC) was kept in liquid form changed to gas. The gas leaked through the plant's vent. Since the city was too crowded; thus it was very easy to affect large number of people. The plant was instantaneously closed after the disaster. The compensation settlement for the victims' families took years to finalize and, eventually, in 1989, Union Carbide agreed to pay $470 million in compensation for the Indian victims. In the next decade, an Indian battery manufacturer purchased the Union Carbide plant in India in 1994 (Wikipedia, 2004). Finally, Dow Chemical Company purchased Union Carbide in 2001 for $10.3 billion.

India, with a growing population of over one billion individuals, is one of the largest economies in the world; and the foreign businesses are attracted to this market due to the large population. For the last few years the Indian economy has been growing extensively due to the rapid introduction and availability of new technology to their educated and English-speaking workforce. The multinational companies are outsourcing in India, which ushers the economy to provide employment; and accordingly it will boost the economic power. India's economic policies are formulated to magnetize capital influxes to the country. These policies directed the economy to have rapid growth in the influxes of foreign investments (Business in India, 2004).

Every culture and every country have their own norms and mores; as such, one must consider that doing business in India could be entirely different from other nations. So, foreign companies need to be aware of the Indian culture and practices in order to be successful in the local culture. Indians are usually delighted to do business with foreigners as they consider it an advantage to their economy. For most Indians, written contracts are the valid legal documents for business settlements; however, generally verbal negotiations make up a substantial part of the business settlements. Usual business agreements are approved after drawn-out negotiations, and when dealing with the government, it is expected to have long delays. Even though the political parties are not directly involved in the businesses, it is important for foreign businesses to satisfy the political parties' needs, especially the party that is currently in power. The political party governs the country; therefore, the party leaders make the final sanctions on the new ventures (Business in India, 2004).

Although Indian business policies are favorable toward foreign businesses, there are a few risks that international companies might face. First, there is the sovereign risk. It is highly unlikely for foreign businesses to have this risk; however it is recommended to evade investing in the very northern tips of the country, since there could be potential terrorist attacks. Second, there is the political risk. Political instability is one of the major issues in India that is causing some suffering. Even though the political instability may not directly affect Indian economy, it delays many of the economical processes. The political instability might slightly affect the foreign investors because of a lack of accurate policies. Third, there is the commercial risk. Just like in every other country, foreign businesses face some commercial risk in India as well. Since not all the products can be promptly sold, companies need to study the supply and demand situation of that product. There are many research institutions in India to conduct such supply and demand studies. These are obvious risks that foreign businesses face, but these are not as critical as they may appear to be and the success of many foreign businesses in India attests to this phenomenon (Investment Risks, 2004). Foreign companies need to ensure that the parent company and the subsidiaries in India are treated equally, especially with the safety standards. They should make the extra effort to assure that all the company processes are set up appropriately, and are followed to the fullest extent as designed for safety measures. In the Bhopal case, many people believe that the Union Carbide organization is responsible for the disaster, since they did not use the same safety devices in India as they used in other Union Carbide plants outside of India (Wikipedia, 2004 and DeGeorge, 1995).

Who is really responsible for the Bhopal disaster? "The accident was caused by the introduction of water into MIC holding tanks. The resulting reaction generated large volumes of toxic gas, forcing the emergency release of pressure. The gas escaped while the chemical 'scrubbers' which should have treated the gas were off-line for repairs" (Wikipedia, 2004). The inquiry on the disaster proves that the safety devices were not completely implemented and practiced in the Union Carbide plant in India compared to other Union Carbide plants. There are also claims that the safety devices were reduced to decrease the operating costs. Furthermore, Union Carbide had sent new technology for operation to India that was never tested to ensure its productivity and safety (Wikipedia. 2004).

Union Carbide blames Indians for the disaster by claiming that they were disrupting the company. Indians and other independent critics claim that Union Carbide was not implementing and using the same safety devices for the plant in India as they were in other Union Carbide plants. Yet, others point to the Indian officials for the inadequate management, and for not supervising the process closely to avoid such unfortunate disasters. The workers were blamed for insufficient training, and the government also was blamed for not imposing appropriate safety devices (DeGeorge, 1995). If Union Carbide, the management, workers, and the Indian government accurately managed their tasks, this disaster could have been completely avoided. Multinational corporations need to learn the cultures of all the countries that they do business with, and work accordingly to provide appropriate safety awareness training and education. It is also their responsibility to ensure that their foreign branches are running smoothly and safely.

When companies do business with developing countries, they should not always expect the developing nation to have the same economic systems as their native country. Every country has its own economic system, political system, and other local customs that influence its infrastructure. It is the foreign company's obligation to follow the country's rules while enforcing high ethical standards and safety measures. Even though there are international laws, they are not always enforced, nor are they always enforceable to the extent needed. The United Nations does not always have appropriate measures in place to enforce these laws; and there are no international police forces available to ensure that all the business processes between two countries are conducted correctly, ethically and legally. As such, in international business, ethics and high ethical standards play a critical role. However, it can be challenging to determine which country's ethical rules need to be followed. It is best to keep in mind that the basic ethical standards tend to be universal and thus are the same for almost all countries. Therefore, following the basic universal rules without violating the local norms can guide businesses to be conducted properly. Multinational companies usually do not try to act immorally. Conversely, when they try to follow the rules and the regulations of their native country in a foreign nation, their actions and processes could be immoral to the locals (DeGeorge, 1995). Basically, the multinational companies should ensure that all their institutions and subsidiaries hold the highest safety standards. Any potential harm that the company causes the foreign country, the parent company needs to take responsibility as quickly as possible in order to remedy the situation as much as possible under the circumstances. When conducting businesses in foreign countries, managers need to assure that institutions employ highly skilled and loyal employees, ensure high safety standards, understand the culture of that country, and behave accordingly, and ensure that all stakeholders are satisfied. These techniques will allow organizations to be victorious in foreign countries and avoid such disasters as the Bhopal and Chernobyl incidents which killed thousands of innocent individuals.

Bibliography:

Business in India, 2004. *Doing Business in India*. Retrieved on 06/01/2004 from the following URL: *http://www.indiaserver.com/biz/dbi/dbi.html*

Business in India, 2004. *Investment Risks in India*. Retrieved on 06/01/2004 from the following URL: *http://www.indiaserver.com/biz/investment-risks-india.html*

De George, R. (1995). *Business Ethics*. (4th ed.) New Jersey: Prentice Hall. Pages 473-503.

Doing Business in India (with description). Retrieved on 06/01/2004 from the following URL: *http://www.asiatravelinfo.com/india/doingbusiness.asp*

Pictures of Bhopal Victims, 2004. Picture viewed from the Bhopal Medical Appeal. Retrieved on 06/02/2004 from the following URL: *http://www.bhopal.org/pictures/bodies.jpg*

Ryan, M., (1995). "Personal Ethics and the Future of the World." *Varied Directions International*. (800) 888-5236. Video narrated by Meg Ryan.

Wikipedia, 2004. *Bhopal Disaster*. Wikipedia: the free encyclopedia. Retrieved on 05/28/2004 from the following URL: *http://en.wikipedia.org/wiki/Bhopal_Disaster*

Questions for Discussion:

1. Who is legally responsible for the Bhopal disaster? Who is morally responsible? Could the disaster have been avoided? If yes, how? Discuss.

2. Does the fact that Union Carbide owned a higher percent of the plant make any difference on who should take responsibility for the Bhopal disaster?

3. Was the compensation for the Bhopal victims' and their families fair and sufficient, provided that they will never enjoy another moment with their loved ones who were killed? Why or Why not?

4. What are some lessons that could be learned from the Bhopal and the Chernobyl disasters?

5. Should international businesses focus on the ethical rules since the basic ethical standards seem to be the same for all countries? Why or why not?

6. How could multinational companies enforce their safety standards?

7. Is it beneficial to implement more international laws for international business? If yes, should the foreign companies follow the international laws regardless of where the business is located?

8. What is the role of the government in ensuring the safety of its citizens? What can governments do to prevent such disasters as the Bhopal and the Chernobyl incidents from taking place in their countries?

Case 2.3: Nike and Commercial Speech

The U.S. Supreme Court had agreed in January 2003 to decide if sneaker and apparel maker giant, Nike, was engaging in protected free corporate public affairs speech in a recent campaign to defend its business practices overseas. The eventual decision also will emerge as a significant court ruling testing the limits of the commercial speech doctrine, which can extend constitutional protection to a firm's marketing, promotional, and advertising activities designed to persuade consumers to buy products and services.

The case revolves around Nike's massive advertising campaign to explain working conditions at its plants overseas in the face of allegations that the company's expensive products are made in sweatshops. Nike's troubles began when several media outlets ran stories about conditions in factories under contract with Nike in China, Vietnam, and elsewhere. The stories contended that the workers were paid below minimum wage, abused verbally and sexually, and exposed to dangerous working conditions, including working with hazardous chemicals.

San Francisco consumer activist Marc Kasky sued Nike, contending its advertising campaign to defend itself was inaccurate and deceptive. He especially took issue with statements by Nike chairman Philip H. Knight at a college appearance that Nike had the best factory conditions. Mr. Kasky also took issue with Nike's similar statements made to reporters and letters to editors and letters to college presidents and heads of athletic departments. Nike also took out full-page ads in college newspapers emphasizing the company's good corporate citizenship and humane labor standards. Certain company assertions, Mr. Kasky charged, including one that Nike paid more than double the minimum wage in countries where its products are produced, and another that workers are protected from physical to sexual abuse, amounted to false advertising. Mr. Kasky's suit also contends that Nike's statements that it provides free meals, housing, and healthcare to its workers were false, and that the workers' pay stubs actually showed that the company was deducting fees for those benefits.

A trial court in California agreed with Nike's contention that such statements are protected by the First Amendment right to free speech, and threw out Mr. Kasky's lawsuit; and a state appeals court upheld the ruling. However, in May of 2002, the California Supreme Court, in a split 4-3 decision, ruled that the company's efforts to defend itself before critics of its practices overseas amounted to "commercial speech," which applies when a company seeks to promote and defend its sales and profits and makes factual representations about its own products and operations. The California court held that Kasky could sue pursuant to a state consumer protection law because Nike's publicity was commercial speech, meaning the company could be sued for deceptive advertising. As opposed to political or public affairs speech, commercial speech, as determined by the Supreme Court, only is protected as free speech under the First Amendment if the speech is truthful and non-deceptive.

Over the recent years, the Court generally has granted commercial speech more First Amendment protection. Nonetheless, the line that separates commercial speech from non-commercial speech, especially political and public affairs speech, which are given the highest degree of First Amendment protection, is not clear. As a matter of fact, the California Supreme Court noted that commercial and non-commercial speech could be "inextricably intertwined" in Nike's statements defending its labor standards. Political speech typically concerns political campaigns as well as positions on public affairs issues, and has educational and informative purposes; whereas commercial speech, such as advertising, possesses the monetary motive to sell products and services.

The U.S. Supreme Court thus was asked to determine whether corporation's full free speech rights to defend themselves and their labor practices without fear of being sued for deceptive advertising. In addition to businesses and advertising agencies, some two dozen news organizations, fearing that lawsuits against companies would keep company executives from talking freely have supported Nike in court filings. The U.S. Chamber of Commerce urged the Supreme Court to give companies more free speech protections. Supporters of the Kaksy suit, however, argued that rather than chilling protected speech, the decision will deter false, deceptive, and misleading speech. Nike asserted that if the Supreme Court does not overrule the California court, there could be a flood of lawsuits against companies for statements they made in the public debate in defense of their business practices. Despite the importance of the case, the U.S. Supreme Court after hearing oral arguments nonetheless dismissed the Nike case without a decision, thereby leaving the decision up to the California Supreme Court, which had ruled that a consumer group could sue Nike for false and deceptive advertising. As a result, Nike agreed to settle the lawsuit and to pay $1.5 million to a workers' rights group, the Fair Labor Association, which will use the money to improve factory condition, strengthen workplace monitoring, and conduct worker programs. The Association, which was formed in 1999, promotes a conduct based on fair international labor standards, monitors labor practices, and makes public reports. Many legal and business people, however, had hoped that the U.S. Supreme Court would settle the speech issue; and the case was expected to set a major precedent.

Bibliography:

Business Week, 4/28/03, pp. 69-70; *Miami Herald,* 1/11/03, 4/24/03, pp. 1C, 3C, 4/28/03, p. 8B, 6/27/03, 9/13/03, pp. 1C, 2C; *Sun Sentinel,* 4/24/03, p. 3A; *Wall Street Journal,* 6/30/03, 1/10/03.

Questions for Discussion:

1. How should the U.S. Supreme Court have decided the case? Should the California Supreme Court's decision have been struck down as unconstitutional? Are Nike's statements political speech or commercial speech? Discuss.

2. Pursuant to Utilitarian ethics, which legal approach produces the "greater good" for society? Discuss.

3. What should Nike be doing in order to be a "socially responsible" company? Discuss.

Case 2.4: Chinese Organ Transplants and Sales

The New Times reported that kidneys, livers, corneas, and other body parts from executed Chinese prisoners are being transplanted into U.S. citizens and permanent residents who otherwise would have to wait years for organs. Many of the patients come back to the U.S. for follow-up care, which Medicaid or other government programs pay for.

The transplants in China, which doctors in both countries say are increasing, have presented the U.S. medical establishment with an ethical dilemma. Should U.S. doctors treat patients who have received organs from executed Chinese prisoners; and, if so, would they be tacitly condoning the practice and encouraging more such transplants? Yet, should they rebuke patients who, often in desperation, participate in a process that some transplant advocates condemn as morally wrong?

Executed prisoners are China's primary Bibliography: of transplantable organs, though few of the condemned prisoners, if any, consent to having their organs removed. Some of the unwitting donors may even be innocent, having been executed as part of a surge of executions propelled by accelerated trials and confessions that sometimes were extracted through torture.

The U.S. transplantation society states that decisions to donate organs must be made freely and without coercion or exploitation of any sort. It opposes any organ donations by prisoners, even to their relatives, because the circumstances of incarceration make it impossible to ensure that the decision is not unduly influenced by secondary benefits, such as an improved diet, that a prisoner may stand to gain.

U.S. doctors, however, say that there is little they can do to stop the flow of prisoner organs to the U.S., because China's supply is growing, just as is the U.S. demand. More transplantable organs are available in China, because more people are being executed. This year, 5,000 prisoners or more are likely to be put to death during a nationwide anti-crime drive. Many of them will be stripped of their vital organs, though there is no available data to say exactly how many. Chinese government policy allows the harvesting of organs if the prisoner or the prisoner's family has given written consent, or if the body is not claimed. In practice, however, the rules are often ignored, and illegal harvesting tolerated.

China, moreover, has made great strides in transplant techniques, having performed 35,000 kidney transplants since its first successful one in 1961. As a result, transplant centers have opened around the country, some with special wards catering to high-paying patients. Hospitals welcome foreign patients, because they pay as much as 10 times the price local patients pay for the same operation.

The demand for organs is growing at such a rapid rate that the Wall Street Journal reported in January of 2007 that online "middlemen" broker to match ailing customers with scares, but legal, organs. The online organs are priced at anywhere from 60% to 400% of their typical costs.

The Wall Street Journal reported in April 2007, however, that China may now be beginning to reconsider its liberal organ transplant and sales policy. The moral issue has emerged as to whether it is fair for wealthy foreigners to be able to get organ transplants in China when there may not be enough organs for Chinese citizens. Yet, the Journal also reported that organ sales have become a big "cash cow" for Chinese hospitals; and the government has not yet banned organ sales.

Bibliography:

Batson, Andrew, and Oster, Shair (2007). China reconsiders fairness of 'transplant tourism.' *The Wal Street Journal*, April 6, pp. A1, A9.

The Informed Reader (2007). Growing organ-supply shortfall creates windfall for online brokers. *The Wall Street Journal*, January 12, p. B4.

Smith, Craig (2001). Chinese organ transplants pose quandary in the U.S., *New York Times*, as reported in the *Sun Sentinel*, November 11, p. 11A.

Questions for Discussion:

1. Is the practice of Chinese prisoner organ transplantation moral pursuant to ethical egoism, ethical relativism, Utilitarianism, and Kantian ethics? Why or why not?

2. Should the government of the United States of America set rules on the usage of the prisoner organ transplantation issue? Discuss advantage and disadvantages to business and international relations.

3. Should the government of China ban the practice because it is unfair to Chinese? Why or why not?

Case 2.5: Organ Donations—The Dutch "Big Donor Show"

The Sun-Sentinel newspaper of Ft. Lauderdale, Florida reported in May of 2007 that a new and very controversial television show has appeared on Dutch national TV. The show is called the Big Donor Show, and its purpose, according to the Dutch network that produces and airs it, is to highlight the crisis in organ donations. The network is a publicly financed television network, called BNN. The program is like a game show contest. For example, in one show, a 37 year old woman who suffers from an inoperable brain tumor, and who wants to donate a kidney before she dies, will choose the recipient from among three contestants. The program has been criticized as immoral and unethical. The Dutch government has been asked to intervene to ban the program, but the government declined, explaining that it would be impermissible government censorship to stop the broadcast, regardless of how distasteful or even unethical the show might be. The network has defended its decision to air the show since its intent is to draw attention to the hundreds of people who die each year for the lack of a kidney transplant. One member of the Dutch parliament condemned the show as illegal, objectionable, unfitting, and unethical, especially the competitive element to the program. A network representative responded by saying it is even more tasteless and shocking to have people die for lack of organs and to have people waiting for organs "playing a lottery."

The network identified the woman donor as "Lisa." No other information about her was provided. During the show, she will hear interviews with the three candidates, their families and friends, before choosing who will get her kidney. Viewers can also vote for a candidate by means of a text message system, but the final determination will be the donor's. Lisa intends to donate one kidney while she is alive, and may donate other organs during her death under the Dutch government's normal allotment system. There is, of course, no guarantee that the recipient "winner" will get the organ since, as with any transplant, the donor and the recipient must be medically compatible and the recipient must be capable of receiving the kidney.

The director of the Kidney Association welcomed the attention the show has brought to the problem of organ donations, but he called on the network to cancel the show now that it has gained publicity, saying the show was "not the way" to solve the problem. He also pointed out that there are about 1,500 people waiting on the organ donation list for more than four years; and so he said that something has to be done to bring attention to the dire need for more donated organs.

Bibliography:

Max, Arthur, "New TV prize: A kidney," The Sun-Sentinel, May 31, 2007, p. 19A.

Questions for Discussion:

1. Discuss some of the legal issues—constitutional free speech, Federal Communications Commission "indecency" rules, and contract public policy—involved if this show were to be broadcast in the United States.

2. Is the show immoral pursuant to the ethical theories of ethical egoism, ethical relativism, Utilitarianism, and Kantian ethics? Discuss.

3. Does this show create value for the network pursuant to the principles of Value Driven Management? Why or why not?

4. Is the show unfitting and tasteless? Why or why not?

5. What would you propose as a solution to the shortage of organs for donation? Why?

(Postscript: On June 2, 2007, the Sun-Sentinel newspaper reported that the Dutch television organ donation "game" show was a hoax! A representative for the show stated that the woman "donor" was not actually dying of a brain tumor (though the prospective recipients are real patients who do need transplants). The representative for the show stated that the show's creators wanted to bring pressure on the government to reform organ donation laws and to raise awareness as to the need for donated organs. The representative pointed out that 200 people die annually in the Netherlands while waiting for a kidney and that the average waiting time is more than four years. So, now the questions emerge as to whether the show's creators acted in legal and in a moral manner by producing this hoax organ donor "game" show. What do you think?)

Case 2.6: Bribery and International Business

Tad Benson is worried. A salesperson for American Machinery, Inc., he has been placed in charge of negotiating an important sale of heavy construction equipment to the government of a small but rapidly developing nation. Deeply in debt, financially overextended, American has staked its future on penetrating foreign markets. The president of American Machinery has been assiduously trying to interest the government of this foreign country to make a major purchase. Tad's potential contract for American is not only a very large one; but also it could open the door to even bigger sales in the future. If he lands the contract, Tad's promotion in the firm is virtually certain. If American does not obtain some very large orders soon, it very likely will have to close a material part of its operations, which will cause many workers to be laid off, and which also will be disastrous for the local communities adversely affected.

Tad has been convinced he would succeed until he speaks with a high level government official who is involved in the negotiations. Tad's bid is looked upon very favorably, in price and quality, the official explains, and it is in fact the lowest bid. However, to Tad's surprise, a $100,000 "commission fee" to the official now will be necessary to legally secure the contract. If Tad does not pay the fee, the official "regrets" that the contract will go to a competitor. The official assures Tad that the payment of the "commission fee" is proper locally.

Tad knows that the sale is critical to the well-being of his company and its stakeholders. He also believes that the company's customers would get the "best possible deal" by buying American's equipment; and he knows that $100,000 is a trivial sum compared to the potential profits represented by the contract.

Yet, although he is aware that such payments are common and accepted practices in many countries, he always has felt that they were wrong; he has never before used them to secure a deal; and he is aware there may be serious legal ramifications to making such a payment.

Bibliography:

DeGeorge, Richard T. (1999). *Business Ethics* (5th edition). Pearson Prentice Hall.

Questions for Discussion:

1. Is it legal for Tad to pay this commission fee or is it an illegal bribe under the Foreign Corrupt Practices Act? Discuss.

2. Is it moral for Tad to pay this bribe pursuant to the doctrines of ethical egoism, ethical emotism, and ethical relativism? Discuss.

3. Is it moral for Tad to pay this bribe pursuant to the doctrines of Utilitarianism and Kantian ethics? Discuss.

Case 2.7: The Legality and Morality of the Salt Lake City Olympic Bribery Scandal

In December 1998, the U.S. Justice Department announced that it was reviewing allegations that Olympic organizers in Salt Lake City might have engaged in bribery of International Olympic Committee members as part of a successful effort to bring the 2002 games to Utah. Attorney General Janet Reno at the time acknowledged that Justice's Criminal Division had launched an inquiry after the Salt Lake Organizing Committee (SLOC) admitted paying tuition, expenses, and fees for several relatives of IOC members. Investigators at Justice are trying to determine whether the SLOC violated the Foreign Corrupt Practices Act, which prohibits the bribery of foreign officials. In addition, tax fraud could be part of the case if the Justice Department investigators were to determine that tax exempt money had been misused by buying gifts or funding scholarships for relatives of members of the IOC.

The issue of vote buying arose because of the disclosure of scholarship payments made to six relatives of IOC members by Salt Lake City officials during their successful bid to play host to the 2002 winter games. The SLOC has said the payments, which amounted to slightly less than $400,000, came from a privately financed fund that was started in 1991. Moreover, Justice investigated Intermountain Health Care, Utah's largest health care provider, which confirmed that it gave free surgical services worth $28,000 to at least two people associated with the IOC. The surgery included knee replacement surgery for an IOC member, and plastic surgery to smooth the bags under the eyes of one person associated with the IOC. The price to stage the 2002 Winter Games was at the time already up to $1.4 billion; and the SLOC's bid process cost $13 million. Tax forms filed by the SLOC did not include entries for the scholarship program. Cash payments ranging from $5,000 up to $70,000 to IOC members from Africa and Latin America also were investigated, as well as a Utah land deal, arranged by Committee officials that turned a quick $60,000 profit for IOC member Jean-Claude Ganga of the Republic of Congo. Expensive gifts, including a pair of shotguns, worth $2,000, for IOC President, Juan Antonio Samaranch, were also reportedly given. Finally, a Salt Lake ethics panel looked into possible use of Committee credit cards to pay for "female escorts" for IOC members. IOC rules forbid members from accepting anything worth more than $150 from bidders.

Marc Holder, an 80 year old lawyer, a Swiss IOC member, member of the IOC's Executive Board, and former head of the International Ski Federation, stated that he believed that several IOC members and their agents had been involved in vote buying the past 10 years; and he said he thought 5 to 7 percent of IOC members, at the time numbering 115, were open to bribery. He also said that there was one agent of an IOC member who boasts that "no city has ever won the Olympic Games without his help." Agents promise, according to Holder, to deliver blocs of IOC votes.

Frank Joklik, president of the SLOC, apologized and accepted full responsibility for the scholarship program run by the group that won the bid for the games. The program provided the $400,000 in tuition and other assistance to 13 individuals, including six relatives of IOC members, mostly from Africa. Only one recipient of the scholarship fund had been identified so far, the daughter of an IOC member from Cameroon, Africa. It was also reported that the son of a Libyan IOC member listed the Salt Lake bid committee's address on his application to Brigham Young University.

Holder has used the word "bribe" to describe the scholarship fund. "With hindsight, I believe this program should not have been part of the bid campaign," Joklik said. Yet, he said he still supported giving academic aid and athletic training to youngsters from developing countries, professing the "humanitarian" and "educational" purposes thereto; but acknowledged that "it should not be done in a way that might possibly appear to influence improperly the voting of IOC members." Nonetheless, Joklik steadfastly maintained that it was not the SLOC's intent to bribe IOC members. In January of 1999 Jolik, and Dave Johnson, the committee's senior vice-president, resigned under pressure. Both denied personal knowledge of these activities.

Holder, moreover, raised the scandal to global proportions when he claimed irregularities in the election campaigns awarding the Summer Games to Atlanta in 1996 and Sydney in 2000 and the Winter Games to Nagano in 1998. He charged that the Olympic selection process is riddled with corruption, with agents demanding up to $1 million to deliver votes. Officials in Beijing, moreover, accused Sydney of buying the 2000 vote.

According to interviews and news accounts, Salt Lake City decided it would concentrate its courting of delegates from Africa and Latin America. The feeling was that finalists, Ostersund, Sweden, and Sion, Switzerland, likely had the support of most European IOC members, and that Quebec's bid might neutralize Salt Lake City's support in North America. A Quebec City newspaper quoted a 2002 bid official who said at least three agents claiming IOC ties offered to swing the vote away from Salt Lake City, which eventually won by a 54-14 vote margin. Ironically, Salt Lake City did not need the African votes; and because the balloting is secret, SLOC could not even be sure it had gotten the votes it is accused of paying for.

The scandal tarnished the reputations of Salt Lake City and Utah, ignited opposition to letting the city play host to the Games, and has provoked "second thoughts" by at least one major corporate sponsor. The allegations already have jeopardized a $50 million pledge of sponsorship from US West Inc., a telecommunications company, which withheld its first payment of $5 million, until it gained more information on the scandal. Local organizers and the U.S. Olympic Committee feared that it would be difficult to raise the remaining $200 million needed to meet the budget.

After an extensive Justice Department investigation, two former executives of the SLOC were indicted in the summer of 2000 on fraud, bribery (for violating the Foreign Corrupt Practices Act), and conspiracy theories for orchestrating a wide-ranging bribery scheme of Olympic officials in order to secure the Winter 2000 games for Salt Lake City, Utah. Thomas Welch and David Johnson were the Salt Lake City Olympic Organizing Committee officials named in the indictment; and they were accused of paying more than $1 million in cash and bogus contracts to IOC officials in an effort to "buy" votes. Welch was the head of the committee of civic leaders that put together the city's bid for the winter Olympics, and Johnson was his deputy.

However, less than three months before the Games began, a federal judge dismissed all the charges. An internal IOC probe did lead to the dismissal of 10 IOC members. Nonetheless, the federal government appealed the judge's decision, and in April of 2003, a federal appeals court reinstated the case against Welch and Johnson, stating that the government deserved a chance to put the case before a jury. However, in December of 2003, another federal judge dismissed the criminal case against the two Salt Lake civic leaders.

This judge, U.S. District Court Judge David Sam, was especially bitter to the federal government. He declared that in his 18 years on the federal bench, he had never seen a case so devoid of "criminal intent or evil purpose." The judge further stated that the evidence never met the legal standard for bribery, and that the case "offends my sense of justice." The judge formally acquitted the two men, which means the government cannot appeal again, because retrying them would amount to illegal "double jeopardy." The two men had faced up to 75 years in prison, although they probably would have received far less if actually convicted. Even if the case had reached a jury, the prosecution would have had a difficult time, since proof of evil intent or bad motive is an indispensable element to a case of bribery and fraud.

The legal case, as well as the "scandal-plagued" Salt Lake City Winter Olympics, is now finally over.

Bibliography:

McAdams, Neslund, and Neslund (2000). *Law, Business, and Society* (6th edition), p. 80; *Herald*, 12/18/98, 4/23/03, 12/6/03; *New York Times*, 12/24/98; *Sun Sentinel*, 11/16/01; *Washington Post*, 7/21/00.

Questions for Discussion:

1. Do you agree with the ultimate legal conclusion to the case? Why or why not?

2. Did the SLOC act in a moral manner pursuant to the ethical doctrines of ethical egoism, ethical relativism, and Utilitarianism? Discuss.

3. Did the companies that contributed to the SLOC organizing fund act in a socially responsible manner? Discuss.

4. Did the actions of the SLOC "pass" the "test" of Value-Driven Management? Why or why not?

Case 2.8: Academic Honesty, Bribery, and Ethical Relativism[6]

In the United States, bribery is illegal and frowned upon by society. In some other countries, however, there is a culture of doing business through what many in the U.S. would deem immoral, that is, bribery. This culture may even extend bribery to government officials under the rationale that such payments are "just what our culture expects." If the culture is pervasive with this attitude, bribery can reach into the depths of the educational system as well.

To illustrate, take the case of Professor Usborn, a U.S. citizen who is a full-time professor at a private U.S. university, is given an opportunity by his university to teach for a year in a Third World country called Cheatsa. Professor Usborn studies the country prior to visiting, and learns that the culture is one of corruption and bribery. He has never been offered a bribe in the United States, and certainly looks down on any sort of bribery.

When he enters Cheatsa, he is met by the Dean of his department from the National University of Cheatsa. During the ride to his new residence near the university, the Dean tells him: "We have had a lot of foreigners come and teach here. We know much about your cultures, but one thing you must understand is that you are not here to change our culture. You are here to participate and enrich yourself in our culture. Professors here make very little money, and the way we survive is to accept small tokens of appreciation from our students. It would not be a good example for you to insult our culture and refuse gifts of appreciation."

Professor Usborn was confused by his host's words; but he soon learns that professors at the university accept payments and gifts from students near the end of a semester. He also learns that some professors make it clear to students that their grades will be determined based on their gifts.

Professor Usborn attends a reception at the U.S. Embassy; and also attending is the U.S. Cultural Affairs Officer. He takes the opportunity to discuss the corruption present in Cheatsa. The embassy officer tells him that any U.S. citizen that bribes a government official would violate U.S. law. He then says: "You know, this is a corrupt country and we can't make a dent in it. Sometimes there is a fine line between bribery and just giving a token holiday or birthday gift."

Toward the end of the semester, Professor Usborn is approached by a student who had been performing poorly. The student asks the professor when his birthday is. Professor Usborn tells him that it happens to be in two weeks. The student then asks what the professor's favorite color is. Professor Usborn answers "red," and then asks why. The student answers that he is only "curious."

Soon, other students begin coming to Professor Usborn and tell him that they understand he has a birthday in two weeks. The final exam for the class will be conducted a week after the professor's birthday.

About ten days later, Professor Usborn begins receiving wrapped packages with birthday cards. The gift from the student who asked what color he likes is a small package wrapped in red. Inside is a red ruby ring. Professor Usborn is shocked. The student explains that his father is the director of a government owned ruby mine; and his father had the ruby ring made especially for the "American" professor.

Soon gifts are heaped upon Professor Usborn. Some contained envelopes of U.S. dollars; others contained bottles of expensive Scotch Whiskey. All of the gifts make very clear who the donors were.

---

[6]Contributed by Gary Waldron, Nova Southeastern University.

Remembering the words of the Dean that foreigners should not insult the culture of the country, Professor Usborn is unsure what to do about the gifts, some of which are worth hundreds of dollars. He finds himself feeling sorry for the one student who has performed poorly and who gave him the ruby ring.

After the final exam, he comes upon this student's paper. It is a clear "F." In the National University of Cheatsa, if a student receives an "F," he or she is expelled from school. Professor Usborn goes to the Dean to discuss the situation. The Dean tells him: "There is only one alternative—keep the gift, and if you feel bad about changing the grade then give him another test, and let him practice on it until he passes. This is our culture, I told you already. Besides, all of the other American professors have accepted gifts and went home happy to have experienced another culture different than their own."

Bibliography:

BBC News report on education corruption: retrieved on December 2007 from: *http://news.bbc .co.uk/2/hi/uk_news/education/6729537.stm*.

Cavico, Frank J., and Mujtaba, Bahaudin G. (2008). Legal Challenges for the Global Manager and Entrepreneur. Dubuque, Iowa: Kendall-Hunt Publishing Company.

International Herald Tribune/Europe, *Russia sets out to fight corruption in education with a new standardized test* (February 2, 2007): *www.iht.com/articles/ap/2007/02//03/europe/EU-GEN-Russia-Education-Reform.php*

Osipian, Ararat L., International Higher Education, *Higher Education Corruption in Ukraine: Opinions and Estimates*, Fall 2007, No. 49 : *www.bc.edu/bc_org/avp/soe/cihe/newsletter/ Number49/p20_Osipian.htm*.

United States State Department site on foreign corruption: *www.usdoj.gov/criminal/fraud/fcpa*.

Questions for Discussion:

1. Is there a difference in "token" birthday gifts and the ruby ring? Why or why not?

2. Considering the culture of corruption in Cheatsa's education system, should Professor Usborn take any birthday gifts? Why or why not?

3. How does the U.S. Foreign Corrupt Practices Act (FCPA) come into play here, if at all? Discuss.

4. Do the Embassy Cultural Affairs Officer's comments help Professor Usborn in making his decision? Why or why not?

5. Does it make any difference that giving the student an "F" will have him expelled from the university? Why or why not?

6. Is there any ethical philosophy that can justify Professor Usborn retaining the student's gifts? What should Professor Usborn do if the philosophy of ethical relativism is applied in this situation? Discuss.

7. If Professor Usborn accepts the gifts, what do you think his attitude will be when he returns to his U.S. university to continue teaching? Discuss.

8. Most people believe that U.S. education is free from corruption; but many people obtain "fake" degrees from on-line sources and use them to get jobs. Does this fact weaken our moral resolve that education remain corruption free? Why or why not?

3. Whistleblowing

Case 3.1: Whistleblowing at a Florida Bank

In 1992, David Cray joined the Largo, Florida, office of NationsSecurities, the brokerage subsidiary of the then NationsBank, and was given clients previously handled by brokers who had left the firm. Soon after his arrival, stated Cray, he was confronted by angry customers who had discovered that they owned mutual funds and not the special bank accounts that they had been promised by his predecessors. Cray consequently became convinced that the holders of NationsBank certificates of deposit had been sold Nations Securities mutual funds without being told that the investments were risky and not federally insured.

Accordingly, in the spring of 1994, said Cray, he began to make suggestions to his managers about cleaning up sales practices. Then he went to their managers; and finally he wrote to NationsBank president Hugh McColl. A few days later, suspecting that his job was in jeopardy, Cray took his story to newspapers in several Florida cities, including St. Petersburg and Tampa. Shortly after the stories appeared, said Cray, a NationsBank manager asked for his keys and sent him home.

Prompted by the newspaper reports, federal and state regulators began to investigate NationsSecurities sales practices. Thousands of investors demanded their money back and instituted a class action suit. A similar suit in Texas was settled for $30 million.

When Cray was terminated, his $100,000 salary, which he earned for most of his 16 years as a broker, ended. Within weeks, moreover, Cray's wife lost her job selling insurance to banks. Cray suspects that her job loss was related to his situation. Furthermore, Cray stated that the job offers he had from several national securities firms while working at NationsBank evaporated once he "blew the whistle."

Since his termination, Cray has gone into business for himself as a broker as the Cray Financial Group. Commencing the business was very costly, he related, as well as a material drain on Cray's and his wife's savings and investments. He struggled for business and was preoccupied with legal affairs. Yet, he stated and thought he did the "right thing."

Cray did file an arbitration lawsuit, claiming wrongful discharge, to the National Association of Securities Dealers; and he "won" in the sense that the panel ruled that he should be reinstated to his former position, which was a remedy he did not seek. Cray, however, was awarded no monetary damages by the arbitration panel.

Nonetheless, Cray stated that "I did what I had to do," and that he was "optimistic."

Bibliography:

Cavico, Frank, 2004. "Private Sector Whistleblowing and the Employment-At-Will Doctrine: A Comparative Legal, Ethical, and Pragmatic Analysis," 45 *South Texas Law Review* 543.

Jacobs, Margaret, 1998. "Arbitration Policies Are Muting Whistleblower Claims," *Wall Street Journal,* August 6, pp. B1, B4.

Longo, Tracey, 1996. "The Cost of Rebuilding a Career," *Kiplinger's Personal Finance Magazine,* February, p. 140.

Questions for Discussion:

1. Would David Cray's whistleblowing be protected by a typical state private sector whistleblower statute? Why or why not?
2. Was David Cray morally required to "blow the whistle" based on DeGeorge's ethical whistleblowing principle? Discuss.
3. Was David Cray treated in a moral manner? Discuss.
4. Did he do the "right" thing? Discuss.

4. Employment-At-Will

Case 4.1: Employment-At-Will and Red Lobster Employee Review Panels

Most employers steadfastly adhere to the traditional, established, general rule of employment—the employment-at-will doctrine—which holds that an employer can discharge an employee at-will for no reason, no good reason, or even a morally bad reason. The restaurant chain Red Lobster, however, by means of its internal "law," has taken itself out of the protective confines of the conventional legal doctrine, because at Red Lobster, an employee can only be terminated or sanctioned if an employee review panel determines that the penalty was fair and just.

In one particular case, noted in the *Wall Street Journal*, an employee review panel at one of the Red Lobster restaurants determined that a waitress had been unjustly fired, and thereby overruled the termination decision of a manager. The review panel included a general manager, a server, a hostess, and a bartender, all of whom had agreed to volunteer to review the circumstances of the waitress's firing, and who had been told to do simply what they believed was fair.

Other employers are also beginning to allow their employees to have their dismissals or other sanctions appealed to panels of their co-workers. These companies feel that such panels are a way of reducing workplace tensions, especially racial, ethnic, and religious tensions, as well as to limit employee lawsuits.

In the Red Lobster case, the waitress, Ruth Hatton, was fired for allegedly stealing a guest comment card from a Pennsylvania Red Lobster where she worked. Ms. Hatton was then an employee of 19 years at Red Lobster.

Red Lobster does not adhere to the employment-at-will doctrine; rather the company allows its employees who have been fired or disciplined to appeal to panels of co-workers, who hear testimony and can overturn management decisions and even award damages. So, instead of suing, the waitress called for peer review, which took place three weeks after the firing. Ms. Hatton said that the peer review option was "cheaper" than instituting a lawsuit. She also said that she "liked the idea of being judged by people who know how things work in a little restaurant."

The Red Lobster manager, who supervised over a hundred employees, and who fired the waitress, testified that she fired Ms. Hatton after an irate customer complained to her and her supervisor. The customer somehow learned that Ms. Hatton had removed her comment card from the box. The customer thus felt violated that her card was taken from the box and consequently her complaints about the waitress and the food had been ignored. Based on a company rulebook, the manager stated that Ms. Hatton had violated a company policy forbidding the removal of company property. The waitress, 53 years old, explained that the customer, a black woman, had requested a well-done piece of prime rib, and then complained that the meat was fatty and overcooked. The waitress also testified that she politely suggested to the customer that "prime rib always has fat on it." The waitress also stated that she thought, based on her experience with black customers in working-class areas, that the customer might have confused prime rib and spare rib. Ms. Hatton then had the meat cooked some more. Yet when the customer remained displeased, the waitress offered her a free dessert. Apparently still unhappy, the customer soaked the meat with steak sauce and then shoved away her plate. Finally, the woman or her companion then filled out a comment card, paid the bill, and left.

Ms. Hatton, consumed by curiosity, she said, next asked the hostess for the key to the comment box. She said she read the card, then pocketed it, intending to show it to the manager, who earlier, because of heating problems at the restaurant, had worried that the prime rib was overcooked, not undercooked. Ms. Hatton testified further that she forgot about the comment card and inadvertently threw it out. The hostess, a 17 year old student employed at Red Lobster for the summer, testified that it was not a "big deal" to give the waitress the key, and that "a lot of people would come up to me to get it."

In the employee review panel's deliberations, the panelists attempted to balance the facts that a minority customer's feelings had been hurt and that an unofficial policy forbidding employees to go into the comment box had been violated, against the panel's belief that Ms. Hatton had not intended to steal company property. All the panelists had peer review training and were being paid regular wages and travel expenses. Several panelists criticized the manager for not placing an official rebuke in Ms. Hatton's file, and leaving the controversy at that. Others thought that the manager was being too sensitive to the race aspect of the case, perhaps by pressure from corporate headquarters. Accordingly, after an hour and one half of deliberations, the panel unanimously restored Ms. Hatton's job. The unofficial policy against reading the contents of a comment box, they reasoned that it had not been consistently enforced at the restaurant. Nonetheless, because the policy had been violated, the panel did not grant the waitress the three weeks of lost wages that she sought. Ms. Hatton's years of experience at the restaurant also emerged as a factor in the decision. When she returned to work, Ms. Hatton stated that the manager treated her professionally, and when the manager transferred to another state, Ms. Hatton contributed to her going-away gift. The waitress concluded that "the process worked," and the panel "took my claim seriously."

Bibliography:

Jacobs, Margaret A., "Red Lobster Tale: Peers Decide Fired Waitress's Fate," *Wall Street Journal*, January 20, 1998, pp. B1, B4.

Questions for Discussion:

1. Has Red Lobster acted in an ethically egoistic manner in abrogating the employment-at-will doctrine and substituting the employee review panel process? Discuss.

2. Do you agree with the panel's decision to overturn the "unfair" and "unjust" discharge of the waitress? Why or why not?

3. Is the concept of an employee review panel moral pursuant to Utilitarian and Kantian ethics? Discuss.

Case 4.2: Employment-At-Will, Southland Corporation, and the "No Resistance" Dilemma

Mr. Wiley has worked for a 7-11 Store in the past eight years and knows many of his customers by name. One day, several teenagers came in to the 7-11 Store and were stealing beer by putting the bottles into their pockets and bags. Teenagers stealing products from the convenience store has become normal in this area, and people do it every week. Mr. Wiley is the store manager who noticed what these teenagers were doing. He had an elderly customer at the counter and wanted to solve this dilemma without putting her in any danger. So, he went close to the boys, and quietly asked the teenagers to leave the beer back on the shelf and leave the store. The teenagers started a fist-fight and started hitting Wiley with bottles. Almost all the teenagers escaped; however, Wiley was able to catch and hold one of the thieves until the police arrived.

Mr. Wiley is considered to be a hero in his community because he was concerned about the safety of his customers and the value of his stockholders. So, he put his own life in danger, and caught the thief at the front of a witness. However, the company has a policy that explicitly states, "Non-resistance should be taken during a robbery situation and employees who violate this policy will be terminated." Wiley had read, understood, and signed this written policy. You are the district manager and in charge of this situation.

Bibliography:

CBS News, 1996. Rob Stafford of CBS on "60 Minutes." December 19th 1996.

Questions for Discussion:

1. As the boss, district manager, do you terminate Wiley? Why or why not?

2. How do you see this dilemma in terms of the various stakeholders (can there be two rights to choose from)?

    • *Individual Vs. Community*—will you consider the impact of your decision for the individual or the community?

    • *Short term Vs. Long term*—will you be concerned about the short term benefits of your decision or long term?

    • *Truth Vs. Loyalty*—will you consider your decision based on truth or loyalty?

    • *Mercy Vs. Justice*—will your decision seek justice for the violation of this law or be merciful?

3. Did Mr. Wiley have a moral obligation pursuant to the ethical principle of Last Resort to rescue this customer and/or prevent this crime?

4. The fact that "non-resistance" policy is an invitation to thieves is well known to the upper echelons of Southland Corporation. Yet, they are more concerned about the lives of their employees and customers than they are about their products; ergo they asked their associates to leave heroic acts of stopping crime to pro-

fessionals at the police department. Research has also shown that "no-resistance" policy has saved more lives than attacking the robbers. The facts are that Mr. Wiley was fired because the organization's rules and guidelines needed to be followed in order to reduce deaths and injuries. Based on utilitarian and Kantian theories of ethics, was it moral for the organization to terminate Mr. Wiley? Were there any other options available for management of Southland Corporation? Discuss and support your views.

5. Outsourcing

Case 5.1: Outsourcing Downsizing

Downsizing is not an unusual business occurrence in today's ever-changing and fast-paced global economy, where outsourcing and off-shoring are now part of the standard corporate practice and vocabulary. Yet what emerges as a most interesting phenomenon is exactly who is doing the downsizing. Inc magazine in December of 2007 reported that today, many companies are outsourcing their human resource departments, in particular the frequently contentious, emotional, and fraught with legal period act of terminating employees. Inc magazine mentioned a San Francisco Bay company called TriNet that is the HR consultant for about 1500 small companies, but is really the de facto HR department for these companies. The company's main responsibility is to structure severance packages and to provide and document information so companies can limit their legal liability; but the company will also coach their clients on how to fire people, and in addition will also step in and fire employees themselves. This is just one example. Inc magazine reported that in the past small companies have relied on professional business consultants to manage payroll and benefits, but now these organizations, which Inc calls "professional employer organizations" or PEOs, are now outsourced to manage more complex business responsibilities such as recruitment, performance reviews, and especially terminations. Inc magazine noted that outsourced terminations are now coming at a time when many companies are experimenting with new, perhaps more impersonal, ways to fire employees. Yet as the magazine noted, many companies are fearful of the legal consequences of termination, especially being sued for wrongful termination, and thus they conclude that it is better to be impersonal and to outsource the discharges to the "professionals." In one illustration provided by the magazine, an outsourcing professional will meet with the CEO and key managers of a firm to "rehearse the script" for the downsizing day events. Then the professional will sit in on the meeting where the discharge of the employee is effectuated, and the professional will take notes, and also, if necessary, keep the CEO and managers "on message" and make sure they "follow the script." Since the HR consultants are technically independent contractors, they provide a degree of legal separation and isolation from the company that has retained them. Despite the perceived advantages of the outsourcing of HR, Inc magazine reported on one disadvantage, as stated by the CEO of a recruiting firm, and that is that a company could be perceived as "cold-hearted" or even "clueless," which would place that company in a much more difficult position to attract and to retain good employees.

Bibliography:

Charkin, Max, "Meet Rebecca. She's Here to Fire You," Inc. Magazine, *http://www.inc.com/magazine*, retrieved December 4, 2007.

Questions for Discussion:

1. Discuss the legal, ethical, and practical implications in outsourcing HR functions, especially terminations and downsizing.

2. Does outsourcing the HR department make sense for a small business based on the principles of Value Driven Management? Why or why not?

Case 5.2: Outsourcing, Immigration, and the U.S. H-1B Visa Program

Business Week magazine reported in March of 2008 a very controversial use of the H-1B immigration visa program in the United States. The visa program was initially established to permit companies in the United States to import workers from other countries, particularly workers in short supply, such as those in the technological, scientific, and engineering fields. However, Business Week reported that the federal government just released data from 2007 indicating that offshore outsourcing companies, particularly from India, are the ones that have most extensively taken advantage of the visa program. In fact, Business Week related that Indian outsourcing firms were granted nearly 80% of the visas approved for 2007. This information immediately generated heated controversy. Business Week reported a communication from Senator Chuck Grassley (R-Iowa) which stated that "the H-1B visa program is not working out as it was intended." The two top firms securing visas in 2007 were Infosys Technologies and Wipro, both Indian companies, which had 4,559 and 2,567 approved visas, respectively. The H-1B visa is a very valuable one which allows these companies to bring workers to the U.S., where the companies have substantial business operations that provide technical support and other services to corporations, and which services complement services provided from India. Business Week also reported that of the top ten recipients of the visa in 2007, six are based in India, and two others, though headquartered in the U.S., have most of their operations in India. Microsoft and Intel are the only two U.S. technological companies in the top ten. Microsoft had 959 visa approvals, and Intel received 369.

Critics such as Senator Grassley as well as Senator Richard J. Durbin (D-Ill.) contend that foreign outsourcers are abusing the visa program. These critics contend, as related by Business Week, that the visa program was supposed to benefit the U.S. economy. The idea was for U.S. companies to bring in foreign workers, especially software programmers and computer scientists with unique skills and knowledge, thereby enhancing innovation and productivity and improving competitiveness. However, critics now declare that the program is actually undermining the U.S. economy by eliminating jobs in the United States. What is happening, critics assert, is that the foreign outsourcing companies are bringing low-cost workers to the U.S., training them in the offices of U.S. clients, and then rotating them back home in a year or two, so they can provide the same services and/or technical support from abroad. Business Week related a communication from Senator Durbin that stated that "valuable high-tech jobs are on a now one-way superhighway overseas." Consequently, these senators want to make the visa program's criteria more restrictive, such as by requiring companies to hire U.S. workers first and also to pledge that the visa workers will not displace U.S. workers. Yet, U.S. technological companies, as reported by Business Week, want the Congress to increase the visa cap from 65,000 a year to at least 115,000. They say that more visas are necessary so the U.S. can attract top talent. Bill Gates is expected to again testify before Congress as to the need for more such visas. Business Week reported the following statement by Gates: "It makes no sense to tell well-trained, highly skilled individuals—many of whom are educated at our top colleges and universities—that the U.S. does not welcome or value them." Currently, the visa program is open to any company with U.S. operations, regardless of where the company is headquartered. The outsourcing firms, as reported by Business Week, deny they are abusing the program, and also state that they are helping U.S. companies remain competitive, particularly by allowing them to reduce costs and concentrate on their core competencies. The foreign firms also state that the jobs they fill in the U.S. are higher skilled than those in India, and involve sales and custom software development. Infosys, for example, has approximately 9000 employees in the U.S., including 7500 on H1-B visas; and it has 88,000 employees worldwide. Business Week also noted a difference in approach between U.S. and foreign companies using the visa program. That is, the U.S. firms frequently try to keep the visa workers in the U.S., whereas the foreign outsourcing firms usually employ the workers in the U.S. on a temporary basis. Business Week also reported that many U.S. workers oppose any expansion of the visa program, since they believe this visa program allows companies to hire cheap employees from abroad. Americans need jobs, they declare, especially when the economy is deteriorating.

Bibliography:

Herbst, Moira, "Guess Who's Getting The Most Work Visas," Business Week, March 17, 2008, pp. 62-64.

Questions for Discussion:

1. Is the H-1B visa program moral pursuant to Utilitarian ethics? Why or why not?

2. Is it moral pursuant to Kantian ethics? Why or why not?

3. Should the H-1B visa program be limited only to U.S. firms? Why or why not?

4. Do you agree with the senators' recommendations for reforming the program? Why or why not?

5. Should the visa cap be increased or decreased? By how much? Why?

6. Should the visa program be abolished completely? Why or why not?

7. How should a U.S. company approach this issue using the principles of Value-Driven Management (VDM)? Discuss.

8. How should an Indian outsourcing company approach this issue using the principles of VDM? Discuss.

6. Immigration

Case 6.1: Illegal Immigration: The States' Legal Response

Business Week magazine reported that the United States confronts an increasingly difficult problem—legally, morally, and practically—and that is how to deal with the estimated 9 million-plus immigrants who live in the U.S. on a more or less permanent basis.

Due to post-September 11 security concerns, some states and federal agencies have determined to crack down on illegal immigrants. For example, California Governor Arnold Schwarzenegger immediately decided upon attaining office to repeal a law granting illegal immigrants access to driver's licenses. Three other states, Alabama, Florida, and Virginia, are working with the Department of Homeland Security to deputize local police to arrest illegal immigrants they confront in the course of routine police work. Three more states have bills pending that would deny in-state college tuition rates to undocumented students. In several states as well as Washington, D.C., some politicians and anti-immigration groups are pushing legislation that would deny illegal immigrants public services, such as schools and health care, and require the local police to enforce the nation's immigration laws to the "letter." The Miami Herald reported in February 2007 that a Florida state representative introduced a bill in the state legislature to fine companies with "illegal" employees and to strip them of state tax "breaks" and benefits. Fines would range up to $25,000 per violation, and sanctions include taking tax "breaks" from farms, liquor licenses from restaurants, and construction licenses from contractors.

Yet, at the very same time, there are efforts by certain states and municipalities as well as businesses to integrate illegal immigrants into "mainstream" U.S. life. For example, Business Week reported in April of 2007 that one county, Montgomery County, pays about $700,000 a year to a non-profit organization that provides employment services, such as hiring halls, English language classes, and legal advice, to immigrants, about 60% of whom are in the country illegally. These efforts recognize the essential facts that these undocumented immigrants are here to stay and even pay taxes, such as Social Security taxes. Accordingly, the feeling is that it is best for everyone to get these people "out of the shadows." Thus, 11 states now issue driver's licenses to illegal immigrants. Moreover, Florida may follow suit, because in April of 2004, then Governor Jeb Bush endorsed a bill to do so there. Moreover, hundreds of cities and local police departments accept a Mexican government-issued I.D. called the *matricula consular* as valid for everything from bank accounts to driver's licenses. In addition, a growing number of financial institutions allow an undocumented alien to obtain a mortgage and open an account using the *matricula*.

Therefore, despite the conflicting policies, many government entities as well as many businesses are engaging in a policy of *de facto* legalization. Some parts of the government are helping illegal aliens in some areas, but enforcing immigration laws in other areas. The situation is further complicated by the increasing political power of Hispanics, as reflected perhaps in President Bush's recent proposal for a partial amnesty program.

The conflicting policies are most apparent concerning driver's licenses, which is a cornerstone for building a life in the United States. *Matricula* holders can secure driver's licenses in 11 states, and a few states will grant them with an I.R.S. I.D. Yet most states require documents that only those here legally can obtain, such as a Passport or a Social

Security number. The issue is highly divisive due to heightened national security concerns. In Florida, although there is a bill to provide licenses to illegal immigrants, the Governor is insisting that illegal immigrants first identify themselves and then be fingerprinted before getting a license. There are literally dozens of bills on the driver's license issue before the various state legislatures, and they are about equally divided as to the easing and stiffening of requirements to get licenses.

The *matricula* itself, however, may be equally as controversial. It first was issued in 2002 by Mexican consulates in the U.S. The document includes name, address, and a photo. Nationwide, according to the Mexican government, almost 1000 cities as well as almost 1000 police departments recognize the document. Moreover, the U.S. Treasury Department a year ago endorsed the document as an easy way for illegal immigrants to open bank accounts. Nevertheless, critics of illegal immigration condemn the use of the *matricula* as encouraging more illegal entry.

U.S. business, however, feels that it cannot ignore millions of potential consumers, even illegal ones. Consequently, some 150 banks, including at least 19 major ones, such as Bank of America, now encourage illegal immigrants to open bank accounts using the *matricula*. Wells Fargo, for example, is setting up 23,000 new *matricula* accounts a month nationwide, according to a bank spokesperson.

The Internal Revenue Service certainly does not ignore illegal immigrants. Rather it requires them to pay taxes; and consequently the IRS has created a special individual tax payer identification number beginning with a "9" for tax payers who do not qualify for a Social Security Number. The Wall Street Journal reported that the tax liability for the "9" filers, most of whom are here illegally, totaled almost $50 billion between 1996 and 2003.

The debate as to how to deal with the ever-growing and now semi-permanent numbers of illegal aliens has challenged the U.S. for many years. The debate is now even more intense due to the intensified security concerns as a result of "9-11" and the War against Terror.

Bibliography:

Boodhoo, Niala, and Feinhard, And Beth (2007). Bills target undocumented workers. *Miami Herald*, February 7; pp. 1C, 4C.

Grow, Brian, (2004). "Aliens: A Little Less Alienated," *Business Week*, May 10, pp. 62-64.

Javers, Eamon (2007). The divided States of America. *Business Week*, April 16, p. 68.

Jordan, Miriam (2007). Even workers in the U.S. illegally pay tax man. *The Wall Street Journal*, April 4, p. B4.

Questions for Discussion:

1. What are the advantages and disadvantages of illegal immigration to the United States' citizens and the community? Discuss and explain your arguments.

2. How should the government—the federal government as well as the states—deal with the difficult problem of illegal immigration—legally, morally, and practically? Discuss.

3. How should business address the issue of immigration and their inclusion in the workplace? Discuss.

Case 6.2: Pesos por Pizzas

The New York Times in January 2007 reported that a large pizza chain in Dallas, Texas, called Pizza Padron, initiated a controversial promotion called "Pesos por Pizzas," in which customers can pay for pizzas with Mexican pesos. There are 59 Pizza Padron establishments in five Southwestern and Western states. Many customers of the chain travel regularly to Mexico, and then they return to the U.S. with Mexican currency, which now can be used to purchase pizza. The customers are given their change in U.S. currency or coins. The promotion, however, now has emerged as another "hot-button" in the immigration debate in the United States. The company's Dallas headquarters had received almost 1000 email messages when the practice became publicly known; some messages were supportive but many called the policy unpatriotic. Several "emailers" and phone callers have called for a boycott of the chain. The New York Times reported that the president of the company, Antonio Swad, stated he was surprised by the outcry. He related that the peso policy was only an effort to reinforce the company's "brand promise" to be the "premier Latino pizza chain." He further related that this was a business decision; and that the Latino population was a significant part of the company's customer base. He also asserted that the United States was "not going to be like it used to be." It is going to be different, he said; and the U.S. has an "opportunity to be better," he also said. Mr. Swad is of Italian and Lebanese heritage; he was born and raised in Columbus, Ohio; and he does not speak Spanish. He opened his first pizza business in Dallas in 1986; and saw an opportunity in the growing Latino population in his neighborhood. He soon changed the name of the business from Pizza Pizza to Pizza Padron; hired bi-lingual staff; and offered Mexican style pizzas. Pizza Padron became a franchise in 2003. From 10-15% of the business from the five Dallas area stores has been in pesos. Despite the criticism, he stated he would continue the promotion, at least for the near future. One critic who seeks to limit immigration expressed concern that Hispanics could create a "parallel mainstream" in the United States. A co-founder of a Hispanic-American public relations organization, as reported by the New York Times, stated that he did not see the policy as a major business trend, but did view it as a "symbolic acknowledgement of the importance of the large and growing Hispanic market." He also said from a business standpoint, the issue is not whether the customers are legal or illegal immigrants, but whether they have money. He also said that the customers also spend U.S. currency on the Mexican side of the border. The policy is clearly for the convenience of the customers since banks offer a better exchange rate than Pizza Padron, which as of this writing gives an exchange rate of 12 pesos per dollar.

Bibliography:

Kovach, Gretel C., "Pizza Chain Takes Pesos, and Complaints," *The New York Times*, January 15, 2007, p. A8.

Questions for Discussion:

1. What are the legal ramifications to the "Pesos por Pizzas" practice? Discuss.

2. Is the pizza chain being "unpatriotic," as some have claimed? Is it leading to a "parallel" Hispanic "mainstream" in the United States? Why or why not?

3. Is the pizza chain acting morally pursuant to the doctrines of ethical egoism, ethical relativism, Utilitarianism, and Kantian ethics? Discuss.

4. What would a Value Driven Management analysis of "Pizza por Pesos" indicate to the pizza chain as the "value-maximizing" course of conduct? Discuss.

Case 6.3: Clash between U.S. Immigration Law and Labor Law

The *Miami Herald* newspaper in January of 2008 reported a very important U.S. federal appellate court decision that places employers in a very difficult situation. Although federal immigration law prohibits and punishes employers from hiring illegal (or undocumented) workers, the District of Columbia appellate court ruled that nonetheless employers pursuant to federal labor law are legally obligated to bargain with the unions that represent the employees. The Herald emphasized that the case emerges as yet another of the "unresolved paradoxes" of U.S. immigration policy. The court did admit that the result might seem "somewhat peculiar indeed" to compel an employer, based on the National Labor Relations Act, to bargain with a union representing employees that the Immigration Reform and Control Act would require the employers to discharge. The case dealt with a company in Brooklyn, New York, called Agri Processor Company, which is a kosher meat manufacturer. In 2005, the company's workers voted 15-5 to join a union, the United Food and Commercial Workers. Company management, however, refused to bargain with the union because management "discovered" that illegal immigrants dominated their workforce. The company placed the Social Security numbers provided by the employees who voted into the Social Security Administration's database, and determined that the most of the numbers were either nonexistent or belonged to other persons. Consequently, the company argued to the National Labor Relations Board that undocumented workers should not legally count as employees who were protected by the National Labor Relations Act. The National Labor Relations Board rejected the company's argument, ruled that even if illegal, undocumented employees could have a collective bargaining vote, and ordered the company to bargain with the union. The company then appealed the Board decision to the federal appellate court in the District of Columbia, which has jurisdiction over all federal regulatory agencies. The company contended that the 1986 Immigration and Reform Control Act made it illegal for a company to knowingly hire undocumented workers. The court agreed with the National Labor Relations Board, however. The court noted, the *Herald* reported, that the authors of the immigration law explicitly stated that the law was not intended to undermine or to diminish labor protections in existing law. Also, the court noted that Congress in enacting the immigration law did not indicate any intention to change the National Labor Relation Act's coverage of employees. The court concluded that it was "entirely reasonable" to include illegal workers within the meaning of "employee" under federal labor law. The *Miami Herald* noted that estimates indicate that six million companies in the U.S. employ up to seven million illegal immigrants.

Bibliography:

Doyle, Michael, "Rulings diverge on laborer rights," *The Miami Herald*, January 9, 2008, p. 3A.

Questions for Discussion:

1. Do you agree with the appellate court's legal conclusion that it is "entirely reasonable" to include undocumented workers within the meaning of "employee" for the purposes of labor law? Why or why not?

2. Is the appellate court's decision a moral one pursuant to Utilitarian ethics? Discuss.

3. Is the appellate court's decision a moral one pursuant to Kantian ethics? Discuss.

4. From the employer's perspective, how should this paradox be resolved using the principles of Value Driven Management? Discuss.

7. Discrimination

Case 7.1: Challenges Facing Retailers: Wal-Mart's Gender Discrimination Case

A federal discrimination lawsuit has been filed against Wal-Mart, the nation's largest employer, accusing the company of violating civil rights law by favoring men over women in promotions and pay.

The plaintiffs' lawyers want the lawsuit to include all 700,000 women who worked at Wal-Mart from 1996 to 2001, which would make this lawsuit by far the largest employment discrimination case in U.S. history. The lawyers intend to file their motion for class certification in April of 2003.

The lawsuit was originally filed in 2001 in federal court in San Francisco. The suit is predominantly based on one statistic compiled by the plaintiffs' experts. In 2001, the lawsuit claims, women made up 65% of Wal-Mart's hourly employees, but only 35% of the company's managers.

The lawsuit also claims wide disparities in pay. One of the plaintiffs' experts, a university statistics professor, found that full-time women hourly employees working at least 45 weeks at Wal-Mart made about $1,150 less per year than men in similar jobs, a 6.2% gap. Women store managers, the professor found, made an average of $89,280 a year, $16,400 less than men. Another expert for the plaintiffs, a sociology professor, found that women made up 89.5% of Wal-Mart's cashiers, 79% of department heads, but only 37.6% of assistant store managers, and 11.5% of the company's store managers. The lawsuit also claims that among the other 20 large retailers, 57% of the managers are women. Hourly jobs at Wal-Mart pay an average of about $18,000 a year, while the average managerial job pays $50,000.

One of the lawyers for the plaintiffs contends that there are enormous disparities in the rate of promotions for men and women. He declares that there is "strong evidence" that the company is "mistreating" women, because they are women.

Wal-Mart officials, however, have condemned the lawsuit as "baseless," asserting that the lawsuit reflects efforts by the lawyers to "squeeze" a company that has very "deep pockets." Wal-Mart has 3,300 stores, including Sam's Clubs, and annual revenues of more than $230 billion. The company's vice-president for communication stated that the company does not discriminate against anyone, including women; and she also questioned the statistics put forth by the plaintiffs' lawyers. She said that the company would provide its own statistical report to the judge in March. She said, finally, that women's lack of interest in managerial jobs helped to explain the lower percentage of women managers. As an illustration, she related that when Wal-Mart posted notices company-wide in January inviting workers to apply to become management trainees, only 43% of those who expressed interest were women. She also stated that it was her belief that women did not want to work the odd shifts, such as working all night long, Saturdays, and Sundays.

Yet one of the plaintiffs, in a deposition, stated that a man was promoted to a manger's position over a more qualified woman candidate because "he has a family to support." Another woman plaintiff testifies that a department manager in South Carolina explained to her that Wal-Mart paid men more because the Bible states that God created

Adam before Eve. Another woman plaintiff related that one of the male managers told her that being a manager "maybe is not something for women because it means you have to be away from home a long time each day." The plaintiffs' lawyers contend that promotions at Wal-Mart often rely on favoritism and the "buddy network."

This new sex discrimination lawsuit is just one of a growing number of legal challenges to working conditions at Wal-Mart, which has more than one million workers in the United States. So far the lawsuits have made little legal headway; but there are many lawsuits pending, including 40 that accuse the company of pressuring or forcing employees to work unpaid hours off-the-clock. Wal-Mart officials deride all these lawsuits.

The nation's largest private employer, Wal-Mart Stores, Inc. currently is being sued by six former employees who contend that the company discriminates against them based on sex. The lawsuit, originally filed in 2001, seeks a judicial order ending the allegedly discriminatory practices at the company as well as lost wages, though the lawsuit does not list a dollar amount. Yet, what really concerns the company is the fact that a federal judge in San Francisco, Judge Martin Jenkins, will soon be hearing arguments by the women plaintiffs that the suit should be elevated into a class action lawsuit involving all current and former female employees in the U.S. since December 1998. Such a judicial certification would add 1.5 million plaintiffs to the case, and make the lawsuit against the nation's largest retailer the largest civil rights suit ever, and potentially costing the company tens, if not hundreds, of millions of dollars.

The female plaintiffs contend that the Arkansas-based company discriminated against them in pay and promotions because of their gender. They argue that the company's tight central control of its stores and one million employees in the U.S. means that a Wal-Mart "culture" favors men over women in pay and promotions as well as status. The lawsuit includes statements from women across the country who claim they were subject to unfair treatment. Some eventually were promoted to management, but nonetheless they still claim that they were kept from moving up to levels they deserved because they are women. They also contend that department employees were segregated by gender—men in electronics and sporting goods, and women at the registers—and also that the majority of managers were men. One woman, a female cashier, was turned down for a merit raise by a manager, who explained that the men were at the company to make a career whereas the women were merely housewives who needed to make some extra money in retail. The plaintiffs state that 2/3rds of the company's hourly employees are women, yet they make up only a small percentage of its salaried managers. They also contend that women earn 5% to 15% less than men in the same jobs. The plaintiffs also say that their data indicates that only 14% of Wal-Mart store managers—the top jobs at local stores—are women. Moreover, they say that women in Wal-Mart's management are paid less. In fact, male store managers average a salary of $105,682—18% more than the $89,280 female managers average. Finally, the women plaintiffs point out that the average proportion of women in managerial positions at the country's largest retailers is some 20 percentage points higher than at Wal-Mart.

The company acknowledges that there have been individual instances of employees being treated unfairly, but it denies that any discrimination filtered down from headquarters in Arkansas. The company also says it pays its employees fairly, but that women do not apply for promotions as readily as men do; and that women who do apply are more likely to get promotions than men. The company also says that it is working diligently to increase the number of positions in management. The company notes, moreover, that men and women managers earn about the same when store size and profitability are taken into account. In nine out of ten stores, the company points out, men and women earn roughly the same salary in similar hourly job categories. Finally, the company notes that when men and women are paid differently, in about one-half the stores, men are better paid, but in the other stores, women are better paid.

Some of the nation's largest retailers, such as Publix, Albertsons, RadioShack, and Dollar General Corp., have also been confronting a multitude of lawsuits alleging that the companies were/are using low-level managers to do the work of regular employees, so as to avoid paying overtime wages. For example, in mid 1990s, Publix settled a gender discrimination case out of court for $85 million. Other retailers have had similar cases which are, at times, settled quickly to reduce the negative publicity.

Lawsuits demanding the payment of overtime wages to white-collar employees have tripled since 1997, according to the Administrative Office of the U.S. Courts. White-collar workers have filed 102 group overtime suits in 2003, compared to 31 in 1997. Groups that sued included managers with few managerial duties who had been told they were ineligible for time-and-a-half pay after 40 hours. The essence of the lawsuits is that the managerial titles of the employees has been misused and abused by the retail employers.

Wal-Mart now faces 30 overtime-related lawsuits on behalf of workers in 28 states. Assistant managers, who filed lawsuits in Michigan and California seeking back pay and damages, contend they spend much of their days on the same tasks assigned to hourly employees legally entitled to overtime pay.

The suits claim there is very little difference between the job duties of the assistant managers and the hourly employees, especially the nighttime assistant managers. According to one legal document, the managerial employees are "simply glorified stockers" who unload trucks, move products, and stock the shelves.

The retailers deny any legal wrongdoing. Pursuant to federal labor law, managers may be entitled to overtime if more than 40% of their time is not spent managing or supervising, or if their jobs do not include decision-making.

As businesses seek to control labor costs to stay competitive, the practice of excluding low-level managers from overtime pay has increased materially, and not only in the retail sector, but also in the restaurant, insurance, and financial services sectors. The practice has been exacerbated in recent times by the weak economy and also concomitantly by the large pool of workers very anxious and eager to secure and keep their positions. Labor costs, of course, can have a large impact on what firms charge for their products and services, especially in the retail sector, particularly in the retail sector where shoppers are always looking for bargains. Wal-Mart, for example, attempts to maintain labor costs at a slim 8% of sales, compared to 9-10% for other large-store retailers. The company also encourages its store managers to reduce labor costs each year by about 0.2-0.3%, according to legal documents. In 2003, Wal-Mart posted sales of $256 billion and net profit of $9 billion.

The Labor Department, in 2003, attempted to revise overtime rules, in part to try to clarify the numerous legal questions concerning exactly who is entitled to overtime pay. The new rules ensure overtime pay to managers and supervisors earning less than $22,660 a year, and deny it to those administrators earning more than $100,000 annually. The rules also exclude a number of employees within that range from claiming overtime.

In another lawsuit, involving RadioShack, the plaintiff managers, who are required to work at least 52 hours a week, contend that they spend most of their time selling merchandise and that they possess very little real supervisory authority. Approximately 40% of the company's roughly 7000 managers have joined the lawsuit. RadioShack, as a matter of fact, had settled a similar lawsuit in California state court in 2002 for about $20 million on behalf of 1200 managers. The company, however, did not admit any wrongdoing in settling the California lawsuit. Under California law, managers who spend less than 50% of their time supervising other employees and doing other administrative tasks are entitled to overtime pay. In January of 2004, three assistant managers filed a lawsuit in California, contending that they were illegally denied overtime pay. These lawsuits are seeking class action status.

Similarly, in 2002, a Dollar General manager filed a lawsuit in federal court, claiming that she worked up to 90 hours a week without receiving overtime pay, bonuses, vacation or sick time. In January of 2003, the federal court certified the lawsuit as a class action for those employees who wished to join the suit.

In 2000, Wal-Mart settled for $50 million an overtime-related lawsuit in Colorado on behalf of 67,000 hourly workers.

Wal-Mart disputes its assistant managers' assertions. The company contends that its managers' time is largely utilized by interviewing job candidates, composing schedules, and engaging in other supervisory responsibilities. A company spokesperson declared that the company is very cost-conscious and thus would not require its most expensive workers to spend the bulk of their time on hourly tasks.

Yet, in order to save money, and to stay within a store's labor budget, Wal-Mart district managers have encouraged store managers to send hourly workers home early. Consequently, many assistant managers, who are required to work at least 48 hours a week, claim they may have to stay on the job for as much as 75 hours a week, in order to compensate for the hourly employees sent home. Of course, if hourly workers are sent home, and a store becomes busy, customer service suffers. For example, as reported by one Wal-Mart executive, who when shopping at a store one Friday afternoon, found impossibly long lines at the register, and, upon inquiring, was told that the store had over spent its labor budget for the month and the district managers had sent workers home.

Another Wal-Mart assistant manager, who stated she was required to work more than 48 hours a week, and who spent most of her time on routine tasks performed by hourly workers, changed her work status, at her own request, to an hourly employee.

In another store, in Michigan, an assistant manager stated that in order to keep the stores on budget, as many as a third of the employees were sent home in the middle of their shift. This manager also stated that in addition to telling the hourly employees to go home, the assistant managers were expected to perform the tasks of the hourly employees. Some days, she stated, she spent a full eight hour shift at the cash register. Although she believed her job was to train, mentor, and supervise employees, she stated that she spent less than 30% of her time with these managerial functions.

The average store manager at Wal-Mart earns about $100,000 a year; assistant manager salaries range from about $30,000 to more than $45,000 a year; and full-time hourly workers make about $9 an hour. Wal-Mart employs about 17,000 assistant managers in the United States.

The lawsuits reveal that the assistant managers are often placed in a difficult position. In order to get the required work done, they either have to compel hourly employees to work "off the clock," naturally creating another set of potential legal problems, or they have to pick up the slack themselves, thereby putting in very long and under-compensated hours. The assistant managers also relate that it is futile for them to complain to store managers, because the store managers have a very strong incentive to keep labor costs low; and that half of a store manager's compensation comes in a bonus tied to store profits.

Wal-Mart Stores, the world's largest retailer, confronting lawsuits alleging gender discrimination in pay and promotions, abuse of overtime pay, and unfair treatment of workers, announced in June 2004 a series of reforms to promote women to management and to install a new pay system that would be fairer to employees.

In one sex discrimination lawsuit, now seeking class action status, the company is accused of paying women less than their male counterparts, as well as segregating women into lower paying non-managerial positions. The company also has been accused of compelling employees to work off the clock, and for forcing assistant managers to perform the tasks of hourly employees but without paying them overtime pay. Wal-Mart also has recently experienced fierce opposition from some communities attempting to block the company from building stores in its neighborhoods.

Chief Executive Lee Scott announced at the company's annual meeting that executive bonuses, including his own, would be cut 7.5% this year and 15% next year if the company does not promote women and minorities in proportion to the number that apply for management positions. He stated, as an example, that if 50% of the people applying for the job of a store manager are woman, the company will make sure that 50% of the people receiving those jobs are women.

He also announced changes in job classifications and pay structure for employees that would help keep pay fair and enable the company to stay competitive in wages. As part of the pay reform, the company commissioned a study of its hourly positions as well as local and national market conditions. One objective of the reforms is to minimize the discretion managers have in setting pay and salary levels. Wal-Mart also created a compliance office that now has 140 people working to ensure that the company follows laws, rules, and procedures. The company has 1.5 million workers worldwide and they are likely to be hiring another 400,000 employees in the next four to five years based on historical growth trends.

The details of the pay plan remain sketchy so far, but apparently workers will be divided into seven classes. Starting wages would be clearly defined. There would be a pay cap per class, which could be a disadvantage for long-time workers. Merit raises, moreover, would be limited to about 5% of store employees. In addition, annual raises would be set at a flat rate, not a percentage of salary, which might be another negative consequence for veteran employees. Workers with a "standard" evaluation would get 40 cents an hour more, whereas those with "above standard" evaluations would get 55 cents more. One observer predicted that the pay plan would save the company money in the long-run because it would increase the turnover of senior employees.

Some critics were skeptical, however, with one saying that the reforms did not seem like a "huge improvement" for the company's employees. The United Food and Commercial Workers Union is particularly skeptical. One union organizer relates that Wal-Mart workers were told by management that the new pay plan was "just like a union contract." So far, the union has failed to organize a single Wal-Mart store.

Bibliography:

Business Week, March 3, 2003, pp. 63, 66, June 14, 2004, p. 39.

The Miami Herald, June 5, 2004, pp. 1C, 3C.

Sun Sentinel, May 27, 2004, pp. D1, D8, June 5, 2004, p. 10b.

Wall Street Journal, May 26, 2004, pp. A1, A2, June 4, 2004, p. A8.

Questions for Discussion:

1. How should these lawsuits be resolved—legally, morally, and practically? Discuss.

2. Is it legal for Wal-Mart to engage in proportion gender-based hiring or is this policy an impermissible quota and thus illegal reverse discrimination under the Civil Rights Act? Discuss. Even if it is legal, is such a policy moral? Why or why not?

3. Is it moral pursuant to ethical egoism, Utilitarian, and Kantian ethics for executive bonuses to be tied to increased diversity hiring and promotion efforts? Discuss.

4. Does curtailing the discretion of managers to set pay and salary scales "pass" the Value-Driven Management "test"? What about the proportional hiring reform? Why or why not?

5. Discuss how other retailers such as RadioShack, Albertsons, and Publix have responded to such unfair practices which hinder the progress of women from rising to the top positions at the same rate as their male counterparts.

6. What are some best practices that companies outside of the retail industry have used to make sure their hiring and promotional decisions are fair to all individuals?

Case 7.2: Age Discrimination and Pilots—U.S. v. International Law

The *Miami Herald* newspaper reported in November of 2006 that a recent change in an international law regarding the mandatory age of pilots has brought to the attention of the public, the airline industry, and government regulators the always contentious issue of the mandatory retirement age for pilots, which has been established in the U.S., for almost a half a century, by government edit at age 60.

Many pilots, particularly those reaching 60, say that it is time to change the rule, which was promulgated by the Federal Aviation Administration (FAA). The *Miami Herald* reported that several pilots have been lobbying members of Congress to get the mandatory retirement rule changed. In November of 2006, a new international rule went into effect, which permits foreign pilots to fly up to age 65, as well as to fly into the United States so long as they have co-pilots who are no older than 59. The change was implemented by the International Civil Aviation Organization, which is a United Nations agency. The rule affects pilots in all but four countries: the U.S., France, Pakistan, and Colombia.

Currently, there is legislation pending in Congress that would replicate the international policy for the United States. The proposed law would allow pilots between the ages of 60-65 to fly if their second pilot is younger than 60. As a response to pressure from the pilots as well as from members of Congress, the FAA has commissioned a panel of aviation experts and medical authorities to determine whether the age requirement should be relaxed. Proponents of the rule state that there is a growing body of medical data to indicate that safety risks from older pilots are non-existent. However, opponents of changing the rule contend that any change could be disastrous to the flying public.

What is most interesting is that the retirement issue has produced deep and vocal divisions within the airline industry and even among pilots. American Airlines, for example, as well as the Allied Pilots Association, which represents 10,000 American Airline pilots, oppose the change. Also opposed is the Air Line Pilots Association, which is the nation's largest pilots' union, with 61,000 members from 40 airlines. The communications director for the Allied Pilots Association said the main reason to oppose any change is safety. He explained that since the 60-year-old retirement rule was promulgated, not a single accident has been attributed to the subtle or sudden effect of aging. Moreover, a spokeswoman for American Airlines stated that the rule has served the industry well; and that American Airlines thus does not support changing the rule. However, Southwest Airlines and the 5,300 member Southwest Airlines Pilots Association as well as Jet Blue Airways, with 11,000 crew members, have called for a repeal of the age limit. Southwest's chairman stated that the skills of airline pilots do not arbitrarily end at age 60.

The *Miami Herald* related that advocates of the repeal have drawn support from research showing that medical advances over the past several decades have considerably improved health and vitality. According to one study noted in the *Miami Herald,* a male pilot nearing 60 when the FAA rule was enacted could expect to live to nearly 76. Today, the life expectancy for a 60 year old pilot is 80.2 for men and 83.5 for women. A representative for the AARP also noted that the older pilots are the ones with the most experience. However, to complicate matters, many of the pilots are concerned that their pension plans could be adversely affected by changing the retirement age. Also, younger pilots may have a stake in preserving the retirement age since it would remove older pilots, and thereby offer promotion opportunities. The Air Line Pilots Association has officially supported the retirement rule since 1980. However, the *Miami Herald* related that a poll released in 2005 showed a divided membership, with 56% favoring the current age rule and 42% advocating change.

Bibliography:

Montgomery, Dave, "U.S. pilots battle over low age cap," *The Miami Herald*, November 23, 2006, pp. 1C, 2C.

Questions for Discussion:

1. Should U.S. law be changed to conform to international law regarding the mandatory retirement age for pilots? Why or why not?

2. Is the U.S. law illegal age discrimination? Why or why not?

3. Is the U.S. law immoral age discrimination pursuant to Utilitarian and Kantian ethics? Discuss.

4. How would a major airline approach this issue using the principles of Value-Driven Management? Discuss.

Case 7.3: Accommodating Muslim Employees: The Pork Product Sale and Taxi Liquor Controversies

It is estimated that about ten million people in the United States are Muslims. Some of these individuals are first or second generation Americans, and others might have migrated to the United States during their college period or professional working adult years. Thousands of these American Muslims are working side by side with people of diverse religious beliefs in the corporate arena, government, transportation industry, the retail environment, etc. Most employers are, of course, doing all that they can to accommodate the needs of their religiously diverse employees as these associates serve their religiously diverse customers. As most managers and entrepreneurs know, the U.S. Civil Rights Act prohibits discrimination based on religion and imposes a legal obligation or duty on employers to make a "Reasonable Accommodation" to their employees' diverse religious beliefs and practices. This case discusses two such dilemmas that Muslim employees face in the American workplace: 1) dealing with pork and pork-related products; 2) producing, selling, serving, or being a part of a team that serves alcohol products.

The *Miami Herald* newspaper reported in March of 2007 a religious controversy, originally reported in the Minneapolis Star, involving Target Corporation and certain Muslim employees in its Minnesota stores. Target is reassigning its Muslim employees who are cashiers but who refuse to scan or ring up bacon and other pork products, such as pepperoni pizza, due to religious reasons. The cashiers have been reassigned to other jobs in the stores. The Muslim employees would call other cashiers to deal with the pork products, or in some situations, would actually ask customers to scan the pork products themselves. When Target's reassignment response became known publicly, the newspapers reported that some customers called to complain, and a few even called for a general boycott of Target. Initially, Target had asked the Muslim employees who were cashiers and who were offended by the pork products to wear gloves or to transfer to other areas of the store. A Target spokesperson, as related by the newspapers, stated that the company's response was a "reasonable solution for our guests and team members." The newspapers also reported that it remained unclear whether the affected employees' wages would be impacted by any job transfers or reassignments, though generally cashier positions can be entry level, or lower-paying positions at most retailers.

Target is attempting to balance the religious rights of its employees with customer demands for service. The U.S. Civil Rights Act not only prohibits discrimination based on religion but also imposes a legal duty on employers to make a "reasonable accommodation" to its employees' religious beliefs and practices. However, an employer is not legally obligated to make any accommodation if it would be an "undue burden" or "undue hardship" to do so. The newspapers reported that some Muslims in the Twin Cities area said that Target was "overreacting to public pressure," and that the stores should be able to accommodate the religious beliefs of Muslim cashiers without disrupting service. The papers also reported that a professor of Islamic law at the University of Minnesota stated that the controversy "is being blown way out of proportion." The professor asserted that pork products represent a very small percentage of the store's overall products; and thus an accommodation could have been made.

From a religious perspective, and for the past 1,400 years, Muslims have been prohibited from eating pork. Muslims believe that the pig is an unclean animal, and thus consider it a sin to eat pork. Some Muslims feel so strongly about the issue that they not only will not touch, let alone eat pork, but also consider it sinful to sell pork products, because to do so would be to encourage as well as aid and abet others to commit sinful acts. Yet some Islamic scholars maintain that Islam does prohibit consuming pork, but not touching or scanning it. Target has stated that it has tried to accommodate its employees' religious beliefs, but so far unsuccessfully; and thus the company is now reassigning the cashiers and other employees to other jobs.

Moreover, the *Wall Street Journal* reported in March of 2007 another religious controversy involving Muslims. This controversy, also arising in Minneapolis, arose when taxi drivers at the Minneapolis-St. Paul International Airport, about 3/4s of who are Muslims, have begun to refuse to transport passengers carrying alcohol. The Journal reported that one woman traveler, returning from France with wine, was turned down by five cabs in succession. The Journal also reported that refusals for transportation service now number approximately 100 per month, and also that "heated altercations" have ensued. In an attempt to accommodate the religious beliefs of the cab drivers, the Journal reported that the Metropolitan Airport Commission has proposed a two color top-light pilot project in order to indicate which cab drivers would accept passengers with alcohol. Some Islamic scholars maintain that Islam prohibits the consumption of alcohol, but not its transportation. Yet, as reported in the *Wall Street Journal*, the Minnesota chapter of the Muslim American Society issued a "fatwa," that is, a religious decree, forbidding drivers in their community from carrying alcohol in order to avoid "cooperating in sin."

Most interestingly, the *Wall Street Journal* reported that these controversies arose in Minnesota because that state now has a very large immigrant population (in the "tens of thousands") from Somalia, many of whom are Muslims.

Bibliography:

Opinion, "Shariah in Minnesota"? *The Wall Street Journal*, March 24-25, 2007, p. A10.

Serres, Chris, and McKinney, Matt, "Target stores reassign Muslim cashiers who avoid pork," *The Miami Herald*, March 19, 2007, p. 3A.

Questions for Discussion:

1. What is the reasonable accommodation that Target should make to its Muslim employees' religious beliefs? What would be an "undue burden" or "hardship" for Target in this situation? Discuss.

2. What is the moral solution to this pork product controversy? Discuss from ethical perspectives.

3. How should the socially responsible retail company deal with its employees' religious beliefs and practices?

4. How should this pork product controversy be resolved from a Value Driven Management analytical standpoint? Discuss.

5. What is the reasonable accommodation that airport should make to its Muslim cab drivers' religious beliefs? What would be an "undue burden" or "hardship" for the airport in this situation? Discuss.

6. What is the moral solution to this airport–taxi controversy? Discuss from ethical perspectives.

7. How should the socially responsible airport authority deal with its employees' and its cab drivers' religious beliefs and practices?

8. How should this airport–taxi controversy be resolved from a Value-Driven Management analytical standpoint? Discuss.

9. Some people (non-Muslims) believe that they should not work on Sundays since their religious beliefs discourage them from doing so as this is their family and worship time. How should employers deal with these employees?

Case 7.4: Wal-Mart Sex Discrimination Lawsuit— U.S. Court of Appeals Decision

The *Wall Street Journal* and the *Sun-Sentinel* newspaper of Ft. Lauderdale reported in February of 2007 that Wal-Mart, the world's largest private employer, now must confront a class action lawsuit alleging that more than 1.5 million female workers were discriminated against regarding wages and promotions due to their gender. A federal appeals court, specifically the 9th Circuit U.S. Court of Appeals, ruled in a 2-1 holding that a decision by a federal district court judge to allow the lawsuit should be upheld, and thus the lawsuit should proceed to a trial, thereby exposing the giant retailer to potentially billions of dollars in damages. As reported in the *Sun-Sentinel*, the appeals court ruled that the evidence presented in the district court trial, which included anecdotal and statistical evidence in addition to factual evidence and expert opinions, "present(ed) significant proof of a corporate policy of discrimination and support plaintiff's contention that female employees were subjected to a common pattern and practice of discrimination." The federal district court judge ruled in particular that there was sufficient anecdotal evidence of discrimination for the lawsuit to proceed as a class action one. Wal-Mart had argued that there should individual hearings for each plaintiff to ascertain if any discriminatory practices were committed. That is, the company argued that the individual women plaintiffs should sue individual stores. The federal district court judge rejected Wal-Mart's assertions. The appeals court did note, however, that the class was very large, but the judge writing for the majority stated, as quoted in the *Sun-Sentinel*, that "mere size does not render a case unmanageable." Also, the appeals court stated that the class action suit would be a better vehicle for legal redress since individual lawsuits would be, as quoted in the *Wall Street Journal*, "clogging the federal courts with innumerable individual lawsuits." A dissenting judge on the court of appeals stated that the individual women plaintiffs should file individual lawsuits so as to safeguard Wal-Mart from paying women who do not deserve any money. Moreover the dissenting judge stated that individual lawsuits would ensure that the aggrieved women obtain the compensation they deserve. The lawsuit was originally filed in 2001 by six female employees of Wal-Mart who alleged that that the company systematically paid its female employees less than male employees with similar qualifications, and that the company frequently overlooked women for promotions. The plaintiffs' statistical evidence demonstrated that Wal-Mart paid women employees 5% to 15% less than men in comparable positions. The federal district court judge not only agreed with the plaintiffs, but also ruled that the lawsuit could apply to all women who worked at Wal-Mart since December 1998. The *Wall Street Journal*, reporting in February of 2007, reported that the number of women potentially eligible to be in the class has now risen to almost two million.

Wal-Mart stated that it would petition the Court of Appeals to rehear the case with all 15 9th Circuit judges. Wal-Mart, as reported in the *Wall Street Journal*, declined any talks of settlement; and further stated that it would pursue an appeal to the U.S. Supreme Court if necessary. A company attorney was quoted in the *Journal* stating that the legal process was going to be a "long one," and that the company was "very optimistic" in securing redress from the Court of Appeals' decision. The attorney also related that Wal-Mart's own review found no significant difference in pay between men and women at 90% of its stores. The company has steadfastly stated that it did not and does not have a policy of discriminating against women. The company said that the courts mistakenly looked at company wide data, and not data from individual stores; and that pay and promotion decisions are made at the local store level by individual managers. The company asserted that the data shows that individual stores did not discriminate against women. Moreover, regarding the class action status of the lawsuit, the company contended that class action status was not appropriate because its 3,400 stores, including Sam's Club warehouse out-lets, operate like independent businesses.

The dissenting judge in the Court of Appeals decision declared that the size of the class would compel Wal-Mart to settle the lawsuit. Since the potential damages are "stratospheric," a "rational defendant will settle even the most unjust claim," stated the judge in his dissent, as reported in the *Wall Street Journal*.

Bibliography:

Kravets, David, "Lawsuit moves forward," *Sun-Sentinel*, February 7, 2007, pp. 1D, 2D.

McWilliams, Gary, and Zimmerman, Ann, The *Wall Street Journal*, February 7, 2007, p. A3.

Questions for Discussion:

1. In the early 1990's, a similar gender case was settled out of court by Publix Super Markets in the Tampa Bay area of Florida. The Publix case involved over 100,000 female employees and the company agreed to pay about $85 million dollars to set-tle it. Why didn't Wal-Mart managers learn from the case of Publix? What could have Wal-Mart managers learned from the improvements Publix made to enhance the promotional opportunities for female employees? Discuss.

2. Discuss the legal issues involved in this sex discrimination lawsuit. Specifically, how much evidence would be necessary to find a company wide pattern of discrimi-nation? Was the decision to certify this lawsuit as a class action one correct? Why or why not?

3. Discuss the moral issues involved in this lawsuit? Is Wal-Mart being treated fairly? Is it being forced to settle an "unjust" case? Why or why not?

4. Using the principles of Value-Driven Management, how should Wal-Mart respond to this lawsuit? Discuss utilizing stakeholder analysis.

Case 7.5: The Don Imus Legal and Moral Controversy

On April 7, 2004, Don Imus verbalized a racial slur towards the African American female Rutgers basketball team players, calling them "nappy-headed hos." This discriminatory comment perpetuated a significant reaction from the public that led large corporations to pull their advertising business from CBS, as well as resulting in Don Imus' termination of employment. In 1996 Don Imus' *Imus in the Morning* radio show was picked up by MSNBC cable television, by which he continued his controversial "shock-jock" version of news and sports commentary programming. On April 7, 2007, he verbalized a sexist and racial comment towards the predominantly African American Rutgers basketball team. Consequently, the negative public reaction that ensued produced tremendous media coverage, and brought out several well known African American public figures, including, Rev. Al Sharpton, Rev. Jesse Jackson, and Oprah Winfrey, to condemn Imus. Initially CBS suspended Don Imus' show for two weeks. A few days later, he publicly apologized several times for his remarks, not only to the media, but also to the famous public figures and the basketball players themselves. Nevertheless, several large corporations pulled their advertisement business from CBS; and consequently CBS terminated its contract with Don Imus on April 11th, 2007. As a result, in May of 2007, Don Imus filed a lawsuit against CBS, stating that he was terminated without "just cause," and emphasizing that according to his contract, he was hired to be "controversial and irreverent." In addition, the lawsuit further stated that a five second delay was implemented into his programming, thereby allowing CBS to censor him upon their discretion.

There are numerous legal issues surrounding Don Imus and his comment made to the Rutgers female basketball team. Important issues are the meaning of the "shock jock" clause in Imus' contract and whether this clause makes what he said legally permissible. Another issue is whether CBS had "just cause" to terminate Imus, who, in the network's opinion, it did have "just cause" for termination. The underlying legal issue that is entering litigation is whether or not CBS or Imus breached the contract that had been established by both parties. On May 4, 2007, it was announced that Don Imus would file a $40 million lawsuit against CBS for breach of contract. Imus and his attorney, Martin Garbus, argue that CBS provided a clause in the contract that proved that CBS was "creating a shock jock," and thus that Imus was doing exactly what CBS wanted him to do. Garbus also argues that CBS and MSNBC had a delay but which gave them the opportunity to block offensive words before they are broadcast. However, neither of these networks used the delay button to block what Imus said. CBS admits that the company, that is, CBS Radio, acknowledges that Artist's (Imus') services to be rendered hereunder are of unique, extraordinary, irreverent, intellectual, topical, controversial and personal character and that programs of the same general type and nature containing these components are desired by company and are consistent with company rules and policies. The contract that CBS has with Imus also states that CBS can terminate Imus for "just cause." Therefore, the contract situation appears to be a case of ambiguity in the contract, meaning that there was not a clear definition of what controversial and irreverent topics would be considered impermissible. In addition, there was no definition of what is to be considered "just cause," which is what CBS is claiming the termination is based on. Did CBS terminate Imus because of the comments that he made or the reaction of the people? One could question CBS's motives because their initial punishment toward Imus was only a two week suspension. Following Imus' comments, seven of his sponsors pulled their ads or suspended advertising to protest his comments. Only following the revocation of the ads did CBS terminate Imus.

Upon analyzing the Don Imus controversy one can see several negative consequences caused by the inappropriate and racial comment made on his morning show. Those directly involved in this incident include Don Imus, the female Rutgers basketball players, and CBS. Those indirectly involved include Don Imus' family, the families of the players, African-American women and minorities, groups that fully support freedom of speech, such as hip-hop artists, CBS's corporate sponsorship, the Federal Communications Commission, and society at large. Don Imus has been a notable shock jock for over the last 30 years with his popular New York based "Imus in the Morning" radio show. He has made a living with his irreverent, sarcastic, and insulting comments regarding all issues and people. His recent termination and discontinuation of his show will obviously create a negative financial situation for him and his family. In addition, the loss of his identity and notoriety may cause emotional distress as a result of being ostracized by his peers and broadcasting industry. In addition, the current litigation with CBS alleging that they terminated the contractual agreement with Imus without "just cause" may create psychological and physical stress to the popular DJ, in addition to several months of legal battles and attorney fees. Due to Imus' racial remark on April 4th, the players were significantly insulted on simulcast cable television's MSNBC. The racial discrimination and personal attack on these women was perceived as humiliating and degrading to their personal character and ethnic and racial background. The public awareness of this incident has brought repeated attention to this insult, which is likely to continue for some time, and not only in the context of news, but in trendy entertainment venues; and now the case has ended up in the court system. This repeated attention, regrettably, is likely to continue the stigma of humiliation and discrimination upon the female players for some time to come. On a positive note, these African American, female players may take advantage of this attention and forum to promote the removal of inappropriate, indecent and profane language utilized in different forms of media. The leveraging of this unfortunate experience could be the beginning of FCC reform, as well as a message to the African American public that demeaning derogatory remarks towards women will not be tolerated from anyone including their own community. Negative results from Imus' misconducts include CBS's loss of millions of dollars from the discontinuation of his show and cancelled ads by high-profile advertisers, such as Procter & Gamble, General Motors, and American Express. This incident likely will result in thousands of consumer inquiries to the FCC that will initiate a close investigation of CBS's radio communication practices. This negative media attention, as well as the attention brought on by the lawsuit instigated by Don Imus, could significantly decrease CBS's credibility in the short-term. Favorably, CBS's quick termination of Don Imus as a result of the public outcry showed sensitivity and empathy to the African American community, and may have restored some credibility lost with the American public. This may be a good opportunity for CBS to be a pioneer in promoting respectful and professional communication practices that encourage diversity and family values. Don Imus has five children; four from his previous marriage and one from his current wife to whom he has been married to for 13 years. His publicly confessed poor judgment regarding his racial commentary, which surely must have placed emotional stress on the family, as well as creating financial insecurity. Since the incident, several of the family members of the Rutgers team have expressed insult and disgust towards the verbal assault upon their children. Along with their children, they have taken this attack personally. Positively, these parents are voicing their concern towards the defamation of black women, and accordingly are actively encouraging a change in societal behavior in the media and in their own community. Don Imus' comments were directed towards the Rutgers players; however, their impact clearly affected a huge minority community, as well as society-at-large. People of all colors, religion, and ethnicity felt the outrage, as the comments left any group or upstanding individual vulnerable to public insult and embarrassment.

The FCC prohibits any obscene, indecent, or profane language on the radio, specifically during the "safe harbor" times between 10pm and 6am; however, it does not monitor programming or performers. The FCC enforces these rules through a system of radio listener complaints. Therefore, it is likely that the initial flood of complaints to the FCC will eventually subside as people become immune to the derogatory communications commonly heard on the radio. The result may be that negative attention and possible censorship of the radio medium will be short-lived, unless the public makes this now very controversial issue a permanent object of attention. Although society as a whole many have experienced a brief negative impact by Imus's action, this action has encouraged needed attention towards this controversy; and therefore may have created a "fresh look" at where the United States is heading regarding the permissible limits of freedom of speech, and especially the effect of certain controversial speech on the country's younger, future generations. The dialogue that ensued after the incident by all segments of society could be construed as a "healthy conversation" that brought up several interesting points. Points that included FCC reform, freedom of speech, reality television, the media, hip-hop culture, and prison values. It is safe to assume that a large segment of the listeners obtained value from the *Imus in the Morning Show,* whether through affirmation with his views, curiosity towards the programming, or "enjoyable disgust" by his irreverent chatter. Yet it is safe to assume that there is also an equally large cultural segment that would never listen to his show as it violates standards of morality and decency. This fact is evident by the comments made by several community spokespersons, such as the Reverends Al Sharpton and Jesse Jackson, Oprah Winfrey, and others. However, even though every person has a right to choose which radio programming to listen to, the mere existence of such programming can be offensive and devaluing to some. The complexity arises in that his racial slur offended even Imus loyal listeners. Even among those with a great tolerance for controversial dialogue and who fully support protected speech, many radio and television listeners were offended by Imus' racist diatribe.

CBS was the contractual owner of Don Imus and the *Imus in the Morning Show,* as well as the supplier through its relationship with MSNBC and radio affiliates. Although the network principals and affiliates would vehemently disagree in public with Don Imus's many political and social views, it could be argued that there was an express or at least a tacit agreement concerning this type of contentious programming due to the network's contractual arrangement with Don Imus. It can also be assumed that CBS was concerned with the consequences of supporting such programming, and thus implemented a five second delay during the programming of the show. The corporate responsibility statement of CBS, it should be underscored, states, "*Responsible programming and diversity are initiatives that we take very seriously at CBS Corporation.*" Due to the fact that the five second delay was not utilized by CBS producers, therefore permitting the racial derogatory statement to be aired, could indicate that the true values or purpose of CBS through the programming of this show was to appeal to a segment of the external culture for the purpose of generating revenue and ratings. Under the precise rules of the FCC, which specifies in detail the specifications of obscene, indecent, or profane language, it is arguable that the comment made by Don Imus did not qualify as a violation in any of these three categories.

In 1968, Don Imus entrepreneurially began a very successful career marketing his coarse and controversial wit on the airwaves. He has effectively branded himself as a broadcaster who is known for his frank and unpretentious social and political commentary, as well as unusual pranks. Don Imus achieved his fame through the public dissemination of his personal values and opinions; and accordingly it very easy to understand what drives him as he is in the business of "letting you know" exactly what he thinks. One very significant value, therefore, to Mr. Imus and other "Shock Jock" broadcasters is to promote the debate of freedom of speech and the permissible limits to program censorship. Don Imus and other daring broadcasters definitely test the limits of free speech as well as societal norms. Though Don Imus may have demonstrated an evident lack of judgment with his choice of words, it could be argues that he was basically "handed a license" to do so in conformity to his contract with CBS. CBS was aware of the possibility of a "Freudian slip," and thus could have implemented the five second delay that the network had failed to be used. Therefore, it could be argues that CBS could have possibly been at greater fault for airing the racial slur. The CBS Corporation does have a corporate responsibility policy where the network places its efforts and commitment on community outreach, public service announcements, responsible programming, and diversity. According to CBS, these are initiatives that they take seriously and are also what they feel are the "core" of what it means to be a public trust. CBS has also established the CBS Business Conduct Statement, which is a statement of ethical and legal standards that all CBS employees and directors must abide by. Based on CBS's social responsibility policy and the definition of social responsibility, CBS has a responsibility to protect the welfare of society as it pertains to the media and television. Initially, CBS suspended Imus for two weeks for the comments he made toward the Rutgers female basketball team, which would have enabled him to return to the airways and possibly make further offensive comments in the future. To exercise truly social responsibility, it could be argued that CBS should have terminated Imus immediately following his comments, not following the reactions of the public. It consequently could appear that CBS was only trying to ameliorate the business ramifications of the controversy by trying to appease the growing uproar of the public. In addition, CBS's termination followed seven sponsors pulling their ads from the Imus' show. Those sponsors include General Motors, Staples, Inc., GlaxoSmithKline, Sprint Nextel, PetMed Express, American Express, and Procter & Gamble. Consequently, it could be argued that CBS terminated Imus due to the financial detriment that was caused due to these sponsors pulling their ads as well as the negative reaction of the public, because CBS' termination of Imus followed the loss of sponsorship as well as public protest, not his on-air actions. In addition, Imus' show operated with a five second delay and neither CBS nor MSNBC chose to block Imus' comment, which inaction could imply that they thought that his comments were acceptable. Accordingly, it could be argued that CBS did not take socially responsible actions to protect the welfare of society. Instead, the network allowed

Imus comments to be aired therefore jeopardizing the welfare of society and as well as the individuals at which he directed his comments, the Rutgers female basketball team. Imus, it should be noted, has made negative comments toward African Americans in the past. For example, he has called Bill Rhoden, an African American, *New York Times* sports columnist a "quota hire" and labeled Gwen Ifill of PBS' "Washington Week" as "a cleaning lady." Ifill is also an African American. However, Imus did not limit his negative comments to just African Americans. Imus has referred to Rush Limbaugh as a "fat, pill-popping loser" and refers to Arabs and Muslims as "rag-heads."

Nevertheless, in August of 2007, CBS reached a settlement with Don Imus, reportedly paying him $40 million; and in return Imus' lawyer said that Imus would drop his $120 million breach of contract lawsuit against CBS. Now Imus has more leeway to seek a return to radio elsewhere; and as a matter of fact, the media reported that he was already in talks with WABC radio. Yet, to complicate matters further, one of the members of the Rutgers women's basketball team sued Don Imus and CBS as well as MSNBC for defamation in August of 2007, claiming that Imus' sexist and racist comments about the team were false and slanderous and impugned and damaged her character, chastity, and reputation.

Bibliography:

Brookins, Simone J. and Winchester, Junelle, Research Paper for Management 5015 (Web2), Huizenga School of Business and Entrepreneurship: "The Don Imus Controversy: Legal and Ethical Issues," June 2, 2007.

Perry, Claudia, "Just how low will shock radio go? Please stay tuned," *The Star-Ledger* (New Jersey), August 15, 2007, p. 2.

Questions for Discussion:

1. Did Don Imus act in a legal, moral, and socially responsible manner? Why or why not?
2. Did the CBS network act in a legal, moral, and socially responsible manner? Why or why not?
3. Did the MSNBC network act in a legal, moral, and socially responsible manner? Why or why not?
4. Did CBS' response to this controversy pass the Value-Driven Management test? Why or why not?
5. How should CBS respond to Imus' lawsuit based on the principles of Value-Driven Management? Discuss.
6. Do you agree with CBS' settlement of the Imus breach of contract case? Why or why not?
7. How would you decide the defamation lawsuit? Why?
8. How should CBS and MSNBC respond to the defamation lawsuit using the principles of Value-Driven Management as the decision-making model? Explain.

Case 7.6: Gay Rights, the U.S. Congress, and the Employment Non-Discrimination Act

The United States Civil Rights Act protects against discrimination in employment based on gender, but not discrimination based on sexual preference, orientation, or gender identity. That is, gay, lesbian, transgender, transsexual, cross-dressing, gender identity questioning, and sexually transitioning employees are not protected by the federal statute. The federal courts, although interpreting the Civil Rights Act to include sexual harassment as a form of sex discrimination, have been very reticent to construe the statute to include gender identity as a type of illegal sex discrimination. However, there are now approximately 31 states in the U.S. that, to vary degrees, prohibit discrimination in employment based on sexual orientation and gender identity. Moreover, there is now, as reported by the *Miami Herald* newspaper in September of 2007, a proposed federal law being debated in Congress, called the Employment Non-Discrimination Act (ENDA), which would place discrimination based on sexual orientation and gender identity in the workplace on the same legal level as discrimination based on sex as well as race, color, national origin, religion, age, and disability. Religious and "traditional values" organizations are lobbying against the bill, declaring that it would not only make homosexuality but also confusion about one's sexual identity a protected class under civil rights laws. Despite opposition from conservative groups, the bill has 165 co-sponsors. Proponents of the bill argue that no one should be discriminated against in employment, and perhaps denied a livelihood, because of their sexual preference and identity. The bill's chief sponsor is Massachusetts Democrat Representative Barney Frank, who is openly gay. Another openly gay member of the House, and also a primary sponsor of the bill, Representative Tammy Baldwin of Wisconsin, stated that the bill would protect people from bias based on "irrational prejudice." The bill, she stated, would ensure that an employee is not treated unfairly because she is a woman with masculine characteristics or mannerisms or a man with feminine characteristics or mannerisms. Another House sponsor of the bill argued that there is a strong economic argument for its passage since U.S. employers cannot afford to leave any talented people out of the workplace. However, one House opponent of the bill contended that it would be too far-reaching and place unnecessary burdens on employers and employees. This opponent asked if there is even a need for such a law, since the evidence of gender identity discrimination actually occurring at the workplace is not clear. Another opponent, representing religious groups, argued that the bill would create problems and confusion for religious groups when they make hiring decisions, and also that the bill if it became law would further entangle the government into religion and religious affairs. A vote in the House of Representatives was expected in the late fall of 2007.

In November of 2007, the U.S. House of Representatives passed the Employment Non-Discrimination Act, which is the first federal prohibition on discrimination in employment against gays, lesbians, and transsexuals. However, some gay rights supporters criticized the House for not including transgender employees under the law's protection. The term "transgender" encompasses workers who are transsexuals, cross-dressers, and people whose outward appearance does not match their gender at birth. The law passed by the House would make it illegal for employers to make decisions regarding hiring or firing or promoting or paying employees based on their sexual orientation. The law would exempt the military and religious organizations. Transgender employees were dropped from the law's protection because of fears that the bill would not pass the House vote with transgender protections. The vote in the House was 285-184. However, for the Act to become law, it must also pass the Senate, where passage is predicted to be much more difficult. Nonetheless, Senator Edward Kennedy (D-Massachusetts) plans to introduce a similar version of the House bill in the Senate. Even if the Senate also passes the Act, President Bush has threatened to veto it; the Bush administration and its Congressional supporters contend that the law would contravene constitutional and religious rights as well as engender a new wave of dubious discrimination lawsuits. The House vote indicates that any presidential veto will not be overridden.

Bibliography:

Hotakainen, Rob, "Job bill fueling gay-rights debate," *The Miami Herald*, September 16, 2007, pp. 21A, 23A;

Miga, Andrew, "House approves work protections for gays, lesbians," *Sun-Sentinel*, November 8, 2007, p. 3A.

Questions for Discussion:

1. Should the Senate also pass the Act? If so, should the President veto it? Why or why not?

2. Is the Act constitutional? Why or why not?

3. Is it moral based on Utilitarian and Kantian ethics? Why or why not?

4. Was it moral to exclude transgender employees from the Act's protections? Why or why not?

5. What are some of the problems—legal and practical—that an employer would confront with such a law; and how should these problems be handled? Discuss.

6. Does the Act pass the Value-Driven Management test? Discuss.

7. Even in the absence of a federal and state law prohibiting discrimination based on sexual preference, orientation, and gender identity, how should a socially responsible employer deal with this challenging issue? Discuss.

8. Product Regulation, Pricing, and Marketing

Case 8.1: "Guerrilla Marketing": The Boston "Bomb" Scare

In 2007, as related in the *Wall Street Journal*, Turner Broadcasting Systems, a Time Warner, Inc. division, retained the services of a New York advertising company, Interference, Inc., for a "guerrilla marketing" advertising campaign in order to promote a show on Turner's Cartoon Network. The promoters of the advertising campaign produced a so-called "guerilla marketing" stunt that caused a bomb scare in Boston, Massachusetts. The two men hired by Interference set up bill board boxes around Boston to promote the show. The result, as described by the Journal, was that most of Boston was "seized up," with highway, subway, and river traffic halted, and thousands of people inconvenienced and stressed out. The two men apparently placed about 40 blinking boxes promoting the "Aqua Team Hunger Force" television show near roads, bridges, depots, and other locations. Turner alerted the city's police department in nine other cities where the boxes were also placed, some of them since January 15, and Turner informed the police of their locations. None of the other cities reported any scares; but in Chicago, police worked overnight to remove 20 boxes from elevated train tracks and store fronts.

Now, the two men have been arraigned on criminal charges, and Time Warner is trying to reach a settlement with the city of Boston to compensate the city for its emergency services. The two defendants arraigned were Sean Stevens, 28, and Peter Berdovsky, 27, who were charged with disorderly conduct and with violating a Massachusetts law, passed after the 2001 anthrax scare, that makes it a felony to place a hoax device with the intent to cause "anxiety, unrest, fear, or personal discomfort." A conviction carries a sentence of a maximum prison term of five years. The attorney who represented the two men, as reported by the *Wall Street Journal,* asserted that the requisite intent was lacking. The attorney stated too that he hoped that the judge would dismiss the charges. He also declared that the government's response was an overreaction. The two men were hired by Interference to set up the light boxes and signs, and were paid $300 each for the 40 boxes. Imprinted on each box, as described by the *Journal,* was an angry-looking cartoon character from the television show, which was making an obscene hand gesture. Time Warner is also facing a criminal investigation by the Massachusetts Attorney General's office. "Guerilla marketing" is a term for marketing activities which employ unconventional advertising stunts meant, as termed by the *Wall Street Journal,* to "fly below the radar of the big media." The purpose, according to the *Journal,* is to create a "counter-cultural buzz" about products. The *Journal* reported that Turner is in "talks" with the Massachusetts officials, and was prepared to offer a monetary settlement.

One director of executive education condemned the stunt as an "inexcusable" and "irrational" act, as related by the *Journal.* A professor of marketing ethics condemned the marketing practices for creating devices that appeared to be threatening to public safety. A spokesperson for Turner stated that if the company believed that anyone would have perceived this marketing campaign as a threat, the company would not have done it. The spokesperson said that the marketing campaign was merely a promotion for a television show. One media consultant, however, stated that despite all the bad publicity and expense, the Turner network made out well due to the added publicity. The New York advertising agency, he related, may look very irresponsible for the "bomb" scare "guerrilla marketing" campaign, but Turner has received much more publicity than normally it would have been gotten for a cartoon advertising campaign.

The *Sun-Sentinel* newspaper of Fort Lauderdale, Florida reported in February of 2007 that Turner Broadcasting Systems and the advertising agency agreed to pay $2 million in compensation for planting the devices, and that the head of the cartoon network resigned due to the "gravity" of the situation. The *Sun-Sentinel* also reported that in May of 2007, the two men who planted the electronic devices apologized in court for causing "such anguish and disruption to so many people." They also performed community service at a rehabilitation center and prosecutors then said they would not pursue charges against the two men.

Bibliography:

Lavore, Denis, "Boston men apologize for scare," Sun-Sentinel, May 1, 2007, p. 8A. Levitz, Jennifer, and Steel, Emily, "Boston Stunt Draws Legal, Ethical Fire," *The Wall Street Journal*, February 2, 2007, p. B3; Weber, Harry R., "Turner executive resigns," *Sun-Sentinel*, February 10, 2007, pp. 1D, 2D.

Questions for Discussion:

1. Discuss the legal issues involved in the "bomb" scare. Was criminal intent lacking? Was the government's legal response an "overreaction"? Why or why not?

2. Did Turner Broadcasting and Interference, Inc. act in a moral manner? Discuss.

3. Did the "bomb" scare produce more value overall for Turner Broadcasting? Discuss using the Value-Driven Management decision-making model.

4. What exactly is "guerilla marketing"? Discuss and provide examples and rationales therefore.

Case 8.2: Pizza Hut's "Book It" Program: Childhood Literacy or Obesity?

The *Miami Herald* newspaper reported in 2007 a most interesting reading incentive program sponsored by Pizza Hut, called "Book It." The program has rewarded students in more than 50,000 schools across the United States to reward young readers with free pizzas. The program now extends to about 22 million children a year. So far, the program has given away more than 200 million pizzas. For example, as reported in the *Miami Herald,* in Miami Dade County, there are 145 participating public and private schools. Pizza Hut states that the program is the largest reading motivation program in the United States. It is conducted annually in approximately 925,000 classrooms from October 1 through March 31. There is also a two month program for preschoolers. Schools and teachers that participate in the program set a monthly reading goal for each child; and those students who achieve the goal receive a certificate they can redeem for a free Personal Pan Pizza. Families frequently accompany the student winners to Pizza Hut, and where they all celebrate the child's reading success, and where they often also purchase food and beverages, thereby increasing Pizza Hut's business. As noted in the *Miami Herald,* one elementary school in Montana had about 300 students collectively read 30,000 books a year with Book It's help, according to the school's principal. The program has attained a Presidential citation; and its advisory board includes members from prominent education groups, including teacher unions and the American Library Association.

However, now the program, as reported in the *Miami Herald,* is being criticized by child development experts on the grounds that it promotes bad eating habits, childhood obesity, and turns teachers into corporate promoters. The newspaper reported that a Harvard psychologist and founder of the Campaign for a Commercial-Free Childhood condemned the program as promoting "junk-food consumption to a captive audience. . . in the name of education." This expert also stated that the program "undermines parents" since the program uses family visits to Pizza Hut "as an integral component of raising literate children."

The director of the Pizza Hut program stated that the company is proud of the program; and she related, as reported in the *Miami Herald,* that the company has received hundreds of emails from participants in the program who praise the program, and who state that Book It helped them get started with reading. A Pizza Hut spokesperson also stated that teachers find the program "an enjoyable way to build interest in reading." The spokesperson furthermore stated that the program is helping teachers do their jobs. The aforementioned principal of the Montana school related that he did not have any negative comments about Book It; and he stated that although there are legitimate concerns about childhood obesity, the program and the schools are not causing obesity in children. Another principal at a Florida elementary school stated that the program not only provides a means to persuade children to read books as opposed to playing video games. In addition, he stated that the program encourages "family togetherness." He stated finally that the positive effects of the program outweigh any negative consequences.

Bibliography:

Crary, David, "Critics blast Pizza Hut pies as prize for young readers," *The Miami Herald*, March 3, 2007, p. 4A.

Questions for Discussion:

1. What are the legal concerns in the Book It program? Discuss.
2. Is the Book It program moral pursuant to Utilitarian ethics? Why or why not? Do agree with the principal that the positive effects outweigh any negative consequences? Why or why not?
3. Is the program moral pursuant to Kantian ethics? Why or why not?
4. Is it a good example of Corporate Social Responsibility? Why or why not?
5. Does it pass the Value-Driven Management test? Why or why not?

Case 8.3: Advertising: The "In An Absolut World" Controversy

FOX News online reported in April of 2008 that the Absolut Vodka Company apologized for a market campaign that featured an advertisement that depicted the Southwestern part of the United States as part of Mexico. The advertising campaign, called "In An Absolut World," showed an 1830s era map when Texas and California as well as several other Southwestern states were part of Mexico. Mexico lost that huge territory in the 1840 war between the U.S. and Mexico and the War of Texas Independence. Many Mexicans still resent the loss of their territory to the United States. The ads had only been used by the company in Mexico, but they still generated a great deal of controversy in the United States, which currently is very concerned with illegal immigration and border security, particularly with Mexico. The immigration issue is certainly a heated and controversial one in the United States. Some U.S. citizens feel that the U.S. is being "overrun" by Mexicans. Many U.S. consumers consequently called for a boycott of Absolut products. Moreover, calls for a boycott began to appear on Internet sites and blogs, especially those of conservative political commentators. As a result, as reported by FOX News, an Absolut spokesperson stated that the ad was neither meant to offend or to disparage anyone, nor to advocate any alteration in borders, nor lend support to any "anti-American" sentiment, nor to intend to reflect any immigration issues. The Absolut spokesperson also said that the advertisement was designed for a Mexican audience, and, as related by FOX News, was supposed to "recall" a time in Mexican history that the Mexican people would feel was more "ideal." The company has apologized for the ad, and is no longer running it in Mexico. FOX News reported that there are currently estimated to be 12 million illegal (or "undocumented") immigrants in the United States, the vast majority of whom are from Mexico. There is still no plan for comprehensive immigration form in the U.S. since the President and the Congress cannot agree on a solution to the problem. The Absolut brand is owned by a Swedish company, which will soon be acquired by the French company Pernod.

Bibliography:

FOXNews.com, "Vodka Maker Apologizes for Ad Depicting Southwest as Part of Mexico," *http://www.foxnews.com/story/0,2933,346964,00.html*, retrieved April 6, 2008.

Questions for Discussion

1. If this advertisement was marketed in the United States, could it be deemed illegal pursuant to the Federal Trade Commission's rules against deceptive, false, misleading, or unfair advertising? Why or why not?

2. Is this advertisement a moral one pursuant to Utilitarian ethics? Discuss.

3. Is it a moral one pursuant to Kantian ethics?

4. Was this a wise advertisement for the company to use based on the principles of Value Driven Management? Should the new French owner of the brand continue to use the ad? Why or why not?

9. *Securities Regulation and Insider Trading*

Case 9.1: Enron: A Reason for Ethical Reform in Business Education and Practice[7]

The collapse of Enron, one of the largest bankruptcies in United States history, led to thousands of employees losing their life savings in pension plans tied to the energy company's stock (The Washington Post, 2002). For instance, the Texas State Employees Retirement Fund (TSERF) reportedly lost an estimated $63 million in Enron investments (Associated Press, 2002) as Enron stock price declined steeply from about $80 in 2001 to less than $1. Consequently, the United States Congress held several hearings to determine reasons for this gigantic fall, and took corrective action on the unpleasant situation. High profile Enron executives, including Kenneth Lay (Chairman and CEO), and Andrew Fastow (CFO), went to testify at the U.S. Capitol. CNN (2002) reported that former Enron vice chairman J. Clifford Baxter was found dead in his car in a Houston suburb in an apparent suicide, effectively "frustrating" the lawsuit filed by Enron shareholders against him and Ken Lay at the U.S. District Court in Houston. Moreover, the U.S. Securities and Exchange Commission (SEC) charged the former Chief Financial Officer, Andrew S. Fastow, with fraud, and he and his wife, Lea Fastow, were subsequently jailed for 12 months for filing false tax returns (Accountancy Age, 2004).

Formed in July 1985 as a result of the merger of Houston Natural Gas and InterNorth of Omaha, Nebraska, Enron was popularly known as one of the world's leading energy, commodities, and services companies (The Washington Post, 2002). Revenues were $101 billion in 2000 across three core businesses, namely wholesale services, energy services, and global assets (Enron, 2004). Enron Wholesale Services engaged in worldwide wholesale businesses, including the marketing and delivery of physical commodities and financial and risk management services. Enron Energy Services was its retail business, which provided integrated energy and facility management outsourcing solutions to commercial and industrial customers worldwide. Enron's Global Assets included pipelines, Portland General Electric, international power, and pipeline and distribution operations. Enron was run by some of the top "brains" in business and good employees.

On December 2, 2001, Enron Corporation along with certain of its subsidiaries filed voluntary petitions for Chapter 11 reorganization with the U.S. Bankruptcy Court for the Southern District of New York. The consequence of this bankruptcy filing was devastating to many stakeholders; and would spur a new business era in the U.S.A. and its worldwide trading partners. Hardly did a day go by without the news media airing the infamous corporate collapses in the U.S. Arthur Andersen, then the auditor of Enron, was subpoenaed by the U.S. Congress for its role in Enron's catastrophic collapse, especially the shredding of competent evidential matter. Coincidently, around the same timeframe, Tyco, MCI-Worldcom, and other once fine companies intensified the broken trust for Corporate America by filing for bankruptcies. Lay-offs were at an all time high, and the U.S. unemployment rate was forecasted to reach 6.5% in January 2003.

---

[7]Coauthored with Dr. Akwasi A. Ampofo.

In the light of the above, several allegations were made against Enron Corporation, its leadership, and its conduct of business. Firstly, Enron admitted to hiding billions of dollars of liabilities (debt) in Special Purpose Entities (SPEs) giving the flimsy excuse that "everyone does it" (Wolk et al., 2004). Moreover, J.P. Morgan, Chase & Co revealed that it had nearly $2.6 billion exposure as a result of Enron's use of SPEs (Wolk et al., 2003). Against this background, research showed that hundreds of respected U.S. companies have an estimated $2 trillion in off-balance sheet subsidiaries. Further, 29% of 141 CFOs responded to a survey that some of their company's debt was not reflected on the balance sheet. Unbelievably, Enron had about 3500 SPEs and nearly 50% of its business off-balance sheet. Also, the SPEs were staffed, housed, and mainly funded by Enron itself. Thus, the economic risks on the underlying transactions of the SPEs were essentially Enron's. As a result, those SPEs needed to be included in Enron financial statements, since Enron was on the "hook" for the SPEs economic failures. Enron failed to fully account for its true liabilities.

On June 3rd 2004, National Public Radio (NPR) aired taped telephone discussions among several Enron employees, which were just made available to the public, discussing how they are ripping off and fooling their electricity customers. The British Broadcasting Corporation (BBC) reported that Enron manipulated the power market to make extra money out of California's energy crisis in 2002. The Associated Press (2001) reported Enron Corporation of Houston as among a handful of a new generation of independent electric power brokers and producers that had reaped high revenue increases from California's power shortages and higher natural gas prices nationwide. CBS news collaborated that Enron held back about 55% to 76% of its energy production in an effort to drive up prices, an allegation that Enron denied as preposterous and which it said never happened.

Further, the BBC noted that Enron embraced new technologies, established new methods of trading in energy and seemed to be a shining example of successful corporate America. The company's success was based on artificially inflated profits, dubious accounting practices ("creative" accounting), and fraud. Several news reports blamed Enron's leadership team on extravagant spending and noncompliance with auditors. Ken Lay told a different story, "Enron engaged in real time audit procedures with its auditors on every significant structured finance vehicle. It has always been Enron's policy to be open with its accountant, Andersen." All these allegations, media reports, findings, and denials have cast a dark cloud over the integrity of Enron and its leadership, as well as the business, accounting, and legal communities.

Consequently, the post-Enron U.S. business climate is far more regulated. For one, section 404 of the Sarbanes Oxley Act (2002) requires written certification of internal controls by the CEO and CFO of all publicly traded companies. The Act also imposes very harsh criminal penalties for non-compliance. In addition, external auditors of those companies will affirm such certifications in the audit report. Further, the creation of the Public Company Accounting Oversight Board (PCAOB) implies loss of self-regulation by the accounting profession, leading to the evolution of Generally Accepted Accounting Principles/Auditing Standards (GAAP/GAAS) to Federally Accepted Accounting Principles/Auditing Standards (FAAP/FAAS). Moreover, the U.S. Financial Accounting Standards Board also issued two statements on disclosure of guarantees and indemnities of debt obligations (Financial Accounting Standards Board Interpretation 45), and consolidation of variable interest entities (Financial Accounting Standards Board Interpretation 46) to tighten financial reporting and protect investors.

In retrospect, Enron and its leadership did not heed certain powerful and profound wisdom referenced by Smith (2003), including "Ethical values provide the foundation on which a civilized society exists (p.47)." "Unethical behavior is a dagger in the heart (p.48)." Moreover, the American President Abraham Lincoln said, "Honor is better than honors." John Adams wrote, "The preservation of liberty depends upon the intellectual and moral character of the people." Jones (2002) said it best: "Ethics don't always pay but lack of it always hurts." Applying the subtle truths in these "pearls," could free the corporate criminals from the grips of jail, and save hard-earned jobs, reputation, and integrity.

Role and Impact on Accounting Profession

The collapse of Enron Corporation has been portrayed as the result of accounting fraud and greed (Culp and Hanke, 2003). Research by AICPA (2003) revealed that business decision-makers see CPAs among most to blame for the corporate accounting scandals. Further, forty percent of business decision-makers (half of investors) think CPAs are willing to "cut corners" for clients (AICPA, 2003). Arthur Andersen's involvement in the Enron scandal, including the shredding of evidential matter, cost it and the accounting profession dearly. It was quite disheartening to see the world's #1 accounting firm in 2000 reduced to dust and barred from practicing accountancy in the state of Texas and before the Securities and Exchange Commission (U.S. SEC). In addition to one partner at Andersen committing suicide, great damage has been done to the image of accountants worldwide and many employees have lost their jobs and livelihoods. Lack of ethics, therefore, really hurts (Jones, 2002).

Bibliography:

Accountancy Age (2004). Andersen and the Enron saga. [Online]. Available: *http://www.accountancyage.com/Specials/1127252*

American Institute of Certified Public Accountants, (2000). Code of Professional Conduct. [Online]. Available: *http://www.aicpa.org/about/code/sec50.htm*

Associated Press (2002). *Enron investments cost state funds $63 million.* [Online]. Available: *http://www.chron.com/cs/CDA/story.hts/special/enron/dec01/1187536*

CNN (2002). Enron's bankruptcy causes aftershocks on Main Street, Wall Street and in Washington. [Online]. Available: *http://www.cnn.com/SPECIALS/2002/enron/*

Culp, C.L. and Hanke, S.H. (2003). A Policy Analysis: Empire of the Sun: An Economic Interpretation of Enron's Energy Business. The Cato Institute. [Online]. Available: *http://www.cato.org/pubs/pas/pa-470es.html*

Enron, (2004). *Company Snapshot.* [Online]. Available: http://www.enron.com/corp/pressroom/factsheets/company.html

Institute of Management Accountants, (1983). *Standards of Ethical Conduct for Management Accountants.* [Online] Available: http://www.imanet.org/ima/sec.asp?TRACKID=&CID=191&DID=323

IFAC (2004). *The Code of Ethics for Professional Accountants.* [Online]. Available: http://www.ifac.org/Ethics/

Jones, D. (2002). *Ethics don't always pay, but lack of them always hurts: Core values from top aid success.* McLean, Virginia: U.S.A. TODAY.

Mintz, S.M. (1997). *Cases in Accounting Ethics & Professionalism*. Third Edition. U.S.A.: Irwin/McGraw-Hill Company.

Washington Post (2004). *Ex-Enron Official Pleads Guilty: Investor Relations Executive Admits to Insider Trading*. [Online]. Available: http://www.washingtonpost.com/wp-dyn/business/specials/energy/enron/

Wolk, H., Dodd, J., and Tearney, M. (2004). *Accounting Theory: Conceptual Issues in a Political and Economic Environment (6th ed.)*. ISBN: 0-324-18623-1

Sarbanes Oxley Act of 2002. Sections 302 and 404.

Smith, L.M. (2003). A fresh look at accounting ethics (or Dr. Smith goes to Washington). Accounting Horizons, Vol.17; Iss.1, pg 47-48. Sarasota, Florida.

Questions for Discussion:

1. Using the Rational Ethical Decision-Making Model, discuss the statement that "creating artificial power shortages in California to raise prices" was a sub-optimal decision for Enron's profitability.

2. Andrew S. Fastow's actions as former Chief Financial Officer of Enron were in violation of aspects of the AICPA Standards of Professional Conduct (*www.aicpa.org*). Discuss this statement with examples.

3. Discuss the behavior of the former Enron leadership from the perspective of Kohlberg's Moral Development Theory.

4. Andrew S. Fastow's actions as former Chief Financial Officer of Enron was in violation of aspects of the International Federation of Accountants' Code of Ethics (*www.ifac.org*).

5. Discuss the statement that "the use of special purpose entities (SPE) was a necessary evil for Enron." (Hint: Find out what SPEs are.)

6. Identify and examine at least three changes in the global business environment following the collapse of Enron or other companies in your country.

7. Discuss Jones' (2002) statement that "Ethics don't always help but lack of it always hurts," from the perspective of business ethics education and practice, borrowing examples from this case and other pertinent material.

8. Discuss separation of auditing from consulting business from the viewpoint of AICPA Standards of Professional Conduct.

9. Suppose you were a Staff Auditor at Arthur Andersen and you were instructed to "shred" Enron documents. How would the AICPA, IMA, or IFAC code of ethics become handy in that scenario? Explain the dissenting views on the internal resolution protocol advocated in the any one of the codes of ethics.

10. Explain your perspectives on reforming the accounting profession using the theories of ethics.

11. Rushworth Kidder, President of Institute for Global Ethics and author, said, "*Ethics in* its broader sense, deals with human conduct in relation to what is morally good and bad, right and wrong. It is the application of values to decision-making. These values include honesty, fairness, responsibility, respect and compassion." Discuss this statement in relation to one of AICPA, IMA, or IFAC Code of ethics.

Case 9.2: Martha Stewart—Conspiracy and Insider Trading

In June 2003, Martha Stewart was indicted on charges of conspiracy, obstruction of justice, perjury, and securities fraud, all linked to a personal stock trade she made in 2001, for which the Securities and Exchange Commission is also bringing civil insider trading charges against her.

She pleaded not guilty to all the charges and declared that she would fight them all. However, she also announced that she was stepping down as chairwoman and chief executive of the media and merchandising company she founded, Martha Stewart Living and Omnimedia, though she will continue to serve as the company's "chief creative director."

The indictment depicted Martha Stewart as attempting to conceal the circumstances of the sale of nearly 4000 shares of ImClone Systems, a transaction that the government says she made after learning that her close friend, Samuel Waksal, the company's founder, and his daughter were selling their own stock. It is most interesting to note that the government's criminal case focuses less on the trade itself than the elaborate cover-up the government alleges occurred afterwards.

According to the indictment, Martha Stewart lied to investigators by telling them that she and her stockbroker had previously agreed to sell the shares if their market value fell below a certain price. Moreover, the government alleges that she altered a phone message from the broker in her assistant's computer immediately following a lengthy conversation with her attorney. The essence of the government's case is that Martha Stewart lied to government investigations, specifically to the FBI and the SEC, by making up fictitious reasons and conversations regarding the sale of her shares of stock so as to hinder the government's investigation as well as to deceive the public, investors, and shareholders, including those of her own firm who also are suing her.

The SEC's civil complaint accuses Martha Stewart of insider trading, based on the information that she is said to have received from Douglas Faneuil, assistant to her stockbroker, Peter Bacanovic, who was also indicted on criminal charges, including perjury, and who was also named in the SEC's case. He too pleaded not guilty. The SEC contends that Martha Stewart should have known that she was receiving material, confidential, inside information, and thus acting illegally, when the assistant broker, Faneuil, told her the Waksals were selling their ImClone stock. The SEC regards Martha Stewart as a "tipee" who received inside information from the "insider" Waksal. The SEC is also seeking to have her barred from serving as a director of any public company, including her own, and to limit any executive role in a company. The government can proceed criminally against her on the obstruction of justice and fraud charges, even if the government does not accuse her of the criminal offense of insider trading.

If convicted, Martha Stewart faces up to several years in prison and the possibility of a very substantial fine. A recent Justice Department directive discourages assigning white-collar criminals to house-arrest, and thus time in prison is a very likely prospect for Martha Stewart if found guilty. The government's criminal case, based principally on obstruction of justice and perjury, is thought by experts to be easier to prove than insider trading charges.

Since the investigation of Martha Stewart was made public a year ago, the company's business has declined in every division.

Previously, Waksal pleaded guilty to felony insider trading charges and Faneuil pleaded guilty to a misdemeanor. Waksal was sentenced in June of 2003 to 87 months in prison and ordered to pay a fine and back taxes of $4.3 million. The sentencing judge underscored Waksal's "lawlessness and arrogance." The judge also mentioned Waksal's lack of social responsibility and the very small percentage of his immense wealth that he contributed to charitable and community causes. Waksal did not, and to date has not, publicly implicated Martha Stewart. Prosecutors have argued that Stewart dumped 4,000 shares of ImClone stock on a tip from stockbroker Peter Bancanovic that the Waksal family was planning to sell.

Waksal's difficulties began when he learned that the FDA was about to reject his company's application for an anticancer drug on which he based the future of his company. According to the indictment, as well as the SEC complaint, when Bacanovic learned from Faneuil that the Waksals were trying to sell their stock, he tried to call Stewart, but she was on an airplane to Mexico, so Bacanovic, who was also traveling, left a message with her assistant, and directed Faneuil to tell her of the Waksal sales when she returned the call. When Stewart, a former stockbroker herself, heard the news, she immediately told him to sell all her ImClone shares.

Martha Stewart, by selling her shares, "saved" herself at least $45,000 over what she would have had if she sold on the day after the FDA news became public. The price of the shares of stock of her company has plummeted, and consequently Martha Stewart and the investors in her company have lost millions.

Martha Stewart ultimately was convicted by a jury of perjury and obstruction of justice in 2004. The jury found that she lied under oath to government investigators and prosecutors when she, in the jury's mind, concocted that fabricated story about an agreement existing with her broker to sell her ImClone shares when the price reached a certain point. The jury also believed that she obstructed justice by changing her computer logs to support her story. Bacanovic, the senior broker also was found criminally liable. The judge, however, had earlier dismissed the government's securities fraud case, which, apparently, the judge felt was too novel and attenuated to support a conviction. Of course, Martha Stewart was not found guilty of trading on inside information because the government, in an exercise of prosecutorial discretion, decided not to bring that criminal charge. In order to sustain such a charge criminally, the government would have been forced to convince a jury, "beyond a reasonable doubt" that a conspiracy existed among the insider-Waksal and the ultimate tippee-Martha Stewart involving both the senior and junior brokers. The government apparently believed that it could not meet this very high legal burden of proof and persuasion. The Securities and Exchange Commission, however, proceeded civilly against Martha Stewart for the civil wrong of trading on inside information. Martha Stewart was sentenced to a five month term, serving one month in prison. She ultimately settled the civil case with the SEC, paying a substantial fine.

Yet the irony of the case against Martha Stewart is that she has been deemed a felon, and soon will be sentenced, for covering up and lying about circumstances which may not have been a crime, or, at the least, which the government chose not to prosecute for evidentiary reasons. Moreover, the ultimate irony to the case is that the FDA is reconsidering ImClone's anticancer drug application due to a recent medical study indicating that the drug may in fact have certain cancer-fighting properties. As a matter of fact, a European study in 2003 found that the cancer drug, Erbitux, does appear to be effective, helping some of the sickest colon cancer patients live longer. At that time, ImClone stock surged on the news.

Bibliography:

The *Miami Herald,* June 5, 2003, pp. 1C, 4C; June 11, 2003, pp. 1C, 4C.

The *Wall Street Journal,* June 5, 2003, pp. C1, C9, June 11, 2003, pp. A1, A8.

Questions for Discussion:

1. How should the Martha Stewart case be resolved on appeal? Discuss.
2. Was Martha Stewart treated in a moral manner? Discuss.
3. Was Dr. Waksal treated justly? Should social responsibility be a factor in sentencing? Discuss.
4. How would an ethical egoist have handled the Martha Stewart situation? Discuss.
5. How would a Machiavellian have handled it? Discuss.

10. Antitrust and Merger

Case 10.1: Exxon-Mobil Merger

Exxon and Mobil, the two largest oil companies in the U.S., announced in December 1998, that they were merging. Exxon, already the largest oil company in the U.S., agreed to buy Mobil, the next largest, for $80 billion in stock, to form the world's biggest corporation, on a scale rivaling that of many nations. The merger, most interestingly, would reunite the two largest pieces of John D. Rockefeller's Standard Oil Trust, which was broken up in 1911 in the nation's most celebrated antitrust case. Following the merger, the new company will control more than 1/4 of the industry market (25.3%) with Royal Dutch Shell next (18.1%) followed by British Petroleum (10.1%). Exxon and Mobil representatives strongly asserted that they confront global competition as well as plunging energy prices, making their merger and the resulting savings a necessity. The companies stated that they could save $2.8 billion within three years. Lee Raymond, the chairman and chief executive of Exxon, who will add the title of president of the combined company, stressed that further efficiency, not massive size, was his goal. He and other analysts said they considered Mobil's $80 billion price to be fairly high, but reasonable considering the benefits. He predicted the purchase would have no effect on his company's profitability in the first year and would begin adding earnings per share after that time. Exxon intended to trade 1.32 shares for each Mobil share, leaving Exxon shareholders owning 70% of the resulting company, to be called Exxon Mobil.

The merger, which would create a corporate behemoth, certainly will be scrutinized very closely and carefully by government antitrust regulators. Oil exploration and drilling interests would not necessarily present antitrust problems because competition in these areas is brisk; but in retailing and marketing operations, the combination, some analysts contend, would be like Ford and General Motors merging, because Exxon and Mobil have significant overlapping retail and refinery businesses in the U.S. and Europe. As a matter of fact, Exxon and Mobil have become the dominant rivals in some refining and retailing markets, such as the Northeast, particularly New Jersey, Washington, D.C., and Texas. In the U.S., the deal would come under the purview of the Federal Trade Commission. The agency has blocked a number of mergers, for example, the combination of Staples and Office Depot, but has approved other big mergers, for example, Boeing's acquisition of McDonnell Douglas. The Federal Trade Commission, moreover, recently approved a significant joint venture between Shell and Texaco, and is now considering the proposed merger of British Petroleum and Amoco. Yet, some antitrust experts see so many anticompetitive consequences of combining the nation's two largest oil and gas companies that they predict the government will refuse to approve the deal in any form. Exxon and Mobil, however, will argue that the combination is necessary for them to compete globally against such giants as Royal Dutch Shell, and foreign producers such as Saudi Arabia, Mexico, and Venezuela. Another impetus driving the merger is the plunge in crude oil prices, which have hit 12 year lows on London and New York markets, dropping below $12 a barrel. Exxon and Mobil firmly believe that only the truly massive will survive in such worldwide competition; and that the world oil over-capacity problem is so grim that the federal government regulators will pass the merger.

One challenge for Exxon and Mobil is to demonstrate how the consumer will benefit from the merger, at least in the short run. Consumers might worry, for example, that the combined company would cut back on refining, which in theory could boost the price of gasoline, heating oil, and other fuels. In addition, some analysts contend that arguments about global competition are not persuasive in a business that is highly regional, down to gas stations that compete against one another from across the street. The big worry is that further concentration in the industry can lead to fewer choices and higher prices for consumers. Still, the combined company would represent just 4% of global oil production capacity; but their total share of U.S. gasoline sales was about 20% last year.

In addition to serving their branded gasoline stations, which will rise to a total of 48,000 stations worldwide, their refineries supply independent retailers with gasoline, heating oil, and other fuels. These independents could face fewer choices too if a combined Exxon-Mobil were to streamline or close refineries.

Employees, however, could pay the greatest cost for the merger, because experts estimated that between 9,000 and 20,000 employees out of 123,000 worldwide are likely to find themselves without jobs.

The new company is to be based at Exxon's current headquarters near Dallas; and Mobil's headquarters in Fairfax, Virginia, would become the center for refining and sales, while Houston would be home to exploration, production, and chemicals. The sheer size of the merger is daunting. In 1997, Exxon earned $4.7 billion and Mobil $2.2 billion.

While Exxon has been cautious about developing new oil and natural gas Bibliography: abroad, Mobil has operations ranging from Indonesia to the Persian Gulf and the Caspian Sea. The merged company will have 21 billion of barrels of proven oil reserves, and its equivalent in natural gas, about 1% of the worldwide total.

Mobil chairman and CEO, Lucio Noto, is known as an international salesperson and diplomat. He would become vice-chairman of the new company. In particular, he enjoys a very good relationship with Middle Eastern leaders, especially Saudi Arabia, which has indicated it may be willing to open its borders to foreign exploration.

The deal, of course, was subject to approval by shareholders as well as government regulators, all of whom approved the merger.

Yet one government regulator apparently has had "second thoughts" about approving the merger. The *Herald* reported in May of 2004 that Joseph Romm, who was the principal deputy assistant energy secretary in the Clinton Administration, feels that in retrospect the government may have erred in allowing Exxon to take over Mobil. He stated that it "probably" was a "mistake" to allow the two oil companies to merge. At the time, oil prices had collapsed, and the industry was in trouble, so mergers seemed like a good idea, he stated.

The *Herald* also reported on a General Accounting Office study that examined eight major oil industry mergers between 1994 and 2000, and found that six of them led to higher gasoline prices. The report of the GAO, which is the investigative "arm" of Congress, stated that market concentration had increased substantially in the oil industry, partly because of the mergers, and that increased market concentration generally led to higher wholesale gasoline prices. Consumers thereby face higher gasoline pump prices today as a result of all the oil industry mergers in the last decade, stated the GAO report. Specifically, regarding the Exxon-Mobil merger, the combination of these two companies, at the time numbers 1 and 2 in the industry, added up to five cents to the price of a gallon of gasoline sold by the merged company.

Bibliography:

Borenstein, Seth, and Moritsugu, Ken, (2004). "Study: Mergers led to high gas prices," *Miami Herald,* May 28, p. 4C; *see also Business Week,* October 16, 2000, p. 55; *Miami Herald,* December 2, 5, 12, 1998; *Sun Sentinel,* December 1, 2, 28, 1998; *Wall Street Journal,* November 30, 1998, December 1, 1998.

Questions for Discussion:

1. Is the former Clinton Administration energy official correct? That is, was the government's legal approval of the Exxon Mobil merger a "mistake"? Why or why not?

2. Is the merger a moral one pursuant to Utilitarian ethics? Why or why not?

3. What should a "socially responsible" merged Exxon Mobil be doing for the community and society as a whole? Discuss.

4. Did the merger "pass" the test of Value-Driven Management? Why or why not?

Case 10.2: AT&T–Bell South Merger—Justice Department and Federal Communications Commission Approval

In October of 2006, the *Miami Herald* and *Sun-Sentinel* newspapers of Florida reported that the U.S. Department of Justice approved unconditionally AT&T's $78.5 billion merger with Bell South. The resulting merger would create the largest provider of telephone, wireless, broadband, and Internet services in the United States. It is important to underscore that the Justice Department, despite the gigantic size of the merger, the Justice Department found no potentially adverse effects on competition, and thus no antitrust problems. Assistant Attorney General Thomas O. Bartlett, who heads the Justice Department section that examines proposed mergers, stated that AT&T's acquisition of Bell South, as reported in the *Miami Herald,* "is not likely to reduce competition substantially." Moreover, AT&T's General Counsel, James D. Ellis, related that the DOJ's approval underscores the benefits of the merger.

The Federal Communications Commission (FCC) is also expected to approve the merger, despite strenuous objections from the two Democrat members of the Commission. There are three Republicans on the Commission, and the chairman, Republican Kevin Martin, already has circulated an order recommending approval. Nevertheless, the Commission stated that it would delay its vote in order to look at more closely the antitrust ramifications of the merger. One particular FCC member, Jonathan S. Adelstein, a Democrat, as reported in the *Miami Herald,* condemned the merger as "a reckless abandonment of DOJ's responsibility to protect competition and consumers." He also declared that the DOJ "took a dive on one of the largest mergers in history." The Commission's other Democrat, Michael Copps, also as reported in the *Herald,* condemned the DOJ for "pack(ing) its bags and walk(ing) out on consumers and small businesses by refusing to impose even a single condition in the largest telecom merger the nation has ever seen." Some consumer advocates have declared that the DOJ's approval of the merger demonstrates that the government is seeking to reconstitute the old "Ma Bell" telephone monopoly, which was broken up in 1984 into seven regional telephone firms and one long-distance provider after a lengthy antitrust court contest in order to promote competition. By including Bell South, the new AT&T would consist of four former "Baby Bells" as well as the long-distance building. Some consumer groups fear that the merger with leave consumers with fewer telecom choices as well as inflated prices for goods and services. As a result of the merger, the Bell South as well as the name of the two companies' wireless venture, Cingular, will be phased out.

If the merger ultimately is approved, AT&T would gain total control over the nation's largest cellular provider, Cingular Wireless, which presently serves 57.3 million customers. AT&T's General Counsel stated that the company is focused on bringing more video choices and "next generation" broadband services to as many consumers as possible, and that the merger with Bell South would help the company more quickly deliver these benefits to consumers. One goal of the merged company is to provide "one stop shopping" for telecom customers, especially large business clients with far-flung operations. Companies and consumers that now get their local phone as well as Internet service from Bell South will not get it from AT&T, though an exact name for the AT&T wireless service has not yet been picked.

AT&T is based in San Antonio; and Bell South is based in Atlanta. The combined company would have operations in 23 states; it would generate $117 billion in revenue and operate 68.7 million local phone lines across 22 states. The merger will give AT&T total control over the nation's largest cellular phone provider, Cingular Wireless, which now serves 57.3 customers. The merged company would employ about 309,000 people before any job cuts. AT&T estimates that about 10,000 jobs would be phased out over three years. Both AT&T's and Bell South's shares rose 0.6% at the end of the trading day the announcement was made, which was a 19 cent gain for the former to $32.96 a share, and a 24 cents gain for the latter to $43.44 a share.

Existing competition consists of Verizon Communications, which dominates the eastern United States, and Qwest, which is the phone company for most of the Rocky Mountain and Northwest regions of the county. The AT&T and Bell South merger, however, will create the largest U.S. provider of telephone, wireless, and broadband Internet service. Cable companies, however, are expected to increase their efforts to siphon off local and long-distance service telephone customers away from traditional telephone companies, such as AT&T.

In December 2006, the FCC unanimously approved the merger, which was the last major regulatory hurdle for the largest telecommunications merger in the U.S. history. The FCC, however, did impose one condition, called "network neutrality," which means the merged telecommunications giant must treat all Internet "traffic" neutrally.

Bibliography:

Dunbar, John, (2006). AT&T's Boyout of Bell South clears hurdle. *The Record*, December 30, p. A-11.

Dunbar, John, "Consumer groups say buyout of Bell South will cut competition," *Sun-Sentinel*, October 12, 2006, pp. 1D, 2D.

Dunbar, John, "Telecom Behemoth Ok'd," *The Miami Herald*, October 12, 2006, pp. 1C, 6C.

Weber, Harry R., "AT&T merger gets OK," *Sun-Sentinel*, October 12, 2006, pp. 1D, 2D.

Questions for Discussion

1. Do you agree with the Justice Department's approval of this merger? Do you agree with the Assistant Attorney General as to the lack of harmful, anticompetitive consequences to the merger? Do you agree with AT&T's General Counsel as to the benefits of the merger? Why or why not?

2. Should the Federal Communications Commission also approve the merger? Do you agree with the two Democrat members of the Commission? Should any conditions be placed on any FCC approval? Discuss.

3. Is the merger a moral one pursuant to Utilitarian and/or Kantian ethics? Discuss.

4. Does the merger pass the Value-Driven Management test? Discuss.

5. What should this giant, merged telecommunications company be doing in order to be a socially responsible firm? Discuss.

Case 10.3: Starbucks: A Socially Responsible but Monopolizing Company?

The national newspaper, *USA Today,* reported in December of 2006, an important anti-trust lawsuit instituted against coffee giant Starbucks by the owner of a small coffee shop in Seattle. The essence of the lawsuit is that Starbucks is a monopoly company that engages in predatory and abusive tactics to maintain and expand its monopoly; that is, Starbucks, it is alleged, is a monopolizing company in violation of Section 2 of the Sherman Anti-Trust Act. Specifically, the lawsuit alleges that Starbucks illegally maintains its monopoly by barring other coffee houses from prime downtown Seattle high-rise locations as well as other locales with such predatory tactics as long-term and exclusive leases with property owners. The lawsuit also contends that Starbucks engages in such unethical, and therefore monopolistic, practices to drive other coffee houses out of business, such as buying coffee sellers, and "flooding" neighborhoods with new Starbucks stores to such a degree that the sales from existing Starbucks shops were "cannibalized."

A spokesperson for Starbucks, as reported in *USA Today,* denied that the company has done anything improper. The spokesperson also stated that the company would defend itself. The company has grown, related the spokesperson, but so has the coffee industry, all of which ultimately benefits the consumer as well as the company's competitors. One of Starbucks' attorneys asserted that the company is committed to doing business in a respectful, ethical, and responsible manner in the communities in which it serves.

The lawsuit is expected to emerge as an important anti-trust one, as it will help clarify two critical areas in monopolization law: first, exactly what is a monopoly (geographically and product-wise); and second, what tactics are so abusive, unethical, and predatory, even if legal, to make the maintenance of that monopoly the legal wrong of monopolizing trade or commerce in violation of the Sherman Act. In particular, it is a challenge in today's truly global economy to exactly ascertain what a monopoly entails geographically.

The Seattle lawsuit, moreover, is seeking class action status; and *USA Today* reports that so far dozens of coffee sellers in Washington, California, Illinois, and other states have reported similar problems with Starbucks.

It is important to note a fundamental principle of anti-trust law, and that is that a monopoly is not inherently illegal, assuming it was lawfully established. However, intentional wrongful acts undertaken to maintain or expand one's monopoly, such as in the Microsoft case, render the legal monopoly company into an illegal monopolizing ones. The purposeful wrongful acts, again it must be stressed, do not have to be illegal in and of themselves; rather, they need "only" be predatory, abusive, and/or unethical, for example, blocking rivals from entering a market, or driving them from a market by unfair competition, thereby limiting consumer choices. In the lawsuit, Starbucks is accused of paying property lessors two to three times the rental market price for leased space, thereby forcing small coffee owners to relocate or to close their businesses. Starbucks is thus accused of "locking up" favorable coffee shop locations in Seattle and neighboring locales. However, proving that a company has intentionally abused its monopoly power is a difficult evidentiary burden to overcome, as evidence of intent is notoriously difficult to demonstrate factually and legally. Where exactly is the line to be drawn between abusive and unethical competition and "mere" "tough" and "hard-hitting" competition? It is expected that the Starbucks case will help to clarify that crucial distinction in anti-trust law.

Of course, before a company can be a monopolizing company, it must first have a monopoly, but the courts have not provided definitive guidelines as to what percentage of a market can equate to monopoly status. Market share monopoly figures range from 50% to 100%; yet there is even a case where a company had a 100% market share and it was not deemed to be a monopoly since it did not have the essence of monopoly power, that is, the power to raise and lower prices at will, and the power to exclude potential competitors from the market. Actually, in one location in Seattle, within a two mile radius of downtown, Starbucks has 59 stores, and thus has attained, according to the lawsuit, a "Starbucks-only zone" that excludes coffee rivals.

In the Starbucks case, if the market is deemed to be gourmet coffee, as alleged by the plaintiffs suing the coffee giant, then Starbucks possesses a monopoly-like 73% market share. However, Starbucks contends that the market for coffee is a more general and generic one, and Starbucks only has a 7% share of that larger market. So, is the market coffee or gourmet coffee? Is the market defined by type and range of product sold, by business region—globally, nationally, locally, or very, very locally by high-rise office space? That crucial "market definition" issue will have to be determined in the lawsuit first, and that issue could be the deciding factor, because if Starbucks does not even have a monopoly, then it legally cannot be a monopolizing firm. Even if Starbucks has a monopoly, there is nothing inherently wrong with long-term and exclusive leases as well as with non-competition clauses in contracts. Under the leases, the landlords promise not to rent space to competing coffee shops; only Starbucks can sell coffee in a building or mall. Starbucks is also accused of "poaching" customers, specifically by offering free Starbucks coffee outside the locations of competing coffee shops. Yet, are such practices committed by a monopoly company so unfairly uncompetitive to be deemed predatory, abusive, and/or unethical. One key legal test to ascertain whether a company has transgressed that impermissible monopolistic line is to examine whether there is any "economic sense" to the business practices. If there is no economic sense for the practices, then the likelihood is that they will be deemed illegal predatory actions designed to eliminate and exclude competitors and thereby to harm the consumers in the long-run.

Starbucks has long been regarded as a very efficient, effective, profitable, as well as a socially responsible company. Its stock has been a favorite of Wall Street. The company opened its first store in Seattle in 1971; and now has grown to over 12,000 outlets globally. It employed 115,000 people, and had $7.8 billion in revenues in 2006. It hopes to expand to 40,000 outlets worldwide. In 2003, Starbucks purchased Seattle's Best Coffee and another gourmet firm for $72 million; and then it closed all of Seattle's Best 22 stores. Yet Starbucks also has been praised for developing the mass market for gourmet specialty coffee, as well as for educating the consumer. The company has been praised for its social responsibility and environmental efforts, for example, by only buying coffee beans at a fair price from Third World producers, and for funding health and education centers in Central American countries. The company donates millions to charities. Yet now the socially responsible company is being castigated as a corporate bully that harms the small business person. Now it is being sued as an illegal monopolizing firm.

The market for specialty coffee shops is a growing one, with about 23,000 coffeehouses now in existence, according to *USA Today*. Starbucks, as noted, dominates the specialty coffee market with a 73% market share. Its closes rivals are Caribou Coffee and

Peet's Coffee and Tea. However, if the gourmet market is defined to include Dunkin Donut (27%) and Krispy Kreme (5%) as well as Tim Hortons (2%), then the Starbucks' "gourmet" market share falls to 43%, which is not a monopoly percentage.

Therefore, according to the lawsuit, Starbuck's strategy and tactics are to completely dominate the gourmet coffee market, to exclude competitors, and to maintain its monopoly, thereby resulting in monopolistic and illegal anti-trust behavior.

Bibliography:

Iwata, Edward, "Owner of small coffee shop takes on java giant Starbucks," *USA Today*, December 20, 2006, pp. 1B, 2B.

Questions for Discussion:

1. Does Starbucks have a monopoly? What is the relevant geographic and product market? Discuss.

2. Is Starbucks a monopolizing company? Are its actions intentionally predatory, abusive, and unethical, and designed to maintain its monopoly? Discuss. Is it therefore an anti-trust violator?

3. Should the fact that its "tough" competitive actions are legal in and of themselves be controlling? Why or why not?

4. Is Starbucks a moral company pursuant to Utilitarian and Kantian ethics? Discuss.

Case 10.4: Sirius-XM Satellite Radio Merger—U.S. Justice Department Approval

The *Wall Street Journal* as well as the *Miami Herald* and *Sun-Sentinel* (Ft. Lauderdale) newspapers reported in February of 2007 a major new telecommunications merger—the proposed $4.84 billion combination of Sirius Satellite Radio and XM Satellite Holdings. The merger was announced as a "merger of equals," with shareholders of both companies owning approximately 50% of the combined company. However, Sirius will turn over $4.57 billion of its stock to XM shareholders which is a substantial premium to the value of their shares. The XM shareholders will get 4.6 shares of Sirius stock for every share they own, based on closing market figures, and Sirius shareholders should get a 22% premium. Sirius' chief executive, Mel Karmazin, will lead the combined company. XM chairman Gary M. Parsons will remain in that role; and XM CEO, Hugh Panero, will stay on as CEO until the deal is finally consummated. XM has about 7.6 million subscribers; and Sirius has more than 6 million. Currently, both companies charge about $13 per month for a subscription. Howard Stern is a major personality on Sirius; and Oprah Winfrey is a major personality on XM. The new entity would have more than $2.3 billion in debt.

In order to legally effectuate the merger the companies will have to convince antitrust regulators at the Justice Department as well as the Federal Communications Commission (FCC) that the merger will not create a monopoly or substantially lessen competition. The merger deal could thus confront very serious legal regulatory hurdles. The key problem for the companies is that there are now only two competing satellite radio companies; and they are merging! The merger at first impression certainly seems to threaten competition and to create a monopoly. The companies will argue that satellite radio competes for listeners with broadcast radio, and in addition that there are several other ways which consumers can obtain music, news, and sports, such as from iPods and computers, and from downloads from cell-phones. The crucial legal question is to define the relevant market. If satellite radio is viewed as a unique technology, and thus the market is narrow; then the combination of the only two competing firms in that market will clearly fail the merger test of Section 7 of the Clayton Act. Pursuant to that statute, a merger will only be approved if there is not a reasonable probability that the merger will substantially lessen competition or tend to create a monopoly in a *relevant market*. How the Justice Department (and ultimately perhaps the courts) define the relevant market is absolutely critical to the legal disposition of this case on merger review. A key question will be whether the merging companies can impose "a small but significant and nontransitory" price increase on consumers without forcing them to move to other products or services. If the companies can, then that imposition of a price increase means that the merged company has market power, which is an important ingredient to possessing a monopoly. However, if due to any price increase, consumers will switch to other products or services and the profits of any price increase will be negated, the pertinent market is broader since it includes other products and/or services, and the probability of competition being lessened or a monopoly being created are reduced. One factor particularly important to the FCC is whether the two companies will be able to provide the present level and scope of products and services if the merger is disapproved.

XM's chairman, Gary M. Parsons, declared that satellite radio is only still a "small player" in the audio entertainment market, which he described as highly competitive, involving multiple parties, and rapidly evolving technologically. That is, the combined companies not only compete with each other, but rather, he argues, with traditional radio and a growing number of digital audio sources. He also attempted to allay fears about prices by explaining that the combined company could not grow "unless it meets consumer expectations on both price and programming." The merger is also expected to significantly reduce costs due to achieving efficiencies and eliminating unnecessary duplication. Research also will be combined, which presumably will lead to more advanced products and services. Synergies produce value, say company spokespersons. The combined companies would no longer have to engage in expensive bidding wars for audio and technological products. Automotive revenue sharing and programming contract renewals would no longer be subject to bidding wars too. However, one fundamental present problem is that Sirius and XM radio receivers cannot receive each others' signals. However, the companies are now working on developing a receiver that could receive both signals from satellites. But the consumer may have to purchase the new technology. Right now, major league baseball games are available only on XM, but a mechanism is being worked out to allow Sirius listeners to get baseball games. The same situation exists with National Football League games, which are only available on Sirius. Until the merger is approved, the companies have stated that they will provide full services to their current subscribers. The merger should provide, in the words of the *Wall Street Journal,* "simplification" and "one stop shopping" to the satellite radio business. One area of duplication that could be reduced is the providing of rock-n-roll music, since both companies cater to specific areas and time periods. Yet consumers could be concerned because during the transition period and the perhaps long regulatory process, the radio transmitters they buy could become obsolete. The concern is exacerbated since many new cars already have satellite radios built in, and these may become obsolete too. It also takes a long time for the automotive industry to adopt its production lines to the installation of new radio technology. But factory installed models on brand new cars may already be out of date.

Industry experts state that it is too early to determine how the merger will affect subscription prices. The merger could, and arguably should, bring down the price of providing service; yet at the same time the merger could give the combined company more power to set prices since it will be the only U.S. satellite radio provider and thus a monopoly. Consumers, of course, are worried about higher prices. The combined company could also provide the consumer with more listening choices due to its size and economic power, said one industry expert. Traditional broadcast radio is, of course, free. Yet according to the *Wall Street Journal* the growth of both companies has slowed and the expectations as to future growth and the size of the satellite market have been curtailed. In 2005, as a matter of fact, the *Journal* reported that both companies lost money—$1.5 billion for that year, and $1.4 billion for the year before. These companies, however, are the only two companies licensed by the FCC to offer broadcast satellite radio services in the United States. Nonetheless, as reported in the *Wall Street Journal,* the companies are confident that the audio entertainment market has so materially changed in the last decade that their merger ultimately will be approved.

AT&T's merger with Bell South was in fact recently approved by the Justice Department and the FCC. Yet one legal point seems very clear; and that is if the Justice Department rules that there is a distinct market for satellite radio, the merger will fail, based on the precedent of the Office Depot–Staples merger, where the Federal Trade Commission ruled that the market was narrowly defined as office supply "super-stores" and not any store that sold office supplies; and thus the proposed merger of the number one and two office supply super-stores, leaving a "dwarfish" Office Max, failed the merger test in the Clayton Act. Naturally, Sirius and XM will argue, as did Office Depot and Staples, that their combined company competes with all forms of audio-entertainment. However, intense opposition to the merger is expected. As a matter of fact, the *Sun-Sentinel* newspaper of Fort Lauderdale, Florida, reported in June of 2007 that 47 Democratic and 25 Republican members of Congress sent a letter to the Justice Department, the FCC, and the FTC condemning the proposed merger as "devastating" to consumers.

One final and most interesting point is that the FCC may approve the merger conditioned on the combined company adhering to FCC indecency rules, which currently neither company has to adhere to since they are pay subscription services as opposed to free services with licenses granted by the FCC. If that "decency" stipulation is a legal condition to the merger, what happens to the now satellite radio (and totally uncensored) "shock jock" Howard Stern!

The U.S. Justice Department (DOJ) in March of 2008 approved the $5 billion merger of Sirius Satellite Radio with XM Satellite Radio Holdings. Moreover, the transaction was approved by the DOJ without conditions. The approval came in about a year after the two companies announced the deal. The DOJ stated that the merger would neither harm competition nor consumers. However, the merger still requires the approval of the U.S. Federal Communications Commission, which could disapprove the merger, approve it, or approve it with conditions. The DOJ based its decision on the facts that the two companies are not competing today, since consumers must purchase equipment that is exclusive to either Sirius or XM, and that customers who subscribe rarely switch service providers. Actually, many consumers do not even choose a service; rather, it is already pre-installed on the cars they buy. Another factor behind the approval was the argument long asserted by the two companies that there is already ample competition provided by other types of audio entertainment, including traditional radio, high-definition radio, Internet radio, broad band radio, and music software such as Apple's iTunes, and music devices such as Apple's iPod. Furthermore, mobile phones with Internet connections will soon be able to offer similar services to satellite radio, and thus even offer more competition to the market. The DOJ stated that such competition would mean that the merger would not harm consumers in the long-term.

The merger had received shareholder approval in November of 2007. The companies have stated that the merger will save hundreds of millions of dollars in operating costs, and that the cost savings will eventually benefit consumers. However, Senator Herb Kohl (D.-Wis), chairman of the Senate Judiciary Committee's sub-committee on antitrust, stated that the merger would produce a monopoly in satellite radio, and consequently asked the FCC to block it. The companies have promised that the merged firm will offer listeners more pricing options and greater choice and flexibility in the channels they receive. Moreover, the companies promised that they would offer pricing options that would range from $6.99 a month for 50 channels, up to $16.99 a month for expanded services. Currently, both companies charge consumers $12.95 a month for a basic subscription. At the end of 2007, the *Wall Street Journal* reported that Sirius had 8.3 million subscribers, and XM had nine million subscribers. Yet some consumers fear that if the two companies are allowed to merge, they will raise their monthly fees. The companies contend that if the merger is permitted the new merged company will emerge as a very strong competitor in the rapidly evolving audio entertainment market, and thus the consumer will benefit with more choices and better pricing. The merger would combine the only two satellite radio companies in the U.S. and create a company with 17 million subscribers. Now, subscribers to either Sirius or XM receive broadcasts only one of the two services with their satellite radios; but an XM radio statement indicated that radios owned by its current subscribers would not need to be replaced in order for the customer to continue to receive radio transmissions. The *Wall Street Journal* reported that the merger was given very little chance of succeeding a year ago due to the fact that it would create a satellite radio monopoly; but nevertheless the DOJ gave its approval. One point is clear now, and that is the DOJ's favorable decision should put considerably more pressure on the FCC to make a decision. The head of the FCC, Chairman Kevin Martin, was initially opposed to the merger, but, as reported by the *Wall Street Journal,* he may be coming around to approve the deal since the merged company is promising to offer "a la carte pricing" which allows consumers to subscribe to individual channels instead of the full lineup of channels, which option Chairman Martin has long called for in the cable television industry. The *Wall Street Journal* predicted that it is now considered "unlikely" that the FCC will go against the DOJ ruling. Yet one FCC condition to the merger may be a requirement that the merged satellite radio company provide free channels to environmental, educational, and religious groups. If the merger is fully approved, such approval may give hope to other communication companies, such as DirecTV and Echo-Star, that their mergers will be approved too.

Bibliography:

Dunbar, John, "Justice approves Sirius deal despite opposition," The *Miami Herald,* March 25, 2008, pp. 1C, 5C; Goldman, David, "XM-Sirius merger approved by DOJ," CNNMoney.com, March 24, 2008, *http://money.cnn.com/2008/03/24/news/companies/xm_sirius*; McBribe, Sarah, and Schatz, Amy, "XM, Sirius Move Closer to Improbable Merger," *Wall Street Journal,* March 25, 2008, pp. B1, B2.

McBribe, Sarah, "How Serius-XM Deal Would Affect Listeners," *The Wall Street Journal*, February 21, 2007, pp. D1, D7; McBride, Sarah, "Sirius and XM Agree to Merge, Despite Hurdles," *The Wall Street Journal*, February 28, 2007, pp. A1, A13; Peterson, Molly, "Sirius-XM deal draws static," *Sun-Sentinel*, June 19, 2007, p. 2D; Rowley, James, "Sirius-XM merger faces major hurdle over antitrust issues, experts say," *Sun-Sentinel*, February 23, 2007, p. 3D; Schatz, Amy, and Wilke, John R., "Sirius-XM's Fate Hinges on Definitions," *The Wall Street Journal*, February 21, 2007, p. B4; Sutel, Seth, "For Consumers, Mixed Signals," *Sun-Sentinel*, February 21, 2007, pp. 1D, 8D; Sutel, Seth, "Heavenly Match," *The Miami Herald*, February 20, 2007, p. 9B.

Questions for Discussion

1. Do you agree with the Department of Justice's legal decision to approve the merger and without any conditions? Why or why not?

2. Is this merger a moral one pursuant to Utilitarian ethics? Why or why not?

3. Is it a moral one pursuant to Kantian ethics? Why or why not?

4. Does the merger pass the test of Value-Driven Management? Why or why not?

5. What should a merged Sirius-XM satellite radio company be doing for society in order to be a socially responsible company? Discuss.

6. Is the proposed merger legal? Why or why not? Specifically, how should the "market" be defined, and why is this determination critical under antitrust law?

7. Is the merger moral pursuant to the ethical theories of Utilitarianism and Kantian ethics? Why or why not?

8. What should a "socially responsible" merged satellite radio company be doing for society? Discuss, providing examples.

9. Does the proposed merger pass the Value-Driven Management test? Why or why not?

10. Is it fair for the FCC to condition the merger on the combined company's adherence to agency "decency" standards, which means that radio personality Howard Stern is now censored to a degree or off the airwaves? Why or why not?

Case 10.5: The European Union and Microsoft: The 2007 European Court Antitrust Ruling

The *Wall Street Journal* and the *Sun-Sentinel* (of Ft. Lauderdale) newspaper reported in September of 2007 that the European Union (EU), in a significant legal ruling, adjudged Microsoft (MS) Corporation to be an antitrust violator. Specifically, the second highest court in the EU, called the European Court of First Instance, hearing the nine year EU case against MS on appeal, concluded that the European Commission was correct in concluding that MS was an antitrust violator that used and abused its market dominance and near monopoly position in desktop computers to expand its reach into server software and media players during the 1990s. In particular, the court upheld the findings that MS improperly bundled its media player with its Windows operating system, and that MS denied competitors the information, called "protocols," necessary to make their computers and servers work more smoothly with MS's hardware and software. The independent makers of media players were particularly harmed by MS, the EU court declared. The court also upheld the record fine of 497 million euros, approximately $613 million, which was first imposed against MS in 2004. Now, MS must either comply with the 2004 court order by EU regulators, which includes a provision mandating that MS must share its code with rivals as well as sell copies of its Windows without the Media Player, or appeal. The European Court of First Instance has 13 judges; it sits in Luxembourg; and it considered the MS appeal for 18 months. Under EU antitrust law, a refusal to license copyrighted material is abusive and illegal if a dominant company seeks to do so without legitimate business justification and to eliminate competition and if the competitor wants to make a new product and not just a copy. The EU decision was criticized for possibly impeding innovation and discouraging competition, thereby eventually harming consumers. MS's supporters argued that the decision will make it more difficult for companies to design products with new features. Also, it was pointed out that today consumers have more technological choices then when the initial case was brought against MS. Moreover, other industry experts stated that the decision would mean that large multinational technology companies would have to adhere to different legal standards internationally, thereby engendering confusion and expense. One European regulator, however, praised the EU decision since this commissioner declared that the consumer was suffering at the hands of MS. In Europe, MS has a 95% market share in operating system software. Note that the European Union has persisted in its antitrust case against MS, even though the U.S. Department of Justice settled its antitrust monopolizing case against the company in 2001. It is also interesting to note the differing rationales between U.S. and EU antitrust law. That is, U.S. law is intended to protect competition, whereas EU law is designed to protect competitors. The former thus has an ultimate consumer benefit purpose superseding any competitor interest. MS had in fact removed its Media Player on one version of Windows, but no one purchased that one since a version with the Media Player was still available at the same price. An attorney for MS did state that the company may be willing to provide its "protocols," but that the company wanted to charge for them; whereas the EU stated that the information should be free. MS has long argued that its competitors do not want to use its information to make new products or anything novel, but only to make copies which they can "drop into" Windows. The company is expected to appeal the latest

EU decision to the EU's highest court, which is a process that could take years. Thus, the MS and EU saga is expected to continue. In the meantime, MS, which has plenty of cash, has put the fine money in an escrow account—just in case!

Bibliography:

Clark, Don, "Microsoft Ruling Raises Stakes for Big Tech Firms," *The Wall Street Journal,* September 18, 2007, p. A10;

Forelle, Charles, "Microsoft Defeat in Europe Court Rewrites Rules," *The Wall Street Journal,* September 18, 2007, pp. A1, A10;

White, Aoife, "EU court upholds Microsoft decision," *Sun-Sentinel,* September 18, 2007, pp. 1D, 2D.

Questions for Discussion:

1. What is the preferable rationale for antitrust law—protecting competition or protecting competitors? Why?

2. Did MS act illegally pursuant to the EU's antitrust law? Why or why not?

3. Was the EU court decision a moral one pursuant to Utilitarian and Kantian ethics? Discuss.

4. Using the principles of Value-Driven Management, should MS submit to the EU court decision or appeal the case? Discuss.

Case 10.6: Microsoft and the European Union (2008): Microsoft Fined $1.35 Billion

The European Union (EU), in February of 2008, fined Microsoft Corporation (MS) a record $1.35 billion for failing to comply with a 2004 antitrust order. The fine is the largest the EU has ever imposed against a single company in an antitrust case. The 2004 ruling required Microsoft to turn over technical documentation regarding a media player investigation. Moreover, in 2007, the EU said that Microsoft was charging too much for the documentation it did release. Specifically, the EU declared that MS charged "unreasonable prices" to software developers who wanted to make products compatible with the Windows Desktop operating system. Microsoft had originally set a royalty rate of 3.87% of a licensee's product revenues for patents, and also insisted that companies who wanted communication information, which it said was highly secret, pay 2.98% of their products' revenues. However, in October of 2007, Microsoft agreed to license the new technical information for $14,000, which amount was well below what it originally had asked for. MS also offered a reduced royalty of 0.4% for a world-wide patent license.

Microsoft said it was reviewing the EU's actions. An appeal is an option for the company. The *Wall Street Journal* reported that a Microsoft spokesperson said that the fine had concerned past issues which have been resolved. Moreover, Microsoft pledged to improve its competitors' programming abilities to make software for Windows that competes with Microsoft's own products. The *Miami Herald* reported that MS had in fact made available 30,000 pages of previously secret software code for Windows on its website; it also reported that one expert on European law stated that the European Union has placed Microsoft in a nearly impossible position, because the company was told to make its technical information available at reasonable prices, but there is no way to measure reasonableness when there does not exist any market. Nonetheless, the *Wall Street Journal* reported that the EU's antitrust investigation of Microsoft is far from over since the EU antitrust chief opened in January of 2008 two new antitrust investigations against Microsoft. The investigations will focus on whether Microsoft's Internet Explorer browser is illegally bundled into Windows and whether other programs, including Microsoft Office, work sufficiently well with its competitors' products and services. The EU has long alleged that MS has withheld critical "interoperability" information for desktop PC software, of which MS is still the world's leading supplier, in order to damage rivals that make software for servers that help computers connect to one another and to expand into new markets. To further complicate matters, the EU will have to approve Microsoft's deal to acquire Yahoo. Microsoft clearly does not need problems in Europe as it seeks to gain control of Yahoo.

Bibliography:

CNN Money, "EU fines Microsoft record $1.3 billion," *http://money.cnn.com/2008/02/27/technology/eu_microsoft*, retrieved February 27, 2008; Emlin, Shelley, "Microsoft fined $1.35B," *The Miami Herald*, February 28, 2008, p. 2C; Forelle, Charles, "EU Fines Microsoft $1.35 Billion," *The Wall Street Journal*, February 28, 2008, p. B2.

Questions for Discussion:

1. Do you agree with the EU's decision to fine MS on legal grounds? Do you agree with the new EU legal investigations? Why or why not?
2. Is the decision a moral one pursuant to Utilitarian ethics? Why or why not?
3. Is it a moral one pursuant to Kantian ethics? Why or why not?
4. How should Microsoft respond to the EU's legal actions using the principles of Value-Driven Management? Discuss.

Case 10.7: Miller-Coors Merger

The *Wall Street Journal* and the *Miami Herald* and *Sun-Sentinel* newspapers of southeast Florida reported in October of 2007 a major merger in the U.S. beer industry. The country's second and third largest brewers, Miller and Coors, announced that they are planning to combine their U.S. brewery operations. Pursuant to the merger, the companies stated that they will conduct all of their U.S. business through the combined company. The objective is to help both companies compete in the struggling U.S. beer market against industry leader Anheuser-Busch, which commands a very powerful presence with marketing and distribution. Its top selling brand is Bud Light, and its U.S. operating profit margin is about 24%, compared to margins of less than 10% for both Coors and Miller.

The result of the merger will mean that 80% of the U.S. beer market will be possessed by just two companies. Miller Brewing is owned by SAB Miller and now has 18% of the beer market, while Molson Coors Brewing has almost 11% of the market. Anheuser-Busch has almost one-half of the market. The combined company will have $6.6 billion in annual revenues. There are, however, many small brewers, and thus some industry experts, who assert that the beer market is more competitive now than it was years ago. The *Wall Street Journal* reported that the volume of beer produced by these small independent beer makers increased 11% in the first half of 2007. Furthermore, imported brands of beer are becoming even more popular with consumers. The result, according to the *Wall Street Journal,* is that the large U.S. brewing companies are struggling. Also, some legal experts contend that government regulators actually may look upon the merger favorably because the merged Miller-Coors might offset the market dominance of Anheuser-Busch and accordingly allow the merged companies to better compete against Anheuser-Busch. The merger of Miller and Coors, which is technically a joint venture, is intended to be completed in 2008. Miller will have a 58% economic interest in the venture, and Coors will have a 42% share, but each company will have equal voting interests, and each will have five members on the combined company's board of directors.

The merger is expected to produce huge cost savings for the two companies. The *Wall Street Journal* reported that the merger is expected to yield approximately $500 million in savings. Distributors in particular should save money since they now will be able to deal with one company instead of two. The savings in part will go to expanded marketing and promotions around the brands. One potential problem of the merger, according to some industry experts, is the "cannibalization" one; that is, both Miller Lite and Coors Light are both in the premium light beer category. As such, do the two types of beer have different attributes? Will beer drinkers recognize the distinction? Regarding geography, however, the two companies' merger is said to be complementary since Coors is predominantly based in the western part of the U.S. and Miller is very strong in the mid-west, and is actually the leading beer in Chicago.

As to the employees of the two firms, one industry leader, Anheuser Busch chief executive August Busch IV, predicted "significant transition confusion" for the two companies. In addition to streamlining production and reducing shipping distances, the *Wall Street Journal* reported that savings are to be achieved from "consolidating" corporate employees.

At the time of the announcement, Molson-Coors' stock rose 10.5% to $57.68, and SABMiller shares rose 1.43% to $30.33, but the price of Anheuser-Busch stock fell 46 cents to $51.57, an almost 1% drop. Peter Coors, vice chairman of Molson-Coors, will serve as chairman of the new company, Molson-Coor's CEO Leo Kiely will be he new CEO of Miller-Coors. Last year, Anheuser-Busch sold 102.3 million barrels in the U.S. in 2006; and experts predict that the merged Miller-Coors will sell 69 million barrels. What is most interesting is that the Miller-Coors merger could prompt the long-rumored merger of Anheuser-Busch and a company outside the U.S., in particular InBevNV, based in Belgium, the world's largest brewer by volume. Anheuser-Busch actually has very little presence outside the United States, though it has some presence in China, India, and Mexico; and overseas is where the greater opportunities for growth reside. Anheuser-Busch is the world's number three beer maker by volume after InBevNV and SABMiller. SAB Miller is very strong internationally but the Wall Street Journal termed its U.S. Miller operations as its "weak link."

The merger most certainly will be closely reviewed by the U.S. Justice Department and the Federal Trade Commission since it combines the U.S. operations of the second and third largest U.S. brewers. The principal merger test in the U.S. is found in Section 7 of the 1914 Clayton Act, which maintains that a merger will be deemed illegal if there will be a reasonable probability of a substantial lessening of competition in a relevant market or if there is a tendency to create a monopoly. There is still vigorous industry competition; however, Anheuser-Busch is still the dominant entity in the market, and the Bush Administration has generally not blocked large mergers, even horizontal ones of competitors at the same level in the marketing chain. Thus, some legal experts say that most likely the merger will not be challenged by the government.

Bibliography:

Fredrix, Emily, "Miller, Coors to join forces," *The Miami Herald*, October 10, 2007, p 3C; "Miller, Coors to merge U.S. operations," *Sun-Sentinel*, October 10, 2007, p. 3D; Kesmodel, David, and Ball, Deborah, "New Alliance to Shake Up U.S. Beer Market," *The Wall Street Journal*, October 10, 2007, p. A1.

Questions for Discussion

1. Should the U.S. government seek to block this merger on antitrust grounds? Does this merger pass the Clayton Act merger test? What exactly is the "beer market"? Is it a competitive one with this merger? Is it even more competitive now? Or is the relevant market a broader "spirit market," combining sweet cocktails and other drinks popular with young drinkers, such as Smirnoff Ice? Discuss.

2. Is this a moral merger pursuant to Utilitarian ethics? Why or why not?

3. Is it a moral one pursuant to Kantian ethics? Why or why not?

4. What should a socially responsible merged company be doing for society? Discuss.

5. Does the merger pass the test of Value Driven Management? Why or why not?

Case 10.8: Microsoft-Yahoo Merger

In February of 2008 Microsoft Corporation announced that it made an unsolicited bid to takeover Internet search company Yahoo for $44.6 billion. The proposed merger of the two companies emerges as Microsoft's most serious challenge to Google, Inc.'s dominance of the very lucrative Internet search and advertising business. In response to the offer, Yahoo officials stated that they would carefully and promptly consider Microsoft's offer. Microsoft Chief Executive Steve Ballmer, however, stated that he would not take "no" for an answer. He also stated that he was confident that the merger was the "right path" for both companies. Microsoft hopes to convince Yahoo shareholders to support the deal so as to make it more difficult for Yahoo's board of directors to reject the offer. Microsoft had previously made an offer to purchase Yahoo in 2007, but that offer was rebuffed, because Yahoo officials said at the time that the company was better off going alone. Yahoo's chief executive, Terry Semel, who had rejected the Microsoft's offer, now has resigned under shareholder pressure. The new CEO of Yahoo is co-founder Jerry Yang, who is also one of Yahoo's largest shareholders.

Microsoft's offer to the Yahoo shareholders was $31 per share. The offer was a cash and stock one. Yahoo's stock has been steadily decreasing, and fell to a four year low in January 2008. The stock, after reaching a high in October of 2007 of $34.08, had fallen 46%. A new Yahoo management team has been trying to turn the company around, but problems were predicted through 2008. Microsoft's announcement immediately raised Yahoo's share price by almost 50%, while competitor Google's share price dropped by 9%. Microsoft's shares immediately after the announcement fell 6.6% to $30.45.

Microsoft has been a very profitable company, reporting a 79% increase in its profit for the last quarter in 2007; but its online division lost $245 million last year. Yahoo also has been struggling to attract more advertisers, even though its Web site attracts one of the biggest audiences. Its profit has declined for five consecutive quarters, engendering plans to lay off 1000 employees in early 2008, which is a 7% reduction of its work force of 14,3000 employees. Microsoft believes that it can save money by merging with Yahoo by eliminating overlapping operations and laying off workers. Microsoft has announced that it expects to save $1 billion in cost savings. However, no precise numbers were indicated as to how many employees would lose their jobs in the merger.

Microsoft, in addition to securing the approval of the Yahoo board of directors and shareholders, will have to obtain approval from government anti-trust regulators in Washington, D.C. and the European Union. A Justice Department official already has stated that the Justice Department is "interested" in reviewing the merger. The *Wall Street Journal* has predicted that the merger would ultimately secure government approval, both in Europe and the United States.

If the merger is accomplished, the deal will represent the largest acquisition in Microsoft's history, towering over the acquisition in 2007 of online ad service company, eQuantive, for $6 billion. Microsoft views Yahoo as its best opportunity to combat Google, which has leveraged its dominance in Internet search and advertising business to mount a challenge to Microsoft in the computer software and computer interaction business. Presently, Google controls almost 60% of the U.S. search market; and it has been widening its lead too, despite strenuous efforts by second-place Yahoo and third-place Microsoft. By combining companies, Microsoft and Yahoo would have a one-third share of the U.S. Internet search market.

Microsoft made $14.07 billion in profit for fiscal year 2007; its total revenue was $51.12 billion. Microsoft is headquartered in Redmond, Washington, and has 83,945 employees. Yahoo made $660 million in profit in 2007 on total revenues of $6.97 billion. It is headquartered in Sunnyvale, California, and has 14,300 employees. There is no guarantee that Yahoo would be willing to sell to Microsoft, but the Yahoo board of directors and management will likely face intense pressure from shareholders to merge with Microsoft, especially because Yahoo's stock and profits have been steadily declining.

The online search market is expected to increase dramatically in the future as more and more people get their news and entertainment on the Web as opposed to television and radio and newspapers and magazines. Globally, advertisers are anticipated to double their spending on the Internet in the next three years. By 2010, the online ad market is expected to reach $80 billion. Although Microsoft still is the world's most successful and valuable technology company, its dominant position will be undermined unless it can establish a more loyal Internet customer base as well as produce more online ad revenue. If the merger is accomplished, one thing is certain, and that is the Internet search business will markedly change since Microsoft combined with Yahoo would emerge as a much more formidable presence as well as a fierce competitor to Google.

Note that the *Wall Street Journal* reported on February 11, 2008 that Yahoo had rejected Microsoft's merger offer. The reason for the rejection was that the Yahoo board of directors thought that Microsoft's buyout offer "massively undervalues" Yahoo. The *Journal* reported that as a result Microsoft is expected to increase its original $31 per share offer; yet the *Journal* reported that Yahoo is demanding $40 a share, which would increase the value of Microsoft's original cash and stock offer by more than $12 billion. Microsoft is also expected to put pressure on large Yahoo shareholders to pressure the Yahoo board of directors to negotiate with Microsoft for an acceptable price for the company.

Bibliography:

CNN Money, "Microsoft bids $45 billion for Yahoo," *http://money.cnn.com/2008/01/02/ technology/Microsoft_Yahoo*; Delaney, Kevin J., Guth, Robert A., and Karnitschnig, Matthew, "Microsoft Makes Grab for Yahoo," The *Wall Street Journal,* February 2–3, 2008, pp. A1, A5; Guth, Robert A., Delaney, Kevin J., and Karnitschnig, Matthew, "Yahoo's Rejection Pressures Microsoft to Mull a New Bid," The *Wall Street Journal,* February 11, 2008, pp. B1, B3; Liedtke, Michael, "Microsoft makes pitch for Yahoo," *Sun-Sentinel,* February 2, 2008, pp. 1D, 2D; *Miami Herald* Wire Services, "Microsoft offers $42B for Yahoo," The *Miami Herald,* February 2, 2008, pp. 1C, 2C.

Questions for Discussion:

1. Is the proposed Microsoft-Yahoo merger a legal one pursuant to anti-trust law? Why or why not?

2. Is it a moral one pursuant to Utilitarian and Kantian ethics? Discuss.

3. Does the merger pass the test of Value-Driven Management? Why or why not?

4. What should a "socially responsible" merged Microsoft-Yahoo be doing for society? Discuss.

Case 10.9: Supreme Court Anti-trust Price-setting Decision[8]

The *New York Times* and *Wall Street Journal* reported in June of 2007 a very significant U.S. Supreme Court anti-trust decision—*Leegin Creative Leather Products v. PSKS (dba Kay's Kloset)* (127 SCt. 2705 (2007). For nearly 100 years, since 1911, pursuant to the Sherman Act Section 1, prohibiting restraints for trade, it has been deemed illegal by the Court for a manufacture and a retailer to fix, that is, to set or to agree to set, the minimum price for which goods could be sold. *See Dr. Miles Medical Co. v. John D.Park & Sons Co.* (31 S.Ct. 376 (1911) (U.S. Supreme Court ruled that under §1 of the Sherman Act, 15 U.S.C. § 1, for a manufacturer to agree with its distributor to set the minimum price the distributor can charge for the manufacturer's goods.)) Such an agreement was branded by the Court as a *per se* restraint of trade, and thus an automatic violation— criminally and civilly—of anti-trust law. However, in a very significant decision, the Court rules that it is no longer automatically illegal for a manufacturer to agree with a retailer or a distributor to agree to set minimum retail prices for goods and services.

The decision will afford manufacturers and retailers materially more power to set retail prices and to restrict the flexibility of discounters. However, the parties on the marketing chain are not totally free to set minimum prices. Although a vertical minimum price fix, also called a resale price maintenance agreement, is no longer a *per se* restraint, it is still governed by the Rule of Reason, which is another very important anti-trust rule. According to this rule, even if a restraint of trade is not automatically illegal, if it is an "unreasonable" restraint of trade, it can still be deemed illegal. The test for ascertaining an unreasonable restraint of trade, however, is by no means a precise one. Basically, it is a weighing test; that is, if the results of the restraint of trade, such as a minimum price-fix, benefit competition and ultimately the consumer, then the restraint of trade, though still a *restraint* it must be noted, would be a legal restraint and accordingly not a violation of anti-trust law. The Rule of Reason, moreover, is applied by the courts on a case-by-case basis. Clearly, the new interpretation by the Court is very favorable to the parties on the marketing chain who set prices vertically. Now, instead of being accused of a legal wrong for which there was no defense (though naturally the government would need sufficient evidence of the agreement to fix prices), the price-fixing vertical prices can now argue that their restraint of trade is a "good" one since it benefits the consumer and is thus reasonable and legal under the Rule of Reason.

The Court's decision was a 5–4 one. Five justices of the Court agreed with the nation's major manufacturers that this new interpretation of the Sherman Act, at least in some instances, could result in more competition and better services. One example, as reported in the *New York Times,* would be the case where a minimum price agreement could make it easier for a new producer to enter the market since it and retailers would be assured of recouping their investments in manufacturing, marketing, and distributing the product. While writing the majority opinion, Justice Kennedy with a stroke of the pen eliminated the 100-year-old precedent by proclaiming: "*Stare decisis, we conclude, does not compel our continued adherence to the per se rule against vertical price restraints. As discussed earlier, respected authorities in the economics literature suggest the per se rule is inappropriate, and there is now widespread agreement that resale price maintenance can have procompetitive effects.*" *Leegin* at 2721. It can also be argued (Williams, 2007) that the Court's decision

[8]Contributed by Stephen C Muffler, Nova Southeastern University

could provide a degree of protection for luxury brands since they now can ensure by means of the vertical agreement that their products are sold at a price that is consistent with the company's brand message.

However, the four dissenting justices agreed with consumer groups that striking down the old rule could result in less competition and thus significantly higher prices for consumers. *Id* at 2725-2737. One dissenting justice, Justice Stephen Breyer stated, "*The only safe predictions to make about today's decision are that it will likely raise the price of goods at retail and that it will create considerable legal turbulence as lower courts seek to develop workable principles. I do not believe that the majority has shown new or changed conditions sufficient to warrant overruling a decision of such long standing. All ordinary stare decisis considerations indicate the contrary.*" *Id* at 2737. The Justice also warned that the decision would create problems for the federal courts as they attempt to apply the Rule of Reason to individual vertical price-fixing cases. *Id* at 2734-2735. Justice Breyer also stated that the decision could translate into a higher annual average bill for a family of four of about $750 to $1000; consequently he criticized the majority's opinion by stating: "*Putting the Court's estimate together with the Justice Department's early 1970's study translates a legal regime that permits all resale price maintenance into retail bills that are higher by an average of roughly $750 to $1000 annually for an American family of four. Just how much higher retail bills will be after the Court's decision today, of course, depends upon what is now unknown, namely how courts will decide future cases under a "rule of reason." But these figures indicate that the amounts involved are important to American families and cannot be dismissed as "tiny."* *Id* at 2736. However, many economists believe that the "give and take" of the market will hinder efforts to artificially set higher minimum prices for products. As one economist, as reported in the *Wall Street Journal*, stated, "if you raise price, you sacrifice volume." Yet other economists state that the ameliorating effects of the market might not prevent "higher end" goods or goods in short supply from being increased in price pursuant to the Court's ruling.

The case before the Court involved an appeal of a judgment of $1.2 million against Leegin Creative Leather Products after it cut off Kay's Kloset, a suburban Dallas retail store, for refusing to honor Leegin's no discount policy. Leegin's retailers were required to agree to a no discount policy, which was part of the company's marketing strategy to sell a line of fashion accessories and small leather goods through small boutiques which could offer specialized service.

Finally, it should be noted that horizontal price-fixing, that is, by competitors at the same level on the marketing chain, such as two manufacturers, is still branded by the courts as a *per se* Sherman Act Section 1 violation. *Texaco Inc. v. Dagher* (126 S.Ct. 1276 at 1279 (2006) ("*Price-fixing agreements between two or more competitors, otherwise known as horizontal price-fixing agreements, fall into the category of arrangements that are per se unlawful.*")). Also, some states pursuant to their own anti-trust laws, still consider vertical price-fixing to be an automatic legal violation. However, still legal is a situation in which a manufacturer unilaterally "suggests" the minimum prices for which its goods are to be sold and then if a retailer refuses to abide by the suggestion, then for the manufacturer to unilaterally decide not to deal with that retailer. This situation is known as the Colgate Doctrine, and is different from a price-fix since there is no explicit agreement as to the minimum price among the parties. Thus, the Supreme Court's decision potentially legalizing vertical minimum price fixes is a momentous one indeed.

Bibliography:

Anderson, Mark, "Vertical Agreements under Section 1 of the Sherman Act: Results in Search of Reasons," 37 University of Florida *Law Review* 905 (Fall 1985).

Cavico, Frank J. and Mujtaba, Bahaudin G (2008). *Legal Challenges for the Global Manager and Entrepreneur.* Dubuque, Iowa: Kendall-Hunt Publishing Company.

Labaton, Stephen, "Supreme Court Lifts Ban on Minimum Retail Pricing," *The New York Times,* June 29, 2007, pp. C1, C2.

Leegin Creative Leather Products v. PSKS (dba Kay's Kloset), 127 S.Ct. 2705 (2007).

McWilliams, Gary, White, Joseph B., and Bravin, Jess, "Split Court Ends Ban on Retail-Price Floor," *The Wall Street Journal,* June 29, 2007, p. A2.

Texaco Inc. v. Dagher, 126 S.Ct. 1276 (2006).

Williams, James S., "Brand Integrity: Lessons From Leegin," *Apparel News,* Volume 63, Number 35, August 17-23, 2007, pp. 1–2.

Questions for Discussion:

1. Which is the morally preferable legal rule pursuant to Utilitarian ethics—the old *per se* doctrine or the now prevailing Rule of Reason test—when it comes to vertical price-setting by manufactures and distributors and/or retailers? Why?

2. How does the "Per Se" legal analysis differ from the "Rule of Reason" analysis? Which one would businesses prefer to apply if they are a defendant in an anti-trust action? Why?

3. As to vertical price restraints, how does the US Supreme Court ethically reason that the "Stare Decisis" (that is, "let the precedent stand") principle will not restrict it from abandoning the "Per Se" legal test under anti-trust law in light of evolution of the U.S. free market economy? Discuss.

4. What if a clothing manufacturer completely refuses to sell its brand products to a retailer at any price? Would the Supreme Court's decision conclude that such a "refusal to sell" by the manufacturer would result in a "Per Se" violation of US antitrust laws? Why or why not?

5. What other instances can you think of in which a vertical minimum price fix would be one beneficial for the consumer and thus legal pursuant to the Rule of Reason? Provide examples with brief explanations thereof.

11. Executive Compensation

Case 11.1: Stock Options—United Health Group's CEO, William McGuire

United Health Group, Inc, the largest health insurance provider in the United States, announced in October 2006 that an independent inquiry found that stock options over the past twelve years were backdated. As a result, Dr. William McGuire, 59, resigned as chairman and will resign in December of 2006 as CEO of United Health Group, Inc. During his 15 years leading the company, McGuire brought about a 50-fold expansion of the company's customers to more than 70 million people in the United States. The stock price also increased 85-fold. McGuire also accumulated about $1.6 billion in stock options, based on the value of options as of December 2005. The company has an affiliation with AARP, and provides a Medicare HMO and drug coverage for seniors. Dr. McGuire became president and CEO in 1989, and was named chairman and CEO in 1991. He is credited with leading the company, particularly by means of a series of acquisitions, from a regional health insurer into one of the largest U.S. managed care companies.

However, according to certain security regulators, McGuire could face criminal charges for obtaining millions from the stock options that might have been backdated to raise their value. He also might face civil actions, including one from the company's shareholders. An internal investigation conducted by an outside law firm found inadequate controls at the company. In particular, the investigation revealed that there may have been a conflict of interest between McGuire and the lead board member who helping to rewrite his compensation package. The key fact was that McGuire was central to the process that set many of the option dates "at or near" the lowest price in a quarter or year, thereby raising his potential profits over a twelve year period. McGuire, however, contends that the pricing dates were set in advance. A re-pricing of McGuire's options from 1994 to 2002 based on the high closing price of each year would deny him a profit of $155 million, according to one report. From 1994 through 2005, McGuire gained $333 million from stock options. He still would be left with about $1 billion in options, which would vest immediately upon his retirement. He also signed certificates granting backdated options to employees. One legal expert, as related in the Wall Street Journal, stated that the SEC will want to determine if the company's directors were deceived in any way. Another issue the SEC is likely to examine is whether the company's past financial statements did not adequately record compensation expenses, thereby misleading investors as to the state of the company's earnings.

Options provide their recipients the right to purchase a stock at a price, called the "strike price," that most companies, including United Health, inform shareholders will be the "fair market value" on the day of the grant. Backdating options involves a company surreptitiously pretending that the grant was made at an earlier date, so that the strike price can be lower and thus the profits for the recipients of the options can be greater. In Dr. McGuire's case, the independent report stated that the stock options were issued on one day, but priced as if they had been issued earlier, when the stock price was lower, which increased their value, but which also meant that the options "were likely back-dated," according to the independent report.

No charges—civil or criminal—have been filed as of this writing; but the company did say that the IRS is now asking for documents pertaining to the compensation of some executives back to the year 2003. United Health has agreed to re-price McGuire's options granted between 1994 and 2002 to the highest price of the year, which the *Wall Street Journal* stated would reduce his potential benefit by probably $100 million. At the end of 2005, McGuire had $1.6 billion in options. Moreover, the company stated that its board of directors had adopted certain changes, including limiting pension benefits, as well as eliminating many "perks," such as post-retirement health insurance. Furthermore, one board member and United Health's general counsel have resigned. Nonetheless, as a result of the disclosures, the company's shares dropped almost 2.5% in a two month period. So far, for the year 2006 as of October, the company's shares have dropped 21%.

Dr. McGuire, nevertheless, could leave the company, the *Wall Street Journal* reported, with $1.1 billion in stock options, retirement payouts, and other benefits. That amount would be in addition to the approximately $530 million that Dr. McGuire earned since 1992 running United Health. Dr. McGuire's employment agreement provides that any departure not deemed a firing will be construed as a "retirement," meaning that almost all of his options immediately vest, related the *Wall Street Journal,* and continue in force for another six years. Moreover, Dr. McGuire will begin to receive a pension of more than $5 million per year (which his wife would receive one-half of if she outlives him). Furthermore, the contract, according to the *Wall Street Journal,* takes a fairly narrow view as to what constitutes grounds for firing, that is, either a felony conviction or the repeated failure to remedy a serious problem despite repeated notices demanding that he solve the problem. In addition to the yearly pension, the Wall Street Journal reported that Dr. McGuire would receive a lump sum pension of $6.4 million, lifetime health care coverage for himself and his wife, health care coverage for his children until the age of 25, possession of the company plane for personal business on the same terms as before, a company paid office and secretary for three years, and an allowance for security and tax and financial planning services. In addition, United Health will pay any taxes—federal and/or state—caused by the payment of these "golden parachute" benefits to Dr. McGuire.

The United Health–McGuire situation is certainly not the only stock option backdating circumstance. Actually, as of October, 2006 more than 30 senior executives or directors at 16 companies have resigned due to stock option problems. Moreover, at least 135 companies have reported stock option investigations, either internally, or by the Securities and Exchange Commission or the Department of Justice's criminal division. In Dr. McGuire's case, his lawyer stated, as reported in the *Wall Street Journal,* that McGuire is an expert in health care, but not in the legal and accounting issues regarding stock options. Moreover, his lawyer stated that McGuire sought out, received, and relied on the expert advice of others.

Bibliography:

Bloomberg News, "Insurer's CEO may be charged," October 18, 2006, p. 3D; Forelle, Charles, and Bandler, James, "How Did United Heath's McGuire Get Some Options Twice," *The Wall Street Journal*, October 20, 2006, pp. B1, B9; Forelle, Charles, and Maremont, Mark, "United Health's McGuire Could Leave With $1.1 Billion," The *Wall Street Journal*, October 17, 2006, pp. B1, B10; Freed, Joshua, "Stock options behind many firings," *The Miami Herald*, October 17, 2006, pp. 1C, 4C; Moore, Duncan, "No. 1 health insurer's CEO resigns in wake of inquiry," *Sun-Sentinel*, October 17, 2006, pp. 1D, 2D.

Questions for Discussion:

1. Discuss the legal issues involved in the granting of backdated stock options.
2. Even if legal, was Dr. McGuire's "golden parachute" moral? Discuss.

Case 11.2: Executive Compensation, Tax Deductibility, and Social Responsibility

Business Week magazine reported in November of 2006 an interesting development regarding executive compensation and a law passed during the Clinton administration in order to curb excessive executive compensation. At that time, companies were allowed to deduct all compensation for their top executives. However, President Clinton took the lead in the promulgation of a law that allowed companies to deduct compensation amounts over $1 million but only if executives managed to meet specified performance goals. *Business Week* reported that the law has not had the effect that President Clinton intended. *Business Week* related that over the law's first decade, average compensation for chief executives at companies listed in the Standard & Poor's 500 stock index dramatically increased from $3.7 million to $9.1 million. One problem with the Clinton law is that it has allowed companies to take tax deductions for executive pay goals, such as, according to *Business Week*, "individual achievement of personal commitment" (for BellSouth Corp.), "improving customer satisfaction" (for Dell, Inc.), for maintaining a workplace that is "fun" (AES Corp.). One way that "fun" was measured by the board of directors was to send to the employees an annual survey. One question asked how the employees felt their co-workers were doing company-wide in relation to four core principles: fun, fairness, integrity, and social responsibility. One executive was measured on the criterion of ensuring that the employees demonstrated "social responsibility." One problem with the criteria, as noted by *Business Week*, is that they are very vague. For example, the criteria might say that the executive will be judged on "earnings per share" or "operational revenue," but these terms are not spelled out, and the detailed definitions are worked out by the compensation committees, and in private. Moreover, the board's compensation committee typically can choose one factor of a combination of objectives in order to ascertain an executive's performance. Furthermore, the performance requirements were not applied to the award of stock options to executives. Another unintended consequence of the Clinton law was in essence to establish $1 million in compensation as the "minimum wage" for an executive, since the law's requirements for performance criteria for tax deductibility only applied to amounts over $1 million. Of course, some companies can simply ignore the law, and thereby forgo the tax deduction, and pay their executives whatever the board deems appropriate. As a result of the apparent abuse of the Clinton administration law, *Business Week* reported that the IRS is now more strictly monitoring compliance. Moreover, the Securities and Exchange Commission in 2007 will be enforcing its new executive pay rules which require more disclosure and justification of executive compensation.

Bibliography:

Epstein, Keith, and Javers, Eamon, "How Bill Clinton Helped Boost CEO Pay," *Business Week*, November 27, 2006, pp. 64–65.

Questions for Discussion:

1. Do you feel that the Clinton administration law created a $1 million "minimum wage" for executives? Why or why not?

2. Is the law a moral one pursuant to Utilitarian ethics? Discuss.

3. How should the performance goal of ensuring "social responsibility" be defined and determined? Discuss.

4. What about the objective of "fun"? Discuss.

5. How should a company approach the issue of executive compensation using the principles of Value-Driven Management? Discuss.

12. Human Resources

Case 12.1: The Psychopath in the Corner Office[9]

Tom, Barb, and Frank were having lunch, and their "chit chat" eventually turned to the latest office gossip. Barb brought an issue up by asking, "Did you guys hear about that meeting with the new stock brokers that Ed had?" Both Tom and Frank responded that they hadn't. "From what I heard, Ed was just like that guy played by Alex Baldwin in the movie *Glengarry Glen Rose*. He just ripped into them from one side to the other." Tom then said, "You know that doesn't surprise me. There is something about him that shows he is not comfortable in his own skin. But he's the consummate 'player' with the senior executives, so either he's Dr. Hyde or the greatest actor to ever work on Wall Street." Frank said he thought Ed was considered the "rising star" in the brokerage, and had caused the sales revenue to rise higher and faster than any of their peers. They then talked about what little they really knew about Ed, where he came from, his credentials, personal life, etc. All they knew was that he had joined the firm about a year ago, right after the merger had occurred, and right in the middle of all that organizational turmoil that they were trying to put behind them. Many of their best friends were "let go" back then; and it was painful to talk about it, even now. Amazingly, Ed had flourished magnificently in all that disruption. Several of the executives he worked closely with had been caught violating serious SEC laws and lost their jobs and licenses. Ed, however, came out "smelling like a rose."

Six months later, Nathan, the Vice President of Personnel for the brokerage, was having lunch with his friend Jack, who happened to be a lawyer for one of the city's largest law firms. Nathan happened to have Ed on his mind for a number of reasons, and he wanted to try and get some free legal advice that Jack didn't mind "throwing his way" over lunch or over a few drinks, given their long friendship. He told Jack that Ed now had a "corner office"; but a few complaints had been made to him regarding Ed's dealings with people, both inside the firm and outside it. Checking into Ed's credentials, he learned that Ed in fact did not have an MBA from the Ivy League business school he claimed, but rather from some "degree mill" with an Ivy League sounding name. He had claimed he was married, but he didn't mention that he had already been divorced three times. His previous employer had gone into bankruptcy. One employee had overheard him tell another broker that he thought it completely normal to lie to people. In the turmoil of the merger, nobody checked these things out; and consequently Ed's background was never closely investigated. All personnel knew was that he had the "blessing" of the president, and had some large accounts that he was bringing with him; and the president knew that one of Ed's clients was a well known billionaire. Nevertheless, one question that concerned Nathan was whether the firm was exposed to any legal liability. Jack's opinion, without knowing all the details, was that there was a potential negligence action that could be brought against the firm, arising out of Ed's misfeasance, malfeasance, or even criminal behavior. Yet that legal exposure, of course, was the same for all its employees.

What really concerned Nathan, however, was how to prevent Ed's behavior inside the firm from harming the firm. It would be impossible now to fire him for not telling the

---

[9]Contributed by Don Valeri, Canadian Lawyer and educator.

firm his MBA was from a non-Ivy League business school, especially because the president considered him a "rising star." What the president didn't know was that Ed's overly aggressive and sharp behavior was starting to cause a few managers to consider quitting. Three brokers that Ed had overtaken had recently "jumped ship" to the firm's competitors after getting "stabbed in the back" by Ed. Yet there was talk that Ed was going to be made a VP in a year or so. As Jack heard more and more of Ed's case, he began to realize that underlying Ed's behavior might be some very serious psychological issues.

The problem in this case is that the issues are more than "just" legal and personnel ones. There could be a serious moral leadership problem in this firm. Unfortunately, at this time there is no easy or clear solution to this case. If one was Nathan, though, one's options would include: 1) Wait for Ed to "self destruct." That option, however, might take years, and would leave a lot of destruction behind it for people and the firm. 2) Take the precautionary steps needed to remove or terminate Ed. This path is even more problematic. The president may favor Ed, and consequently might be disinclined to fire him after personally hiring him and raising him to VP status. To do that, the president will have to admit he made a mistake, and that might be hard for him to do. Ed has likely ingratiated himself to the president, and accordingly the president may feel he "owes" Ed something in return. There also may be some sort of mentor relationship here. Furthermore, the worst possibility is that Ed knows of some "skeleton in the closet" of the president's, or even in others' "closets," with which Ed could use in a harmful manner someday. In other words, in an office "political war," he may be very difficult to get rid of. Combining with other senior executives to remove him may fail, or worse, even backfire. Whistleblowing to the board of directors is also risky, as well as problematic, since many of directors owe their seats to the president, and thus will be reluctant to want to get involved in this situation until it adversely affects the firm, financially or legally, or impacts the president in some harmful manner. The board members are likely to see this as just another "personality conflict." Ultimately, only the president can remove Ed. Yet that discharge may not ever happen until the president has to choose between Ed and saving his own job. 3) Slowly and quietly educate the president about the dangers of having people on board with the psychological make up of someone like Ed. At some point, hopefully, the likelihood is that the "light will go on," and then he will be forced to make a decision. At that point, one should also know whether the president has the leadership capabilities that entail integrity and "moral backbone."

Bibliography:

Paul Babiak and Robert D. Hare. *Snakes in Suits: When Psychopaths Go to Work* (2006). Regan Books/Harper Collins.

Hervey Cleckley and Emily S. Checkley (1980). *The Mask of Sanity* (5th edition).

Robert D. Hare (1999). *Without Conscience: The Disturbing World of Psychopaths Among Us*. Guilford Press.

Questions for Discussion:

1. What are the legal issues in arising out of this case? How should they be resolved? Discuss.

2. What are the ethical issues arising out of this case? How should they be resolved? Discuss.

3. Is Ed what psychologists now call a "high functioning" or "successful psychopath"? Should the firm be concerned if he is? If so, what should it do, if anything, at this point in time? What would you advised Nathan?

4. Is Ed acting in a Machiavellian manner? How should one respond to such Machiavellian tactics in the workplace? Discuss.

5. Of the three aforementioned options in the case, which one is the most efficacious? Why?

Case 12.2: Office Romance—Legal and Ethical Issues

Office romance is a very prevalent, contentious, and difficult human resource (HR) issue today—legally, morally, and practically. All employers—large and small—eventually will have to deal with the challenge of employees who date, fall in love, and then fall out of love and break up—perhaps in a bitter and inimical manner. The extent of the potential problem was underscored by the *Miami Herald* newspaper which reported in February of 2007 that 43% of U.S. workers admitted dating a co-worker. Of course, many of these relationships lead to marriage and have "happy endings," and some relationships that end leave the former romantic partners as still "friends," but unfortunately many other relationships end acrimoniously, degenerate into antagonism and recriminations, and then even worse, lead to lawsuits.

Employers certainly do not want to be liable when office romances "crash and burn." Accordingly, employers have taken several proactive measures to avoid liability. One measure is called formally a "consensual relationship agreement," or more informally a "love contract." Such a contract is used mainly for senior executives. In a "love contract," the intimate couple can disclose their relationship, and also, most importantly for the employer, expressly state that their relationship is voluntary and consensual. The contract also typically will state that the intimate co-workers have read the company's sexual harassment policy, and that they are free to break up without any adverse impact to their jobs. The signed original "love contract" is usually filed with the company's HR department. Unrequited love is always problematic; yet whether a "love contract" is the solution is still a matter of debate.

All employers should be proactive and accordingly have policies on relationships and dating among co-workers. Employers should also ensure that all the employees are aware of such policies. The policies must underscore to employees that there are appropriate legal as well as ethical standards of conduct at the workplace. The employees should also be advised that there may be career repercussions when they commence a relationship. For example, an employer can (and perhaps should) have a policy that when two employees in the same department start dating, one might need to be transferred to another department. Similarly, a policy may state that employees on the same work team cannot date and form romantic relationships. In a more extreme policy, one dating employee may have to resign or be discharged from the company. At the very least, employers should seriously consider policies that prohibit managers from dating subordinate employees. Another policy is to have managers and supervisors report dating type relationships; but not to require such reporting by lower level employees. Of course, one must define "relationship." Such a policy typically would not require the reporting of a "mere" date. Yet the *Wall Street Journal* reported in 2005 that only 12% of companies that were surveyed by the American Management Association had written guidelines on office dating. The *Wall Street Journal* also reported in 2005 that most major companies do not fire employees involved in consensual affairs where neither partner directly reports to the other. It also reported that some companies, such as IBM and Xerox, have formal policies that allow relationships between employees who are not on the same management hierarchical chain.

The primary objective of such policies and measures is to shield employers from liability pursuant to sexual harassment and gender discrimination laws if the office romance later degenerates into a workplace dispute. Presumably the romance was commenced by the employees based on their own free will without any claim of coercion or intimidation for sex, which of course is the genesis of many sexual harassment lawsuits. Employers also want to minimize morale problems at work, especially charges of favoritism, and concomitant disruption, as well as negative publicity—externally as well as internally, which can all affect the bottom line of the business. Furthermore, an executive's failed office romance may impair the executive's ability to lead the company. Employers today are especially sensitive to office romance due to the potential of workplace sexual discrimination and sexual harassment claims, particularly since the U.S. Supreme Court has ruled that an employer may be absolutely liable for an executive, manager, or supervisor who sexually harasses a subordinate employee in the managerial hierarchical chain. Sexual harassment is premised on a workplace environment that is hostile, offensive, or abusive sexually. The legal standard for what constitutes a hostile sexual environment is a very subjective one too. Employees can sue an employer for allowing a hostile sexual environment to occur and also for not stopping the offensive sexual behavior. The problem for the employer is exacerbated when the relationship was originally consensual but now one party wants to break it off, but the other party still persists in making now unwelcome romantic advances. Furthermore, even though the federal civil rights act does not protect against discrimination based on marital status, about two dozen states and many municipalities have laws that ban discrimination on the basis of marriage. A legal problem in such a state or city might arise if a married employee who has an affair is terminated, but an unmarried employee who has an affair is not discharged. The married employee could well claim illegal discrimination based on his or her marital status. Another legal problem for employers is that employees are entitled to privacy rights—pursuant to constitutional law for government employees, but also pursuant to tort law for all employees. An employer who too intrusively investigates its employees' romantic relationships or discharges employees for such relationships may be sued for intentionally violating the employees' privacy rights.

To complicate matters further from a practical vantage point, the employee having the romantic relationship with a senior level executive may perceive that due to the relationship with the executive he or she may think he or she has, or be perceived as having, more power and influence beyond his or her official job status and authority. Employers thus want to take steps to not only avoid legal liability but also to ensure that office romances do not hinder job performance. The productivity and teamwork adversely affected may not only involve the romantically involved employees but also their co-workers. Accusations of conflict-of-interest, whether real or perceived, have the potential to disrupt and negatively impact the workplace. Damage to the value of merit as a core principle for promotion can be another very negative consequence. Office romances can be a major distraction at work, even without charges of favoritism and conflict-of-interest.

Yet it is difficult to have an effective total ban on dating since human nature and sexual attraction may overcome any employer policy. People will still get romantically involved at the workplace regardless of any policy. People meet other people most frequently at work. Total prohibitions of relationships may drive them "underground." "Turning a blind eye," moreover, means that the employer has lost an opportunity to provide guidelines and to counsel the dating couple. Of course, dating employees may attempt to keep their relationship secret; yet secrecy can be difficult to achieve in certain workplaces, particularly where the corporate culture is one of openness and informality and where the employees work long hours together. Employees who date and form relationships, whether secretly or openly, should be very scrupulous about keeping their romantic relationship out of the office. One company, Southwest Airlines, as reported in the *Wall Street Journal* in 2005, not only employs over 1000 married couples, but also explicitly allows consensual office romantic relationships. However, the airline also has a policy and a process that affords an employee who objects to a particular office romance to complain to the HR department or to a manager, who in turn is obligated to find a remedy if the office romance negatively impacts the company's "culture." One would presume that the company's culture would demand at a minimum professional and ethical behavior at the workplace.

One particularly well publicized office romance case dealt with former Boeing Company Chief Executive Harry Stonecipher, 68, whose extramarital affair with a 48-year-old female executive resulted in a great deal of adverse publicity for Boeing, and which consequently resulted in Stonecipher's termination by means of a forced resignation. At the time, as reported in the *Miami Herald,* Boeing's board chairman explained that "the CEO must set the standard for impeachable professional and personal behavior." Business ethics, therefore, extends to more than "mere" corporate concerns, but also the personal life of top executives. One fact that made the Stonecipher case particularly troublesome, and which surely contributed to the CEO's ouster, was that he was brought in to clean up the company's ethics after a company and Air Force conflict-of-interest contracting scandal. His dalliance was thus a major embarrassment to Boeing. In Stonecipher's case, the board of directors was tipped off to the romance by an anonymous whistleblowing employee who sent the board a copy of an explicit email that the CEO had written. The whistleblower, it appears, had intercepted an email between the pair. Apparently, Stonecipher met the employee, who was a vice-president and a long-time company employee, at a company retreat. At the time of the forced resignation, opinion was divided as to whether the Boeing board did the "right thing." The board's investigation of Stonecipher, however, did not reveal that the affair caused Stonecipher to influence his paramour's career prospects at Boeing, which clearly would have been unethical. Polls show, nonetheless, that a majority of people in the U.S. think that extramarital affairs are immoral. Thus, an executive having an extramarital affair may raise a character issue for the executive and his or her partner as well as the company. One commentator suggested that Stonecipher was so quickly terminated because the board did not want the personal email to be made public. It is interesting to note for the record that the infamous, and now deceased, Ken Lay of Enron married his secretary (who, since Lay died before he was formally sentenced, inherited the bulk of his estate, as opposed to the Enron victims, because Lay, though convicted, was not technically "sentenced").

Certain concluding points are very clear: drawing the line between personal and business affairs is never easy; employer scrutiny of office romance surely will increase; consequently, employers not only will have to get involved with workplace romances, but they also will have to manage office romances, very carefully too. Employers may choose to "look the other way" when employees date, but that "head in the sand" approach is shortsighted and very risky. Employers must always keep in mind that office romances can "crash and burn," and consequently be prepared to act accordingly to contain the damage to the firm and its stakeholders.

Bibliography:

Forman, Ellen, "Love in the workplace," *Sun-Sentinel*, February 14, 1999, pp. 1A, 14A; Hymowitz, Carol, and Lublin, Joann S., "Many Companies Look the Other Way at Employee Affairs," *The Wall Street Journal*, March 8, 2005, pp. B1, B6; Hymowitz, Carol, "Personal boundaries shrink as companies punish bad behavior," *The Wall Street Journal*, June 18, 2007, p. B1; Roberts, Dan, and Maitland, Alison, "CEOs now face more scrutiny," *The Miami Herald*, March 22, 2005, p. 2C; Rose, Barbara, "Companies are learning to accept office romances," *Sun-Sentinel*, March 13, 2005, pp. 1E, 2E; Rosenberg, Joyce M., "Cupid's arrow can be deadly in the office," *The Miami Herald*, Business Monday, February 12, 2007, p. 12; Selvin, Molly, "In love in the office? Sign on the dotted line," *The Miami Herald*, February 14, 2007, p. 3C; Shellenbarger, Sue, "Employees Often Ignore Office Affairs, Leaving Co-Workers in Difficult Spot," *The Wall Street Journal*, March 10, 2005, p. D1; Shellenbarger, Sue, "Getting Fired for Dating a Co-Worker: Office Romance Comes Under Attack," *The Wall Street Journal*, February 19, 2004, p. D1.

Questions for Discussion:

1. Discuss the legal, moral, and practical issues involved in office romance.
2. Specifically, what office romance policies do you believe are the most efficacious—legally, morally, and practically? Why?
3. In the Boeing-Stonecipher case, was the CEO treated in a moral manner? Why or why not?
4. Did the Boeing-Stonecipher whistleblower act in a moral manner? Why or why not?
5. Does the Southwest Airlines' office romance policy pass the test of Value Driven Management? Why or why not?

Case 12.3: Transgender and Transsexual Employees: Legal and Ethical Issues

The issue of transgender and transsexual and sexually transitioning employees is emerging today as an important and very challenging employment issue—legally, morally, and practically—for business. The issue has been thrust into the "public eye" as well as the federal courts by two noteworthy cases—one a public sector employment case and the other a private sector one, though with religious ramifications.

The first case, reported in the *Wall Street Journal* in March of 2007, dealt with a man, aged 55, a business professor at a Methodist evangelical religious school in Michigan, who was discharged when school officials told him that his "womanly appearance" violated the school's requirements of "model Christian character" and "Christian behavior." He thought there is no requirement that an employee be a Methodist. The professor was ordered to dress and to act like a man. Nevertheless, the professor began to wear loose clothing, manicured his nails, and started hormone therapy, and in time he developed breasts. The school had ordered him to work from home, teaching online (taking a 20% pay cut), and ordered him not to appear on campus with female clothing, female makeup, or any outward exhibitions of feminine appearance or behavior. However, as admitted by the professor, he visited the campus twice, wearing a college T-shirt and female makeup. He was then dismissed. The professor is now contesting his dismissal pursuant to federal anti-discrimination laws. He has not yet had any gender altering surgery. He is married and the father of three; and his wife of 35 years, who is a nurse, plans to stay with him. The case is further complicated due to the fact that the professor's doctor has diagnosed him with "gender-identity disorder," which means a person is suffering from uncertainty about one's sexuality and where one's sexual identity differs from one's body. The case is expected to draw attention to, and further refine, two important legal principles—the freedom of religious organizations to operate without government intrusion and the rights of employees of such organizations to be treated in a non-discriminatory manner with regard to gender. The case could also involve a claim made under the Americans with Disabilities Act, particularly whether the courts will recognize the professor's diagnosed disability as a legal disability, and if so what the employer's accommodation to such a disability should be. The courts, it is important to note, have long recognized an exception to the Civil Rights Act that allows religious organizations to uphold their religious beliefs. For example, the Catholic Church has been allowed to exclude women from being priests. Yet, this exception has not been precisely defined by the courts; and thus the exact issue as to whether legal anti-discrimination protections would encompass the case of a teacher of secular subjects at a religious school.

In the second case, a public sector case, as reported by the *Miami Herald* newspaper and *Newsweek* magazine in March of 2007, the city of Largo, Florida discharged its long-time (14 years) city manager, Steve S., when he informed the city commissioners that he was going to have a sex change operation, was currently undergoing hormone treatments, and now wanted to be called "Susan." He said, as reported in the *Herald,* that he chose the name Susan because that is the name his mother would have called him if he had been a girl. He also stated that he has always felt that a female "presence" was trying to come out. He is married and has a child, and presently he and his wife have no plans to divorce. His wife in the past has been very supportive and actually has helped him pick out dresses. He must live as a man for at least a year, as that is the medical protocol for a person contemplating a sex change operation. He now has to run with a sports bra due to the hormone therapy. He also ventures out on weekend trips as "Susan," and at times men buy drinks for him. His wife is worried about his safety. Steve's confidential memo about his plans to the city commission was leaked, however, to the local media, and quickly the story spread through the national media. The *Miami Herald* reported that the city commissioners were "aghast," and that they faced a "barrage" of calls and emails, many from, as the *Miami Herald* described Largo, the "close-knit religious community." The five commissioners terminated the manager, explaining that they doubted his integrity as well as his ability to lead the city and its 1200 employees. Steve/Susan now is represented by the National Center for Lesbian Rights. However, he/she is not certain about suing, and is hoping that the city commission reverses its decision. As the city manager, Steve served as an employee-at-will and thus was subject to dismissal by the commission. However, the dismissal of even an at-will employee cannot violate the Civil Rights Act or, since the employer here was government, the U.S. Constitution, which protects freedom of expression of government employees as part of their 1st Amendment free speech rights. Freedom of speech and expression, however, are not absolute constitutional rights and the courts use a balancing test to weigh the public sector employee's interest in speech and expression against the government employer's interest in managing its workforce efficiently and thus serving the public interest.

In addition to Constitutional protections, the Civil Rights Act, which prohibits discrimination based on sex, is also at issue. The courts, however, have not interpreted the anti-sex discrimination provisions in the U.S. Civil Rights Act to encompass discrimination based on sexual preference or orientation, though there is a developing body of case law dealing with same-sex sexual harassment, and there are some cases in the federal courts which have held that people that are changing their sex are protected by sex discrimination law. There is also a noteworthy U.S. Supreme Court case in which the court ruled that an accounting firm engaged in gender stereotyping, and thus illegal sex discrimination, by denying a woman employee a partnership because of her "macho" male behavior. There is also, as reported in the *Wall Street Journal,* a federal district court case in which the court ruled that a city in Ohio illegally fired a transsexual firefighter. The rationale given by the court was that the U.S. Civil Rights Act protects a person who does not act or identify with his or her gender. Moreover, approximately one-third of the states in the U.S. now outlaw discrimination based on sexual orientation or preference. According to the *Miami Herald* newspaper, in 2007, seven states had laws that prohibit the discharge of an employee based on his or her gender identity. Florida does not have such a law. There is a proposal in the U.S. Congress, called the national Employment Non-Discrimination Act, which would prevent employees from being fired because of their sexual orientation and gender identities. Currently, federal civil rights law does not offer any protection to transgender employees. *Newsweek* magazine reports, though, that eight states (but not Florida) and the District of Columbia do offer such protection. Moreover, *Newsweek* reports a study by the Human Rights Campaign that states that 122 of Fortune 500 companies include gender identity as part of their employment non-discrimination policies. Similarly, in the private sector, the *Sun-Sentinel* newspaper of Ft. Lauderdale in 2006 reported that 85% of the Fortune 500 companies bar discrimination based on sexual orientation and preference. Boeing, for example, has a very extensive policy of anti-sex discrimination which goes so far as to prohibit discrimination against people based on "gender identity," a new legal and human resource term which signifies not only gay and lesbian employees and those transitioning from one sex to another, but also workers who might be abused or ridiculed for not acting male or female enough. Another company that was one of the first to include "gender identity" or gender expression as a rule in its internal corporate polices was Lucent Technologies. Thus, even though the law may not support gay, lesbian, bisexual, transsexual, and transgender employees, many companies today are beginning to provide such protection by means of their own internal company rules and regulations. The corporate employment situation has now moved far beyond acknowledgement of gay and lesbian employees, to the promulgation of expansive sexually based non-discrimination policies, offering domestic partner benefits, as well as support for "gay pride" events and the active recruitment of gay employees. Of course, companies are now under very practical pressures to hire and retain competent employees in a very competitive global business environment. Companies are also cognizant of the fact that a solid portion of their customer base, approximated at 10%, are gay, lesbian, bisexual, transsexual, and transgender employees. Today, as reported in the *Sun-Sentinel* newspaper, the Gender Public Advocacy Coalition notes that in 2006 approximately 166 major corporations now have gender identity and gender expression provisions in their corporate policies.

One point is clear, and that is that even if the law is unclear and unsettled and perhaps developing, the workplace today is surely a more inclusive environment that recognizes all types of individuals—and for their contributions and not their sexual status. Diversity, always an important issue—legally, morally, and practically—for companies has now been expanded to encompass sexuality and gender issues.

Bibliography:

Joyce, Amy, "Support for gay workers is increasing, survey says," *Sun-Sentinel*, October 2, 2006, p. 9; Negrete, Figueras, "Town rocked by sex-change case," The *Miami Herald*, March 4, 2007, p. 1A; Rothaus, Steve, "Publicity surrounding sex change is unusual," *The Miami Herald*, March 4, 2007, p. 1A; Sataline, Suzanne, "Who's Wrong When Rights Collide," *The Wall Street Journal*, March 6, 2007, p. B1; Waddell, Lynn, and Campo-Flores, Arian, "A Case of Gender Blues," *Newsweek*, March 12, 2007, p. 51.

Questions for Discussion:

1. Discuss the legal issues—constitutional as well as statutory—federal and state—involved in the two cases. Specifically, how should the two cases be resolved legally? Explain your decisions.

2. Should federal civil rights law be amended by Congress, or interpreted by the federal courts, to include sex discrimination protections to cover gay, lesbian, transgender, transsexual, sexually transitioning, and gender-identity-suffering employees.

3. Have the terminated employees, even if legally dismissed, been treated in a moral manner? Discuss, utilizing ethical theories and principles.

4. What would a Value-Driven Management analysis indicate as the value-maximizing approach to each case from the perspectives of the employers? Discuss, utilizing the stakeholder VDM model.

Case 12.4: Employment At-Will, Mass Layoffs, and Rehires: Circuit City's "Wage Management Initiative"

The Miami Herald and *Sun-Sentinel* (Ft. Lauderdale) newspapers reported in March of 2007 a very large layoff plan for the giant electronics retailer, Circuit City, which is the second largest electronics retailer after Best Buy Company. The plan is being called the "wage management initiative." What makes the Circuit City "initiative" controversial is the fact that it has terminated 3,400 of its highest paid salespeople, but then plans to hire replacements at a lesser salary. Furthermore, the company has stated that the terminated employees can apply for their old jobs, but now at the lower pay scales. The terminated employees will receive severance pay. It also should be noted that the affected salespeople were not given the option to take a pay-cut; rather, they were terminated, and then told they could reapply for their old jobs. There is, though, a 10 week waiting period before they could apply for their old jobs. The affected employees were employees-at-will and thus not protected by any contract regarding their employment tenure with the company. According the newspapers, a company spokesperson stated that the jobs that were eliminated paid "well above" the market average. Circuit City pays approximately $10 to $11 an hour, on average, as reported in the newspapers. An industry expert, as related by the *Miami Herald*, stated that entry-level pay for such sales positions is about $8 an hour for inexperienced workers. The newspapers also reported that the layoffs would reduce 2008 expenses by $110 million, and reduce annual spending in 2009 by $140 million. Both papers reported that the reason for the mass layoffs was financial, specifically that the company is trying to save money after reporting its first loss in six quarters in December of 2006. The company's stock has fallen 21% over the past 12 months, the papers reported; but after announcement of the "restructuring," the stock went up 1.9% as reported in the *Herald*. Apparently, the company's financial problems are being caused by the poor sales of flat-panel televisions. (The *Sun-Sentinel* article used the word "plummeted.") Circuit City had to greatly reduce the prices on TVs during the 2006 holiday season due to intense competition from Wal-Mart, Home Depot, and Costco, all of whom began selling flat-screen TVS for less.

However, there could be some negative consequences for Circuit City from the "restructuring." First, the layoffs could have a negative impact on sales as the new sales personnel get adjusted to the company and its products and learn their jobs. Second, as the *Herald* noted, the retailer could be "risking a public backlash" from consumers. Another risk is that employee morale would be damaged. For all these reasons, customers might start avoiding Circuit City stores. Actually, one customer, as reported by the *Herald*, stated that he would no longer shop at Circuit City since the company was not willing to pay its employees a "living wage." One industry expert, as reported in the *Herald*, stated that the company's strategy was "quite cold" and not "in the best interest of Circuit City as a whole." One strong point to Circuit City has been that its sales people have long been regarded as very knowledgeable, which gave the company a competitive edge over other large retailers, especially Wal-Mart. Some companies do have two-tiered wage systems, such as Caterpillar Company, with new hires making less, but, as noted in the *Herald*, terminating employees and then offering to rehire them at a lesser wage is "very rare."

Business Ethics: The Moral Foundation of Effective Leadership, Management, and Entrepreneurship

It is most interesting to note that the CEO of Circuit City, Philip Schoonover, was paid $8.52 million in 2006, including a salary of almost one million dollars. (To compare, the CEO of Best Buy was paid $3.85 million, including a salary of $1.7 million.)

Bibliography:

Anderson, Mae, and Simon, Helen, "Circuit City cuts jobs, wages," *The Miami Herald*, March 29, 2007, pp. 1C, 4C; Clother, Mark, "Higher pay means no job," *Sun-Sentinel*, March 29, 2007, pp. 1D, 2D.

Questions for Discussion:

1. Did Circuit City act legally? Why or why not?
2. What would the legal result be if the terminated "better-paid" employees were predominantly over 40 years of age? Discuss.
3. Did Circuit City act morally pursuant to Utilitarian and Kantian ethics? Discuss.
4. Do you agree with the expert who said the company's strategy was "quite cold"? Why or why not? Do you agree with this expert who said that the company initiative was not in the best interest of the company as a whole? Why or why not?
5. Is it fair for the CEO to be paid such compensation when the salaries of the salespeople are being reduced? Discuss.
6. What exactly is a "living wage" for employees of large electronic retailers? Discuss.
7. Do Circuit City's actions pass the Value Driven Management test? Why or why not?
8. Is Circuit City a socially responsible company? Why or why not?

Case 12.5: Employer E-Mail Systems and Unionization

The *New York Times* reported in December of 2007 that the National Labor Relations Board (NLRB), a federal regulatory agency empowered to regulate labor relations in the United States, has ruled that employers now have the right to prohibit their employees from using the employers' e-mail systems to transmit union-related messages. The decision, as noted by the *Times,* certainly will hinder pro-union and organizing messages by employees as well as union efforts to maintain communications between the unions and their membership. The decision was a 3-2 one, reflecting a Republican v. Democratic split on the Board. The Board ruled that it is now legal for an employer in the U.S. to prohibit union-related e-mails so long as employers have a policy forbidding employees from sending e-mail for non-work-related solicitations for outside organizations. The *Times* deemed the ruling to be a "significant setback" to labor unions in the United States. The unions, as reported by the *Times,* contended that e-mail systems have become a "modern day gathering place where employees should be able to communicate freely with co-workers to discuss work-related matters of mutual concern." Yet now employers can prohibit union-related email as part of an overall non-solicitation policy. The case before the NLRB, the *Times* reported, involved a newspaper in Eugene, Oregon, The *Register-Guard,* and e-mail messages transmitted by a newspaper employee who was also the president of the Newspaper Guild at the paper. The employee sent three messages about marching in a town parade, and she also urged employees to wear green to show support for the union during contract negotiations. The majority on the NLRB explained that an employer has a "basic property right" to regulate the use of its e-mail systems, including restricting employees' use of what is, the Board underscored, company property. Labor leaders, the *Times* reported, naturally attacked the decision, condemning it as yet another in a series of rulings that have favored employers and undercut employees. The *Times* reported that the general counsel of the AFL-CIO condemned the decision by declaring that the "Bush labor board has again struck at the heart of what the nation's labor laws were designed to protect—the right of employees to discuss working conditions and other matters of mutual concern." The *Times* also pointed out that labor unions in the U.S. continue to struggle to reverse their membership decline. Unions represent only 12% of the workers in the United States, down from 35% in the 1950s. The two Board members who dissented argued that the employees' interest in freely communicating with other employees about union activity and other matters of joint concern should, pertaining to e-mail systems, supersede the employer's property interest. Of course, personal, non-work-related, e-mail messages, such as for-sale communications and wedding announcements, should still be permissible, based on the Board ruling and court precedent regarding conventional ground bulletin boards, as opposed to group or organizational postings, such as union messages. Moreover, an exception for organizational messages on behalf of charities should also be permissible.

Bibliography:

Greenhouse, Steven, "Labor Board Restricts Union Use of E-Mail," *The New York Times,* December 23, 2007, p. 28.

Questions for Discussion:

1. Do you agree with the National Labor Relations Board legal determination? Why or why not?

2. Is the NLRB decision a moral one pursuant to Utilitarian ethics? Why or why not?

3. Is the NLRB decision a moral one pursuant to Kantian ethics? Why or why not?

4. How would you balance the values of employers, employees, and unions utilizing the principles of Value Driven Management? Discuss.

13. Accounting

Case 13.1: A CPA Firm's "Ethical Crossroads"[10]

As was customary on Fridays, Emery Johnson and his junior partner, Tom Fuller, were having lunch at their favorite restaurant. As busy Certified Public Accountants (CPAs), their Friday lunches provided them with time to discuss their business as well as a few relaxing hours away from the office. Today, however, the discussion was not enjoyable; in fact, it was somber. In looking over their financial statements, Emery had noticed a disturbing trend: although billings had steadily increased, the balance in accounts receivable had grown even faster. Furthermore, a comparison of the accounts receivable aging for the last six months indicated that the percentage of past due accounts (over 60, 90, and 120 days) had increased each month. In discussing the reason for the dismal collections, their consensus was that the slowed economy had resulted in decreased donations to their many non-profit clients. Thus, most of these clients were slow in paying their accounting fees. Emery and Tom concluded that if collections did not quickly improve, a substantial bank loan would be needed. Johnson & Associates, Inc. is a small CPA firm located in the Cleveland, Ohio area. It specializes in attestation engagements for non-profit organizations. The firm was founded in 1979 by Emery Johnson, CPA. His goal was to build a loyal client base by delivering quality but reasonably priced auditing and review services to the non-profit niche. Emery knew from the outset that a successful CPA had to build a reputation based on competence and integrity. He also was aware that he had to develop trusting relationships with his clients, and that the firm's services had to be delivered in a timely manner. Determined to grow the firm, he was willing to put in the long hours and hard work needed to accomplish his goal. So far, Emery's efforts had been successful. The annual performance and satisfaction survey completed by the clients regularly indicated a perception of Johnson & Associates as a highly competent CPA firm that charged fair prices and exhibited a high level of integrity. Moreover, as Emery's reputation in the non-profit niche grew, so did his business; by 2007 the firm had about 75 audit and review clients that generated annual billings of over $1.5 million. During the years of expansion, Emery had hired a small staff of auditors. Last year he had decided that the size of the workload and the firm's profitability and continued growth justified taking on a partner. When Tom Fuller, the firm's sole audit manager, mentioned that he was being recruited for the controller position at one of the firm's largest clients, Emery countered with an offer of a 30% partnership.

Emery Johnson had earned a bachelor's degree in finance in 1970 and a master's degree in accounting in 1976. Both degrees were from a nearby state university. A few years later, he passed all four parts of the CPA exam. After working his way up to the manager level at a national CPA firm, he decided to open his own practice. Tom Fuller, upon graduating from college with a degree in accounting, had worked for three other firms prior to being hired by Johnson & Associates. After taking an extensive review course, he had, shortly before joining Emery's firm, finally succeeded (on his fourth attempt) in passing the CPA Exam. Over the years, Tom's responsibilities had steadily increased, and

---

[10]Contributed by Dr. Josephine Sosa-Fey and Dr. Donald L. Ariail, Texas A&M University–Kingsville.

after four years he had become the firm's audit manager. When Emery made him a lucrative partnership offer, Tom promptly accepted. Since Emery was the CPA he most respected—a highly competent accountant and a man of great integrity—Tom felt the partnership to be a perfect business marriage. Sherry James had graduated with a master's degree in social work from a state university in Georgia. After working for a number of years as a social worker, she founded Women's Helping Hand, Inc. (WHH) as an IRS designated 501 (c) (3) non-profit organization. WHH offers counseling services for women in abusive relationships and provides temporary shelter to them and their children. By 2007, WHH had provided critically needed help to thousands of victims of domestic abuse. Being just as passionately dedicated to the organization's mission as she was on the first day of business, Sherry has been worried for several months about the organization's prospects for survival. Private contributions (the organization's sole source of revenue) were down by 20% from last year, and this negative trend is expected to continue for another year. WHH has been a client of Johnson & Associates from the outset. The firm provides an annual review of the financial statements for a fee of $5,000. Having been happy with the timely services and fair billings of the firm, and being well known and respected by Cleveland's non-profit community, Sherry's many referrals have been instrumental in the firm's rapid growth. During a recent, prior to year-end, planning visit to WHH, Tom was in Sherry's office looking over the records (that he would soon be reviewing) when the following discussion took place:

Sherry: "Tom, I think this year I would like your firm to do an audit instead of just a review."

Tom: "Oh? Why do you think you need an audit?"

Sherry: "At a recent conference, I sat next to the head of one of the large non-profits, and she mentioned that they were in the process of having their financial statements audited by one of the Big Four CPA firms. I just thought that if an audit is what the successful non-profits have done, maybe that's what we need."

Tom: "Well, we've been doing your annual review for many years, and never have found anything questionable. Of course, we certainly want to provide WHH with the level of assurance service needed. I'll tell you what . . . Let me discuss it with Emery, and I'll get back to you."

Sherry: "That's fine, Tom. Give my regards to Emery."

Prior to leaving WHH, Tom let Sherry know that an audit would require more extensive procedures than were needed in a review. Consequently, an audit would take longer to complete and would, therefore, cost considerably more than a review. A brief discussion then took place regarding the potential audit fee. When Tom got back to the office, he headed straight for Emery's office and asked him if he had a few minutes to talk about the WHH account. He proceeded to tell him about his conversation with Sherry.

Emery: "As far as I can remember, we've never found anything wrong during our reviews of WHH. Does she know that the fee for performing an audit will be around $19,000?"

Tom: "You're right. We've never found anything that was even slightly questionable. In the last ten years our reviews haven't resulted in even one adjusting entry. As far as I know, WHH doesn't need an audit for any regulatory, statutory, or legal reason."

Emery: "Did you try to pinpoint where the idea of the audit came from? It's not uncommon for organizations to upgrade engagements from a review to an audit."

Tom: "As far as I know, WHH is not seeking any financing that might require an audit. Moreover, an upgrade to an audit is unlikely to have the slightest impact on donations. I can't think of any business or financial reason for WHH to need an audit. WHH's internal controls are sound, and the financial statements are prepared in accordance with FASB 117."

Emery: "I also can't think of any benefit the client will receive by having an audit instead of a review, except maybe peace of mind. There's a lot to be said for peace of mind, and she's certainly entitled to it, and so are we. Even though WHH, like most of our non-profits, is experiencing a cash flow crisis, it does have a $25,000 CD that it can draw from. As long as she knows how much it will cost, I don't have a problem with changing the engagement to a certified audit."

Tom: "Yes, she's aware of the increased cost for an audit. I gave her a copy of our latest fee schedule and briefly discussed an audit fee range of between $17,000 and $21,000. While she was shocked by the amount, she did mention that they could tap into their emergency savings and would, as usual, be able to promptly pay us."

Questions for Discussion:

1. CPAs are faced with ethical decisions on a daily basis regarding upholding the profession's ethical standards. What should be Emery's response in accordance with the AICPA's Principles of Professional Conduct? (Refer to: http://www.aicpa.org/about/code/sec50.htm).

2. Does the firm need an ethical justification to upgrade their services from a review to an audit?

3. Does the client need to receive an increased benefit from having the audit performed? Is "peace of mind" a justifiable benefit? Whose "peace of mind" are Emery and Tom concerned about?

4. If he accepts the client's reason for the audit, is Emery immorally taking advantage of the trust and goodwill created with the client over their long business relationship? Do the partners have an ethical obligation to dissuade the client from hiring them to perform what appears to be an expensive and unnecessary upgrade in services?

5. Can Emery and Tom ignore the client's trust in them and perform attestation services that provide WHH with little to no benefit? (Refer to AICPA Professional Standards, ET Section 51.)

6. Should Emery and Tom consider the potential negative consequences for WHH if the organization uses its emergency funds to pay the audit fee?

Case 13.2: Over-Billing: An Accountant's Legal and Ethical Quandary[11]

Bill Wyatt, a management accountant at Horizon Real Estate Management Company (Horizon), has been feeling ill since having lunch with Mark Brown, his friend and one of the company's best leasing agents. He has a pretty good idea of what made him sick, and it wasn't the food.

The narrative commences with John and Margaret Jacobs. John Jacobs is a dentist in Atlanta, Georgia. While his parents provided for his earlier college education, he used school loans to pay for dental school. During the years John attended dental school, he and his wife, Margaret, had struggled to make their mortgage payments and still have money for food and other living expenses. All of this was accomplished on Margaret's salary as a dental hygienist. At long last, John finished school and started working in the office of a local dentist. After gaining about two years of practical experience, John and Margaret decided to become entrepreneurs by opening their own dental practice. They would start the practice with John as the sole dentist and Margaret as the dental hygienist/office manager. A review of their finances made it apparent that they would have to borrow the money needed to lease office space, buy necessary equipment, and cover other initial start-up costs. Moreover, their CPA had warned them that many small businesses fail because the owners rely too soon on the cash flow from the business for their personal living expenses. Therefore, the business cash flow plan also provided for their living expenses during the first six months of operation. Based on their CPA's projection, John and Margaret sought financing from various sources. Margaret's uncle provided a portion of the funds. When the bank turned them down for a business loan, the balance of the funds came from a loan secured by their home that virtually wiped out the equity they had accumulated during 10 years of ownership. Once the start-up funds were covered, John ordered the necessary equipment, and he and Margaret began looking for office space. After two unsuccessful weeks on their own, they decided to seek the help of a real estate professional. As they discussed their options, John remembered that Bill Wyatt, a close friend in his Sunday school class, worked at Horizon. The following Sunday, John asked Bill for his help:

John: "As you know, I'm starting my own dental practice. Margaret and I have been looking without success for a dental office. Can you help us find a good location? We have limited funds and will be starting the practice on a tight budget."

Bill: "I'm sure that Horizon can find something for you. I won't be directly involved, since I'm the assistant controller, but I can put you in touch with Mark Brown, one of our best leasing agents."

John: "That's great! Please ask him to call me tomorrow."

Bill Wyatt is the assistant controller at the home office of Horizon. Over the past seven years, he has worked his way up the ladder in the accounting department. In addition, since earning a degree in accounting he has pursued a professional designation as a Certified Management Accountant (CMA). Several months ago, he passed the last part of the

[11]Contributed by Dr. Donald L. Ariail, Dr. Josephine Sosa-Fey, Miguel Valdez, and Laura E. Yanez, Texas A&M University–Kingsville.

exam, and just last week received the CMA Certificate that is proudly displayed on his office wall. He is hoping this achievement will, in the near future, give him a shot at being promoted. If not, the CMA designation will certainly be a plus in applying for a controller position with another mid-sized company.

The Horizon Real Estate Company has been in business for over 15 years. During that time, it has maintained its home office in Atlanta, Georgia while expanding to a total of 30 offices located throughout the state. The revenues of the business are derived from commissions earned from managing rental properties: residential (21%), commercial (36%), and resort (43%) properties. The accounting and finance functions are centralized in the home office, and the lines of responsibility in accounting flow from the bottom up as follows: staff accountants, senior accountants, assistant controller (Bill Wyatt), controller (Jack Cooper), chief financial officer (Rick Hogg), chief executive officer (Ken Alexander), and finally, the Audit Committee of the Board of Directors.

Soon, however, an ethical quandary begins to emerge. Mark found John and Margaret a great deal on an office. Due to another dentist having previously leased the space, floor plan modifications were not needed. In addition, no other general dentistry practice was located within a three mile radius. Further, both a periodontist and an orthodontist had offices in the same building. These fellow practitioners would be great referral sources. Thus, John and Margaret happily signed a year's lease that required a deposit of $6,400 and monthly rentals of $3,200. John's practice rapidly expanded. Before the end of six months, it became apparent that they had drastically underestimated their office space requirements. The growing practice needed at least twice the square footage.

Due to John's busy schedule, Margaret scheduled a meeting with Mark Brown to discuss their office space problem.

Margaret: "We've really done well at this location and are getting referrals from our periodontist and orthodontist colleagues. Our problem is that we've done so well that we need twice the space we now have. Can you find us another location under your company's management so that we can move without breaking the lease and losing our deposit?"

Mark: "Margaret, I'm really glad the business is doing so well! Give me a few days to look at our inventory of properties. I'll see if another office with sufficient square footage is available." About two days later, Mark called Margaret with good news.

Mark: "I think I've found the perfect office space for you. Dr. Williams, the dermatologist next door to you, is moving at the end of the month. We can double your space without your having to move."

Margaret: "That sounds great! We're worried about moving from a location that has worked so well for us."

Mark: "When can we get together to discuss the details?"

Margaret: "How about tomorrow afternoon? John has appointments all day, but I should be able to get away for an hour or so around 2:00 p.m."

Mark: "Good! I'll see you then."

When Margaret arrived for the meeting, Mark was ready with a floor plan prepared by Horizon's architect, and he had also drawn up a new lease that showed a monthly rent of $6,400—twice the amount of the old lease.

Margaret: "Mark, the floor plan looks great! Of course, John and I will need to carefully review it. We probably will want to make some minor changes."

Mark: "That's fine; I just wanted to give you a general idea of what can be done with the expanded space."

Margaret: "If we take this additional space, I think that it will suit us very well. In addition, it should be good for both the property owner and Horizon. By the time we take over the new space, we will have been here for six months. As you are aware, we have always paid our rent on time. And, most importantly for the owner and Horizon, there won't be any loss of rental income. I understand there's a lot of vacant space in this area of town. If I sign the new lease, can't we get a break on the rent?"

Mark: "I see your point. You and John have been great tenants. Let me talk to my boss and the owner, and I'll get back to you tomorrow."

The next day, Mark called Margaret and reported that the property owner was willing to rent the combined space for $5,200 a month, saving John and Margaret $1,200 per month. A lease was drawn up in the name of John's professional corporation, and Margaret (a corporate officer) came by later in the day and signed the new lease. Some months later, Mark had lunch with Bill Wyatt; and that is when Bill's ethical quandary really began.

Mark: "John Jacobs gave his notice today."

Bill: "Really, I didn't know anything about them moving. I thought that they were doing great in the medical building you found for them."

Mark: "Well that's true. However, Margaret came by this morning and gave us a written notice. She said that they had already found another location in a newly constructed building where they will get six months of free rent, will not have to make a deposit, and will only pay monthly rentals of $4,800."

Bill: "How long have they been renting through us?"

Mark: "By the time they move out, they will have been in that location for 18 months: 6 months under the initial lease and 12 months under the revised lease. By the way, after Margaret gave me the notice, I pulled their lease and noticed something really strange. As you know, we negotiated a new lease with them when they expanded into the larger space. The new lease was for $5,200 per month. I had originally drawn up the lease at $6,400 per month—twice the amount they had been paying for the first 6 months. For some reason the unsigned lease for $6,400 was in the *active files*. After a lot of digging, I found the signed lease for the correct amount of $5,200 in the *dead files*. I hope that we sent you guys in accounting the right lease!"

When Bill got back to his office, he checked the accounts receivable ledger for the Jacobs' account and was shocked to discover that the lessee had been mailed monthly invoices for $6,400. And, surprisingly, Jacobs had regularly paid each bill throughout the term of the lease. Consequently, Horizon had over-billed and over-collected a total of $14,400 during the last 12 months. It appeared that the wrong lease had been sent to his department. No one, including himself, had noticed that the lease was unsigned. Bill, concerned about this oversight, went directly to Jack Cooper's office and told him the entire story. He then asked Jack how best to correct this error:

Bill: "I feel terrible about this situation, and I'd like to ask for your assistance in correcting it as quickly as possible. What would you say is the best way to do it?"

Jack: "Look, Bill, this is the real world. We've got to play hardball if we want to stay in business. The Jacobs are leaving, the rent is paid, and no one knows about any problem. As far as I'm concerned, there is no problem."

Bill: "Jack, we made an honest mistake; we have to make it right!"

Jack: "If these people were stupid enough to overpay, they don't deserve a refund. We don't want to lose our 10% commission on this overage and, more importantly, the owner will probably sue us if we tell him to write a refund check. We can't afford to stir up this hornet's nest."

Consequently, Bill is confronted by an ethical dilemma. Actually, Bill is sickened by this situation. He has been friends with the Jacobs for a long time, and does not want them or anyone else cheated. He vividly remembers their years of financial hardship: tight budgets and large school loans, while John was in dental school, and then he recalls the Jacobs going deeply in debt to get the business started. Bill wants to do the "right thing."

Questions for Discussion:

1. Should Bill reveal the billing error to the Jacobs? How does the Institute of Management Accountants (IMA) Code of Ethics address such communications by CMAs? The IMA Code of Ethics is available at: *http://www.imanet.org/about_ ethics_statement.asp.* As per the IMA Code of Ethics, what procedure should Bill follow in pursuing a resolution to this ethical issue? Why?

2. This billing error appears to have been an accident. How would the ethical and legal situation be different if Horizon had purposely overcharged the Jacobs? Does the fact that the bills were *mailed* to the lessee affect the legal or consequences of this situation? Discuss.

3. Are the Jacobs legally owed the amount of the overcharge? Why or why not?

4. What appears to be the ethical culture at Horizon? How should the ethical culture affect Bill's decision regarding his future with Horizon?

5. What would be some of the consequences of the Jacobs' subsequently discovering the overcharge? How would this affect their relationship with Bill?

6. If this over billing was made public, how would this affect Horizon's reputation? What if it came to light that over-billing was a regular practice at Horizon?

7. Should Bill's personal relationship with John and Margaret affect his ethical decision? Why or why not?

8. Should the amount of the overcharge be a factor in Bill's ethical decision? What if the overcharge were for $1,000, or $500, or as low as $100? Discuss.

14. File Sharing

Case 14.1: Digital File Sharing: Music Industry Wins Copyright Infringement Lawsuit

Copyrighted digital files, especially songs and movies, are shared illegally over "peer-to-peer" file sharing networks that connect computer users over the Internet. Many millions of people around the world have file sharing software on their computers which they use to illegally share, download, and copy copyrighted works. It is widely assumed, moreover, that many people will continue to download music and movies from the Internet, regardless of any court decisions or legislative prohibitions. The *Miami Herald* reported in October of 2007 that the number of people sharing files online at any given time has increased 69% to almost 9.4 million since 2003. Professor Lee Burgunder in his book, *Legal Aspects of Managing Technology*, states that the number of illegal downloads by 2004 was approximated to be as high as five *billion* tracks a year. The entertainment industry has naturally responded to this illegal activity.

In order to stop the illegal file sharing and to protect their valuable copyrights to music and movies, the entertainment industry first attempted to proceed against the file sharing networks, attaining success in shutting down the Napster file sharing network with its central server system. Furthermore, the U.S. Supreme Court ruled in 2005 in a unanimous decision, *Metro-Goldwyn-Mayer Studios, Inc. v. Grokster, LTD,* that even file sharing companies that do not have central server systems, such as Grokster, could be held liable legally for copyright violations but only if their products encourage consumers to illegally share songs and movies. The Court ruled that file sharing and other technology companies could be sued by the entertainment industry if a court determines that their products encourage consumers to use the products to pirate music and movies. The burden, however, will be on the entertainment industry, principally the music companies and movie studios, to convince a judge and/or jury that a technological company is encouraging such theft. The lower federal courts, therefore, will have to decide, on a case-by-case basis, what constitutes illegal "encouragement." In the *Grokster* case, in which 29 movie studios and record labels confronted companies that give away file sharing software online, the Supreme Court overturned an earlier ruling of the Court of Appeals which was in Grokster's favor. In the earlier appeals court decision, the Court of Appeals upheld the file sharing companies because the file sharing software also could be used for legal purposes. Nonetheless, the Supreme Court held that lawsuits could proceed against technology providers, but only those that actively and deliberately market their products as a means for consumers to avoid paying for movies, songs, CDs, and DVDs, as well as television programs. As opposed to the former Napster, which effectuated the file sharing through a central server system and was thus the "middleman," Grokster and other "peer" software companies permit users to connect to one another directly, without passing through a central system. The Supreme Court also stated that a technology company could not be sued merely because it later finds that consumers used its products to violate the law. The Court, however, did not provide any standards to determine when a technology company was encouraging or inducing or causing consumers to use its products in an illegal manner so as to violate copyright law.

Consequently, instead of suing the file sharing services, another response of the entertainment industry to combat file sharing has been to sue individual file sharers for copyright infringement. The music industry in fact has already sued hundreds of people who have been downloading and uploading songs online, and has reached settlements with many of them. The *Miami Herald* and the *Wall Street Journal* reported in October of 2007 that the music industry has sued more than 26,000 people that they contended illegally shared music online in contravention of copyright laws.

In one case, however, instead of a settlement, the music industry pursued a legal action in court for copyright infringement against a private individual who decided to fight the music industry in court. The majority of people sued have settled, with the *Wall Street Journal* reporting that the average settlement paid to the music industry is $5,000. Yet in the one case that went to trial, the *Wall Street Journal* and the *Miami Herald* newspapers in October of 2007 reported that the music industry had prevailed in a significant legal victory when a federal district court jury in Duluth, Minnesota ruled that a private person intentionally and illegally shared music online, and then awarded damages of $222,000 for the copyright infringement. The defendant file sharer and losing party was Ms. Jammie Thomas, a single mother of two, who makes $36,000 a year, and who denied that the Kazaa file sharing account was hers. The prevailing plaintiffs were the six major recording companies, who accused her of illegally offering 1,702 songs for sharing on the Kazaa file sharing network. One of the songs was Journey's "Don't Stop Believing." The lawsuit, however, focused on only 24 songs. The jury found that Thomas willfully violated the copyright on all of them, and determined that that she must pay damages of $9,250 per song, for the total of $222,000.

One issue before the jury was whether there was sufficient evidence to pinpoint Thomas as the computer user who made the files available for sharing. The jury was convinced that there was sufficient evidence to demonstrate the connection between specific users and those engaged in illegal file sharing activity. This case is noteworthy since it was the first copyright infringement file sharing case tried before a jury. The plaintiff music companies included EMI Group, Sony, Bertelsmann, Vivendi, and Warner Music Group. These companies typically ask for subpoenas from the federal courts to an Internet service provider to determine the specific person behind the file sharer's Internet protocol address. In the Thomas case, the *Wall Street Journal* reported that Thomas used the name "Tereastarr," which was the same name that Thomas used to log into her computer and several websites, such as MySpace. Regardless of the jury verdict, Thomas stated that she does not have the money to pay the judgment.

One very important aspect to the lawsuit was the fact that proof was not deemed necessary that the songs made available online by Thomas were actually downloaded by anyone else. It is very interesting to note, as reported by the *Wall Street Journal* and the *Miami Herald*, that the judge in the case, U.S. District Court Judge Michael Davis, was planning on instructing the jurors that the music companies would have to prove as part of their case that someone actually downloaded and copied the songs in order to prevail on their copyright infringement claim. However, the attorney for the music companies argued, and cited precedent for the proposition, that merely making the songs available could be construed as copyright infringement. As a result, the judge changed his mind and did not issue an instruction that actual downloading and copying were critical elements to the legal wrong of copyright infringement. Legal experts, however, state that the actual use issue is not settled.

One legal expert, as reported in the *Miami Herald*, stated that the damages assessed by the jury were disproportionate to the legal wrong of violating the copyright on the 24 songs, particularly since Thomas was "only" accused of offering the songs, and for free too. Actually, she could have purchased the songs legally for only 99 cents on a legal music download site. Indeed, one business related response by the entertainment industry to all the illegal file sharing has been the development of new, subscription-based online services for legally distributing music and movies to consumers.

Another interesting aspect to the private copyright infringement litigation instituted by the music industry is that the lawsuits are actually costing the record companies more money than they are bringing in by settlements and now by a court victory. Nonetheless, the Recording Industry Association of America has stated that the entertainment industry wants to "send a message" that file sharing and downloading music are legal wrongs, and risky ones too. Of course, many of the lawsuits were against people who offered a very large number of songs and movies on their file sharing folders, but the entertainment industry has also demonstrated that it is willing to proceed against smaller file sharers who "only" downloaded a few hundred files. The industry intent, of course, is for the lawsuits and the threat thereof to act as deterrents to even the smallest copyright infringers that they are not "safe" from legal action. However, because there was some backlash by the public because some of the alleged perpetrators were "only children," the entertainment industry is now taking measures to warn individuals that file sharing is illegal, and to warn file sharers that their actions are being monitored and could result in copyright infringement lawsuits against them.

The Thomas legal decision is expected to give force and credence to the entertainment industry's attempts to stop illegal file sharing; yet the practice of file sharing—illegal as well as legal—continues to increase. Now, the entertainment industry, and the music companies in particular, are predicted to increase their efforts to stop illegal file sharing by means of copyright infringement lawsuits brought against individual file sharers.

Bibliography:

Birdis, Ted, ""File-Sharing Bust," *The Miami Herald*, June 28, 2005, pp. 1C, 5C.

Burgunder, Lee (2007). *Legal Aspects of Managing Technology* (4th edition). Mason, Ohio: West's Legal Studies in Business Academic Series/Thomson-West/Thomson Higher Education.

Cavico, Frank J., and Mujtaba, Bahaudin G (2008). *Legal Challenges for the Global Manager and Entrepreneur*. Dubuque, Iowa: Kendall/Hunt Publishing Company.

Freed, Joshua, "Music piracy: Legal issues remain in doubt," *The Miami Herald*, October 6, 2007, pp. 1C, 3C.

Gomez, Lex, "Ethical Responsibility, At Issue with Grokster, Applies to Others Too," *The Wall Street Journal*, June 27, 2005, p. B1.

McBride, Sarah, "Music Industry Wins Digital Piracy Case," *The Wall Street Journal*, October 5, 2007, p. B4.

Metro-Goldwyn-Mayer Studios, Inc. v. Grokster, LTD., 125 S.Ct. 2764 (2005).

Piccoli, Sean, and Young, Chris, "Court Strikes at File Sharing," *Sun-Sentinel*, June 28, 2005, pp. 1A, 6A.

Schatz, Amy, McBride, Sarah, and Wingfield, Nick, "Grokster, Streamcast Can Be Sued Over Online Piracy," *The Wall Street Journal*, June 28, 2005, pp. B1, B4.

Questions for Discussion:

1. Do you agree with the decision in the Thomas case? Why or why not?

2. Do you agree with the judge's not giving an instruction to the jury that copyright holders have to prove that the materials offered were actually used? Should proof of actual file downloading and copying be essential to a copyright violation, or is simply making songs available online a copyright violation? Why or why not?

3. Does the federal district court jury decision stifle innovation and creativity in the technological fields? Why or why not?

4. Is the federal district court decision a moral one pursuant to Utilitarian and Kantian ethics? Discuss.

5. Pursuant to the principles of Value Driven Management, should the music industry be instituting these lawsuits against private parties for copyright infringement, even though they are losing money on the litigation? Why or why not?

APPENDIX B

Forms, Surveys, and Applications

A. Introduction

The purposes of this section are to provide the reader with appropriate and relevant material that can be used in training and surveying a population, ethically reflecting, and/or making better moral decisions.

1. Utilitarian Theory

As one knows, "Utilitarianism" refers to a systematic theory of moral philosophy that determines morality by focusing on the consequences of actions. Actions are not good or bad in themselves; they are judged right or wrong solely by virtue of their consequences. A utilitarian, after identifying the action for ethical evaluation, determines those people directly and indirectly affected by the action. The utilitarian then attempts to ascertain consequences of the action, good and bad, on the affected parties. In the most challenging aspect of this ethical theory, the utilitarian then strives to measure and weigh the good as compared to the bad consequences. If the good consequences outweigh the bad, the action is moral; if the bad consequences outweigh the good, the action is immoral. A quantification form is enclosed in this section for practical usage.

2. Personal Business Ethics Score Instrument

Researchers have been trying to create the best method of obtaining true information from respondents, without making them feel guilty or putting them in a position where they would have to state what they would do in each situation. To do this most effectively, the majority of researchers have agreed that scenarios are a convenient method of measuring the respondent's approval or disapproval of each situation, without requiring them to state what they themselves would do in each situation by themselves. Social research often requires that people reveal personal information about themselves, which might be unknown to their closest friends and family members, and this is not always an easy task. The "Personal Business Ethics Scores" questionnaire can be used for research; and this questionnaire is based on prior research conducted in the field of business ethics. This instrument contains 11 short scenarios dealing with specific moral situations. These scenarios have been used by researchers to determine the Personal Business Ethics Scores of managers, executives, and leaders.

PBES SCENARIOS

The Personal Business Ethics Score

1. Electrical-equipment price conspiracy
2. Conflict with superior's ethics
3. Insider information of stock split
4. Sharp selling of used cars
5. Use of inferior products
6. Padding the expense account

7. Promotion of less capable based on connections

8. Pressure in newspaper for advertising

9. Auditor overlooks a bribe

10. Pirating employees to learn competitors secrets

11. Recommending questionable bonds

The Personal Business Ethics Scores (PBES), included in this section, measures one's level of commitment to personal integrity and honesty in business decisions and to the laws governing business. The scores derived from the scenarios are measured on a Likert five-point scale, 1 (strongly approve) to 5 (strongly disapprove). The PBES scores for the 11 scenarios could range from a low score of 11 to a high score of 55. The low score represents a low sense of personal business ethics, and a high score represents a high sense of personal business ethics.

The original Clark instrument was written in the 1960s. Certain details of the scenarios have been updated by past researchers to accurately reflect today's conditions. All moral scenarios are relevant to the business dealings of individuals and companies in the current environment. Topics such as making illegal payments, insider trading, nepotism or favoritism to certain individuals during promotions, selling inferior products, and environmental issues are the topics of daily newspaper and television discussions. Some of these issues are national; yet others are international and thus can affect everyone in the world. It appears as though nepotism, love of personal power and gain, tribalism, and other bribery evils are universal situations often representing unfair practices. Individuals, logical and realistic human beings, desiring to keep their jobs and their friends, may deviate from their moral standards to conform with the pressures of society. The dilemmas in this survey are relevant to such practices; and the survey thus measures the respondents' level of commitment to personal integrity in such situations as well as their observance of the laws governing business.

This questionnaire was presented by the original author to a panel of five faculty members in the marketing department at University of Southern California. These faculty members concluded that the scenarios were valid for the two scales. A standard test-retest reliability check was made of each of the two scales. The test was twice administered to a group of 40 subjects with a three-week interval between test administrations. The test-retest reliability coefficient for the PBES was .76, which manifests an acceptable degree of reliability. The test-retest reliability coefficient for the SRS was .86, which represents a high degree of reliability.

More complete information on this instrument, its history, and how it can be applied to different populations using statistical analysis can be obtained from a dissertation published by UMI Dissertation Service titled "Business Ethics Survey of Supermarket Managers and Employees." It was completed by Bahaudin G. Mujtaba in 1997. The following is the reference information for the original instrument by Clark (1966) and the updated instrument by Mujtaba (1997):

- Clark, J. W., & Clark, S. J. (1966). Religion and moral standards of American businessmen. Cincinnati: Southwestern Publishing Co.

- Mujtaba, B., 1997. "Business Ethics Survey of Supermarket Managers and Employees." UMI Dissertation Service. A Bell & Howell Company. UMI Number: 9717687. Copy-

B. Utilitarian Quantification Form

The essence of utilitarianism is to quantify consequences-good and bad-into numerical units of pleasure and pain. If there are more positive than negative consequences, the action is moral; conversely, if the negative numbers predominate, the action is immoral. The purpose of the utilitarian analysis herein is to determine whether a specific course of action is moral as determined by its impact on the relevant stakeholders. Accordingly, affected categories or stakeholders may be designated and included as in the following form.

Stakeholders	Pain	Pleasure	Details/Reasons
Owners			
Customers/Consumers			
Competition			
Shareholders			
Employees			
Suppliers/Distributors			
Local Community			
Government			
Society			
Families			
Males			
Females			
Minority			
Management			
Potential Employees/Students			
Immigrants			
Business and Industry			
Total Scores			
Difference in Scores			

C. Business Ethics Survey

This study is primarily concerned with the Business Ethics view of managers and non-managers in different cultures. You are not required to record your name and the information you provide will be totally confidential. Please check/circle the appropriate sections; and your cooperation deserves my heart-felt thanks and gratitude.

A. What is your gender?   1. ____ Male   2. ____ Female

B. What is your age?
1. ____ 16-25   2. ____ 26-35   3. ____ 36-45
4. ____ 46-55   5. ____ 56 or above

C. How would you describe yourself?
1 ____ White
2 ____ Black
3 ____ Hispanic   4 ____ Asian/Pacific Islander
5 ____ American Indian/Alaskan Native
6 ____ Other (please specify) _____

D. Where were you born?
1. _____

E. How many years have you lived in the United States of America?
1. ___ Never lived in the USA   2. ___ 1–5 years
3. ___ 6–10 years   4. ___ 11–19 years
5. ___ 20 or more years

F. What is the highest academic schooling you have acquired until the present time?
1. ___ Less than twelve years
2. ___ High School Diploma or Equivalent.
3. ___ Two years of College or Institute Training
4. ___ Bachelors Degree   5. ___ Masters Degree
6. ___ Doctorate Degree
7. ___ Other (please specify)_____

G. How long have you worked with your current employer?
1. ___ Less than one year   2. ___ 1–5 years   3. ___ 6–15 years
4. ___ 16–30 yrs.   5. ___ 30 or more years

H. Have you ever worked in a management position?

    1. ___ Yes   2. ___ No

I. How many years of management experience do you have regardless of industry?

    1. ___ zero or less than one year   2. ___ 1–5 years   3. ___ 6–10 years

    4. ___ 11–15 years   5. ___ 16 or more years

Direction: Please circle the answer which best expresses your judgment of each case.

1. A number of high-ranking executives of several electrical companies were convicted and sentenced to jail for conspiring to fix the prices of heavy electrical equipment. Their defense counsel argued that they sought to rationalize a chaotic pricing situation. **What is your evaluation of the action of these executives?**

    1. Strongly Approve   2. Approve   3. Undecided

    4. Disapprove   5. Strongly Disapprove

2. Saxon is a sales representative of Ajax Tool Company. Saxon has been instructed by Maynard, Vice President of Sales, to adopt a sales policy Saxon considers unethical. Maynard and Saxon have discussed the policy at length and it is apparent Maynard thinks the policy is quite ethical. Maynard orders Saxon to follow the policy, and Saxon reluctantly does so. **What is your opinion of Saxon's actions?**

    1. Strongly Approve   2. Approve   3. Undecided

    4. Disapprove   5. Strongly Disapprove

3. Stone, a member of the Board of Directors of Scott Electronic Corp., has just learned that the company is about to announce a 2-for-1 stock split and an increase in the dividends. Stone personally is on the brink of bankruptcy. A quick gain of a few thousand dollars can save Stone from economic and social ruin. Stone decides to take advantage of this information and purchases stocks now to sell back in a few days for a profit. **What is your opinion of Stone's actions?**

    1. Strongly Approve   2. Approve   3. Undecided

    4. Disapprove   5. Strongly Disapprove

4. Chuckwell sells used cars for an Auto Company. Although Chuckwell feels that the cars sold are reasonably priced, in the sales talk Chuckwell is forced to match the extravagant claims and tactics of competitors. The company engages in such practices as setting back the speedometers, hiding major defects, and putting pressure on prospects to close a deal on their first visit. Chuckwell knows that the company could not survive without such practices. Although, Chuckwell dis-

agrees with such practices, nevertheless, Chuckwell follows these practices. **What is your opinion of Chuckwell's actions?**

1. Strongly Approve 2. Approve 3. Undecided
4. Disapprove 5. Strongly Disapprove

5. The Reed Engineering Firm faces a very competitive situation in bidding for a large contract to construct a new store for a large discount chain. Inasmuch as the firm is seriously in need of the work, Pennings, a partner in the firm, suggests that Reed submit a bid which will certainly be low, and then make its profit on the use of inferior materials. Pennings is certain this can be done without arousing the suspicion of building inspectors. Pennings argues that any firm which is awarded the contract will have to do that since the bidding will be so competitive. Reed, senior partner, agrees, stating that it is not an infrequent practice anyway. **What is your opinion of Penning's actions?**

1. Strongly Approve 2. Approve 3. Undecided
4. Disapprove 5. Strongly Disapprove

6. BeeBee is a sales person for Sweet Soap Company. With commissions, BeeBee's salary is $36,000 per year. BeeBee usually supplements this to the extent of about $1,800 per year by charging certain unauthorized personal expenses against the expense account. BeeBee feels that this is a common practice in the company; and if everybody is doing it, BeeBee should do it also. **What is your opinion of BeeBee's actions?**

1. Strongly Approve 2. Approve 3. Undecided
4. Disapprove 5. Strongly Disapprove

7. Shaw, Treasurer of Lloyd Enterprises, is about to retire and contemplates recommending one of two assistants for promotion to treasurer. Shaw is sure that the recommendation will be accepted, but also knows that the assistant not recommended will find his/her promotion opportunities seriously limited. One of the assistants, Musta, seems most qualified for the new assignment, but the other assistant, Perwiz, is related to the president of Lloyd's biggest customer. Though Shaw hates to do it, Shaw recommends Perwiz for the job because the relationship with the customer will help Lloyd's. **What is your opinion of Shaw's actions?**

1. Strongly Approve 2. Approve 3. Undecided
4. Disapprove 5. Strongly Disapprove

8. Kraft, editor of the Daily News, is troubled. Kraft has just received a visit from Cramer, a public relations executive with the Aztec Department Store. Aztec is a big advertiser in the Daily News, and its continued purchase of advertising space is very important to the paper. Recently, Aztec sold a large quantity of appliances

which proved to be defective, and refused to exchange the merchandise for better quality products. The Daily News at the present time is running a series on local business firms. Cramer wants to be sure that a story on the Aztec will contain no mention of this unfortunate occurrence. Kraft is troubled; but in order not to offend this important advertiser, Kraft agrees not to mention the sale of defective appliances. **What is your opinion of Kraft's actions?**

1. Strongly Approve   2. Approve   3. Undecided

4. Disapprove   5. Strongly Disapprove

9. Schall, a Public Accountant, has been called in to audit the books of the Lakewood Trucking Company in anticipation of a public sale of stock. In the course of the audit, Schall discovered an item that is puzzling: a $20,000 advertising expense paid to a Chicago Advertising Company. This was a one-payment expense three years ago, and no further business has been done with the Chicago firm. When questioned by Schall, Wallen, President of the Trucking Company, readily admitted this money was used as a bribe to pay a union official. "It was a question of paying up or going out of business," Wallen explained. However, due to an employee empowerment program, Wallen sees no possibility of this situation recurring and asks Schall not to mention this in the Auditor's Report. Since the firm seems well managed, Schall agrees to ignore this. **What is your opinion of Schall's actions?**

1. Strongly Approve   2. Approve   3. Undecided

4. Disapprove   5. Strongly Disapprove

10. Piser, President of Piser Fashions Co., has heard rumors that a competitor, Sunset Fashion, is coming out with a new line of spring styles which in all likelihood will sweep the market. Piser cannot afford to wait until the new styles come out and hires Bishop, plant supervisor of Sunset. Although Bishop is not a designer, in the capacity of plant supervisor Bishop has become thoroughly familiar with the new Sunset line. It is understood that Bishop will reveal the full details of the new Sunset styles to the new employer, Piser Fashions Co.. **What is your opinion of Piser's action?**

1. Strongly Approve   2. Approve   3. Undecided

4. Disapprove   5. Strongly Disapprove

11. Sarwar is a sales person for Fare and Shear, stockbrokers. Sarwar has been instructed to recommend to customers Electric Power Co. Bonds, because the brokerage firm is carrying a heavy inventory of these bonds. Sarwar does not feel the bonds are a good investment under present circumstances; and is reluctant to recommend them. However, after some thought, Sarwar decides to follow the company directive and recommend the bonds. **What is your opinion of Sarwar's actions?**

1. Strongly Approve   2. Approve   3. Undecided

4. Disapprove   5. Strongly Disapprove

D. Age Discrimination and Cultural Values Survey[12]

This study is primarily concerned with the view of age from the perspective of individuals socialized in different cultures. You are not required to record your name and the information you provide will be totally confidential. Please check/circle the appropriate sections; and your cooperation deserves heart-felt thanks and gratitude.

A. What is your gender?   1. _____ Male   2. _____ Female

B. What is your age?
    1. _____ 16–25   2. _____ 26–39   3. _____ 40–49
    4. _____ 50–59   5. _____ 60 or above

C. How would you describe yourself?
    1 _____ White   2 _____ Black   3 _____ Hispanic
    4 _____ Asian/Pacific Islander
    5 _____ American Indian/Alaskan Native
    6 _____ Other (please specify) _____

D. Which country have you lived in most of your life?
    1. ___ USA   2. ___ Jamaica   3. ___ Turkey
    4. ___ Afghanistan   5. ___ Other (specify): _____

E. How many years have you lived in the United States of America?
    1. ___ Never lived in the USA   2. ___ 1–5 years
    3. ___ 6–10 years   4. ___ 11–19 years
    5. ___ 20 or more years

F. What is the highest academic schooling you have acquired until the present time?
    1. ___ Less than twelve years
    2. ___ High School Diploma or Equivalent
    3. ___ Bachelors Degree—Specify discipline: _____
    4. ___ Masters Degree—Specify discipline: _____
    5. ___ Doctorate Degree—Specify discipline: _____
    6. ___ Other (please specify)_____

---

[12]Taken from the authors' book entitled, *"Age Discrimination in Employment,"* 2006.

G. Which country do you currently reside in?

1. ___ USA   2. ___ Jamaica   3. ___ Turkey

4. ___ Afghanistan   5. ___ Other (specify): _____

H. How long have you worked with your current employer?

1. ___ Less than one year   2. ___ 1–5 years   3. ___ 6–15 years

4. ___ 16–29 years   5. ___ 30 or more years

I. What industry do you work for currently?

1. ___ Education

2. ___ Government

3. ___ Private sector

4. ___ Retail

5. ___ Health

6. ___ Other (please specify)_____

J. Have you ever any had diversity training (workshop) with your past or current employers?

1. ___ Yes   2. ___ No

K. Have you even had any ethics training (workshop) with your past or current employers?

1. ___ Yes   2. ___ No

L. Have you ever had an ethics course in an academic setting (community college, college, graduate school, professional school, etc)?

1. ___ Yes   2. ___No

Age and Cultural Values Questionnaire

Direction: Please answer based on the perspective of the country where you have lived most of your life. For example, if you have lived in Jamaica, Turkey, or Afghanistan most of your life, but are currently living in the USA, then answer these questions from the perspective of Jamaica, Turkey, or Afghanistan. Please keep in mind that for the purpose of research in the USA, "older workers" are those individuals who are 40 years of age or older.

12. Do "older workers" get more respect than "younger workers" in your country?

a. Yes _____

b. No _____

13. Do "older workers" get more respect than "younger workers" from managers and employers in your country?

    a. Yes _____.

    b. No _____.

14. Do you prefer to work with:

    a. "Older workers" (those who are 40 years of age or above) _____.

    b. Younger workers (those who are less 40 years of age) _____.

    c. All workers—I have no preference on age _____.

15. Do most managers in your culture prefer to work with:

    a. "Older workers" (those who are 40 years of age or above) _____.

    b. Younger workers (those who are less 40 years of age) _____.

    c. All workers—They have no preference on age _____.

16. Based on your observations, do most managers in your country believe:

    a. "Older workers" are more productive than younger workers _____.

    b. Younger workers are more productive than "older workers" _____.

    c. All workers are equally productive _____.

17. Is it more difficult for "older workers" to find jobs in your country?

    a. Yes _____.

    b. No _____.

18. Is it more difficult for "younger workers" to find jobs in your country?

    a. Yes _____.

    b. No _____.

19. Have you ever seen evidence of age discrimination toward "older workers" by managers in your country?

    a. Yes _____.

    b. No _____.

20. Have you ever seen evidence of age discrimination toward "younger workers" by managers in your country?

    a. Yes _____.

    b. No _____.

21. Is age discrimination against "older workers" legally wrong in your country?
    a. Yes _____.
    b. No _____.
    c. Do not know _____.

22. Is age discrimination against "younger workers" legally wrong in your country?
    a. Yes _____.
    b. No _____.
    c. Do not know _____.

23. Is age discrimination against "older workers" regarded as morally or ethically wrong in your country?
    a. Yes _____.
    b. No _____.
    c. Do not know _____.

24. Is age discrimination against "younger workers" regarded as morally or ethically wrong in your country?
    a. Yes _____.
    b. No _____.
    c. Do not know _____.

25. Is age discrimination against "older workers" regarded by you personally as morally or ethically wrong?
    a. Yes _____.
    b. No _____.

26. Is age discrimination against "younger workers" regarded by you personally as morally or ethically wrong?
    a. Yes _____.
    b. No _____.

27. Do you have any comments on age issues, discrimination, and older workers that you would like to share?

_____

_____

_____

_____

_____

_____

_____

_____

_____

_____

_____

_____

_____

_____

_____

_____

E. Personal Ethics and the Future of the World

The video titled *Personal Ethics and the Future of the World* is narrated by Meg Ryan (Ryan, 1995) and produced by Varied Directions International. It provides a view of the basic ethical dilemmas and solutions for personal reflections and better decision-making. As such, this video and others that provide a similar forum for discussion are great tools for business ethics training. The message of this segment is that scandals, "ripoffs," and immoral behaviors happen in the society, and the solution belongs to each and everyone. *Your actions and behavior matter,* and what individuals do will decide what happens to the future of the world. People have various kinds of challenges and these challenges will either be beneficial to us or destroy the society. However, many people believe that the real solution lies in our own personal ethics. Let us see what ethics is and what it means to us personally.

Most dictionaries state that "ethics" is telling right and wrong. Yet we know it is a little more difficult than that when applied in daily activities. For example, one's friend threw a rock through a school window and vandalized a school building, then he tells you about it. Now, you are aware of the situation. The principal of the school asks you, "Who did this?" "What do you do?" Well, you have an ethical dilemma that you need to resolve: *Loyalty to your friend or truth?* You have to choose between a right and possibly another right decision based your opinion or cultural upbringing with regard to loyalty: two right decisions to you personally—loyalty or truth. Throughout your life, you have always been taught that being loyal to your friends and family members are parts of one's honor. So, you either have to tell the truth or be loyal, but cannot be both which is a "tough" personal choice; yet you will have to make a choice that you can live with and believe in.

Could there be a relationship between loyalty and telling the truth? How about the loyalty of all the people in Germany to Hitler? How about the loyalty of the soldiers in China as the students were being killed and physically hurt in Tiananmen Square? Maybe ethical challenges need practice and training just like martial artists who continually practice their basics to strengthen their bodies and minds. Based on their practice to condition their bodies and minds, they can respond to situations much better, and accordingly they will be more in control of their lives by making quick and effortless decisions.

Many American teenagers (45%) believe and rely on their own experience to make ethical decisions. However, that may not always be enough when we are making decisions that affect others in the society. For example, one boss wanted to try an experiment that was very dangerous and interesting. You know that if you don't follow the order, you will lose your job. However, you also know that the experiment is very dangerous and can put many lives in danger. The risks are great. So, what should you do? In the case of the Chernobyl radioactive fallout in the nuclear power plant, the people decided to stay quiet, and the experiment went very wrong. In this one experiment, people stayed quiet and did not speak to anyone about the problems and concerns in the experiment. However, on April 9, 1986, the worst industrial nuclear disaster took thousands of lives and damaged the environment around it. The Chernobyl nuclear disaster affected people around the globe. Perhaps, this could have been avoided if people spoke up regardless of personal consequences.

F. Universal Principles

There are certain principles that are common to all people (Ryan, 1995). For example, killing another person is wrong no matter where you are. The following are some common ethical principles that one should remember, value, teach, or share, and follow in one's daily life.

1. *Self-respect.* Learning to respect yourself; and learning to value yourself is the first universal principle. Learn to know yourself is part of respecting yourself. Make decisions that show the beautiful you. Express yourself, the true you; happiness and results will follow. Always make decisions based on who you are and what you believe in. The truth will rise to the top; and the truth will always set you free. As Einstein said, "My head is my office." Make your best office or files to be your own head and mind, which will enable you to make consistent decisions. *Self-respect creates self-confidence in oneself.*

2. *Respect for reality.* Learn to respect reality. Admit the truth, be honest, and have integrity regardless of the situation and cost. The Chernobyl disaster in the Soviet Union went very wrong because people didn't have respect to see reality and the possible consequences of their decisions. Many children and people in that environment died. In the real world, what can go wrong often may go wrong. Radiation didn't stop at the borders of Soviet nation, but it spread and already affected others throughout the world.

3. *Respect for community.* You are not alone; and all your decisions have a "domino effect." You are part of a community. Help people get out of bad situations and instill the type of hope in people that will inspire them and provide them the aspiration to show their inner-self. Get people off drugs and gangs, and stop wars that have destructive affects on people and communities, which shows that we live in an interdependent world. Strive for win-win globally.

4. *Respect for life.* Learn to make decisions that respect all forms of life, such as plants, environment, people, and animals. The Exxon Valdez oil spill in Alaska affected

people, birds, fish, sea mammals, and the environment for many, many years. Set and clarify your priorities and your decisions will become easier based on your values. The ship's captain, Joseph Hazelwood, left the bridge and legally he was not wrong; however, morally, he was responsible and should not have left the bridge. Ethics and morality, like the Value-Driven Management framework, go well beyond the law, and consider all stakeholders involved in the situation.

5. *Respect for the future.* Learn to act in such away that every actions enhances the world for you and the future generations. Years ago, people could not make decisions that would affect so many people, but today each and every decision can have a profound affect on people, business, environment (which includes all forms of life), and the future generations. You can be part of the ethical solution by committing yourself to consider the future generations that will be living on earth. If it was not for improvements and commitments of our distant ancestors, we would probably still be living in caves. As human beings, we have the brain capacity to distinguish right from wrong and make the future brighter for coming generations, and that ability is what sets us aside from animals.

Bibliography

Ryan, M., (1995). *Personal Ethics and the Future of the World.* Video produced by Varied Directions International. (800) 888-5236. Narrated by Meg Ryan.

Bibliography

Adler, Mortimer J. (1987). *Aristotle for Everybody*. New York: Macmillan Publishing Co., Inc.

Adler, Mortimer J. (1985). *Ten Philosophical Mistakes*. New York: Macmillan Publishing Co.

Agular, Francis J. (1994). *Managing Corporate Ethics*. New York: Oxford University Press.

Alsop, Ronald. (2003). Right and wrong. *The Wall Street Journal*, September 17, P. R9.

Anders, George, "Business Schools Forgetting Missions"? The Wall Street Journal, September 26, 2007, p. A2.

Anderson, Elizabeth. (1993). *Value in Ethics and Economics*. Cambridge, MA: Harvard University Press.

Ang, Audra. (2004). China bans Nike commercial. *The Miami Harold*, December 7, p. 5C.

Apuzzo, Matt, "Airlines admit price-fixing," Sun-Sentinel, August 24, 2007, pp. D1, D2.

Arlow, P. (1991). Personal Characteristics in College Students' Evaluations of Business Ethics and Corporate Social Responsibility. *Journal of Business Ethics, 10*, 63–69.

Arlow, P., & Ulrich, T. A. (1980). Business ethics, social responsibility and business students: An empirical comparison of Clark's study. *Akron Business and Economic Review*, pp. 17–22.

Arlow, P., & Ulrich, T. A. (1985). Business ethics and business school graduates: A longitudinal study. *Akron Business Review*, 13–17.

Arlow, P., & Ulrich, T. A. (1988). A longitudinal survey of business school graduates' assessments of business ethics. *Journal of Business Ethics, 7*, 295–302.

Arnst, C. (1996). The bloodletting at AT&T is just the beginning. *Business Week*, p. 30.

Associated Press, "Energy Drinks Under Fire," The Wall Street Journal, August 22, 2007, p. D4.

Babbie, E. (1992). *The practice of social research* (6th ed.). Wadsworth Publishing Company.

Badenhorst, J. A. (1994). Unethical behavior in procurement: A perspective on causes and solutions. *Journal of Business Ethics, 13*, 739–745.

Badaracco, Jr., Joseph L. (1997). *Defining Moments: When Managers Must Choose Between Right and Right*. Boston, MA: Harvard Business School Press.

Ball, Jeffrey. (2006). As Exxon Pursue African Oil Charity Becomes Political Issue. The *Wall Street Journal*, January 10, pp. A1, A10.

Barker, E. (1959). *The Political Thought of Plato and Aristotle*. New York: Dover Publications, Inc.

Barro, Robert J. (2002). The State of the Union: Bush Mostly Got it Right. *Business Week*, February 25, p. 30.

Barry, Bruce. (2007). Speechless: The Erosion of Free Expression in the American Workplace. San Francisco: Berrett-Koehler Publishers, Inc.

Baumhart, S. J. (1961). How ethical are business-men? *Harvard Business Review, 39*. pp. 6–9.

Baxter, D. G., & Rarick, A. C. (1987). Education for the moral development of managers: Kohlberg's stages of moral development and integrative education. *Journal of Business Ethics, 6*, 243–248.

Beauchamp, T. L., and Bowie, Norman E. (2004). *Ethical theory and business* (7th edition). Upper Saddle River, N. J., Pearson Prentice Hall.

Beauchamp, T. L. (1988). Ethical theory and its application to business. In T. L. Beauchamp & N. E. Bowie (Eds.). *Ethical Theory and Business* (3rd ed.) (pp. 1–55). Englewood Cliffs, NJ: Prentice Hall.

Becker, H., & Fritsche, D. (1987). Business ethics: A cross-cultural comparison of managers' attitudes. *Journal of Business Ethics, 6*, 289–295.

Beltramini, R. F. (1984). Concerns of college students regarding business ethics. *Journal of Business Ethics, 3*, pages 195–200.

Beauchamp, Tom L. (1982). *Philosophical Ethics*. New York: McGraw-Hill Book Company.

Beecher, Jonathon & Bienvenu, Richard. (1983). *The Utopian Vision of Fourier*. Columbia: University of Missouri Press.

Behrman, Jack N., (1988). Essays on Ethics in Business and the Professions. Englewood Cliffs, NJ: Prentice Hall.

Belicke, Dan. (2006). A social strategist for Wal-Mart. *Business Week*, February 6, p. 11.

Bendixen, Mike, Abratt, Russell, and Jones, Preston. (2007). Ethics and Social Responsibility in Supplier-Customer Relationships. *Journal of Applied Management and Entrepreneurship*, January, pp. 3–23.

Bird, Otto A. (1967). *The Idea of Justice*. New York: Frederick A. Praeger, Publishers.

Berstein, Aaron. (2005). A Major Swipe At Sweatshops, *Business Week*, pp. 98–100.

Bishop, T. R. (1992). Integrating business ethics into an undergraduate curriculum. *Journal of Business Ethics*, 11, 291–299.

Blanchard, Ken and O'Connor, Michael. (1997). *Managing by Values*. San Francisco, California: Berrett-Koehler Publishers, Inc.

Bok, Derek. (1990). *Universities and the Future of America*. Durham, North Carolina: Duke University Press.

Bowie, Norman E. & Freeman, Edward R. (1992.). *Ethics and Agency Theory: An Introduction*. New York: Oxford University Press.

Boatright, John R. (2007). Ethics and the conduct of business (6th ed.). Upper Saddle River, N.J. Pearson Prentice Hall.

Brenner, S. N. (1992). Ethics programs and their dimensions. *Journal of Business Ethics*, 11, 391–9.

Brenner, S. N., & Molander, E. A. (1977). Is the ethics of business changing? *Harvard Business Review*, 55, 57–71.

Bromiley, P., & Marcus, A. (1989). The deterrent to dubious corporate behavior: Profitability, probability and safety recalls. *Strategic Management Journal*, 10, 251–271.

Brown, M. K. (1994). Using role play to integrate ethics into the business curriculum: A financial management example. *Journal of Business Ethics*, 13, 105–111.

Brandt, Richard B. (1992). *Morality, Utilitarianism, and Rights*. Cambridge: University of Cambridge Press.

Bravin, Jess, "Court Hears School-Diversity Cases," The Wall Street Journal, December 5, 2006, p. A2.

Bray, Ilan. (2005). A Company's Threat: Quit smoking or leave. *The Wall Street Journal*, December 20, p. D1.

Brinton, Crane. (1990). *A History of Western Morals*. New York: Paragon House.

Bronowski, J. and Mazlish, Bruce. (1962). *The Western Intellectual Tradition*. New York: Harper & Row, Publishers.

Brown, Marvin T. (1990). *Working Ethics*. San Francisco: Jossey-Bass Publishers.

Brugger, Walter (ed.), & Baker, Kenneth. (1974). *Philosophical Dictionary*. Spokane, Washington: Gonzaga University Press.

Buchholz, Rogene A. (1979). *Fundamental Concepts and Problems in Business Ethics*. Englewood Cliffs, New Jersey: Prentice Hall, Inc.

Business Week. (2002). Material Published on the May 5th 2002 and October 26th 2002. *Business Week*.

Byrne, John A., "After Enron: The Ideal Corporation," Business Week, August 26, 2002, pp. 68–74.

Byrnes, Nanette, and Sassen, Jane, "Board of Hard Knocks," Business Week, January 22, 2007, pp. 36–39.

Capell, Perri, "Why Weight-Discrimination Cases Pose Thorny Legal Tests," The Wall Street Journal, October 2, 2007, p. B4.

Carr, A. Z. (1994). *Is business bluffing ethical?*. In J. Drummond & B. Bain (Eds.), Managing business ethics (pp. 26–38). Butterworth-Heinemann Ltd.

Carmichael, S., & Drummond, J. (1989). *Good business* (1st ed.). Published in London.

Carroll, A. B. (1975). Managerial ethics: A post-Watergate view. *Business Horizons*, 2, 75–80.

Caruso, David B. (2006). KDC's recipe soon to be trans fat-free. Sun-Sentinel, October 31, p. 30.

Cava, A. (1990). Teaching ethics: A moral model. *Business and Economics Review*, 36(3), 10–13.

Cavalier, Robert J. (ed.), Govinlock, James (ed.) and James P. Sterba (ed.). (1989). Ethics in the History of Western Philosophy. New York: St. Martin's Press.

Cavanagh, F. G. (2006). *American business values*. (5th ed.). Upper Saddle River, New Jersey: Pearson Prentice Hall.

Cavanagh, F. G., Moberg, J. D., & Velasquez, M. (1995). Making business ethics practical. *Business Ethics Quarterly*. pp. 398–418.

Cavico, F. J. (2001). Business plan and strategies as legally protected trade secrets and University of Miami. *Business Law Review*, pages 1–66.

Cavico, Frank J. (2004). Private Sector Whistleblowing and the Employment at Will Doctrine: A Comparative Legal, Ethical, and Pragmatic Analysis. *45 South Texas Law Review*, Pages 543–645.

Cavico, Frank J. (1992). Employment at Will and Public Policy. 25 Akron Law Review. page 497.

Cavico, F. & Mujtaba, B. G. (2008). *Legal Challenges for the Global Manager and Entrepreneur.* Kendall Hunt Publishing Company. United States. ISBN: 978-0-7575-4037-0.

Center for Business Ethics. (1986). Are corporations institutionalizing ethics? *Journal of Business Ethics*, 5, 85–91.

Chap, J. (1985). Moral judgment in middle and late adulthood: The effects of age appropriate moral dilemmas and spontaneous role taking. *International Journal of Aging and Human Development*, 22, 161–171.

Chappell, Tom. (1993). *The Soul of a Business: Managing for Profit and the Common Good.* New York: Bantam Books.

Cheng, Roger, "I Can See You," The Wall Street Journal, November 27, 2006, pp. R6, R7.

Clark, J. W., & Clark, S.J. (1966). *Religion and moral standards of American businessmen.* Cincinnati: Southwestern Publishing Co.

Clark, Robert W. & Lattal, Alice Darnell. (1993). *Workplace Ethics: Winning the Integrity Revolution.* Lanham, MD: Rowman & Littlefield Publisher, Inc.

Conlin, Michelle, "More Micro, Less Soft," Business Week, November 27, 2006, p. 42.

Coy, Peter, "It's Not Business' Business," Interview with Robert Reich, IdeasOutsideShot, Business Week, September 30, 2007, p. 86.

Covey, Stephen R. (1992). *Principle-Centered Leadership.* New York: Simon and Shuster.

Crary, David. (2007). Critics blast Pizza Hut pies as prize for young readers. *The Miami Herald*, March, 2007, p. 4A.

Cunningham, G. Watts. (1924). *Problems of Philosophy.* New York: Henry Holt & Company.

Danner, Patrick, "Group: Chain's mercury alerts mislead," The Miami Herald, November 30, 2006, pp. 1C, 6C.

DeGeorge, Richard T. (2006). *Business Ethics* (6th ed.). New Jersey: Pearson Prentice Hall.

DeGeorge, Richard T. (1993). *Competing with Integrity in International Business.* New York: Oxford University Press.

DeGrazia, Sebastian. (1989). *Machiavelli in Hell.* Princeton, NJ: Princeton University Press.

Delaney, Kevin J., "Google: From "Don't Be Evil" to How to Do Good," *The Wall Street Journal*, January 18, 2008, pp. B1, B2.

Delaney, Kevin J. (2005). Google outlines philanthropic plan. *The Wall Street Journal*, Oct. 12, p. B5.

De Nisi, Angelo S. and Griffin, Ricky W. (2008). *Human Resource Management*. Boston; Houghton Mifflin Company.

DesJardines, Joseph R. (2007). Business, ethics, and the environment. Upper Saddle River, New Jersey: Pearson Prentice Hall.

Diamond, Randy. (2002). McGreevey signs law requiring smart guns. The Bergen Record, December 24, pp. A1, A7.

Dickerson, Marla. (2006). Hidden tax' helps stifle Mexico's development. *Sun-Sentinel*, p. 20A.

Donaldson, Thomas. (1989). *The Ethics of International Business*. New York: Oxford University Press.

Donaldson, Thomas (ed.), Werhane, Patricia, and Cording, Margeret. (2002). *Ethical Issues in Business—A Philosophical Approach* (7th edition). Upper Saddle River, New Jersey. Pearson Prentice Hall.

Dowling, Bob, "The Robin Hood Robber Baron," Business Week, November 27, 2006, p. 116.

Dunbar, John. (2006). AT&T's buyout of BellSouth clears hurdle. The record, December 30, p. A–11.

Durant, Will. (1965). *The Story of Philosophy*. New York: Washington Square Press, Inc.

Dworkin, R.M. (1991.). *The Philosophy of Law*. Oxford: Oxford University Press.

Dwyer, Paula, and Carney, Dan. (2002). "Year of the Whistleblower," *Business Week*, pp. 107–109.

Emerging Market Indicators. (2006). "Bribery," *The Economist*, p. 106.

Engardio, Pete, and Roberts, Dexter, "How To Make Factories Play Fair," Business Week, November 27, 2006, p. 58.

Engardio, Pete. (2004). Global Compact, Little Impact. *Business Week*, July 12, pp. 86–87.

Engardio, Pete, "Beyond The Green Corporation," Business Week, Special Report, January 29. 2007, pp. 50–64.

Ferrell, O.C., Freedrich, John, and Ferrell, Linda. (2008). *Business Ethics: Ethical Decision-Making and Cases* (7th ed.). Boston, Houghton Mifflin Company.

Ferrell O.C. and Gardiner, Gareth. (1991). *In Pursuit of Ethics: Tough Choices in the World of Work*. Springfield, Il.: Smith Collins Company.

Fischer, John Martin. (1986.). *Moral Responsibility*. Ithica, New York: Cornell University Press.

Fisher, Colin, and Lovell, Alan. (2006). *Business ethics and values* (2nd ed.). Pearson Prentice Hall.

Flew, Anthony. (1984). *A Dictionary of Philosophy* (2d edition revised). New York: St. Martin's Press.

Flint, Joe, Branch, Shelly, and O'Connell, Vanessa. (2001). "Breaking Longtime Taboo, NBC Network Plans to Accept Liquor Ads," *The Wall Street Journal*, December 14, pp. B1, B6.

Fox, Adrienne, "Corporate Social Responsibility Pays Off," HR Magazine, August 2007, pp. 43–47.

Fox News, "Italian Priest Persuades Red Bull to Pull Christmas Ad," http://www.foxnews.com, retrieved December 4, 2007.

Fowler, Geoffrey A., and Marr, Merissa. (2006). Disney and the Great Wall. *The Wall Street Journal,* Feb. 9, pp. B1, B2.

Fowler-Hermes, J., (2001). "Appearance-based Discrimination Claims Under EEO Laws." *The Florida Bar Journal.* April 2001, p.32 f.

Frankena, William K. (1973). *Ethics* (2d edition). Englewood Cliffs, New Jersey: Prentice-Hall, Inc.

Freedman, A. (1990). *Business ethics survey of hospitality students and managers.* DBA Dissertation at Nova Southeastern University.

Freeman, R., & Gilbert, D. (1988). *Corporate strategy and the search for ethics.* Englewood Cliffs, NJ: Prentice-Hall.

Freeman, Edward R. (1991). *Business Ethics: The State of the Art.* New York: Oxford University Press.

French, Peter A. (1995). *Corporate Ethics.* Ft. Worth, Texas: Harcourt, Brace, and Company.

Friedman, M. (1994). *The social responsibility of business is to increase its profits.* In A. W. Wines and A. Stevens (Eds.), *Reading in business ethics and social responsibility* (pp. 137–141). Iowa: Kendall and Hunt Publishing.

Friedrich, Carl Joachim. (1963). *The Philosophy of Law in Historical Perspective.* Chicago: The University of Chicago Press.

Fritzche, D. J. (1995). Personal values: Potential keys to ethical decision making. *Journal of Business Ethics* 14, 909–922.

Frost Jr., S.E. (1962). *Basic Techniques of the Great Philosophers* (revised edition). New York: Doubleday & Company, Inc.

Garver, Eugene. (1987). *Machiavelli and the History of Prudence.* Madison, Wisconsin: The University of Wisconsin Press.

Gellerman, S. W. (1986). Why 'good' managers make bad ethical decisions. *Harvard Business Review,* 64, 85–91.

Gilligan, C. (1982). *In a different voice: Psychological theory and women's development.* Cambridge, MA: Harvard University Press.

Gilligan, C. (1977). In a different voice: Women's conception of self and morality. *Harvard Educational Review,* 47, 481–517.

Gini, Al. (2005). *Case studies in business ethics* (5th ed.). Upper Saddle River, N.J., Pearson Prentice Hall. Green, Ronald M. (1993). The Ethical Manager: A New Method for Business Ethics. New York: Macmillan Publishing Co..

Givray, Henry S., "When CEOs Aren't Leaders," Business Week, September 3, 2007, p. 102.

Goodman, Cindy Krischer, "PepsiCo CEO defines good work," The Miami Herald, September 11, 2007, pp. 1C, 4C.

Goodman, Cindy Krischer, "Volunteering through work isn't always so voluntary," The Miami Herald, November 8, 2006, p.1C.

Green, Hardy, "Are B-Schools a Blight on the Land," Business Week, November 5, 2007, p. 90.

Greenhouse, Linda, "Justices 5–4, Limit Use of Race For School Integration Plans," The New York Times, June 29, 2007, pp. A1, A20.

Guelzo, Allen, "The Stuff of Democratic Life," The Wall Street Journal, November 22, 2006, p. A14.

Guthrie, W.K.C. (1975). *The Greek Philosophers.* New York: Harper & Row, Publishers.

Guthrie, W.K.C. (1971). *Socrates*. Cambridge: Cambridge University Press.

Guthrie, W.K.C. (1988). *The Sophists*. Cambridge: Cambridge University Press.

Grassian, Victor. (1981). *Moral Reasoning*. Englewood Cliffs, New Jersey: Prentice-Hall, Inc.

Hadzsits, George Depue. (1963). *Lucretius and His Influence*. New York: Cooper Square Publishers, Inc.

Hamlyn, D.W. (1988). *A History of Western Philosophy*. London: Penguin Books.

Hampshire, Stuart. (1983). *Morality and Conflict*. Cambridge, Massachusetts: Harvard University Press.

Hardin, Russell. (1988). *Morality within the Limits of Reason*. Chicago: The University of Chicago Press.

Hare, R.M. (1989). *Essays in Ethical Theory*. Oxford: Oxford University Press.

Hare, R.M. (1981). *Moral Thinking: Its Level, Methods and Point*. Oxford: Clarendon Press.

Harman, Gilbert. (1977). *The Nature of Morality: An Introduction to Ethics*. New York: Oxford University Press.

Hart, H.L.A. (1994). *The Concept of Law* (2nd ed.). Oxford: Clarendon Press.

Heller, Agnes. (1981). *Renaissance Man*. New York: Schocken Books.

Henderson, David R. (2007). Sirius Business. *The Wall Street Journal*, February 28, 2007, p. A15.

Henderson, Steven, "School integration revisited," The Miami Herald, December 5, 2006, p. 6A.

Henderson, Verne E. (1992). *What's Ethical in Business?* New York: McGraw-Hill, Inc.

Hitchens, Christopher. (2007). *God is not great*. New York: Twelve Hachette Book Group, USA.

Hobhouse, L.T. (1906). *Morals in Evolution*. New York: Henry Holt & Company.

Hoffman, Kathy Barks. (2005). Health policy imperils jobs. Sun-Sentinel, February 9, p. 1D.

Hoffman, W. Michael & Moore, Jennifer Mills. (1984). *Business Ethics: Readings and Cases in Corporate Morality*. New York: McGraw-Hill Book Company.

Holmes, Robert L. (1993). *Basic Moral Philosophy*. Belmont, California: Wadsworth Publishing Co.

Holmes, Stanley, and Zellner, Wendy. (2004). The Costco Way. *Business Week*, April 12, pp. 76–77.

Homes, Stanley, and Smith, Gerri. (2002). For Coffee Growers, Not Even A Whiff of Profits. *Business Week*, Sept. 9, p. 110.

Hosmer, Larue Tone. (1987). *The Ethics of Management*. Homewood, Illinois: Richard D. Irwin, Inc.

Hulliung, Mark. (1983). *Citizen Machiavelli*. Princeton: Princeton University Press.

Hume, David. (1957). *An Inquiry Concerning the Principles of Morals*. New York: Macmillan Publishing Company.

Iwata, Edward. (2006). Owner of small coffee shop takes on java titan Starbucks. USA Today, December 20, pp. 27–28.

Jackall, Robert. (1988). *Moral Mazes: The World of Corporate Managers*. New York: Oxford University Press.

Jay, Anthony. (1994). *Management and Machiavelli*. Oxford: Pfeiffer and Company.

Jentz, Gayloard A, Miller, Rober Leroy, Gross, Frank G. (2007). *West's Business Law* (10ᵗʰ ed.). Thomson West.

Jewell, Mark, "Doughnut to be healthier," The Miami Herald, August 28, 2007, p. 4A.

Johnson, Tim. (2005). Taking care of older parents is law of land. *The Miami Herald*, Feb. 9, p. 17A.

Jones, W.T. (1975). *A History of Western Philosophy* (2d edition revised). New York: Harcourt Brace Jovanovich, Publishers.

Jones, Gareth R. and George, Jennifer M. (2003). *Contemporary Management.* (3ʳᵈ Ed.). New York, NY: McGraw Hill.

Kabel, Marcus, "Wal-Mart trucks make environmental progress," The Miami Herald, July 18, 2007, p. 3C.

Kaczor, Bill. (2006). Layers' ads will first need approval of Bar. Sun-Sentinel, November 3, p. 10B.

Kane, Robert. (1994). *Through the Moral Maze: Searching for Absolute Values in a Pluralistic World.* New York: Paragon House Publishers.

Kant, Immanuel. (1959). *Foundation of the Metaphysics of Morals*. New York: The Bobbs-Merrill Company, Inc.

Kavka, Gregory S. (1986). *Hobbesian Moral and Political Theory*. Princeton, New Jersey: Princeton University Press.

Kenny, M. and Mujtaba, G. B. (2007). Understanding Corporate Entrepreneurship and Development: A Practitioner View of Organizational Intrapreneurship. *Journal of Applied Management and Entrepreneurship*, Vol. 12(3).

Kesmodel, David, "FTC Criticizes Ruling In Whole Foods Case," The Wall Street Journal, August 22, 2007, p. A4.

Kingsley, Michael. (2004). In Defense of Excess. *Time*, March 15, p. 67.

Koch, G. C., Gable, W., & Ellig, J. (1993). *Introduction to Market Base Management*. Fairfax, VA: The Center for Market Processes.

Koenig, David, "Whole Foods acquires rival," Sun-Sentinel, August 29, 2007, p. 3D.

Kohlberg, L. (1984). *The Philosophy of Moral Development*, San Francisco: Harper and Row.

Kohlberg, L. (1972). A cognitive-developmental approach to moral education. *The Humanist*, 4, 13–16.

Kohlberg, L. (1969). Stage and sequence: The cognitive-developmental approach to socialization. In D. Grosling (ed.), *Handbook of socialization theory and research*, Chicago: Rand McNally.

Koenig, David, "Whole Foods acquires rival," Sun-Sentinel, August 29, 2007, p. 3D.

Kuper, Lavrance. (2006). *Ethics—The Leadership Edge*. Cape Town, South Africa: Zebra Press.

Lavine, T.Z. (1984). *From Socrates to Sartre: The Philosophic Quest*. New York: Bantam Books.

Lewis, Seth. (2006). Protect yourself. *The Miami Herald*, Feb. 20, pp. 4–5.

Lippman, Walter. (1964). *A Preface to Morals*. New York: Time Incorporated.

Bibliography

Louden, Robert B. (1992). *Morality and Moral Theory*. New York: Oxford University Press.

Lozano, Juan A. (2006). Enron ex-CEO Sentenced. *The Miami Herald*. Oct. 24, pp. 1D, 2D.

Lozano, Juan A. (2006). Judge vacates lay's fraud conviction. *The Miami Herald*. Oct. 18, pp. 1C, 2C.

Lyons, David. (1989). *Ethics and the Rule of Law*. New York: Cambridge University Press.

Machiavelli, Niccolo. (1950). *The Prince and the Discourses.* New York: Random House, Inc.

MacKinnon, B. (2007). Ethics: theory and contemporary issues. 5th ed. Thomson, Wadsworth. United States.

MacIntyre, Alasdair. (1966). A Short History of Ethics. New York: Macmillan Publishing Company.

Mackie, J.L. (1990). *Ethics: Inventing Right and Wrong*. New York: Penquin Books.

Madsen, Peter (ed.). & Shafritz, Jay M. (ed.). (1990). *Essentials of Business Ethics*. New York: Penguin Books USA, Inc.

Maher, Kris. (2004). Global Companies Face Reality of Instituting Ethics Programs. *The Wall Street Journal*, Nov. 9, p. B8.

Makower, Joel. (1994). *Beyond the Bottom Line*. New York: Simon & Schuster.

Mandel, Michael J., "And The Enron Award Goes To...Enron," Business Week, May 20, 2002, p. 46.

Mansfield, Harvey C. (1995). *Machiavelli's Virtue*. Chicago: University of Chicago Press.

Mattingly, Garret. (1965). *Machiavelli. Renaissance Profiles*. Plumb, J.H. (ed.). New York: Harper & Row, Publishers, 1965.

McGrath, Elizabeth Z. (1994). *The Art of Ethics: A Psychology of Ethical Beliefs*. Chicago: Loyola University Press.

McKay, Betsy. (2007). Why Coke aims to slake global thirst for safe water. *The Wall Street Journal,* March 15, 2007, p. B1.

McNatt, Robert. (2000). Chripter: Not quite so equal. *Business Week*, Nov. 13, p. 14.

Miller, Richard W. (1992). *Moral Differences: Truth, Justice and Conscience in a World of Conflict*. Princeton, NJ: Princeton University Press.

Miller, Roger LeFoy and Jentz, Gayloard A. (2007). Business law today (7th ed.). Ohio, Thomson-West.

Mills, Bill. (2007). Divided court rejects school diversity plans. CNN.com; http://www.cnn.com/2007/law/06/28.

Moore, G.E. (1989). *Principia Ethica*. New York: Cambridge University Press.

Morris, Tom. (1997). *If Aristotle Ran General Motors: The New Soul of Business*. NY: Henry Holt and Company.

Mujtaba, B.G. and Cavico, F.J. (2006). Age discrimination in employment: cross-cultural comparison and management strategies. BookSurge Publishing, United States.

Mujtaba, B. & Mujtaba, L. (2004). Creating a Healthy Learning Environment for Student Success in the Classroom. *The Internet TESL Journal.* Vol. X, No. 2, February 2004. The article can be retrieved via the following URL link: http://iteslj.org/ or: http://iteslj.org/Articles/Mujtaba-Environment.html.

Mujtaba, B.; Griffin, C.; and Oskal, C., (July 2004). Emerging Ethical Issues in Technology and Countermeasures for Management and Leadership Consideration. *Journal of Applied Management and Entrepreneurship.* Vol. 9, No. 3.

Mujtaba, B. (1997). Business Ethics Survey of Supermarket Managers and Employees. UMI Dissertation Service. A Bell & Howell Company. UMI Number: 9717687. Copyrighted by UMI. UMI: 300 North Zeeb Road. Ann Arbor, MI 48103. Phone: (313) 761-4700. (800) 521-0600.

Mujtaba, B. G. (1996). Ethics and morality in business. *Journal of Global Competitiveness,* Vol. 4 (1). ISBN 1071-0736. pages 339–346.

Murphy, Jeffrie G. and Coleman, Jules L. (1990). *Philosophy of Law: An Introduction to Jurisprudence* (revised edition). Boulder, Colorado: Westview Press.

Nash, Laura L. (1990). *Good Intentions Aside: A Manager's Guide to Resolving Ethical Problems.* Boston: Harvard Business School Press.

Norman, Richard. (1991). *The Moral Philosophers: An Introduction to Ethics.* Oxford: Clarendon Press.

Nuttall, Jon. (1993). *Moral Questions: An Introduction to Ethics.* Cambridge, U.K.: Polity Press.

Oakley, Justin. (1993). *Morality and the Emotions.* New York: Routledge.

O'Connell, Vanessa. (2002). "Landmark TV Liquor Ad Created by D.C. Insiders," *The Wall Street Journal,* January 3, pp. B1, B3.

O'Toole, James. (1996). *Leading Change: The Argument for Values-Based leadership.* New York: Random House.

Overbye, Dennis. (2007). Free will: Now you have it, now you don't. the New York Times, January 2, pp. F1, F4.

Patron, Rachel. (2007). Rulers must be realists. Sun-Sentinel, May 4, p. 23A.

Paul, Ellen Frankel, et. al. (editors). (1994). Cultural Pluralism and Moral Knowledge. Cambridge: Cambridge University Press.

Pellegrino, Edmund D. (1989). Character, Virtue and Self-Interest in the Ethics of the Professions. *Journal of Contemporary Health Law and Policy*, No. 5, 53f.

Piasecki, Bruce, "Social responsibility: the new key to global success," The Record, August 12, 2007, p. B–2.

Piper, Thomas R., Gentile, Mary C., and Parks, Sharon D. (1993). *Can Ethics Be Taught?* Boston: Harvard Business School.

Plato. (1952). *Gorgias.* Indianapolis: The Bobbs-Merrill Company, Inc.

Plato. (1990). *The Republic.* Translated with Introduction and Notes by Francis MacDonald Cornford. Oxford: Oxford University Press.

Pohlman, R.A. and Gardiner, G.S. (2000).*Value Driven Management, How to Create and Maximize Value Over Time for Organizational Success.* (New York) Amacom.

Poole, Ross. (1991). *Morality and Modernity.* New York: Routledge, Chapman & Hall, Inc.

Posner, Richard A. (1990). *The Problems of Jurisprudence.* Cambridge, Massachusetts: Harvard University Press.

Pounds, Marcia Heroux, "More employers try to stub out smoking habit," Sun-Sentinel, November 18, 2007, pp. 1A, 23A.

Pound, Roscoe. (1954). *An Introduction to the Philosophy of Law* (revised edition). New Haven: Yale University Press.

Pressman, Aaron. (2005). Activist Funds Make Waves. *Business Week*, Oct. 24, pp. 124–25.

Rachels, James. (1986). *The Elements of Moral Philosophy*. New York: McGraw-Hill Publishing Company.

Rosenblatt, Joel, "Former HP chief pleads not guilty in spy case," Sun-Sentinel, November 11, 2006, pp. 1D, 2D.

Russell, Bertrand. (1972). *A History of Western Philosophy*. New York: Simon & Schuster.

Ryan, M. (1995). "Personal Ethics and the Future of the World." *Varied Directions International*. (800) 888-5236. Narrated by Meg Ryan.

Rugaber, Christopher S., "Web-ad deal clears U.S. antitrust hurdle," The Record, December 21, 2007, p. B–5.

Russell, Bertrand. (1957). *Why I Am Not a Christian*. New York: Simon & Schuster, Inc.

Scheffler, Samuel. (1992). Human Morality. New York: Oxford University Press.

Shellenbarger, Sue. (2004). Getting fired for dating a co-worker: office romance comes under attack. *The Wall Street Journal*, February 19, p. D1.

Shellenbarger, Sue. (2005). Employers often ignore office affairs. *The Wall Street Journal*, March 11, p. D1.

Schneewind, J.B. (ed.). (1990). *Moral Philosophy from Montaigne to Kant*. New York: Cambridge University Press.

Schwarneberg, Robert. (2006). Suit over loft bed falls short. *Star-Ledger*, August 16, pp.13,16.

Serra, Dan, "New 401(k) plan promotes social responsibility," Sun-Sentinel, Your Business, December 4, 2006, p. 11.

Sharp, David J. (2006). *Cases in business ethics*. Sage Publications, Thousand Oaks, California.

Sherman, Mark. (2007). Race-based school programs reined in. *The Miami Herald*; June 29, 2007. pp. 1A, 2A.

Singer, Marcus G. (1958). *Moral Rules and Principles. Essays in Moral Philosophy*. Edited by A.I. Melden. Seattle: University of Washington Press.

Singer, Peter. (1993). *Practical Ethics* (2d edition). Cambridge: Cambridge University Press.

Slote, Michael. (1992). *From Morality to Virtue*. New York: Oxford University Press.

Smith, Sasha. (2001). Spying: How far is too far. *Fortune Small Business*, June, p. 85.

Smalley, Suzanne, "Ben & Jerry's Bitter Crunch," Newsweek, December 3, 2007, p. 50.

Snoeyenbas, Milton, Almeder, Robert, and Humber, James (eds.). (1992). *Business Ethics*. Buffalo, New York: Prometheus Books.

Solomon, Robert C. (1993). *Ethics: A Short Introduction*. Dubuque, Iowa: Brown & Benchmark.

Solomon, Robert C. (1992). *Ethics and Excellence: Cooperation and Integrity in Business*. New York: Oxford University Press.

Sorell, Tom & Henry, John. (1994). *Business Ethics*. Oxford: Butterworth-Heinemann.

Solberg, J., Strong, C. K., & McGuire, C., Jr. (1995). Living (not learning) ethics. *Journal of Business Ethics*, 14, 71–81.

Solomon, R. C. (1994). *New world of business: Ethics and free enterprise in the global 1991's* (2nd ed.) (pp. 33–78). Published by Rowman and Littlefield Publishers, Inc.

Special Report, "How To Fix Corporate Governance," Business Week, May 6, 2002, pp. 69–78.

Stephenson, H. B., Galbraith, S., & Grimm, R. B. (1995). Ethical congruency of constituent groups. *Journal of Business Ethics*, 14, 145–158.

Sterba, James P. (ed.). (1988). *Morality in Practice* (2d edition). Belmont, California: Wadsworth Publishing Company.

Stout, David. (2007). Use of race in school placement curbed. The New York Times. Website: http://www.nytimes.com/2007/06/28.

Strauss, Leo. (1958). *Thoughts on Machiavelli*. Chicago: The University of Chicago Press.

Sullivan, Robert J. (1989). *Immanuel Kant's Moral Theory*. New York: Cambridge University Press.

Thomas, Geoffrey. (1993). *An Introduction to Ethics: Five Central Problems of Moral Judgment*. Indianapolis: Hackett Publishing Company.

Thomas, JR., R. (2001). From Affirmative Action to Affirming Diversity. *Harvard Business Review* on Managing Diversity. Originally published in the 1990 edition of Harvard Business Review.

Thomson, Todd S. (2006). Green Good for Business. *Business Week*, May 8, p. 124.

Thorne, Debbie M., Ferrell, O.C., and Ferrell, Linda (2008). Business and Society: A Strategic Approach to Social Responsibility. Boston, Massachusetts: Houghton Mifflin Company.

Thurn, Scott. (2007). Behind Outsourcing: Promise and Pitfalls, *The Wall Street Journal*, February 26, 2007, p. B3.

Toffler, Barbara Ley. (1991). *Managers Talk Ethics*. New York: John Wiley & Sons, Inc.

Tong, Vinnee, "Aquafina to clear up source of contention," The Record (Bergen County, New Jersey), July 28, 2007, p. A9.

Trevino, Linda K. and Nelson, Katherine A. (2007). *Managing business ethics*. Haboken, N.J. John Wiley and Sons, Inc.

Tuleja, Tad. (1985). *Beyond the Bottom Line*. New York: Penguin Publishing Co.

Velasquez, Manuel G. (1992). *Business Ethics: Concepts and Cases* (3d edition). Englewood Cliffs, New Jersey: Prentice Hall.

Walker, Elaine, "Burger King limits advertising to kids," The Miami Herald, September 12, 2007, pp. 1C, 6C.

Watson, Charles E. (1991). *Managing with Integrity*. New York: Praeger.

Weinreb, Lloyd L. (1987). *Natural Law and Justice*. Cambridge, Massachusetts: Harvard University Press.

White, Erin and Patrick, Aaron O. (2007). Shareholders push for vote on Executive pay. *The Wall Street Journal*, February 26, 2007, pp. B1, B3.

White, R. (2002). Do employees act like they think? Exploring the dichotomy between moral judgment and ethical behavior. *Public Administration Quarterly, 25*, 391–412.

Wilbur, James B. (1992). *The Moral Foundation of Business Practice*. Lanham, MD: University Press of America, Inc.

Williams, Bernard. (1985). *Ethics and the Limits of Philosophy*. Cambridge, Massachusetts: Harvard University Press.

Williams, Bernard. (1981). *Moral Luck*. Cambridge, U.K.: Cambridge University Press.

Wilson, James Q. (1993). *The Moral Sense*. New York: Macmillan, Inc.

Windham, Christopher. (2004). J&J to Give Away New AIDS Drug. *The Wall Street Journal*, March 29, p. B6.

Wong, David B. (1986). *Moral Relativity*. Berkeley, CA: The University of California Press.

Workplace Visions, (2007). Social Responsibility and HR Strategy. *Society for Human Resource Management*, No. 2, 2007, pp. 2–8.

World Bank Institute, 2007. Internet Course: "CSR and Sustainable Competitiveness." Retrieved on January 27, 2007 from: www.infoworldbank.org/etools/wbi_learning/index.

Don't Quit

When things go wrong as they sometimes will.
When the road you are trudging seems all up hill.
When funds are low and debts are high.
And you want to smile, but you have to sigh.

When care is pressing you down a bit.
Rest, if you must, but don't quit.
Life is queer with its twists and turns.
As everyone of us sometimes learns.

And many a failure turns about
When he might have won had he stuck it out:
Don't give up though the pace seems slow—
You may succeed with another blow.

Success is failure turned inside out—
The silver tint of the clouds of doubt.
And you never can tell how close you are.
It may be near when it seems so far:

So stick to the fight when you are hardest hit—
It's when things seem worst that you must not QUIT.

(Unknown)

Author Biography

Frank J. Cavico

Dr. Frank J. Cavico is a Professor of Business Law and Ethics at the H. Wayne Huizenga School of Business and Entrepreneurship of Nova Southeastern University in Ft. Lauderdale, Florida. He has been associated with the University as a full-time faculty member since 1988, and has an adjunct since 1985. He has been involved in an array of teaching responsibilities, at the undergraduate, master's and doctoral levels, encompassing such subject matter areas as business law, government regulation of business, constitutional law, administrative law and ethics, labor law and labor relations, health care law, and business ethics. He was the principal faculty member in the creation of the required Huizenga School MBA law and ethics course: "The Values of Legality, Morality, and Social Responsibility in Business"; and he presently serves as Lead Professor for that course. In 2000, he was awarded the Excellence in Teaching Award by the Huizenga School; and in 2007, he was awarded the Faculty Member of the Year Award by the Huizenga School. His fine record is manifested by numerous research endeavors, principally law review articles, in the broad sectors of business law and ethics. His most recent law review publications examined trade secret law, the law of intentional interference with contract, a comparative legal and ethical analysis of "whistleblowing" in the private sector, the tort of intentional infliction of emotional distress in the private employment sector, and the covenant of good faith and fair dealing in the franchise business relationship. In 2005, he published, together with his faculty colleague and co-author, Dr. Bahaudin Mujtaba, a textbook on business ethics, Business Ethics: Transcending Requirements Through Moral Leadership. Since then, he and Dr. Mujtaba have published three other books: Age Discrimination in Employment, Legal Challenges for the Global Manager and Entrepreneur, and Business Law for the Entrepreneur and Manager. They also have published several scholarly articles. Dr. Cavico discharges substantial service responsibilities at the Huizenga School, principally by serving as the Chair of the Faculty Executive Committee and Chair of the Faculty Rank, Reappointment, and Promotion Committee, as well as Lead Professor for several law and ethics courses.

Drs. Cavico and Mujtaba have created a scholarship at the Huizenga School of Business, The Business Ethics and Global Corporate Social Responsibility Scholarship, to which they donate a portion of their royalties from the sale of all their books, which sum is matched by their university.

Dr. Cavico holds a J.D. degree from St. Mary's University School of Law and a B.A. from Gettysburg College. He also possesses a Master of Laws Degree from the University of San Diego School of Law and a Master's Degree in Political Science from Drew University.

Dr. Cavico is licensed to practice law in the states of Florida and Texas. He has worked as a federal government regulatory attorney and as counsel for a labor union; and he has practiced general civil law and immigration law in South Florida.

Dr. Cavico is married; and he and his wife, Nancy, a Registered Nurse and adjunct nursing professor, reside in Lauderdale-by-the Sea, Florida. Nancy holds a BSN Degree as well as a Legal Assistant Certificate from Nova Southeastern University. They co-authored a law review article on nursing malpractice law as well as one on the nursing profession and the employment at will doctrine.

Bahaudin G. Mujtaba

Bahaudin G. Mujtaba is serving as the Chair for Management Department and is an Associate Professor in Nova Southeastern University's H. Wayne Huizenga School of Business and Entrepreneurship in Fort Lauderdale, Florida. Bahaudin has worked as an internal consultant, trainer, and teacher in the corporate arena. He also worked in retail management for 16 years. As a consultant, he coaches, trains, educates, and develops managers. In his capacity as a consultant and trainer, Bahaudin has worked with various firms in the areas of management, diversity management, cross-cultural communication, customer value/service, and cultural competency.

His Doctorate Degree, from the H. Huizenga School of Business and Entrepreneurship of Nova Southeastern University, is in Management, and he completed his dissertation research on the topic of business ethics in management. He has two post-doctorate specialties: one in Human Resource: Management and another in International Management. He has been listed in the publications of *Who's Who in America, Who's Who in Management,* and *Who's Who in the World.* Bahaudin is the author and coauthor of over sixteen professional and academic books.

During the past 25 years he has had the pleasure of working in the United States, Brazil, Bahamas, Afghanistan, Pakistan, St. Lucia, Grenada, Thailand, and Jamaica. He was born in Khoshie of Logar province and raised in Kabul, Afghanistan. Bahaudin and his family moved to Pakistan for one year during the Soviet invasion of Afghanistan in the early 1980s and then moved to the United States when he was a teenager. This diverse exposure has provided him many insights in ethics, culture, leadership, and management from the perspectives of different firms, people, and countries. He is grateful for such opportunities in the past years and looks forward to learning each and every day.

Contributors' Biographies

1. **Dr. Donald L. Ariail,** a Certified Public Accountant, is Assistant Professor of Accounting at Texas A&M University-Kingsville, System Center San Antonio. He has published numerous articles on taxation and has presented papers at both national and international conferences. He also was recipient of the 2006 KPMG Outstanding Dissertation Award presented by the Gender Issues and Worklife Balance Section of the American Accounting Association. Prior to entering academia in 2005, he was the owner of a successful local CPA practice in Atlanta, Georgia and had worked in the Public Accounting profession since 1972. He is the holder of a Doctorate Degree in accounting from the H. Wayne Huizenga School of Business and Entrepreneurship of Nova Southeastern University.

2. **Dr. Elizabeth Danon-Leva** received her Doctorate in International Business Administration at Nova Southeastern University. She has published papers in several conference proceedings, books, and journals, and works as a business consultant and Adjunct Professor in International Business and Management. Her research interests include business ethics, leadership, cross-cultural studies, and change management.

3. **Joe Durden,** a Certified Public Accountant, is the owner of Samuel J. Durden, CPA, PC, a CPA firm located in Fayetteville, GA. The firm specializes in attestation engagements for non-profit organizations. He is currently seeking a Doctoral Degree in accounting from the H. Wayne Huizenga School of Business and Entrepreneurship of Nova Southeastern. His dissertation will research the integration of accounting history into financial accounting courses. He holds a Masters in Business Administration from Kennesaw State College located in Kennesaw, Georgia and undergraduate degrees in Accounting and Finance from Armstrong State College located in Savannah, Georgia.

4. **Dr. John Wayne Falbey** is a faculty member and Program Chair for Real Estate Development at the H. Wayne Huizenga School of Business and Entrepreneurship, Nova Southeastern University; He is a member of the Florida and Colorado Bar Associations. Dr. Falbey also is Managing Member and President of The Falbey Group, LLC, a real estate development firm in Florida. He has been actively engaged in real estate development for more than thirty years.

5. **Stephanie C. Ferrari** is a Web Developer at the H. Wayne Huizenga School of Business and Entrepreneurship of Nova Southeastern University. She received her Bachelor of Science Degree in Computer Science and completed her Master of Business Administration Degree at Nova Southeastern University. Stephanie currently teaches Online Communications and Internet Competency for the Huizenga School's doctoral programs. She and her husband, Silvano Ferrari, also own and manage a Precision Tune Auto Care franchise in Lauderhill, Florida.

6. **Dr. William Freeman** has worked in the nonprofit and cause-related arena for over two decades. Currently, he is an adjunct professor in the Master's of Nonprofit Management program at George Mason University in Arlington, Virginia. He is

an Examiner with the Malcolm Baldrige National Quality Program (2005-2006), certified in the Balance Scorecard methodology and organizational change implementation. Freeman received his Doctoral Degree at Nova Southeastern University's H. Wayne Huizenga School of Business and Entrepreneurship. He earned a MBA from Southeastern University in Washington, DC.

7. ***Gina H. Harris*** is currently the Director of Claims for a Professional Liability Insurance Group. She graduated from Nova Southeastern University's Masters of Management with a focus on Leadership Program at the School of Business and Entrepreneurship. She has a Bachelors of Business in Marketing from the University of Miami. She was inducted into Huizenga School's International Honors Society. She is interested in the topics of workforce diversity management, power bases, leadership, teamwork, and coaching.

8. ***Dr. Matthew G. Kenney*** is a graduate of Nova Southeastern University's H. Wayne Huizenga School of Business and Entrepreneurship. He is the founding director of the Entrepreneurship Academy, and also serves as an adjunct professor for Franklin University's MBA program and Colorado Technical University.

9. ***Dr. Stephen C. Muffler*** has been practicing business law, both transactional and litigation, for over 15 years as a member of the Florida Bar. He attained his Bachelor's Degree in Criminal Justice from the University of Missouri-St. Louis in 1990 and his Juris Doctorate from Nova S.E. University in 1993. He went on to earn his Masters of Law (LLM) in international law from University of Miami in 1996. He started his career with the Florida Bar assisting in the investigation and prosecution of ethical complaints against Florida attorneys. He phased into private practice in Fort Lauderdale and teaches business law and ethics as an adjunct professor for Nova S.E. University. He also donates his time as an appointed city official holding the post of Chairman of the Citizens' Police Review Board for the City of Fort Lauderdale for the past 5 years. This municipal board reviews professional complaints against city police officers and recommends the appropriate sanctions, if any, to the city manager. He has written numerous published articles dealing with business law and criminal justice.

10. ***Dr. Miguel A. Orta,*** a native of Cuba, has been teaching Import/Export Management, Comparative Management and International Negotiations, International Legal Environment, and Law, Ethics, and Society for Nova Southeastern University. Miguel has a BA in Political Science and Mass Communications from Florida State University, A Juris Doctor from Duke University and a Masters in International Business from Nova Southeastern University. As founder of American Strategic Consultants, he has conducted market research, feasibility studies, and business planning for the development of international enterprises in Venezuela, Colombia, Argentina, Brazil, Ecuador, Mexico, and Panama. He is presently involved in strategic planning for Chinese, Indian, Malaysian, and Thai companies entering the United States and Latin American markets. During the 1990's, he served as a special business and trade consultant to Fernando Color de Mello, the first democratically elected president in Brazil after the fall of the military dictatorship.

11. ***Cuneyt Oskal*** was born in the third largest city of Turkey, called Izmir. After he graduated from the department of engineering sciences at Aegean University in Izmir, Turkey, he enrolled in the one-year intensive M.B.A. program of Istanbul University in the department of Business Administration. Then, he had an opportunity to work for the Turkish Army Force as a Chemical Engineer for about two years. After his military service, he completed a Master's Degree in Management Information Systems at Nova Southeastern University. Cuneyt is currently working for N.S.U. as a Webmaster, and is also teaching college computer technology classes as an adjunct professor.

12. ***John W. Palma, Jr.*** graduated from the Charles E. Schmidt School of Science at Florida Atlantic University with a Bachelor of Arts in Psychology. His interests include history, behavioral finance, and the psychological consequences of wealth, status, and power.

13. ***Dr. Randolph Pohlman*** has written two books, entitled *"Understanding the Bottom Line: Finance for Non-financial Managers and Supervisors"* and *"Value Driven Management: How to Create and Maximize Value Over Time for Organizational Success."* Dr. Pohlman was a senior executive at Koch Industries, the second largest privately-held company in the U. S. He was recruited to Koch via Kansas State University, where for more than ten years, he served the college in a variety of administrative and faculty positions, including holding the L. L. McAninch Chair of Entrepreneurship, and served as Dean of the College of Business. Dr. Pohlman is an active presence in the South Florida community serving as a Trustee and member of the Board of Governors for the Greater Miami Chamber of Commerce. He served as a member of the 2004 GMCC Cutting Edge Award Committee, and was Chief Judge for the 2002, 2003, and 2005 GMCC Cutting Edge Awards. He also serves on the Board of Governors and is a Trustee for the Greater Fort Lauderdale Chamber of Commerce. He is on the Board of Directors of the International Assembly for Collegiate Business Education (IACBE). In addition, Dr. Pohlman serves on the Board of Directors for two companies: Clark Consulting and Viragen, Inc. He currently serves as Dean of the H. Wayne Huizenga School of Business and Entrepreneurship at N.S.U.

14. ***Dr. Josephine Sosa-Fey,*** a Certified Manager, is Lecturer of Management at Texas A&M University-Kingsville, System Center San Antonio. She received a doctor of Business Administration Degree from the H. Wayne Huizenga School of Business and Entrepreneurship at Nova Southeastern University. Her doctoral dissertation was on ProQuest's 2002 Top Ten Best Seller List. She has authored refereed articles in the *International Journal of Business and Public Administration,* the *Journal of Business and Leadership: Research, Practice and Teaching,* and the *Journal of Studies in Conflict & Terrorism.* She also has presented and published numerous refereed papers in national and international conference proceedings.

15. ***Miguel Valdez*** is a student in the College of Business at Texas A&M University-Kingsville, System Center San Antonio.

16. **Dr. Don Valeri,** B.A. (Hons), LL.B., M.B.A., Ph.D., is a lawyer located in Vancouver, British Columbia. He currently teaches business law and business ethics. His doctoral research was in leadership studies, with an emphasis on servant leadership and other forms of ethical leadership.

17. **Dr. Gary Waldron** is a professor, attorney and international educator with extensive experience in higher education, grant proposals, practice of law, litigation, project consulting, and emerging markets education/training. Currently, he is an Adjunct Professor at Nova Southeastern University, Huizenga School of Business. Significant skills in design, development and implementation of curricula for law and business students in Eastern Europe, completing seven years as a Visiting Professor of Law. Teaching experience includes: business law, contract law, international commercial arbitration, international law, civil comparative law, and business ethics. He acted as an advisor to university administrators and senior faculty on management of programs in education reform. He was an advisor on the USAID Business Management Education for Ukraine Project, sponsored by the University of Minnesota; and Senior Legal Adviser to FMI on the USAID project in Ukraine advising government officials on commercial law. Professor Waldron received both a Doctor of Jurisprudence and a Master's Degree in Education from Indiana University. He is a member of the Bars of California and Indiana.

18. **Laura Yanez** is a student in the College of Business at Texas A&M University-Kingsville, System Center San Antonio.

Index

Index

E

M

N

O